the PRIMARY ENGLISH ENCYCLOPÆDIA

The Heart of the Curriculum

Margaret Mallett

David Fulton Publishers
London

David Fulton Publishers Ltd
Ormond House, 26–27 Boswell Street, London WC1N 3JZ

www.fultonpublishers.co.uk

First published in Great Britain in 2002 by David Fulton Publishers

Note: The rights of Margaret Mallett to be identified as the author of this work has been asserted by her in accordance with the Copyright, Designs and Patents Act 1988.

British Library Cataloguing in Publication Data
A catalogue record for this book is available from the British Library.

ISBN 1 85346 777 4

Typeset by Book Production Services, London
Printed and bound in Great Britain by The Cromwell Press Ltd, Trowbridge, Wilts.

Contents

Foreword

I was talking recently with a group of very keen Primary PGCE students about the teaching of literacy and language. One of them made the remark that, 'It's really interesting all this stuff, but there's so much of it, isn't there? How can I possibly read all these books? This student was right: there is an awful lot of 'stuff' to read about primary English. Wouldn't it be good if there were one volume where you could start to gain an understanding of this enormous field? To be really useful, such a volume would have to do a number of things. It would have to be as comprehensive as possible so it readers could find most of what they needed within its pages, but it would also have to whet the appetite of these readers and inspire them to pursue some topics in much greater depth by reading elsewhere. The task of producing such a volume seemed as if it might be beyond one person, yet Margaret Mallett set about doing just that and the book you now have in your hands is a tribute to her success.

What you have here *is* an encyclopaedia: it contains most of the information that teachers of primary English need to know. If you want to learn what adverbial clauses, mass nouns or limericks are, the book will tell you. If you want some preliminary information about the *Warnock Report*, cue-systems in reading or the EXEL project, the book will tell you. But this is much more than a catalogue of knowledge in the area. Margaret also set herself the aim of producing a book which 'soars above the requirements of the day to capture some things of enduring importance about the Primary English classroom'. So she includes entries (or essays) which try to, and do, inspire their readers to a much rounder and fuller vision of what is possible in primary English teaching and what the real goals of this might be.

So, in future, my answer to students such as the one quoted will be simple: 'Have you tried the Primary English Encyclopaedia? And I will make the recommendation in the certain knowledge that the book will not only answer her immediate questions, but will also lure her deeper into the fascination of teaching English to primary pupils.

David Wray
Warwick University
January 2002

Acknowledgements

I would like to thank all the children, teachers and student teachers with whom I have worked and who have made me feel that English is one of the most exciting elements of the Primary Curriculum.

I very much appreciate the generosity of the authors and publishers who allowed me to illustrate some entries with pictures from their work. Full acknowledgement is given on the pages where the work appears.

I am grateful to Jennifer Shepherd, Paula Woodhead and Jan McGillivray and the children of Castlecombe Primary School in Mottingham, Kent for allowing me to use the writing samples with the entries on alliteration, poetry and special educational needs. My thanks go also to Elaine Shiel and the children of Primary 3, Corstorphire Primary School, Edinburgh for the writing about Cocoa the Brown Bear which appears with the entry on shared writing. Sele First School allowed me to include two poems about the Angel of the North and I thank the children and teachers involved. Michelle Coles and Abbie and Rowan kindly allowed me to include Abbie's 'Edward the Lion' poem and Rowan's piece under the play and recount entries.

My colleagues at Goldsmiths College have been a great inspiration and include, most recently, Clare Kelly, Michelle Coles, Chris Kearney, Celia Burgess-Macey and Colton Paul. I have also benefited over the years from the insights of the other members of the editorial team working on the journal *English 4–11* (The English Association, Leicester) – John Paine, Susanna Garforth, Henry Pearson, Pauline Hilton and Brenda Marshall, Clare Kelly and Angela Wilson read selected entries and made helpful comments. Neither are responsible for any errors that remain. But, above all, I would like to thank my husband, David Mallett: this task would not have been accomplished without his encouragement and practical help.

About this Encyclopaedia

The idea for this book arose out of conversations with student teachers. They felt that in a time of great change, with many new challenges and demands, they needed a reference book which gave them easy access to key concepts and ideas about language, literacy and literature in the vast landscape of Primary English. It needed to be comprehensive, they thought, but should also 'give us a bit of inspiration'.

This encyclopaedia tries to meet these wishes. There are already many useful guides and handbooks but these are organised round themes or, perfectly properly, concentrate on one aspect of English, be it talk, drama or literacy. This book provides a different kind of support, in an essentially accessible form, across the whole area of Primary English. Of course no one author can be an expert on everything in such a large and important area and readers are constantly referred to other books and resources to expand their knowledge and understanding. Like other encyclopaedias the present work aims to be 'a first port of call'. It covers the subject knowledge teachers need (or gives clear advice about where to obtain it) and there is much about how English is planned, carried out and assessed within the current statutory frameworks. But teachers have wider intentions and interests than the statutory frameworks. So there are entries on the history of children's literature, on theories of language development and some different views of what good English teaching involves.

The alphabetical format means key words and concepts can be easily found. However, I have been concerned that this should not fragment the English curriculum and appear to avoid the complexities. So I have written what I hope is a unifying introduction – *Primary English: The Heart of the Curriculum*. This gives an overview which sets out some of the enduring principles on which excellence in the primary English classroom are properly based and draws out the significance of the relationship between the four language processes.

The Audience

My audience includes student teachers on both BA (Ed), GRT and PGCE courses, new teachers and teachers returning to the classroom after a career break. However, I hope the encyclopaedia will be a valued reference book for all who are interested in and concerned about primary English. I have tried to encompass as much as possible of what someone, wherever in the world they work, would want to know (or know where to find out) when setting out to teach English in an exciting and well-informed way to children in the first eleven years of their lives.

The Entries

In selecting the entries I have kept in mind the great amount of subject knowledge teachers need. There are times when we like to check our understanding of key concepts and the entries contain some succinct definitions of grammatical and literary terms. Sometimes what seemed straightforward at first is more complicated on further research and reflection and I have not sought conformity in entry length. Thus the size of the entries varies according to my judgement of the space needed. Some entries – definitions of parts of speech 'prepositions' and 'pronouns' and explanations of technical terms like 'ellipsis' and 'onomatopoeia' – will aim to give information briefly and clearly. Others like 'cohesion', 'genre' and 'portfolios' will need more space. I have tried to give glimpses into the work of the many scholars, teachers and authors whose work has enriched my teaching. Sometimes a brief quotation or paraphrased insight will persuade you it is worth seeking out particular books to read more deeply into a topic. I have taken up a simple approach to cross referencing. Other relevant entries on each topic are set out under the 'See also' heading.

Extended Entries

Seventeen of the entries – Bilingualism, Book making, Drama & English, Early Years Language and Literacy, Fiction: choosing and using, History of Children's Literature, History of English teaching in the Primary School, Information and Communications Technology and English, Junior Years Language and Literacy, Language acquisition, Literacy Hour, Non-fiction Reading and Writing, Reading, Speaking and Listening, Special Educational Needs in language and literacy, Visual Literacy and Writing have a special status in terms of space and format because they are crucial to the understanding of good English teaching. Here issues will be identified and explored. Where space allows, some 'vignettes' from the classroom will be included as well as enriching background material. Here I have drawn on all I have learnt from the children, students, colleagues and teachers with whom I have worked over many years. I want to communicate the enjoyment as well as the hard work that accompanies children's development as talkers, listeners, readers and writers.

Further Information

While long lists are avoided, readers are directed, at the end of each entry, to key texts and resources. The bibliographies there will supply the reader with suggestions for further research.

Who's Who in Primary English

Passing time and changing emphases can mean that we lose sight of those who have made a lasting contribution. Some of these teachers and scholars are included alongside today's influential 'voices'. The list is one person's selection with a eye on space – my apologies go to those not included in spite of their achievements. In making my choices I have concentrated on those who have contributed to the practice and understanding of the classroom teacher. Children's writers are too numerous for inclusion in the Who's Who and are mentioned instead under entries like 'picture books', 'poetry' and 'novels'.

It cannot be said too often that however many official reports and books we have – lively and worthwhile English work can only be realised in the classroom by the imagination, planning and pedagogic skill of a creative and reflective practitioner. The introduction to this book places English work at its most inspirational at the very heart of the curriculum.

Margaret Mallett
Goldsmiths College Education Department
January 2002

Introduction

Primary English:
the heart of the curriculum

This short introduction soars above the requirements of the day to capture some things of enduring importance about the Primary English classroom. Successful schools, and we must be encouraged by this, interpret current requirements in terms of their fundamental beliefs about English, language and literacy in the primary years and their judgement about the needs and priorities of their pupils.

The first thing to remember is that becoming an enthusiastic speaker, listener, reader and writer is essentially a social and collaborative process – it needs the involvement of other human beings. Everything we know about young children shows they learn actively and with others. Think of children when they first come to school: they are generally competent users of spoken language and ready to learn and share their thoughts, feelings and ideas with others. They are inquisitive creatures not rock-bound sponges. They question, wonder, laugh, object, enjoy and constantly try to make sense of a shared world. The good practitioner builds on the excitement and enthusiasm of the younger children to energise speaking and listening, to develop reading and to encourage writing through the primary years. A classroom which is alive and purposeful will be one where teachers and children collaborate and share activities.

Oracy and literacy, using language to think and learn, is central to every lesson and helps organise nearly every experience, whether in or out of the classroom. What, then, is distinctive about English lessons? Let me say at this point that I am aware that some teachers, particularly of the very young, prefer to think in terms of 'language and learning' more broadly. Nevertheless, even in the earliest stages we can detect an 'English' perspective. English is associated with those times when we consider, evaluate, savour and enjoy language as a phenomenon in its own right. We study our mother tongue – its structure and functions and the ways in which it varies. Texts are the materials which we use for all these things. They may be spoken or written and found in many different media; they may be one of the great variety of non-fiction texts now available. But, above all, English is the special home of imaginative literature in all its forms – picture books, short stories, novels, poetry and play scripts.

Although English has a content – the study of language and literature – it is essentially to do with processes, about becoming able to talk insightfully about texts and issues, to read thoughtfully and critically and to write with purpose and coherence. We want children to become passionate about using their language. The more we can link language work to real tasks and real purposes the better – lists, letters and posters for a school event is a simple example. Of course, there are some essential and challenging things to teach and learn about language as a symbolic system – about parts of speech, sentences, cohesion, word meanings and so on. Children have to be helped with the conventions of paragraphing, spelling and punctuation if the content of their work is to reach the audience it deserves. But there is everything to be gained from hanging on to a sense of playfulness in language study – round rhythm, rhyme and puns, for example.

The stories children read draw on experience, good and bad, of the real world, but they also draw on the inner world of the imagination to explore what could be or might be as well as what is. The best writing for children gets to the centre of the human situation. When they talk about a story, relate it to their own experience, think about behaviour, attitudes and views, they use all their faculties of thought and feeling. Fiction has a unique power to help children assimilate knowledge and understanding by drawing on their experience of life, enriched by the memory of all the other books they have read. Here, English has something in common with other subjects which help us represent and assimilate experience – drama, music and art. Teachers and children can be comforted in an uncertain world when they share what human beings have in common. Stories bring them in touch with people who have problems over relationships with friends and family, who have fears about growing up or who are feeling the confusion which occurs when a family is moving home or breaking up. Fiction allows us to reflect on all this at a distance from the rawness of our own circumstances. We should not expect children to like everything they read. In fact we want them to be critical readers, able to give evidence for their opinions. The discussion about issues can lead to children's own writing – in which they can maintain, if they wish, this distance from direct experience. The teacher and the other children provide a natural and empathetic audience for each other's writing.

The spirit of English can permeate the whole curriculum. By this I mean more than that we use language to learn in every subject. The things we do in English lessons can help us bring a personal perspective to other areas of the curriculum. The creative exploration of fiction can sometimes infuse a special life and energy into history, science or geography lessons. For example, if an ethical issue, such as the use of the environment or use of the world's resources arises in geography or science, teachers might inform the discussion by turning to texts like *The Whales' Song* by Diana Sheldon or *Where the Forest Meets the Sea* by Jeannie Baker. Here the essentially human response and the interest in texts nurtured in English lessons can be drawn on. Thus the collaborative, community atmosphere of the best English lessons, where everyone's voice is valued, benefits all areas of the curriculum. Where the sharing of enjoyments, insights and observation exists, the bigger purposes of becoming literate shine out and the hard aspects, the chores of learning if you like, are seen as more worthwhile.

None of this would be possible without the vital role played by teachers. They create contexts for learning, choose resources, respond to children's achievements and assess and intervene to help children make progress. Good teachers are responsive to what works well and flexible in adapting to what needs to be changed. There is a cycle and a rhythm to good English teaching: planning and teaching is followed by evaluation and record keeping, and then the fruits of the evaluation feed into the next cycle of planning. A momentum builds. Current assessment requirements include summative testing – to provide snapshots of what a child knows and can do at a given time. Teachers know that we need a richer profile to complement these results with more formative judgements which pinpoint where special help may be needed and help us celebrate achievements.

Part of being a reflective practitioner involves enriching our professional understanding with research findings. This can be built on our own classroom evaluations or on the published research of others, where we are entitled to take a critical approach. The English Co-ordinator has a crucial role, providing leadership and encouragement and a cooperative approach to curriculum development so that all teachers are involved. Just as children enjoy collaborating over their learning, so teachers benefit from interaction with colleagues – sharing, reflecting and discussing issues together. Not everyone will agree all the time – there is stimulation in sharing different views – but there needs to be trust and understanding between colleagues and agreement on the most important aspects of policy and practice.

It is hard to imagine good English practice that does not have a constructive and imaginative approach to those learning English as a second or additional language. There will always be concern too for supporting the progress of children with special language and literacy needs. Partnership with parents and families, an essential part of a school's culture, is particularly important in helping these young learners.

From all this you will gather that I believe that the best English lessons can have a special atmosphere. How is this atmosphere created? It seems to do with giving value to worthwhile activities. Teachers and children often have rituals which symbolise the sharing and enjoyment of reading and telling stories – in one classroom by a child holding the 'story wand', in another the 'story mouse'. Another class was joined by William the bear when children read their stories aloud. For older children a regular time for reading the class novel, for reading out their own writing or for silent reading is enough to give the activity status and value.

If you ask me what I think is the greatest challenge for teachers, it is helping children become competent writers. Teachers have the task of helping children feel confident when faced with a blank page. It involves helping them with difficult things like finding a theme, developing and keeping control of a piece of writing and turning ideas into a structured and coherent account or a satisfying story. Above all, it is about helping children find their 'voice' so that what they write is recognisably their own.

While ideas about English lessons in the primary school will change, I believe that these fundamental features will survive even as each new generation of primary teachers interprets their work in new ways. Increasingly, the expectation is that teachers will have a high level of subject knowledge. Resources will become more diverse and richer, ways of working will change – no doubt with greater use of computers and visual technology. But the good English classroom will always be a fertile ground for new ideas, have an energy about it and be a place where interesting things happen where there is a creative and reflective approach. This is not to underestimate the sheer hard work involved for teachers and children during periods of change. We can have huge lists of what should be achieved but it is the teacher in the classroom who motivates, interests and, above all, values and respects their pupils. Some aspects of teaching and learning may be transformed by technology but we will always need the skill and commitment of teachers, who are themselves good models of how to be confident and articulate speakers, sympathetic listeners and enthusiastic readers and writers.

For me, nothing is closer to the heart of English than the sheer enjoyment of teacher and children talking deeply and intently about a book, poem or a play. They savour the highlights, muse on the characters, admire the author's skill in developing the plot and using just the right word, phrase or image. Often they return to the text to find the evidence to support a point, they respond to the views of others and perhaps move on to further activities – drama or writing – to help assimilate new insights and ideas. Every faculty is brought into play – heart as well as mind – and the very act of sharing helps organise thinking and all the language processes are brought together. Often children's insights surprise us and make us see a story in a new way. Of course children and teachers need quieter times as well – to perfect handwriting or to finish tasks. But we savour those occasions when children's sheer creative energy spills over into talk, writing and drama – times when minds imagine, ideas flow, pens skip across the page or fingers fly over the keyboard – and we hope that children will remember these times.

A

Abbreviation

See also acronym, apostrophe and ellipsis

This is the shortened or contracted form of a word or phrase. Frequently used abbreviations or contractions include don't (do not), can't (can not) and haven't (have not). Children need careful teaching about the difference between possessive apostrophes and those used to indicate contraction. Sometimes the abbreviation becomes a word in its own right, for example pub, plane or fridge, and in these cases the apostrophe has been dropped. Other abbreviations are acronyms like SAT (standard assessment test) and NATE (the National Association for the Teaching of English). Useful abbreviations of Latin terms include: e.g. for example (exempli gratia); i.e. that is (id est); etc. and so on (et cetera); N.B. note especially (nota bene). The best account of 'abbreviation' known to me is in McArthur's Oxford Companion.

McArthur, Tom (1992) *The Oxford Companion to the English Language* Oxford: Oxford University Press.

Abstract noun

See also clause, grammar, noun, parts of speech, sentence

This is a noun which names a state or condition (melancholy), a quality (mercy), a concept (feudalism) or an action (favouritism). Such nouns are 'abstract' because you cannot perceive the phenomena they denote with your senses.

Accent

See also language variety, speaking and listening

This is the aspect of language variation to do with pronunciation. All spoken language, including standard English, is spoken with an accent. Pronunciation varies according to a speaker's geographical and social origin. For example, I come from the north of England and pronounce 'bath' and 'path' with a short 'a' while my husband, a southerner, pronounces them with a long 'a'. People speaking in a second or additional language often have a distinctive accent. 'Received' pronunciation refers to the accent historically associated with BBC announcers (although regional accents are heard increasingly) and the well educated. But language is dynamic and pronunciation like other aspects – dialect and vocabulary – changes with each generation of users and many well-educated people speak with a regional accent and are proud to do so.

Acronym

See also abbreviation

An acronym is made up of the initial letters of a related sequence of words and pronounced as one word. Examples include NATE (National Association for the Teaching of English) and UKRA (United Kingdom Reading Association).

Acrostic

See also poetry, verse

This describes a poem or puzzle where the first letter of each line, read sequentially, spells out a word or phrase. In a double acrostic, the first and last letters of each line spell out a word or phrase.

Adjective

See also adjectival clause, grammar, parts of speech

Adjectives are words that modify nouns or pronouns or complement verbs.

- the *yellow* dress
- it is *spacious*
- those gloves look *attractive*

'Simple' adjectives include words like 'large', 'small' and 'red' while what are termed 'derived adjectives' are created by adding a suffix (-able, -ful, -ish) to a noun or verb, for example, 'readable', 'restful' and 'foolish'.

Adjectives (and adverbs) have comparative and superlative forms. Comparative forms include:

- hard – harder
- challenging – more challenging

Superlative forms include:

- large – largest
- impressive – most impressive

Adjectival clause

See also clause, grammar, parts of speech

An adjectival clause modifies a noun.

> The girl, *who was flushed with pride,* rose to receive the bouquet.

Adventure stories

See also history of children's literature

In Victorian times, adventure stories tended to reflect the traditional world of men and boys. The action often centred on dangerous journeys and exciting events on land and at sea. John Rowe Townsend (1990) locates the roots of children's adventure stories both in Daniel Defoe's *Robinson Crusoe* and the historical novels of Sir Walter Scott. *Treasure Island* by Robert Louis Stevenson introduced a vivid new kind of adventure story for children which broke away from the moralistic flavour of earlier books. The action is exciting and the characters are fully rounded mixtures of good and bad qualities. *Treasure Island,* which Stevenson wrote in 1881 to amuse his stepson during a wet August in Scotland, is still in print. Another book, H Rider Haggard's *King Solomon's Mines,* also written in the 1880s, had considerable influence on later writers of adventure stories. For more detail about the early history of adventure stories, I recommend John Rowe Townsend's *Written for Children,* Victor Watson's *Cambridge Guide to Children's Books in English,* and Peter Hunt's *Children's Literature: An Illustrated History.*

There are fashions in children's reading choices as in other things. At the beginning of the twenty-first century children seem to favour stories set in magical worlds of the imagination: R.L. Stine's Goosebumps series, Roald Dahl's fantasy tales and J.K. Rawling's Harry Potter books. Nevertheless, stories of young people facing up to physical danger – sometimes touching the improbable but staying within the confines of the physical world – are still enjoyed. Historical novels for children often contain the elements of hazard faced up to with courage and resourcefulness that we associate with the best adventure stories. Rosemary Sutcliff's novels still interest and excite young readers in the later primary years. *The Eagle of the Ninth* (Oxford University Press, 1954) tells the story of a dangerous venture, north of Hadrian's Wall, to find out the truth about the disappearance of the Ninth Legion and to recover its lost Eagle. Two other much read historical stories, again for the 10–12s, are Marita Conlon-McKenna's *Under the Hawthorn Tree* (Puffin) – the tale of the dangerous journey to find help made by three courageous children during the Irish famine of the 1840s – and Berlie Doherty's *Street Child* (HarperCollins, 1993) which tells the true story of a boy who escaped from a workhouse in the 1860s and whose circumstances inspired Dr Barnado to set up his homes. Cynthia Harnett's ever-popular book, *The Wool Pack,* is set in an earlier period, fifteenth-century Winchester and the Cotswolds. (A new edition was published by Egmont books in 2001.)

Not all adventure stories are historical novels. The impact on people of natural disasters are described in Andrew Salkey's books: *Hurricane* (1964), *Earthquake* (1965) and *Drought* (1966). Enid Blyton wrote adventure stories in the 1940s and 1950s – *The Famous Five* series for example – which were formulaic but created a predictable world which some children still find reassuring whatever the reservations of some adults. Still in print is Arthur Ransome's *Swallows and Amazons* series which has strong male and strong female characters and involves children from the town in sailing adventures in the Lake District during their summer holidays. Twelve books were published between 1930 and 1947. Unlike contemporary authors writing in the category often termed 'realistic', Ransome does not involve us in issues like the tensions between parents and children. Subtle nuances in developing relationships are explored in *Walkabout* (Penguin, 1963) – James Vance Marshall's powerful story of some children's survival after an aeroplane crash in the harsh physical environment of the Australian outback. *Walkabout* and other children's novels of the second half of the twentieth century, like for example Anne Holm's *I am David* (Egmont Books, 1989) and Ian Seraillier's *The Silver Sword* (Penguin, 1983), are not just adventure stories but quality works which tell us profound things about the human condition. Another kind of survival story – Robert O'Brien's *Z for Zachariah* (Penguin 1998) – relates the events in Ann's life in the form of a diary when she discovers she is the sole survivor of a nuclear holocaust.

The traditional adventure story is thrilling because the characters face life-threatening situations. In the later part of the twentieth century there had been many books which included some element of fear and mishap but with a light touch. Teachers have their own favourites which they include in the book collection. Two examples are Beverly Cleary's amusing tale *Ramona Quimby Aged 8* (Oxford University Press, 2001) – which, not surprisingly, appeals to girls about age 8 years – and Willard Price's *Arctic Adventure* (Vintage Books, 1993) liked by girls and boys of about ten years. The latter is one of a series telling about the travels of young Hal and Roger to different countries. Their mission is to collect wild animals for their father's zoo and in the story about the arctic visit the brothers face freezing temperatures and lack of food.

Annotated booklists for different ages and abilities are available from the Book Trust, Book House, 45 East Hill, London SW18 2QZ Tel. 020 8516 2977. www.booktrust.org.uk

Hunt, Peter (ed.) (1995) *Children's Literature: An Illustrated History* Oxford: Oxford University Press.

Townsend, John Rowe (1990, sixth and definitive edition) *Written For Children* London: The Bodley Head.

Watson, Victor (2001) *The Cambridge Guide to Children's Books in English* Cambridge: Cambridge University Press.

Adverb

See also adverbial clause, connectives, grammar, parts of speech

These are words which modify or give extra meaning to other parts of speech – to verbs, another adverb or an adjective. So: an example of an adverb modifying a verb is – 'She ran *swiftly*', of another adverb – 'She ran *very* swiftly, and an adjective – 'Her shorts were *really* elegant'. What are termed 'sentence adverbs' – 'happily', 'regrettably' – modify the whole sentence as in '*Happily*, she came first in the race'.

Adverbs can be divided into groups:

Time:	soon, tomorrow, immediately
Frequency:	occasionally, sometimes, often
Place:	inside, near, here
Manner:	effectively, skilfully, swiftly

Adverbs can also function as connectives.

Adverbial clause

See also adverb, clause, grammar

Like adverbs, adverbial clauses modify, elaborate or qualify verbs.

In the following sentence, 'after the children had put on their coats' modifies the verb 'ran'.

'*After the children had put on their coats* they ran into the playground'.

Similarly 'when we left the school' is an adverbial clause modifying 'There was a hail-storm' in the sentence below.

'There was a hail-storm *when we left the school*.'

Adverbial clauses, like other clauses, usually have a subject and verb, as in the examples above.

Adverbial phrase

See also adverb, adverbial clause, clause, grammar

An adverbial phrase is a group of words functioning the same way as a single adverb.

So in the following sentence 'in an encouraging way' is an adverbial phrase.

'He looked at me *in an encouraging way.*'

However, in the next sentence 'encouragingly' is an adverb modifying the verb 'looked'.

'He looked at me *encouragingly*.'

An adverbial phrase, like other phrases, is a group of words acting as one unit. Unlike a clause, a phrase does not have a verb and subject.

Advertisements

See also environmental print, genre, National Curriculum, National Literacy Strategy, persuasive genre, visual literacy

Advertisements on bill boards, in magazines and newspapers, on the radio and on screen are a powerful part of the environmental print which surrounds us. Children notice pictures and format from an early age and soon become sensitive to their cultural associations: advertisements reflect what we most value, fear and desire. They transmit strong social meanings which we may absorb unconsciously. They can be for 'good' purposes – to draw our attention to the merits of worthwhile events, places of interest and institutions. While the profit motive seems a less worthy purpose, some advertisements recommend products in an honest and reasonable manner and the competitive spirit they encourage is an aspect of a free society. Reading and reflecting on the visual impact of advertisements and on the linguistic devices – persuasive vocabulary, puns, alliteration – has long been part of the English programme for older primary school pupils. In the United Kingdom, the National Literacy Strategy introduces the analysis and making of advertisements in Year 4, Term 3. But younger children are also interested in the effects of this kind of text. I remember seeing a teacher work with seven year olds making posters about caring for the environment. The work had arisen from a shared reading of Julia and Charles Snape's picture book *The Giant*. Working in pairs, the children simply did not want to leave their work to go out to play, so absorbed were they in communicating their own environmental concerns to others. Another exciting project on advertising involving young children is written up in Carolyn White's chapter 'Somebody Makes a Choice' in *Visual Images* (Callow, 1999). The work took place in Australia and began with the teacher videoing a selection of television advertisements aimed at children. After watching the commercials the children were given task cards and asked to work in pairs. The cards gave each pair one of four tasks: record the colours used; describe the music; describe the characters; record who speaks and what is said. Just beginning to write, the children either asked the teacher to scribe for them or used pictorial representations to record the information. The teacher wrote a summary of the findings in each of the four categories on large pieces of paper for display. White points out that the work was spread over four weeks and was quite challenging for her exuberant five year olds. After studying several commercials, including one advertising McDonalds, the children and their teacher produced a list (see box on p. 6) of what a children's commercial needs to be effective. White was interested that the children picked out 'magic and pretending things' as a key ingredient – the McDonald's advertisement was set in a fantasy land showing children following Ronald McDonald along a yellow brick road to find something scrumptious to eat. I have referred to this project in some detail as it shows there are ways of involving quite young children in understanding persuasive texts. Indeed, at the end of the work, one child revealed that what he had learnt was much more than superficial: 'when you advertise, somebody makes a choice' – hence White's chapter title.

If children are to understand the impact of this kind of material we need to build up resources. These include collections of advertisements for the book corner – examples from magazines and newspapers and from radio and television advertisements on cassettes and video film. The book corner computer is important when it comes to children's work on their own creations: software programs like Banner and BannerMania can help children make professional looking posters of any size. Once the resources are in place we need imaginative projects and tasks to get the children thinking through the issues. The ideas in the list below would be suitable for guided reading or writing in the Literacy Hour or for work outside it. I find three things helpful to keep in mind. First learning about advertisements and commercials as kinds of persuasive text is something revisited at different stages through the primary years. Each 'revisit' takes the pupils' understanding further. So teachers adapt ideas for different age groups. Second, wherever possible, it is best for children to design publicity and advertising material for real use. Thirdly, we can help focus children's work by providing task cards, carefully selected resources and helpful ways of presenting their findings.

English work round advertisements

- analysing an advertisement for a newspaper or magazine as an example of persuasive text, attending to choices at text level (format), sentence level (syntax) and word level (vocabulary).
- designing and writing advertisements to promote a school event or an imaginary product.
- experimenting with language and design for advertisements for different media – screen, radio, magazine or bill board (See Sealey, 1996 pp. 30–32 for an exciting case study – children making a radio advertisement for their school).
- presenting print advertisements to the group showing how linguistic and visual features combine to make an impact on a targeted audience (See *Grammar for Writing*, p. 147).
- acting out advertisements designed for television.
- improvisation round the making of an advertisement involving children taking up the roles of business people paying for the advertisement and of the producer, editor and actors. (A Year 6 class known to me carried out a project like this. Teacher and children greatly enjoyed researching what was involved in each role and the final presentation was shown to the school.)
- examining ethical aspects of advertising (some of these became apparent in the Year 6 case study referred to above).
- studying advertising aimed at children (see example from Australia described above in which five to six year olds studied commercials). Older primary children often enjoy analysing advertisements aimed at children younger than themselves. Whatever the age group, it is helpful for them to work out some categories to guide their analysis.
- making advertisements for constructive and worthwhile reasons for the book corner or posters to advertise a school function.
- market research using questionnaires and interviews might usefully precede making posters to publicise school events. What would encourage pupils to support the events and how might this be incorporated into the publicity material?
- specific topics like looking at the use of verse in advertisements and comparing verse for profit and poetry for aesthetic purposes.
- using advertisements in developing children's visual literacy and showing, for example, the effectiveness of visual images and how the visual and the linguistic aspects link. Children could be shown a TV advertisement and, in pairs, write down what they notice about aspects like choice of colour, style and image, the appearance of the characters and the way the product is packaged. Then they could discuss how far the language – name and description of product and what people say – matches or extends the visual aspects.

Examining advertisements and commercials and writing their own helps children develop critical abilities in several ways. It certainly draws their attention to how writing can be used to manipulate the reader and change attitudes and behaviour – often purchasing behaviour. We are surrounded by advertisements in every media type and children should understand the negative as well as the more positive implications (Wray, 1995, p. 90). This kind of work also shows them how purpose and sense of audience interact. The purpose of an advertisement is to affect the perception of a product or event of a target audience. It is a way of helping children imagine how they might reach and impact on 'the wider community' which is one of the audiences children are expected to write for in the later primary years (National Curriculum English Orders, EN 3, paragraph 11).

Now that a range of different media are, more than ever, part of our daily experience this kind of work helps develop children's visual literacy and draws their attention to how text and pictures link.

A children's commercial needs:

- Bright colours
- Magic and pretending things
- A catchy song or music with a beat

(Based on the list five year olds made with the teacher's help after a study of television advertisements used in the commercial breaks between children's television programmes (White in Callow, 1999, p. 45).)

Banner and *BannerMania* TAG (01474 357350).

DfEE (1998) *The National Literacy Strategy Framework for Teaching* London: DfEE (see Year 4, term 3, Writing Composition, para. 25).

DfEE/QCA (1999) *English, The National Curriculum for England* London: DfEE.

DfEE 0107/2000 The National Literacy Strategy Guidance *Grammar for Writing* (p. 147).

Sealey, Alison (1996) *Learning About Language: Issues for Primary Teachers* Buckingham and Philadelphia: Open University Press.

White, Carolyn (1999) 'Somebody makes a choice' in Jon Callow *Visual Literacy: visual texts in the classroom* NSW, Australia: Primary English Teaching Association.

Wray, David (1995) *English 7–11: Developing Primary Teaching Skills* London: Routledge, chapter 6.

Affix

See also morpheme, prefix and suffix

An affix is a morpheme attached to a word which may be a prefix (*dis*appear, *un*inspiring) or a suffix (read*ing*, like*ness*).

Agreement (or concord)

Agreement is to do with the relationship between number, person and gender.

> That *dog seems* to be hungry (number agreement).

> *I* bruised *myself* (person agreement).

> *She* managed to prepare lunch *herself* (gender agreement).

There is a more detailed explanation under 'concord' with copious examples in McArthur, 1992 pp. 254–5.

McArthur, Tom (1992) *The Oxford Companion to The English Language* Oxford: QPD and Oxford University Press.

Alliteration

See also assonance

This refers to the repetition of sounds in a sequence in prose or poetry for emphasis or effect. The term refers to consonants and the repeated letters are often the initial letters of words or in the stressed syllable of a word. For example, in Shakespeare's *The Tempest* we have the stirring lines:

> 'Full fathom five thy father lies'.

The under eights love the alliteration in Adrian Henri's poem about hedgehogs in danger – *H25*. The first line is 'Hedgehogs hog the hedges' and the second verse begins 'With halts for hungry hedgehogs'. (*The Ring of Words* edited by Roger

McGough and illustrated by Satoshi Kitamura.)

As well as a device in literary texts, alliteration is used in tongue twisters – 'Peter Piper picked a peck of pickled peppers', similes – 'as good as gold', proverbs – 'waste not, want not', advertisements – 'super sizzling sausages' and newspaper headlines – 'Saucy Sue Soaks up the Sun'. The language of newspapers and advertisements has long been in the English programme of older primary children and this is reinforced in the National Literacy Strategy objectives.

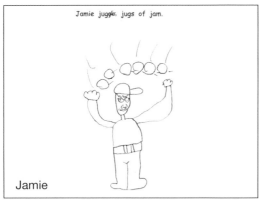
Jamie

Vanessa

Vanessa and James (Reception class at Castlecombe Primary School) heard the teacher read John Foster's alliterative poem 'Zoo Dream' before typing their own illustrated alliterative sentences.

Alphabet

See also consonant, Early Learning Goals, dictionary, horn book, non-fiction reading and writing, phoneme, reading and vowel

An alphabet is the set of symbols used in a system of written language. In English, there are twenty six letters in the alphabet of which five are vowels 'a', 'e', 'i', 'o', 'u' and twenty-one are consonants 'b', 'c', 'd', 'f', 'g', 'h', 'j', 'k', 'l', 'm', 'n', 'p', 'q', 'r', 's', 't', 'v', 'w', 'x', 'y', 'z'. As there are 44 phonemes (units of sound) and only 26 letters of the alphabet, some sounds are represented by combining letters. The National Literacy Strategy provides a structured programme to teach children all the sound symbol correspondences.

From medieval times up until the eighteenth century children learnt to read with the help of alphabet books. Many early primers consisted of a flat piece of wood with a sheet of paper covered by a layer of transparent horn – hence their name – horn books. The alphabet was accompanied by prayers as reading and religion were linked. By the nineteenth century illustrators were producing beautiful alphabet picture books, for example Kate Greenaway's *A Apple Pie* (1886).

The twentieth century brought some excellent alphabet books and friezes. Favourites for the nursery/reception age group include John Burningham's *ABC* (Jonathan Cape, 1964), Dick Bruna's *b is for bear* (Methuen, 1971) and Brian Wildsmith's *ABC* (Oxford University Press,

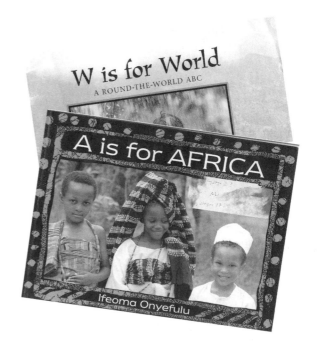

A is for Africa by Ifeoma Onyefulu and *W is for World* by Kathryn Cave, both published by Frances Lincoln, are photographic alphabets which also teach children about distinctive environments and the people who live in them.

1995). Some of the books are enjoyed as toys – Robert Crowthers's *The Most Amazing Hide-and-Seek Alphabet* (1977) is delightfully playful as the child pulls a tag to find which animal is hiding behind each letter. Children up to about eight years enjoy two life-enhancing geography alphabet books: K. Cave's *W is for World* (Frances Lincoln with Oxfam, 1998) and I. Onyefulu's *A is for Africa* (Frances Lincoln, 1997). Both books teach about different environments in the strong context of photographic alphabets.

The alphabet provides a major way of organising information and children need to be helped to find their way round dictionaries, encyclopaedias, indexes and catalogues, whether in print or electronic.

Analogy

See also metaphor, simile

Analogy is used to explain or describe the nature of something by comparing it to something else. Thus it often takes the form of a simile or metaphor. We might say to someone – 'Think of life as a journey through time, sometimes the way may be rocky and difficult, at other times we may pass through cool meadows and rest beneath shady trees'.

Children make use of analogy, bringing what is known to something new, when they try to spell or read words new to them. Sometimes analogy does not work when children try, for example, to make plurals in line with examples known to them – 'mouses' is not the plural of 'mouse'. But, even so, the attempt to bring existing knowledge to new situations is a sign of genuine learning and experiment and should be encouraged.

Anaphoric reference

See also cataphoric reference

We use 'anaphoric reference' when we look back to an earlier word or words in a sentence to discover the meaning of a word or phrase. So in the sentence – 'Although the children were tired after the morning's work they could still enjoy

the afternoon story' – the second part of the sentence makes sense in the light of the first.

Anecdotes

See also narrative, speaking and listening, story telling

These are short accounts usually of an event or something that happened to the teller or writer or someone known to them. From the earliest stage young children enjoy telling others about significant events: what they did yesterday; what happened when their pet or favourite toy was lost; what the squirrels were doing in the park last Saturday. Often what they relate is chronologically ordered and this helps them develop a sense of the narrative form (Mallett, 1997). Reading and listening to literature is a strong context for the sharing of pertinent anecdotes. We value all the connections children make in their talk and writing between what they read and events and situations in their lives. The teacher's skill lies in his or her constructive and imaginative response to children's anecdotes. A number of children in a Year 6 class were responding to the teacher's reading of Anthony Browne's picture book *The Tunnel* (Puffin, 1989) by sharing anecdotes about sibling relationships. The teacher focused the discussion by asking the children how their experiences were similar to and different from those of the children in the book. This nudged the anecdotes into a higher gear and, as often happens, the anecdotes were developed into a satisfying written piece.

When children write journals or diaries in or out of school they draw on anecdotes. These 'vignettes' from real life are more interesting when writers include their own attitudes, opinions and response. Here we can hardly have a better model than the writing in *Anne Frank's Diary* (Puffin, 1997).

Mallett, Margaret (1997) *First Person Reading and Writing in the Primary Years* Sheffield: NATE.

Animals (in children's stories and information texts)

See also history of children's literature

Animals have been a favourite element in many children's stories and information books over the centuries. In *Aesop's Fables* (told to if not originally intended for children) the stories about animals which embody human characteristics of envy, greed, insensitivity and wickedness are used to bring about moral awareness.

A landmark book is Anna Sewell's *Black Beauty*, first published in 1877, to draw the attention of adults to the plight of cab horses. Sewell uses the device of telling the story in the form of an autobiography of a horse and it soon became evident that children had a strong empathetic attachment to the story.

Very different from *Black Beauty* but also loved by children are Rudyard Kipling's *Jungle Books* (1894–5) in which the animals speak to Mowgli (John Rowe Townsend thinks this is an acceptable convention which gives the animals a necessary dignity) and Kipling's *Just So Stories* first published in 1902. Children love to hear these mythic versions of how the camel got its hump, the leopard its spots and the rhinoceros its folded skin.

In her very interesting analysis of *The Wind in the Willows* by Kenneth Graham Julia Briggs remarks on the anthropomorphic approach to animals and while appreciating the exuberance of the characters also notes that 'women and lower classes are silently excluded from this Arcadia' (Hunt, 1995, Chapter 7, p. 181). If you are prepared to consider good retelling – Inga Moore has brought out a wonderfully illustrated abridged version in two volumes: *The River Bank* and *The Adventures of Mr Toad* (Walker Books). Older primary children might appreciate William Horwood's sequels to *Wind in the Willows* which illustrate more current issues. For example, *The Willows and Beyond* includes the same characters now faced by pollution of the River and the threat of housing development on the land of the Wild Wood.

Beatrix Potter's books, for example *The Tale of Peter Rabbit* (1902) – and Alison Uttley's *The Squirrel, the Hare and the Little Grey Rabbit* (1929) create a world where animals talk, wear clothes and have a social life similar to human beings. Townsend and others believe Potter's

work superior: her illustrations are based on the scientific drawing she made of animals (Townsend, 1995). But I have a personal soft spot for the Little Grey Rabbit stories which I received regularly as welcome gifts when I was a child. I still recall the smell of the glue on the binding and the shiny smoothness of the little pages.

It is true that the humanised animal story can descend into cosiness and we can tend 'to distinguish between "good" animals – usually meaning nice furry ones – and "bad" animals which are slimy or snappy and generally uncuddleable' (Townsend, 1995, p. 95).

In seeking an explanation for animal fantasies being one of the most endearing and enduring categories of children's fiction, I turn again to Townsend: it may be because of the essential innocence of animals who only know how to be the animal they are (Townsend 1995, p. 213). Of course there are some deliciously evil animal characters – the weasels in the Grey Rabbit books, Manny Rat in Russell Hoban's *The Mouse and his Child* and General Woundwort in *Watership Down*.

One of the most original animal stories of the second half of the twentieth century is *Watership Down* – Richard Adams' extremely successful first book which is enjoyed by adults as well as children. Here we have a strong story about the dangers a community of rabbits meet in their search for a new warren. The rabbits have their own fascinating language and culture and the story is underlain by some profound ethical issues. The book explores issues about leadership, loyalty to friends and endurance for a cause. Two animal books concerning issues about animal welfare and its conflict with the interests of human beings (although not equalling the epic *Watership Down* in literary stature) are enjoyed by children of about nine years. The first, *Mrs Frisby and the Rats of NIMH* by Robert O' Brien, tells two intertwined tales of a field mouse whose home is at risk from a plough and of rats who have escaped from a laboratory. The issues are dealt with in a way children can understand. The second, *The Midnight Fox* by Betsy Byars, brings alive powerfully a young boy's conflict between loyalty to a vixen who trusts him enough to show him her young and the relatives – farmers who have given him hospitality and friendship. This entry can only mention a few of the animal stories that are such a big part of most school collections. But I would like to mention the books about farm yard and other animals by Dick King Smith. *The Sheep-pig, Dodos are Forever, Daggie Dogfoot* and *The School Mouse* and many others tell exciting stories with humour and compassion and are often about succeeding against the odds and making the best use of any talent you have.

The assumption that children enjoy factual books about animals has long been established: Thomas Boreman's *Description of Three Hundred Animals,* first published in 1730, went into seven editions and books like this have been published ever since.

Today software, CD-ROMs (using sound as well as visual effects and text to bring alive animal habitats), and the Internet join the ever-popular large-print encyclopaedias of animals and the traditional information books often concentrating on one species. The life cycles of creatures can be presented in narrative form and, with its similarity to story, is a sympathetic start to the world of information books for the very young. Quite a lot of books for the under sixes are structured by questions. *Are you a Snail?* in Kingfisher's Up the Garden Path series brings humour and excellent illustrations to the task of identifying a snail's characteristics. Animals that speak and dress are also used as a device to draw children into books imparting facts. For example, a mother and baby seagull have a conversation about the water cycle in MacDonald Young Book's *The Drop Goes Plop.* 'Genre confusion!' warn the purists – but children seem to find the imaginary journey exhilarating and they remember the basic information well.

The growing feeling that we should respect animals is not only apparent in the hundreds of guides to caring for pets but also in books raising questions about our wider treatment of animals like Miles Barton's *Why Do People Harm Animals* (Gloucester Press). Anna Sewell's concern for animal welfare lives on.

Hunt, Peter (ed.) 1995) *Children's Literature: An Illustrated History* Oxford and New York: Oxford University Press. (Chapter 7, Section on Animals' Lands.)

Townsend, John Rowe (1995 edition) *Written for Children* London: The Bodley Head. (Chapter 10, Articulate Animals.)

Anthology

See also poetry, short stories

An anthology is a collection of poems, songs, short stories or prose extracts, often by different authors and published in one volume. Collections of poetry and short stories are a most important resource in the Primary English lesson. Some poetry anthologies are tried and tested over time and still enjoyed – *The Oxford Book of Children's Verse* (Peter and Iona Opie); *Peacock Pie* (Walter de la Mare); *The Young Puffin Book of Verse* (Barbara Ireson) – while the many exciting newer ones – including *Island of the Children, an Anthology of New Poems* (Angela Huth); *Thawing Frozen Frogs* (Brian Patten); *Mind Your Own Business* (Michael Rosen) – cover every aspect of life at school and home and of course the inner world of the imagination. Short story collections often concentrate on a particular genre like fairy stories – *The Faber Book of Favourite Fairy Tales* (Sara and Stephen Corrin) – myths and legends – *King Arthur and His Knights of the Round Table* (Roger Lancelyn Green) – and folk tales from different cultures – *Anancy – Spiderman* (James Berry).

Useful also are the anthologies teachers make – collections of poems and extracts and annotated notes and book reviews gathered over the years to support their English work. Children make collections too – they like to hand-write and illustrate favourite poems on themes like Animals, People and Food and to place their anthology in the book corner.

Phinn, Gervase (2000) *Young Readers and Their Books: Suggestions and Strategies for Using Texts in the Literacy Hour* London: David Fulton (excellent sections on poetry anthologies for different age groups).

Antithesis

This is used as a more powerful alternative to the word 'opposite' as in the following sentence.

'This mechanistic approach to children's Art is the antithesis of all I believe in.'

Antonym

An antonym is the opposite in meaning of another word. For example, mean and generous, fast and slow, tall and short.

Apostrophe

See also punctuation

The apostrophe is used in three ways.

* to mark the omission or elision of letters and sounds as in *don't* (do not)
* to indicate a plural form, especially in abbreviations as in *NQT's*
* to mark possession in nouns *the boy's hat; the teachers' notebooks*

N.B. Use of punctuation changes along with other aspects of language. The use of an apostrophe to indicate a plural in the second example above is still 'correct' but becoming less universal. Email has led to a modification of the use of punctuation.

Apposition

When a noun or noun phrase is in apposition to another, it comes next to it and explains or in some way modifies it. Usually either one can be missed out without changing the broad meaning of the sentence. *Mr Blair* and *the British Prime Minister* are in apposition in the following sentence. 'Mr Blair, the British Prime Minister, sought re-election in 2001'. The terms 'partial apposition' or 'weak apposition' are sometimes used where only one of the nouns or noun phrases can be omitted. For example, in 'Mrs Wilson, until recently the acting deputy head teacher, left the school at the end of the summer term', *until recently the acting deputy head teacher* cannot stand alone without some modification.

Apprenticeship approach to reading

See also big shapes, metaphor, miscue analysis

The apprenticeship approach to the teaching of reading has been clearly explained in Liz Waterland's booklet published in 1988. Waterland's approach is based on the work of Frank Smith and Kenneth and Yetta Goodman. Kenneth Goodman famously referred to reading as a 'psycholinguistic guessing game' in which contextual clues are of great importance. Some critics of this approach, including Joyce Morris (1979), Katharine Perera (1980) and Marilyn Jager Adams (1991), consider that it underestimates the importance of word recognition skills and the development of strategies to understand large units of text in becoming a fluent reader.

The apprenticeship approach has gone out of favour in its more extreme form. Nevertheless, Frank Smith's insistence on the importance of the teacher as model reader continues to influence good practice and Goodman's diagnostic reading test – miscue analysis – continues to be used, usually in modified form, in many classrooms.

Waterland, Liz (1988) (second edition) *Read With Me: An Apprenticeship Approach to Reading* Stroud: The Thimble Press.

Appropriateness in language

See also language variety, register

This is a linguistic term referring to the fact that language varies according to the situation in which it is used. Children soon learn that the way in which they talk to Grandma at home is different to the way in which they talk to their friends in the playground. Likewise some forms that may be appropriate in speech are not appropriate in written texts.

Argument

See also genre, persuasive genre

Argument is a text type setting out the case for or against something. In the later primary years children are encouraged to develop their writing by following a rational theme to support or refute a case. Examples include: case for and against school uniform, sports days or fox hunting. Not only do children have to set out one view point, they also have to anticipate what might be said in opposition.

For a most thought-provoking account of young children's use of argument see chapter 8 'Developing Control of the Argument' in Riley and Reedy, 2000.

Riley, Jeni and Reedy, David (2000) *Developing Writing for Different Purposes* London: Paul Chapman.

Art and English

See also advertisements, Bible, book making, Carnival (and literacy), comics, History and English, illustrations, picture books, sacred texts, visual literacy

Art activities are an excellent context for learning a vocabulary to talk about making and creating things, to evaluate visual and tactile qualities, to develop understanding of how the visual and the verbal relate and to make explicit children's ideas about how to make imaginative use of their experience.

There is much potential for linking art with literacy both in and outside the Literacy Hour. The picture books which are widely used and enjoyed in the primary classroom provide many opportunities for children to begin to appreciate such artistic concerns as form, colour and composition alongside a written text. There is more about this under the 'picture books' entry.

Books can help children begin to understand about artists from different times and cultures. In the case of younger children, the books are often narratives. The story of Van Gogh's life as a painter is told in Laurence Anholt's *Camille and the Sunflowers* (Frances Lincoln); the book is a starting point for experiments with colour using different media. But it also leads to a search for words to describe the many different yellows and golds the artist used, and it invites the exploration of the characters' feelings about the paintings. By the later primary years children will begin to understand the social and cultural factors which can affect the work of an artist. The

story of Faith Ringgold shows the struggle of a black, woman artist from Harlem to achieve recognition for her work. Her story is told in *Faith Ringgold* by Robyn Montana Turner (Little, Brown, & Co) and children will appreciate that Faith's images – which vary from pictures of her slave grandmother to paintings of current figures like Michael Jackson – tell of the artist's personal history. Many exciting suggestions for children's own writing – biographical and autobiographical – and for their own art work can be triggered by this book and others are available in the Art and Literacy section of *Find That Book*.

Poems are often good starting points for children's pictures and some literature links well with the creation of timelines or friezes with illustrations. I have often seen the journey of Edward Lear's 'jumblies' represented in a lively and humorous frieze ('The Jumblies' in *A Book of Nonsense,* Dragon's World Publishers). Another favourite poem for inspiring art work is Robert Browning's *The Pied Piper of Hamelin.* A student of mine, working with nine year olds, asked them to create their impression of the landscape in the place where the children were taken by the piper. To get them underway, she showed them how different illustrators had imagined the land. Other teachers prefer not to show children other illustrations until after they have completed their paintings. I am still wondering which is the most fruitful way round. Perhaps children need more help than we sometimes appreciate to find ways of building illustrations from a poem or story and to understand that they are not limited to representational works but that an abstract picture might better capture mood and atmosphere.

Carnival is a context in which many media and many ways of celebrating blend – visual (costume making, dance, masks, masquerade), aural – (music) and verbal (poetry, improvisation and story). The Lambeth Schools Carnival Group have produced a pack of resources to support art, music and writing activities (details are below).

Book making also links English and Art in an interesting way: the complementary roles of written text and illustration come into strong relief and children are usually eager that their book should be aesthetically pleasing as well as being a successful story or non-fiction text.

Carnival in the Curriculum (2001) Lambeth Schools Carnival Group. (This is a pack costing £25 and containing instructions for making costumes and masks and ideas for all kinds of activities – art, music and language; from 13 Helix Gardens, Brixton, London SW2 2JJ.)

Find that Book: Making links between literacy and the broader curriculum (1999) Lewisham Professional Development Centre. (Tel. 020 8314 6146.)

Article

See also determiners

In English there are two articles: *the* – the definite article; *a/an* – the indefinite article.

The definite article can be used with any common noun – singular (the teacher) and plural (the teachers).

It also forms part of some proper names – *the British Museum*.

The indefinite article 'a' is used before consonant sounds – *a cat* and the indefinite article 'an' before vowels – *an apple*.

Assessment

See also miscue analysis, portfolios, primary language record (The), reading, record keeping, SATs, speaking and listening, writing

Rather than viewing assessment as something that always takes place at the end of episodes of work, it is helpful to see it as part of the whole cycle of learning. Assessment is an umbrella term for all the ways in which we evaluate children's progress. Our assessment of the pupils, whether it is built up through cumulative observation or is the result of a more formal set of tests of specific attainments, should feed back into the next cycle of planning and teaching. There are a number of possible formats for recording the results of assessment evidence. In assessing the children's progress, we are of course also evaluating the effectiveness of our teaching strategies and results will indicate if and how we need to modify these. This dynamic approach informs the assessment sections of the extended entries on each of the four language processes: Speaking and Listening, Reading and Writing.

There are some useful terms to keep in mind when selecting ways of assessing children's progress in English and indeed in the other primary curriculum subjects. One important distinction is between formative and summative kinds of assessment. Teachers make formative assessments as part of the everyday work of the class. This kind of assessment concentrates on a child's developing abilities and often diagnoses where help is needed. Comments on what the teacher has observed inform the pupil's profile. A great strength of this kind of assessment is that it is integrated with teaching and learning and feeds easily back into planning. For example, after a focus on fairy tales as a genre we might ask the children to write their own modern fairy tale. Their writing would be helpful and satisfying as part of their work and would also help the teacher see how far each individual had understood and applied features of the genre in their own writing.

Summative assessment comes at the close of a phase of work and in the United Kingdom, at the end of the Key Stages at seven years and eleven years. Records of summative assessments form the basis of reports for future teachers and for parents and provide snapshots of what a child has achieved at a particular age or stage. The descriptions of levels of achievement in the UK National Curriculum guide teachers in making summative assessments and standardised tests, for example the National Curriculum SATs in reading and writing, add information to the profile.

Where teachers wish to compare children's results with the average attainment, in reading for example, of a large number of pupils of the same chronological age, they use a standardised test. Norm tests provide a reading age which may be higher or lower than a child's chronological age. If we want to know how far a child has progressed in acquiring particular skills we use a criterion referenced test. The National Curriculum Levels of Achievement are criterion referenced since they compare a particular child's performance against the descriptions of each level of attainment.

Diagnostic tests are carried out to identify a child's particular difficulties in for example reading and writing. Where a child is judged to be eligible for a statement of special educational need diagnostic tests are carried out by an educational psychologist. These formally administered tests guide teachers in preparing and implementing an appropriate remedial programme. The miscue analysis entry explains how teachers can carry out a useful diagnostic reading test less formally.

Assimilation and accommodation

See also prior knowledge

Assimilation, the adaption of new material to an existing system, and accommodation, the adjustment of existing structures to new material are complementary processes in Jean Piaget's adaptive model of learning. To explain how an individual learns Piaget uses the analogy of the digestive system. When we eat something it has to be assimilated – changed by gastric juices in the mouth and stomach to become capable of being used by the body. At the same time, the digestive organs have to make adjustments to receive the food and allow for its passage through the organs of digestion. So it is with new learning: we have to present it in the right way for the young learner and it has to be capable of being absorbed into the young learner's existing frameworks of knowledge. The 'presenting new information in the right way' is crucial and at the heart of the teacher's professional skills.

One thing to take account of is the prior knowledge a learner brings to a new topic. Skilled teachers are able to help children organise their prior knowledge, often by inviting carefully orchestrated discussion. What we sometimes find is that children have concepts and understandings but do not yet control the formal vocabulary to refer to them. Part of the teacher's role is to help children move from what Piaget called 'spontaneous concepts' (those we acquire in the course of living – 'stone', 'food', 'water') to 'scien-

tific concepts' (usually acquired in formal contexts – 'igneous rock', 'vitamins', 'water cycle'). Vygotsky took over Piaget's classification of concepts and suggested how they could be exploited in classroom learning (Vygotsky, 1962/1986). For an account of how an understanding of 'spontaneous' and 'scientific' concepts can help us plan and reflect on lessons – in this case an interesting lesson about 'Rocks' to ten year olds – see Chapter 2 'Systematic learning: what is involved?' in Mallett and Newsome, 1977. This reminds us (at a time when work in United Kingdom primary schools can be rather subject orientated) that all good teaching has to begin with children's existing concepts – there is no other sensible place to start.

Educational theories come in and out of fashion but over a long teaching career I have found Piaget's adaptive model extremely helpful to keep in mind in my planning and teaching of both children and students. For a clear introduction to the work of Piaget, Bruner and Vygotsky and some helpful suggested applications to the classroom, I recommend David Wood's book *How Children Think and Learn*.

Mallett, Margaret and Newsome, Bernard (1977) *Talking, Writing and Learning, 8–13* Schools Council Working Paper 59. London: Evans/Methuen.

Vygotsky, L.S. (1986 edition with an introduction by A. Kozulin) *Thought and Language* Cambridge, Mass: The MIT Press.

Wood, David (1988) *How Children Think and Learn* Oxford: Blackwell.

Assonance

See also alliteration

This is the term used to refer to the repeated use of a vowel phoneme in poetry or prose for aesthetic impact or to enhance meaning by drawing attention to particular words. Examples include: 'handstand', 'easy to please', 'plain Jane'.

Atlas

See also geography and English, non-fiction reading and writing

An atlas is a book of maps and communicates visually. It is often best to start with simple map making when children are very young. They can begin to make maps of the classroom and the journey to school so the principles of the representation of space and distance are established. Then when they are ready for map books teachers can chose from a number of good first atlases for the under sevens including Longman's *Keystart First Atlas;* Franklin Watts' *Step by Step: Maps and Globes* and Wayland's *Big Book of Mapwork 1* which begins with maps from fairy tales.

The next stage is to look at clear maps of one country – Longman (Book Project) have an *Atlas of the British Isles* suitable for the 7–9 age range.

In the later primary years children are ready to understand more sophisticated cartography and the quality of the design and of the supporting materials are important. CD-ROM altases enable children to explore the world using multi media – interactive maps and video clips. The new technology can be motivating and empowering, but children need to be taught how to get the best out of it. Dorling Kindersley's CD-ROM package My First Amazing World Explorer is often bought for the under nines – but older children, particularly those with special literacy needs, can use it to acquire map skills in an enjoyable way. But the provision for older children should also include materials of the challenge of Dorling Kindersley's *World Reference Atlas* (which includes statistical charts) updated in 1998 and also in the 1995 PC and Apple versions. For many purposes, an ordinary atlas of good quality like *Philips Junior Atlas* will serve the need. *Going Places,* the Schools Library Service booklet, provides an annotated list of map books and atlases for different age groups. Maps can provide a reading challenge. It is best not to have maps with too small a scale or too much density of information. The best maps for the under elevens are not cluttered with more information than necessary. The organisation of the atlas is important as is the quality of the index which needs to have a good way of differentiating the names of towns, rivers and mountains. Children may need help with interpreting keys and symbols. Locators and comparitors will help children with world location and comparative size. There needs to be a good mix of colour maps, diagrams and statistics.

Mallett, Margaret (1999) *Young Researchers: Informational Reading and Writing the Early and Primary Years* London: Routledge (pp. 135–6).
Schools Library Service (1997) *Going Places: Resources for Geography.* Hertfordshire: Schools Library Service.

Attainment Targets

See also assessment, criterion referenced assessment, National Curriculum, SATs

Attainment Targets describe the standards children are required to meet in English and in all other subjects as they follow The National Curriculum Programmes of Study.

In English there are three Attainment Targets: Speaking and Listening, Reading and Writing. Primary children are normally placed at one of the first six National Curriculum English levels and it is hoped that as many children as possible will achieve a level 2 or above at the end of Key Stage 1 and at least a level 4 at the end of Key Stage 2. As each level in each Attainment Target is described in terms of criteria, this approach to assessment is described as 'criterion referenced'. It is also 'norm referenced' in the sense that expectations are linked to the likely achievements of other children of the same age.

Audio books/tapes/cassettes

See also book area corner

Audio books/tapes are cassettes containing the taped version of a printed book. Cassettes of children's stories are often bought together with the book for use in school. This gives an opportunity for children to hear sustained reading of a text and some children benefit from following the print version as they listen to the story being told. The strategy should, of course, be used as well as and not instead of reading out loud to children. Sometimes audio cassettes are included in packages like the Story Sacks series for the very young produced by Child's Play (0845 603 0220). *The Old Lady Who Swallowed A Fly* which won an Alcuin Award from the European Parents' Association is a typical story sack containing an audio cassette of the song and other favourites, a doll of the Old Lady into which bean-filled creatures like the spider and the fly can be stuffed and a board game bringing together words, pictures and memory.

As well as these commercial cassettes, teachers often build up resources by making their own recordings of favourite books. Older children sometimes make recordings for younger ones and sometimes parents will be prepared to translate stories into their children's home languages. There is a strong case for having a listening area with easily used tape recording and play back equipment and a good range of stories within the classroom, perhaps as part of the book corner.

Audio tapes of a child involved in shared reading can be added to their English portfolio to provide extra evidence of progress.

Audit (of Primary English)

See also English Co-ordinator, planning

English audits are carried out as part of a school's general cycle of curriculum improvement but are particularly needed when a new English Co-ordinator takes over, after an OFSTED Inspection or when new statutory requirements have to be put in place. During an English audit every aspect of the English curriculum is reviewed including resources and the school library, teaching approaches, assessment and record keeping. The auditing process leads to an action plan and to setting literacy targets.

The Co-ordinator might well begin by examining the school's English policy and noting where it needs updating or improving. The next stage is to identify some key questions about what needs to be found out and to note ways in which the evidence will be obtained and then presented to others. The most effective way of gaining a picture of the state of the school's

English work is by making careful observations during sensitively conducted visits to all the classrooms and talking to the teachers and the children. This helps show up any mismatches between what is written down in the policy and what actually happens. Sometimes teachers are asked to fill in questionnaires about their practice and views. This can generate a lot of work and the question sheet is best kept short!

The English Co-ordinator needs to liaise with the head teacher, the Co-ordinators of the two Key Sages and the Special Needs Co-ordinator. In a very useful analysis of the whole auditing process, Merchant and Marsh point out that peer observation in particular can be 'unnerving' for teachers. It is justified as probably the most powerful way to bring about professional development but it needs to be carefully managed (Merchant and Marsh, 1998, Chapter 3).

Once evidence has been collected from observations, discussions, questionnaires, reports, SATs results and English portfolios the next stage is to give feedback and work towards improvement of any areas shown to need attention. The Co-ordinator with energy and vision tries to create a good working atmosphere in the meetings and a sense of excitement about the changes – whether in teaching, assessment or improving the school library and in investing in new technology like software, CD-ROMs and the Internet. Realistic literacy targets should be agreed and supported by an action plan to ensure the development of good English practice in the school. The secret is to make the implementation of improvements a combined effort involving all the teachers in a constructive way. Tyrrell and Gill include an interesting case study in *Co-ordinating English at Key Stage 1* in which a Co-ordinator gains respect by allowing others to observe her own practice in a area which has been shown through the audit to need support. Teachers needed some help with 'modelling' how books work and helping children to understand book language. We are shown the steps by which the Co-ordinator demonstrated in her own classroom how children could be helped to enjoy a story *and* learn about reading and print as the use of speech marks, commas and capital letters were 'modelled'. The big book used was Joy Cowley's *Mrs Wishy Washy* (Story Chest) which has a welcome touch of humour about it. (Tyrrell and Gill, 2000 pp. 17–19.)

Tyrrell, Jenny and Gill, Narrinderjit (2000) *Co-ordinating English at Key Stage 1* London: Falmer Press (pp. 12–14 and 17–19).

Merchant, Guy and Marsh, Jackie (1998) *Co-ordinating Primary Language and Literacy* London: Paul Chapman (Chapter 3).

Authors of children's books – *see* history of children's literature

Autobiography

See also anecdotes, biography, genre, first person writing, letters

An autobiography is a first person account written by the subject which may seek to justify, explain or excuse as well as to inform. The boundaries between fact and fiction can become blurred as a writer selects and shapes particular incidents. What we get is one person's version of what happened and how they felt about it. 'Some autobiographies come near to being works of fiction and many works of fiction have autobiographical aspects' (McArthur, 1992, p. 98).

There are not many full length autobiographies for readers under eleven years but two good examples are Roald Dahl's *Boy: Tales of Childhood* (Puffin) and *Anne Frank's Diary* (Puffin, 1997). A case study of Year 6 children using these is under the 'first person writing' entry.

Autobiography is sometimes used in information books on recent history, see for example the *In Grandma's Day* series published by Evans in the late 1990s. Each book is organised round the memories of one person's life in the 1930s and 1940s. Reading about the memories of a real person living through dramatic times (for example as an evacuee in the Second World War) in the twentieth century gives children a different perspective on history. Such texts can also be used in English or the Literacy Hour to compare the features of first and third person accounts. For the mature ten year old and older children, the

autobiographical novel based on the diaries of Tittiana Vassilieva, *A Hostage to War* (Collins), is a powerful account of a young girl's courage during the famine caused by the Nazi invasion of the Soviet Union. The first person voice of the diaries (translated by Anna Trenter) speaks movingly of hunger, fear and the ceaseless toil of Tania as she faces work on the farms and factories of the Third Reich.

Where we want children to compare autobiography with biography, Roald Dahl's autobiography, *Boy*, might be compared with Chris Powling's short biography – *Roald Dahl* in Evans' *Tell Me About Writers* series.

Fictional autobiographies use the first person 'voice' as a literary device. There are always reasons for the choice of 'voice'. It may suit the author's purpose to show a set of events very powerfully from one character's viewpoint or to give an impression of spontaneity. Far from being easy to write in the first person, it is in fact a very sophisticated kind of writing which has to be carefully crafted to succeed. In *The Midnight Fox* (Puffin, 1980), for example, Betsy Byers wants the readers to share the intensity of the urban boy's experiences in the countryside. The use of Tyke's 'voice' in *The Turbulent Term of Tyke Tyler* by Gene Kemp (Penguin, 1979) gives the narrative energy and immediacy and draws the reader in more than a third person account might have done. Letters are an important kind of first person writing that can be a powerful literary device. They are used, to great effect, in Simon James' *Dear Greenpeace* (Walker Books, 1991) for children of about 6–8 years and, for older children, in Beverley Cleary's *Dear Mr Henshaw* (Puffin, 1983) and Harry Horse's *The Last Polar Bears* (Viking, 1993). Children whose roots are in countries far away from where they live often see letters as a way of bridging the distance between friends and relatives. For children of about nine plus, *Jazeera's Journey* by Lisa Bruce (Methuen, 1991) shows how letters can link lives, in this case the lives of Jazreera in England and her grandmother in Asia.

Reading books like those mentioned above can be a helpful starting point for children's own writing (see more about this under 'first person writing').

McArthur, Tom (ed.) 1992 *The Oxford Companion to the English Language* Oxford: Oxford University Press.

Mallett, Margaret (1997) *First Person Reading and Writing in the Primary Years* Sheffield: NATE.

Auxiliary verb

See also modal verb, parts of speech, verbs

An auxiliary verb adds meaning to another verb, as in the following:

'They *have* descended'.

'He *is* going'.

'*Can* you sing?'

In these examples 'have', 'is' and 'can' are auxiliary verbs and 'descended', 'going' and 'sing' are the main verbs.

The most frequently used verbs which can function as auxiliaries are 'be', 'have' and 'do'.

B

Ballad

See also poetry, verse

A ballad is a long poem or song telling a story. Traditionally, ballads were narrative poems sung to a simple musical accompaniment, passed down through the generations and adapted and changed by different singers. The old ballads tell stories about brave deeds or the momentous events of a particular community. The ballad was at its most popular in the late Middle Ages, especially in the border counties of Scotland and England. Sometimes a distinction is made between 'high' ballads about heroes like Sir Patrick Spens and 'low' ballads reflecting popular culture. Growing up in the North East, I often heard dialect ballads like The Lambton Worm – about a community threatened by the emergence of a monster from a weir–sung at gatherings and parties.

From the sixteenth century onwards printed poems called 'broadside ballads' about recent events became popular in England. (It is probably from this tradition that the folk songs of Bob Dylan and modern pop songs come.) But these coexisted with the continuation of 'high' ballads including the 'literary ballads' which were narrative poems written by established poets whose work took on some of the form and spirit of the old ballads. The ballads of the Romantic period include, for example, Coleridge's literary ballad – The Ancient Mariner (*Lyrical Ballads,* 1798). Scott's Proud Maisie and Keat's haunting La Belle Dame sans Merci are also well-known ballad poems.

In the primary years children over about eight years enjoy hearing ballads read out loud because of the exciting (albeit often ultimately sad) events, the strong rhythm and the repetition of words for dramatic effect. As part of the Literacy Hour text level work in Year 5, term 2 children consider the features of ballads and narrative poems. Of course we want them to respond to a good story most of all but children can also appreciate the short regular verses and rhyme scheme of a ballad. The pattern can take many forms, but traditionally the ballad stanza is a quatrain in alternate four and three stress iambic lines. Many of us can remember by heart the first stanza of Sir Patrick Spens and this is a good example of the classic ballad form.

> 'The king sits in Dumferling towne,
> Drinking the blude-red wine:
> 'O whar will I get a guid sailor,
> To sail this schip of mine?'

Children can be helped to acquire a vocabulary to enable them to discuss the characteristics of the poems. In his book *Young Readers and their Books* Gervase Phinn suggests we talk about features like for example the mood, theme, metre and figures of speech. We can also consider why particular words are used and how the characters are brought to life. The first verse of Sir Patrick Spens shows us the typically abrupt start ballads often have and the use of stark 'to the point' dialogue. Talking about all this will help children write their own ballads to read out loud and arrange in a book. A good place to start if you want to introduce a study of ballads is with a dramatic poem like, for example, The Highwayman by Alfred Noyes. This and other stirring ballads, like The Pied Piper of Hamelin by Robert Browning, are included in *The Oxford Book of Story Poems*. Some ballads are only found in general poetry collections and teachers often build up their own anthology over the years.

Of course the term 'ballad' is now often used to describe modern narrative poems which do not conform to the traditional stanza format. You will find help to extend interest and understanding of modern ballads with able, older primary children in Robert Catt's chapter in Fisher and Williams 2000. He concentrates on ballads and narrative poems on animal themes by present day poets, for example Charles Causley's I Saw a Jolly Hunter and My Mother Saw a Dancing Bear. Catt stresses the importance of careful reading of the poems out loud by teacher and children to communicate subtle meanings. His classroom examples indicate the importance of encouraging a 'community of enquiry' – a context in which children share with each other and the teacher their understandings and response to what are often heart rending and disturbing themes. Looking again at Catt's analysis of his work reminded me that teachers themselves, including myself, need much more than a superficial knowledge of ballad poems to develop work of high calibre.

Enjoying ballads

(Based on Holly Anderson's 'Follow the Piper' TES Primary, p. 47. 22.1.1999).

- Tell the children the story first.
- Share any interesting background e.g. *Pied Piper of Hamelin* based by Browning on a fourteenth-century legend.
- Compare different editions and their illustrations (Browning's poem is in his complete works, in a colourfully illustrated version published by Ginn, in *The Everyman Children's Classic,* illustrated by Kate Greenaway).
- Discuss particular sections and suggest how they illuminate character.
- Draw attention to choice of word and phrase and their effect.
- Improvise parts of the story – in *The Pied Piper of Hamelin* teacher in role as piper, perhaps.
- Script dialogues (e.g. between the children at different points in the story).
- Talk about deeper meaning/moral of the poem.

Catt, Robert (2000) '"Jolly good I said": using poetry with older children' in Robert Fisher and Mary Williams (eds) *Unlocking Literacy: A Guide for Teachers* London: David Fulton.

Phinn, Gervase (2000) *Young Readers and their Books: Suggestions and Strategies for Using Texts in the Literacy Hour* London: David Fulton (see p. 106 for Phinn's poem based on the Northern legend – The Legend of the Lambton Worm).

Baseline assessment

See also assessment, early learning goals, portfolios, Primary Language Record, the

Baseline assessment refers to the assessment, including language assessment, all children in England take at the start of their statutory schooling. These assessments, which are taken a few weeks after children begin in Reception classes, vary in different LEAs but must be in line with the National (QUA) Baseline Assessment scales. Teachers need to understand the requirements of the Early Learning Goals and the desired outcomes at the end of the Foundation stage when children will go on to Year 1. Assessments may be based on what teachers already know about the children or they can be based on planned assessments within the context of everyday classroom activities. The language aspects concentrate on early reading behaviour, letter knowledge and phonological abilities which might include saying or singing rhymes. Many teachers consider it helpful to have the information these early assessments provide and the tasks can be carried out in such a way that the child experiences little or no stress.

Even so, many early years teachers are concerned about the possible narrowing effect on the Foundation Years Programme that the existence of a simple summative set of tasks might encourage (Marian Whitehead, 1997, p. 180). The baseline assessments or something like them are likely to remain. We can help by also using approaches to monitoring assessment which go beyond the summative and sample the full range of children's language experience and knowledge (see for example the CLPE Primary Language Record, 1988).

Whitehead, Marian (1997, second edition) *Language and Literacy in the Early Years* London: Paul Chapman.

bias (in children's books)

See also factual genres, history of children's literature, reading

All books have a bias in the sense that they draw on an author's distinctive view of the world in general and on the story or topic in particular. But when we say a book is 'biased' we usually mean that there is some unwelcome favouring of one perspective over another in a way that distorts 'the facts'. Of course general agreement on what 'the facts' are, particularly in the more controversial and sensitive topics, is sometimes problematic.

When it comes to children's books, there are two main kinds of unwelcome bias. First, there might be a bias in the whole book collection towards texts by authors from one culture and where the characters and settings favour one approach to the world and human experience. Individually, such books may be excellent – they may meet important criteria like having powerful stories and convincing characters. Any book that is good of its kind and suitable for the age group is welcome. Rather, it is the possible omission of the work of authors from all parts of the globe, authors who can share with readers some different experiences and perspectives, that concerns us. This is why I support all those who feel teachers should be helped, in their college days and beyond, to acquire and continue to develop expert knowledge about the full range of books and resources for the age groups they teach. The handbook I find particularly useful when developing library collections is *A Multicultural Guide to Children's Books 0–16+* edited by Rosemary Stones. There are excellent lists under categories like picture books, myths and legends, poetry and fiction and non-fiction for different age groups as well as articles by authors and publishers. Helpful reviews of new books and software appear in a number of journals including, *The Times Educational Supplement,* *The School Librarian, Books for Keeps* and *Language Matters.*

The second kind of bias is to do with the content and attitudes expressed in particular books. I am thinking about stories or non fiction texts that offer a stereotyped view – in language or illustration – of gender, race or social class. Many of us are uneasy with the notion of censorship but none of us would offer children books and resources that were offensive to any of the groups that make up our society.

Stones, Rosemary (1999) *A Multicultural Guide to Children's Books 0–16+* London: Books for Keeps Tel. 020 8852 4953.

Bible, the

See also parable, sacred texts

The Bible is a collection of sacred books divided by Christians into two parts – The Old Testament and The New Testament. It is studied not only because of its religious significance but also as literature – it contains writing of many kinds including prose, poetry, epistles and prophecy. So great has been the influence of the Bible on Western culture that knowledge of the scriptures is important in understanding the work of many authors and poets, for example George Eliot, John Milton and William Blake.

Since the times of these writers we have become a much more plural society and there are stories for children based on other holy books as well as the Bible (see 'sacred texts' entry). The stories from both The Old Testament and The New Testament are used in Religious Education but also have a place in English lessons as powerful tales and parables with profound insights about the human situation. The best versions manage to communicate the deeper meanings. In a thought-provoking article in *Books for Keeps,* Ralph Gower urges us to seek retellings of holy books which retain the significance of the stories and therefore the approval of Jewish, Christian and Muslim believers. He considers, for example, that John Ryan's *The Very Hungry Lions* (Lion Publishing, 1999) gets nearer to the importance of the Daniel story to Jewish people than some of the other retellings for the very young. We need to look at the details added by authors to the tales and also at the illustrations, and ask ourselves whether these are distractions or helpful aids to understanding and reflecting. Children under eight years would find some of Mary Auld's retellings of Old Testament stories appealing – *Noah's Ark* for example (Franklin Watts). Walker Books' 'Bible Stories' series includes the dramatic tales – *Jonah and the Whale, The Amazing Story of Noah's Ark* and *Joseph and His Magnificent Coat of Many Colours* – all well written and illustrated by Marcia Williams in a colourful cartoon style that works well. *The Usborne Children's Bible* (written by Heather Amery for Usborne) draws stories from both The Old Testament and The New Testament and would be good for reading out loud to five to seven year olds. The younger end of this age group would also enjoy sharing two traditional tellings of the Christmas story – Heather Amery's board book (illustrator Norman Young) *Christmas Story* (Usborne) and Georgie Adam's picture book (illustrator Anna Leplar) *The First Christmas* (Dolphin).

Older primary children (and children in the early secondary years) might find *The Lion Graphic Bible* scripted by Mike Maddox and illustrated by Jeff Anderson (Lion Publishing) a vigorous if startling retelling. In comic strip, different formats are used to separate parables and dreams from the main text – very useful if children and teacher are considering the language and imagery of parables. Some might not like the very up to date language in the speech bubbles. Perhaps, too, the comic strip form can sometimes miss the more subtle connotations of some stories. This version could be used alongside a scholarly work like *The New Encyclopaedia of the Bible* which is edited by John Drane and provides comprehensive coverage of Bible history.

I was encouraged, by Ralph Gower's recommendation in his *Books for Keeps* article, to look at two collections (both from Macdonald Young Books) which take us beyond Bible stories. These are Sybil Sheridan's *Stories from the Jewish World* (which includes recent historical experience in the Holocaust) and David Self's *Stories from The*

Christian World which tells of the life of Francis of Assisi and of later important figures, including Adjai Crowther, the first black African bishop. Apart from their merit as powerful tales which illuminate aspects of human experience, the use of biographical material makes these source books helpful texts for the nine to eleven year olds following the National Literacy Strategy in the United Kingdom.

Gower, Ralph 'Biblical books for children' in *Books for Keeps* March 1999 No.115.

McArthur, Tom (1992) *The Oxford Companion to English Literature* London: QPD with Oxford University Press (pp. 116–24).

Bibliographic cue-system

See also cue-systems, phonics, reading, spelling

The bibliographic cue-system is less universally acknowledged than the other three which are semantic, syntactic and grapho-phonic (see separate entries). It comes into play when children use their existing knowledge of different written texts to identify the text they are reading. After tuning into whether it is fiction or non-fiction they might decide on assigning the text to a narrower category – for example a short story or a biography.

The bibliographic cue-system begins to be used at an early age. Very young children use their developing experience of books to understand features of the cover title and author and the relationship between pictures and text.

Big Books

See also Literacy Hour

For many years Big Books, about 50 x 36 centimetres, have been used to develop young children's literacy. The National Literacy Strategy has brought them to the fore as a major resource in the shared reading part of the Literacy Hour and publishers have responded to this need by producing books for Key Stage 1 and Key Stage 2. Some books are written specially in large format. Others are enlarged versions of smaller format books and many of these have proved successful resources for class-based work, for example Jenny Baker's rain forest book *Where the Forest Meets the Sea* (Walker Books), Manning and Granstrom's *What's Under the Bed* (Franklin Watts) and a number of Walker's Read and Wonder titles – *Big Blue Whale* and *Spider Watch*. However, books with a lot of print on each page, with tiny labelled diagrams or many small, detailed and delicately coloured pictures may not survive the expansion so well. Children have to be able to see the print and pictures easily and to read headings, labels and diagrams if they are to benefit from the teacher's demonstration.

Big books come in all genres – stories, poetry, reference and information books. The important thing to check is that they are good examples of their kind with clear inviting language and illustrations that link well with the written text. Mallett, in an article 'Non-fiction in the Literacy Hour' (*Books for Keeps*, 1998) reminds us to choose at least some books that have a touch of humour to enjoy sharing. Children learn about the features of each kind of book, often joining with the teacher in reading out loud. Teachers will draw attention to text-level aspects – the setting, characters and plot in fiction and the distinctive global organisation – headings, information boxes, retrieval devices – of the different kinds of non-fiction text. In both fiction and non-fiction there will be a focus on the links between illustration and written text, on the author's choice of vocabulary and on helping children use their knowledge of context and sentence structure to make meaning from print. A Big Book may be at the centre of the literacy work for a day or a week, inspiring interesting reading and writing activities in the guided and independent group work which follows the shared reading and writing slots.

In Chapter 2 of his book *Young Readers and Their Books,* Gervase Phinn (2000) sets out some annotated Big Book recommendations for different ages and stages. Some publishers of Reading programmes build in progression. For example Cambridge Reading's Big Books Literacy Packs are organised so that children in Reception and Year 1 are not overwhelmed with too many retrieval devices all at once. Thus *Dinosaur* is an information story about one particular species – the Maiasaur – from egg to adults but with information boxes to introduce non-narrative text. *Coral Reef* for the end of Year 2 features contents page, an index and good clear labelled diagrams. Children and teachers can also make their own Big Books to join the selection. Indeed enjoying Big Books can lead to exciting shared writing. At Goldsmiths College in South London Carol Eagleton, a primary specialist in Art, helped student teachers over a number of years to make Big Book resources with their pupils based on the approach in Don Holdaway's influential book – *The Foundations of Literacy* (1979).

For a thorough and inspiring account of how to plan and carry out work in the shared reading parts of the Literacy Hour see Chapter 3 in Graham and Kelly's *Reading Under Control.* They advise against doing too much on a text all at once and remind us that 'First and foremost, you are modelling the pleasure and rewards to be gained from the overall reading of a text'.

In its Big Book form, the pictures of the Tasmanian rain forest in *Where the Forest Meets the Sea* by Jeannie Baker, reproduced by permission of the publisher Walker Books (1987), inspire lively discussion about environmental issues and often encourage children's own writing.

<table>
<tr><td>

Recommended Big Books

For Key Stage 1

Splish, Splash, Splosh Mick Manning and Brita Granstrom, Franklin Watts, about the water cycle

What Babies Used to Wear Anne Witherington and Bobbie Neate. Longman. Pelican Big Books

My Cat Likes to Hide in Boxes (a comic poem) by Eve Sutton. Puffin

Dinosaur Roar by Paul and Henrietta Strickland. Puffin

The Big Hungry Bear by Don and Audrey Wood. Child's Play International (some visual aids are available – a red story sack with mouse strawberry and wooden knife and an audiotape version of the story with music)

For Key Stage 2

World War 11 Anthology, various authors selected by Wendy Body. Longman Pelican Big Books

An Encyclopaedia of Greek and Roman Gods by Brian Moses. Longman Pelican Big Books

Words Borrowed from Other Languages by Sue Palmer. Longman Pelican Big Books

History from Photographs by Kath Cox and Pat Hughes. Wayland/ MacDonald

Rain Forest by Meredith Hooper. Cambridge Reading

</td></tr>
</table>

Graham, J. and Kelly, A. (2000, second edition) *Reading Under Control* London: David Fulton.

Holdaway, Donald (1979) *The Foundations of Literacy* Sydney: Ashton Scholastic.

Mallett, Margaret (1998) 'Non-fiction in the Literacy Hour' in *Books for Keeps* September No. 112.

Phinn, Gervase (2000) *Young Readers and Their Books* London: David Fulton.

'Big shapes'

See also 'bottom-up' reading approaches, interactive reading model, reading, 'top-down' approaches to reading

'Big shapes' refers to the larger textual structures which provide a framework for the reading process; the term tends to be associated with 'top-down' approaches and the search for meaning. Barrs and Thomas explain the term, on page 6 in *The Reading Book,* as follows. 'These large overarching textual structures – such as different kinds of narrative structures, and the structures that relate to different genres – and the way these are reflected in the rhythms and tunes of written language, are a most important source of knowledge which readers have to draw on, in addition to their sense of the unfolding meaning of a text, to support their reading.' The importance of recognising 'the tune on the page' suggested by these writers has had great influence on good practice. The 'big shapes' aspect of reading is recognised in the text-level objectives of the National Literacy Strategy *Framework for Teaching* (DfEE, 1998).

However, important as sensitivity to these 'big shapes' is, there are, as Barrs and Thomas make clear, other important aspects of reading. There needs to be careful teaching of the 'smaller shapes' as well: letter- and word-level work, phonetic information and letter-sound correspondence. Good initial teaching of reading manages to orchestrate strategies to develop the different aspects of reading and to integrate the best of both 'top-down' and 'bottom-up' approaches. For clear, practical advice about combining the different aspects in classroom routines I recommend Graham and Kelly's analysis in Chapter 3 of their book *Reading Under Control.* They emphasise the role of story telling and reading stories out loud in drawing children's attention to the bigger shapes of literacy – developing their contextual and semantic understanding – while showing also how graphic and phonic work fits into the programme.

The term 'big shapes' can be used more generally to refer to larger structures in bodies of knowledge. Margaret Meek uses it in Chapter 7 of *Information and Book Learning* when considering the challenge of learning history in school and making sense of history texts. 'The problem for readers begins with the writers' difficulties in relating the "big shapes" of historical time to the minutiae of any given event.' Although we have more information sources than ever and the printing techniques to reproduce original documents, she fears we may still lack enough 'interpretative text' to fit bits of information together to achieve some overall coherence.

Barrs, Myra and Thomas, Anne (eds) (1991) *The Reading Book* London: Centre for Language in Primary Education.

Graham, Judith and Kelly, Alison (2000, second edition) *Reading Under Control* London: David Fulton.

Meek, Margaret (1996) *Information & Book Learning* Stroud: The Thimble Press.

Bilingualism

See also dual-language texts, equal opportunities, language variety, mother tongue, multiculturalism, multilingualism

People who are bilingual can operate in two languages. While in Britain and the United States operating in one language, monolingualism, is the norm about half the world's population is bilingual 'and kinds of bilingualism will present in every country of the world '(McArthur, 1992, p. 126).

Definitions of bilingualism vary from equal competence in both languages as speakers, readers and writers, to much greater competence in one language or incomplete competence in either. Skutnabb-Kangas offers the following definition of being bilingual as able to 'function in two (or more) languages, either in monolingual or bilingual communities, in accordance with the sociocultural demands made on an individual's communicative and cognitive competence by these communities and by the individual herself, at the same level as native speakers, and being able positively to identify with both (or all) language groups (and cultures) or parts of them' (Skutnabb-Kangas 1984, p. 90). This very full definition reinforces the notion that taking

on a language involves taking on a culture. The high level of linguistic and cultural competence described in Skutnabb-Kangas' definition is our ultimate aim for young children entering our schools as learners of English as an additional language. There are, however, a number of important and quite complicated issues here. Even the terminology is problematic and the terms themselves change: 'English second language learners' (ESL), and 'bilingual children' became in the 1990s 'children with English as an additional language'. In her book *Making Sense of a New World* Eve Gregory points out that teachers in some countries avoid using the term 'bilingual' because it might 'deflect attention from the fact that children need help as they go about learning in a new language' (Gregory, 1996, p. 8). Gregory goes on to suggest that the term 'emergent bilinguals' is appropriate to refer to children who are at the very beginning of the journey that will take them to the level of competence in Skutnabb-Kangas' definition. Such children may come from very different cultural and linguistic backgrounds but have in common that they are usually the first in their family to receive formal education in their new country and do not speak the language of the host country at home.

There are issues about how far official requirements for a prescribed curriculum and frequent testing in Britain are helpful to emergent bilinguals. The official attitude is that children should control their new language as speakers and listeners, readers and writers as soon as possible. The intention is good – that these children should maximise their opportunities in their new society. However, if they are to maintain the very real linguistic and cultural advantages of being bilingual, they need also to be encouraged and enabled to continue to use and develop their competence in their mother tongue. These are complex issues – for example some parents want the emphasis to be very much on their children's swift acquisition of the language of their 'host' country. The books mentioned below explore these issues further, often like Gregory (1996) sharing case studies of the progress of particular children. Drawing on them, I now offer some pointers to good practice in supporting emergent bilinguals at school and classroom level.

- *Positive attitudes.* A young bilingual benefits from a school culture that recognises becoming bilingual as positive – as leading to increased linguisitic awareness and cultural sensitivity. The whole school community can benefit from the knowledge and expertise of emergent bilinguals and their parents. Nevertheless, the teacher plays an important role in helping children to become bilingual and helps coordinate formal and informal learning (Gregory, 1996, p. 8).

- *Knowledge and understanding.* Educators need to have as much knowledge as possible about the spoken and written forms of the languages represented in the communities whose children they teach and about the cultural context. Whitehead (1997) acknowledges that we are unlikely to have the linguistic skills and cultural experiences to meet all language needs. The knowledge we need is the kind which supports our professional expertise, see for example Baker (1995) for advice for parents and teachers. We can also encourage the participation of parents, grandparents, older siblings and members of local linguistic groups. Indeed to be effective practitioners we need to know about the children's literacy experiences at nursery schools, play groups and in religious settings in their communities.

  Our efforts to become informed about all this communicates to emergent bilinguals and their families the respect we feel for their languages and cultures.

- *Interaction with peers.* Emergent bilinguals benefit greatly from learning alongside their monolingual peers and the benefits are mutual. The recent trend has been away from setting up withdrawal units where children tended to learn English through de-contextualised exercises. One encouraging thing is that what seems beneficial to emergent bilinguals is also good practice for all children: conversation round practical tasks in science, mathematics and technology (children link language and meaning through a general sense of the context); games where instructions and activities are linked and repeated; stories in a shared and interactive context; writing for real audiences and purposes. For a more detailed analysis of these issues see Wiles, 1985.

- *Story telling and listening.* The telling of stories with dramatic expression, gesture and story boards and other props like dolls, boxes and hats helps children learn their new language in an enjoyable way. The very young also learn well through the rhythms of rhymes, songs and verse (see Hester, 1983 for helpful suggestions).

- *Reading and listening to stories.* When they have stories read to them children experience structured language as opposed to the relatively unstructured language of everyday conversation. This structure which basically consists of a beginning (providing a setting for a story and an introduction to characters), a middle (where things happen and a plot develops) and an end (at which point conflicts and problems are resolved) is sometimes termed a 'story grammar'. The text children hear is stored as a resource for retelling their own stories. Fox (1988) and Dombey (1988) have contributed to our understanding about this. The language resource that written stories provide is valuable to all children and not least to emergent bilinguals (Gregory, 1996).

- *Learning to read.* Young children learning to read in a second or additional language need careful help over coordinating the cueing systems. We have to remember that contextual cues may not be as available to them as to other children – even now that we have universal supermarkets and global news programmes. Monolingual children are more secure in the idiom of their language and quickly grasp 'knife and fork' and 'fish and chips'. Children whose first language is in another script have to learn a new set of symbols. Word order in a language also relies on culturally acquired knowledge. As Gregory, 1996 shows, young readers in a second language usually catch up quickly, but we still need to be aware of their needs.

- *Dual-language texts.* These are often traditional stories and criteria for selections are discussed under the entry of this name. The best are a helpful resource but we need to check the quality of the language and illustration. Dual-language labels and signs are sometimes helpful, but other languages can also be brought into high status curriculum areas like mathematics and geography. Whitehead encourages children, parents and teachers to write their own bilingual texts using all the available technology of computers, printers and photocopiers, laminating machines and cameras. As well as producing dual-language versions of stories, poems and songs we can extend our enterprise to anecdotes about the children's lives, games, birthday cards and letters. Such collaborations could also lead to helpful multi-language materials for real purposes and audiences. (Whitehead, 1997 p. 80).

- *Multicultural resources.* All children deserve the very best books and resources from across the world. If we have in our class children whose roots are in a particular country we seek out the best stories from that place. Here we would be helped by Rosemary Stones' book *A Multicultural Guide to Children's Books.*

Baker, C. (1995) *A Parents' and Teachers' Guide to Bilingualism* Clevedon: Multilingual Matters.

Edwards, V. (1998) *The Power of Babel: Teaching and Learning in Multilingual Classrooms* Stoke-on-Trent: Trentham Books.

Gregory, Eve (1996) *Making Sense of a New World: Learning to Read in a Second Language* London: Paul Chapman.

Hester, Hilary (1983) *Stories in the Multilingual Primary Classroom: Supporting Children's Learning of English as Second Language* London: ILEA (alas, out of print at present but obtainable by libraries).

McArthur, Tom (1992) *The Oxford Companion to the English Language* London: OPD for Oxford University Press.

Skutnabb-Kangas, T. (1984) 'Multilingualism and the education of minority children' in Skutnabb-Kangas, T. and Cummins, J. (eds) *Minority Education* Clevedon: Multilingual Matters.

Stones, Rosemary (ed.) (1999) *A Multicultural Guide to Children's Books 0–12* Books for Keeps with Reading Language and Information Centre.

Whitehead, Marian (1997 edition) *Language and Literacy in the Early Years* London: Paul Chapman (see pp. 78–80).

Wiles, S. (1985) 'Language and learning in multi-ethnic classrooms: strategies for supporting bilingual students' in Wells, G. and Nicholls, J. (eds) *Language and Learning: An Interactive Perspective* London: The Falmer Press.

Wyse, Dominic and Jones, Russell (2001) *Teaching English, Language and Literacy* London: Routledge (see Chapter 29 'Supporting black and multilingual children').

Biography

See also factual genres, genre, non-fiction reading and writing

The author of a biography usually writes about the life story of another individual in the third person. Along with autobiography, biography is one of the more literary kinds of non-fiction. At best, as Margaret Meek argues, it is '… an encounter with a life and ideas' (Meek, 1996).

The National Literacy Strategy *Framework for Teaching* brings in biography during the first term of Year 6 (10–11 year olds). However, children can appreciate this kind of writing from an early age and often encounter short biographical accounts in history and religious studies texts. If you want to introduce children to some short, illustrated biographies you might find useful Evans Brothers' *Tell Me About* series which includes biographies of writers for children such as Enid Blyton, Roger Hargreaves, Beatrix Potter and Roald Dahl. The author of the last of these, Chris Powling, does not hide the more eccentric aspects of Roald's nature 'he was an outsider – someone who never behaved as other people expected him to'. The cruel things that happened to Dahl – the illness of one of his children and his wife – are included as well as his achievements. Children above about eight years would manage most of the books in this series.

Biography can link history and English helping us to see the private as well as the public person (Hoodless, 1996). Some biography-type books for children introduce biographical details of famous people through story. Hodder and

Stoughton's 'Little histories' series is suitable for children of about seven years and older and titles include *My Uncle Was Sir Francis Drake* and *Remember, Remember the Fifth of November* both by Rob Childs. Josephine Poole's beautiful subtle picture book *Joan of Arc,* illustrated by Angela Barrett, would be enjoyed from about eight upwards (Hutchinson) Older primary children will be ready for more conventional biographies, for example Leon Ashworth's *Queen Victoria* and Neill Tongue's *I Have a Dream: the Story of Martin Luther King* (Franklin Watts).

History books often tell of the deeds and policies of prominent people but biography can help show how ordinary lives were lived at different times. For children over ten years, Raymond Briggs' comic strip biography *Ethel and Ernest: A True Story* (Jonathon Cape) shows the ups and downs of domestic life in the period leading up to the 1930s. Briggs catches how his parents are affected by the impending war and by the changes it will bring for people like them. Children appreciate the background detail and the moving story of the main characters.

Film and televisual texts can spark an interest in the lives of both famous and ordinary people at different times. Channel 4 Learning's 'Famous People' series includes presentations of the lives of Grace Darling, Neil Armstrong and Ghandi.

Letters, photographs, timelines, maps, posters, theatre programmes are all used in biographies and autobiographies to complement, illuminate and extend the written text. Children can be helped to see all of these as identifying typical features of the genre and learn to use them in their attempts at biographical writing.

Hoodless, Pat (ed.) (1996) *History and English: Exploring the Links* London: Routledge.
Meek, Margaret (1996) *Information and Book Learning* Stroud: The Thimble Press.

Blank verse

See also free verse, poetry

Blank verse is a form of poetry which has rhythm and metre but not rhyme. It is often in iambic pentametres – lines of ten syllables with an unstressed/stressed syllable pattern. This pattern is evident in the following lines from Shakespeare's *A Midsummer Night's Dream* spoken by Oberon Act 1V, Scene I.

'I did then ask of her her changeling child:
Which straight she gave me, and her fairy sent
To bear him to my bower in fairy-land'.

Children are unlikely to write in blank verse in the primary years, but by age 10 or 11 they may encounter it in their first forays into Shakespeare's work and in some classic poetry.

Blend

See also cluster, phoneme, phonics

The noun 'blend' is a synonym for a cluster of sounds while the verb 'blend' refers to the process of merging phonemes when someone decodes a word.

Blurb

See also modelling (of language processes), reading

The 'blurb' is the writing on the back and flaps of the book cover which tells potential readers about the content and style of the book and often provides bibliographic detail about the author. We can help children to scan the 'blurb' to find out if they want to read a particular book. Information about the kind of book they have picked up, and whether they have read some of the author's other works is useful and makes them active selectors of what they read. However, children must also realise that 'blurb' does not mention weaknesses as well as strengths as a review does since authors and publishers want us to read and buy their books and are likely only to put positive things about them. We need to remember this when we read 'This is the best book on…' or 'Highly acclaimed, this book will…'.

Book area/corner – see reading area/corner

Book making

See also Art and English, blurb writing

Making books is an enjoyable and meaningful way for children to learn about reading and writing and has an important place across the curriculum. The actual making, decorating and illustration of the books links English to Art and to Craft Design and Technology. At Goldsmiths College, book making has long been considered to be of great value and students and children have made and continue to make an exciting range of books of all shapes and sizes and on all possible topics. Stories of all kinds, poetry books, big books and the full range of non-fiction texts appear again and again in the book making workshops. More recently we have added electronic books to our repertoire. The covers have been varied and inviting – some in the shape of animals real and fantastic – dragons, unicorns, bears, lions and foxes – others made to look like houses, castles, footballs, birthday cakes, pizzas and household objects like disks, telephones, plates, rubbish bins and chairs. With the help of Carol Eagleton, a primary teacher with a specialism in Art, students and children have been helped to use a range of fabrics – wall paper, silver foil, cloth, sandpaper and fur to make the illustrations arresting. We have found children and students are most inventive and love making little doors, wheels that turn, unusual games and pop-ups to add fun and interest. Very young children need direct teaching about folding and cutting and of course safety rules should be observed by everyone and perhaps displayed in the form of a chart. From time to time teachers and children enjoy making hard-covered books that are bound, glued or stitched but it is less time consuming to make simple concertina and origami books (see *You Can Make Your Own Book* by Paul Johnson, Addison Wesley, 1998 in small and big book format).

As well as individual children making books with the help of an adult, other contexts include children working in pairs or groups and even as a whole class where the different tasks will be shared out. Older primary children making class magazines or newspapers enjoy taking up roles as editors, feature writers, illustrators and proof readers.

Book making whether the text is hand written or word processed is hugely motivating and satisfying – but there are a number of other important reasons to encourage children in this activity.

Most importantly, making their own books involves children in the kind of talk and reflection that help them understand how books work – bringing into conscious focus the nature and conventions of written language. They take on the role of author which involves them in important choices. When writing a story, for instance, they need to decide on the setting, plot and characters and whether to tell the tale from the point of view of one character or in the third person. If the latter, might they include direct speech? Often this brings energy to the tale and helps with characterisation as well as providing the teacher with an excellent opportunity to reinforce paragraphing and speech marks. And indeed, book making is a good context in which to attend to transcriptional aspects of writing as children usually care enough about their book to want it to be above reproach in spelling, punctuation and general presentation.

Book making can make an important contribution to a young writer's understanding of genre. Stories and non-fiction texts are organised differently because they have different purposes. While a story follows a time sequence and builds momentum as it proceeds, a non-fiction book is usually non-narrative and is organised according to the dictates of the subject. Children learn to divide the main topic into smaller topics and aspects and to use sub-headings to indicate this. They learn also about the retrieval devices – contents page, index and glossary – which help the reader find their way round the book. The kind of illustrations a book has identify it with a genre and book making helps children understand what is appropriate and how illustrations complement and sometimes extend the written text. Thus actually writing a non-fiction book teaches a child more about the distinctive genre features than anything else can do.

On those occasions where a hard-back book is created with a dust jacket, children have the opportunity to use a different kind of writing – the 'blurb' to promote their work and some brief biographic details.

Because it is a relatively sustained task, book making is an excellent context in which to encourage children to plan their writing, make a rough draft and then re-read and refine the draft into the final copy. The word processor has made this much easier and discussion round the computer with other children or the teacher about how to improve the draft is particularly valuable.

I have already mentioned that the attention of a child making a book can be drawn to the fact that the purpose of a piece of writing is linked to certain genre features: a story, for example about a journey, might be to thrill, move or just simply enjoy while a non-fiction book, on boats and ships perhaps, would need to provide accurate and interesting ideas and information. The other fundamental aspect of any piece of writing is the intended audience since the interests, age and ability of the likely readers also has a considerable effect on how the book is written and illustrated. Older primary children often enjoy producing books for the younger children in the school. Sometimes teachers arrange for the older and younger children to meet up before the book making starts to agree on the sort of book that is wanted and then again at the end of the project to share the work.

Every writing task has the potential to involve the other three language processes – reading, talking and listening. But the sustained nature of the book making activity and the high level of interest that usually accompanies it makes this a particularly rich context for language development. Child and supporting adult (or other members of the group) discuss each decision, listening carefully to each other's views and the writing is constantly reviewed by being read back to each other. Once the book is made children often like to read it to the class or a group and again this gives rise to further talk and questions.

Helpful books for teachers which develop these points further include Paul Johnson's *Children Making Books* and D. Smith's *Through Writing to Reading*. For advice about non-fiction

book making and a detailed account of a child working with her teacher and her mother (who took the photographs) on a pizza recipe book – see my *Young Researchers*. A lively, information filled and entertaining book for children aged about nine to eleven is Powling and Anderson's *The Book About Books*. As well as good sections on whether electronic books will replace paper ones and what makes a classic, there is a helpful attempt to explain how an author creates a book.

It is important to help children to share the books they have made with their class, with other classes in assembly and with a wider audience by displaying them on open evenings. The computer, printer and photocopier all make it easier for children to make more than one copy of their book so that they can take it home as well as enjoy having it in school. In one school I know two children made such an interesting book on dragons that six copies were made for group reading. Books made by children are often placed in the classroom collection in the reading corner. Sometimes they are included in the library.

Johnson, Paul (1995) *Children Making Books* Reading: Reading and Language Information Centre, University of Reading.

Mallett, Margaret (1999) *Young Researchers: Informational Reading and Writing in the Early and Primary Years* London: Routledge (see chapter 4).

Powling, Chris and Anderson, Scoular (2001) *The Book About Books* London: A & C Black.

Redfern, Angela and Edwards, Viv (1997) *Practical Ways to Inspire Young Authors* Reading: Reading and Language Information Centre, University of Reading.

Smith, D. (1994) *Through Writing to Reading: Classroom Strategies to Support Young Authors* London: Routledge.

Book review

See also portfolios, writing area/corner, reading diaries, writing

A book review is a written evaluation of a text. It usually gives a brief outline of the events in a story or novel (or an indication of the scope and coverage of a non-fiction work) and goes on to comment on strengths and possible weaknesses.

Reviews of children's books, software, CD-ROMs and websites – both fiction and non-fiction – appear in journals, for example *Books for Keeps, Language Matters* (CLPE), *English 4–11* (The English Association) and *The School Librarian* and professional papers like *The Times Educational Supplement.* There are also a number of websites featuring teacher reviews (see under Further Information).

Teachers ask children to write reviews of books and resources, sometimes in a reading diary (see separate entry) and sometimes they ask for a longer review for display or for a class book. Always being expected to write a review after reading a book or using a resource becomes tedious. On the other hand we do want children to reflect on what they read and to develop some criteria to judge quality.

There should be a list on file of the main reading each child does each term, but I would be inclined to ask for a full length review only from time to time and to try to vary the tasks and set them up in interesting ways.

Suggestions for Reviews of Books and Resources

- Very young children like writing their short reviews inside the shape of an animal or object in the story. I have seen a colourful display of such reviews of Eric Carle's *Bad-tempered Ladybird* written in the ladybird shapes the children had drawn themselves.
- Children very much appreciate it when a teacher or student teacher does some writing specially for them. Where the whole class has enjoyed a shared reading of a novel or story the teacher could join the children in writing a review and make a display with the story, novel or picture book in the centre. If the book has been written recently and

reviews are available in *Books for Keeps* or another journal, older children might appreciate a published review on display as well. Sometimes publishers or book shops will be prepared to send a poster or other publicity material to enliven the display.

- Choose an author the children like and display children's reviews of all or some of his or her books. Ask the children to say why they prefer one particular book by this author. I have seen this done with the work of Dick King-Smith, Roald Dahl, Anne Fine and Michael Rosen.
- Ask the children if they have a favourite kind of story, for example – animal stories/poems, horror stories, amusing tales, fairy tales or traditional stories from different cultures. Choose a different kind of story for review every few weeks and ask the children to read out their work.
- Have a focus on a particular aspect of stories – plots, settings, characters – and ask older children to compare this aspect in books by different authors. After reading out the reviews there could be a class discussion.
- Formats for writing reviews including headings for setting, plot, characterisation, illustrations, language, would you recommend this to a friend? and so on – can help some children get started but can become rather mechanistic if the same one is used too often. Rather than always presenting children with a given format, they might enjoy planning their own with sub-headings to organise their writing. One child asked to do this suggested giving each book a star rating from one star to five 'on excitement'.

So far, I have had reviews of fiction in mind but I find both boys and girls enjoy evaluating non-fiction texts – both print and CD-ROMs if the task is set up in an interesting way. For example, I asked children from a Year 5 class (nine year olds) to read and make notes on two non-fiction picture books based on the same theme. Each of the books was based on the true tale of Mary Anning, a young girl who discovered a dinosaur skeleton at Lyme Regis: *Stone Girl, Bone Girl* by Laurence Anholt (1998) illustrated by Sheila Moxley (Doubleday) and *The Fossil Girl: Mary Anning's Dinosaur Discovery* by Catherine Brighton, presented in cartoon format.

The children noted:

- that although each writer had gone to the same sources, each had chosen to emphasise different parts of the story.
- the style of illustration was matched by the language used to tell the story.

The books were displayed together with the children's reviews on a table in the literacy corner.

The books and then the reviews were read out loud and led to a class discussion about fact and opinion and the advantages and possible disadvantages of using a cartoon format.

We often invite authors of poetry and fiction for children to visit our schools but it is worth asking good non-fiction authors if they would tell the children about their work.

BBC ONLINE: Education: Schools Online. Look and Read: Spywatch – website is http://www.bbc.co.uk/ education/lookandread/lar/index.htm

British Educational and Communications Technology Agency (BECTA) – a large database of information and reviews of resources by teachers; website is http:// www.becta.org.uk

Homerton College, Cambridge Teachers evaluating educational multimedia – http://www.teem.org.uk/

The Virtual Teacher's Centre (part of the National Grid for Learning) includes 'Literacy Time' which provides teachers' reviews of print and electronic texts – website is http://www.vtc.ngfl.gov.uk/resource/literacy/index.html

The Fossil Girl: Mary Anning's Dinosaur Discovery by Catherine Brighton, Frances Lincoln, tells the true story of a young girl's discovery of the first complete Ichthyosaur fossil in lively comic strip form.

Stone Girl, Bone Girl: The Story of Mary Anning by Laurence Anholt and illustrated by Sheila Moxley, published by Doubleday, a division of Random House, tells the same story as that in *The Fossil Girl* but emphasises Mary's family relationships and the influence of other 'curiosity' collectors on her hobby. Children of about eight or nine enjoy the challenge of comparing the two tellings.

Book Trust

The Young Book Trust section of Book Trust is a resource and information centre which houses a large number of children's books. Its priority is 'bringing books and readers together'. Members receive regularly updated and helpfully annotated book lists for specific age groups and abilities, for example 'Beginning to Read 5–8', 'Newly Fluent Readers 6–10 and 'Confident Readers 8–11'.

The Young Book Trust also awards book prizes and supports research into children's reading and literature. One major recent initiative was a five-year pilot called Bookstart which pioneered the provision of books for the very young. Parents were encouraged to read with their children.

Young Book Trust; Tel. 020 8516 2977
Website: www.booktrust.org.uk

Books for Keeps

An international children's book magazine principally providing reviews of books and other materials, fiction and non-fiction from pre-school to 12+. Contents also include author interviews, articles on all aspects of writing for children and a useful briefing page covering news, letters and book prizes. There are six issues a year and the editor is Rosemary Stones.

Tel. 020 8852 4953
E-mail: booksforkeeps@btinternet.com

'Bottom-up' reading approaches

See also big shapes, interactive reading model, 'top-down' reading approaches

'Bottom-up' approaches are based on the assumption that reading is initially learned by manipulating the smallest units of language – letters and words. Traditional phonics teaching was based on this approach. In contrast, what are often called 'top-down' approaches, concentrate on prediction and guessing and on young learners searching for meaning rather than just decoding words.

For a clear explanation of how 'bottom-up' and 'top-down' approaches can be combined to promote an 'interactive' model of reading see Chapter 2 in Jeni Riley's book *The Teaching of Reading.*

Riley, Jeni (1996) *The Teaching of Reading* London: Paul Chapman Publishing

Boys and English – see gender

Brainstorming – see concept mapping

Breakthrough to Literacy

See also reading, reading schemes

Breakthrough to Literacy, developed by David McKay *et al.* for publication in 1970, is a reading programme based on children's own experiences and language. It consists of banks of words, letters and punctuation marks which are arranged in pockets and can be displayed on a wall at a height children can easily reach. The children have sentence makers – small stands in which they can build up sentences which become their first reading materials. Children compose sentences about their lives and the programme is therefore associated with what has been termed 'the language experience approach' to reading and writing. I remember teachers who liked the programme very much, but others found it difficult to keep track of all the word bank items and found organisation rather labour intensive.

The small reading books are colour graded according to readability and while some retell traditional tales, many of them are on topics close to the children's experience like 'The Loose Tooth' and 'In the Park'. The developers of the programme visited primary schools and asked the children what they would like their reading books to be about.

Some teachers still use the word banks and sentence makers to help children understand the concept of a word and a sentence. However, the programme is unlikely to be used alone as it has too little emphasis on phonological aspects of reading to be in tune with current United Kingdom practice.

Bristol Language at Home and School Project

See also early years Language and Literacy, research (into Primary English)

Directed by Gordon Wells, this longitudinal study carried out during the 1970s and 1980s showed a strong link between young children's familiarity with story and their later success in reading and writing. Wells argues that having books read to them at an early age helps children understand about the de-contextualised nature of print, something that does not become evident in encounters with environmental print. Stories take us away from our immediate context and serve as a bridge to the abstract.

The analysis of a large number of recordings of preschool children and parents talking suggested that ordinary family activities often provided excellent contexts for literacy learning. Parents who use writing often during the day – notes, letters, shopping lists and so on – provide strong models of literacy and their children do particularly well as writers when they get to the later primary years.

The project generated many articles and books. *The Meaning Makers: Children Learning Language and Using Language to Learn* (Hodder & Stoughton, 1987) is particularly helpful and inspiring to teachers of the primary age range. It follows a representative sample of children from their first words to the end of the primary years. The transcripts of children, parents and teachers talking and the telling classroom vignettes make this a useful and enjoyable read.

British Educational and Communications Technology Agency (BECTA)

This Internet site <http://www.becta.org.uk> is a huge database which can be searched by subject or key stage. It includes reviews by teachers, advisers and librarians on books and resources. There are links to the National Grid for Learning/Virtual Teacher Centre.

Bullet point

See also paragraphing

This is a device used in text books and in word processed accounts to set out a related sequence of information or list.

For example, in *The Framework for Teaching* (DfEE, 1998) Year 4, Term 1 handwriting entry number 16 is set out as follows using two bullet points:

'16. to know when to use:

- a clear neat hand for finished, presented work;
- informal writing for everyday informal work, rough drafting, etc:'

It is helpful for children to learn about bullet point format and to use it in some of their non-fiction writing. Over use of the device, however, risks disorganising a piece of writing.

Bullock Report

See also history of English teaching, language across the curriculum, LINC materials, subject knowledge

The Bullock Report, *A Language for Life,* was presented in 1975 by the Committee of Inquiry set up by the Secretary of State for Education and Science, Margaret Thatcher, in 1972. Chaired by the historian Sir Alan Bullock the committee investigated all aspects of the teaching of English as a mother tongue, advised on how practice might be improved (and the role that initial and in-service training might play) and made recommendations about how children's levels of attainment might be monitored.

The tone of the report, which was over 600 pages in length, was optimistic and constructive. The committee recommended that teachers in both primary and secondary schools should have informed views on how children make progress in learning to talk, read and write and work towards a whole-school language policy.

Although we now have in the United Kingdom a more prescribed approach to teaching English than the Bullock Committee envisaged, many of their recommendations continue to influence our thinking and practice. For example, the importance of talk in learning in every lesson, the contribution parents can make by taking an interest in children's reading and writing and the recognition of Language Study and Subject Knowledge as important parts of English work all have their roots in the views underpinning the Bullock Report.

Cambridge Reading

See also reading schemes

This up-to-date reading programme, first published by Cambridge University Press in 1996, provides a wide range of books covering all the genres mentioned in the National Curriculum and The National Literacy Strategy *Framework for Teaching*. It spans an age range from Nursery/Reception to Year 6 and many of the reading books are by well-known writers and illustrators. In line with the 'Searchlight' model which informs current United Kingdom official frameworks, the programme includes phonics and reading skills, aims to develop a sight vocabulary and recognises the importance of reading for meaning and enjoyment.

Capitalisation

See also full stop, punctuation, sentence, proper noun

This term refers to the consistent use of capital letters to begin the first word of a sentence and the first letter of a proper name, for example of a person or city. But are the rules for capitalisation in English clear cut? In his detailed account, Tom McArthur (1992) comments that some people prefer to capitalise the first letter of the first word of a phrase following a colon others keep to lower case. Convention favours the latter option but the former is not judged to be 'wrong'. Is it the 'Earl of Essex' or the 'earl of Essex'? Either is acceptable but more people feel easier with the former when designating an actual title.

While we need to understand that use of punctuation changes as do other aspects of language and that there are some areas of dispute, we can agree that by about seven children should have been taught the following:

- English is one of the languages that has two interlocking systems of letters – upper case and lower case.
- Sentences always begin with a capital letter and end with a full stop.
- Names of people, cities, countries, titles, days and months and so on begin with a capital letter.
- 'I', referring to the writer, is capitalised.

McArthur, Tom (1992) *The Oxford Companion to the English Language* Oxford: QPD with Oxford University Press.

Caption

This is usually a title or short explanation introducing a diagram or picture.

Case study approach to research – see under research

Carnival (and literacy)

See also Art and English, diary, non-fiction reading and writing

Carnival is a celebration which uses many art forms – dance, art, costume making, drama and masquerade. In Britain carnivals take place in towns and cities in the summer months and the largest is Notting Hill Carnival. Cultural influences from Africa, Asia, Europe, the Americas and the Caribbean are combined. Lambeth Schools Carnival Pack is an excellent starting point for a school carnival.

There are rich opportunities for channelling the excitement and enthusiasm Carnival generates into literacy activities – talking and improvised drama and stories and poems. In her article

'The Carnival's coming to town' (*The Guardian* 17.7.01) Celia Burgess Macey suggests children could be encouraged to develop their autobiographical writing abilities in Carnival diaries as well as non-chronological reports.

Carnival in the Curriculum (2001) Lambeth Schools Carnival Group. A pack of information, activities, resources for costume making and card masks, colour illustrations and ideas costing £25 from 13, Helix Gardens, Brixton, London SW2 2JJ.

Burgess-Macey, Celia 'The Carnival's Coming to Town' in *The Guardian*, Tuesday 17 July 2001, p. 48.

Cartoon – see comics

Catalogue

A catalogue is a list of items, often in the form of a booklet, which sets out for example items for sale or for mail order. Bibliographic catalogues provide the contents of a library or libraries.

Cataphoric reference

See also anaphoric reference

This is a forward reference in a text. So in – 'If he wanted to, Harry could concentrate for long periods' – 'he' is cataphoric.

Cassettes – see audio books/tapes/cassettes

CD-ROM (Compact Disk-Read Only Memory)

See also fairy tales, fiction, information books, Information Communication Technology (ICT) and English, non-fiction reading and writing, and visual literacy

CD-ROMs are disks which are read by a computer system and usually combine a number of media – text, video and sound. They have 'hot-links' which allow the user to move from one piece of text to another by clicking on a word or phrase. Children need help in navigating successfully and retrieving information from a vast store. As Lydia Plowman (1998) puts it: 'The main navigational problem is knowing when all the relevant information on a given topic has been seen and how it relates to the structure of the multimedia document.' Visualising the mainly invisible structure of the text in its entirety requires some experience and sophistication.

Educational CD-ROMs need to achieve the right balance between educational and entertainment aspects. Some CD-ROMs have little educational content despite their title. CD-ROMs should not just be books on a screen but should allow users to explore pathways and make good use of sound, animation and video. Marian Whitehead urges us to be selective about the 'reading books' on CD-ROM we select – they should not 'simply replicate dreary primers and mask meaningless text with visual tricks and loud music' (Whitehead, 1997, p. 170). Useful general criteria for judging quality are emerging. I have developed the following questions based on the criteria the British Interactive Multimedia Association uses for its annual awards (BIMA 01733 245700).

Does the CD-ROM:

- Match with the needs of the age group it is intended for
- Engross and entertain the young learner
- Make imaginative use of the technology
- Prove a suitable medium for the subject
- Enable the user to navigate easily
- Provide quality search systems and bookmarks
- Offer quality content – taking account of accuracy, comprehensiveness, creativity and interest
- Offer quality images and audio experiences

CD-ROMs are well established as resources for the primary curriculum (see John Garvey, 2000 for a detailed account). They are used for teaching reading – for example the Dr Seuss's ABC ('Living Books' series) and Nursery Rhyme Time (Sherston) – and are part of the fiction collection in class and school libraries. But perhaps their impact on children's research across the curriculum has been most significant. The information in a set of space-consuming print encyclopaedias can be placed instead on a disk for easy storage. Publishers of children's reference books – dictionaries, atlases, encyclopaedias and thesauruses – have been producing CD-ROM versions for some time. 'My First Amazing World Explorer', for the under nines, has an interactive picture atlas, games and activities to teach about map skills and it includes enjoyable extras like a jigsaw and a sticker map (Dorling Kindersley). 'Oxford Children's Encyclopaedia' from Oxford University Press is an easily used electronic resource with a huge range of information for children from about eight years upwards. Like similar electronic reference texts, it offers video-film and animation to extend what is described in writing. For example, you might see part of a frog's life cycle – the laying of eggs and tadpoles emerging from the spawn – in short film extracts. Being able to see machines working and animals moving makes viewing a CD-ROM highly motivating for many children, and a different sort of experience to reading print. Nevertheless, we should remember that reading books remains a distinct experience and electronic interactive media complement rather than replace books. In fact many publishers offer a CD-ROM together with a book as a package. Two-Can Publishing (Zenith Entertainment plc) have an exciting range of combined resources in their Interfact series. The electronic extension activities link extremely well with each sub-topic. For example in *Water,* the double spread on 'Shipshape and Seaworthy' has a disk link which allows the young learner to control a fleet of cargo ships, to learn about how ships float at sea and how you have to judge the right weight of cargo if the vessel is to be seaworthy.

Garvey, John (2000) '"Incredibly Creative Tools": using ICT and multimedia' in Fisher, Robert and Williams, Mary (eds) *Unlocking Literacy: A Guide for Teachers* London: David Fulton.

Plowman, Lydia 'Reading multimedia texts: Learning how CD-ROM texts work' in *Language Matters* Spring 1998.

Whitehead, Marian (1997 edition) *Language and Literacy in the Early Years* London: Paul Chapman.

Centre for Language in Primary Education (CLPE)

See also Primary Language Record (The), record keeping

This professional development centre for teachers in nursery, primary and special schools is based in Southwark, London. It has had considerable influence on primary English, language and literacy and assessment and record keeping throughout London, more generally in the United Kingdom and in other countries, particularly the United States.

It is well established in three areas. First, it has an excellent library of books and resources and is well known for the quality of its own publications, not least *The Primary Language Record Handbook* and *The Core Book: A Structured Approach to Using Books Within the Reading Curriculum.* Second, it links closely with schools and offers a wide range of consultancy services and professional courses. Thirdly, the staff carry out classroom based research, one recent initiative being a spelling project which is described and evaluated in *Understanding Spelling* by Olivia O'Sullivan and Anne Thomas (CLPE, 2000). Another research study draws on research in Year 5 classrooms on the links between the study of literature and writing development and a main outcome was *The Reader in the Writer* by Myra Barrs and Valerie Cook (CLPE, 2001).

Centre for Language in Primary Education website is www.rmplc.co.uk/orgs/clpe/index.html

Chapbooks

See also history of children's literature

Chapbooks were inexpensive works of popular literature sold by itinerant pedlars from the sixteenth to the nineteenth centuries in Europe and America. They usually contained ballads, romantic stories, folk and fairy tales. Up until the start of the eighteenth century their often bawdy humour made them suitable reading only for adults. But by about 1800, children's chapbooks containing nursery rhymes, alphabets, prayers, riddles and stories were increasingly sold. By the end of the eighteenth century children's chapbooks were small – about 4 x 2 ¹/₂ inches (10 by 6 cm) – and about 16 pages in length. The leather covering of the earlier adult chapbooks was replaced with rough paper, rather like sugar paper. There is a detailed account of the form and history of children's chapbooks in Carpenter and Pritchard, 1984. These authors comment that many chapbooks whether for adults or children were not only poorly printed and spelt but they were also sometimes written 'with little or no regard for the dramatic shape and highlights of the story' (*ibid.* p. 107). But nevertheless there were some important contributions made by the tradition of chapbooks. They were the only form of imaginative literature accessible to a large number of poor people. Their existence also ensured the tradition of nursery rhymes and fairy tales was continued into the nineteenth century. Some publishers, Rusher of Banbury in the nineteenth century for example, produced small children's books of some merit (*Jack the Giant Killer*) with woodblock illustrations, sometimes hand coloured. Those seeking more information about the place of chapbooks in the history of children's publishing would enjoy Chapter 2 in Peter Hunt's *Children's Literature: An Illustrated History* which also includes a number of interesting illustrations showing the different formats of chapbooks at different times.

Carpenter, Humphrey and Prichard, Mari (1984) *The Oxford Companion to Children's Literature* Oxford and New York: Oxford University Press.

Hunt, Peter (1995) *Children's Literature: An Illustrated History* Oxford: Oxford University Press (Chapter 2).

Chart

A chart is a type of diagram or table often with a numerical element. Children learn that the kind of illustrations used in a book or resource help identify it with a particular genre. For example, charts in geography texts may show variations in temperature or population while in history they may take the form of timelines and family trees.

The verb form of chart as in 'The explorer's next task was to chart the island' means to make a map of an area or, more generally, as in 'We need to chart our progress over the next few weeks' to construct a plan of action.

Child-centred learning

See also big shapes, creative writing, hobbies and English, *Plowden Report*

Child-centred or progressive models of learning, following the theories of Rousseau, Dewey and Froebel, afford experience and discovery a central position. At the heart of this philosophy, especially in its more extreme forms, we have a horticultural metaphor which views the adult's role mainly 'as provider of a rich soil in which to watch the child bloom' (Czerniewska, 1992). In the first half of the twentieth century, English teaching in the primary years leaned towards a 'basic skills' model and children spent much time on grammar and spelling exercises. In the 1960s, partly as a move away from what many saw as a mechanistic attitude to learning which regarded young children as 'sponges' soaking up teaching input, there was a move towards recognising the needs, interests and preoccupations of the young learners. The 'personal growth' model of language development shows how a child-centred approach can be used in English. The teacher's role was to provide experiences in a motivating environment, to provide quality resources including story books and to be an audience to children's talk and writing. Rather than fit the child to the curriculum, child-centred teachers adjusted the programme to the needs of individual children. If you want to get a flavour of this approach I suggest you read John Dixon's book *Growth Through English*. The Plowden Report (1967) celebrated the talking and writing that came out of the best classrooms during this child-centred period.

Current approaches favour a more structured approach to the teaching of English in which teachers intervene to support children's progress in all aspects of language development. Most children need systematic help to become readers and writers and contexts for speaking and listening need to be carefully planned and set up.

It is worth retaining some things of value from a child-centred approach. A child's special interests, abilities and precoccupations are an important consideration. The spoken language reveals these and its role in learning is central in childcentred approaches; it has a very important role in any English programme and across the whole curriculum as a tool for learning. It is also wise and motivating for children to have choice about some of the writing they do in the classroom. Sometimes, it is helpful for them to concentrate on compositional aspects – the content and flow of their writing, attending to the transcriptional aspects in a later draft (Frank Smith, 1982). 'Differentiation' in teachers' planning helps us take account of the needs of particular children and the current emphasis on involving them in monitoring their own progress in reading and writing is very much in the spirit of a child-centred approach.

Czerniewska, Pam (1992) *Learning About Writing* Oxford UK and Cambridge USA: Blackwell.

Dixon, John (1967) *Growth Through English* Oxford: Oxford University Press with NATE.

Smith, Frank (1982) *Writing and the Writer* London: Heinemann.

Child Language Acquisition – see Language Acquisition

Children's literature – See history of children's literature and adventure stories, advertisements, animals, autobiography, ballad, Bible, biography, classics, comics, dual-language texts, factual genres, fairy tales, folk tales, haiku, historical novels, horror, illustrations, legend, library skills, multimedia, myths, newspapers, novel, parable, picture books, playscripts, poetry, reading corner, reading range, sacred texts, science fiction, short stories, traditional tales

Children's literature awards

There are a large number of awards and prizes for the best fiction and non-fiction for children. News of these is available on websites in professional journals like the *TES* and in specialist journals on children's literature like *Books for Keeps* and *The School Librarian*. Below is a selection of some of the best known.

Awards for fiction include:

The Smarties Book Prize is divided into three age ranges – 5 years and under, 6–8 years and 9–12 years.

The Blue Peter Book Awards are in three categories – 'Special Book to Keep Forever', 'The Book I Couldn't Put Down' and 'Best Book to Read Aloud'.

Grinzane Junior Award is an international children's book award – the first winner, in 2000, was Emma Chichester Clark for her picture book *I Love You, Blue Kangaroo*, Andersen Press.

2000 Special Educational Needs Book Award gives a prize to the book the panel consider most successfully provides a positive image of children with special needs.

Guardian Children's Fiction Award selects the best children's novel.

The Carnegie Medal is a Library Association Award (in memory of Andrew Carnegie, the great benefactor of libraries) for the author of what is judged to be the most outstanding book for children of the previous year.

The Kate Greenaway Medal, The Library Association, is awarded to a book with outstanding illustrations.

Sainsbury's Baby Book Award complements the Bookstart programme which gives out books at the 8-month health check and is sponsored by Sainsbury's and co-ordinated by the Book Trust.

Exelle Awards for Black Publishing include a prize for the best children's book in a multicultural context.

Books for Children Mother Goose Award goes to an outstanding illustrator of children's books.

The Keith Barker Millennium Children's Book Award is a special award given by The Schools' Library Association in memory of the contribution of Keith Barker who was reviews editor of *The School Librarian* for many years.

The Signal Poetry Award

The Children's Book Award is run by the Federation of Children's Book Groups and awards prizes for the Picture Book Category, The Shorter Novel and The Longer Novel and an Overall Winner.

Awards for non-fiction include:

- *The Times Educational Supplement* Information Book Award (Junior–9 years and under).
- *English 4–11* (The English Association) *Picture Book Award* given for an outstandingly good informational picture book for children aged 4–7 years and one for children aged 7–11 years each May. Website: www.le.ac.uk/engassoc/
- *Earthworm Children's Award* (Friends of the Earth) for the best book of the year on environmental issues.
- *The Science Book Prize* (The Science Museum, London) for an outstanding science book for the under 8s.
- *Junior Aventis Prize for Science Books* for an outstanding science title for the under 14s.

Finally, *The Eleanor Farjeon Award* is presented by The Children's Book Circle (e-mail: jo.williamson@harpercollins.co.uk) for distinguished services to children's books.

Choosing books and resources – see audio books/tapes/cassettes, CD-ROM, core books, creation stories, fairy tales, fiction, folk tales, history of children's literature, Information and Communications Technology (ICT) and English, information stories, legend, myths, non-fiction reading and writing, picture books, reading range, traditional tales

Chorus

See also poetry, rhyme, rhythm, verse

The noun 'chorus' can refer either to a group of singers or to the part of a poem or song which is repeated after each verse. Its origin is in Ancient Greece where a 'chorus' (khoros) of actors or singers gave the commentary in plays. A similar role is found in Elizabethan drama – the chorus in Shakespeare's *Henry V* draws us into the action. Used as a verb, if people 'chorus' something they say it together.

Children usually learn about the function of a chorus by singing songs in music lessons and reading and writing poems with this feature. Poems with a chorus that children enjoy performing are *The Pied Piper of Hamelin* by Robert Browning (1842) and *Goblin Market* by Christina Rossetti (1862). T.S. Eliot's *Old Possum's Book of Practical Cats,* published by Faber Paperbacks in 1974, includes several poems where the chorus contributes to the energy and message – *Macavity: the Mystery Cat, The Old Gumble Cat* and *The Rum Tum Tugger.*

Chronological non-fiction

See also factual genres, information story, narrative, non-fiction reading and writing

Chronological non-fiction (or narrative non-fiction) is a term used to refer to any text which is organised mainly on a time sequence basis. The most commonly encountered kinds of chronological non-fiction in the primary and pre-schools years are 'information stories', 'procedural' kinds of writing (including recipes and instructions for experiments in science) and early autobiographical writing.

Circle time

This refers to times when a whole class of young children at the Nursery or Reception class stage sit with the teacher in a circle to share news, opinions and feelings. Sometimes, to help with understanding of 'turn taking' conventions, the teacher will hand an object like a toy or ball to whoever is invited to speak. Where this is working well the atmosphere is relaxed and non-threatening and listening to others is praised as much as spoken contributions.

Class discussion – see collaborative learning, discussion text, Drama and English, plenary, Speaking and Listening

Class reader

See also fiction, narrative, novel

The class reader is the novel or short story chosen by the teacher to read aloud to the class over a period of time. The children may or may not have their own copies of the text to follow the reading. In the United Kingdom, the structured nature of the Literacy Hour has led to older primary children in particular hearing short extracts rather than having the experience of enjoying the whole text. There are important reasons for finding time to read a whole work to the class. Above all listening to and discussing a quality work of literature brings the class together as a community of readers and listeners and places the emphasis on enjoyment and sharing. I have often heard children make insightful comments about the boy's conflict of loyalty in Betsy Byers' *The Midnight Fox* – should he care most about his hospitable farming relatives or about the vixen who has trusted him with a glimpse of her young? Younger children love talking about dangers in the environment and about family relationships when hearing Dick King Smith's *The Hodgeheg*. The discussion which accompanies the reading is often of high quality – there are few better contexts for sharing thoughts, ideas and feelings. Just listening to a fine plot unfolding, interesting characters developing and savouring the setting in which the author places the story is educative. Less forward readers listen to language and imagery in books which they are not yet able to tackle independently. The shared context is also helpful to young learners for whom English is a second or additional language. Response can be deepened through carefully chosen writing and drama activities – for further suggestions see under 'fiction'. Sometimes just reading and talking about the story is enough but for further suggested activities see under 'fiction' in this book and in Graham, 1997, Graham and Kelly, 2000 and Marriott, 1995.

Graham, Judith (1997) *Cracking Good Book* Sheffield: NATE.

Graham, Judith and Kelly, Alison (2000, second edition) *Reading Under Control* London: David Fulton.

Marriott, S. (1995) *Read On: Using Fiction in the Primary School* London: Paul Chapman.

Classics (of children's literature)

See also fiction, history of children's literature, picture books

Classics are books with lasting appeal. But what qualities are needed to achieve this endurance in books for those under eleven years? It would be brave to set out criteria, not only because they might be challenged, but also because I believe works of undoubted value and originality would slip through them. So what follows is no more than some observations about what seems to help a book earn classic status.

Classics link the generations – parents often want to share what they enjoyed with their own children. And parents often instinctively choose to share powerful stories that are not 'time bound'. They may be set in a distinct period but their imaginative appeal seems to set them above a particular time so that children of different generations can enjoy and respond to them.

No-one would deny the importance of a gripping, page-turning story but classics, in addition, tell us something universal about the human situation – about conflict, confusion and loss, and about achievement against the odds, kindness and love – very often through the eyes of the growing child. This is what I think Julia Eccleshare (2001) has in mind when she refers to a book capable of 'tapping into the constants of childhood and of parent/child relationships' (p. 9).

The best books create a strong setting – a coherent world – for the events and characters they create. These imaginative worlds, sustained throughout a story, are valuable achievements in their own right but also create wonderful refuges for the young reader – an escape sometimes from the harshness of the real world. Of course the imaginary worlds created in books are often far from bland or cosy but often full of challenge and danger as readers of *The Hobbit, The Borrowers* and the Harry Potter series know. Perhaps the point is that it is easier to face virtual dangers than real ones.

Of course a large number of books having these qualities have been written over the years, but those works which are consistently recognised as classics have some of them to an unusual degree.

There is debate about which children's books justify being called 'classic' and people disagree about the merits of particular works. Teachers, scholars of children's literature and children themselves would, if invited, produce different lists of the 'ten best classics', although I would expect the same three or four books to appear in most selections. My own list? *Black Beauty* by Anna Sewell, *Alice in Wonderland* by Lewis Caroll, *The Secret Garden* by Frances Hodgeson Burnett, *The Wind in the Willows* by Kenneth Grahame, *The Tale of Peter Rabbit* by Beatrix Potter, *The Lion, the Witch and the Wardrobe* by C.S. Lewis, *The Silver Sword* by Ian Serraillier, *Carrie's War* by Nina Bawden, *Tom's Midnight Garden* by Philippa Pearce, *The Iron Man* by Ted Hughes. I found it difficult to stop at ten.

Publishers produce editions of established classics alongside more contemporary books which seem to have classic potential. It is interesting to see which titles are included in publishers' lists – Puffin Modern Classics (*The Borrowers* by Mary Norton, *Stig of the Dump* by Clive King) and Oxford University's Oxford Children's Modern Classics (*Flambards* by K.M. Peyton and *Eagle of the Ninth* by Rosemary Sutcliffe). If you want to learn more about the best contemporary books you would enjoy Tony Watkins and Zena Sutherland's chapter in Hunt (1995). For a most interesting analysis of the role of publishers in sustaining interest in the classics and helping establish newer classics, see Julia Eccleshare's article in *Books for Keeps,* 2001. While welcoming publishers' initiatives which keep outstanding books in print, she hopes this will never be at the expense of promoting good contemporary literature.

Eccleshare, Julia (2001) 'The proliferation of modern 'classics' in *Books for Keeps* No.126, January.

Watkins, Tony and Sutherland, Zena (1995) 'Contemporary Children's Literature, 1970–present in Hunt, Peter (ed.) *Children's Literature: An Illustrated History* Oxford: Oxford University Press.

Classroom assistant

Those wishing to be classroom assistants can complete a training course covering all the areas in which they contribute. These include: helping to prepare materials, displays and organise resources; joining in team planning discussions; supporting the work of individual children and small groups; recording children's progress. Classroom assistants are very important in English lessons. In the Literacy Hour they help by filling in observation grids during shared reading for use by the teacher in the plenary. Many assistants become very skilled at their work and this allows the teacher to use his or her expertise to the full.

Clause

See also adjectival clause, adverbial clause, grammar, sentence, subject knowledge

A clause is a group of words containing a verb. It can sometimes stand on its own as a simple sentence or it can be a structure within a sentence as in 'because I wanted to' in 'I went to the party because I wanted to'. There can sometimes be two clauses, capable of existing independently, joined by a conjunction as in: 'I went to the party and I had a good time'. The clauses in this example could become short sentences: 'I went to the party'. 'I had a good time'.

Clause analysis involves breaking down a sentence into its constituent clauses. So let us consider how the following sentence – 'When they departed, they discovered that their coats had been left behind' – might be broken down. 'They discovered' is the main clause; 'when they departed' is an adverbial clause of time modifying the verb 'discovered'; 'that their coats had been left behind' is a subordinate noun clause, object of the verb 'discovered'.

Although there has been a move back towards the study of grammar as part of English work, few would advocate formal clause analysis in its extreme form in the primary years. One issue is whether studying clause analysis would have a beneficial effect on children's writing. There are some interesting tasks round clauses and sentences for children in *The Primary Grammar*

Book by Bain and Bridgewood. If you are teaching in England or Wales you need to consult the National Literacy Strategy *Grammar for Writing* guidance document.

In the United Kingdom teachers are required to have knowledge about sentences, phrases and clauses as an underpinning to their teaching. For a clear account, see Chapter 7 in Angela Wilson's book *Language Knowledge for Primary Teachers*.

Bain, Richard and Bridgewood, Marion (1998) *The Primary Grammar Book: Finding Patterns – Making Sense* Sheffield: NATE.

Grammar for Writing National Literacy Strategy. DfEE 2000.

Wilson, Angela (2001, second edition) *Language Knowledge for Primary Teachers: A Guide to Textual, Grammatical and Lexical Study.* London: David Fulton.

Cliché

This is a phrase or idea which has lost its impact because it has been overused. Some metaphors – 'the apple of his eye' – and similes – 'as good as gold' – come into this category. However, the favourite sayings of a culture tell us much about values, beliefs and attitudes. Our shared knowledge of what they mean can be a quick route to communication and it is quite difficult to avoid clichés altogether. Indeed the sheer familiarity of some much-used phrases can sometimes serve a useful function – by helping us through upsetting or difficult situations. We find ourselves saying 'it may be for the best' or 'there are other fish in the sea' to comfort others. In written form, except for direct speech, clichés tend to be tedious ('In this day and age'; 'explore every avenue'; 'the bottom line'). I recently reviewed a book which aimed to help children write stories. It recommended that young writers used linking phrases like 'out of the blue' and 'suddenly I heard a loud noise…' This will help you control the adventure story genre, it claimed. I doubt it! Children are capable of thinking of phrases of their own which have more energy and originality than these exhausted notions.

Cloze procedure

See also cue-systems, Gap Reading Comprehension Test, grammar

'Cloze' stands for 'closure'. It refers to a reading task in which children 'guess' the words needed to fill the gaps deliberately omitted from a text. So the procedure is used not only to assess children's prediction abilities but also as a diagnostic tool showing where teachers can fruitfully intervene to give finely tuned help to a young reader (for example to help them understand how verbs and objects need to agree). Cloze procedures can also be used to measure readability of a text.

Sometimes in cloze procedures, the words to insert in the various gaps are given at the foot of the passage, at other times young readers have a free choice of words. Teachers may choose to construct their own cloze exercises or use published examples. The words omitted may be a particular part of speech – adjectives or conjunctions perhaps. Or every nth word is missed out but here the remaining text must provide enough semantic and syntactic support to enable its successful completion. During the task children use their knowledge of syntax and semantics to fill in the omitted words. Syntactic knowledge helps a young reader sense whether, for example, the word will be a verb or a noun and to tune in to subject-verb agreement when deciding whether nouns are singular or plural. Teachers often model the process for the children by thinking through the prediction task out loud – 'this word would make sense and sounds right'. The Directed Activities Round Texts used in the Literacy Hour include group work round cloze texts. Where children talk in a group about their decisions the task becomes a truly reflective activity.

Of course more than one word can often be appropriately placed in a gap. Older primary children can be asked how the meaning of a passage may be changed with each alternative. Consider the following sentence:

The ———— entered the room and began to stroke the dog to quieten it.

Our syntactic knowledge tells us that the space has to be filled with the name of a person, a proper noun, but consider how the context interpretation would vary depending on which one of the following alternatives was chosen: cleaner, child, burglar, vet. As meaning develops during the reading of the passage, some of our earlier decisions might need to be altered.

Now that English work is often informed by a media education perspective, cloze procedure approaches can be extended in a number of interesting ways, for example to deconstruct visual texts. In an advertisement made up of a series of images, we might substitute one of them and discuss with the pupils what difference this makes to the meanings conveyed by the series (Frank Potter, 1994).

Potter, Frank (1994) 'Media education, literacy and schooling' in Wray, David and Medwell, Jane (eds) *Teaching Primary English* London: Routledge.

Cluster

See also blend, consonant, phoneme

Sometimes called a blend, a cluster is a group of sounds that run together, for example, spr (spread) or gr (greet).

Code of Practice

See also Special Educational Needs (SEN) in language and literacy

The *Code of Practice* (DfEE, 1994) was set out by the 1993 Education Act and required that children with Special Educational Needs should normally be educated in mainstream schools. It reinforced the principle established by *The Warnock Report* (1978) that, where appropriate, children should be given a statement of special educational needs. It insisted on the importance of early identification of children's difficulties and the drawing up of an Individual Education Plan (IEP). Primary schools have a Special Educational Needs co-ordinator (SENCO) who liaises with the class teacher and the English co-ordinator over formulating an IEP for children with special needs in reading and writing.

Cohesion

See also register

Cohesion helps create what linguists call 'textuality' – the sense that what we have is a text rather than a random group of sentences. Angela Wilson describes how the careful writer ensures that 'each bit of their meaning is somehow bound into the whole so that readers or listeners can follow their drift, and can see the connections between one sentence or one part of the text and another' (Wilson, 1999, p. 83). Cohesive links or ties can be achieved at sentence level by using conjunctions (and, but) and adverbs (soon, there). At text level, one way of achieving cohesion is by using pronouns (such as he, she, they) which help a reader make referential connections to earlier parts of the text. There is an abundance of connectives and cohesive ties which are used differently according to the particular kind of text. A procedural text, like a set of instructions to use machinery, might achieve cohesion by numbering or bullet pointing the steps. There is another kind of cohesion called lexical cohesion which in literary texts is sometimes achieved by using vocabulary creating images linked to a particular theme. An example of this kind of linkage is found in the repetition of hot, firey imagery in *The Firework-Maker's Daughter* an exciting novel for children of about nine years upwards. When Lila entered the Grotto of the Fire-Fiend: 'red fire and flame licked and crackled at the rocky roof', 'a wide carpet of boiling lava spread' and 'mighty hammer and anvils rang with the rhythm of a great fire-dance' (by Philip Pullman, Corgi Yearling Books, 1996).

There are a number of ways in which teachers can help children understand more about cohesion so that they have the opportunity to bring that understanding to their own writing. For example, a text can be cut up, perhaps into paragraphs, and a pair or group of children asked to put the story together in the right order. Sometimes the end of the story is omitted and here children enjoy creating their own ending making it of a piece with the rest of the text. In their helpful resource book, *The Primary Grammar Book,* Bain and Bridgewood include interesting activities to help children learn how to create cohesion in a text, including using both co-ordinating connectives (where the clauses linked together are of equal status) and subordinating connectives (where one clause functions as part of another one). Many students also find *The Grammar Book* for secondary pupils useful to support their own understanding of grammatical terms (Bain and Bain, 1997).

The practical activities in *The Primary Grammar Book* are useful in achieving the National Literacy Strategy objectives. As Key Stage 2 gets underway, cohesiveness in writing comes to the fore. From Year 4 onwards the sentence and text level work in the NLS *Framework for Teaching* supports children's developing sense of cohesion. In Year 4 term 3, sentence level work includes using connectives – adverbs and conjunctions – to structure an argument, reinforced at text level where children assemble and sequence points to convey a point of view. Using connectives both to link clauses in sentences and to link sentences in longer texts is a sentence level objective in Year 5, term 3 and this meshes with the writing tasks – writing a letter of protest, constructing an argument – at text level. By the final term of Year 6 children are helped to divide whole informational texts into paragraphs and to comment on how the paragraphs are sequenced and how appropriate connectives are used to link one paragraph to the next.

Bain, R. and Bain, E. (1997) *The Grammar Book* Sheffield: The National Association for the Teaching of English.

Bain, Richard and Bridgewood, Marion (1998) *The Primary Grammar Book* Sheffield: The National Association for the Teaching of English.

Crystal, David (1987) *The Cambridge Encyclopaedia of Language* Cambridge: Cambridge University Press.

McArthur, Tom (1992) *The Oxford Companion to the English Language* Oxford: Oxford University Press.

Wilson, Angela (1999) *Language Knowledge for Primary Teachers: A Guide to Textual, Grammatical and Lexical Study* London: David Fulton (Chapter 7).

Collaborative learning

See also book making, constructivism, critical discourse, discussion, discussion text, Drama and English, Information and Communications Technology (ICT) and English, language and thought, metacognition, plenary, speaking and listening, zone of proximal development

The term 'collaborative learning' refers to any activity in which pupils or students work together, but it is particularly associated with pupil-led group talk. Using talk to plan, reflect on and evaluate learning was a favoured strategy in many classrooms in the 1970s and 1980s. While good practitioners have always included contexts for group discussion, before the publication of *Language, the Learner and the School* by Douglas Barnes, James Britton and Harold Rosen in 1967, talk exchanges in many classrooms consisted mainly of pupils' responses to the teacher's questions. This book created much excitement and there were many courses on language and learning which emphasised collaborative talk as a way of using language to learn across the whole curriculum. Douglas Barnes wrote the 'Language and Learning' unit for an Open University Education course which set out the principles underpinning the approach and provided examples of good practice. The well-known 'Role of Language in Learning' course (affectionately referred to as 'the role course') was established at The London Institute of Education. Where collaborative talk was well planned and organised the benefits were clear – not least children became much more motivated and there was a new energy in many classrooms. Children are after all social beings who thrive on cooperation with others. However, there was sometimes a lack of a clear focus and some felt that children spent too much time over relatively unstructured conversations. There was also a growing appreciation of that part of Vygotsky's work which drew attention to the role of the teacher in directing children's work and 'modelling' certain kinds of thinking by talking through ideas and solutions to problems alongside the pupil.

Now, in the United Kingdom and in other parts of the world as well, there has been a move towards more structured contexts where the teacher is very firmly at the centre. There is some concern, particularly amongst early years practitioners, that our more prescriptive frameworks may not provide enough opportunity for collaborative talk round activities.

However, the thoughtful practitioner can fulfil current requirements and provide for children's talk. Indeed many of the purposes for talk to meet the requirements of the National Curriculum can only be met by pupils having the chance to contribute to small group talk. In an interesting research project, small groups of children were asked to draw up some ground rules for collaborative talk. Some sensible rules emerged, for example that you should think before you speak, respect the contributions of others and be prepared to change your mind (Mercer *et al.* 1999). In this research children's increasing awareness of their own learning and how it can be improved (metacognition) is valued and exploited.

I end with some ways in which we can bring collaborative pupil-led talk fruitfully into English work. First, when we read to the whole class from a novel, short story or other literary text there is often an issue or aspect of characterisation of interest and importance. Where appropriate, the teacher can stop reading, divide the children into groups and ask them to discuss the issue. Often it is helpful for one child to act as scribe and to make some notes. Then the groups feed back comments, conclusions and questions to whole group discussion. The teacher's role in weaving together the different contributions is highly skilled. He or she also helps initiate pupils into a 'critical discourse' – a questioning, speculating kind of discussion. Terry Phillips puts it like this: '"Facts" are taken-for-granted hypotheses; they can be reflected upon in small group discussion, unpacked and turned into amazing new ideas' (Phillips,1994). A second context is talk round the computer. Children can work jointly on cloze procedures and other language activities, but the teacher needs to monitor this carefully – just working together using the computer does not necessarily lead to useful talk and collaboration. For a very helpful analysis of how we can organise this see Chapter 5 'Developing Exploratory Talk' in Grugeon *et al.* 1998. A third context arises

when we ask children to write as a group. The computer may be used for group writing or the children can hand-write their work. Shared writing is built into the Literacy Hour but mainly involves teacher and children constructing a text. Sometimes pupils benefit from working on a writing task with their peers in pairs or a small group. Book making and making class journals and magazines lend themselves to collaborative work. Under the Drama entry the many ways in which children can collaborate round improvisations and texts is covered.

Grugeon, Elizabeth, Hubbard, Lorraine, Smith, Carol and Davies, Lyn (1998) *Teaching Speaking and Listening in the Primary School* London: David Fulton.

Phillips, Terry (1994) 'The dead spot in our struggle for meaning: learning and understanding through small group talk' in Wray, David and Medwell, Jane (eds) *Teaching Primary English: The State of the Art* London and New York: Routledge .

Collective noun

See also noun, parts of speech

A collective noun refers to a group of things or people – crowd, herd, flock or team. As this category of noun is singular, strictly speaking, it matches with a singular verb as in 'The crowd moves forward'. However, as we think of the collective noun as plural in meaning, many find it acceptable to use it with a plural verb – 'The crowd move forward.'

Colloquialism

This refers to any expression which is informal and non-standard – for example 'She ain't at home'.

Colon

See also punctuation

The colon is a punctuation mark with four main uses:

- it can introduce a list of items. 'We need for

the writing corner: a computer, lined paper, sugar paper, pens, pencils and crayons.'

- it may replace a comma when speech or a quotation is used. 'The school dentist told the children last week: "Clean your teeth morning and evening".'
- it indicates a semantic link between two parts of a sentence. 'The ants are all over the school yard: they must have a nest near by.'
- it can replace a conjunction like 'and' or 'but' to create a crisp or even dramatic effect. 'I asked for your assignment: you did not hand it in.'

Colour coding

See also reading, reading corner

Colour coding is an organisational device used in class libraries or in the book or reading corner to indicate either type of book (fiction, poetry, information, reference) or what Cliff Moon calls 'the readability of texts'.

Moon, Cliff (published yearly) *Individualised Reading* Reading: Reading University Reading and Language Information Centre.

Comics

See also illustrations, journalistic writing, magazines, pop culture, visual literacy

Comics are a category of popular literature mainly, although not exclusively, for children. As well as weekly comics we have all seen the annuals that feature particular comic strip characters – these appear in book shops as Christmas approaches. I remember my sister and I eagerly awaiting the arrival of *The Rupert Bear Annual*. The comic strip cartoon format is well known: pictures show a series of events which may be humorous or tell a story. Often there are stock characters and young readers acquire a cumulative insight into how they are likely to behave and react. Although some comic strips only have pictures, there is usually a brief text at the bottom or top of each illustration and distinctive speech balloons coming from the characters' mouths. Noises – 'Boom!!', 'Smash!!', 'Crash!!' – are included with multiple exclamation marks and visual effects.

Comics became widely available reading matter in the first part of the twentieth century. Those that remained popular after the Second World War included *Beano, Buster* and *Dandy* – in which the events and characters are entertaining but one-dimensional – and the comics read by older boys, *Wizard, Hotspur* and *Rover*. Some comics originally included quite long prose stories but by the end of the 1960s 'the comic across all age groups had demoted the word in favour of the picture' (Hunt, 1995). The dominance of the visual has intensified now that children watch more and more animated cartoons on television and use interactive texts on CD-ROMs.

Worth a mention when considering the history of the comic are two 'quality' publications – *Eagle* and *Girl* – which came out in the early 1950s. Both comics aimed to include a balance of fact and fiction as well as comic strips and show that a cartoon strip format in itself does not imply trivial treatment of an issue or a story. (Modern picture books sometimes use a comic strip format to tell stories of some profundity – for example Briggs' *When the Wind Blows* about nuclear war, for older children and adults). *Girl* was a particularly interesting case in the history of comics as the editor, the Reverend Marcus Morris, tried to 'blur gender boundaries and modernise the self image of girls' (Hunt, 1995). To this end there were stories about female pilots and detectives. However, when the original editor moved on *Girl* resorted to the more traditional themes in girls' magazines – school stories, ponies and nurses. It was claimed that market research showed girls themselves wanted this change of emphasis. Another development was the emergence of the 'horror comic'. This came from America and led to much disquiet. Concern over the violent content of some of the comics led to a voluntary 'Comics Code' in America and to the Children and Young Persons (Harmful Publications) Act in Britain.

Of course comics, like other kinds of popular fiction, are culturally situated and tell us, amongst other things, something about how men and women, boys and girls are regarded in our society. If you want to learn more about the relationship between popular fiction, reading behaviour and gender you would find Jenny Daniel's 'Girl Talk', Chapter 2 in Styles *et al.*, 1994, of great interest. Once children leave the cosy world of *Postman Pat* and *Jack and Jill* – comics for the very young – the type of popular literature they choose is gender related. Boys tend to read comics for sheer entertainment and more than one generation has enjoyed characters like Dennis the Menace and Keyhole Kate. But the stories in *Bunty* and *Judy* involve the girls who read them in moral dilemmas and relationship issues. Daniels believes the 'social realism' in girls' reading material leads to greater emotional maturity. So while the home reading of many boys locks them into the narrow genre of their comics, girls' reading is more likely to make them aware of human motivation. On the other hand girls are more likely to be influenced by advertising and nudged too soon into the world of adult preoccupations.

While children, like adults, are entitled to read for entertainment in their leisure time, it is important they understand the limitations of some reading material. And there is also a problem with stereotyping of different groups in our society in some comics – parents and teachers would not want to condone the reading of violent and stereotyped material. It is all the more important, then, that we introduce children to as wide a range of reading as possible in school and encourage critical reading. Boys are perfectly capable of reflecting on their reading if given encouragement and opportunity. After reading some back copies of the now discontinued comic *Roy of the Rovers,* ten-year-old Tom remarked that although he found them entertaining 'You know Roy will always win and do brave things for the team.' The very features of familiarity and predictability of boys' comics which appeal to boys also make them a limited kind of reading. The suggestions below are activities which aim to help children to develop their critical thinking about comic strip texts:

Children can be asked to:

- analyse use of character, setting, plot and language in comics brought from home. Or, if you feel some children might resent this invasion into their private reading choices, another idea is to suggest they examine critically comics for children younger than themselves – for example *Twinkle, Jack and Jill* or *Postman Pat.*

- add text and speech bubbles to their own version of Ronald Briggs' wordless comic strip picture book – *The Snowman* (1979). Then they might discuss whether the narrative was best driven by pictures alone or with written text added. Other wordless books can give rise to interesting and quite profound discussion about how pictures alone can create a story, for example Shirley Hughes' wonderful wordless story of a little girl's flying fantasy *Up and Up* (1979). Another successful wordless book is Pat Hutchin's *Changes, Changes* (1970) in which a man and woman make a house out of building blocks and then change it to a fire engine, a boat, a truck, a train and then back to a house again.

- look at some of the Rupert Bear cartoon strips with the prose story but without the rhyming couplets and then write their own verses. Later their efforts can be compared with what Albert Bestall, one of the authors of the Rupert Books, wrote.

- compare the impact of a print comic strip and a film cartoon.

- examine story and picture books in comic strip format, for example – Catherine Brighton's lively comic strip version of the Mary Anning story *The Fossil Girl: Mary Anning's Dinosaur Discovery* (Frances Lincoln) for children of about eight years and above. A Year 5 teacher (9–10 year olds) helped children to compare Brighton's version of the dinosaur find with Laurence Anholt's prose text in *Stone Girl, Bone Girl* (Doubleday-Transworld Publishers).

- talk about books containing different kinds of text including comic strip. An outstandingly good example is *Chips and Jessie* (1985) which includes letters, prose and cartoon strips to tell five stories about two friends and their family and pets by Shirley Hughes.

- look at the use of comic strip and cartoon characters in non-fiction–reference and information books. There are lots of examples. Snoopy and Charlie Brown from Schulz's cartoon *Peanuts* are used in *The Charlie Brown Dictionary* (Random House). The interesting thing here, pointed out by Tom McArthur, 1992, is that the publishers rely on children knowing that life is perplexing for Charlie Brown. Only if they know this are they able to appreciate the humour. Children like the colourful cartoon stories in the M.Y. Bees series (Macdonald Young Books) which explain the water cycle, the plant cycle and life cycles of animals. Sam Godwin's *The Case of the Missing Caterpillar* uses speech balloons when the ladybird characters tell the story of the butterfly's life cycle. Children might like to try this format for some of their writing and to discuss the impact of direct speech.

Daniels, Jenny (1994) '"Girl talk": the possibilities of popular fiction' in Styles, Morag, Bearne, Eve and Watson, Victor (eds) *The Prose and the Passion* London: Cassell.

Hunt, Peter (ed.) 1995 *Children's Literature: An Illustrated History* Oxford, New York: Oxford University Press.

Mallett, Margaret 'Gender and genre: reading and writing choices of older juniors' in *Reading*, UKRA Vol. 31, No. 2, July 1997.

Watson, Victor (2001) *The Cambridge Guide to Children's Books in English* Cambridge: Cambridge University Press.

Comma

See also punctuation

A comma is a punctuation mark which is used to separate different parts of a sentence where this would be helpful in making meaning clear. So it is used:

- to mark off things in a list before the conjunction. 'I suggest you bring plums, apples, pears, strawberries and grapes.'
- to indicate an aside, instead of using dashes or brackets. 'The girls, sheltering underneath the tree, will begin the races just as soon as the rain stops.'
- to separate clauses in a sentence. 'As soon as we got into the car, which was waiting on a yellow line, she found the homework was missing.'
- to introduce direct speech instead of a colon. 'He pleaded, "I want to take the dog for a walk"'.

Command

Sentences in the imperative mood express a command. 'Sit down!' Sometimes a pronoun is added. 'You sit down!' Commands often end in an exclamation mark to add impact.

Common noun

See also abstract noun, grammar, noun, parts of speech, proper noun

A common noun refers to things and people as an example of what the word in question denotes – a village, a hamster or a teacher. (A proper noun, on the other hand, refers to particular identities and names and begins with a capital letter – James, Newcastle or July.) Common nouns can be abstract (love, beauty, joy) or concrete (pencil, rock, train). Some common nouns can be described as countable (having a singular and plural form like book and books), others as uncountable (mass nouns which are usually singular like relief, electricity and wool).

Communication skills – see Drama and English, speaking and listening, and writing

Communicative competence/ competence and performance

See also appropriateness in language

This is the ability to adjust our use of language to particular social situations. We might say, 'Shut up' to a whining sibling but we are more likely to say, 'Please be quiet' to an adult talking in a library where we are trying to work. Both requests are grammatically sound but they are appropriate in different circumstances.

The linguist Noam Chomsky distinguished between 'competence' – knowing the rules of grammar – and 'performance' – knowing how to use the knowledge in actual situations. (A similar sort of distinction was made by Ferdinand de Saussure between 'langue' and 'parole'.) The anthropologist Dell Hymes used the term 'communicative competence' to cover both knowledge and social use of language.

Crystal, David (1987) *The Cambridge Encyclopaedia of Language* Cambridge: Cambridge University Press. See Section 65, 'Linguistics'.

Competence – see communicative competence

Complement

In its everyday sense 'complement' refers to things that go well together as in 'The study of letters as evidence in history and the work on different types of letter in the Literacy Hour complement each other.'

In language study, the word or words needed to complete the meaning of another word are the complements. Let us look at the following sentence which exemplifies the function of a complement.

'Jatinder is very strong.'

The subject is 'Jatinder' and 'is' is the verb. But there is no object. 'Very strong' is the complement. Usually complements tell us more about the subject. There are complements for each part of speech (see McArthur, 1992) but they very often occur after verbs like 'be' and after other linking verbs – 'become', 'seem' and 'get'.

In the following examples the complements are underlined.

Leone seemed <u>confident</u>.

Jim became <u>faster at running</u>.

Sally is <u>an acquaintance of mine</u>.

McArthur, Tom (1992) *The Oxford Companion to the English Language* London QPD for Oxford: Oxford University Press.

Composition

See also grammar, vocabulary, writing

Compositional aspects of writing – getting ideas, selecting vocabulary and grammar – were distinguished from transcriptional aspects by Frank Smith (1982). Smith believed that there was a strong case for allowing young writers to take the risks involved in the creative aspects of writing and to organise their thoughts and ideas before tidying up the transcriptional or secretarial aspects – neat writing, spelling and so on in a later draft.

Smith, Frank (1982) *Writing and the Writer.* London: Heinemann.

Compound sentence

See also sentence

This is a sentence consisting of two main clauses. The following compound sentences are punctuated in different ways to link the two clauses:

* using a conjunction – in the following sentence 'but' – together with a comma. 'Mr Smith pushed the notes through the door, but no-one heard the package fall on the mat.'
* using a conjunct – in the following sentence 'however' – and semi-colon. 'I was concerned that Mary felt unwell on the morning of Sports Day; however, she had recovered by noon in time to enjoy the egg and spoon race.'

A compound sentence is capable of being presented as two simple sentences.

Compound word

A compound word is formed by joining two words as in sandpit, daytime and headache.

Comprehension

See also prior knowledge

To comprehend something is to understand it. When we read, our level of comprehension is dependent on a number of factors including our existing understanding or 'prior knowledge' of the subject and the level of attention to the passage we achieve. The noun 'comprehension' used in the context of the classroom often refers to an exercise in which pupils or students read a passage of prose or a poem and then write down the answers to questions about it.

The issue here is – does answering questions about a text develop children's reading ability? This partly depends on the nature of the questions. If an opinion backed by evidence from the text is invited we could argue that it does. On the other hand, requests for fairly obvious information are unlikely to help a young reader make progress. Children in the United Kingdom answer comprehension-type questions as part of the Year 6 Reading SATs so teachers need to give their pupils experience of this kind of task. One danger is that too much of children's time might be spent in answering rather mechanistic questions about a text and not enough time in sharing their thinking and response to literature with the teacher and children in lively discussion.

Concept mapping

See also assimilation and accommodation, metacognition, prior knowledge

This is a method of accessing and organising prior knowledge, often when a new topic is being introduced. The teacher might begin by placing headings on a chalkboard or computer white board and then ask children to 'brain storm' round each heading. So if we wanted to start work on traditional tales, we might begin with headings like – fairy tales, folk tales, creation stories and legends. Sub-headings under fairy tales might include – 'oral tradition', 'written versions – Perrault, Grimm and Anderson', 'rags to riches theme', 'modern versions/post-modern tellings'. Or children themselves might make headings and make links between them with arrows. It is the discussion of what has been jotted down that is so helpful at the start of new work. This involves the young learners in the planning and development of the work. In their book 'Literacy in the Secondary School' Lewis and Wray suggest that concept maps and brainstorming have a place not only at the beginning

of a topic, but also at the end when the fruits of thinking and reading will have modified the original map. In fact the comparison of the 'before' and 'after' maps can provide evidence for assessment purposes and can be used in the later primary as well as the secondary years. Pupils could add to their original maps what they have discovered in a different coloured pen. The advantage of this is that pupils get a sense of the development of their own thinking and knowledge (Lewis and Wray, 2000).

Lewis, Maureen and Wray, David (2000) *Literacy in the Secondary School* London: David Fulton.

Concepts – see functions of language, language acquisition, language and thought, spontaneous and scientific concepts

Concepts of print

See also baseline assessment, Early Learning Goals

Children need to understand some basic concepts about print before they can learn to read and write. Marie Clay, the New Zealand reading expert, devised a series of questions which a teacher can ask a young child to establish what they know. This structured assessment is called the 'Concepts about Print Test'.

But as Graham and Kelly (2000) point out, Clay's books *Sand* and *Stones* make the assessment quite tight – there is a formal score sheet and children are asked to correct deliberate errors. So many teachers prefer to formulate their own questions and use a book of their own choice.

Marie Clay's work has had great influence and helped teachers identify what needs to be known about print before children can learn to read. Some of the principles underpinning her work have influenced Baseline Assessment frameworks in Britain. However, her books are quite challenging and before turning to them students might find it helpful to look at Graham and Kelly's modified version of the test. Amongst other things, children are asked to show the teacher which parts of a book we read, the pictures or writing, whether they understand the purpose of punctuation marks and have a concept of directionality.

Clay, Marie (1979) *Sand: The Concepts About Print Test* London: Heinemann.

Clay, Marie (1979) *Stones: Concepts About Print Test* London: Heinemann.

Clay, Marie (1985) *The Early Detection of Reading Difficulties* Auckland: Heinemann.

Graham, Judith and Kelly, Alison (2000, second edition) *Reading Under Control* London: David Fulton. See Chapter 4 'Monitoring and Assessing Reading'.

Conferencing

See also speaking and listening, process approach to writing, writing

Conferencing refers to the conversations between teacher and pupil and between pupil and pupil to support children's writing. The notion is associated with Donald Graves and the 'process' approach. Conferences can take place before, during and after the writing is completed. At the planning stage children can be helped to make their aims explicit. First drafts – hand written or word processed – can be discussed and improvements suggested as well as features praised. After the writing is completed a child can review the result with the teacher or another pupil. When choosing samples to include in a child's Language Portfolio there is an opportunity for a broader review of what has been achieved. Sometimes children will mention writing that has been done at home. It is useful to record which kinds of writing the child has enjoyed and to set targets for future progress. In 'Monitoring and Assessing Writing' Liz Laycock suggests that teachers might mention the writing they enjoy – letters or stories perhaps. Sometimes a small group of children enjoy a shared reviewing of their writing over a period of time.

Graves, Donald (1983) *Writing: Teachers and Children at Work* New Hampshire: Heinemann.

Laycock, Liz (1998) 'Monitoring and Assessing Writing' in Graham, Judith and Kelly, Alison (eds) *Writing Under Control* London: David Fulton.

Conjunction

See also punctuation

A conjunction is a part of speech which connects words, phrases or clauses. There are two main kinds: co-ordinating conjunctions and subordinating conjunctions.

- Co-ordinating conjunctions (including and, but, or) connect units of equal status as in: 'Amanda was very tall for her age *but* she was not at all self-conscious'. Where adjectives are of equal status the last in the list can be preceded by 'and' as in:
  'The apples were large, red and juicy'.
- Subordinating conjunctions (including if, because, although) connect a subordinate clause to the main clause as in: 'I am going to the open air theatre tomorrow if it does not rain.'

Connective

See also adverb, adverbial clause, adverbial phrase, cohesion, conjunction

A connective is a linking word or phrase that can be a conjunction – 'if', 'as' and 'but' – or an adverb – 'finally', 'however' and 'then'. Connectives which are adverbs or adverbial phrases and clauses help make texts cohesive. For example, they may indicate consequences – 'therefore'; explanation – 'in other words'; or opposition – 'however'.

While connecting conjunctions join clauses within a sentence, connecting adverbs make a meaning bond between clauses that remain separate sentences.

'I intended to go *if* it stopped raining. (conjunction).
'I had already seen the film. *Nevertheless* I decided to join her.' (adverb)

Punctuation can also act as a connective sometimes, as the dashes do in the sentence:
'Helen – late as usual – gave the keynote lecture.'
For more examples, see DfEE (2000) *Grammar for Writing*, p. 187.

Connotation and denotation

Connotation or affective meaning refers to the fact that some words or terms may bring about an emotional response in individuals or groups. For example, the connotation of the word 'examination' might be an optimistic one for high-achieving individuals and groups – a chance to show what they know and to excel, while for others the word may be associated with anxiety and stress.

Denotation is a contrasting term purely to do with cognitive meanings and refers in an emotionally neutral way to objects and ideas. We may denote the 'blueness' of an object precisely by describing the colour as 'sky blue'. (Of course particular colours may well have a personal and emotional connotation for individuals or for whole cultures, for example red for good fortune in China and white for mourning in India.)

Consonant

See also cluster, digraph and phoneme

All the letters of the alphabet that are not vowels (a, e, i, o, u) are consonants and usually occur at the beginnings and ends of syllables. Note that letter 'y' can function as both a vowel (ay, ey, oy) and a consonant. When forming a consonant, the speaker interrupts the air flow with lips and tongue.

Constructivism

See also assimilation and accommodation, language and thought

This is a theory of learning in which it is claimed that we form mental representations or 'constructions' from our experience of the world. Learning involves the continual building of these constructions so that our mental picture of the world becomes more complex and more coherent. It is not just a matter of adding to our knowledge as new experience sometimes requires us to reshape or even abandon our existing ideas because they no longer fit with the evidence – human beings had to rethink the notion that the earth is flat. This links with Piaget's notion of 'accommoda-tion' of new information by our existing structures. As Herne *et al.* (2000, p. 3) put it: 'Learning is about understanding things differently – not just remembering more information.'

The constructivists see learning as essentially active, as a constant making sense of experience in the world. So a school programme which made the pupils relatively passive would not provide the opportunities to interact, interrogate and collaborate which seem to follow as desirable from a constructivist point of view.

Herne, Steve, Jessel, John and Griffiths, Jenny (2000) *Study to Teach: A Guide to Studying in Teacher Education* London: Routledge.

Contents page – see retrieval devices

Contextual understanding – see big shapes

Co-ordinator of English – see English Co-ordinator

Copying

See also handwriting, non-fiction reading and writing, writing

There are contexts in English in which children copy as a part of their learning. I want to look at the more positive aspects of copying before turning to some problems. In the early years children are often helped to trace or copy letters of the alphabet, and this not only helps them become familiar with the letters but also gives practice in holding and controlling a pencil or crayon. There is wide use of handwriting books which help children to practise the key movements of letter formation by either tracing over letters or copying them underneath the printed version. But, as Anne Washtell points out in 'Routines and Resources', it is important to talk to the children about these activities and what they find easy and difficult so that it is not just a passive activity (Graham and Kelly, 1998).

As children move through the primary years

they copy words from dictionaries and other reference sources and sometimes lists of tasks and titles from the board or screen to help organise their work. New technology is helping to save both teachers' and children's time. For example, in the primary school where I have been a governor for many years the classrooms now have 'interactive white boards' and children can download what the teacher has written onto their personal laptops. The word processor makes editing and proof reading quicker. Nevertheless, there will always be a place for children sometimes making a hand-written fair copy of their most important work.

Now to the more troubling aspects of copying. The issue of passive copying, particularly from non-narratively organised information books, has long been recognised by teachers (p. 100 in Mallett and Newsome, 1977), inspectors (OFSTED, Annual Report, 1993, p. 8) and researchers (Wray and Lewis, 1992, Mallett, 1999). Children carrying out research using secondary sources were often asked to put the information in their own words. But once an author has organised information and chosen a structure and a vocabulary, it is very difficult to rewrite their work unless the information can be changed and enriched by new ideas and facts. Trying to make a synthesis from several different sources is extremely challenging, even for older students.

What then might help? Here are some suggestions which my students and I have found useful. (These are also discussed under the non-fiction extended entry.)

Ask children to:

- spend some time discussing what they already know about a new topic, with the teacher as a class or in small groups, so that their 'prior knowledge' is organised into a framework to receive the new information actively.
- take some of their own questions to secondary sources (Mallett, 1999).
- talk to teacher and other pupils about all the new ideas and information.
- make notes on the particular topic, if possible from several sources, and write the final

account from the notes.
- make notes on information from pictures and diagrams as well as from written text and construct their own diagrams from information in written sources.
- write in a different genre to the source used – for example the source might be a report on Tudor food in an information book and the writing task could involve using the information to make a Tudor menu or recipe (Lewis and Wray, 1996, call this 'genre exchange').

Teachers can help by:

- choosing, and where appropriate displaying, lively resources of different readability levels – both print and electronic – to enthuse young learners
- including visual materials in book, poster and CD-ROM form, as a source of information
- feeding in new experience relevant to the topic – a video-film, a visit from an expert, an outing, classroom research – to sustain interest and so that the secondary materials are not the only inspiration for children's writing (See Mallett, end of Chapter 3, 1999, for an interesting challenge to the information in a book – six year olds found their classroom snails preferred a different diet to that recommended in the text they were using!)
- making opportunities for talking about and sharing new ideas (Riley and Reedy, 2000)
- making writing tasks interesting and, where appropriate, using 'scaffolding' techniques like 'conferencing' (planning and discussion between teacher and pupil or pupil with pupil partner) or writing frames (outline structures of different generic forms) to support young learners (Lewis and Wray, 1996).

Lewis, Maureen and Wray, David (1996) *Writing Frames: Scaffolding Children's Non-fiction Writing in a Range of Genres* Reading: Reading University Reading and Language Information Centre.

Mallett, Margaret (1999) *Young Researchers: Informational Reading and Writing in the Early and Primary Years* London: Routledge.

Mallett, Margaret and Newsome, Bernard (1977) *Talking, Writing and Learning 8–13* Schools Council Working Paper 59. London: Evans/Methuen.

Riley, Jenni and Reedy, David (2000) *Developing Writing for Different Purposes: Teaching about Genre in the Early Years* London: Paul Chapman.

Washtell, Anne (1998) 'Routines and resources' in Graham, Judith and Kelly, Alison (eds) *Writing Under Control: Teaching Writing in the Primary School* London: David Fulton.

Wray, David and Lewis, Maureen (1992) 'Primary children's use of information books' in *Reading* UKRA, Vol. 26, No. 3.

Core books

See also audio books/tapes/cassettes, CD-ROMs, creation stories, fairy tales, fiction, folk tales, individualised reading, reading schemes, non-fiction reading and writing, novel, short stories, traditional tales

'Core books' refers to the heart of the collection of reading materials for each year group in the primary school. The collection in British schools includes books and materials covering the different kinds of fiction and non-fiction genres required by the National Curriculum English programmes and the National Literacy Strategy Framework. Sets of books from reading schemes and programmes may be included. The English Co-ordinator meets with classroom teachers to decide on how the core collections should be developed and the best new texts added. Experienced teachers have a sense of what children are likely to enjoy. There are many good publishers' collections of 'core books'. Often these have been chosen on sound principles and include many quality texts. However, choosing books for the children we teach is one of the great pleasures for most practitioners and it is satisfying for teachers to be active in creating their own collections.

Two of the most useful guides to beginning and developing a collection are Cliff Moon's *Individualised Reading* programme and Ellis and Barrs' *The Core Book*. Cliff Moon's guide, which is revised every year, divides large numbers of books into broad categories to match children's different reading stages. Each stage in Moon's system has a colour code: below stage 1 is red; stage 1 is yellow; stage 2 is white and so on. Teachers sometimes add other symbols which mean, for example, the book is within the capability of an older but less forward reader and of reasonably mature content. Of course matching child and resource by 'readability' criteria is not a mechanistic procedure. Teachers take account of children's interests and sometimes their prior knowledge of a topic when helping them select texts. I remember a group of six year olds who had been enjoying some work on mini-beasts talking with great interest about the cross section of a spider in a book intended for nine year olds and above – Ted Dewan's *Inside the Whale and Other Animals* (Dorling Kindersley, 1992).

The Core Book: A Structured Approach to Using Books Within the Reading Curriculum sets out the principles underpinning the creation and development of a core collection. The accompanying lists of quality texts are placed under suggested age ranges and in categories like traditional tales, picture books, stories and information books.

In their chapter 'Resources for Reading', Graham and Kelly (2000) include an interesting section on core books, making it clear that these are the books which show children the pleasure of reading. They recommend that we include books with significant stories that will connect with children's feelings and interests (*The Patchwork Quilt* by V. Flourney and J. Pinkney), books with prediction opportunities (*All in One Piece* by Jill Murphy) and books with secrets (*The Very Hungry Caterpillar* by Eric Carle).

Ellis, Sue and Barrs, Myra (1997) *The Core Book: A Structured Approach to Using Books Within the Reading Curriculum.* Accompanied by *The Core Booklist* compiled by Lazim, A. and Moss, E. London: Centre for Language in Primary Education.

Graham, Judith and Kelly, Alison (2000) *Reading Under Control* London: David Fulton, Chapter 2 'Resources for Reading'.

Moon, Cliff (published yearly) *Individualised Reading* Reading, Berkshire: Reading and Language Information Centre.

Count noun (also called countable noun and unit noun)

See also collective noun, common noun, grammar, noun, parts of speech

A countable noun can be singular or plural (for example, mother/mothers; dictionary/dictionaries) unlike a mass or uncountable noun which is usually only used in the singular (for example, health; furniture).

Couplet

See also onset and rime, poetry

This term refers to two consecutive lines of poetry or verse which rhyme and, or, are of the same length. Sometimes couplets stand alone at the end of a poem, but they can be the form throughout the poem. The Rupert Bear Books courageously tell whole stories in rhyming couplets with an alternative prose narrative.

> 'Next morning, Rupert wakes to hear
> A strange sound come from somewhere near...
> He peers outside the tent and blinks
> "It's frogs! They're everywhere!" he thinks'.
> (*Rupert and the Raft,* Rupert, The Express Annual,
> Exeter: Pedigree Books, No. 63, 1998, p. 47)

A teacher working with nine year olds provided some prose passages from one of the Rupert Books and asked the children to write their own couplets. Then they compared their efforts with those in the book. The children took up a playful approach and produced some interesting results with the touch of humour this verse form can often encourage. This also proved a good context for reinforcing onset and rime patterns and punctuation knowledge.

In Shakespeare's plays, couplets are sometimes used to signal that a courtly character is in reflective mode, especially as a scene comes to an end.

> 'I will go tell him of fair Hermia's flight
> Then to the wood will he tomorrow night
> Pursue her: and for this intelligence
> If I have thanks, it is a dear expense;
> But herein mean I to enrich my pain
> To have his sight thither and back again.'
> (Helena speaking at the end of Scene i, Act I *A Midsummer Night's Dream,* William Shakespeare).

Cox Report

See also History of English teaching, *Kingman Report*, LINC materials, National Curriculum

At the time the National Curriculum was first set up, Professor Brian Cox chaired the committee which produced *English for Ages 5–16* (known as the *Cox Report*) for the Department of Education and Science in 1989. The committee was asked to focus on teaching English in England and Wales, but their remit did not extend to Scotland and Northern Ireland.

The recommendations had to take account of the model of English language teaching in the Kingman Report (1988) and the format of the assessment model required by the National Curriculum. Nevertheless, the report reflected many of the views of teachers, linguists and educationists who recognised the subtlety of the processes by which children acquire language. Teachers warmed to the report's acknowledgement that literature is central in successful English teaching and that language is socially situated and used for a diversity of purposes. Further, the needs and contributions of those in British society having a mother tongue other than English were sympathetically analysed. But the report also introduced systematic teaching and assessment of spelling and punctuation, teaching about the forms and functions of language and the expectation that children would be helped to acquire standard English in writing by the end of the primary years.

Because teachers needed considerable subject knowledge to carry out the recommendations in the 1989 *Cox Report,* a government-funded in-service training project called *Language in the National Curriculum* or LINC was established and headed by Professor Ronald Carter. Professor Carter and his team produced 500 pages of in-service training materials designed to help teachers carry out appropriate language study with their pupils. About 400 training courses were set up attended by about 10,000 teachers. But the Government at that time decided to suppress the materials, saying that the materials were not suitable for classroom use. Of course the materials were not for direct classroom use: they were to help teachers acquire the extensive knowledge about language they needed in order to fulfil the requirements of the National Curriculum. There was also a feeling, exploited in parts of the press, that the Government felt that the materials did not sufficiently privilege Standard English. Yet, as Brian Cox argues in his book *Cox and the Battle for the English Curriculum* 1995, the LINC materials 'adopted a balanced and moderate position towards controversial issues like the teaching of grammar and the place of Standard English and dialects in the curriculum'. (Cox, 1995, p.18). No wonder that Peel and Bell use the metaphor of a volcano to suggest the devastating force with which language issues can break into the public domain. The LINC materials did not disappear into oblivion; they were commercially produced and are available from Nottingham University. Not only did the in-service materials flourish – several LINC related books emerged and the BBC produced LINC TV programmes. There was a political decision in the early 1990s to rewrite the 1989 English Curriculum and the revised version was finalised as part of a slimmed down national curriculum in 1995. Cox regarded the new English orders as having an unfortunate tone and emphasis and making 'the teaching of English seem dull and mechanical'. Nevertheless he considered that teachers could still carry out good practice if they enriched the new curriculum with insights from the 1989 Cox Curriculum (Cox, 1995).

Since Cox wrote this book the whole National Curriculum, including the English Curriculum, has been revised – in 2000. The English Curriculum has become even more slimmed down and at Key Stages 1 and 2 there has been a move towards teaching phonics as a major part of the reading programme. A National Literacy Strategy is now in place which has set out objectives for each term of each year from Reception until Year 6 in a document called *The Framework for Teaching* (DfEE, 1998). The publication of guidance like that in, for example, *Grammar for Teaching* (DfEE, 2000) shows the trend towards a grammar-based approach to the teaching of writing.

Perhaps one of the main legacies of the Cox Curriculum for the Primary years is the emphasis on the power of story and narrative. To give something of the flavour of the Cox Report and to remind us of the role of narrative in becoming literate – something recognised in the current frameworks in which we work – I end this entry with a direct quotation.

'Young children hear stories either told or read from a very early age and, as soon as they have the skill they read themselves. In this way, they internalise the elements of story structure – the opening, the setting, character, events and resolution. Similarly, they come to realise that, in satisfying, well structured stories, things that are lost will be found, problems will be solved, and mysteries will be explained and so on.' (DES, 1989, para. 17.28)

Cox, Brian (1995) *Cox on The Battle for the English Curriculum* London: Hodder & Stoughton.
Peel, Robin and Bell, Mary (1994) *The Primary Language Leader's Book* London: David Fulton

Creation stories

See also Bible the myths, sacred texts, traditional tales

Creation stories are tales about the origin of the earth and all its physical features, people and creatures. In that these stories deal with and try to explain a great human concern – how did we begin? – they can be broadly placed with myths. We learn much about a culture different from our own by reading its creation stories. But a sensitive approach is needed and indeed 'myths and legends which carry a culture's religious beliefs will be handled and presented differently from a light hearted folk tale' (p. 27, *A Multicultural Guide to Children's Books*).

If you want a beautifully illustrated story about why day follows night I recommend *The Coming of the Night: a Yoruba creation myth from West Africa* retold by James Riordan (Frances Lincoln, 1999). Creation stories are included in Anita Ganeri's collection *Out of the Ark: stories from the world's religions* (Macdonald, 1994). Ann Pilling keeps the flavour of the oral tradition in her retellings in *Creation: Stories from Around the World* (Walker Books, 1997). I was encouraged to seek out *When the World Began: Stories collected in Ethiopia* told by Elisabeth Laird and illustrated by Yosef Kebede, Emma Harding, Griselda Holderness and Lydia Monks (Oxford University Press) when I noticed Valerie Coghlan's very positive review in *Books for Keeps* (2001, No. 124, p. 25). As Coghlan points out, the vivid stories give us a glimpse into 'foibles of human nature common to people of all nationalities'. It also communicates to children the strong story telling tradition of Ethiopia.

Ted Hughes' *How the Whale Became and Other Stories* is a classic for younger children while older primary children enjoy the intriguing stories in print and on tape in his anthology *The Dreamfighter and Other Creation Tales* (Faber and Faber).

Stones, Rosemary (ed.) (1999) *A Multicultural Guide to Children's Books* London: Books for Keeps.

Creative writing

See also child-centered learning, process approach to writing, writing

'Creative writing' (sometimes termed imaginative, free, personal and intensive writing) is associated with the 'personal growth' model of English teaching of the 1970s and 1980s. To some extent this approach was a reaction to the emphasis on grammar exercises in the 1950s and 1960s. Often the starting point for creative writing was a story, music, drama, painting or poetry. More contrived 'stimuli', as they were often called, included lighted candles, displays of unusual objects and tape recordings of strange noises (Basil Maybury's book, *Creative Writing for Juniors* Batsford 1967, describes some of the more bizarre approaches). In some classrooms children were helped to find a 'voice' to express feelings as well as thoughts and ideas and writing was produced which was spontaneous and individual in character. In others, however, there was an approach welcoming 'free expression' without any profound engagement with ideas or very much concern about spelling, handwriting or punctuation. For an interesting account of the history of writing in the classroom before the 1980s see Pat Pinsent's chapter in Graham and

Kelly 1998. We are invited to join Mary, an imaginary teacher in the 1960s and 1970s, as she copes with the changing approaches to supporting children's writing.

At the beginning of the twenty-first century unstructured approaches to writing are out of favour in the United Kingdom. Story writing is still an important and enjoyable part of the English curriculum but children are usually helped to plan, draft, edit and proof read their work. There has also been a move towards encouraging, in addition to story writing and personal writing, informational kinds of writing in the Literacy Hour and outside it.

Teachers interested in developing their own creative writing abilities enjoy the courses on writing poetry, stories and drama for radio and television at the Arvon Foundation which has houses in Devon and North Yorkshire.

Avron Foundation, The Arts Council of England. Website: www.arvonfoundation.org
Pinsent, Pat (1998) 'From copying to creation' in Graham, Judith and Kelly, Alison (eds) *Writing Under Control* London: David Fulton.

Creoles

See also bilingualism, grammar, language acquisition, language variety

These are languages which have come about through contact between speakers of different languages. The first stage in the development of a Creole is a 'pidgin' – a means of communication with a much narrower range of functions than the two languages it has come from. Pidgin speakers used the vocabulary of the new language, embedding it in the syntax of their original language. It is important that we recognise pidgins as creative solutions to a problem: new language varieties which have come into being to serve the human need to communicate in often difficult and changing circumstances. Most pidgins have arisen out of colonisation and are based on European languages like English, Portuguese and Spanish. Pidgins either die away because their function is no longer needed or, where they become the mother tongue of a community, they develop into

Creoles. The stages by which a pidgin changes to a Creole – including the expansion in structural linguistic resources in grammar, vocabulary and style – are clearly described by Crystal, 1987.

There is likely to be some conflict between a Creole and the language from which it is derived. The original language often enjoys status through its association with wealth and education while the related Creole may have its roots in slavery.

There has been renewed interest in both pidgins and Creoles because of the light they shed on language acquisition and language change and indeed on issues to do with whether there is a universal grammar underpinning all languages. In an interesting analysis, Tom McArthur examines some current political issues, for example, the role and function of pidgins and Creoles in the transition of some countries into post colonial societies.

Crystal, David (1987) *The Cambridge Encyclopaedia of Language* Cambridge: Cambridge University Press.

McArthur, Tom (1992) *The Oxford Companion to the English Language* Oxford: QPD and Oxford University Press.

Criterion referenced assessment

See also assessment, National Curriculum

Where an assessment involves setting a pupil's performance against explicit criteria we describe it as 'criteria referenced'. For example, the National Curriculum English levels of attainment in Speaking and Listening, Reading and Writing list descriptions for performance at each level and assessment is therefore criteria referenced.

Critical discourse

See also advertising, argument, collaborative learning, reading, fiction, language and thinking, metacognition, non-fiction reading and writing, persuasive genre, reflective reading

When we help children to control 'critical discourse' we help them to think deeply and evaluatively about information and issues whether they are speaking, listening, reading or writing.

I believe a good place to begin is with group discussion. We can help raise the level of discussion by the way we focus it and by the way we intervene to comment on children's contributions – 'Why do you say that?' 'Could there be another way of looking at this?'

When we help children to evaluate information, from whatever source, we need to help them distinguish between what is a relatively objective 'fact' and what is an opinion. They need this ability to make progress in the distinctive kinds of reading and thinking appropriate to each academic subject. Helping them to evaluate will also make them less vulnerable to persuasion by advertising and the mass media. Under the 'advertising' entry there are suggestions for work to extend children's knowledge and understanding of language to persuade.

Thinking now about reading – we do not always need to read in full critical gear. One sign of a mature reader is that they read flexibly according to the nature of the reading task. They may swiftly scan a text for a date or name, skim to get the main 'gist' of the content. But they need to be able to bring their intellectual faculties into full gear if the task demands the need to understand and evaluate information or an argument. One of the clearest accounts of the different kinds of reading is given by Lunzer and Gardner in *The Effective Use of Reading*. The quality of the texts affects how easy or difficult it is to get our thoughts round the information and arguments. Information books which lack coherence and present 'the world in bits' do not invite us into a critical discourse (Meek, 1996).

Children who have managed to employ a critical discourse in discussion and in reading may still find it difficult to find a critical 'voice' in their writing. One of the most useful series of research studies to help here was carried out by Bereiter and Scardamalia in Ontario in the 1980s. These researchers remind us that successful writers have to do two things: first they call up from memory the content of what they want to write and then they use their knowledge of discourse types to compose the text. No wonder all of us find writing so difficult! Bereiter and Scardamalia have suggested some ways to help young writers using what they call 'prompts'. These 'prompts' include brainstorming ideas before starting to write, making a plan of headings, listing key words and phrases to develop an argument and, interestingly, to write the last sentence early on to focus the rest of the writing. Some of these strategies may help move children on from just memorising content and setting it down to actually transforming the content into a coherent argument or discourse (Bereiter and Scardamalia, 1987). Of course an interest in and commitment to the subject of the writing helps a great deal. Using some of the 'prompts' suggested by Bereiter and Scardamalia, Reedy helped six year olds produce satisfying pieces of writing on the ethics of keeping animals in zoos (see Riley and Reedy, 1999, pp. 147–60). I wholeheartedly recommend this account to anyone concerned with helping children enter into the discourse of reasoned argument.

My analysis so far is mostly relevant to informational kinds of language. There are also different levels of engagement with fiction. Sometimes children, like older students and adults, enjoy reading a highly predictable book by a popular author. Their critical faculties will move to a low gear – but even young children can notice the limitations of an undemanding text. How, then, do we help children enter into the discourse of demanding, quality literary texts? Two scholars and teachers have helped particularly here. Aidan Chambers in a number of his books, including *Tell Me,* shows the educative energy of conversation between developing readers and a mature reader who loves literature. By gentle encouragement and nudging, perhaps some questioning, the children learn how to read and think about different literary texts and the different layers of meaning in those texts. This is one of the books my students and I return to again and again as it shows so powerfully how a teacher can initiate children into the critical literacy that enables them to enjoy more and more literary forms.

Margaret Meek argues that the texts themselves can teach. She has considered how young children come to understand and use the language of books and concludes tha author tells a story teaches a young re enjoy and respond. In her book *Texts Tha*

Meek pinpoints 'intertextuality' as one of the devices picture book authors use to draw in and extend the abilities of the young reader. Intertextuality is the way a text draws on and refer to other texts. She shows how Janet and Allan Ahlberg's *The Jolly Postman* combines a number of texts with which children will be familiar – letters, fairy tales, post cards, invitations and recipes – and brings together a number of shared cultural understandings between author and young reader.

As children listen to or read more they have the opportunity to become sensitive readers of literature. They learn, for instance, to relate closely to the author, appreciating sometimes teasing humour and learning to fill the space between words and deducing meanings that are hinted at. The evaluative abilities that are developed enable them to share their insights and enjoyments with others by adopting the critical discourse of mature readers.

Bereiter, Carl and Scardamalia, Marlene (1987) *The Psychology of Written Composition.* Hillsdale, New Jersey: Lawrence Erlbaum.

Meek, Margaret (1988) *Texts That Teach What Readers Learn* Stroud: The Thimble Press.

Meek, Margaret (1996) *Information and Book Learning* Stroud: The Thimble Press.

Mills, Colin (1994) 'Texts That Teach' in Wray, David and Medwell, Jane (eds) *Teaching Primary English* London: Routledge.

Riley, Jeni and Reedy, David (1999) *Developing Writing for Different Purposes: Teaching About Genre in the Early Years* London: Paul Chapman.

Cross-curricular projects

See also Art and English, child-centred learning, creative writing, English projects, Geography and English, History and English, language across the curriculum, Physical education and English, Religious Education and English, Science and English

Cross-curricular projects, topics or themes in which the boundaries between the different subjects blur, are particularly associated with the late 1960s, the 1970s and the 1980s in the

United Kingdom. The *Plowden Report*, published in 1967, celebrated the richness of children's response in talk, writing and art work in the best primary project work. Favourite topics for younger children included – the Seasons, Ourselves, Food, Growth, Places and Pets. For older children, work was often round topics like – Change, Travel, Predators, Festivals, Town and Country, Buildings and Environmental Issues. Each topic included English in the form of stories, personal writing, writing in role and drama and at least one other subject. The Seasons would be likely, for example, to include a geographical and science aspect and the perceptions of poets and writers as well as the children's feelings about them. A topic like Buildings might combine history with literature. The principles behind this way of organising teaching come from the work of educational philosophers like John Dewey who put first-hand experience at the heart of the educational process for young children. Although John Dewey did not himself deny the existence of separate subjects, many had the impression that the *Plowden Report* 'saw subjects as rather contrived ways of viewing the world' (Riley and Prentice 1999).

The best primary project work was lively and imaginative and involved children in worthwhile first-hand experience and in careful research from secondary sources. If you want a flavour of the vitality of children's talk and writing from broad-based project work you might look at two books – both outcomes of Schools Council Projects in the 1970s – Connie and Harold Rosen's *The Language of Primary School Children* and Mallett and Newsome's *Talking, Writing and Learning*. One of the 'contexts' in Chapter 2 of the second of these research studies was a description and evaluation of an exciting study of Ships and the Sea from historical, musical and literary perspectives. As Primary Research Officer on the project, I was involved in travelling round the country to collect evidence of good practice during this research. I particularly remember visiting a school in Kinver, Shropshire and finding that it was the myth and folklore of the sea – especially monsters, pirates and mermaids – that seemed to appeal most to the imaginations of these nine

year olds. One of the images that I remember most is in the first few lines of one of the many poems, lyrics and stories the children wrote.

> 'Frolicsome are the waves that reach the far shore
> The swift eye of a sailor scans the sea.
> A strange and wondrous voice rings like a crystal bell–
> A maiden fair on the azure sea.'

Another project involved a class of ten year olds in a two-day field trip to a village, Craster, on the north eastern coast. A visit to the kipper factory, an examination of the landscape and seascape and interviews with local people about perceptions of their current lifestyles and occupations gave a geographical perspective. An exploration of the ruins of nearby Dunstanborough Castle provided opportunities for historical research as well as poems and story writing.

I have included these two 'snapshots' of project work because they give some idea of the richness and vitality of the work when it was planned and carried out by excellent practitioners. There was a freedom to take advantage of special interests and extend the research of individual children. There was a welcome recognition that language was the medium for learning across the curriculum. Contexts for collaborative talk and writing and for sharing the fruits of investigation arose easily. Perhaps English work fared particularly well as the broad content of many projects gave much scope for writing stories and for improvised drama. History, science and drama often benefited from an English perspective – feelings as well as thinking were brought into play. For example, in the Ships and the Sea project the children wrote sympathetic pieces 'in role' which revealed their understanding of the hard routines and conditions of sailors through the centuries.

However, there was also work described as 'project work' which lacked a clear focus and did not give enough time to helping children with spelling and language study. Many teachers also felt that by the end of the primary years children should have made a start in acquiring the ways of thinking and ways of validating evidence associated with each of the main school subjects. As early as 1978 official surveys were expressing concern about the lack of coherence in some thematic approaches (DES, 1978) and in 1984 Alexander pointed to the danger of work being *ad hoc* and 'whimsical'. While there was often much scope for differentiation, teachers identified a core of work for everyone and then created programmes for different groups and individuals, matters to do with progression sometimes did not fare so well. While each project might have been well planned and evaluated, how each built on the last and moved the children forward was often less clear. The arrival of a subject-centred National Curriculum changed the emphasis of primary teachers' planning and at the beginning of the twenty-first century project work crossing subject barriers is less common. English is regarded as a separate subject and much of the teaching is prescribed and takes place in the designated time we call the Literacy Hour.

Nevertheless, there is official recognition of the benefits of linking subjects within the newer frameworks and educational philosophies. *The Framework for Teaching* encourages links between literacy teaching and other areas of the curriculum. 'For example, during the Literacy Hour, pupils might be searching and retrieving from information texts used in science, writing instructions linked to a technology topic, studying myths, autobiographies or stories linked to a unit in history' (p. 13).

It is also true that good early years work, whatever the lesson, needs to help the children get a personal foothold. In an inspiring account, Riley and Reedy describe how a class of Year 1 children are helped to write about keeping animals in zoos as part of a bigger science topic on Living Things. A shared reading of Anthony Browne's picture book *Zoos* (1992) had led to some passionate discussion about whether animals were 'happy' in zoos. Because the children's sympathetic imaginations had been put into full gear they were able to write with some energy about their viewpoints. The uniting of science and English in this was most successful in developing children's thinking and writing. At a time when we are trying to improve children's

writing and to make opportunities for extended writing an English perspective can put warmth and commitment into some kinds of writing across the curriculum. Let me end by recommending an account of a special project carried out with older primary children in 2001 which brought together science, art and creative writing. In their inspirational book *Let Our Children Learn* Brown, Foot and Holt describe how children's intellectual curiosity about natural objects they had chosen resulted in some life-enhancing writing, drawing and book making (Brown, Foot and Holt, 2001). Projects like this one show that the spirit of cross-curricular work lives on even though the educational context in which we teach and learn has changed.

Alexander, R. (1984, 1988) *Primary Teaching*. London: Cassell.

Brown, Tony, Foot, Michael and Holt, Peter (2001) *Let Our Children Learn* Nottingham: Education Now Publishing Co-operative.

Department of Education and Science (1978) *Primary Education in England* London: Her Majesty's Stationery Office.

Dewey, John (1938) *Experience and Education* New York: Collier-Macmillan.

Mallett, Margaret and Newsome, Bernard (1977) *Talking, Writing and Learning 8–13* Schools Council Working Paper 59. London: Evans/Methuen.

National Literacy Strategy *Framework for Teaching* 1998 DfEE.

Riley, Jeni and Prentice, Roy (1999) *The Curriculum for 7–11 Year Olds* London: Paul Chapman.

Rosen, C. and H. (1974) *The Language of Primary School Children* Harmondsworth: Penguin Books.

Cross sections – see diagrams

Cue-systems

See also big shapes, grammar, miscue analysis, phonics, reading

The use of a number of cue-systems in making sense of print is associated with the psycho-linguistic models of reading of Kenneth Goodman and Frank Smith. They reacted against the mechanistic decoding methods of the first part of the twentieth century, and while they did recognise that understanding of grapho-phonic correspondence played a part, they put the search for meaning at the centre of the reading process. In *The Reading Book,* Barrs and Thomas illuminate the psycho-linguistic approach and show how it can inform classroom practice.

There are three generally accepted cue-systems important in learning to read – semantic (or context), syntactic and grapho-phonic. Some teachers and linguists add a fourth – the bibliographic cue-system.

The semantic cue-system helps the young reader to tune into what makes sense, drawing on their knowledge of the text, any illustration and their wider experience of the topic.

The syntactic cue-system brings into gear a child's sensitivity to what sounds right grammatically and what is likely to come next.

The grapho-phonic cue-system keys into the young reader's knowledge of sound–symbol correspondences, visual understanding of letter combination and sight vocabulary. In spite of many exceptions there are quite a lot of times when this cue-system will help a child work out a new word.

The bibliographic cue-system draws on all that we know about texts, including the concepts about print – directionality of print, distinguishing between illustrations and text and so on – assessed in Marie Clay's well-known test. Our cumulative experience of fairy tales take us into an imaginary world where the laws of science are not obeyed, where numbers like three and twelve are significant and where wishes are granted. The kind of language used and the illustrations are distinctive and help us link the text to the fairy tale genre. We develop a different set of expectations about information books which have a particular global structure with sub-headings, retrieval devices and labelled diagrams.

Information from these cue-systems is successfully blended in fluent reading. Bussis *at al.* (1985) use the metaphor of an orchestra to stress that all must be in harmony although different instruments may be dominant at particular times. In the same way, one cue-system might come into prominence because it is the best one to tackle a particular word or phrase.

The 'searchlight' model of the National Literacy Strategy suggests we think of cue-systems as searchlights beamed on the text.

Miscue analysis is a diagnostic reading test which assesses how well young readers are using each cue-system.

Barrs, Myra and Thomas, Anne (eds) 1991 *The Reading Book* London: Centre for Language in Primary Education.
Bussis, A *et al.* (1985) *Inquiry into Meaning: An Investigation in Learning to Read* Hillsdale, NJ: Lawrence Erlbaum Associates.

Cultural diversity and resources

See also bilingualism, carnival, dual-language texts, language variety, multiculturalism

The children in British classrooms now reflect the diversity of cultures, religions and languages in our world. The wide range of literacy experience in which many children from minority communities engage has been researched by scholars like Eve Gregory (Gregory, 1996). Global travel and media coverage of events across the world make children more aware than ever before of the different environments in which human beings live. It would be surprising if all this did not affect work in English lessons. For it is in English lessons, above all, that children's whole experience inside and outside the classroom is the rich material on which we work. Books and other materials are a starting point for discussion, art work and writing and writers and illustrators of children's books have begun to reflect this wide diversity of experience. Children whose roots are in different part of the world need to see themselves reflected in both stories and information books. In her introduction to the latest edition of *A Multicultural Guide to Children's Books*, Rosemary Stones welcomes the increase in fine picture books designed as dual language editions. Mantra, for example, publish dual language versions of outstanding picture books including *Amazing Grace, Badger's Parting Gifts, Owl Babies* and *Can't You Sleep, Little Bear?*

Of course we do not want recipe-written books, but rather as Graham and Kelly put it 'good stories which naturally and in an unforced way give our children a sense of themselves having a place in a diverse world' (Graham and Kelly, 2000, p. 24).

AIMER (Access to Information on Multicultural Education Resources) Database – contact aimer.online@reading.ac.uk. Website is http://www.ralic.reading.ac.uk

The Centre for Language in Primary Education's *Finding Yourself in a Book* (1999) lists books that reflect the cultural and linguistic diversity of children in Southwark schools. E-mail: info@clpe.co.uk

The Reading and Language Information Centre's *The Other Languages* (1996) provides information for teachers about linguistic and cultural diversity. Available from RALIC, The University of Reading, Bulmerche Court, Reading RG6 1HY.

Graham, Judith and Kelly, Alison (2000 edition) *Reading Under Control* London: David Fulton.

Gregory, Eve (1996) *Making Sense of a New World* London: Paul Chapman.

Mantra website is: http://www.mantrapublishing.com

Stones, Rosemary (1999) *A Multicultural Guide to Children's Books 0–16* London: Books for Keeps and Reading: Reading and Language Information Centre.

Curriculum Development Plans – see audit

Curve of distribution – see norm referencing

D

Dash

See also compound word, hyphen, punctuation

This is a punctuation mark which signals either a pause or an aside or which separates dates. (The dash to link compound words like story-time or cue-systems is called a hyphen.)

Considering pause first, in the following example the dash shortens the number of words needed. So we can write:

> 'The teacher went into the classroom – it was totally deserted' instead of something like
> 'The teacher went into the classroom and found it was totally deserted.'

We can show children that a dash can be used to create a more dramatic impact than a comma, as in:

> 'After so much rain there could only be one outcome – floods.'

Emphasis can also be achieved, as in:

> 'He wore scarlet robes – a very vibrant scarlet.'

When used as an aside, as in the following sentence, a pair of dashes provide an alternative to commas or brackets:

> 'Not one child sat waiting for her – every one of them had measles – so she returned to the staff room.'

Dashes can be inserted between dates '2001–2002' or words 'The Paris–Dakar Rally' replacing the word 'to'.

Finally, a dash can be used where the writer chooses to miss out the middle letters of a swear word 'D–n!' or not to make fully explicit a well known name as in 'T–y B–r'.

Debates – see collaborative learning, discussion, discussion text, Drama and English, group discussion, plenary, prior knowledge, speaking and listening

Decoding skills

See also 'bottom-up' approaches to reading, phonics, reading

Decoding skills are to do with the ability to translate letters into sounds. Phonic methods put this ability at the centre of the reading process. However, the English language is not entirely phonically regular so in current approaches to reading in the United Kingdom the graphophonic cue-system is only one of the systems children are taught to use, the others being semantic (context), syntactic and bibliographic.

The National Literacy Strategy *Framework for Teaching* and the guidance in *Progression in Phonics* set out a programme for teaching phonological aspects of reading. For further help in understanding the issues and for help in planning here, I recommend *Sound Practice* by Layton *et al.*

DfEE (1998) *The National Literacy Strategy Framework for Teaching*. London: DfEE.

DfEE (1999) *The National Literacy Strategy. Progression in Phonics* London: DfEE.

Dombey, Henrietta and Moustafa, M. (1998) *Whole to Part Phonics: How Children Learn to Read and Spell* London: CLPE.

Layton, Lyn, Deeny, Karen and Upton, Graham (1997) *Sound Practice: Phonological Awareness in the Classroom* London: David Fulton.

Deep structure – see transformational grammar

Definite article

See also determiners

The definite article is the term used to describe the word 'the' which introduces a noun phrase.

So in 'The term has begun well and everyone is full of energy', 'the' is the definite article linked to the noun 'term'.

'The' is also used to introduce comparative adverbs and comparative adjectives. In the following sentence – 'The longer the document the less likely I am to read it' – 'the' introduces the comparative adjective 'longer' and the comparative adverb 'less likely'.

Denotation – see connotation and denotation

Design and Technology and English

See also book making, language across the curriculum, procedural or instruction genre

There are two aspects here. First we use language to teach and learn in every lesson – to plan, explain, question, discuss and evaluate. In a subject with a strong practical element it is important to communicate intentions and justify decisions. When it comes to reading and writing, a number of non-fiction genres are perfectly suited to use in the context of practical work. This range of material includes instruction manuals with procedural text. Dorling Kinder-sley's book *What's Inside?* shows how everyday things are made. An excellent book (in print and on CD-ROM) which seems to appeal to different age groups is David Macaulay's *The Way Things Work* (Dorling Kindersley). This explains the structure and function of a range of machines and implements using beautifully labelled and annotated diagrams. Then there are books which use technology to create pop-ups, windows and simple mechanisms linking technology with book making.

But English also has a role to play in Design & Technology through story, poetry and make believe. Fiction can create an exciting context for making things characters need. Teachers some-times ask children to design a boat for Edward Lear's 'jumblies' which will be more effective than a sieve! ('The Jumblies' in *A Book of Nonsense,* Dragon's World Publishers). The Lewisham Centre's *Find that Book* resource file suggests

work round a large number [...] including Verna Aardema's [...] *Kapiti Plain* (younger chi[...] moving picture to illustrate [...] Ted Hughes' *The Iron Man* (older [...] helped to control the iron man's eye m[...] using a computer). There are imaginative sug[...] tions for using picture books – children might, for example, help the resourceful Mrs Armitage improve her bicycle further (Quentin Blake's *Mrs Armitage on Wheels*) or help design false teeth, glasses and a wig for the giant in Raymond Briggs' *Jim and the Beanstalk.*

The Lewisham Centre resource is well worth consulting for inspiration on linking texts in the Literacy Hour with Design & Technology. To give just two examples, it is suggested that in Year 3 children make puppets and use them to tell myths, legends, fables and parables and that Year 6 pupils might assess how the different technolo-gies – printing, video and celluloid – affect the message conveyed in classic fiction adapted for television and film.

English can humanise Design & Technology showing how things can be made to help people and make particular people happy. There is nothing like a work of fiction to help children feel empathy for characters and this can be exploited in making connections between hand, head and heart in work linking English and Design & Technology.

Find that book: Making links between literacy and the broader curriculum Lewisham Professional Devel-opment Centre, 199 (Tel. 020 8314 6146).

Desk-top publishing

See also Information and Communications Technology (ICT) and English, word processing

This refers to the use of software installed in a personal computer and used for graphic design, editing and printing. Desk-top publishing pack-ages suitable for children, for example *Microsoft Publisher,* have greatly increased presentation choices, enabling the production of a range of professional-looking publications including leaflets, newspapers, greeting cards, posters and

own books. Clearly this helps children
erstand the formats appropriate to different
nres. Teachers can combine desk-top
publishing software with CD-ROM software –
for example Dorling Kindersley's CD-ROM
version of *The Jolly Postman* which provides
templates for letters and e-mails to fairytale characters (Garvey, 2000).

Garvey, John (2000) '"Incredibly creative tools" using
ICT and multimedia' in Fisher, Robert and Fisher,
Mary (eds) *Unlocking Literacy* London: David
Fulton.
Walker, Sue (1993) *Desktop Publishing for Teachers*
Reading: Reading University Language and Infor-
mation Centre.

Determiner

A determiner is used with a noun or noun phrase
and modifies the reference of that noun or noun
phrase. Determiners include:

articles	*a drawing,*	*the dictionary*
demonstratives	*this packet,*	*these apples*
possessives	*my jacket,*	*their pockets*
quantifiers	*some sugar,*	*both hands*
numbers	*seven days,*	*fifty coins*
question words	*which car?,*	*which size?*

Developmental writing – see Early Learning Goals, emergent writing, writing

Dewey system

Most school libraries use a version of the Dewey
system of categorising books. Children are taught
from the earliest stages to look in the reference
files, now often computerised, to find the allo-
cated number of a particular book and then
locate it on the shelf. Simplified Dewey systems
often use colour to help children track down
different subjects – history, geography and
science. Older children can be asked to make task
sheets or wall charts with simple instructions on
finding a book to help younger children use the
system.

Diagnostic assessment – see assessment, formative assessment, miscue analysis

Diagrams

See also CD-ROM, factual genres, illustrations, Internet,
non-fiction reading and writing, visual literacy

While 'table' and 'chart' suggest a numerical
element, 'diagram' raises the expectation of illustrations showing structures like part of a machine
or vehicle or processes like food chains or life
cycles. Computer technology now provides the
opportunity to see machines and parts of the
body working. For a detailed analysis of visual
forms in electronic texts like the Internet and
CD-ROMs I recommend Tina Sharpe and Elizabeth Dieter's chapter 'Visual literacy and the
Internet' in *Image Matters,* an interesting publication from Australia edited by Jon Callow, 1999.
There are two things to remember about
diagrams and other visual forms. First they are,
like written texts, culturally situated – our
cultural experiences affect how we view them.
Second, visual kinds of literacy need to be taught
– particularly the relatively new electronic forms.

But will electronic forms make print texts
redundant? I think not – for one thing print texts
are in some respects more flexible in that they can
be carried to many locations. And reading a book
is a distinct experience. So, rather than replacing
books and print diagrams, new technology has
energised book production and made possible
highly effective computer-enhanced diagrams
and illustrations, particularly in children's information and reference books.

What qualities make a good diagram, particularly for children? Apart from accuracy, clarity
and attractiveness, good labelling like that in
David Macaulay's book *The Way Things Work* (in
print and on CD-ROM, Dorling Kindersley) is
essential. There also needs to be good linkage
between diagrams and the accompanying written
text. If children look at and talk about quality
diagrams they are more likely to be inspired to
construct their own in a clear manner.

Cross-sections are a particular kind of diagram
often encountered in texts written for primary

school children. They are a feature of texts in several subject areas: history where the internal structure of the buildings of a period may be studied, for example a medieval or Tudor house; geography when soil layers or rock structures may need to be shown; science where the internal structure of part of the human or an animal body needs to be revealed. If you want to introduce cross-sections to the under eights in an entertaining way, I recommend Manning and Granstrom's *What's Under the Bed* (Franklin Watts, in small and big book format), a highly original story about the imaginary journey of two children and their cat through the layers of the earth right through to the burning centre. The big book version would be particularly helpful in showing how a key works – there is a splendid example of a key on the page showing the structure of an ant colony.

How much detail should a cross-section show? Of course it all depends on your purpose. One of my students worked with six year old on a series of lessons on mini-beasts and noted that they found the simple, uncluttered cross-section of a spider in French and Wisenfield's *Spider Watching* (Walker Books) very helpful at the beginning of the work. However, when their questions about the spider's structure became more detailed, she brought in Ted Dewan's *Inside the Whale and Other Animals* (Dorling Kindersley, 1992). They needed a lot of help in understanding the enormously detailed cross section of the spider but became deeply absorbed and asked the teacher to read the labels and annotations about the spider's tarsal claws and spinnerets. So, where children have got some foothold in a topic they can tackle difficult text and diagrams, with help of course, to feed their curiosity.

I find older primary children enjoy Stephen Biesty's work, in print or on CD-ROM, in which everything – pictures, labels, annotations and longer written accounts – is beautifully interrelated. A teacher using Biesty's *Incredible Cross Sections: Castle* in Year 6 history work praised the great attention to detail Biesty shows – for example on page 11 even a small corner of the cross section shows how castles were built and the workers' authentic tools. Opposite the picture Biesty

provides the fruits of his extremely conscientious research, telling us about the nature and origins of the materials used to build the castle, the structure and function of the different tools and even the procedures necessary to get permission to build the castle in the first place. The sheer fun and wit of the pictures draws the young readers in, but they find that the information both pictorial and written is far from superficial.

Callow, Jon (1999) (ed.) *Image Matters: Visual Texts in the Classroom* Marrickville, Australia: PETA, The Primary English Association.

Dialect

See also language variety, standard English (For issues to do with pronunciation see accent. What counts as a language rather than a dialect is a difficult issue to do with politics as well as linguistics, see Creoles for a discussion of languages which have developed under special circumstances.)

The term 'dialect' refers to a language variety which has a distinctive grammar and vocabulary. Regional dialects are part of an often rich home culture and identify speakers with a particular part of the country and a particular social group. Many children have done their first learning before coming to school in a non-standard but grammatically consistent dialect form. Standard English is a dialect which has acquired a special status for historical and cultural reasons.

The National Curriculum English Orders and the National Literacy Strategy *Framework for Teaching* require teachers to help children acquire standard forms in both speech and writing. The intention is that all children should learn to control the forms which enjoy a high status in our society and will help propel them through the gateway to better examination results and better occupational prospects. It is also true that speaking in standard English means more people will understand – not because standard English is linguistically or grammatically better but because, for historical and cultural reasons, it has acquired a high status here and abroad and is spoken and understood by a large number of people. There are important issues here. Many teachers feel concern about seeming to criticise the language of a child's home. A sensitive approach would be to explain to the children it is a matter of adding to their language repertoire rather than replacing their first dialect. But how far does this notion of appropriateness help – particularly in the case of younger children who may still get the impression that there is something unacceptable about their speech? In a very interesting analysis, Rebecca Bunting argues that 'the addition of standard English to a child's repertoire must affect the meaning and status of their first dialect, not only psychologically but cognitively too' (Bunting, 2000, p. 65).

I am not going to pretend there are any easy answers here, but I think the controversy is less troubling when it comes to written language. If I may bring in a personal observation here – I learnt as a child a wealth of Geordie songs, sayings and social history which remain part of my self-image, but I am glad I was helped to control standard forms in writing quite early on in my school career.

Three areas where support may be needed to help children make their writing conform to standard English are as follows:

- Subject–verb agreement, particularly in the case of the verb 'to be' where 'we was' is non-standard and 'we were' is standard.
- Special dialect words like 'canny' and 'bairn' (Geordie dialect words meaning respectively 'sweet' and 'young child') are appropriate in direct speech where the speaker uses a dialect form but not normally appropriate in general prose passages.
- Use of double negatives in some non-standard dialects are appropriate in the direct speech of someone using a dialect form or in a dialect song, dramatic improvisation or poetry.

We can take a positive approach to language variety by on the one hand helping children to control standard forms and on the other making opportunities in drama and poetry writing for the enjoyment of their first dialect.

Older primary children enjoy studying their local dialect through song, drama and folk tale. They can look at other dialects in picture books, for example Allan and Janet Ahlberg's *Burglar Bill*

and Antony Browne's different voices belonging to members of different families in his *A Walk in the Park*. In Chapter 2, pages 6–12 of their book *Primary English: Knowledge and Understanding* Medwell *et al.* suggest that intending teachers look at the lexical and grammatical features that show Dickon, in Frances Hodgeson Burnett's *The Secret Garden,* is speaking in a Yorkshire dialect. This kind of task can be adapted to use with older primary children and would give the message that regional dialects are worthy of study and interesting language forms in their own right.

Bunting, Rebecca (2000) *Teaching About Language in the Primary Years* London: David Fulton.

Medwell, Jane, Moore, George, Wray, David and Griffiths, Vivienne (2001) *Primary English: Knowledge and Understanding* Course book meeting 4/98 Standards. Exeter: Learning Matters.

Dialogue books/journals

See also diary

These are booklets which accompany the books children take home, to read either on their own or with an adult or older child. Teacher and the adults at home can keep in touch by making a comment when they want to about the child's preferences and progress. Dialogue books are best introduced as a school policy with an agreed format so that there is continuity as the child moves through the school. Children often appreciate feeling part of the dialogue (instead of just being written about!) and many teachers encourage them also to write in the dialogue book if they wish.

Diary

See also autobiography, carnival (and literacy), dialogue books, first person writing, reading diaries

A diary or journal can just be a calendar of engagements or quite a detailed chronological record of the writer's experiences, observations, feelings and attitudes.

Such private writing is usually done at home but some teachers reserve a space when children write in a diary, perhaps once or twice each week.

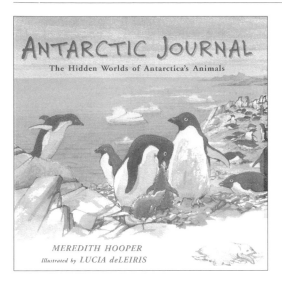

Front cover of *Antarctic Journal: The Hidden Worlds of Antarctica's Animals* by Meredith Hoope, illustrated by Lucia deLeiris (Frances Lincoln, 2000). Introduces children from about eight to eleven to writing nature diaries and combines meticulous first person observations with superb illustrations and sketches done on site.

This reinforces the notion that some people write for themselves, perhaps to record and make sense of all the experiences a human being has. Children under seven years are often encouraged to write their news in a special book or jotter. But this kind of writing is usually shared with the rest of the class, often at the beginning of the school day. The more private diary writing of older children can be a refuge from a perplexing world and it may not be claiming too much to say that it may encourage the development of a strong inner life. Writing a diary in school must always be an option and not something imposed. It is important that the teacher keeps the diaries in a safe place. Occasionally children may express a wish to share a particular entry with the teacher or the class or even to make the diary interactive by asking the teacher to write comments and reactions. Children sometimes like to give their diary a name – Anne Frank called her diary 'Kitty' – and enjoy choosing a title like *My Secret Journal* or *The Life and Thought of…* The content is up to the children and many like to include photographs, cartoons and drawings. It can be pointed out that the pictorial aspects should not make the diary look too much like a scrapbook.

How can we help children who want to write a journal but find it difficult to start? It might help to think of what an imaginary pen friend would like to know – about pets, hobbies and special places. Steiner and Phillips (1991) remind us that details about names and why they were chosen can make an interesting beginning. For those who need further help, they go on to suggest a sort of writing frame under headings like: Today I did; Today I felt; Today I felt sad/happy about; What I liked best about today. I have known of small groups of children who have enjoyed diary writing in the literacy corner and have produced their own agreed format. A small group of ten year olds in one school known to me decided they wanted to write their autobiographies. These turned out to consist of several chapters and the children were quite keen to read out particular parts of their books to the class. There are further practical suggestions for personal diary keeping in Mallett (1997).

So far the more private kind of diary has been considered. There are more open diaries and journals, the most usual being the reading diaries children keep to record their reading choices (see separate entry). However, some teachers of older primary children encourage the keeping of current affairs dairies and nature diaries. Current affairs diaries are usually written up once a week by 9–11 year olds. Each child selects an item from a newspaper from home or from a collection in the literacy corner, writes up a summary and includes a personal response. Time is found for them to read out their work and to start a discussion with others. This is an excellent way to develop aspects of children's literacy since it encourages children to look closely at particular models of writing with a clear purpose in mind. This journalistic sort of writing and discussion is emphasised in the National Curriculum English and the National Literacy Strategy programmes for Year 4 onwards.

Nature diaries provide a context where English and Science perspectives can be mutually enriching, as the response of pupils to natural phenomena is encouraged. Younger children enjoy writing entries about the development of tadpoles, caterpillars or birds visiting the school bird table. Several schools have an Internet site to share children's observations. If the diaries are a home project teachers need to inform the parents about what is required and gain their co-opera-tion. A simple format needs to be agreed, but children need to be conscientious in recording the date and time of observations and labelling drawings. Younger nature diarists may find Angela Wilkes' advice about keeping nature logs in *The Amazing Outdoor Activity Book* (Dorling Kindersley, 1996) helpful.

Mallett, Margaret (1997) *First Person Writing in the Primary School: Enjoying and Reflecting on Diaries, Letters, Autobiographies and First Person Fiction* Sheffield: NATE.

Steiner, Barbara and Philips, Kathleen (1991) *Journal Keeping with Young People* USA Teacher Ideas Press, Libraries Unlimited, Inc.

Dictionary

See also alphabet, non-fiction reading and writing

A dictionary is an alphabetically organised refer-ence text which defines and gives the meaning or meanings of words. Some dictionaries provide further information, for example about the root and origin of the word and a guide to its pronun-ciation. The main purposes of a dictionary are to check spelling, to confirm that a word is being used appropriately or to find a synonym.

There is a wide variety of print and electronic dictionaries for children of different ages.

Word books for the very young are not, strictly speaking, dictionaries as they are often organised thematically rather than alphabetically. But they do foster an early interest in words and in ideas – see Janet and Allan Ahlberg's *The Baby's Catalogue*. They also help children see how illus-tration and written text link to make meaning. Young children find Richard Scarry's colourful and detailed word books most entertaining – for example *Cars and Trucks and Things That Go* (Collins). *Collins First Word Book* provides bright double spreads of objects in familiar settings like the kitchen, garden and bathroom, surrounded by appropriate vocabulary. Words are helpfully embedded in phrases in *My Oxford Picture Word*

Book – and there is now *My Oxford Word Box*, a CD-ROM combining stories with games, rhymes and word families. Alphabet books are an early introduction to alphabetic organisation (see under separate entry 'alphabet') and therefore are natural forerunners to first dictionaries. Many first dictionaries display the alphabet in upper and lower case round each page; *Ladybird First Picture Dictionary* highlights the letters dealt with on each double spread. A selection of early dictio-naries has an important place in the early years classroom and might include *Chambers First Dictionary*, Dorling Kindersley's *My First Dictio-nary* and *My First Oxford Dictionary*. For group or class based word level work with children aged six years and under *The Oxford Reading Tree Dictionary* is now in Big Book format. Teachers of the under sevens are familiar with the detailed and advanced questions young children some-times ask. Dictionaries and encyclopaedias intended for the younger age range sometimes do not give adequate coverage and explanation. Therefore it is wise to provide also a good dictio-nary intended for an older age group which teacher and child can use together when appro-priate.

In the middle primary years, from about age seven to nine, there are good print dictionaries by the main publishers of children's reference books and an increasing number of electronic versions. Good print dictionaries for this age range include *The Usborne First Dictionary* which includes puzzles and some excellent spelling tips. The National Literacy Strategy *Framework for Teaching* requires children to move towards dictionaries without illustrations. There are many splendid illustrated dictionaries for chil-dren up to the end of the primary years and some children will continue to feel more comfortable with these. *The Oxford Young Readers' Dictionary* which has over 6,000 entries is a good non-illus-trated dictionary for the over sevens. Most chil-dren's dictionaries for the over sevens have 'bold print' head words, phrases and parts of speech, but this one is particularly clear, partly because of the choice of bold print on cream coloured paper. The 'using this dictionary page' is lucid and inviting.

Dorling Kindersley's *Incredible Amazing Dictionary* has 1,000 words and offers games and puzzles to practise dictionary and alphabet skills. *Word Bank* (TAG 01474 357350) and *Crossword Creator* (MacLine/WindowsLine (020 8111/ 1177) help children compile their own personal dictionaries and the second of these includes *Roget's Thesaurus*.

As children reach the later primary years, their grip on certain genre features of dictionaries – the use of phrases as well as sentences, the provision of several, often numbered, meanings and abbreviations – strengthens. As we would expect, in general illustrations become fewer and written entries becomes longer. However some children, and not only those with special learning needs, continue to benefit from carefully chosen illustrations. I have found children like using *Usborne Illustrated Dictionary* which looks inviting and has a particularly helpful user's guide to parts of speech, and hints and guidelines on forming plurals and using apostrophes. *Collins School Dictionary* suits abler eleven year olds and gives good guidance on grammar and pronunciation. I like the generous spacing in this dictionary; each 'sense' is given on a new line. Another good dictionary for the last year of the primary school and into the secondary years is the *Oxford School Dictionary* which has over 40,000 head words, with plurals, tenses, nouns as appropriate and word origins for all root words. The format is plain and clear and new vocabulary, including words like 'internet' and 'virtual reality', are clearly explained.

Specialist dictionaries – for example Dorling Kindersley's *Dictionary of Science* – often provide a good browse – but lack of A–Z organisation in some of them makes them seem more like encyclopaedias.

Teachers and librarians develop criteria for choosing print and electronic dictionaries for particular age groups. Some of the general criteria are similar to those we use for information texts and I have indicated something about what to look for in referring to particular texts above. The best print dictionaries are easy to use and in a clear and inviting format while electronic books, in addition, need to communicate information which may not be linear in a helpful way. If there are illustrations and diagrams these need to be appropriate, clear and well labelled. Written explanations need to be lucid and the words contextualised. It is worth checking that a new purchase covers the vocabulary children are likely to want to check across the curriculum. Clear explanations of new words to describe new technological concepts like 'Homepage', 'Image map' and 'HyperText links' are now required. I would also ask myself if the print or electronic dictionary was likely to encourage browsing and an interest in words. This means including some unusual and interesting words. You just need to look in children's picture books to find some fascinating words which have a strong imaginative appeal, for example 'rumpus' in Maurice Sendak's *Where the Wild Things Are* (The Bodley Head), 'exultation' (of larks) in Patricia MacCarthy's *Herds of Words* (Pan MacMillan) and 'migration' in Karen Wallace's *Think of an Eel* (Walker Books).

New dictionaries in different media and format, and for all age groups, are published constantly. I have given some examples in the analysis above, but anyone updating their dictionary selection would find it helpful to look at the titles from some of the main publishers of children's reference books which include: Collins (020 8741 7070), Dorling Kindersley (020 7836 5411), Global Software Publishing (01480 496666), Kingfisher (020 7903 9999), Oxford University Press (01865 556767) and Usborne (020 7430 2800).

Digraph

See also phoneme, phonics

Digraphs are two letters that make one sound or phoneme in a word. There are two kinds: consonant digraphs (ch, ph, sh, wh) and vowel digraphs (ai, ay, ie, au).

Diphthong

See also phoneme, phonics

This describes two vowel sounds which create a new sound within a syllable. The tongue moves to change the pronunciation of one vowel sound to another as, for example, in hear, height and rain.

Direct and indirect speech (or direct and reported speech)

See also dialect, punctuation, quotation marks, speech marks

Direct speech is the written down utterance of a person and speech marks are used to indicate what was actually said – '"Please put the science equipment back in the cupboard as soon as the lesson is over", he said to the classroom assistant.' Tom McArthur indicates how we can vary the reporting verbs – 'said, commented, cried, enquired, observed, replied, retorted, screamed, whined and yelled'. Adverbs can help convey something about the speaker's manner – 'demurely, happily, mysteriously' and so on (McArthur, 1992, p. 314). We can help children vary their choice of vocabulary by pointing out the possibilities. Reading interesting conversations in stories can be an inspiration to children in their own attempts at writing direct speech. We can explain that what people actually say is often an indication of character and attitude.

Indirect speech provides an account of what someone has said, written or thought and is written in the third person – 'He asked the classroom assistant if she would please put the science equipment back in the cupboard as soon as the lesson was over.'

Units 4 and 16 in *Grammar for Writing* are concerned with the conventions of speech punctuation, with suggestions for activities.

Grammar for Writing DfEE 2000.
McArthur, Tom (1992) *The Oxford Companion to the English Language* Oxford: Oxford University Press.

Directed Activities Around Texts (DARTs)

See also cloze procedure, EXIT model, note taking, summary

DARTs help children learn about the structure of texts and the features of print, particularly if they are carried out in a supportive context. The under sixes enjoy simple sequencing games made by photocopying and cutting up sections of a suitable text and asking children to put the story together again. Of course it is the talk round the task that is so valuable. Favourite books for this activity include *Little Rabbit Foo Foo* by Michael Rosen (Walker Books, reissued 1999), *Oi! Get Off Our Train* by John Burningham (Walker, reissued 2000) and *The Jumblies* by Edward Lear (Orchard reissued 1998). Bain and Bridgewood present sequencing tasks of increasing complexity in their book *The Primary Grammar Book*. The emphasis is very much on children becoming able to give reasons, both spoken and written, for the way they order the paragraphs making up a text.

One important activity which helps children use their predictive abilities is 'cloze procedure' which requires one or a pair of young learners to complete texts where words have been deliberately removed. Sometimes the words that have been missed out and are to be inserted are given at the bottom of the page. Alternatively, children can be given a text where more than one word would be semantically and grammatically acceptable to fill the gap. Again, talking with the teacher or another child about why some words fit and others do not makes this a highly reflective activity whether done using a print passage or on the computer.

If you want a book providing suggestions for meaningful games round children's books, particularly for five to seven year olds and inexperienced older readers, you cannot do better than look at Helen Bromley's *Book-based Reading Games*. There is advice about dice games based on cumulative texts, track games on journeys in stories and sequencing games. The children in the case studies returned to the texts independently 'with renewed confidence and interest'.

There are suggestions for using the games with children with special needs, young bilingual learners and reluctant boy readers. UK teachers will find the section on using the games to energise the shared and the group elements in the literacy hour and to meet specific National Literacy Strategy Objectives very helpful.

The approach to using non-fiction texts in the National Literacy Strategy *Framework for Teaching* draws on the Nuffield-funded research of David Wray and Maureen Lewis and on the Extending Interactions with Texts EXIT model (Wray and Lewis, 1997). Teachers in Britain will have worked with the National Literacy Strategy training module which presents the EXIT model – aiming to get children interacting with texts rather than closely paraphrasing them in their writing. Activities include – activating prior knowledge, formulating questions to take to texts and communicating information.

Bain, Richard and Bridgewood, Marion (1998) *The Primary Grammar Book: Finding Patterns-Making Sense* Sheffield: NATE (National Association for the Teaching of English).

Bromley, Helen (2000) *Book-based Reading Games* London: A Language Matters Publication, Centre for Language in Primary Education.

Department for Education and Employment (DfEE) (1998) *The National Literacy Strategy: Literacy Training Pack. Module 6: Reading and Writing for Information* London: DfEE.

Wray, David and Lewis, Maureen (1997) *Extending Literacy: Reading and Writing Non-Fiction* London: Routledge.

Directionality

See also concepts of print, reading

Directionality refers to the reader's understanding of where one starts to read and the direction to go in. This is one of the basic concepts about print assessed by Marie Clay's Early Concepts of Print procedure.

Clay, Marie (1979) (second edition), *The Early Assessment of Reading Difficulties* Auckland: Heinemann.

Discourse analysis

See also collaborative learning, field of discourse, mode, speaking and listening, speech act, tenor

Discourse analysis refers to the systematic categorisation of naturally occurring speech. A highly influential scheme for illuminating classroom discourse or conversation was devised by the linguists Sinclair and Coulthard in 1975. They divided spoken exchanges into three main categories:

- initiation: the teacher might ask: 'What are words called that tell us more about a noun?'
- response: a child might answer: 'An adjective?'
- feedback: the teacher assesses what the child has said: 'That's right. Good!'

This category system helped us understand roles and functions rather than intentions and meanings and it is important to bear in mind that the way the utterances are categorised depends, to some extent, on individual interpretation. (For a helpful review of the history of discourse analysis see Bunting, 2000, Chapter 3.)

Another great influence on language analysis, both spoken and written, in the United Kingdom was the functional approach of M.A.K. Halliday. The 'functions' are essentially social in Halliday's work. He stresses the situational restraints on language in terms of field (topic of the communication), tenor (relationship of participants – relative status, age and roles) and mode (medium for the communication). This functional model led to the 'Language in Use' approach to language study in some secondary schools. Children worked with spoken and written texts arising out of 'real' situations. This functional perspective is still discernible in the language study approach of the National Literacy Strategy see, for example, the work on advertisements in The National Literacy Strategy *Grammar for Writing*.

In the late 1980s, Edwards and Mercer carried out work on the creation of what they termed 'common knowledge' between teachers and children (Edwards and Mercer, 1987).

They were interested in how this 'common knowledge' was constructed and the role of context in its creation. Two kinds of knowledge were identified: 'ritual knowledge' and 'principled knowledge'. Teachers initiate children into the conventions for expressing 'ritual knowledge' which consists of giving a 'right' answer expressed appropriately. 'Principled knowledge' is more to do with carving out an explanation which depends on a well-thought-out understanding of information and issues. The 'rules' of discourse were, according to Edwards and Mercer, learnt mainly in the classroom. Many teacher researchers were encouraged by the work of discourse analysts to tape-record classroom talk in an attempt to make explicit the dynamics of learning. As well as noting the findings of Edwards and Mercer, teachers were also inspired by earlier work on classroom conversations carried out in the 1960s by Douglas Barnes *et al.* These latter researchers suggested that a continuum of questions teachers and children might ask ranged from those that were closed and required a 'right' answer and those that were 'open' and invited an opinion. The analysis was energised by lively transcripts from different classrooms (Barnes *et al.* 1969). This approach to reflecting on classroom discourse reinforced the notion that even knowledge passed on by the teacher or a book has to be constructed anew by the learner. So, while children take on the cultural resources of their society, passed on partly by the school, there should be room for their own creative solution to problems and challenges.

An interest in classroom talk and how it illuminated gender issues was reflected in a number of studies in the 1970s and 1980s. The way teachers – often unconsciously through gesture and facial expression as well as what they actually say – shape the responses of particular children to the possible disadvantage of girls has been studied by researchers like Swann and Graddol (1989).

In the 1970s and 1980s there was an interest in the talk of preschool children in natural settings as well as talk in Nursery and Reception classrooms. Gordon Wells and his researchers on the Bristol University project *Language at Home and School* recorded children's everyday conversations with their parents, caregivers and siblings to try to identify what kinds of language experience led to literacy success later on. The books which

were an outcome of the longitudinal project, *The Meaning Makers* (1987) for example, emphasise the power of spoken language in bringing about learning. The importance of stories, read or told to children, as precursors of literacy is established by this research. The value of talk round written texts, particularly fiction, has been demonstrated by the classroom examples insightfully evaluated in Aidan Chambers' book *Tell Me* (1993).

Teachers continue to be interested in classroom talk but more as a way of learning and evidence of learning than as a way of analysing teacher and pupil roles. Talk episodes may be recorded to show children's progress in social aspects of speaking and listening, like turn taking and responding to the contributions of others, and as evidence of progress in planning, hypothesising and presenting an argument.

Barnes, Douglas, Britton, James and Rosen, Harold (1969) *Language, the Learner and the School* Harmondsworth: Penguin.

Bunting, Rebecca (2000, second edition) *Teaching About Language in the Primary Years* London: David Fulton.

Chambers, Aidan (1993) *Tell Me* Stroud: The Thimble Press.

Edwards, D. and Mercer, N. (1987) *Common Knowledge: The Development of Understanding in the Classroom* London: Methuen.

Sinclair, J and Coulthard, R (1975) *Towards an Analysis of Discourse.* London: Oxford University Press.

Swann, J. and Graddol, D. (1989) 'Gender inequalities in classroom talk' in *Gnosis,* Issue 14, London: LDA.

Wells, Gordon (1987) *The Meaning Makers: Children Learning Language and Using Language to Learn.* London, Sydney, Auckland and Toronto: Hodder & Stoughton.

Discussion

See also collaborative learning, discussion text, Drama and English, plenary, prior knowledge, speaking and listening

This implies an exchange of viewpoints and posing of open rather than closed questions. At every stage, discussion in class and group settings is a major way of making sense of all kinds of information, often derived from reading, in every lesson. It can also be a potent evaluative tool: for example children assess their learning – discussing perhaps the quality of resources used and the success of an episode of improvised drama. In English, fiction is an important starting point for the exchange of views on for example plot, characters, motivation, language use and ethical issues. One of the most useful and exciting books about this is Aidan Chambers' *Tell Me: Children Reading and Talk* (1993, The Thimble Press).

Chambers, Aidan (1993) *Tell Me: Children Reading and Talk* Stroud: The Thimble Press.

Discussion text

See also collaborative learning, genre, National Literacy Strategy, non-fiction reading and writing

This kind of text, one of the six non-fiction genres in the United Kingdom National Literacy Strategy *Framework for Teaching,* presents different viewpoints on a topic. Children can talk about which argument they find most convincing and produce their own discussion texts to present to others. Topics for children's own 'discussion' writing might include the advantages and disadvantages of Sports Days, School Uniform and Keeping Pets.

Displays

See also writing area/corner, libraries, reading environment, writing

Good displays of books and resources and related children's work in the school entrance hall, the library and the classrooms encourage interest in reading and writing. They also invite comment and are a special way of communicating and sharing our knowledge about enjoying reading. All the books we select should of course be good of their kind. The following list brings together what I have seen and read over the years which might usefully be held in mind when displays are set up to promote English work:

Finding a focus

It is best to present something coherent and not overcomplicated

- books/resources by one author/illustrator/ publisher; on one theme – adventure, science fiction, spiders; or a particular kind of book – for example poetry anthologies, short stories or non-fiction.
- different versions of the same traditional tale. (I remember an excellent display made by a Year 5 class and their teacher on different tellings of *Red Riding Hood.* Some of the children's own modern versions of the story were included.)
- one book in the centre of the display and reviews by the class and the teacher surrounding it.
- the ten favourite books of one class together with children's short reviews. (Tyrell and Gill (2000) suggest we call such a display 'A Really Good Book'.)
- favourite books from the childhoods of teachers and other adults in the school.
- Year 5 or Year 6 display for younger children of their favourite early books with annotation on stand up cards.
- new books and books short listed for a prize like Smarties, Carnegie, Kate Greenaway or the *TES* information book award.
- books on a particular country or culture or on a topical event or festival; dual language books.
- books related to film or television.
- books children have made.
- children's writing of a particular kind, attractively mounted.

Creating visual appeal

If you remember displays that impressed you, they tend to be uncluttered, fresh looking and with a focal point

- an eye-catching book cover or an object like a box or vase that fits with the theme of a story might intrigue.
- we can get ideas from shop windows and museums about the grouping of items. Some imaginative teachers use boxes, packing cases, easels and coloured paper or curtain as a back drop – but we do need to avoid a cluttered effect.

- on the whole, well selected books attractively displayed can be enough. If we make displays too elaborate we might not change them as frequently as is wise. As Chambers remarks 'every display has a natural life-span' (Chambers, 1991).

Involving children in the display

- copies of books should be readily available once children have been tempted by the display.
- a lively talk about the displayed resources in assembly can excite children's interest.
- teachers can take the children to visit a display, read snippets from the books and talk to the children about them.
- as well as regular small scale displays, once or twice a year schools often make a large scale set of displays involving parents, teachers and friends of the school in the preparation.

Chambers, Aidan (1991) *The Reading Environment: How Adults Help Children Enjoy Books* Stroud: The Thimble Press (Chapter 5).

Tyrrell, Jenny and Gill, Narinderjit (2000) *Co-ordinating English at Key Stage 1* London: Falmer Press (Chapter 2).

Domestic and family novels

See also classics, fiction, history of children's literature, realism

Domestic and family novels, as we would expect, explore life in the familiar settings of the home, garden, local school and neighbourhood. Two books by Frances Hodgeson Burnett – *The Secret Garden* (1910) and *The Little Princess* (1905) – which explore, amongst other things, relationships with family and friends still have a continuing appeal for children in the primary years. The *William* stories, written by Richmal Crompton from the 1920s right up until her death in 1969, are about a socially privileged little boy. But he seems to have a universal appeal – perhaps it is his pitting himself against his parents and other adults that attracts young readers. Another enduring example of this genre is about people at the other end of the social scale – *The Family from One-End Street* by Eve Garnett

(1937). It follows the everyday happenings in the household of a dustman and his washerwoman wife. Some have criticised it for being condescending. John Rowe Townsend comments 'People from higher up the social scale are terribly nice to the Ruggleses; and the Ruggleses know their place' (John Rowe Townsend, p. 150, 1995). In spite of such reservations the book remains in print and many children seem to enjoy the stable, supportive family world portrayed and the amusing things that happen – Rose burning a petticoat when she does the ironing and Kate losing her hat. As Peter Hunt points out 'the period flavour is so strong that it is very difficult to judge how far the Ruggles family are being patronised' (Hunt, 1995, p. 218).

Perhaps we think of Arthur Ransome's *Swallows and Amazons,* set in the 1920s and 1930s, as adventure stories – but while making the children independent during their holiday activities, Ransome also sets them in a secure middle class world. So while the books are about an escape from everyday family life – the domestic environment remains in the background.

Just because events take place in a homely setting does not preclude the occurrence of dramatic or even fantasy events. The story in Philippa Pearce's *Tom's Midnight Garden* (1958) takes place in a family home and young readers learn about the difficulties of a childless couple when they agree to look after a young relative. And the novel explores in a profound way the nature of friendship. But is is also a story about a series of journeys back to another time. Pearce's story for younger children *The Battle of Bubble and Squeak* also has lively events based round home: two messy gerbils infuriate the adults in the family.

The stories in Nina Bawden's novels are often in domestic and family settings. *Carrie's War* (1973) shows us how evacuees cope with separation from their parents and adjustment to strange domestic circumstances. *The Peppermint Pig* (1975) takes us through a year in the life of the Greengrass family after the father of the household leaves to seek his fortune in America. Bawden's novels support Victor Watson's assertion that family stories need not be cosy (Watson 2001).

Hunt, Peter (ed.), (1995) *Children's Literature: An Illustrated History* Oxford: Oxford University Press.

Townsend, John Rowe (1990 edition) *Written for Children: An Outline of English Language Children's Literature* London: The Bodley Head.

Watson, Victor (2001) *The Cambridge Guide to Children's Books in English* Cambridge: Cambridge University Press.

Drafting

See also compositoning, conferencing, editing, process model of writing, proof reading, transcriptional aspects of writing, writing

Drafting involves taking ideas from a plan and developing them into written text. The work of both Donald Graves (1983) and Frank Smith (1982) has illuminated the role of drafting in the process of children's writing. Graves in particular argues that writing, at any rate that which is likely to go beyond the superficial, involves several different stages from the 'pre-composition' to 'publication' of the fair copy. In the United Kingdom the sequence was often: plan, draft, revise, proof read and present. Shared writing has been a good context in which to model how the writer moves through the stages. The plan can be oral or written down and then, using this, the writer shapes his or her thoughts in a draft either on paper or on the computer. The revision stage offers a chance to reshape ideas and thoughts to better effect and to add in anything missed. Proof reading concentrates on secretarial errors and it sometimes helps to have proof reading partners as it may be easier to spot someone else's mistakes. Finally children present their work in fair copy. Two things have a considerable effect on the content, organisation and style of writing. First, the writer needs to have a clear idea of the purpose of the writing task and second, they need to have a sense of the audience for their work. Bearing these two things in mind is helpful in following the sequence outlined above and bringing writing to final draft.

As the SATs in Reading and Writing at the end of Key Stage 2 require 'first draft' responses children need some practice in planning 'in their heads' and writing a single draft.

There is also an issue over how often we should ask children to take a piece of writing through all the drafting stages. Here we need to have a sense of proportion. While it certainly gives value to writing if some of the work children do is taken through the stages discussed above – plan, draft, revise, proof read and present – there are occasions when a first draft is all that is required. I have found that struggling young writers find too much redrafting de-motivating.

Graves, Donald (1983) *Writing: Teachers and Children at Work* Portsmouth, NH: Heinemann Educational Books.

Smith, Frank (1982) *Writing and the Writer*. Portsmouth, NH: Heinemann Educational Books.

Drama and English

See also genre, play and language and literacy, speaking and listening, writing

In this entry the use of drama and role play as powerful approaches to teaching aspects of English are considered. Drama and role play are important agents for learning in every lesson. Indeed where Drama has its own place in the weekly programme, teachers may use a drama lesson to develop a theme from history, geography, science or other curriculum areas. Where English is concerned, drama and role play have a special value: to develop spoken language in a range of contexts; to explore themes arising from children's experiences, anecdotes and from texts of all kinds; to encourage reading and writing for different purposes and audiences. In doing all this we must remember that language is socially situated and the different kinds and usages have developed to serve different societal purposes. This complexity can be explored through drama.

While the benefits of drama and role play to children's language and learning are undisputed, it is also valuable experience in its own right; it is the intense involvement in the created situations which leads to worthwhile and varied use of language. Feelings as well as thoughts are important in English and improvisation allows the exploration of many human situations that are part of growing up and often include painful episodes like separation from loved ones and difficulties with friends. Drama can also help children explore interesting aspects of cultural diversity where a story or information book might be a starting point.

Good primary practitioners have always used drama to energise English work. It was encouraging to find Drama brought firmly into the 1995 National Curriculum orders and its place has been made even more secure in the 2000 revision. To some extent there has been a softening of the old conflict between drama as a learning process and drama as a product to be presented. It is more helpful to regard these as two complementary aspects, each coming into strong focus at particular times for particular purposes. For example, teachers and pupils studying a play might explore a situation or issue through improvisation. Teachers may also help children to script an improvisation which has stabilised. A scripted improvisation could be the basis for a performance for parents, friends of the school and other children.

Role play in the Early Years (3–6 years)

Children enjoy spontaneous role play from an early age; it allows the expression of feelings, attitudes and opinions in a relatively secure context. Early years teachers build opportunities for role play into their long-term planning and thereby achieve some of the language and literacy objectives in the early learning goals. In the context of imaginative play children can take on different roles. This creates opportunities for using spoken and written language for different purposes and thus makes a considerable contribution to language development.

Young children need space and time for role play. Changing the location of the activity and adding appropriate props increases the range of possibilities. The teacher and nursery team can intervene to link the play with literacy experiences and other learning. They can develop situations out of stories and anecdotes children bring to the classroom. Areas available for role play can be transformed into for example – a cafe, office of a fire station, builders' yard, post office, shop, train station, clinic or garden centre.

With encouragement, young children will attempt writing linked to the theme of the role play. Five year olds learning about fire fighters might have an office with the duty rotas, posters about Fire & Safety, forms to fill in, records of fires extinguished, advertisements for fire equipment, instructions for use of fire fighting aids and some cards and letters of thanks from people they had helped. In fact writing appropriate labels, posters and so on is part of helping the children understand the context for their role play.

A home corner also provides a non-threatening context for all kinds of writing to support role play activities like writing stories to read to dolls, menus for the toys' meals, greetings cards, shopping lists and letters to build into play situations. An outstanding project in which six year olds built much of their talk and writing for a term round the life of Mr Togs (a life-sized doll in charge of the classroom shop) is described and evaluated in *Mr Togs the Tailor* published by the Scottish Consultative Council on the Curriculum in 1987.

Early Years teams become skilled in observing children's role play and judging where to intervene to help the children extend their activity. Four year olds who had listened to a reading of Allan and Janet Alberg's picture book *Burglar Bill* built aspects of the story into their play. To extend the children's reflection on the key issues – do ex-burglars make good parents? – one of the nursery teachers dressed up as Burglar Betty and holding a doll, answered the children's questions in role. This is an example of 'hot seating' which is a technique useful for any age group when teacher or child 'in role' is questioned by others. A student teacher working in the nursery said she will never forget the children's excitement and the profundity of their questions.

Improvisation and drama at Key Stages 1 and 2

Contexts for speaking and listening One challenge for teachers is to find ways of helping children become competent in the range of speech situations they will encounter as adults. Some of these are unlikely to arise naturally in the course of classroom work or to be part of the day-to-day experience of the child. Providing opportunities for dramatic improvisation, which is a development from the role play of younger children, is a valuable way of encouraging children to use different kinds of spoken language for different audiences and purposes. Examples include: persuading local councillors that provision of a park for the village community is a priority; asking the police to help find a lost bicycle; children and adults in conflict over having a family pet. Often inspiration for these comes from a story. For example, one of my students helped children base an improvisation on the theme in James Simon's book *Dear Greenpeace* about a child who is convinced she has a whale in her garden pond. Particularly if you work with older primary children you will find inspiration in Jenny Griffiths' book *An Early Start to Drama*. I have seen a number of very successful series of lessons based on the waste dump idea. For example, people oppose the council's plan to have a chemical waste dump on the boundaries of a small town.

To extend their work and make it worthwhile, sensitive intervention by the teacher is necessary. This can be done by direct support and advice or by the teacher stepping into a role – perhaps as a key figure like a monarch or as a discordant voice such as a dissident peasant. Dorothy Heathcote, a great teacher of drama to all age groups and people of widely varying abilities and needs, showed how a teacher can energise children's improvisation by taking up a role.

Drama is essentially a cooperative activity and helps children listen, collaborate and learn from each other and to be aware of each other's needs. The discussion to plan an improvisation, the improvisation itself and its evaluation all help children to become more confident users of the spoken language.

Drama benefits from having space and some basic resources like an overhead projector, musical instruments, a tape recorder, wooden blocks to create structures and some simple props. However, it can sometimes take place in the classroom. Issues arising from books can be explored in pairs, each child taking up a different role. While the emphasis is on the value of the process, I find children love to show their work to the class. Duologue work can lead to scripting and I have seen this kind of approach used successfully in the Literacy Hour.

Contexts for reading and writing In English, themes often arise from the literature children have been enjoying. This ranges from the picture books of the early years (David McKees *Not Now Bernard*; Valerie Flournoy's *The Patchwork Quilt*) to collection of short stories (*Aesop's Fables*; Jane Kurtz's *Mamo on the Mountain*) and novels (Betsy Byars *The Midnight Fox*; Philippa Pearce's *Tom's Midnight Garden*) for older children. Television and film as well as books, newspaper articles and letters all provide powerful stories to extend and reflect on through drama.

Where the issues in literature are explored through improvisation, children bring a new depth to their reading. Discussion of the plot, characterisation and use of language help children benefit from each other's insights. The planning of how episodes will be acted out and their evaluation contributes to children becoming careful and reflective readers.

Working with texts expands vocabulary in a natural way and is a welcome by-product of children becoming genuinely engaged with the themes they are exploring. Year 5 children, working on improvisations inspired by Barbara Jeffers' retelling of *Brother Eagle Sister Sky*, explored environmental concepts like 'conservation' and 'habitats' and wrote about issues of complexity like the reconciling of the needs of different groups.

Drama creates contexts for many of the kinds of writing both fiction and non-fiction in the National Literacy *Framework for Teaching*. A teacher of a Year 3 class helped children act out parts of Julia and Charles Snapes' picture book *Giant*. The giant in the story is a huge mountain which disappears when the villagers drop litter in the fields on the mountain side and generally adopt a cavalier attitude to conservation. The interesting thing about this work was that the environmental issues led teacher and children to use information texts to develop their work. The children's written response was particularly rich and varied and included posters to try to stop the dropping of litter, letters to the giant to persuade her to come back, poems and reports on caring for the environment.

Many of the literacy strategy objectives were met in an interesting and coherent way including: expressing views about a story, writing simple play scripts, talking about some of the differences between fiction and non-fiction and writing non-chronological reports (text level work, Year 3, Term 1 of *The Framework*).

Conclusion

So, drama and improvisation have an important role in energising English and developing children's language in ways difficult to achieve by any other means. Above all drama nearly always enthuses children and seems to bring about a spirit of cooperation which leads to much hard work and concentration.

There are a number of very good books, chapters and articles on Drama in the Primary classroom including:
Clipson-Boyles, Suzi (1999) 'The role of drama in the literate classroom' in Prue Goodwin (ed.) *The Literate Classroom* London: David Fulton. (This has an excellent annotated list of drama techniques with literacy examples.)
Griffiths, Jenny (1991) *An Early Start to Drama* Hemel Hempstead: Simon & Schuster Education (practical ideas for building drama round issues).
Neelands, Jonathan (1992) *Learning Through Imagined Experience* London: Hodder & Stoughton (helpful on drama's role in language development).
Toye, Nigel and Prendiville, Francis (2000) *Drama and the Traditional Story for the Early Years* London: Routledge/Falmer.

Dual-language texts

See also bilingualism, cultural diversity, multiculturalism, multilingualism

Dual-language books or resources have a text written in English and another language. As well as helping bilingual young learners, having dual-language texts in the classroom increases the awareness of monolingual children of different languages and cultures.

The quality of dual-language texts is as important as in any other book. The story must meet criteria of exciting plot, good characterisation, convincing setting and successful illustrations. Format is also important and the two languages should have equal status.

The main problem with dual-language books is that we may find it difficult to judge the quality of the translation.

In their article in the 1999 edition of *A Multicultural Guide to Children's Books* Viv Edwards and Chris Routh observe that there have been few recent additional titles to dual-language book lists. This seems to be because of high origination costs and relatively small print runs. However, there has been a trend to take good quality picture books in English and to publish dual-language versions. Magi Publishing, for example, has dual-language versions of established picture books like for example *Amazing Grace, The Whales' Song, Owl Babies* and *Badger's Parting Gifts* (Magi website – www.littletiger.okukbooks.com). Other good publishers and suppliers of dual-language books include Zero to Ten (Tel. 01753 578 499), Milet (website – www.milet.com) and Mantra (website – www.mantrapublishing.com).

As well as initiatives from publishers, projects involving parents, teachers and children have contributed to multicultural resources. For example, the Multilingual Word Processing Project based at the university of Reading has exploited the new technologies to produce learning materials in a range of languages. The Fabula Project is a European funded project to promote literacy in 'languages of lesser diffusion' in the European community. The Fabula multimedia software which has been produced by teachers, children, software designers and researchers has the potential to be used with any language with a roman script. It enables the creation of bilingual storybooks by inserting text and scanned illustrations into simple templates. There are also features like speech bubbles, sound effects and language links to explore the texts and glossaries.

Fabula Project at Reading and Language Information Centre. Tel. 0118 931 8820. Website: http//www.fabula-eu.org

Specialist book shop – Heffers Children's Book Shop, 20 Trinity St, Cambridge CB3 3NG.

Stones, Rosemary (ed.) (1999) *A Multicultural Guide to Children's Books 0–16+* London and Reading: Books for Keeps with The Language and Information Centre, Reading, see the chapter on 'Multilingual Resources for Children'.

Dyslexia

See also Special Educational Needs (SEN) in language and literacy

This term means literally word blindness or difficulty with words. It has been extended to refer to a syndrome which includes other symptoms like memory problems, clumsiness and spatial difficulties. Reid pinpoints 'patterns of difficulties relating to the processing of information' as the key symptom (Reid, 1998, p. 2). For a helpful account of the phonological processing difficulties of dyslexics, see Goswami, 1999.

Sometimes dyslexia is developmental and therefore temporary – children just beginning to write often write words in reverse – 'saw' for 'was' or put the wrong beginning consonant – 'doy' for 'boy'.

Children are tested for dyslexia if they are of normal intelligence and general linguistic ability but have severe problems with written language – with reading, writing and spelling. The use of the term 'dyslexia' is controversial and some teachers and educational psychologists prefer to refer to 'specific learning disability'. There are two main positions on 'dyslexia'. First, we have the medical explanation where neurological factors to do with vision and hand eye co-ordination are deemed important. Second,, we have an explanation in terms of social and psychological factors including memory difficulties. What is not in doubt is that some children have considerable problems with learning to read and write and need carefully thought out support.

Multi-sensory approaches seem to have helped children with dyslexia. These include drama in which children make letter shapes as part of the story, handwriting patterns that support spelling memory and making the shapes of letters of the alphabet in paint, sand and clay. As computers provide a multi-sensory and multi-modal forum for the exchange of information they are also helpful and, in Anita Keates' words, 'become (for dyslexic learners) a non-critical friend for life' (Keates, 2000, p. 84). All kinds of ICT, including tape recorders and hand held spell-checkers, are likely to help dyslexic children of all ages.

Goswami, U. (1999) Speech Coding and Dyslexia: The Phonological Representations Hypothesis. *Dyslexia Review,* Vol. 11, 2, 4–7.

Keates, Anita (2000) *Dyslexia and Information Communications Technology: A Guide for Teachers and Parents* London: David Fulton.

Reid, G. (1998) *Dyslexia: A Practitioner's Handbook.* Chichester: Wiley.

The British Dyslexia Association is a national charity which co-ordinates over a hundred independent local dyslexia associations and organises conferences and sells publications. Address is: 98 London Road, Reading, Berkshire. RG1 5AU. Website is: http:// www.bda.dyslexia.org.uk

Early Learning Goals

See also early years language and literacy, emergent writing, speaking and listening, reading, writing

These are the learning objectives for children to reach by the end of the Foundation stage (3–6 years). Since September 2000, early years practitioners have worked within the framework of the Early Learning Goals. If you are a student you may find it helpful to look at the 'Early Years' entry to read about some of the issues in how very young children are provided for in Nursery and Reception classes. The goals for literacy under the heading 'Communication, language and literacy' are a 'prior experience' link with the objectives for Key Stage 1 (see National Curriculum English, Key Stage 1 En 1, 2 and 3). You will find all the early learning goals and other information in DfEE's *Curriculum Guidance for the Foundation Stage.*(DfEE/QCA, 2000). The following list of objectives is a selection from the 'Communication, language and literacy' goals. At the end of the foundation stage most children will be able to:

- sustain attentive listening to and using spoken and written language, and readily turn to it in their play and learning
- use language to imagine and create roles and experience
- link sounds to letters, naming and sounding the letters of the alphabet
- read a range of familiar and common words and simple sentences independently
- know that print carries meaning and, in English, is read from left to right and top to bottom
- show an understanding of the elements of stories, such as main character, sequence of events, and openings, and how informa-

tion can be found in non-fiction texts to answer questions about where, who, why and how
- attempt writing for various purposes, using features of different forms such as lists, stories and instructions
- write their own names and other things such as labels and captions and begin to form simple sentences, sometimes using punctuation
- use their phonic knowledge to write simple regular words and make phonetically plausible attempts at more complex words
- use a pencil and hold it effectively to form recognisable letters, most of which are correctly formed.

Curriculum Guidance for the Foundation Stage, 2000, Qualifications and Curriculum Authority/DfEE.
Early Learning Goals (DfEE/QCA, 1999c).
The National Literacy Strategy: Developing Early Writing. Guidance. DfEE 2001 (to guide the teaching of writing in Reception and Years 1 and 2).

Early years language and literacy

See also baseline assessment, Drama and English, Early Learning Goals, emergent writing, enabling adult, Junior Years language and literacy, parents and families, play and language and literacy, reading, siblings (and literacy), speaking and listening, writing

The term 'early years' has often been used to refer to children up to eight years old. This is still the case in many countries, but in the United Kingdom the term is now applied mainly to three to six year olds in the 'foundation' years. The experiences a child has in the preschool and early school years are likely to affect later development and there has been a lot of debate about how much structured learning there should be. Traditionally much learning during these years was achieved through rich experience through play and discovery with little formal instruction. Recent initiatives affecting the under sixes include the formulation of 'early learning goals' for children entering school (thus creating a foundation pre-National Curriculum for children in under fives settings), the putting in place of baseline assessment shortly after children enter compulsory schooling and the increasing of the range of providers of early years education.

The main issue is whether children aged three to six benefit from the kind of structured learning environments and direct teaching Ofsted recommend in their publication 'The Quality of Nursery Education'. Many respected practitioners and early years educationists believe play based and child directed learning contexts are more appropriate for the age group. Their concern is that direct teaching at too young an age might lead to a lack of self confidence and create anxiety. These issues are discussed in a research report by academics at Durham University who had been working with Reception class teachers (Stout *et al.*, 1998).

It is always helpful to know something about the approach in other countries when thinking about these issues. There is a trend in the French *écoles maternelles* and in Japanese private nurseries towards some literacy teaching and New Zealand, Trinidad and the Republic of Ireland teach reading early as in Britain. But many other countries favour play based programmes for children under six or seven. In Norway, Denmark, Sweden and Finland children learn through play and discovery at nursery, learning to read and write formally only when they start school at seven years. Hungary, Austria and Switzerland favour an oral approach to teaching nursery aged children and musical activities are integrated into the daily programme.

Early years practitioners in the United Kingdom hope the Early Learning Goals can be interpreted in a way that will ensure a rich learning environment for the under sixes. I think this means achieving these within the 'big shapes' of learning. What are the 'big shapes' or priorities for language and literacy? First of all we should recognise that children bring to school many achievements and ways of dealing successfully with new experiences. This is where we begin. We need also to see becoming literate as part of a bigger picture of making meaning, through activities like role play, art and craft and talking and listening in a range of contexts. The nursery or early years team like to plan activities round a theme like Ourselves, Journeys, Growing and so on. This gives a vitality and coherence to all the activities, including language activities. I remember a Reception class who helped the teacher make the home corner into a fire station and who were keen to write the work rotas for the noticeboard and to tell and write stories about rescuing people from fires (Dalton-Vinters and Mallett, 1995).

Language work is nourished by books and resources. Often the adult will take up an opportunity to enrich and inform children's play with a story or information book. Children enjoying play round the idea of Journeys asked for a book that would tell them about how train doors shut and how you make tickets. This project and others are case studies in *Young Researchers* (Mallett, 1999, Chapters 2 and 3). Sharing stories is a particularly enjoyable and important activity: children listen, talk about the characters and link their own experiences with what happens. Early enjoyment of story is the foundation for later literary experience where children need to have sympathetic insight into the circumstances and feelings of others. Sometimes it is enough just to hear the story read and talk about it, but at other times it can lead to role play, early writing and art work.

Good partnership between schools and parents and families is helpful for every aspect of learning, including literacy development. Teachers benefit from knowing about a child's literacy practices and experiences at home. There is more about this under the entries on 'parents and families' and on 'siblings and literacy'. Parents are often extremely supportive and willing to do practical things like displaying books and translating stories into home languages. I remember a student being delighted when the parents of her nursery class sent in photographs of the children as babies so that she could help them to make their own book based on the Ahlberg's *Peepo!*

Even if you are a teacher of older children there are several reasons why you should make yourself knowledgeable about early years education. First, some of the most interesting research about how human beings learn, not least how they learn to speak and develop their language abilities, has been carried out with very young children. From birth to about six years there is 'unparalleled speed and complexity of growth in children's thinking, language, social and cultural awareness and physical skills' (Whitehead 1999, p. 1). Second, the essentially active way in which children learn has implications for a model of learning to serve beyond the very early years. Third, later learning builds on the earliest stages. To take just one example, if teachers of older children are familiar with the kind of programme in good nurseries which emphasises young children's enjoyment and participation in story telling, saying and singing nursery rhymes and sharing picture books of vitality and merit, they can build on this. Finally, the good early years practitioner is a helpful model for the role of the teacher at all stages. We can learn much about the how to observe children, how to relate these observations to our planning, how to intervene sensitively and how to evaluate progress. Not all of the books listed below are referred to directly in this entry, but they would all help extend your understanding of children's language and literacy needs at this crucial early stage.

Browne, Anne (1996) *Developing Language and Literacy 3–8* London: Paul Chapman.

Campbell, Robin (1996) *Literacy in Nursery Education* Stoke on Trent: Trentham Books.

Dalton-Vinters, Julia and Mallett, Margaret (1995) 'Six year olds read about fire fighters' in *Reading* UKRA, April, Vol. 29, No 1.

Mallett, Margaret (1999) *Young Researchers: Informational Reading and Writing in the Early and Primary Years* London: Routledge.

Nutbrown, C (1997) *Recognising Early Literacy Development: Assessing Children's Achievements* London; Paul Chapman.

Ofsted website: www.ofsted.gov.uk

Qualifications and Curriculum website: www.qca.org.uk

Stout, Jane, Tymms, Peter and Thompson, Linda (1998) *Reception Class Teachers: Their Aims, Views and Stories* School of Education, Durham University (Tel. 0191 374 2000).

Whitehead, Marian R. (1997, second edition) *Language and Literacy in the Early Years* London: Paul Chapman.

Whitehead, Marian (1999) *Supporting Language and Literacy Development in the Early Years* Buckingham and Philadelphia: Open University Press.

eBooks

These are books in electronic form held on a computer's database and stored like any other document. To read the text a 'reader' application is used. This displays the text page by page on screen. While eBooks are not expected to replace printed texts they have advantages, particularly for students and researchers who need rapid access to published, copyright information. They can be searched in the same way as a CD-ROM and information can be bookmarked.

Where pay-per-view facilities are available selected pages can be downloaded, viewed and printed, as is the case with CD-ROM.

Edinburgh Reading Tests

See also reading age, Standardised Reading Tests

This group, timed, written series of tests (in four age phases) published by Hodder & Stoughton (1977) covers the age-range from seven to twelve years. The materials are arranged in sentences and paragraphs. Reading behaviour as well as a number of aspects of reading, for example ability to sequence, use of syntax and comprehension are assessed, resulting in a profile of the child's abilities. Therefore as well as providing a summative measure the test has a diagnostic value. It is of course more time-consuming to carry out than a simple word test like the *Schonell Graded Word Test*.

Editing

See also composition, drafting, transcriptional aspects of writing, writing

Editing a draft involves some reordering of words and phrases for particular purposes, for example to reduce the number of words or to sharpen up the argument. Proof reading for transcriptional errors can often be combined with editing.

Most children have learnt by the end of the primary years to check through their 'first drafts' for spelling or punctuation errors but find it much more difficult to improve the compositional aspects of their writing once they have organised it.

By constantly reviewing their work as they write, editing can become a more dynamic activity, embedded into the whole process rather than just something that happens at the end. Teachers can help by modelling the editing process – perhaps on the computer.

Effective Reading Tests

See also reading age, Standardised Reading Tests

Untimed, group and in the form of reading booklets, this four level set of tests (Macmillan, 1986) has a total age-range of 7.3–12.8 years. These tests have a modern format and emphasise comprehension – children answer questions on the different sections of text.

Elaborated and restricted codes

See also language and thought, language variety

In the 1960s the sociologist Basil Bernstein identified two codes or ways of using language which he suggested were part of a general theory of social rules. The elaborated code, as the name suggests, was used in formal or educational settings where a range of linguistic forms made meaning entirely explicit. This kind of language was characterised by the use of subordinate clauses, the pronoun 'I' and the passive tense.

The restricted code was a form of language which was appropriate in less formal settings and in contexts where speakers were members of the same group and therefore did not need to 'spell everything out' to get their meaning across. Features of this use of language were tag questions, liberal use of pronouns and gestures and intonation conveying meaning rather than flexible and creative linguistic forms.

Nobody had much trouble in accepting that language changes according to the formality of the context. The difficulty occurred because the codes became associated with social class. While middle class and educated people were thought to be able to switch codes as appropriate, the poorly educated and lower working class individual controlled only the 'restricted' code. At its crudest, one argument was that as lower working class children spoke a 'restricted language' they were unable to learn properly at school. Terms like 'language disadvantage', 'language deprivation' and 'language deficit' came to be used and Bernstein distanced himself from arguments and conclusions which he considered were distortions of his theory. These issues are discussed in Chapter 3 of *Gender, Race and Class in Schooling* by Chris Gaine and Rosalyn George.

Today the notion that some children arrive at school 'linguistically disadvantaged' is thankfully unacceptable and we believe all but the most severely mentally handicapped children can be taught. Nevertheless, teachers try to help children become as competent and flexible as possible in their use of language to aid their learning.

Gaine, Chris and George, Rosalyn (1999) *Gender, 'Race' and Schooling: A New Introduction* London: Falmer Press.

Electronic books – see CD-ROMs, fairy tales, fiction, Information and Communications Technology (ICT) and English, factual genres, information books, non-fiction reading and writing

Elementary schools

See also history of English teaching

Elementary schools provided free education for children between five and twelve years from 1870 when their establishment was required by the Elementary Education Act.

The curriculum was limited, like that in the voluntary schools, and there was much learning by heart, copying writing and writing to dictation. The government exercised control by the 'payment by results' system in which teachers were paid only if the children passed tests in the three Rs – reading, writing and arithmetic.

The 1944 Education Act brought in age phase organisation of schooling and established primary schools which catered for children from five to eleven years. Children then went on to secondary schools and so the all age elementary schools began to close. The kind of secondary school children went to was now decided by the 11+ examination which often had a narrowing effect on the English curriculum of the later primary years.

Elision

Elision occurs when a speaker slurs or a writer omits a vowel, consonant or syllable. In writing, elision is often indicated by an apostrophe – 'you shouldn't' and 'won't you?'

Ellipsis

See also cataphoric reference, cohesion

'Ellipsis' refers to the missing out of part of a sentence in speech or in writing where the omitted words are implied from the context. In conversation, we often rely on the context to support what we say. A typical exchange might be:

'Where are the umbrellas?'
'At the door'.

The second speaker does not need to say 'The umbrellas are at the door' or even 'They are at the door.'

In writing, ellipsis is less frequent because, in the absence of immediate feedback, we need to be more explicit. Ellipsis can help avoid repetition and yet maintain cohesion. It helps the reader focus on the most important information. So we might have;

'The post was advertised for several weeks and eventually seven people applied. Two were invited for interview.'

We do not need make the second sentence longer by repeating information – 'Two of the seven people who applied were invited for interview.'

In punctuation, ellipsis is indicated by three points and used to indicate part of a quotation has been missed out. So 'Sunday newspapers, the last genre to emerge, have become a significant institution in Britain' (McArthur, 1992, p. 691) in a shortened version might become 'Sunday newspapers ... have become a significant institution in Britain'.

Sometimes the three ellipsis points can have a dramatic effect as in 'The water came nearer and nearer...'. Then the reader is left to draw their own conclusions and a new paragraph begins.

For more examples and further information about 'ellipsis' you might consult Medwell *et al.*, 2001 and McArthur, 1992.

McArthur, Tom (1992) *The Oxford Companion to the English Language* London: QPD and Oxford: Oxford University Press.

Medwell, Jane, Moore, George, Wray, David and Griffiths, Vivienne (2001) *Primary English: Knowledge and Understanding* Exeter: Learning Matters.

E-mail

See also Information and Communications Technology (ICT) and English

E-mail (electronic mail) are messages and documents prepared on personal computers and delivered electronically – that is, using fixed line or satellite communication links. The messages can be read and responded to 'on screen' without the need to prepare a hard copy or to print out and they can be merged into existing documents and productions. Increasingly children are using e-mail as away of communicating within the school or to children in other schools.

As we might expect with a new way of

communicating, e-mail is developing its own conventions and language style which is sometimes at odds with the ordinary rules of grammar and punctuation. Teachers need to remind pupils that while certain simplifications may be appropriate while using e-mail, other writing tasks need to conform to standard forms of grammar and punctuation.

Emergent writing

See also Early Learning Goals, Early years language and literacy, enabling adult, writing

'Emergent', also referred to as 'developmental' or 'early' writing, is a term for how a young child begins to control the process of writing from the earliest stage of the very first marks to beginning to use the conventions of writing to make meaning. At first children have little knowledge about words and sounds and how these are represented by letters. They experiment, imitating the flow and speed of the mature writer and play with the shape and orientation of letters and with punctuation marks like full stops. These early stages are explored by a number of writers including Bissex, 1980, who charts her own child's progress towards writing, Hall who stresses the young child's urge to experiment with different written forms and Temple *et al.*, 1988, who identify some stages in the journey towards becoming a writer. Marian Whitehead describes in detail the interplay between the young child as an active meaning maker, learner and their personal and cultural environment in the journey towards becoming a writer. Here they are helped by the sensitive adult who takes the ideas and feelings children are shaping into narrative forms and acts as scribe – setting the message down in a conventional form (Whitehead, 1997, Chapter 7). Then the child acquires the confidence to write himself or herself.

Alison Kelly is concerned that terms like 'emergent' and 'developmental' might suggest that writing abilities just happen without specific teaching (Graham and Kelly, 1998, p. 73). But early years educators are more likely to argue against mature forms being pressed on young children before they can cope with them. The important thing is that children should build confidence in their ability to write and feel positive about the enjoyment writing can bring.

Bissex, Glenda (1980) *GNYS AT WRK: A Child Learns to Read and Write* Cambridge, Mass.: Harvard University Press.

Graham, Judith and Kelly, Alison (1998) *Writing Under Control* London: David Fulton.

Hall, Nigel (1987) *The Emergence of Literacy* Sevenoaks: Hodder & Stoughton.

Temple, C,. Nathan, R.G., Burris, N.A. and Temple, F. (1988, second edition) *The Beginnings of Writing* Boston, Mass.: Allyn & Bacon.

Whitehead, Marian (1997 edition) *Language and Literacy in the Early Years* London: Paul Chapman. See Chapter 7 'Early representation and emerging writing'.

Emotional literacy

See also response

This refers to a human being's understanding of how to relate to others in a constructive and sensitive way. It also has to do with consciousness of our own needs and the effects on others of our behaviour and attitudes. Many factors are likely to affect the level of emotional literacy an individual develops. One of these factors may be the special insights children develop from cumulative exposure to quality fiction: developing sensitivity to the subtle messages in texts may play a part in helping them grow and develop as responsive human beings. Of course we must be wary of simple linking of cause and effect here – there is no evidence that students of literature and the Arts are morally superior beings!

But let me give an example of how I think fiction may help. A student teacher read *Grace and Her Family* to her eight year old class (Hoffman and Binch, 1995, Frances Lincoln). This wonderful picture book tells the story of Grace's journey to meet her father's new partner and their children and in doing so explores her ambivalent feelings about this second family. The children particularly liked Grace's image of herself 'like gum stretched out all thin in a bubble' as she struggles to find the emotional resources to be part of two families. It showed them how it was possible to reconcile conflicting feelings and tolerate situations they would not have chosen. There are some subtle messages: we see an illustration of Grace reading fairy stories as her stepmother offers her food. The children came to understand that Grace's reading gave her insights into other people's dilemmas and challenges and this helped her with her own problems.

Enabling adult

See also Language at Home and School Project, reading environment, zone of proximal development

Perhaps it is Vygotsky who most powerfully brought the notion of the enabling adult to a form which communicated to the teacher in the classroom (Vygotsky, 1986). Listening to a more mature person thinking through some information or an issue provides a scaffold for the young learner in any subject or area of expertise. This intellectual companionship stretches the possibilities for the young learner. Some parents and caregivers are particularly gifted at encouraging the kind of conversations which help young children to develop and extend their interest in the world around them and to grow intellectually. Gordon Wells and his team of researchers on the *Language at Home and School* project found that these life enhancing conversations occurred in all social groups (Wells, 1987, Chapter 1).

For a detailed and inspiring account of the role of the early years educator in supporting children's literacy progress see Marian Whitehead's analysis in *Language and Literacy in the Early Years,* Chapter 8. Whitehead argues that teaching and demonstrating are important but the good early years educator should also provide 'mothering 'support and like a mother 'desire the success and achievements of their charges and surround them with the incitement to succeed' (Whitehead, 1997, p. 181).

In English, the teacher is a model for children's discussion and for their reading and writing. Aidan Chambers, writing specifically about reading, argues that all the other obstacles

in the way of learner readers can be overcome if they have the help and example of a trusted, experienced adult reader (Chambers, 1991, p. 15).

Chambers, Aidan (1991) *The Reading Environment: How Adults Help Children Enjoy Books* Stroud: Thimble Press (see particularly Chapter 17).

Vygotsky, L.S. (1986 edition) *Thought and Language* Cambridge. Mass.: MIT.

Wells, Gordon (1987) 'The children and their families' in *The Meaning Makers: Children Learning Language and Using Language to Learn* London: Hodder & Stoughton.

Whitehead, Marian (1997) *Language and Literacy in the Early Years* London: Paul Chapman.

Encyclopaedia

See also CD-ROM, factual texts, library skills, non-fiction reading and writing, software, study skills

An encyclopaedia is a reference text in print or electronic form and is normally organised alphabetically. (Some encyclopaedias for young children are organised thematically.) General encyclopaedias for adults (*The Encyclopaedia Britannica* for example) can be huge, scholarly works with a large number of entries spanning every possible subject written by leading experts and arranged in many volumes or on huge computer databases. Here we are concerned with encyclopaedias for children – how we choose encyclopaedias from the many on the market and how we help children of different ages use them.

General criteria for choosing an encyclopaedia would include being up to date and accurate, well written and illustrated and with a content of interest and use to a particular age group. But the very best encyclopaedias have some other qualities. They manage to put across the idea that knowledge is not static but expands: astronomers discover new stars and palaeontologists find new kinds of dinosaurs. Often such discoveries are more than a superficial addition to what we know; one dinosaur fossil recently unearthed suggested that some of these creatures, far from being the green or brown we usually picture, were bright red and orange. Not only does this lead us to picturing the creatures differently, it also makes us think in a new way about camouflage and predators. Further, our attitudes to what is known change. Stephanie Harvey notes that the great contribution of Native Peoples to the development of the American West has transformed encyclopaedia entries on this topic (Harvey, 1998). So a good encyclopaedia explains knowledge that seems fairly secure while giving the impression that there is still much to be discovered and thought about. This welcome speculative approach can be a feature of encyclopaedias for the very young. Angela Wilkes, in *Your World: A First Encyclopaedia* (Kingfisher), shares some theories about how dinosaurs became extinct with her young readers and makes it clear that 'No one knows exactly why'.

Another quality we look for is a capacity to draw a young learner, whether browsing or researching, easily into a particular field of knowledge. Good illustrations are most important. Sixty per cent of the 175 seven to eleven year olds taking part in the Exeter Encyclopaedia project said they looked at photographs, maps and drawings first, mentioning particularly entries on muscles, places, plants, lakes, events, sharks, World War II and Henry VIII. CD-ROM encyclopaedias have strong potential for developing children's visual literacy. Older primary children find the visual aspect of both *Eyewitness Children's Encyclopaedia* (Dorling Kindersley) and *Earth Quest* (an initiative by Dorling Kindserley with the National History Museum) appealing. The second of these explains and demonstrates the movement of tectonic plates, erupting volcanoes and destroying earthquakes. The written text in both print and electronic encyclopaedias also has to inspire. The first part of a lively entry on 'Storms' in Dorling Kindersley's *Children's Illustrated Encyclopaedia* puts the phenomena in an interesting perspective:

> 'About 2,000 thunderstorms are raging throughout the world at this very moment, and lightning has struck about 500 times since you began reading this page. Storms have enormous power: the energy in a hurricane could illuminate more light bulbs than there are in the United States.'

This is a long way from the impersonal language of older encyclopaedias whether for adults or children. We know an encyclopaedia has succeeded if children want to carry their researches into other books.

Valuable as browsing is – savouring the illustrations and dipping into the text – children also use encyclopaedias to find specific information or as a first port of call when beginning a new topic. There are important issues about how we support children's use of reference books. Getting the best out of an encyclopaedia can be a complicated matter. Even the older primary children in the Exeter Encyclopaedia Project had difficulty with the index volume of a multi-volume set of children's encyclopaedias (Wragg, 2000). So some direct teaching about retrieval devices is needed.

Teachers can best help very young children understand about head words and indexes in the context of an interesting task. Five year olds learning about 'Whales' were eager to consult reference books for a much older age group alongside their teacher to find the answers to their questions (Doyle and Mallett, 1994). The 'Whale' work case study shows us that the desire to find out – children's sometimes passionate curiosity about something in particular – supplies the energy and will to learn about 'looking up' procedures. Older children often have time-tabled sessions in the library to learn about library and study skills. However well intentioned, too many 'looking up' exercises outside a context to give them point and meaning can become dreary. This does not rule out times when teachers and librarians can help children understand the organisation of reference books and how to carry out searches in both print encyclopaedias and electronic search systems.

Whether children are using electronic or print encyclopaedias, the important thing is how they use the information they find: perhaps to help them debate an issue in class discussion or to make notes towards a piece of writing which will be further enriched by what is found in other books. Margaret Meek reminds us that children are never too young to read critically and to have opinions about which texts have been most helpful (Meek, 1996).

Doyle, Kathleen and Mallett, Margaret (1994) 'Were dinosaurs bigger than whales?' *TACTYC Early Years Journal*, Vol. 14, No. 2 Spring.

Earth Quest Dorling Kindersley/Natural History Museum (goes beyond superficial information for children who love science).

Encyclopaedia Britannica and *Encarta* (both comprehensive encyclopaedias for teachers' use with a good search engine).

Eyewitness Children's Encyclopaedia Dorling Kindersley (this provides an array of multi-media navigation systems and it links to Dorling Kindersley's Internet site. It has a talking dictionary. Children can easily print screens).

Harvey, Stephanie (1998) *Non-fiction Matters: Reading, Writing and Research in Grades 3–8*. York, Maine: Stenhouse Publishers (see Chapter 8).

Mallett, Margaret (1999) *Young Researchers* London: Routledge.

Meek, Margaret (1996) 'The quick fix: reference books' in *Information and Book Learning* Stroud: The Thimble Press.

Wragg, Ted 'Obscure Reference' article in the *Times Educational Supplement* about The Exeter Encyclopaedia project. (Funded by Encyclopaedia Britannica, this study involved observing the strategies of 175 seven to eleven year olds, from five rural and five urban primary schools in the Midlands and South, as they carried out tasks using encyclopaedias.)

English as an additional language (EAL) – see bilingualism, dual-language texts, equal opportunities, language variety, multiculturalism, multilingualism

English/Language Co-ordinator

See also Art and English, assessment, audit, core books, Design and Technology and English, displays, Drama and English, early years, enabling adult, English language policy and equal opportunities, Geography and English, History and English, Information and Communications Technology (ICT) and English, Junior Years language and literacy, Literacy Hour, Mathematics and English, National Curriculum, parents and families, phonics, Physical Education and English, planning, Primary Language Record, reading, reading corner/area, record keeping, Religious Studies and English, Science and English, speaking and listening, writing, writing area/corner

The large number of '*See also*' entries indicates that the responsibilities of the English Co-ordinator or Subject Manager take in every aspect of language, learning and literacy.

Co-ordinating English is a huge brief, not only are co-ordinators concerned with language and literature in English lessons, but they also reach out to the language activities – speaking and listening, reading and writing – which make possible learning across the whole curriculum. 'Language Co-ordinator' suggests this wide coverage, but as the National Curriculum orders refer to 'English' this entry uses the title 'English Co-ordinator'.

There have always been positions of responsibility for subject areas in the primary school, often referred to as 'scale posts' in the past. Now the expectations resting on all subject co-ordinators have been formalised and their wide-ranging nature made explicit. The tasks involved are nearly always in addition to those of class teaching.

Although it is a demanding one, the role has many satisfactions: seeing children across the whole school develop as language users; convincing children of the pleasure of reading and producing their own stories and factual accounts; selecting a whole range of exciting resources whether print or electronic; supporting students and probationer colleagues as well as collaborating with all the teachers to help them become excellent practitioners; reaching out to parents and the wider community.

The Teacher Training Agency has highlighted four core areas of responsibility for subject co-ordinators: Strategic direction and development of the subject; Teaching and learning; Leading and managing staff; Efficient and effective deployment of staff and resources.

Each of these contains many familiar tasks and so here I have selected some which seem to me of particular importance. My account draws on the analysis of Waters and Martin (1999), Chapter 2: 'Being a Co-ordinator'.

Strategic direction and development of the subject

This aspect of the Co-ordinator's role is to do with putting in place policies and practices to promote good planning and resourcing, staff confidence in teaching the subject, regular analysis of data to monitor progress, set targets and achieve improvement. By creating a sound global framework, Co-ordinator and teachers can then turn with confidence to developing specific aspects of teaching and learning.

Teaching and learning

There needs to be good coverage, continuity and progression and this involves co-ordinators and their colleagues knowing what the National Curriculum English programmes and the *National Literacy Strategy Framework for Teaching* require. I believe the most successful co-ordinators interpret and implement formal requirements in a way that serves the needs of the pupils and teachers in their school. Then there is the huge task of assessment and record keeping to attend to. This must be coherent and systematic, easily manageable and integrated into the teaching cycle. The Co-ordinator's task here also involves initiating and maintaining good communication with parents and the wider community and encouraging their involvement.

Leading and managing staff

This includes communicating with senior management and other subject co-ordinators and supporting all teachers, not least newly appointed and student teachers, in their professional development. Co-ordinators are more likely to succeed if they build an atmosphere of cooperation and trust and deal sensitively with cases where a teacher has to improve an aspect of their practice. The 'audit' entry gives an example of a co-ordinator showing how we meet the requirements for teaching reading while it still remains an enjoyable and life enhancing experience for children and teacher (Tyrrell and Gill, 2000).

Efficient and effective deployment of staff and resources

Co-ordinators need to establish staffing and resource needs, including those to carry out the priorities in the development plan. These needs have to be costed and communicated to senior managers and a share of the school's overall budget negotiated.

Performing well in all of these areas requires organisational, management and motivational skills as well as a great deal of professional and subject knowledge about language and literature. I have formed my own view over the years of what characterises the above average English Co-ordinator. Certainly those who command most respect are themselves excellent practitioners – models of how to plan, resource, organise and evaluate their lessons and to inspire their pupils (Medwell *et al.*, 1998). We are more likely to take notice of what someone advises or demonstrates if we have been impressed by the fruits of their endeavours! I also find teachers are more eager and able to follow an English policy or strive to meet the demands of a development plan if they have been involved at every stage in its creation. Finally, and I have said this before, the Co-ordinator that can energise the other teachers by their enthusiasm, good humour and genuine concern for the progress of both colleagues and children, is of great value to any primary school.

Medwell, Jane *et al.* (1998) *Effective Teachers of Literacy* London: Teacher Training Agency.

Merchant, Guy and Marsh, Jackie (2000) *Co-ordinating Primary Language and Literacy* London: Paul Chapman.

Tyrrell, Jenny and Gill, Narrinderjit (2000) *Co-ordinating English at Key Stage 1* London: Falmer Press.

Waters, Mick and Martin, Tony (1999) *Co-ordinating English at Key Stage 2* London: Falmer Press.

English development plan

See also audit, English Co-ordinator, English/language policy

This is a plan setting out the steps towards good practice often either after an audit or after an inspection which has identified strengths and weaknesses. The development plan will show the stages by which good practice in each aspect of English – planning, resourcing, teaching, record keeping – will be achieved and when. See Chapter 9: 'Producing a development plan' in Waters and Martin, 1999, for detailed lists of what should be included.

Waters, Mick and Martin, Tony (1999) *Co-ordinating English at Key Stage 2* London: Falmer.

English/Language policy

See also English/Language Co-ordinator, English development plan

English policies are written plans setting out a whole school policy on the teaching of all aspects of English and language and learning across the curriculum. Merchant and Marsh put it like this: 'A language policy is essentially a statement of the principles and practices which underpin the content and delivery of the English curriculum' (1998, p. 52).

The policy needs to be written in accessible language so that the most important aspects are clearly communicated to anyone who might need to consult it. All the teachers should be given the opportunity to contribute to the formulation of the policy. Bear in mind it may be one of the first glimpses a new teacher, a new governor or an outside agency like an OFSTED inspection team has of the English and language work in the school. While the policy should do the work of teachers and children justice it must be an honest reflection of what actually happens in the classroom. It therefore needs to be regularly updated. For a detailed account of how a policy document might be organised and the issues it should address, I recommend 'Developing and writing a language policy' Chapter 4 in Merchant and Marsh, 1998. Language policies documents are often written under headings which are likely to include: the school's aims and philosophy; resources and accommodation including the library; the organisation and methodology of the English programme; planning, assessment and record keeping; staffing and the role of the Co-ordinator; language in English lessons and across the curriculum; special educational needs; children learning English as an additional language; parents and the community; equal opportunities and children's entitlement; special achievements and initiatives.

Merchant, Guy and Marsh, Jackie (1998) *Co-ordinating Language and Literacy* London: Paul Chapman.

English projects (themes, topics)

See also advertisements, comics, cross-curricular projects, fairy tales, language variety, picture books

English projects provide an organising theme or topic for sustained work round an aspect of language or literature. Under 'cross curricular projects' I observed that topics across the subject boundaries, once a favourite way of organising some primary school work, are out of favour in the subject centred approach now prescribed by the government. English projects, fortunately, remain a good way of awakening and sustaining children's interest. Sometimes literature used in the Literacy Hour might lead to further work. For example, a class who had looked at a fairy tale in the Literacy Hour enjoyed a deeper study of different kinds of the genre over several weeks. In the Nursery and Reception years a series of activities might take a story or picture book as the starting point. One Nursery class of four year olds were helped to make their own book based on the Ahlberg's picture book *Peepo*.

Older primary children might look at an aspect of language variety – the songs and sayings of the local dialect. Another linguistic topic is word meanings, starting perhaps with the street names and buildings in the area of the school. Language change is another possible focus for sustained work.

English work that is sustained over several lessons often achieves a momentum and goes beyond the superficial. There is currently some concern over the lack of time in the Literacy Hour for extended writing – topic-based English work might help provide a context for committed, sustained accounts.

English schemes – see planning

Enlarged texts – see Big Books

Environmental print

This includes all the written language a child encounters including notices in parks, advertisements on bill boards, shop and restaurant signs, writing on cereal packets and written language on the television and on CD-ROMS. Children often notice the letters that make up their own names and this interest in print needs to be reinforced.

Early years teachers bring much of what the child sees in the way of print in the environment into the nursery and Reception classroom. The home corner might be a shop with all the labels and signs involved or a café with menus, bills and newspapers. Graham and Kelly suggest we help children make notices based on those they have seen in the world outside the classroom (Graham and Kelly, 2000, p. 47). So we might have 'Please keep the reading corner tidy' and 'Please wash your hands after feeding the tadpoles'. All this helps with the building of a sight vocabulary as children become readers and writers. Above all, it shows children the social purposes of writing and its importance in everyday life. For more about how environmental print helps children's understanding of literacy see Hall, 1987.

Graham, Judith and Kelly, Alison (2000) *Reading Under Control: Teaching Reading in the Primary School* London: David Fulton.

Hall, N. (1987) 'Environmental print' in *The Emergence of Literacy* Sevenoaks: Hodder & Stoughton.

Epic poetry

Epic poems tell the story of some great person or event, generally bound up in myth or religion. Some have their origin in an oral tradition, and were handed down from generation to generation.

Epiphany

An epiphany is a special moment of insight when an idea or situation is seen with new clarity. Let me give an example. A teacher read Anthony Browne's picture book *Zoo* to six year olds who had not thought of keeping animals in cages as controversial. When the mother in the story comments 'poor thing' when the tiger is seen pacing up and down its cage they suddenly saw things in a new light. Perhaps, they said, it was cruel to enclose creatures who needed a lot of space (Riley and Reedy, 2000).

Riley, Jeni and Reedy, David *Developing Writing for Different Purposes: Teaching about Genre in the Early Years* London: Paul Chapman.

Equal opportunities

See also bilingualism, gender and language development, multiculturalism, multilingualism

A school's English policy (and policies for other subjects) has a section which sets out how all children whatever their gender, ethnicity or social group will be given equal access to the curriculum. Having a whole school policy helps make equality of opportunity consistent throughout the school. In her useful book *Making Gender Work* Judith Baxter shows how 'a planned cycle of observation, monitoring, and evaluation – of the differentiated needs of all pupils, plus a range of curricular provision' ensures no child is marginalised (Baxter, 2001). Such reflective practice is the key to benefiting all children whatever their age, ability, gender or cultural background. When this aspect of the English policy is monitored we might check some of the following;

- Resources – do the materials in the classroom and the school library reflect the needs and interests of children of both genders, children from ethnic minorities (including emergent bilinguals) and children from a range of different social backgrounds. Are there quality dual-language texts to show we value children's first languages and to encourage family involvement in literacy?

- Research – are the teachers aware of studies which indicate that girls may need encouragement to contribute fully in talk contexts and that some children, particularly boys, may need special help with literacy? For a background to language and equality issues see Chapter 3 in Gaine and George, 1999 and Ofsted, 1993, for evidence of boys literacy underachievement. Are teachers also aware of research into supporting young emergent bilingual children, for example Gregory (1996)?

- Teaching strategies – is there evidence that teachers are putting into practice imaginative approaches, for example setting up drama work where the less confident children, often girls, take on leading roles and providing the more structured writing tasks that seem to motivate reluctant boy writers? (see Baxter, 2001).

Baxter, Judith (2001) *Making Gender Work* Reading: Reading and Language Information Centre.

Gaine, Chris and George, Rosalyn (1999) *Gender, 'Race' and Class in Schooling* London, Falmer Press.

OFSTED (1993) *Boys and English* London: OFSTED.

ERIC (everyone reading in class)

ERIC is an acronym to refer to times when the whole class is enjoying sustained, quiet reading. You might also come across DEAR (Drop Everything and Read), USSR (Uninterrupted Sustained Silent Reading) and SQUIRT (Sustained Quiet Uninterrupted Independent Reading Time). Many teachers simply refer to it as 'reading time'. In Britain it was once fairly common practice to make available regular silent reading times, but this provision has diminished in recent times as the National Literacy Strategy Literacy Hour has not concentrated on this kind of reading context. There is, however, no reason – except for pressure of time – why teachers should not choose time outside the Literacy Hour for this activity. There are several reasons why silent reading is worth preserving. Reading books at home now competes with time on the computer and watching television as well as outdoor pastimes. So if we want the clear message that reading is valuable for its own sake to come through we need to show it is worth making time for in school. Newly independent readers can be helped in reading times to make the transition from reading out loud to reading silently. Graham and Kelly observe that a gentle nudge to 'try reading in your head' is all that is needed, but children must have peace and quiet for this to be viable' (Graham and Kelly, 2000, p. 61). Children of all ages benefit from the time and space to savour a book and read at their own pace. Sometimes the teacher reads as well to stress the importance of a class being a 'reading community' but there will also be times when it is helpful to observe particular children and to

judge their level of concentration and choice of book. The most passionate argument for reading time in school is, for me, made by Aidan Chambers in his book *The Reading Environment*. He reminds us that 'a sacrosanct period is one of those rituals that condition our set of mind' (Chambers, 1991, p. 38). It is the teacher who can encourage and provide the will power for children to enjoy sustained reading. This more than anything else is likely to make a child a committed reader for life.

Chambers, Aidan (1991) *The Reading Environment* Stroud: The Thimble Press.

Graham, Judith and Kelly, Alison (2000) *Reading Under Control* London: David Fulton.

EXEL Project

See also EXIT model, genre, genre exchange, non-fiction reading and writing, research (into Primary English) and writing frames

The Exeter University Extending Literacy Project (EXEL) was funded by the Nuffield Foundation and headed by David Wray and Maureen Lewis. They worked with teachers throughout the country during the 1990s to find ways of supporting children's non-fiction reading and writing. See under EXIT model for their process stages to extend interaction with texts.

They looked for essentially practical answers to questions such as: how can we support children's informational reading and writing so that they are less likely to copy wholesale from books and resources? Although writing frames (skeleton frameworks to help organise a piece of writing) and genre exchange (using information gained from one genre, for example an information book to write in another, for example, a diary entry, menu or advertisement) are not original ideas, Wray and Lewis brought them to a practical level for use in the classroom. Their six categories of non-fiction – recount, report, procedure (instruction), explanation, persuasion (exposition) and discussion – are used in the National Literacy Strategy *Framework for Teaching* (DfEE, 1998).

Their work with Key Stage 2, seven to eleven year olds, is known best but they have also considered younger children's progress in this area of literacy, and in the late 1990s and the early 2000s the project has turned to children in the secondary years. Many teachers feel the strategies are particularly helpful to children with writing difficulties.

Views about how often to use the frames differ and some teachers prefer alternative forms of scaffolding, for example, helping children plan their writing verbally (see conferencing). Used without thought and too often, writing frames can bring about a mechanistic response from young writers. Wray and Lewis themselves consider the frames to be a temporary prop which children eventually give up and have written in depth about how best to use them.

The directors of the project and many of the teachers they worked with have given lectures and workshops to teacher conferences and seminars and a large number of books and articles have been published (for example Lewis and Wray, 1995 and Wray and Lewis, 1997). The work, and particularly the EXIT model has informed the non-fiction approach in The National Literacy Strategy launched in England in 1998.

Lewis, Maureen and Wray, David (1995) *Developing Children's Non-fiction Writing: Working with Writing Frame* Leamington Spa: Scholastic.

Wray, David and Lewis, Maureen (1997) *Extending Literacy: Children Reading and Writing Non-fiction* London: Routledge.

Exclamation

See also punctuation

An exclamation is a sentence which communicates surprise, delight, shock, distress and other strong emotions. For example 'I have passed all my examinations with high marks!' Sometimes an exclamatory phrase functions as a verbless 'sentence'. For example 'How wonderful!'

Exclamatory sentences and phrases, as is evident from the examples above, end with an exclamation mark.

EXIT model

See also Directed Activities Around Texts, EXEL project, non-fiction reading and writing, writing frames

The EXIT Model (Extending Interactions with Texts) was an outcome of the Exeter Extending Literacy Project funded by Nuffield and carried out during the 1990s. The model identifies ten process stages, some of which are preliminary, like the 'activation of prior knowledge' and the 'establishing purposes', some which are to do with learning from secondary sources like 'interacting with the text' and 'monitoring understanding' and others which involve reconstructing what has been learned 'communicating information'(Wray and Lewis, 1997).

This model informs the National Literacy Strategy training materials to help teachers carry out the non-fiction part of the literacy programme. There is no doubt that the activities recommended in this model would help children interact with texts rather than remaining relatively passive readers and writers. But for me there is something missing from the model: there is no explicit recognition of how first hand experience might be integrated with the secondary source input, although it could be part of the 'establishing purposes' category. In my own model of non-fiction reading and writing 'offering new experience' – which may take the form of an activity as in a science experiment, story (told or read) a visit or field trip or a contribution from a visitor – comes after 'organising prior experience' (Mallett, 1992, p. 61 and Chapter 8). In a very interesting analysis of a series of lessons on zoos with a Year 1 class, David Reedy uses Anthony Browne's story *Zoo* to offer a new perspective to the children. The children had never thought that keeping animals in cages might be controversial until the picture book was read to them. A turning point came when they saw the tiger pacing up and down in its cage. This brought the children new energy and commitment to finding out more. Reedy comments 'If we are to motivate children to want to go through the research process, then we must ensure their curiosity is stimulated, by exposing them to new information and ideas that cause them to want to know more' (Riley and Reedy, 2000, p. 145).

Mallett, Margaret (1992) *Making Facts Matter* London: Paul Chapman.

Riley, Jeni and Reedy, David (2000) *Developing Writing for Different Purposes: Teaching about Genre in the Early Years* London: Paul Chapman.

Wray, David and Lewis, Maureen (1997) *Extending Literacy: Children Reading and Writing Non-fiction* London: Routledge

Explanation text

See also genre, non-fiction

Explanation texts, one of the six kinds of non-fiction used in the National Literacy Strategy *Framework for Teaching,* explain a structure like that of a plant, animal or machine or a process like the working of the digestive system or of an engine. David Macauley's book *The New Way Things Work* which has clear, well-annotated diagrams of wheels, levers and all sorts of moving parts, shows both structure and function and is one of those inspirational explanation texts which appeal to a wide age range. The CD-ROM version shows all the moving parts in action.

Expository texts

See also report, explanation text, persuasion, discussion

'Expository' kinds of writing explain, describe or argue a case. Exposition is an impersonal form and the third rather than the first person tends to be used. Writer and reader are sometimes distanced from one another and an impression of objectivity given by use of the passive voice.

Expressive talk and writing

See also speaking and listening, writing

'Expressive' talk and writing was one of the function categories in the model of language developed by Professor James Britton and his team of researchers during the Schools Council 'Development of Writing Abilities' project in the 1970s. Britton observed that most of us use a spontaneous, fairly unstructured kind of speech when formulating action plans or new ways of construing our experience of the world. This he termed 'expressive' language which helped us make a start on organising our ideas. The sort of conversations people have in their homes and in the pub about political initiatives are often like this. Young children's talk is full of their immediate interests, preoccupations and recent activities, and not surprisingly their first writing tends to resemble 'written down' speech in its spontaneity and openness about the mood of the moment. Often the child is not thinking about the needs of an audience but is eager to relate his or her immediate concerns – the visit to see the ducks in the park, the outing to swim in the local baths or the frog-spawn on the nature table. Britton argues that children's writing development begins from this 'expressive' centre, moving on the one hand towards 'poetic' writing (with a form or pattern characteristic of different kinds of fiction) and on the other towards 'transactional' writing (which included all the factual genres). We recognise that a child's writing is moving towards the poetic end of the 'writing continuum' when there are signs of 'the deliberate organisation of sounds, words, images, ideas, events, feelings' (Britton, 1970, p. 177). When a child's writing moves from the expressive towards meeting the demands of the factual, it becomes more explicit. Britton explains that: '…some features that might be omitted from the expressive version because they are implied when we write for someone of similar interests and experiences to our own, have now to be brought into the writing' (*ibid.*). So, for Britton, writing development was at least partly to do with differentiation and increasing control over a greater number of writing types.

'Expressive' writing is not mentioned in current frameworks. As early as 1980 there were fears that too much 'expressive' writing might take time that could be spent on helping children develop other more disciplined kinds of writing (Allen, 1980). And thinking in Britain was influenced by teachers and scholars in Australia who became known as the 'genre theorists' and who felt that narrative genres, and particularly stories and writing with an 'expressive' function, dominated too much in primary schools. They argued that children should be helped to use a much wider range of reading and writing, not least non-fiction kinds. This research and thinking influenced the National Literacy Strategy and *Framework for Teaching* indicates where the different kinds of non-fiction reading and writing fit into the programme.

There is no doubt that some kinds of non-fiction writing were often neglected, or at least unsupported, in the primary school before the 1990s. However, expressive kinds of language have an important role in children's development of language and thinking. We should welcome the expressive touches in children's early writing that show they are trying to make sense of all their experience. Early Years teachers are rightly concerned that children are not nudged too early into mature forms of writing. I believe that children are more likely to become successful talkers and writers if they have the opportunity to explore their experience and ideas in an expressive way.

Allen, D. (1980) *English Teaching Since 1965: How Much Growth?* London: Heinemann Educational Books.

Britton, James (1970) *Language and Learning* London: Allen Lane, The Penguin Press.

F

Fable

See also under history of children's literature and parable

A fable is a story with a moral which becomes explicit at its end. The characters are often animals showing unattractive human traits like pride, selfishness and greed. One of the best known collections is *Aesop's Fables,* often enjoyed by both children and adults. Aspects of the natures of the animal characters, for example the cunning of the fox, have become absorbed into our culture. Sayings like 'sour grapes' also originate from these tales thought to have been written about the sixth century BC by a Greek slave.

Fables are still well-liked forms of children's literature and there are many retellings of single fables in picture book format, for example Beatrix Potter's *The Tale of Johnny Town-Mouse,* Brian Wildsmith's *The Lion and the Rat* (La Fontaine version) and Geoff Patterson's *The Goose that Laid the Golden Egg.* Mary Steel provides a useful annotated booklist in the Signal bookguide entitled *Traditional Tales.* Some of the features of fables are found in both print cartoons and film versions (for example in Beryl the Peril, *Sunday Times)* and in animated cartoons (*Wallace and Gromit, Tom and Jerry*).

DfEE (1998) *The National Literacy Strategy Framework for Teaching.* London: HMSO (see Year 3, Term 2).

Steele, Mary (compiler, 1989) *Traditional Tales* Stroud: Signal Bookguide edited by Nancy Chambers.

Faction

See also under transitional genre

A new term referring to texts, usually for children under eight, which combine features of both story and non-fiction. So we might have a story about the life of a dog or horse together with some panels and information boxes giving information about diet and breeding. Sometimes storybook characters and talking animals appear in these texts and many young readers enjoy the playful approach. Language must change, of course, and we need new words to clinch new concepts but some people, including the present writer, find 'faction' a charmless addition. The books the term refers to vary in quality, but the best in this transitional genre are enjoyed by young readers and listeners who can learn within the familiar story framework. It is now a category under which new children's books are reviewed in well thought of children's literature journals such as *Books for Keeps* where recent examples include the books mentioned below.

Hooper, Meredith (ill.), Allan Curless and Mark Burgess (2000) *Dogs' Night* London: Frances Lincoln. (Dogs climb out of their paintings at the National Gallery.)

Lia, Simone (1999) *Billy Bean's Dream* London: David & Charles Children's Books (a numbers and colours book woven round an exciting story).

Factual genres

See also under atlas, diary, dictionary, discussion text, encyclopaedia, EXEL project, genre, information books, Information and Communications Technology, information story, informational writing, instruction texts, Internet, journals, journalistic writing, maps, narrative non-fiction, Literacy Hour, National Literacy Strategy, non-fiction reading and writing, persuasive genre, procedural or instruction genre, reading, recount, referencing, reports transitional genres, writing

Features of the many genres called factual, informational or non-fiction are discussed under separate entries. Supporting children's reading and writing of non-fiction is covered under the entry 'non-fiction reading and writing'. This section considers the nature of factual kinds of material in general and its relevance to Primary English.

Factual genres describe, explain, organise and explore aspects of the real world we all inhabit. This contrasts with fiction which is less tied to the actual, exploring the possible and the inner world of the human imagination. The differences can be quite difficult to pin down, though generally we can tell to which general category – fact or fiction – a particular piece of written material belongs. Good factual writing often demands imaginative power and the ability to think laterally. Some experts can write speculatively about their field and show the same wonder and curiosity as a young child. Nearly every factual topic carries ethical issues which demand the sort of discussion we often associate with the best work in English lessons. The information explosion brought about by human endeavour and progress together with the technological revolution, the use of powerful computers and the Internet, has transformed the sheer amount and variety of information available to us – a veritable explosion. This has made it all the more necessary to have strategies for selecting and accessing and making sense of and critically assessing all the information now available.

Fiction in all its forms and children's response to it is the beating heart of English and so we can think of factual kinds of reading and writing mainly informing other lessons. But we all know this division is too stark. Just as stories and poems can infuse life and meaning into work across the curriculum, some factual genres have an important place in the English lesson. In the introduction to this encyclopaedia, it is argued that feelings about issues and events as well as thought and reflection are central to learning in English. Teachers draw on all kinds of text in a classroom where there is informed discussion about all the issues that concern human beings. Newspapers and magazines are worth rifling for features and readers' letters on themes like homework, hunting and waste disposal. These can serve as models for children's own letters and oral arguments. Children now often share these reflections using e-mail and the Internet to link with children in other schools.

Factual books and the Internet can often enrich reading stories and novels involving interesting issues. Children reading Dick King-Smith's *The Sheep-pig* asked for information about pigs to do with their breeding, life span and intelligence. Information books were sought on all these aspects and energised the children's response to the story (Mallett, 1992, Chapter 1. Part 3 of *New Readings*, K. Kimberley *et al.*). I observed work in a Year 6 class where factual texts were used fruitfully alongside Ted Hughes' *The Iron Woman* to illuminate environmental issues.

The National Curriculum and The National Literacy Strategy have encouraged teachers to widen the range of texts used in the primary classroom. The six categories of non-fiction included in *The Framework* are recount, report, explanation, discussion, persuasion and instruction (procedural). There are also some literary non-fiction genres, for example autobiography, biography and travel books. In the later primary years, children make progress in the more challenging kinds of factual genres, such as persuasive and journalistic kinds of reading and writing. One of the kinds of factual genre which is mentioned particularly in Year 6, term 2 is the discussion text. This is a text giving more than one viewpoint which children can then talk about, perhaps justifying their own opinion.

Derewianka, Beverley (1996) *Exploring the Writing of Genres* Royston, Herts: UKRA.

Mallett, Margaret (1992) 'How long does a pig live?' in Kimberley, K., Meek, M. and Miller, J. *New Readings: contributions to an understanding of literacy* London: A&C Black.

Mallett, Margaret (1999) *Young Researchers: Informational Reading and Writing in the Early and Primary Years* London: Routledge.

Wilson, Angela (1999) *Language Knowledge for Primary Teachers* London: David Fulton.

Fairy tales

See also history of children's literature, fiction, folk tales, traditional tales

We term 'fairy tales' the kind of traditional tales that tell of magic and talking animals, and of elves, sprites and other 'little people'. But the boundary between fairy tales and folk tales, which also sometimes have supernatural elements, is thin. Some experts on children's literature believe that fairy tales are a category of folk tale. John Rowe Townsend argues that 'folk' refers to the origin of a tale while 'fairy' indicates the nature of the story (Townsend, 1995 edition, Chapter 7, p. 67). Very generally, the characters in folk tales tend to be ordinary people – farm workers, cobblers, seamstresses and woodcutters for example – while fairy tales are usually about kings and queens, princes and princesses and others of noble birth.

Of course it is well known that fairy tales began as oral tales to amuse adults. But by the middle of the nineteenth century, fairy tales collections by Perrault, Grimm and Hans Anderson had been published. The published versions were for child readers and the more shocking elements were toned down.

Primary teachers need some background knowledge and understanding of the history and the features of fairy tales to inspire their classes. One of the most illuminating essays on fairy tales is the introduction by the Opies to their beautifully illustrated book *The Classic Fairy Tales*. For the Opies the defining feature is that a fairy tale 'contains an enchantment or other supernatural element that is clearly imaginary' (I. and P. Opie, *op cit.*, 1974, p. 15). We search out anthologies or books on a single tale where the telling makes a powerful appeal to the young imagination. The illustrations too must intrigue and please.

Two anthologies recommended for the under 8s are *The Walker Book of Fairy Tales* told by Amy Ehrlich (Walker Books) and *First Fairy Tales* retold by Margaret Mayo in rhyme and with much repetition. Vivian French's retelling of seven traditional fairy tales ('Jack and the Beanstalk', 'Hansel and Gretel', 'The Fisherman and His Wife', 'Beauty and the Beast', 'The Elves and the Shoemaker', 'Rumpelstiltskin' and 'Cinderella') is illustrated by Peter Malone with exceptionally fine paintings. French's gift for memorable language makes her creation of the magical worlds well worth reading out loud. Good primary school collections will include fairy stories from different lands. Reading or listening to them tells us about the culture they arose from – its customs, values and beliefs. The Puffin *Classic Fairy Tales* has a good mix of English, Irish, Scottish and Welsh stories. Barbara K. Wilson tells a rather Cinderella-like tale from China about some magic fish bones in *Wishbones: A Folktale from China*. Yeh Hsien finds a wonderful golden fish and feeds it until it grows enormous but her jealous stepmother kills and eats the fish. *Tales from India* retold by Sanjeevini, Navjeet and Misti (illustrated by Daksha and Manju Gregory) is a collection of Indian folk tales adapted for young readers. As well as the books there are also available dual-language cassettes in Gujarati and Punjabi (Mantra, 1984).

Modern fairy tales often challenge traditional gender roles in an entertaining way, for example *Princess Smartypants* (1986) by Babette Cole, *The Paper Bag Princess* by Robert Munsch (1980) and William Jay's *The Practical Princess and Other Liberating Fairy Tales* (Nelson/Hippo) are enjoyed. Children of about eight years (when they will have a grip on the features and conventions of traditional tales) love the idea of dragons saving princes instead of princesses, and princesses wearing paper bags instead of gowns. Older children would appreciate the alternative tellings of well known tales in Alison Lurie's *Clever Gretchen and Other Forgotten Fairy Tales*. For a most entertaining post-modern picture book presenting playful stories round traditional fairy tale characters see John Scieszka's *The Stinky Cheese Man and Other Fairly Stupid Tales* (Puffin, 1992) and by the same author *The True Story of the Three Little Pigs*.

Judith Graham has some helpful suggestions for follow-up activities after ten to eleven year olds have heard *The Stinky Cheese Man and Other Fairly Stupid Tales* – comparing the traditional and revised versions of the fairy tales and later on carrying out their own subversive adaptations to other traditional tales (see pp. 68 and 69, Graham, 1997).

There is a growing software collection with programs that both entertain and raise issues about the conventions of fairy tales. For example children of about five years seem to enjoy the Play and Learn series which includes *Snow White and the Seven Hansels* which combines *Little Red Riding Hood, Hansel and Gretel* and *Snow White and the Seven Dwarfs.* Children do need to know the stories as the game involves avoiding mixing up the events in the tales (Mac/PC, Gauntlet Entertainment, Tel. 01908 575 600).

Graham, Judith (1997) *Cracking Good Books: Teaching Literature at Key Stage 2* Sheffield: NATE.

Opie, Iona and Peter (1974) *The Classic Fairy Tales* Oxford: Oxford University Press.

Phinn, Gervase (2000) *Young Readers and Their Books* London: David Fulton.

Stones, Rosemary (1999) *A Multicultural Guide to Children's Books 0–16+* London and Reading: Books for Keeps with the Reading University Reading and Language Information Centre.

Townsend, John Rowe (1995 edition) *Written for Children* Harmondsworth: Penguin.

Family literacy projects

See also parents and families, siblings (and literacy)

Family literacy initiatives involve working through parents to help their children to make progress in reading and writing and, at the same time, helping the parents' literacy (Bird, 2001). There are a number of interesting initiatives and projects which you can read about in Bird's book for The National Literacy Trust. One such project is based at the Borough of Barking & Dagenham Library Service and benefits from a DCMS/Wolfson Public Libraries Challenge Award. During the period of the initiative, The Family Reading Librarian takes in collections of books to schools. The interesting thing about this is that the collections contain books for different age groups and interests so that when the child takes home a selection there is something for each member of the family.

The Basic Skills Agency has helped put into practice the Government's *Standards Fund Family Literacy Programme* by providing short initiatives in which children and parents are encouraged to engage in joint literacy activities.

These initiatives and others like them work on the principle that parents and children can help each other in becoming more literate. The signs are that they make a difference. However, family literacy initiatives raise complex issues, not least how you help maintain the interest and commitment of families when the initial project ends. We should not underestimate the challenge of helping those who do not usually feel comfortable in a library environment to acquire long term interest in books and other materials.

Barking and Dagenham Library Service (2000) *Annual Library Plan.*

Bird, V. (2001) *National Developments in Family Literacy* London: National Literacy Trust.

Fantasy

See also faction, fairy tales, fiction, history of children's literature

A fantasy is something created out of the imagination and may be a daydream, painting, a story or a poem. James Britton, in his article on the role of fantasy, suggests it is located in 'a third area' between external reality and the inner world of necessity. The child who can inhabit this 'third area' can handle images as play. You need to read this rewarding but quite challenging article yourself. It is worth the effort – not least because it argues for the value of children's play. It suggests that a very young child who can live creatively through play is likely later to be able to enjoy and take part in all the richness of the cultural world including literature, music and art (Britton, 1971).

One of the activities which provides the space for playing with images in school is of course the enjoyment of books and the stories children tell and write. In children's literature 'fantasy' is a category often contrasted with 'realism' which is to do with what has happened or what at least could happen without coming into conflict with the natural laws of nature.

Some of the finest children's books from the middle of nineteenth century onwards belong to the literary genre called 'fantasy'. Charles Kingsley's *The Water Babies* (1863), Lewis Carroll's *Alice* stories (1865), J.R.R. Tolkien's *The Hobbit* (1937), C.S. Lewis's *Narnia* books (1950) Philippa Pearce's *Tom's Midnight Garden* (1958) and more recently J.K. Rowling's *Harry Potter* books of the 1990s and early 2000s. Writing about the *Alice* books, Victor Watson considers they established new possibilities for children's books by creating an imaginative space for writing about the dynamics between adults and children – 'dynamics that might be complex, loving, intimate or problematical, but were no longer just authoritarian' (p. 18, Styles *et al.*, 1992). I recommend John Rowe Townsend's book *Written for Children* if you want to find out more about fantasy literature for children through history: chapters on fantasy thread through the book under chapter titles like 'The never-lands', 'Fantasy between the wars' and 'Modern fantasy'.

Perhaps other fantasies also create the space to think about ideas in an uninhibited way and allow us to experiment with notions unrestrained by the normal rules of time and space. Some books seem to invite the question 'What would happen if – I was very small, very large, I could fly or if I had a magic finger?' I have found children are intrigued by Roald Dahl's short story *The Magic Finger* (Puffin, 1979). The girl in the story uses her magic finger to punish those who annoy her. Children, often powerless in real life, find this satisfying.

The modern picture book is an ideal vehicle for fantasy as the illustrations can provide a second narrative which may complement, extend or even contradict the written text. The idea of a magic implement comes into some of Anthony Browne's books. In *Bear Hunt* (1979), Bear escapes from hunters in the jungle by drawing himself out of trouble with his magic pencil. Children learn how to read a fantasy book by reading with an adult and interpreting the features of the genre. Use of certain symbols in the illustrations may have a special cultural meaning.

My students and I find that even children not normally eager to write, enjoy writing their own stories about having a magic pencil or finger. By inviting this kind of story we are giving children the opportunity of playing with ideas in a highly satisfying way. If we want children's imaginative powers to grow we have to help them exercise them. Children's thoughts flow easily from fact to fiction and this is reflected by a category of books called, rather inelegantly, 'faction' whose main function may be informational but which may also feature storybook elements like talking animals. Many of these books, like the Macdonald Young Books Bees series, are for younger children. But there are books for older primary children of this type as well, for example Ted Dewan's *The Weatherbirds* (Viking, 2000) in which a stork, a parrot, a sparrow, a goose and a dodo undertake an exhilarating journey through the weather of the world. Different weather systems are clearly described and there are wonderful illustrations, including a panorama of New York at sunset. The fantasy elements will not be liked by everyone – some may think they risk 'genre confusion' – but I find that children enjoy the humour.

Britton, James 'The third area where we are more ourselves: the role of fantasy' *English in Education*, Vol. 5, No. 3, 1971 (reprinted in *The Cool Web* Meek, M. *et al.*).

Styles, Morag, Bearne, Eve and Watson, Victor (eds) (1992) *After Alice: exploring children's literature* London: Cassell.

Townsend, John Rowe (1990) *Written for Children* London: Cassell.

Fiction: choosing and using

See also adventure stories, animal stories, Book Trust, class reader, emotional literacy, enabling adult, figurative language, historical novel, history of children's literature, picture books, playscripts, poetry, novel, reading environment, reading response, reading range, shared writing, short stories and subject knowledge

Fiction is literature drawing on invention and the inner world of the imagination, often using figurative language to get meaning across. The books listed below, and particularly Barrs' *Core Books,* give help in choosing good examples of children's picture books, novels, short stories, play scripts and poems as well as taped and electronic books. Journals which regularly review children's fiction include *Books for Keeps, The School Librarian, The Times Educational Supplement, Signal* and *Language Matters*. Annotated and regularly updated book lists for different age groups and abilities are available from the Young Book Trust (Tel. 020 8516 2977). There are also many helpful Internet sites to guide resource selection including: http://www.listening-books.org.uk; www.booktrust.org.uk and http://www.vtc.ngfl. gov.uk/resource/literacy/index.html which is part of The National Grid for Learning and links to many other useful sites.

What is a quality fiction text for children? It might well have some of the following qualities: strong plot, interesting and convincing characters, language that is alive and powerful, layers of meaning, well-described settings providing virtual experience of other environments, relevance to a range of human issues and engaging feelings as well as thoughts. The best books have something profound to say about the human condition and particularly the experience of the growing child – but not in a self-conscious way. In fact, children respond to humour, even if some darker issues are explored. Although nearly every possible topic has been explored in children's fiction, I cannot think of a book which is completely pessimistic – the ending offers at least some hope. Looking at the whole fiction collection we would want to have books that appeal to both genders, which include children who have their roots in every part of the world and avoid unwelcome bias.

By the end of the primary years we hope that children will have become confident and enthusiastic readers of fiction both at home and in school. We have succeeded if children read fiction independently and by choice. The entries on the novel and on emotional literacy aim to explain the distinctive contribution reading quality fiction makes to a child's intellectual and emotional development.

In the United Kingdom, primary teachers work within the frameworks of the National Curriculum English programmes and the National Literacy Strategy; the fiction element of these frameworks assume practitioners have a certain level of language awareness and subject knowledge (see Angela Wilson, 1999). The different genres, both fiction and non-fictions, to be covered are assigned to particular terms in each year group in *The Framework for Teaching*. At whole-text level, there are some questions which can usefully be asked of each work: what kind of text it is; if appropriate, what is important about the plot, characterisation and setting; how the resolution of central conflicts is achieved; whether there are some particular human issues considered in an illuminating way. Sentence-level study will involve drawing attention to kinds of syntactic structures used and use of literary devices like metaphor and simile while word-level work will focus on the vocabulary used and its impact. Statutory requirements must be heeded, but hopefully this will not prevent us from emphasising reading for meaning and pleasure in our daily practice. Response to fiction can be explored and deepened by carefully chosen activities. Benton and Fox (1986) consider that activities before, alongside or after hearing a story, play or poem should be those which lead children deeper into the layers of meaning. Sometimes just to listen or to read and reflect silently is enough, but often the children's response will be developed by a carefully thought out activity. Teachers know best which activities are most likely to interest the children in their class after they have enjoyed a particular piece of fiction. The suggestions in books by Chambers, Graham, Mallett and Marriot and in the list below may be helpful, particularly to students and to beginning teachers. This list is culled from many books and classroom examples. There is some evidence, for example, that greater success is experienced by girls in GCSE English, and that very generally boys lag behind in reading and appreciating fiction. In my experience both boys and girls enjoy the activities listed below where they have been explained and introduced well. I will never forget the power and passion of a discussion about what makes a good friend by a group of ten year old boys and girls after a teacher's lively reading of Gene Kemp's *The*

Turbulent Term of Tyke Tiler. You need to decide at which point to introduce an activity – before, during or after the shared reading. Your choice will be affected by the nature of the actual text, the best ways of working in your particular classroom context and the age, abilities and preferences of the individuals that make up your class. So adapt, extend and ring the changes.

Extending Reading Response

Speaking and listening

- retelling the story
- reading favourite parts out loud
- sharing predictions about how a story will develop
- talking about the issues in a class or group setting
- individuals presenting an opinion on an aspect of the text – characterisation, setting, plot or resolution to encourage further discussion
- if appropriate, talking about and interpreting illustrations
- imagining the content of letters and conversations (could be written down later)
- talking about the writer's use of language and imagery for particular effects
- dramatic improvisation round issues
- tape recording a pretend radio book review programme
- thinking aloud in role – revealing a character's motivations
- hot seating – one child takes up the role of a central character and answers questions from teacher and other children.

Writing

- 'reading journals' (see Judith Graham's photocopiable framework in *Cracking Good Books* or devise your own, consulting the children)
- preparing character dossier with reports, letters and sketches
- creating timelines – chronological charts of events in the story
- scripting part of a story
- sharing own anecdotes after reading an autobiography like Roald Dahl's *Boy*

- alternative fairy stories on the theme of a traditional tale; other kinds of genre exchange, for example making part of a story into a film script with posters advertising the film and a cast list
- poems on a powerful theme in the text
- the story from another character's perspective
- letters between characters, perhaps writing in pairs
- diary entries
- newspaper reports based on an event in a story (favourites are *The Three Little Pigs* and *Red Riding Hood*)
- sequels – these are challenging but older children might enjoy writing a chapter about what has happened a few years after the book ended
- some fiction lends itself to the making of maps of the setting or a journey
- display one author's work together with reviews, cover flap 'blurb' and comments by teacher and children.

Barrs, M. (1997) *The Core Booklist* London: The Centre for Language in Education.

Benton, Michael and Fox, Geoff (1986) *Teaching Literature 9–14* Oxford: Oxford University Press.

Chambers, Aidan (1993) *Tell Me: Children Reading and Talk* Stroud: The Thimble Press. Teaching of English (NATE).

Graham, Judith (1998) *Cracking Good Books* Sheffield: The National Association for the Language in Primary Education.

Mallett, Margaret (1997) *First Person Reading and Writing in the Primary Years* Sheffield: NATE.

Marriott, Stuart (1995) *Read On: Using Fiction in the Primary School* London: Paul Chapman.

Stones, Rosemary (ed.) (1999) *A Multicultural Guide to Children's Books 0–16+* London: Books for Keeps and The Reading and Language Information Centre.

Townsend, John Rowe (1990, 6th and definitive edition) *Written for Children* London: The Bodley Head.

Wilson, Angela (1999) *Language Knowledge for Primary Teachers* London: David Fulton (Chapter 9).

Fiction as a source of information

See also Art & English, History & English, information story, Science & English

We learn much about life at different times and in different environments and about the human condition from fiction. In Primary English, fiction and informational texts can sometimes work together to help children learn.

After enjoying Kenneth Grahame's *The Wind in the Willows,* children sometimes turn to information books about the creatures of the riverbank. I have known cases where older primary children have taken their explorations further – into books about the changes in the natural environment and how we can prevent more damage being done to our riverbanks. The celebration in *The Wind in the Willows* of the natural world is a powerful background to looking at environmental issues because it gives us a sense of the richness we have lost or might lose.

Experienced teachers often find fiction a powerful beginning for other kinds of learning. Just a few other examples known to me of children's interest being sparked by stories include: eight year olds wanting to find out about spiders after reading E.B. White's *Charlotte's Web,* nine year olds investigating pigs and animal welfare after a shared reading of Dick King-Smith's *The Sheep-pig* and ten year olds researching the facts on evacuees during the Second World War after enjoying Nina Bawden's *Carrie's War.*

Things can happen the other way round. Richard Adam's *Watership Down,* a fantasy which gives us a sense of the spirit of the countryside, could be a starting point for or complement informational research. But in an interesting case study by Donald Fry, in Chapter 2 of *Children Talk About Books,* this novel is a way into enjoying fiction for a seven year old who has a preference for factual texts. Seven-year-old Clayton identifies with the interests of his father who works on a farm and reads *Farmer's Weekly.* Father and son enjoy informational reading about animals, agriculture and wild flowers. The teacher praised this at parents' evening but suggested father and son might also read some fiction together to broaden the range of Clayton's reading. In this case a story read by father to son, extended an interest in agriculture and wild life.

Illustration can sometimes link fact and fiction; picture book illustrators in particular often take great care over detail and accuracy. Judith Graham (1996) explores the potential of Alexander and Lemoine's story, *Leila,* about a child searching for her lost brother in the desert, a starting point for research into desert life. Clothes, plant and lifestyle are all portrayed powerfully.

So, there can be some rich interplay between texts of different kinds. But we need a light touch here – mostly stories are worthwhile for their own sake and impart their lessons with gentleness and subtlety.

Fry, Donald (1985) *Children Talk About Books: Seeing themselves as readers* Milton Keynes: Open University Press.

Graham, Judith (1996) 'Using illustration as the bridge between fact and fiction' *English in Education* Vol. 30, No. 1.

Field of discourse

See also brainstorming, register

The 'field of discourse' is an aspect of its 'register' and is concerned with the topic or content of a spoken or written text. There is a close link between the topic or content and the vocabulary used in a text. When easing children into the 'field of discourse' of a new topic teachers often invite 'brainstorming'. Here the words and concepts associated with, for example, volcanoes, the Vikings or electricity are identified and made into a concept map or web.

Figurative language

See also analogy, metaphor, simile

In literary texts, and particularly in poetry, language is often used obliquely to the subject by using devices like imagery and analogy.

Film – see television and literacy, video-film and visual literacy

First person writing

See also anecdotes, autobiography, diary, expressive writing, journal, letters, recount

This is writing from one person's viewpoint and can take the form of a diary or journal entry, a letter, a factual narrative (recount) or a full length autobiography. Writers of fiction sometimes use the first person 'voice' as a device to achieve certain effects – see under 'autobiography'.

First person recounts or narratives are a very important kind of writing in English work where all a pupil's intellectual and imaginative faculties are often brought into play. How we react to and feel about events, people and ideas are relevant in a way they might not be in other subjects. The very first writing children do is often very like written-down speech. James Britton called this 'expressive writing' and considered it was close to the interests and preoccupations of the writer.

The advantages of writing in the first person include the sense of immediacy it gives, the detailed insight gained into one person's way of dealing with life and experience, with events and people and its potential to 'invite the reader in'. But within these very strengths lie some possible limitations. As ten-year-old Hayley remarked, 'everything is shown through only one person's eyes'. Mallett (1997) carried out a series of lessons with a Year 6 class to point up some of the differences between first and third person writing.

After reading parts of Roald Dahl's *Boy: Tales of Childhood* (Penguin, 1984), *Anne Frank's Diary* (Unicorn Books, 1960) and *The Shorter Pepys* (Bell & Hyman, 1985) these were some of the features of autobiographical writing that children and teacher noted:

- A diary entry, letter or full length autobiography is the writer's selection of events and although it is closely based on real experience, the writer chooses how to tell each event, what to emphasise and what to miss out.
- The 'voice' has a friendly, confiding tone, in

some respects like speech.
- Enough detail is included to involve the reader with the situation.
- Events, both sad and humorous, and which illuminate aspects of the human situation, are skilfully described.
- The narrative does not just describe events, it assesses them and their impact on people. The writer's own behaviour and that of others is constantly commented on and evaluated, and thoughts and feelings are of great importance.
- Direct speech can add to the vitality of the writing.

(First Person Reading and Writing in the Primary Years, p. 14.)

When it comes to their own first person writing some children find it difficult to go beyond the rather monotonous listing of events in chronological sequence with over use of the conjunction 'and'. Teachers can help by looking with the children at how skilled writers add interest. Both Roald Dahl and Anne Frank energise their accounts with a lot of direct speech. The writers we want to read do not stick to safe and bland topics and reactions. Anne Frank's diary is fascinating partly because we hear about who fell out with who. The children in the case study liked the chapter in *Boy* where Dahl describes having his tonsils out without anaesthetic on the kitchen table!

A book my students and I have found helpful in inspiring children of between about five and seven years is Martina Selway's *What Can I Write? Rosie Writes Again* (Red Fox, 1998). The children are shown, with a touch of humour, that their everyday experiences are worth writing about. The same age group nearly always respond to Simon James's delightful book *Dear Greenpeace* (Walker Books, 1991) which consists of the letters Emily wrote to and received from Greenpeace about the whale in her garden pond.

Britton, James (1970) *Language and Learning* Allen Lane: The Penguin Press.
Mallett, Margaret (1997) *First Person Reading and Writing in the Primary Years: Enjoying and reflecting on diaries, letters, autobiographies and first person fiction* Sheffield: National Association for the Teaching of English (NATE).

Flash cards

See also reading

Flash cards are pieces of card about 15 cm by 10 cm with 'key' words printed on them in large letters. This resource is associated with the 'Look and Say' method of teaching reading in which children learn a 'key' vocabulary before meeting the same words in a reading book. The approach is class based and children get used to routines in which they say the words when the cards are held up and then find reinforcement in the reading books. Unlike the phonic approaches which emphasised sounds, the Look and Say method stresses the learning of whole words.

In modern practice, the building up of a core vocabulary is maintained, but mechanistic drilling with the flash cards has fallen out of favour.

Flow chart

See also diagrams, visual literacy

A flow chart is a type of diagram which shows the stages involved and the options to choose from in various courses of action.

Folk tales

See also fairy tales, multiculturalism books, traditional tales

Folk tales are a category of traditional tales which are told over time and which communicate the social attitudes, beliefs and customs of a particular culture. Although their roots are in oral tradition, many have now been written down. As Mary Steel writes, 'folk tale' and 'fairy tale' have been used interchangeably by editors, although 'fairy tale' in the title generally indicates that the book is intended for children' (Steele, 1989, p. 5). My students and I find it helpful to join Townsend in regarding 'folk' as referring to the origin of a tale, while 'fairy' refers to its nature (Townend, 1995, p. 67). So 'folk tales' is the larger category and a particular folk tale may or may not be a fairy tale.

Folk tales come from many different countries and alongside a good story tell us something about the cultures in which they are set. The annotated lists of traditional tales in *A Multicultural Guide to Children's Books 0–16+* recommend folk tales for different age-groups. For example, stories from a number of different countries particularly suitable for reading out loud to younger children are to be found in Margaret Mayo's *The Orchard Book of Magical Tales* (Orchard, 1993). Enjoyed from about age seven years upwards are Caroline Ness's tales from the Indian sub-continent *The Ocean of Story: a collection of magical folk tales* (1995) and Berlie Doherty's collection, in which stories from Africa, Canada, Australia and Wales are included, *Tales of Wonder and Magic* (1997). Mary Steele's Bookguide also has an annotated list of traditional tales, including folk tales.

If you want both to increase your knowledge of folk tale as a genre and gain helpful advice about using it in English and across the curriculum, *Tales for the Telling* is a most stimulating and helpful resource. The annotated lists are well organised, often under intriguing headings, for example, 'Stories about a land in the sky', 'Stories in which somebody has a secret name' and 'Stories with an unusual mode of transport'.

Steele, Mary (compiler) (1989) *Traditional Tales* Stroud: Signal Bookguide, edited by Nancy Chambers.

Stones, Rosemary (ed) (1999) *A Multicultural Guide to Children's Books 0–16+* Co-published by *Books for Keeps* and The Reading and Language Information Centre, Reading.

Tales for the Telling: a journey through the world of folk-tales (2000), Newcastle upon Tyne: The Centre for the Children's Book. Tel. 0191 274 3941 (This Education Pack is an exciting guide through the folk tale world which suggests many language activities round folk tales. The Centre for the Children's Book will from 2003 house its collection of children's books in a seven-storey former flour mill in Gateshead.)

Formative assessment

See also assessment, reading, speaking and listening, miscue analysis, writing

This is a kind of assessment which records what a young learner has achieved and how they might be helped to make further progress. It can serve a diagnostic purpose: a miscue analysis provides a profile of a young reader's strengths and limitations. Formative assessments feed into a dynamic cycle of planning, teaching and learning. The results of formative evaluations can be used with test results to provide a summative assessment, a snapshot of where a pupil is at a particular time.

Framework for Teaching (National Literacy Strategy)

See also discussion text, explanation text, genre, fiction: choosing and using, instruction, Literacy Hour, National Curriculum, non-fiction reading and writing, persuasive writing, reading, recount, reports, writing

The National Literacy Strategy *Framework for Teaching,* first published in 1998, provides a detailed scheme of literacy work with term by term objectives, organised into text level, sentence level and word level. This links with the 2000 National Curriculum English Orders for children aged 5–11 years.

There are a growing number of other DfEE National Literacy Strategy publications which give further guidance on particular aspects: for example *Progression in Phonics* (1999), *Grammar for Writing* (2000), *Developing Early Writing* (2001).

Free verse

See also poetry

This is verse without a regular metrical pattern and rhyming system but featuring some conventions of poetry like imagery. Many modern poets favour a form that makes meaning, rather than a fixed rhyme or metre, paramount. Teachers often encourage children to write poetry in this form as it frees them from sacrificing meaning to achieve rhymes. It is important not to give the impression free verse is just cut-up prose.

Full stop

See also drafting, proof reading, punctuation, sentence, transitional aspects of writing

A full stop is used to show the end of a sentence but for a young child the concept of what a sentence is takes time to acquire. We do not speak as we write, and may not always pause at the end of sentences. In a very interesting article 'Developing concepts of sentence structure and punctuation', David Hutchinson worked with a child on a piece of writing which was a retelling of John Burningham's picture book *Come away from the water, Shirley.* The child seemed to be using his speech to develop his account and he used conjunctions where maturer writers would place full stops. 'shirley and her mum and dad were going to the seaside and her dad....' But when researcher and child looked again at the writing the next day, the child spontaneously decided to put a full stop after the title and with gentle nudging was able to add other full stops to the account. This seems to support the idea of separating compositional aspects (content) and transcriptional aspects (spelling and punctuation) and encouraging proof reading, even for the very young (Hutchinson, 1987).

In setting out principles for the teaching of punctuation, Nigel Hall urges us to see punctuation as a means of enhancing the meaning of writing. Hall's research reinforced the approach in Hutchinson's case study which placed the teaching of punctuation in the context of lively writing experiences (Hall, 1998). This is helpful for teachers to keep in mind when working with Year I children (6–7 year olds) who are required in *The Framework* to recognise full stops and capital letters and become able to use full stops in their writing.

Hall, Nigel (1998) *Punctuation in the Primary School* Reading University: Reading and Language Information Centre.

Hutchinson, David (1987) 'Developing concepts of sentence structure and punctuation' *Curriculum,* 8(3): 13–16.

Functional literacy

If someone is said to have achieved 'functional literacy' it means that they have sufficient competence in reading and writing to live and work in their society. It implies, for example, that they will be able to understand print in the environment – notices, labels, road signs – and manage to read well enough to do a job. The term is sometimes used pejoratively as it emphasises the utilitarian aspects of language. Notions of what is needed for 'functional literacy' will change as society and the job culture changes, for example competence on a word processor is now a basic requirement while up to about the late 1980s it was not.

Functions of language

See also accent, communicative competence, dialect, field of discourse, language acquisition, language and thought, language change, language variety, mode, register, standard English, tenor, transformational generative grammar

The functions of language are to do with the purposes for which an individual uses it at a given time and in a particular context. While structural linguists, like Saussure and Chomsky, emphasised language as an autonomous system made up of words, sentences and longer pieces of text, functional linguists, notably M.A.K. Halliday, saw the structures in a language very much as being derived from its functions (Halliday, 1978). So the form language takes is affected by the purpose of the user. We might be encouraging friends to take a holiday, giving a closely argued formal lecture or trying to persuade someone to vote for us: each purpose affects the form our language will take.

The context of the situation in which a language episode takes place also has a considerable effect on the form of what we say. Halliday describes the different aspects of the context. The 'field' is what is written and spoken about, for example children might be talking about the appearance and habits of the classroom snails. The 'mode' refers to the kind of language used (it will be different in a telephone call, an e-mail or a lesson); the children in the example conducted a conversation in which they were beginning to use some scientific terms like 'habitat' and 'tentacles'. Finally, the 'tenor' is to do with the attitudes of participants towards each other – the children looking at the snails were sharing their observations.

There is more about how functional linguists view language variety and language change under these entries. Halliday's model of functions of language in the young child is covered under 'language acquisition'. It is important to mention here that for older children and adults Halliday suggests we make a distinction between two main functions of language: ideational and interpersonal. The ideational aspect is to do with the content, with what we express. The interpersonal aspect refers to the relationship between participants – our language choices are affected by the relative age and status of the language users and the gender of each and the attitudes they might have towards each other based on past encounters.

The functional approach to language has much to offer in the primary years. In the United Kingdom and other countries like Australia there is recognition that children need to learn about and use different kinds of text, spoken and written. A large part of learning about genre is understanding the different social purposes and the effect of different contexts on language forms. In her book *Teaching About Language in the Primary Years,* Rebecca Bunting goes into further detail about the application of the functional model to the classroom (Bunting, 2000, pp. 21–4).

Bunting, Rebecca (2000 edition) *Teaching About Language in the Primary Years* London: David Fulton.

Halliday, M.A.K. (1978) *Language as Social Semiotic* London: Edward Arnold.

G

Gap Reading Comprehension test

See also cloze procedure, reading age, Standardised Reading Tests

This group, written and timed test for the age-range 7.08–12.06 years (Heinemann, 1970) works on the cloze procedure principle. Children fill in missing words in paragraphs with gaps. Supplying the omitted words involves young readers in applying syntactic and semantic cueing systems. They need to ask themselves – what would make sense and sounds and looks appropriate?

Gender & language development

See also equal opportunities, language variety, video-film

Debates about gender and language development are associated with other large issues like the implications of 'sex roles' in society and linguistic differences between women and men.

Proponents of feminist philosophies tend to argue that it is the male dominated use of language which has kept women in a subordinate position in society. In the current climate, with the very understandable concern about boys' literacy needs, we must not forget that women continue to be disadvantaged in the workplace, earning less than men for similar work and still battering at the glass ceiling when it comes to being appointed to senior positions (*Guardian,* 22 August 2000).

Here we are concerned with gender and language issues as they effect schooling. The picture is both interesting and complex. In the 1970s and 1980s, influenced by feminist analyses, teachers were preoccupied with the disadvantages girls might encounter in school. The emphasis was firmly on inclusion and equal opportunities. As one who lived and taught during these times two things stand out in my memory. First, while not wanting to act as censors, teachers were concerned that classroom and school library book collections should not only reflect in written text and illustration the traditional roles of girls and women. Reading schemes in particular were scrutinised for sexual, racial and class stereotyping and publishers responded to criticisms made at this time as the improved resources of today show. Second, there was considerable awareness of girls' disadvantage in talk contexts following the results of research studies, for example that of Swann and Graddol. The latter researchers provided evidence, not only of the tendency of boys to dominate class and group discussion, but also of how teachers sometimes unwittingly encouraged it (Swann and Graddol, 1988).

By the 1990s the focus had shifted to boys and their underachievement, particularly in literacy. Of course, it had been known for a long time that boys are in general slower to develop their reading and writing abilities than girls. But why did this change from a preoccupation with girls' disadvantages to concern about boys' needs come about at this time? One reason seems to be to do with the increasing need in the United Kingdom for schools to meet demanding targets which brought the relative lack of success of boys in literacy to the fore. Both the National Curriculum and the National Literacy Strategy are based on inclusion – on the principle that all pupils regardless of gender, class, ability or culture should participate in every part of the curriculum. But also built into the requirements is the need to differentiate – to provide for an individual's particular needs and abilities in planning and teaching. Rather than concentrate on the needs of one gender to the possible disadvantage of the other, there is increasing recognition that boys and girls have different learning needs. Baxter, for example, in a very helpful booklet *Making gender work* suggests that if both girls and boys are to flourish we need to employ carefully thought out 'differentiated learning strategies and experiences' (Baxter, 2001, p. 3).

When it comes to speaking and listening contexts, teachers need to be aware of their own use of language and their non verbal communication like eye contact and gesture which could effect how children learn and contribute. Both Browne (1996) and Baxter (2001) suggest that allowing another teacher to observe our lessons and to report on boys' and girls' responses and our own teaching style might help us reflect on how we can promote a gender – fair oracy programme. In her very interesting analysis of talk and learning, Browne observes that when they start school many children already show signs of gender identity in the way that they speak and listen to others. Although these are general trends – not all individuals will conform to the pattern – boys often already dominate and expect to be listened to while girls seem more likely to listen to others rather than participating. In planning our oracy work we can bear these tendencies in mind and extend the language experiences of both genders. For example we can support and encourage girls when they make contributions to discussions and praise boys when they listen and make supportive comments about the ideas of others. We need also to be fair in choosing topics to appeal to both genders for discussion. Boys and girls can be invited to take turns at being 'leaders' and 'scribes' in group work and giving presentations to the whole class.

Gender differences in reading are also evident early in a child's school life. Children tend to model their reading behaviour and attitudes on the same sex, older members in their families. Very generally, women read fiction and men non-fiction. The emphasis is still on story in the early years and Nursery and Reception classes tend to experience a mainly female culture, possibly rein-forcing boys' impression that reading is for girls (Millard, 1997). But both boys and girls need to become able to read a range of texts as they grow older – hopefully for their own enjoyment and interest – but also as a way of making progress in school. There is a case for introducing information texts as well as stories from the earliest stages and The National Literacy Strategy has helped by formalising the inclusion of a range of text types. The new emphasis on non-fiction – both print and electronic – promises to improve the attitude of many boys towards reading as an appropriate activity for both genders. It is likely also to help those girls who read only stories to appreciate how quality information texts can satisfy their curiosity and create new interests. In a recent discussion about their teaching practice, student teachers at Goldsmiths College found reading out loud to children inside and outside the Literacy Hour helped children experience a greater range of texts than if all had been left to independent reading. It is in this sort of context that teachers can model the critical, reflective kind of reading children need to develop to expand their thinking. Even older primary children greatly enjoy and learn from the teacher reading a novel or short story out loud – above all, it brings the whole class together, boys and girls, as a community of young listeners and readers.

Gender differences are just as strong if not more so when it comes to writing. To some extent, the same preference for fiction is shown by girls and for non-fiction in the case of boys. Teachers can help by creating a balance between writing tasks, ensuring that both boys and girls have the opportunity for story writing and for the different kinds of non fiction writing. It can be made clear that all aspects of writing are valued so that boys as well as girls take time over presentational aspects as well as the content and style of their work. The emphasis on shared writing in the literacy hour means the teacher can draw on the strengths of both boys and girls. I was interested to read in Baxter's *Making Gender Work* that boys often prefer writing where there is some structure built into the task. I have also found this is the case. For example, in my own small scale research study of one Year 6 class's reading and writing choices two ten-year-old boys commented as follows:

> Dan. I like writing the end of a story when the teacher has read out the first part. It gives you a good start… you don't have to think of a beginning.
> Tom. Yes and it gives you an idea of the sort of thing you can write, like *The Secret Tunnel* was a mystery.

Tom seems to be saying that there are conventions in a particular genre and you feel more confident about controlling them if you have been given some idea of how to proceed. (Mallett, 1997, p. 55.)

When there is a free choice of what to write teachers find boys and girls tend to choose very different stories in setting plot and characterisation. Girls often like to create fantasy situations and are interested in people's and animals' feelings and reactions. As all teachers know, boys on the other hand, very often choose to write horror stories, sometimes showing the influence of their computer programmes and the television programmes they watch. Although we are glad that some children are prepared to attempt a story at all, there have to be some guidelines about what is acceptable. We must protest if a child consistently writes of violent events and weapons. On the whole a constructive approach is best – one which encourages children to think about what they are writing and why they have chosen a particular story line and particular words and phrases.

Baxter, Judith (2001) *Making Gender Work* Reading: Reading and Language Information Centre (site address for the centre's other publications – www.ralic.ac.uk).

Brown, Ann (1996) *Developing Language and Literacy 3–8* London: Paul Chapman (see Chapter 7).

Mallett, Margaret (1997) 'Gender and Genre: Reading and Writing Choices of Older Juniors' in *Reading* UKRA Vol. 31, No. 2, July 1997.

Millard, Elaine (1997) *Differently Literate: Boys, Girls and the Schooling of Literacy* London: Falmer Press.

Swann, J. and Graddol, D. (1988) 'Gender inequalities in classroom talk' *English in Education* Vol. 22, No.1, pp. 48–65.

Genre

See also under autobiography, biography, discussion text, explanation text, expressive talk and writing, faction, factual genres, fantasy, fiction, film, history of children's literature, instructional texts, novel, persuasion, poetry (and sub-categories like epic, ballad, haiku and free verse), realism, recount, reports, television and literacy, text level work, transactional genres, transitional texts, visual literacy. For particular kinds of children's books see under entries like adventure stories, animal stories, fairy stories, school stories, parables and traditional tales

Genres are types or kinds of text. The form of a text varies according to its purpose. At one time the term 'genre' was used to refer mainly to kinds of literature – novels, poems and play scripts and their sub-categories. Now it tends to refer to any type of text whether written, spoken or pictorial.

The National Curriculum English programmes and the National Literacy Strategy objectives are genre based; the assumption is that development in literacy is partly to do with controlling, as readers and writers, the kinds of texts valued in our society. Included are all kinds of fiction and non-fiction in a wider range of media than ever before – in addition to print (books, articles, newspaper letters, flyers, transcripts and posters) we have software, the Internet, CD-ROMs, electronic books, cassettes and video film.

Underpinning the National Curriculum emphasis on genre is the work of a group of Australian academics and teachers who are referred to as 'genre theorists'. Their classroom-based research studies found that teachers encouraged the writing of narratives much more than other kinds of writing like persuasive and explanatory kinds of writing. For essays by different genre theorists see Reid (1987) and for a critical analysis of the work of J.R. Martin, F. Christie and J. Rothery I recommend the last section of Chapter 12 in Wyse and Grant (2001).

Critics of the genre theorists often express concern about the formal teaching of genre their work has sometimes led to. It is also felt that genre is presented as too static a phenomenon. While the characteristic elements of a genre may be organised fairly predictably, we must remember that language is socially situated and dynamic – it changes as a culture changes. Think of the impact on writing forms of the new technologies – the e-mail is a developing form reflecting changes in our working procedures and resources. This more flexible approach to genre is found in the work of Wilson (2001, Chapter 4) and Derewianka (1996).

Derewianka, Beverley (1996) *Exploring the Writing of Genres* published by the United Kingdom Reading Association (UKRA) Minibook Series.
Reid, I. (ed.) (1987) *The Place of Genre in Learning* Victoria: Deacon University.
Wilson, Angela (2001) *Language Knowledge for Primary Teachers* London: David Fulton.
Wyse, Dominic and Grant, Russell (2001) *Teaching English, Language and Literacy* London: Routledge-Falmer.

Genre exchange

See also EXEL project.

This term is used to refer to transforming information read in one form into another. A child might read a non-narrative text about the food eaten by the Saxons and be asked to use the information to create a menu. It is a strategy which helps children draw on information in their writing rather than copying or closely paraphrasing.

Genre theory – see genre

Geography & English

See also atlas, factual genres, information story, narrative, non-fiction reading and writing, visual literacy

In geography lessons the things children learn about include the physical features, and climate of the earth, the places where people live and the environmental challenges that they face. An 'English' perspective helps children get a personal foothold in these topics. Geography, like other subjects, can been linked with English through the Literacy Hour; the same text can be used in either context but in different ways. Meredith Hooper's *River Story* (Walker Books) would help under sevens explore geographical concepts of

time, place and change as the river makes its journey from its source to the sea. In English, the emphasis would be on how the visual and the verbal interact to tell an exciting narrative. Children could talk about the dynamic words to describe the water's movement – 'bubbling', 'trickling', 'bouncing' and 'slipping' – and how Bee Willey's pictures extend our understanding. The ways in which texts can link Geography with English in the literacy hour is given powerful practical illustration in Lewisham's Professional Development centre's excellent publication – *Find that book.*

Resources for geography include books and print atlases, posters and publicity material from travel agents, maps and leaflets about local amenities from local authorities, newspaper articles and letters on environmental issues, CD-ROMs and the Internet. All this links the written word with social purposes children can understand. In the case of younger children especially, we can use fact and fiction flexibly. Indeed many of the books written for them are 'transitional' in the sense that they only have some of the features of the mature genre they are leading towards. For instance when it comes to 'map books' and early atlases there is everything to be gained from selecting those that relate to children's existing knowledge and experience. Wayland's *Big Book of Mapwork 1* begins with fairy tale journeys and continues with simple map making showing streets, following a route and learning about compass directions. This interactive resource encourages children to make their own maps – an excellent way of learning how a map works. The enjoyment of Pat Hutchin's story, *Rosie's Walk,* is often extended by asking children to make a map of Rosie's journey across the farmyard, pursued by a fox. The story can be a starting point for helping children understand directional language. Poetry can also inspire making maps. Teachers sometimes ask children to make a map of the village where Robert Browning's *The Pied Piper of Hamelin* is set, with its town hall, River Weser and Koppelberg Hill. A number of my students have praised Eljay Yildirim's *Aunty Dot's Incredible Adventure Atlas* which uses letters to involve children in a journey round the world.

These are illustrated with clear maps, pictures and photographs that give insight into different cultures. This entertaining book can be the starting point for children's own letters and travel diaries which allow appreciation of personal response and evaluation of places. For more suggestions about map books and atlases, see Mallett, 1999.

There is a long tradition of books which try to help children understand life in another country by following a day or week in the life of a child about their own age. Frances Lincoln's *Child's Day* series is a recent addition to this tradition and covers days in the lives of children in India, Russia, Ghana, Brazil and China. Some of the photographs give the flavour of subtle cultural differences; there is a picture of a class of young children in a Russian school in *Pollina's Day* which communicates powerfully what a serious business learning can be. Two other books, each with an alphabetic organisation, also tell us about our shared world in a warm and sympathetic way. Ifeoma Onyefulu's *A is for Africa* and Kathryn Cave's *W is for World,* both published by Frances Lincoln, introduce interesting vocabulary and ideas with involving photographs. The issues round having connections with two different cultures is a theme often explored in children's picture books and novels. The subtle feelings about both the people and the environments are explored in Hoffman and Binches' *Grace and her Family.*

Geography is concerned with large concepts like time and space, often difficult to explain to children. *Out there somewhere it's time to* by Manning and Granstrom (Frances Lincoln) has an imaginative approach to understanding time differences across the world, by creating contrasts through text and exhilarating illustrations of different environments which include Guilin (in China), New York, Moscow and Newcastle on Tyne. The book has two levels of text: the main text is bold and conversational, the smaller text is more like that of a conventional information book.

Most of the texts mentioned so far linking geography and literacy have been suitable for the under eights. But older primary children also need the encouragement provided by powerful photographs and diagrams and interesting texts and those found in the media and on the Internet become increasingly valuable as children get older. For an interesting account of geography's contribution to environmental education, often through children's involvement with matters of local concern, see John Cook's chapter in Reiley and Prentice (1999) 'Geography: a sense of place'.

Poems and novels also link English and geography. John Agard's poem 'What the teacher said when we asked, 'What Er We Avin for Geography, Miss' entertains but can also invite deep reflection on the subject of geography (in *Can I buy a slice of sky?,* edited by Grace Nichols, Blackie Publishers). Then there are poems about volcanoes and earthquakes that show us the human side of natural disasters. 'Hurricane' from *A Caribbean Dozen* (Walker Books) gives an insight into what it feels like to be caught up in the 'big wind'. Novels and short stories which take us into a distinctive setting or environment very memorably or give us the texture and personal detail of a journey perhaps give the most powerful links between English and geography. Here we would all have our own favourites which might include Anita Desai's *The Village by the Sea: An Indian Family Story,* Beverley Naidoo's *Journey to Jo'bug: A South African Story* and Ian Seraillier's *The Silver Sword.*

Cook, John (1999) 'Geography: A Sense of Place' in Riley, Jeni and Prentice, Roy (eds) *The Curriculum for 7–11 year olds* London: Paul Chapman.

Find that book: making links between literacy and the broader curriculum (1999) Lewisham Professional Development Centre (Tel. 0208 314 6146).

Mallett, Margaret (1999) *Young Researchers: Informational Reading and Writing in the Early and Primary Years* London: Routledge.

Gifted children – see Special Educational Needs

Girls & English – see gender and language development

Glossary

This is a list of specialist or technical words with explanations usually found at the end of the text they support. When children make their own information books a glossary is often appropriate and helps them clinch some important concepts about the topic.

Grammar

See also adjective, adjectival clause, adverb, adverbial clause, auxiliary verb, clause, cohesion, conjunction, participle, parts of speech, phrase, preposition, pronoun, sentence, subject knowledge, verbs

David Crystal suggests the following simple definition of grammar: 'Grammar is the study of how we make sentences.' David Crystal's essentially practical definition is taken up by the NLS *Grammar for Writing* materials for teachers of Key Stage 2. Children will understand this concrete view – that we make sentences out of words just as a carpenter makes things out of wood. If we follow the conventions in putting the words together we can make them do a job. The approach in these materials and in Bain and Bridgewood's resource book *The Primary Grammar Book* is to create resources – words, phrases and sentences which can be split up and reassembled or transformed into different patterns.

The explicit teaching of grammar in the United Kingdom went out of fashion from the 1960s until the National Literacy Strategy launched in 1998 brought it back on the agenda. The new approach involves children in talking about how parts of speech like nouns and verbs function in sentences. This way of teaching and learning grammar is likely to improve children's spelling and punctuating. The requirement that teachers and children control a metalanguage for talking about such matters is bound to encourage a special awareness of language and how we use it. More controversial is the claim that it will improve the quality of children's writing, although this is the belief underlying DfEE's National Literacy Strategy *Grammar for Writing*.

In an interesting article in the *Times Educational Supplement* (22 January 1999), Sue Palmer sympathises with teachers not educated to analyse sentences: '…complex sentences can be a grammatical minefield into which even the most experienced grammarian steps with caution'. She cautions too against getting bogged down in terminology when teaching children, reminding us that knowing what a verb or complex sentence is, is not an end in itself but a way of improving literacy: '…whenever grammatical terminology begins to mystify rather than clarify, it's time to stop using it'.

Bain and Bridgewood distinguish 'teacher knowledge', which is placed under headings called 'reminders', from the teaching objectives which specify what children are to learn. The loose-leaf file format of their book, which contains much useful photocopiable material, makes it flexible to use. It includes the means of making activity cards which help children to explore language at word, sentence and text level through games.

There are a number of books which are helpful to support our own knowledge of grammar including Crystal (1996) and McArthur (1992). Some of the recently published books for secondary children can be helpful for those of us of any age who seek an accessible text and illuminating examples of grammatical rules. Many find Bain and Bain's *The Grammar Book* accessibly written and Mark Smee's *Grammar Matters* takes us through units on words, then sentences and then paragraphs and texts. There are entertaining illustrations and a sense of progression. *Collins School Reference Grammar* is a handy, alphabetically organised, quick reference book for anyone from secondary school upwards. *The Grammar Guide* by John Seely shows that linguistics can be put across in an interesting way.

My own breakthrough came about when I realised that what we need to do when defining phrases and clauses is to ask, just as one would of a word, what is the function of this phrase or clause in the sentence?

Grammar and punctuation knowledge requirements

(based on the Technical Vocabulary list on pp. 69–72 in the National Literacy Strategy *Framework for Teaching*, DFEE, 1998).

Key Stage 1
Reception: capital letter

Year 1: full stop; question; question marks; sentence

Year 2: speech marks; comma; exclamation mark, punctuation, italics

Key Stage 2
Year 3: adjective; bullet points; conjunction; grammar; formal and informal language; noun-collective, common, proper; pronoun, personal, possessive; verb; verb tense; 1st, 2nd, 3rd person

Year 4: adjectives–comparative, superlative; adverb; clause; colon; connective; hyphen; paragraph; phrase; possessive apostrophe; semi-colon

Year 5: standard English and dialect; imperative verb; preposition; speech – direct, reported; subject; rhetorical question

Year 6: asterisk; complex sentence; hypothesis; impersonal language; parentheses – brackets, commas, dashes; voice-active, passive.

Bain, Richard and Bridgewood, Marion (1998) *The Primary Grammar Book* Sheffield: NATE.

Bain and Bain (1995) *The Grammar Book* Sheffield: NATE.

Crystal, David (1997 edition) *The Cambridge Encyclopaedia of Language* Cambridge: Cambridge University Press.

Mannion, Mark (1999) *Collins School Reference Grammar* London: Collins.

Medwell, Jane, Moore, George, Wray, David and Griffiths, Vivienne (2001) *Primary English: Knowledge and Understanding* Exeter: Learning Matters. (This is a course book meeting 4/98 Standards.)

The National Literacy Strategy *Grammar for Writing*, Guidance (2000) DfEE.

Palmer, Sue (1998) Video and teaching notes based on her five programme on sentence grammar in the BBC's *English Express* series.

Seely, John (1999) *The Grammar Guide* London: Heinemann.

Smee, Mark (1998) *Grammar Matters* London: Heinemann.

Grapheme

See also grapho-phonic cue-system

A grapheme is the smallest unit of sound in the form of a written symbol. All the 26 letters of the alphabet are graphemes as are any group of letters which forms one sound, for example the 'ow' in swallow. In short, a grapheme is a written-down phoneme.

Graphology

This is the study of the written form of a language.

Grapho-phonic cue-system

See also cue-systems, graphemes, phonics, phonemes, phonological awareness

This cue-system helps young readers combine phonic and graphic knowledge in decoding text. To help, teachers need to understand the principles. These include knowing that: sounds or phonemes are represented by letters; phonemes are represented by one or more letters; the same phoneme can be represented in different ways; the same spelling may represent more than one sound (DfEE, 1999).

DfEE (1999) *The National Literacy Strategy. Phonics: Progression in Phonics* London: DfEE.

Group discussion – see collaborative learning, discourse analysis, discussion text, Drama & English speaking and listening

Group work – see collaborative learning, guided reading/writing

Guided reading/writing

See also Literacy Hour

Placing children into groups for reading has a long history. Sometimes children of a similar ability or interest were placed together, sometimes more forward readers sat with struggling readers to help them. Children often remained in their reading groups for other literacy activities, including writing. However, there was also a tradition of the teacher hearing each child read as often as possible and OFSTED (1996) found that this was not economic of a teacher's time. It was felt that it was more efficient for a teacher to work with several children of about the same ability who could benefit from the same teaching.

Ability groups for guided reading and writing are now built into the organisation of the Literacy Hour. Group reading requires that six children all read the same text with the teacher present and receive help appropriate to the whole group. Children can learn from the teacher about predicting what might happen next in a story, how the setting is brought alive and how the author uses images. Most importantly they benefit from discussing their response to the story or poem. When it comes to non-fiction, using the retrieval devices, learning to summarise and to 'read' the diagrams can be demonstrated. Many children seem to enjoy the interactive nature of group reading.

Guided group writing follows the same principles: all the children work on the same writing task, possibly arising from the shared reading or writing part of the literacy hour, with the help of the teacher. Just as in the guided group reading context, the teacher can demonstrate planning, drafting and proof reading and point out some of the differences between for example writing fiction and non-fiction. Some difficulties may arise because of the time constraint. Twenty minutes is not long to see even a modest piece of writing through from plan to fair draft. This is where a more flexible approach to how time is spent in the literacy hour would be helpful.

OFSTED (1996) *The Teaching of English in 45 Inner London Primary Schools* London: OFSTED.

Haiku

This is a Japanese poem of three lines with 17 syllables. Traditionally the poem reveals the writer's impression of a scene or an object in a particular season or time.

> 'A pink orchid blooms
> in solitary splendour
> in a silent wood.'

Handwriting

See also Early Learning Goals, Early Years, Language and Literacy, National Curriculum, phonics, spelling

A school's English policy will have a section on their approach to the teaching of handwriting and we need to communicate the school's approach to parents so that they can help. What aims should guide our choice of a handwriting style and approach? Rosemary Sassoon, who has carried out research into all aspects of handwriting and written many practical books on how best to teach it, suggests three main aims to guide us. She believes that children should be able to write legibly, speedily and with a developing individual style. Many primary schools in the United Kingdom favour the cursive style which is simple and aesthetically pleasing.

The National Curriculum English programme for Key Stage 1 also emphasises the importance of well formed and legible handwriting to help children communicate their meaning. At this stage children are to be taught such basics as how to hold a pen or pencil, form letters of regular size and shape, leave regular sized spaces between words, form lower and upper case letters and learn how to join letters. This and other aspects of writing development are addressed in more detail in The National Literacy Strategy *Developing Early Writing* guidance

publication. Designed to complement *Curriculum Guidance for the Foundation Stage,* it sets out a framework for the teaching of handwriting in Reception and in Years 1 and 2 with many suggestions and materials for practical activities.

Good practitioners have often used a multisensory approach in the earliest stages. *Developing Early Writing* reinforces this, suggesting such strategies as sky writing (making letter shapes in the air), making letter shapes to music, making letters in sand and using language to describe shapes, referring perhaps to 'the curly caterpillar shape'. These controlled movements of the whole body help children gain 'gross motor control' and therefore posture and balance. Children also need to develop 'fine motor control' which includes smaller movements of the hand and fingers. Activities here might include cutting out letter shapes or patterns, finger painting and structured play with sand and water.

Children need to be encouraged to sit comfortably in an upright position and to position and grip their pen or pencil well. Left-handers tend to push the writing implement rather than pulling it which can lead to a less smooth action (Graham and Kelly, 1998, Chapter 5). Very simple things can help and are appreciated by young learners – making sure a child's writing book is on the left (tilted to the right so that the writer can see their writing) and demonstrating letter shapes using the left hand. In a useful summary, Ann Browne reminds us to allow left-handers more time to become competent and to help them establish a firm pencil grip (Browne, 1993).

At what age should joined up writing start? Most teachers would introduce it by seven years. *Developing Early Writing* recommends beginning as soon as children can form the separate letters so that spelling patterns can be reinforced.

Handwriting in the National Literacy Strategy approach is linked to both phonics and spelling. When they reach step 2 of *Progression in Phonics* and hear consonant phonemes in the initial position – s, m, c, t, g, h – they will need to learn the letter shapes alongside the sounds. If we learn the pattern of a word, writing it using the correct letter strings can become conveniently automatic and for the same reason there is also a case for introducing the writing of digraphs, (ay, au, ch, wh etc.) as a unit of two letters joined together. Some published handwriting packages link spelling and handwriting. For example *Collins Handwriting* by Peter Smith and Judith Williams, a structured handwriting programme in spiral bound photocopiable books, features lists of simple key words to practice particular letters and letter strings (see a detailed account about the links between spelling and handwriting in Section 4 of *Developing Early Writing)*.

For a helpful account of how to help older primary children with weak handwriting see 'Handwriting', Chapter 16 in Wyse and Jones.

Browne, Ann (1993) *Helping Children to Write* London: Paul Chapman.

Developing Early Writing DfEE manual, 2001, ref: DfEE 0055/200; Tel. 0845 602 2260.

English 4–11 No. 4, Autumn 1998, is an issue on all aspects of Handwriting (The English Association, University of Leicester, Tel. 0116 252 3982).

Graham, J. and Kelly, A. (1998) *Writing Under Control* London: David Fulton.

Sassoon, Rosemary (1983) *The Practical Guide to Children's Handwriting* London: Thames & Hudson.

Sassoon, Rosemary (1990) *Handwriting: the way to teach it* Cheltenham: Stanley Thornes.

Wyse, Dominic and Jones, Russell (2001) *Teaching English, Language and Literacy* London: Falmer.

Hearing impairment

See also Special Educational Needs

Some children suffer from complete hearing loss, others from partial hearing loss and special strategies need to be put in place to support their learning and development.

The trend in the United Kingdom has been to decrease the number of hearing impaired children being provided for in special schools, particularly where the schools are 'out county'. Instead the money is used to put in place support for teachers of hearing impaired children in mainstream classes. This help is either in the form of support from an Adviser in special needs at the local Education authority who assesses and makes recommendations, or withdrawal from classes for special help.

National Deaf Children's Society website: www.ndcs.org.uk

Historical novel

See also adventure stories, biography, History & English, history of children's literature, novel

Good historical fiction helps children develop sensitivity to the different textures of particular historical periods. If we are reading a novel to enrich the study of a period in history, it is best if the story is fixed in a particular time frame to give children a more than superficial understanding. *The Railway Children* by Edith Nestbit informs us about food, housing, transport and the lives of people of different circumstances in Victorian times in the context of a story of adventure and human warmth. A detailed grasp on what life was like in one period helps children know what has been moved on from and contributes to a sense of chronology (Hoodless, 1998).

As well as contributing to the history lesson, historical novels often raise issues about the kind of human dilemmas we discuss in English. D. Oakden's *The Discus Thrower* (Anglia Young Books, 1992), for example, tells us about living in Ancient Greece and raises, in a subtle way, questions about how certain groups including women and slaves were treated in that culture. Rosemary Sutcliff's *The Lantern Bearers* also brings different ways of living, attitudes and beliefs to a human level. History lessons need stories about events arising from the conditions and beliefs of a particular period rather than stories where the historical setting is a superficial backdrop to events that could be set at any time (Cox and Hughes in Hoodless, 1998). In his novel *The Silver Sword* (Puffin, 1956), Ian Serraillier shows us the price of war through the experiences of refugee children searching for their father. Another novel, for older primary children, *When Hitler Stole the White Rabbit* (J. Kerr, HarperCollins, 1993) provides insight into living in Nazi Germany and then in wartime Britain. Novels like these take us beyond wars, treaties and laws and bring the past alive through human dilemmas, attitudes and feelings.

Older children in the primary school are often encouraged to reflect on how the historical background has been woven into the narrative. Reading out loud some of the more demanding novels – Rosemary Sutcliff's Roman stories for example – helps make their insights accessible to children who would find them hard to read on their own. In *Young People's Reading at the End of the Century* (1996) it is observed that children are choosing history novels less frequently, showing a preference for novels based on contemporary themes and for fantasies. Reading them out loud in history or English reminds children how interesting and powerful these novels can be (Collins and Graham, 2001). Ten year olds whose teacher was reading them Nina Bawden's *Carrie's War* told me how much the story of the evacuees had helped them enjoy and understand their history work on the Second World War.

Children's Literature Research Centre (1996) *Young People's Reading at the End of the Century* London: The Roehampton Institute.

Collins, Fiona and Graham, Judith (eds) (2001) *Historical Fiction for Children: capturing the past* London: David Fulton.

Hoodless, Pat (1998) 'Children's Awareness of Time in Story and Historical Fiction' in Hoodless, P. (ed.) *History and English: Exploring the Links* London: Routledge.

Lewisham Professional Development Centre (1999) *Find that Book: Making links between literacy and the broader curriculum.* Tel. 020 8314 6146 (the history section of this book provides notes on using *The Railway Children* and *The Lantern Bearers* in the Literacy Hour and in history).

History & English

See also autobiography, biography, history of children's literature, diary, historical novel, letters, narrative, picture books, story

Old Boney was on the poop deck.
"A narrow squeak", he cried. "Back to France, my men. Back to France!"
Seeing Red by Sarah Garland and Tony Ross (1996) Andersen Press

English and literacy can be successfully linked to most other curriculum areas, as language is an agent of all learning, but for me (discounting Drama which really is part of English) the most fruitful and sympathetic possibilities lie with history. The first point to make is that history is essentially a literate activity which involves establishing evidence and communicating ideas (*Find that book*, 1999). Thus it provides a natural context for particular kinds of discussion, reading and writing. This richness of textual material connects it to the Literacy Hour and to the National Curriculum English programmes. Second an 'English' perspective, often achieved through the use of narrative or drama, can help children begin to understand about the circumstances and lives of people living in a particular period. This analysis starts by looking at non-fiction texts and then at story as a way of bringing the past 'alive' for young historians.

Non-fiction texts for history include primary sources like letters, diaries, documents, inventories and report and secondary sources, for example information and reference books, both print and electronic, autobiographies and biographies. (For a thorough guide to written sources for history see Blyth and Hughes, 1997.) The same non-fiction text might be used in history to increase historical understanding and in the literacy hour to learn about the linguistic features of a kind of writing. So, to give a specific example, a letter sent to a young girl by her soldier brother during the Second World War could be studied for evidence about historical events in history and as an example of informal language in the Literacy Hour (see *Letters to Henrietta* by Nell Marshall, Cambridge University Press).

There are fruitful connections in the other direction as well. For example older primary children who have worked as readers and writers on journalistic kinds of writing in English are well placed to evaluate newspaper sources in history.

Autobiography and biography can be used in both English and history and publishers are commissioning biographies for children to meet Literacy Hour objectives. These introduce children to literary kinds of non-fiction and to the photographs and other illustrations of lives of people in the past. Ginn have published a series of biographies on figures like Mary Seacole, Alfred the Great and Boudicca. 'In Grandma's Day' (Evans series) has first hand accounts of ordinary women describing their lives in the 1930s and 1940s. For further suggestions of examples of stories about historical figures and about ordinary people, see under the 'biography' entry.

When it comes to children's writing, we need to help them begin to control explanation and argument. Research in Australian schools during the 1980s and 1990s suggested that history teaching could be too reliant on recount genres with a narrative structure and urged that other genres should be encouraged, including explanation and argument (Christie, 1989; Derewianka, 1991; Gibbons, 1995).

Nevertheless, story forms in all their variety are a powerful meeting place for history and English. Teachers have known for a long time that novels, short stories and picture books set in the past can help develop historical knowledge and understanding. When a story is carefully chosen and read out loud with vitality and conviction, it will appeal to young imaginations and draw the children into a sequence of events, encouraging curiosity and discussion. Some stories bring part of the past alive in different cultures and periods in a way children can understand. The feelings and motivations of all kinds of people are revealed and children can also be helped to gain a vocabulary to talk about events and issues in history. Children can enjoy the historical aspects of stories from a very early age: Nursery and Reception children are fascinated by the settings, objects and clothes in the Ahlbergs' picture book set in the 1940s – *Peepo* (Penguin, 1981). Two stories, both by Martin Waddell, *The Toymaker* and *Grandma's Bill,* explore differences between the generations. For age seven and above some of the books in the many 'history through story' series publishers produce give a strong sense of lives lived in particular situations and periods through narrative and illustration. For example George Buchanan's *Kidnap on the Canal* tells the story of a boat boy in the nineteenth century and ends with factual notes (1999, Franklin Watts Sparks series). Older primary children both learn about history and enjoy the language and drama of powerful novels like Rosemary Sutcliff's – *Dragonslayer; The Eagle of the Ninth* and the many novels by Leon Garfield, Joan Aiken and Rober Westall (see more about this under 'historical novel' and 'History of Children's literature'). Then there are the stories of the past which children can be helped to create themselves. Gordon Wells describes and evaluates a project carried out by ten year olds who were celebrating the centenary of their school through historical research, drama, writing and painting. One of the most successful activities was making stories for dramatic presentation about life in a school in the late nineteenth century (p. 206, Wells, 1986). This same imaginative reconstruction of the past through careful historical research and story telling is a major theme in the work of Kieron Egan (1986).

While History and English can combine to good effect they are separate areas of knowledge and understanding. Some of the differences in emphasis when we use stories for history and stories for English are quite subtle and worth looking at in a little more detail. In the analysis which follows, I draw on the case study used by Kath Cox and Pat Hughes in their chapter 'History and Children's Fiction' in *History and English*. They share with us some work with Year 2 children round Sarah Garland's *Seeing Red* – a children's picture book set in the eighteenth century and based on a legend that may be partially true (Anderson Press, 1996). It tells the story of Trewenna, a Cornish girl, who saves her village from invasion by the French. She manages this by persuading the other women to join her in showing their red petticoats from the cliff tops to deceive the French soldiers into thinking English redcoat soldiers are lying in ambush. The plan succeeds and Napoleon Bonaparte commands his invasion fleet to return to France.

A major contribution that stories make in history is to support children's developing understanding of chronology through sequencing. So, as is the case in *Seeing Red,* pictures and written text tell of a series of events with pace and energy. This story is set at an identifiable historical time but the teacher needs to reinforce its historical aspects. To understand the events in *Seeing Red* children have to know that England was at war with France two hundred years ago, that Napoleon Bonaparte was a real person and that people used objects like bellows and candlesticks and wore a particular style of clothing. If this story were being used in an English lesson, it would be the power of the story, the characterisation and the language choices made by the author that would be paramount.

What about the significance of the illustrations in picture books used for each subject area? In *Seeing Red* they are integrated into the telling of the events and are a source of insight into aspects of the historical period – landscapes, interiors, dress and distinctive objects. The children in the history case study were shown other pictures including a reproduction of a water colour painting of soldiers in the red uniforms worn at the time. Talk about the illustrations in English would tend to centre on how the pictures added to the dramatic power of the plot and extended our understanding of the qualities of

the characters revealed in the written text.

The language of a story or picture book is important in both history and English, but in different ways. In history children need to learn some of the language of the period: historical vocabulary like 'musket' and 'flintlock pistols' is used in *Seeing Red.*

When the children commented that 'Old Boney' was 'a skitting name', the teacher helped them see the motivation behind this use of a nickname: people try to make fun of their enemies to reduce their terror. In English we would be interested in the effect of choices the author made in vocabulary, syntax, use of direct and indirect speech and choice of 'person' and tense. We would also want to think about the use of language devices like alliteration and use of imagery like simile and metaphor. Think of the power of these images of the petticoats and socks in *Seeing Red* – 'as red as cocks' combs, as red as holly berries, as red as a robin's breast…as red as the jackets of redcoat soldiers'.

Blyth, Joan and Hughes, Pat (1997) *Using Written Sources in Primary History* London: Hodder & Stoughton.

Egan, Kieron (1986) *Teaching as Story telling: an alternative approach to teaching and curriculum in the elementary school* London, Ontario: The Althouse Press.

Hoodless, Pat (ed.) (1998) *History and English: Exploiting the Links* London: Routledge.

Wells, Gordon (1986) 'Stories across the curriculum' pp. 206–13 in *The Meaning Makers: children learning language and using language to learn* London: Hodder & Stoughton.

History of children's literature

See also under adventure stories, animal stories, ballads, chapbooks, classics, comics, creation stories, ebooks, factual genres, fiction, fairy tales, fantasy, folk tales, haiku, historical novels, horror stories, horn book, legend, multi-media, myths, novel, picture books, poetry, realism in children's books, traditional tales, science fiction, short stories

In describing what children's literature has encompassed over the centuries, Peter Hunt writes that it is 'everything from a sixteenth-century chapbook to a twentieth-century computer-based interactive device – everything from a folk tale to the problem novel, from the picture-book to the classroom poem, from the tract to the penny dreadful, from the classic to the comic' (Hunt, 1995, p. ix). While when we refer to 'children's literature' we usually have in mind fiction rather than information texts, I would include literary forms of non-fiction like autobiography and biography. Moreover, while historians of children's books have generally explored writing they considered to have some literary merit many now reach out beyond the established classics to the more popular children's fiction. Fiction, and the response of children to it, will always be central in the English Curriculum. But the emphasis of the current frameworks on genre, on understanding the features of the different types of text, affects priorities in initial teacher education courses so that the careful study of the history of children's literature may be nudged into a marginal position or ignored altogether. Does it matter? There are two main reasons why intending teachers benefit from such study. First, looking at the origins and development of children's literature puts current attitudes and approaches in perspective and reveals the stages in the journey children's literature has made. Second, it helps us to explore concepts of childhood: our society changes, attitudes to children change and all this is reflected in books written for them.

The History of Children's Literature is a huge area of study: there is an immense number of texts for children and also a growing body of writing about them. This entry can only provide a starting point by identifying some landmarks in the story, some important children's books and key texts of criticism and just some of the issues about which people feel passionately. It only touches on children's literature outside the United Kingdom interesting and important as this is, given the limits on space but readers will find help here in Townsend (1990), Hunt (1995) and Watson (2001). At this stage, I want to mention some general works of analysis – often rather large tomes. A book on my 'most acces-sible' bookshelf is *The Oxford Companion to Children's Literature*. I find the alphabetical organisation helpful, particularly when I need information quickly. There was a new printing in 1999, but of the unrevised 1983 edition and so it does not take up developments in the later years of the twentieth century. Brian Alderson has revised F.J. Harvey Dalton's *Children's Books in England* and there is a new, fifth edition of *Twentieth Century Children's Writers* now called *The St James Guide to Children's Writers*. A further valued addition to my bookshelf is Victor Watson's *The Cambridge Guide to Children's Books in English* which provides a critical and appreciative overview of children's books written in English across the world. I like John Rowe Townsend's *Written for Children* because of its distinctive, forceful and sometimes controversial 'voice'. He tells us, in the preface to the definitive 1995 edition, that the book is 'a study of children's literature and not children's reading material'. So don't expect to find here an analysis of 'popular series books and other material of insignificant literary merit'. Townsend does, however, include a brief chapter on the impact of the multi media revolution and recognises that the boundaries between fiction and games and between education and entertainment are becoming blurred. One of my most 'borrowed by students' books – Peter Hunt's *Children's Literature: an Illustrated History* – is good for browsing. As the title promises, it provides important visual images of book illustrations across the time span and has strong sections on comics and other kinds of popular children's literature. The chronology at the back is extremely useful for quick reference. A more recent acquisition is Hunts' *Children's Literature* (2001) which contains thought provoking surveys of the work of forty authors including contemporary authors like Michael Rosen, Quentin Blake, Ann Fine and J.K. Rowling and some short 'Topic' chapters on censorship, gender, drama, film, media and fantasy. Looking further along my 'most accessible' bookshelf I see current and back copies of *Signal,* a journal which contains scholarly and exciting articles about children's books, covering in some cases both the early part of the twentieth century and as far back as the nineteenth century.

Ask any teacher, critic, educationist or librarian to tell you about the history of children's literature and you will find different authors and different aspects of the story emphasised. I hope that you will look at the entries on fairy tales, on picture books, on realism in children's books, on novels and so on in this book and seek out some of the valuable works to which I have referred to nourish and enrich your understanding of this fascinating subject. Now for my brief telling of the story of children's books.

The first books for children

Before Caxton printed the first book in England, *The History of Troy* in 1474, books were hand-written, rare and expensive. The only material for children was books of instruction about manners and behaviour called 'courtesy books'. There were no books for their entertainment. But it is highly likely that children would hear and enjoy the stories intended for adults and passed down by word of mouth. These stories took the form of fables (including those of Aesop), ballads (of Robin Hood and other folk heroes) and folk tales.

Until the end of the seventeenth century, nearly all books for children were school texts often for teaching the alphabet or books of prayers and religious tracts. Townsend reminds us that the Puritans viewed children 'as young souls to be saved' (Townsend, 1995, p. 6); they sought books for their children which combined learning to read with religious instruction. The most well known was *Divine Songs, Attempted in Easy Language for the Use of Children* by Isaac Watts, published in 1715.

What form did these early instruction texts take? From around the sixteenth to the eighteenth century 'hornbooks' provided an ABC in upper and lower case, an invocation to the Trinity and the Lord's Prayer and sometimes lists of spellings. Horn books were made by putting a printed page into a wooden frame (with a handle so that it could be held like a mirror) and covered by a thin layer of transparent horn. The 'battle-dore', which developed from the hornbook, was an early primer. It was a folding piece of card-board with an alphabet and woodcut illustrations of animals and objects. If you want to read more about early children's books and to see some interesting illustrations you would appreciate Gillian Avery's chapter, 'The Beginnings of Children's Reading to c.1700' in Hunt (1995). It ends with 'a glimmer of light amongst the Calvinist gloom', Bunyan's *A Book for Boys and Girls* (1686) – a book of verses with images of animals, activities and everyday objects. There were still religious messages but given with a light touch. In an age where children were regarded as small adults here is the start of a recognition that they might like books with some hint of the visual image and playfulness.

The first commercial publishers of children's books

From about the mid-seventeenth century some London publisher-booksellers began to print and distribute large numbers of cheaply produced books of popular literature for ordinary people. These slim pamphlets were known as chapbooks and were taken round the country by pedlars. At first they were written for adults – romances, ballads and fairy tales like Tom Thumb. The paper was often coarse and the illustrations rough and ready. The tales often lacked literary merit, but this was not always the case and the work of writers of the quality of Bunyan was sometimes published in chapbook form. Margaret Kinnell tells how as a young boy Walter Scott was inspired by chapbook romances from Allan Ramsay's Edinburgh bookshop (Hunt, 1995, p. 27). Sometimes a few pages for children would be included in an adult's chapbook – an ABC or a rhyme with woodblock pictures. Then whole books began to be published for them. John Bunyan's *A Book for Boys and Girls* was produced as a chapbook under a new title – *Divine Emblems*. One of the benefits of the chapbook industry was that it made available children's versions of books intended for adults. By the end of the eighteenth century there were abridged versions of Jonathan Swift's *Gulliver's Travels* and Daniel Defoe's *Robinson Crusoe*. These books had great appeal and, as Townsend points out, themes from both – the imaginary miniature world of the former and the desert island in the latter – have been echoed in many later books.

One publisher was particularly important in establishing a tradition of publishing and marketing of children's books. This was John Newbery of London who with his associates published the first children's version of Charles Perrault's fairy tales. In spite of some negative religious attitudes, the fairytale had come to England from France in the early eighteenth century in the form of *Tales of Past Times Told by Mother Goose* (1729) – a translation of the tales set down by Charles Perrault. Newbery's edition for children soon followed. Chapbook versions became common and at last children had access to imaginative literature in print. This recognition that fairy tales and the inner world of the imagination were valid areas for children's books helped establish a tradition of fairy tales for children in the nineteenth and twentieth centuries. Newbery published school books, story books, fairy tales and poetry collections for children as well as a large number of books for adults. A person of extraordinary energy he also succeeded in other businesses – newspapers and patent medicines, for example. Of all his children's books *Goody Two Shoes* seems to have been particularly popular. Perhaps the tale of a girl triumphing in spite of early hardships – who becomes the Principal of a Dame-school and a benefactor to the poor – accounts at least partly for its strong appeal. Helpful analyses of the contribution of Newbery to children's publishing are found in Chapter 2, 'Mr Locke and Mr Newbury', in Townsend, 1995 and 'A Business of Importance', Chapter 2 in Hunt, 1995. Both writers note Newbery's commercial instincts in making a success of his publishing business. He aimed to distribute widely and he advertised in provincial newspapers.

Children's books in the nineteenth century

This century saw the development of existing genres, the fairy tale and the adventure story, and the emergence of new forms like the school story and the 'new' fantasy. It also saw the emergence of what are now referred to as 'classics' – books with a long term appeal like Charles Dickens' *Oliver Twist* 1838, Thomas Hughes' *Tom Brown's Schooldays* 1857, Charles Kingsley's *The Water Babies* in 1861, Lewis Carroll's *Alice's Adventures in Wonderland* 1865, Mark Twain's *The Adventures of Tom Sawyer* 1876 and Johanna Spyri's *Heidi* (English translation in 1884).

From the beginnings of fairy tales in children's chapbooks in the previous century, sprang many retellings not only of Perraults' stories, but also of the German stories of the Brothers Grimm (1823) and the Danish tales of Hans Anderson (1846). Oscar Wilde's anthology of his original fairy tales, *The Happy Prince,* came out in 1888 and Andrew Lang's expanding series of fairy tale collections began with *The Blue Fairy Book* in 1889.

The century also saw books that are not easily placed in a category. Charles Kingsley's *The Water Babies* 1861 is a moral tale about the working conditions of child chimney sweeps but as soon as Tom enters the water and drowns we are in a world of fantasy. And in 1865 one of the most enduring fantasies of all time came out – Lewis Carroll's *Alice in Wonderland* and, soon after, its sequel *Alice Through the Looking Glass.*

Stories based on experience of the real world weave their way through the century. Here I am thinking of Dicken's *Oliver Twist*, 1838, Frances Hodgson Burnett's *Little Lord Fauntleroy* published in 1886 and an early version of *The Little Princess* under the title *Sara Crewe* in 1887. (Her most loved book *The Secret Garden*, about transformation and rebirth, was published in 1905.) Also under the 'realism' umbrella is that remarkable animal book *Black Beauty* (1887) about the cruelties to which horses were subjected by harsh masters and mistresses.

Adventure stories celebrated a male world of empire building and adventure on land and at sea while girls' books reflected the female world in domestic settings. The writers of boys' adventure stories in the nineteenth century reflected the world of imperialism, approved of kinds of male behaviour and occupation and Christian values. They were particularly influenced by two earlier authors – Daniel Defoe and Sir Walter Scott. The adventure stories of Captain Marryat, including

Mr Midshipman Easy (1836) celebrated life at sea. There were a number of other writers who developed the boys' adventure story in the second part of the nineteenth century. R.M. Ballantyne, for instance, wrote a number of stories including the popular *The Coral Island: A Tale of the Pacific Ocean* in 1858. But perhaps G.A. Henty was the most successful writer in the genre with titles that included *Cornet of Horse*, 1881 and *With Clive in India*, 1884. Henty, a retired war correspondent when he began writing full time for children, sold about 150,000 books annually at the height of his popularity. Henty often prefaced his tales with a letter to 'My Dear Lads', in which he drew attention to the heroic exploits of the story which followed and which had 'helped to create the empire'. Briggs and Butts make an interesting link between the structure of, on the one hand, adventure stories, and, on the other hand, of folk and fairy tales – pointing out that both use 'formulaic elements and stereotyped characters' (Hunt, 1995, p. 151). Robert Louis Stevenson's *Treasure Island* (serialised in the boys' paper *Young Folks* 1881–82) has a folk tale structure with a hero, a challenge/conflict and then a resolution. But, as Townsend observes, it manages to be an exceptionally exciting story and to have characters that combine good and evil qualities – like Long John Silver (not all villain) and Squire Trelawney (not all hero). This complexity of characterisation created a new model for children's writing (Townsend, 1990, p. 46).

Another important genre to emerge in the late nineteenth century was the school story. The best known is Thomas Hughes' *Tom Brown's Schooldays*, 1857. Its exploration of friendship and the tension between the different perspectives of children and adults in the school has had a considerable influence on the school stories written since.

This skim through the nineteenth century would not be complete without mentioning the developments in colour illustration in its later years since here we find the origins of the modern day children's picture book. At the beginning of the century illustrations were still coloured by hand but as mechanical colour printing developed it was brought to a high standard by master colour-printers, like Edmund Evans. A number

of gifted illustrators benefited. Walter Crane illustrated picture books based on nursery rhymes and alphabets for publishers like Routledge and Evans. In *Written for Children* Crane's illustration of the nursery rhyme 'Dickory Dock' from *The Baby's Opera* 1877 is reproduced. It shows two alert little children turning round to look at the mouse running up the grandfather clock (Townsend, 1995, p. 120). Kate Greenaway's pictures in, for example, *The Pied Piper of Hamelin* (1888) and *Under the Window* (1879), established her as a fine illustrator with a distinctive style, even if some found her children rather too perfect and the settings too idealised. Another renowned illustrator, Randolph Caldecott, was particularly good at showing action in his illustrations. If you want an impression of the energy Caldecott brings to his images look at his drawing of John Gilpin clinging desperately to his horse's mane as the creature gallops off in his drawing for Cowper's poem *John Gilpin* (1878) (Townsend, 1995, p. 117).

The history of children's literature is always about perceptions of childhood at particular times. As the nineteenth century came to an end the importance of play, games, dressing up and make believe to children's development was becoming increasingly recognised. This was reflected in books showing the pleasures of imaginative games like dressing up, playing with soldiers and dolls' tea parties all of which provided an opportunity to imitate adult behaviour see (Julia Briggs, Chapter 7, 'Transitions 1890–1914', Hunt, 1995).

Children's books in the twentieth century

Historical events – particularly the two world wars – brought about great societal change which had a profound effect on children's literature. The emergence of the children's librarian, trends in the publishing and marketing of children's books, the growing recognition that children's literature was worthy of scholarly study and could facilitate learning to read and the coming of television and multimedia as dominant cultural mediums, were all momentous developments. The analysis in this section takes account of all this and sometimes I have to step away from straight forward chronology.

However, at first there was little change and the years leading up to the First World War were a good time in the history of children's literature. Rudyard Kipling's *Just So Stories* – much loved, mythical explanations of how the camel got a hump and how the elephant got its trunk and so on – was published in 1902. The recognition of the playful element in childhood, notable in books towards the end of the previous century, was found in J.M. Barrie's *Peter Pan* (1904), Kenneth Grahame's *The Wind in the Willows* (1908) and E.E. Nesbit's *The Railway Children* (1906).

The First World War broke into this period of relative calm and continuity and in the years after the war the most important children's books were mainly in poetry and in fantasy. In his chapter 'Fantasy Between the Wars', Townsend explores the work of Walter de la Mare and Eleanor Farjeon; known mainly as poets, both were also writers of short stories for children (Townsend, 1990). The books from the 1920s which have survived best in spite of their period flavour are A.A. Milne's *Winnie-the-Pooh* (1926) and *The House at Pooh Corner* (1928). Peter Hunt explains their enduring popularity thus: 'Pooh Bear is the optimist (or mystic) everyman, as well as the amiable child. The enchanted forest contains the whole of childhood (with a touch of Arcadian nostalgia), and there is a hierarchy of types of children to identify with – Piglet, Tigger, and Roo; the children are in conflict with the strange and pretentious adults – Rabbit, Owl, and the misanthropic Eeyore – but all is made safe by the presence of Christopher Robin' (Hunt, 1995, p. 202).

The other enduring fantasy published between the wars was J.R.R. Tolkien's *The Hobbit,* 1937. Tolkien reached back into myth and legend in creating a unique imagined land in which the hobbits – creatures about half the size of a human being – live their lives. Critics of children's literature (for example Townsend, 1990, Chapter 21) recognise the influence of Tolkien's work on his friend C.S. Lewis's Narnia series which also creates an alternative world. The first story, *The Lion, the Witch and the Wardrobe,* was published in 1950 and while the books have many admirers and remain in print, some have found the religious allegory oppressive. One successor of these stories creating an imagined world is J.K. Rowling's *Harry Potter* series. I am an admirer of Ursula Le Guin's '*Earthsea'* quartet which also follows the fortunes of a young wizard in a secondary world and helps young readers reflect on moral dilemmas in everyday decisions. They are not easy books to read and understand, but would challenge and interest the ablest readers in the later primary years.

The school story tradition, begun in the previous century, continued and developed during the twentieth century. The Chalet School series by Elinor Brent-Dyer began in 1925 and the books are still in print. In the 1940s and 1950s, Enid Blyton wrote the *Malory Towers* series. William Mayne's quartet of choir school stories beginning with *A Swarm in May* (1955) brings alive the daily life of children whose life centres round singing and the cathedral. Another distinctive world was created in Anthony Buckeridge's *Jennings* books whose picture of prep school life is in the tradition of other great comic writers. By the 1970s many school stories centred on the modern primary school, for example Gene Kemp's *The Turbulent Term of Tyke Tiler* (1977) and Jan Mark's *Thunder and Lightnings* (1974). The latter includes incidents in school although it is not a school story in the conventional sense. For a reference work on the history of school stories for boys and girls see Auchmuty and Wooton, 2000.

The tradition of realistic works begun in the nineteenth century also continued. During the 1930s and 1940s, Arthur Ransome wrote his twelve novels in the *Swallow and Amazons* series about the school holiday adventures of middle class children spent on boats in the Lake District. Another very well liked writer whose stories followed the real life events and challenges of family life was Noel Streatfield whose first book, *Ballet Shoes,* came out in 1936. Around the same time, in 1937, a book about a very different family came out. Eve Garnett wrote *The Family from One End Street* which was about an urban working class family called the Ruggles. Many children enjoyed the humour in the everyday life of the family – Rose, the eldest of the seven children, tries to help her mother with her job as a washerwoman but burns a customer's petticoat. But some teachers and critics found it patronising. Townsend, for example, writes 'Mr and Mrs Ruggles are seen from above and outside' (Townsend, 1990, p. 149).

The Second World War, like the first one, changed society and many of the old certainties no longer existed and this had an effect on children's literature. Some thought the cultural change brought about by the greater availability of television and other media would have a negative effect on reading. But the picture is far less clear cut. Children's television brought excellent serials of children's books and programmes like *Jackanory* which generated interest in talking about and buying books. There were other developments which led to an increase in quality children's books. Significant forces here were two groups of professionals who became very important to the development of quality children's literature. First, knowledgeable and enthusiastic children's book editors were, from the late 1940s and the 1950s being appointed by publishing houses, for example Frank Eyre, John Bell and Mabel George of Oxford University Press and Eleanor Graham and then Kaye Webb at Puffin (Penguin). Publishers continue to have considerable influence – they decide if and when to re-issue the established classics and help create 'modern' classics by the way books are reprinted and marketed. Publishers took advantage of the new consumerism of the 1970s, publishing large numbers of children's books in paperback format. Second, children's librarians were becoming expert not only at making children's books accessible, but also on how particular authors and kinds of books were perceived. If you want to learn more about the development of books and libraries for children you would enjoy Eileen Colwell's autobiography *Once Upon a Time*. She became a librarian in 1921, a time when children were rarely welcome in public libraries (Ray, 2001). Elkin and Kinnell's *A Place for Children* celebrates the achievements of librarians like

Eileen Colwell who have made children's library services so successful in promoting the enjoyment of reading and story telling. *The School Librarian*, the Journal of the School Library Association, remains an excellent journal for all those who care deeply about children's literature. It provides reviews of all kinds of literature, some 'briefing' pages about relevant events – book prizes, exhibitions and so on – and a number of articles exploring current issues and issues of continuing importance.

The post-war years also saw children's literature recognised as both worthy of scholarly attention and as an important agent in helping children learn to read. Two critics and scholars, Margaret Meek and Aidan Chambers, have made a considerable contribution to our understanding of the links between children's literature and literacy. Aidan and Nancy Chambers founded The Thimble Press in 1970 and the journal, *Signal*, which is now read all over the world and contains scholarly articles and reviews of the full range of children's literature. *Tell Me: Children, Reading and Talk* by Aidan Chambers explores the role of talking about books and creating enthusiastic readers. Another landmark publication was *The Cool Web* which aimed to help us to unite the teaching of reading 'with the way readers are made' and with 'the rich profusion of children's books' (Meek, Warlow and Barton, 1977).

One outcome of bringing children's literature under the scrutiny of literary theory was an increasing interest in and concern about social aspects: this was a major preoccupation for many teachers and librarians in the 1970s as they exercised choice over what to buy for primary-aged children. Were we right to take into account, when evaluating children's books, issues to do with sexism, racism and social class? Could a book succeed on aesthetic criteria but fail on social ones? Certainly the children in our schools came from a wider range of ethnic and cultural backgrounds and this was a stimulus to providing the best books from all over the world for all the children. *Books for Keeps*, and its editors, for example, Chris Powling and Rosemary Stones, deserve recognition for the constructive approach taken to multiculturalism both in the journal *Books for Keeps* and for the regularly updated publication *A Multicultural Guide to Children's Books 0–16* now published by Books for Keeps together with the Reading and Language Information Centre, Reading.

The greater sensitivity to the social messages that books might send to young readers stimulated discussion of what is often called the 'Blyton phenomena'. From the 1940s Enid Blyton wrote a huge number of books which included the 'realistic' series *Famous Five* and *Secret Seven,* the *Malory Towers* school stories and short story collections of fairy tales. Children loved them all, unlike critics, librarians and some parents. The books were criticised for racial, gender and social class stereotyping. There was also disquiet about the predictability of the stories and the linguistic shortcomings of the books – narrowness of vocabulary and simplicity of syntax. Huge numbers of articles and books have been published about Blyton. David Rudd has written a critical analysis of Blyton's work and he helps illuminate the appeal it has for children (Rudd, 2000). Certainly the settings for many of the stories are predictable and reassuring. Children can also have the excitement of a fast moving story told simply.

Some adults feel similar sorts of reservations about the work of Roald Dahl, another commercially successful writer for children. There is no doubt that the books, published from the 1960s until Dahl's death in 1990, have been, and indeed are, hugely enjoyed by almost all children. They like the sheer exhilaration of the stories which have a distinctive imaginative appeal. Their themes often involve adults being humiliated while children overcome obstacles and win through to success. Feeling in control, even if vicariously, must be satisfying for children who are usually powerless in an adult world. While teachers and librarians do not, as a few did with Blyton's work, refuse to stock the Dahl books, some prefer to leave children to seek out his work for themselves rather than actively promoting it. Townsend approves of the friendly giant *The BFG* (1982) but considers many of the other books appeal to 'the cruder end of childhood

taste'. He calls *Charlie and the Chocolate Factory* (1964) 'a thick, rich, glutinous candy bar of a book' (Townsend, 1995, p. 249).

No account of children's literature in the twentieth century is complete without some mention of historical fiction – there is more about this under the 'historical novels' entry. Historical novels for primary-aged children fell out of favour towards the end of the twentieth century (see the report of *Young People's Reading in the Twentieth Century, Roehampton*). This is unfortunate as a story set in the past can, like other narratives, help us reflect on human relationships and the human condition. The best books stretch the imagination by showing us the lives of people in different times and circumstances while illuminating life in our own times. Rosemary Sutcliff, for example, explores timeless themes of honour, courage, loyalty and determination both in her earlier books which include *Eagle of the Ninth* (1954) in which a young Roman seeks the lost eagle of his father's lost legion in the wilds of the north of Scotland and her later books like *Song for a Dark Queen* (1978) which explores Boudicca's attempts at revenging her treatment from the Romans. The outstanding novel exploring the Second World War is Ian Serraillier's *The Silver Sword* (1956) which tells the story of the search of three children for their parents during Nazi oppression in Warsaw. Nina Bawden is another children's writer who has brought history alive; *The Peppermint Pig* (1975) tells about the everyday life of a family at the turn of the nineteenth century and *Carrie's War* (1973) explores the life of young evacuees struggling to cope with change and separation when they leave London for a Welsh town in the 1940s.

Some of the best novels of the twentieth century are organised round time-slips: an early example is Alison Uttley's *A Traveller in Time,* 1939. Penelope Taberner slips in and out of her life in an ancient farmhouse in Derbyshire to Tudor times when Mary Queen of Scots was imprisoned. Accounting for its enduring popularity, Townsend writes that the book succeeds because 'of a profound and loving sense of place, and of the endurance of that place in time'

(Townsend, 1990, p. 139). This same strong evocation of a particular place is found in other time travelling novels – Lucy Boston's *The Children of Green Knowe* and Phillipa Pearce's *Tom's Midnight Garden* (1956). I find the cover picture by Peter Farmer for the 1970 paperback edition of the latter book especially evocative in showing the power of a particular place in the memory. Victor Watson gives a fine appreciation of this novel towards the end of his chapter 'The Possibilities of Children's Fiction' in *After Alice*. The book, he writes, 'defines a space in which two people caught up in Time can find each other. The final chapter is a triumph:the boy and the old woman Hattie has become greet each other almost like lovers, accepting age and change and incomprehensible mysteries' (Styles *et al.*, 1992, p. 22).

The last decades of the twentieth century saw the rise and development of the children's picture book. Its roots are found in the nineteenth century illustrators like Crane, Greenaway and Caldecott. Edward Ardizzone was one of the first twentieth century illustrators to make an impact with his action packed 'Tim' series the first of which was *Little Tim and the Seafaring Captain* (1936). It is significant perhaps that an illustrator, Quentin Blake, was appointed the first Children's Laureate (in 1999). His book *Words and Pictures* includes illustrations from much of his best work over the last fifty years. From the 1960s there was a golden age of picture books including the work of Charles Keeping, Brian Wildsmith, Shirley Hughes, John Burningham, Janet and Allan Ahlberg, Anthony Browne and David McKee. The multi-layered meanings and the subtle ways in which written text and illustration relate are discussed under the 'picture book' entry.

Looking back to the years at the end of the twentieth century three things stand out for me: the establishment of the electronic book alongside print books, each offering a distinct experience; the development of the children's picture book as a major art form dominating displays in book shops; the delight in fantasy reaching a climax in the publishing success of J.K. Rowling's *Harry Potter* books.

Into the twenty-first century

The technological revolution, bringing electronic books and all the potential of a multi-media world, began in the twentieth century and is accelerating as the new century gets underway. These huge qualitative developments are bound to have an enormous effect on how childhood is experienced, on the nature of literacy and therefore on the kind of texts written for children. Peter Hollingdale homes in on one societal change, observing that British parents 'have quietly withdrawn children from the freedom of the streets and replaced it by the freedom of the bedroom doubling as an IT temple, with unforeseeable future consequences for imagination, socialisation and physical health' (Hollingdale, 2001, pp. 31–2). There is no doubt that 'book time' will compete more and more with alternatives like television viewing, film and the computer as well as other hobbies and pursuits. And all these changes will have an impact on the way children's literature develops in the future. It seems that adventure stories, whether realistic or in the form of fantasies like the *Harry Potter* novels, are now finding more favour with child readers than historical novels. But does not the great popularity of the *Potter* books show some things have not changed? Children have the same eagerness for stories exploring challenges, conflicts, relationships with others even if these are explored through a parallel fantasy world. Indeed a student group of mine returned from teaching practice convinced that a fantasy world like that created by J.K. Rowling has a helpful 'distancing' effect, making it easier for some children to reflect on and talk over issues to do with relationships, personal behaviour and courage in the face of difficult circumstances.

But, given the speed with which new technology is developing, will the print book survive at all? Is Townsend right in thinking the book is 'a tough old bird' likely to keep going? The definitive edition of *Written for Children* ends with this thought:

> 'Perhaps it is not too wildly optimistic to hope that in the twenty-first century, when all the modern miracles, and some we have not yet dreamed of, have come to pass, a child will still be found here

and there, lying face down on the hearthrug or whatever may have replaced the hearthrug, light years away from his or her surroundings, lost in the pages of a book.'

Centres for Children's Literature

- *British Council Literature Department.* Website:http://www.britishcouncil.org/arts/literature
- *Centre for Language in Primary Education*, London. Tel. 020 7401 3382/3.
- *The Centre for the Children's Book*, Newcastle upon Tyne. Tel. 0191 274 3941.
- *Children's Book Circle.* Tel. 020 7416 3130.
- *Children's Books in History Society.* Tel. 01992 464 885.
- *Harrogate Library Collection of Early Children's Books* (mainly Victorian period). Tel. 01423 863 635.
- *The Library Association.* Tel. 020 7255 0500.
- *The Literacy Centre*, Brighton. Website: http://curric-cat.admin.bton.ac.uk
- *The National Art Library* at The Victoria and Albert Museum, London (mid-nineteenth-century children's books). Website: http://www.nal.vam.ac.uk
- *National Centre for Research in Children's Literature* Roehampton. (The British Library funded study *Young People's Reading in the Twentieth Century* is based at this centre.) Tel. 020 8392 3008.
- *The National Literacy Trust*, London. Website: http://www.literacytrust.org.uk
- *United Kingdom Reading Association* (UKRA). Website: http://www.ukra.org
- *The Wandsworth Collection of Early Children's Books* (history of publishing). Tel. 020 8871 7090)
- *The Young Book Trust* (the children's division of Book Trust – the national charity to promote books and reading). Website:http://www.booktrust.org.uk Tel. 020 8516 2978)

Children's Literature Journals

- *Books for Keeps.* Tel. 020 8852 49530.
- *Carousel* – The Guide to Children's Books. Tel. 0121 643 6411.
- *Children's Book News.* Website: http:www.booktrust.org.uk
- *Children's Books History Society Newsletter.* Tel. 01992 464 885.
- *The Children's Book Handbook*, Young Book Trust (gives details of publishers, prizes, societies and contains both UK and International sections). Website: www.booktrust.org.uk
- *Children's Literature Abstracts.* Address is 5906 Fairlane Drive, Austin TX 78757–4417. USA. Back copies available in university libraries.
- *Children's Literature in Education.* Tel. 01363 772 357.
- *English in Education.* Tel. 0114 255 5419.
- *Growing Point* (no longer published but back copies are available. Has a helpful index system which allows researchers to track references to particular authors and illustrators from 1960–1990.)
- *The Junior Bookshelf* (no longer published but back copies are available from libraries).
- *The School Librarian.* Website: www.sla.org.uk
- *Signal* Tel. 01453 755 566/872 208.

Auchmuty, Rosemary and Wotton, Jan (compilers, 2000 edition) *The Encyclopaedia of School Stories* Aldershot: Ashgate.

Blake, Quentin (2000) *Words and Pictures* London: Jonathan Cape.

Carpenter, Humphrey and Pritchard, Mari (1983, reprinted 1999) *The Oxford Companion to Children's Literature* Oxford: Oxford University Press.

Colwell, Eileen (1998) *Once Upon a Time…Memories of an Edwardian Childhood* (privately printed).

Elkin, Judith and Kinnell, Margaret (2000) *A Place for Children: Public Libraries as a Major Force in Children's Reading* British Library Research and Innovation Report 117. LA Publishing.

Harvey Darton, E.J. (1999 edition, revised by Brian Alderson) *Children's Books in England* London: The British Library & Oak Knoll Press.

Hollindale, Peter (2001) 'Odysseys: The Childness of Journeying Children', *Signal*, 94, January.

Hunt, Peter (ed.) (1995) *Children's Literature: An Illustrated History* Oxford: Oxford University Press.

Hunt, Peter (2001) *Children's Literature* Oxford: Blackwell Publishers.

International Board on Books for Youg People (IBBY). Email is ibby@roehampton.ac.uk

Meek, M., Warlow, G. and Barton, G. (eds,) (1977) *The Cool Web: The Pattern of Children's Reading* London: The Bodley Head.

Prendergast, Sara and Tom (eds of 1999 edition) *The St James Guide to Children's Writers*. Fifth edition of *Twentieth Century Children's Writers* London: St James Press.

Ray, Sheila (2001) 'Books about Children's Books 2000' in *Signal* No. 95, May.

Rudd, David (2000) *Enid Blyton and the Mystery of Children's Literature* London: Macmillan.

Styles, Morag, Bearne, Eve and Watson, Victor (1992) *After Alice: exploring children's literature* London: Cassell.

Watson Victor (2001) *The Cambridge Guide to Children's Books in English* Cambridge: Cambridge University Press.

History of the English language

See also functions of languages, language change, language variety, structuralists model of language

A study of this history is beyond the scope of this book but is considered to some extent under the entries shown above. The books listed below will help those who wish to read more deeply.

Barber, C. (1993) *The English Language: a historical introduction* Cambridge: Cambridge University Press.

Bryson, B. (1990) *Mother Tongue: The English Language* London: Penguin.

Pyles, T. and Algeo, J. (1993, 4th edition) *The Origins and Development of the English Language* London: Harcourt Brace Jovanovich.

Wyse, D. and Jones, R. (2001) *Teaching English, Language and Literacy* London: Routledge (see Chapter 1 'The history of English, language and literacy').

History of English teaching (in the primary school)

See also Bullock Report, Cox Reports, creative writing, elementary schools, English projects, English projects, *Kingman Report*, language across the curriculum, LINC materials, National Curriculum, National Oracy Project, National Writing Project, *Plowden Report*, process approach to writing, projects, progression in phonics material.

The long list above shows that the fascinating and continuing story of the history of English teaching in the primary school underlies many of the entries of this book. Change comes about for many reasons – social, economic and political – and as a result of research by teachers and academics looking intently at what happens in the classroom. My account will be structured by some key landmarks which include reports and other initiatives which have brought about changes in approaches to language and learning and to models of English teaching.

I begin the story with the 1870 Elementary Education Act which led to free education for all children from five to twelve years. At this time the 'skills' model of English teaching held sway. Children were taught in large formal groups and their writing consisted of copying from the board or writing down dictated passages. There was a lot of reciting of poetry and religious texts and an emphasis on spelling, grammar and hand writing drills. The payment by results code, the requirement that children should pass frequent tests in reading, writing and arithmetic in order for teachers to be paid, led to a mechanical and routine driven curriculum.

A landmark in the emergence of English as a subject, encouraging practice in which children's creative language skills were developed, was The Newbolt Report on 'The Teaching of English in England', Board of Education, 1921. Protherough and Atkinson (1994) pinpoint four central concepts in the teaching of English at all levels identified by Newbolt. These were the need for literacy to be at the core of the curriculum, the need to develop children's 'self expression', a belief in the importance of quality literature and a concern for the development of mind and character. By 'self expression' the writers of the report were thinking of a style of teaching where talk and writing drew on children's creativity rather than one where drills and exercises prevailed. As the 1920s got underway, more schools began to encourage silent reading and, to some extent, children's creative skills. But this was in addition to but not instead of grammar teaching by copying models of appropriate language.

The thinking made explicit in the Hadow reports, published in 1931 and 1933, took the more flexible approach to English and language development favoured in the Newbolt report further. As Wyse and Jones note, they read as 'remarkably progressive documents for their time, and the principles of child-centred education that are explicit in their recommendations continued to inform thinking in primary language teaching for the next 50 years' (Wyse and Jones, 1999, p. 9). Not only did the reports recognise the importance of imaginative play for young children, they also identified three approaches to reading: 'look and say', 'phonics' and 'sentence-based', the last of these being more meaning based, and recommended that teachers should draw on all of these in their literacy programme.

By the time the 1944 Education Act was passed (recommending the replacing of 'all age' elementary schools by separate primary and secondary schools) some of the progressive recommendations of the Hadow reports were finding their way into more classrooms. In the 1960s, the Plowden committee investigated how far the Hadow recommendations had been put in place and its report, published in 1967, celebrated existing good practice as well as making recommendations for improvements. In the same year John Dixon published his book *Growth Through English*. This book captured the spirit of the times and the emphasis on creative, imaginative and personal kinds of writing. It explored models of English teaching: the 'skills' model of the elementary classroom, the 'cultural heritage' model typical of English teaching in grammar schools which was based on a canon of quality texts and the 'personal growth 'model in which writing expresses what the writer feels is worth saying (Pinsent, 1998).

The Bullock Report reinforced Plowden's emphasis on the 'process' aspects of speaking and listening, reading and writing. Rather than working through exercises, Bullock urged that children be helped to use language for real purposes and audiences. The report's areas of concern covered, on the one hand, the kinds of language use associated with English lessons – to appreciate literature, to talk about issues of human concern, to write accounts from their experience – and, on the other hand, English and language as a way of learning in every lesson. The report encouraged every school to have a language policy and a teacher with special responsibility for coordinating everything to do with language.

Then, as the 1970s got underway, beliefs about how children were taught English began to change. We must remember that attitudes towards and trends in education do not lie outside more general economic, social and political climates. In the 1970s, economic difficulties and concerns about the amount of government spending led to a reduction in the amount of money available for education and a greater focus on the efficient use of resources.

In 1988 the Education Reform Act was passed; it established a National Curriculum in state primary and secondary schools and gave the government more power to intervene directly in how the curriculum was taught. The National Curriculum brought about considerable change in English and language work. First it took, from the earliest stages, a subject-centred approach to the curriculum. This may have been partly a reaction to Plowden's favouring of the 'integrated day' where a teacher monitors groups of children working on different subjects. The 'integrated day' approach was considered by some to be particularly unsuitable for children beyond the infant stage. They considered the over sevens required a more focused approach which did justice to each school subject (Beard, 1999). 'English lessons' replaced 'language activities' in the official documents. Second it was genre based, that is language development was seen at least partly to do with children, both as readers and writers, coming to control an increasing range of kinds of written material. Third, it identified levels of attainment and put in place an intensive assessment system. These three features have persisted through several versions of the National Curriculum.

The National Literacy Strategy *Framework for Teaching* (DfEE, 1998) built on the National Curriculum English programmes and prescribed English teaching in more detail, setting out objectives at word, sentence and text level for each term from Reception to Year 6. There are many helpful and imaginative suggestions not least for non-fiction reading and writing – often neglected in the past – but the problem with a prescribed programme is that it can take away a practitioner's will to evaluate principles and practice and to deploy them to meet the particular needs of their class. It recommends an essentially teacher-centred approach: direct teaching of the whole class replaced the group and individual work favoured by progressive teachers and given voice in the Plowden Report. Even group work is to be guided by the teacher or in the case of independent groups, structured by carefully formulated tasks. There is research evidence that structured work is sometimes more successful than 'looser' approaches in the later primary years, see for example the finding of Mortimer *et al.*, 1988. However, Mortimer *et al.* insisted they were not imposing a 'blueprint' for every classroom.

The Framework requires that reading is taught by a mix of methods – as recommended as long ago as the 1930s in the Hadow reports – and informed by a model using the metaphor of cue-systems as 'search-lights'. But it is the 'phonic' approach which is given greatest emphasis in the guidance material, for example *Progression Through Phonics* (DfEE, 1999). More recently the emphasis in guidance material – *Grammar for Writing* (DfEE, 2000) and *Developing Early Writing* (DfEE, 2001) – is on helping children become successful writers. (I just wonder if we would help young learners find their 'voices' if we encouraged the kind of writing James Britton termed 'expressive' – writing close to talk which helps to organise new thinking and ideas. This transitional kind of writing is rarely mentioned now. I also believe that reading all kinds of texts to the class is another valuable way of showing young learners the choices available to a writer.)

How will English teaching in the primary years develop in the future? One thing is certain, it will not remain the same: what happens in school responds to changes in our wider society. In the interesting final chapter of her book *The English Curriculum in Schools,* Louise Poulson maintains that further developments in information technology will continue to transform schools and how we define literacy (Poulson, 1998). I believe three things – to some extent already evident – would help English and language teaching in the primary years change and develop successfully: flexibility in how the literacy hour and other national initiatives are implemented; respect for teachers as reflective practitioners whose views on how changes are implemented deserve recognition; and linking curriculum development to the findings of quality research.

Beard, Roger (1999) 'English: range, key skills and language study' in Riley, Jeni and Prentice, Roy *The Curriculum for 7–11 Year Olds* London: Paul Chapman.

Dixon, John (1967) *Growth Through English* Oxford: Oxford University Press for NATE.

Pinsent, Pat (1998) 'From Copying to Creation: the teaching of Writing before the 1980s in Graham, Judith and Kelly, Alison (eds) *Writing Under Control* London: David Fulton.

Poulson, Louise (1998) *The English Curriculum in Schools* London: Cassell.

Protherough, R and Atkinson, J. (1994) 'Shaping the image of an English teacher' in Brindley, S. (ed.) *Teaching English* London: Routledge.

Riley, Jeni and Prentice, Roy (1999) *The Curriculum for 7–11 Year Olds* London: Paul Chapman (see Chapter 4).

Wyse, Dominic and Jones, Russell (2001) *Teaching English, Language and Literacy* London: Routledge (see Chapter 1 'The history of English, language and literacy').

Hobbies & English

See also journal, motivation, newspapers, non-fiction reading and writing

The interests and activities children enjoy out of school can enrich classroom discussion as well as their reading and writing. Very young children enjoy talking about their 'news' and will sometimes be asked to write and draw about such things as going swimming, playing computer games and family outings. Sometimes sharing a book can awaken an interest – it is never to early to become an expert! One of my students was surprised at the range and depth of questions from five year olds when she shared Claire Llewellyn's *My Best Book of Creepy Crawlies* (Kingfisher) with them. I find that seven to nine year olds often have hobbies based round collections of items which they like to label and annotate: wild flowers, shells, fossils and stones. Parents and friends can acknowledge and develop these interests with gifts of books and CD-ROMs.

Children's hobbies and interests provide a route into non-fiction reading and serve as a springboard for enthusiastic writing. Two friends, one aged eight the other nine, were able to enthuse others in their class when the teacher invited them to talk about their shared hobby – reading and learning about fossils and especially dinosaurs (see *Making Facts Matter,* 1992).

Angela Redfern (1994) writes about her success in helping an unenthusiastic young writer gain a sense of purpose when encouraged to write about his passionate interest in hens. When asked about his chickens, Redfern writes 'it was like switching on a light bulb. Once he got started, it became clear that Owen, aged six, knew everything there is to know about keeping chickens and as he gathered momentum he positively glowed.' After much effort, Owen was helped to produce a book for the school library which had sections on 'kinds of chickens', 'food' and 'laying eggs'.

Mallett, Margaret (1992) *Making Facts Matter: Reading Non-fiction 5–11* London: Paul Chapman.
Redfern, Angela (1994) 'Introducing Owen, expert eggstraordinary: the launching of a young writer' in TACTYC *Early Years Journal.* Vol. 14, No. 2.

Home corner – see Drama and English, play and language and literacy

Home–school contacts – see parents and families

Homographs

These are words which are spelt in the same way but whose meaning depends on how they are pronounced. Examples often quoted are 'entrance' and 'bear' as in: 'The entrance to the stock cupboard is near the window' and 'The power of the story to entrance was evident in the children's faces'; and 'The tear is her school blazer was worse than she has thought' and 'The tear rolled down the boy's cheek'.

Homonyms

Homonyms are words pronounced and spelt the same way but which can have different meanings. Examples are 'grounds' and 'bear': 'The school grounds offer pleasing views' and 'The coffee grounds spilled from the upturned cup onto the new carpet'; and 'The bear came menacingly from between the trees' and 'Many were called to bear arms to defend their country'.

Homophones

These words sound the same when spoken, but differ in spelling and meaning.

So we might have 'whales swimming together 'or 'hearing a baby's wails'. Another example is a 'The bear caught a fish' or 'Her bare arms risked sunburn at midday'.

Horn book

This is a book made of wood, with a handle so it can be held like a racquet, on which a sheet of printed paper is mounted and protected by a layer of transparent horn. The horn is held in place with a strip of metal. Horn books were often quite small, about four inches by three inches plus the handle. The printed sheet changed little over the centuries and usually included the alphabet in upper and lower case, the ampersand, the five vowels and the Lord's Prayer. Horn books were used for teaching reading from the sixteenth to eighteenth centuries.

Horror stories

See also fantasy

Many older children like the controlled feelings of fear that horror stories provide. Mallett quotes ten-year-old Natasha's remark that 'horror stories are exciting and you get frightened but nothing actually happens to you' (Mallett, 1997). R.L. Stines's 'Goosebumps' series appeals because of the humour of the tales as well as the scariness.

Mallett, Margaret (1997) *Gender and Genre* in Reading UKRA, vol. 31, No. 2.

Hot seating

A strategy used in drama to help children think deeply about a character's motivations and feelings. One child, or a pair of children, answer questions from the rest of the class, usually in role.

Hyperbole

This refers to statements that are a deliberate exaggeration of the truth, used for effect and not, generally, meant to be taken seriously.

Hypermedia

This describes computer text or linked texts comprising words, pictures and sound which can be freely accessed by the user.

Hyperstudio

From TAG (01474 357350), this is a multimedia authoring tool which enables teachers and children to create interactive books.

Hypertext

This is a term used in computing to describe a facility to jump from one page of text to any one of a number of earlier or later pages.

Hyphen

See also dash

This is a punctuation mark used in two main ways. First, we might use a 'link hyphen' to join words or parts of words together to create a new word: 'spare-part', 'after-hours' or 'green-house'. Over time, as the new words becomes established, the hyphen may be dropped. The second use, a 'break hyphen', is used in a text where a word cannot fit onto a line and has to be carried onto the following line as in: 'After many years of travelling she decided to settled down and raise a family in the hot and dusty outback of Australia.'

'Break hyphens' may also replace commas to separate two closely linked pieces of text as follows: 'Word processing is preferable – particularly for an important piece of course work – as it is usually more legible and professional looking than hand writing.'

A hyphen may also replace two short sentences: 'I think I will travel by rail – there might be heavy traffic on the roads'.

Where break hyphens replace commas or provide an alternative to two short sentences they are often called 'dashes'.

Iconic representation

See also language acquisition, language and thought, visual literacy

This refers to the representation of experience through image. In Bruner's theory of development the 'iconic' stage is reached when children can think by drawing on images. The breakthrough comes when they can conjure up the image of an object which is not physically present – for example of Teddy, upstairs. Experiments have suggested that other primates can think through iconic representation, see for example the introduction to *A First Language* by Roger Brown. After the acquisition of speech we continue to do some of our thinking and representation of experience iconically.

Brown, Roger (1973) *A First Language* Harmondworth: Penguin.

Illustrations – see under diagrams, photographs and visual literacy

Image – see under iconic representation, visual literacy

Imagination (secondary worlds) – see under fantasy, fairy tales

Imperative

Sentences with an imperative as their main verb require the person addressed to carry out some action as in 'Jump now!' In addition to giving a command, the mood of an imperative verb may be a request 'Please give me the racquet', a warning 'Look out!', an entreaty 'Save me!' or an offer 'Have some more!' Often imperatives are in the second person, even if the pronoun is missed out. In 'Look out!', 'you' is implied. Less frequently an imperative can be in the first person (Let's start now) or the third person (Someone tell him to be quiet).

Impersonal language

This is the language of text books and official documents. Sometimes impersonal language is in the passive voice. Thus in a report of a scientific experiment we might find language like: 'The chemicals were heated in a test tube over a bunsen burner until the liquid turned blue'. Impersonal language contrasts with the personal tone usual in a letter to a friend or a more informal 'chatty' account in a newspaper or magazine.

When would we expect children to control impersonal kinds of reading and writing? Children from about age seven or eight onwards are usually able to recognise some of the features of formal as opposed to personal letters. The National Curriculum views control over more impersonal kinds of language as an achievement of the later primary years (DfEE, 1999, English: The National Curriculum, Key Stage 2, 5C). Teachers in the United Kingdom working within the National Literacy Strategy *Framework for Teaching* introduce children increasingly to more formal kinds of reading material in Year 5 and Year 6 (9–11 year olds). By the end of year 6 it is hoped that children will understand some of the features of impersonal language, for example sustained use of the present tense and the passive voice, as both readers and writers. One issue here is to do with insisting on children using adult kinds of writing before they are ready to do so.

The entry on 'expressive talk and writing' invites a consideration of these matter.

Improvisation – see under Drama & English

Indefinite article

This is the 'a' or 'an' we use to introduce a noun phrase. 'A' precedes a consonant as in 'a little lamb' while 'an' comes before a vowel 'an able adversary'. 'An' is sometimes used in words beginning with 'h' as in 'an historian'.

Independent group work

See also collaborative learning, discussion, independent group work in the Literacy Hour, Literacy Hour, speaking and listening

There is a long tradition of organising children in non-teacher-led groups to carry out some of their English work. The structure of such lessons varies but usually there is some input from the teacher before the children start work on their own. The theme for the work might arise from the teacher reading a poem or piece of literature or from showing of a video film – perhaps a dramatisation of a classic like Philippa Pearce's *Tom's Midnight Garden*. On other occasions, the teacher invites the children to discuss and evaluate non-literary materials – advertisements, publicity material or letters to a newspaper on a controversial topic. Although Benton and Fox's influential book *Teaching Literature Nine to Fourteen,* written in the mid-1980s, is out of print, it is worth searching out because their ideas for literature-based work in pairs and groups are still extremely helpful. Just a few of these are – making a book programme using a cassette tape, improvising events mentioned but not described in detail in a book and making a front page of a newspaper featuring a dramatic event in a novel or story. The ideas still inspire lively work and can be brought up to date with the use of computer software. More recently Stuart Marriott's suggestions for group work round fiction in his book *Read On* have proved helpful to student teachers.

Towards the end of a lesson where group work

has predominated, the children are nearly always invited to feed back their thoughts and conclusions to the whole class. The best work of this kind provides the opportunity for children to learn how to work well collaboratively and to develop their spoken language ability. There is recognition of the benefits of this kind of work in the official frameworks which now guide English teaching. The National Curriculum English orders emphasise the need to help children both put forward their own opinions and listen and respond to those of others. The independent group work in the Literacy Hour (see below) can be a context for good collaborative work.

Benton, Michael and Fox, Geoff (1985) *Teaching Literature Nine to Fourteen* Oxford: Oxford University Press.

Marriott, Stuart (1995) *Read On: Using Fiction in the Primary School* London: Paul Chapman.

Independent group work in the Literacy Hour

See also Literacy Hour, reading and spelling

This is an important element in the NLS Literacy Hour. After the class-based 30 minutes, children are placed by ability into about five groups of six pupils. Two of the groups carry out guided reading (or writing) with the teacher's supervision while the other three engage in literacy tasks on their own. It is important that tasks are pitched at just the right level of challenge as the children work independently for twenty minutes. The emphasis of the work may be towards reading or writing although all four language processes – speaking and listening as well as reading and writing – are involved. The degree of collaboration depends on the tasks. Sometimes each child may work through set activities on their own and at other times the children may function as a group. The National Literacy Strategy *Framework for Teaching* has a built in progression. The activities set out below feed in to particular parts of the framework but many of them can be adapted for different ages and stages.

Where the emphasis is mainly on reading, activities include:

- those that link with points made in whole class phonic work. For example, if split digraphs – 'a-e', 'i-e' and 'o-e' have been covered children might be asked to notice these in the words of a book.
- predicting the ending of the story read in the shared reading part of the Literacy Hour
- reading fiction in CD-ROM form and noting features of style and vocabulary.
- reading and noting features of format of factual material on CD-ROM, for example younger children in Year 2 or 3 would enjoy working with Dorling Kindersley's *First Incredible, Amazing Dictionary* – there are games to reinforce alphabet and dictionary skills.
- word games reinforcing a recent focus, for example the tasks on Sherston's *Oxford Reading Tree Rhyme and Analogy* CD-ROM.
- research into the life of the author of the week and their work either in the library or using the Internet.

Where the emphasis is mainly on writing, activities include:

- making a plan for their own writing in the genre used in the class-based part of the hour. This might be for a fable or fairy tale. The time slot is too short for the extended fiction writing older children do, but shorter non-fiction tasks fit well with the twenty minute time scale – menus, diary entries or book reviews.
- using software to encourage some different formats for writing – see some suggestions at the end of this entry.
- spelling games, using dictionaries and word-banks (see Graham and Kelly, 1998 pp. 86–90 for many activities to support spelling development and awareness of words).
- making books on aspects of language like 'homonyms and homophones, the letters of the alphabet and etymology. (See Palmer, 2000 for insight on the letters of the alphabet.)
- reading different kinds of poems and writing their own like haiku, limericks and rhyming and unrhyming poems (see Laycock and Washtell, 1996 for rhyme and alliteration games).

Graham, Judith and Kelly, Alison (1998) *Writing Under Control: Teaching Writing in the Primary School* London: David Fulton (see Chapter, 5 'Transcription: Spelling, Punctuation and Handwriting').

Laycock, L. and Washtell, A. (1996) *Curriculum Bank Key Stage Two Spelling and Phonics* Leamington Spa: Scholastic.

Palmer, Sue (2000) *The Little Alphabet Book* Oxford: Oxford University Press.

Software

Banner and *Banner Mania* TAG 01474 357350 (both support poster making).

ClarisWorks Primary Templates TAG 01474 357350 (story starters, diary format etc.).

My First Incredible, Amazing Dictionary Dorling Kindersley 0207 836 5411.

Oxford Reading Tree Rhyme and Analogy Sherston Software 01666 840433.

Oxford Compendium, Oxford University Press on CD for WINPC (includes the Concise Oxford Dictionary and The Oxford Thesaurus).

Writer's Toolkit SCET 0141 334 9314 (formats for different writing styles including journalism).

Independent reading

See also core books, ERIC, individualised reading, Literacy Hour, reading choices

A child is described as an 'independent reader' when he or she is able to read even a simple text unsupported by a more mature reader. Some newly independent readers continue to read out loud for some weeks, others quickly become able to read silently. This move to controlling the reading process is a considerable breakthrough for the young learner. He or she has a source of pleasure that can be turned to at any time and a means of gaining information without adult help. See entries under core books and individualised reading for information about resources arranged according to difficulty.

Index

See also retrieval devices, factual genres, information books

An index is the 'key' to locating specific information and is an important element in children's non-narrative information books. Bakewell and Williams (2000) conducted a survey and made 21 recommendations for good indexing of children's books. For example, a good index is consistent, avoids passing references and subheadings and deserves a separate page or pages. Much emphasis is now placed on electronic searching. Interestingly these researchers believe that if children think in indexing terms they are likely to search the web more effectively.

Bakewell, K.G.B. and Williams, Paula L. (2000) Indexing Children's Books, Society of Indexers Occasional Papers on Indexing No. 5; £13.00 including postage and packing, from Globe Centre, Penistone Road, Sheffield S6 3AE.

Individual Education Plan (IEP)

See also Code of Practice, Special Educational Needs

Although not mandatory, the Code of Practice since 1994 (DfEE) given local authorities and governing bodies practical guidance on their responsibilities towards children with special educational needs. This includes preparing education plans involving individualised provision for all children at stage 2 of the Code and beyond. This may sit uneasily with current developments stressing the common educational needs of children. For an analysis of the issues see Chapter 2 in Croll and Moses (2000).

Croll, Paul and Moses, Diana (2000) *Special Needs in the Primary School: One in Five?* London: Cassell.

Inference

See also critical discourse, language acquisition, language and thought, metacognition, metalanguage

This refers to the ability to draw a logical conclusion from two or more statements. For example:

Human beings need to eat to survive.
Dr Smith is a human being.
Conclusion: Dr Smith, like all human beings, needs to eat to survive.

This is an example of the 'analytical competence' which the psychologist and developmentalist Jerome Bruner believes is created in the young of literate societies (Bruner, 1966.)

Bruner, Jerome (1966) *Towards a Theory of Instruction* New York: WW Norton.
(N.B. This interest in intellectual development was characteristic of Bruner's early work. Since then he has drawn attention to the power of story and the imagination to enhance making sense of the world – see, for example his book *Actual Minds, Possible Worlds* Cambridge, Mass: Harvard University Press, 1986.)

Infinitive

This is the 'base' form of a verb signalled by the word 'to', so we have: to be, to speak, to sleep, to intervene and so on. In English, sentences must contain a 'finite' verb and the 'infinite' can be made finite by adding the boundaries of person, tense and modality.

Inflection

See also affix, prefix and suffix

Inflection refers to the parts of a word that are added before or after the root. The parts added vary according to the function of the word in a sentence. So the inflections 'ing' and 'ed' added to the stem word 'ask' would give us – 'I was asking' and 'I asked'. Inflection also refers to changes to the spelling of words to suit the need in a sentence. For example 'spoke' is an inflection of the stem word 'speak'.

Information books

See also CD-ROMs, diagrams, encyclopaedia, factual genre, genres, non-fiction reading and writing, visual literacy

The typical children's information book is illustrated, usually on a single topic, like Squirrels, Ships, The Vikings or Volcanoes, and organised non-chronologically. (There are transitional kinds of non-fiction some of which follow a time sequence or mingle fact and fiction, see 'information story', 'faction' and 'transitional genre'.) Some publishers are particularly well known for their information titles, including Dorling Kindersley, Franklin Watts, Kingfisher, Longman, Walker Books and Frances Lincoln.

Crocodiles have varied diets and will eat anything they can

The best information books invite young readers in by using exciting illustrations and lively writing. There is some intriguing information about lifestyle and habitat in *Crocodiles* by Barbara Taylor, Lorenz Books, Anness Publishing, 2000.

Publishers like to present series of books and, with some honourable exceptions, they tend to fit each topic firmly in the series format, each title having the same number of pages and the same style of diagrams. And they love colourful, double spreads! Even a good format can become tedious if encountered too often. This entry examines some of the main features of information books, considers some criteria for selecting them and offers some reflections on their future.

One of the most insightful studies of the structure of typical children's information books was by Christine Pappas (1986). This analysis identified what she terms the 'obligatory elements' of the genre – the things that will always be present in an information book. Teachers would recognise these elements if they looked at one of the information books in their classroom or in the library. The first is 'topic presentation' which introduces the subject matter – 'A squirrel is…'. The second is the 'representation of attributes' and describes the different parts of the subject – 'A squirrel's body is designed to help them move and eat; they have a long tail and sharp teeth which can bite into nuts'. The third element is the 'characteristic events' and, in the case of a squirrel, would include its life cycle, breeding and hibernation and perhaps information about diseases and predators. Pappas suggests that children develop

expectations about the order and nature of these obligatory elements and this helps them develop competence in this sort of reading. There are two optional elements in Pappas' model: 'category comparison' – 'Red squirrels… while grey squirrels…' – and a 'final summary'.

While Pappas has illuminated the global features of an information book others, like Bobbie Neate, have drawn attention to the desirability of their having effective mechanical guiders like subheadings and having retrieval devices such as content pages and indexes (Neate, 1992). The importance of having illustrations aligned with, complementing and sometimes extending the written text is emphasised in Mallett (1999). There are also considerations to do with content. Obviously we need books which provide accurate and up to date information and this can mean that the life of an information book tends to be shorter than that of a storybook. Looking across the whole collection of books in the school, we need to ensure that we have books reflecting history, knowledge and understanding from across the whole world. Here we can draw inspiration from Rosemary Stones' *A Multicultural Guide to Children's Books*.

Apart from criteria based on sound overall structure, helpful guiders and retrieval devices, good linkage between writing and illustrations and useful and comprehensive collection of books, what else should influence our choice of information books?

Of great importance is how the book is written, the way in which language is used to inform and inspire young readers. In her helpful account 'Do the Blackbirds Sing All Day?', Helen Arnold cautions that an information book might be superficially attractive but not relate strongly enough to children's own experience. She urges us to reject books with language so bland and impersonal a computer might have written them! The authorial voice is most important. Arnold asks 'Is it genuine, conveying real interest in the subject?' and 'Can it excite curiosity without indoctrinating? Does it respect rather than patronise the reader?' (Arnold, 1992, p. 131). Both Helen Arnold and Margaret Meek, particularly insightful writers about information books, acknowledge how difficult it is to write them well. You need, argues Meek, to keep the 'big shapes' in mind when writing a history book, not allowing the 'minutiae of any given event' to overwhelm the main ideas. Nor must we allow illustrations of contemporary artefacts, however good, to lessen the amount of interpretative text which is necessary to help young readers fit bits of information together to make a coherent understanding possible (Meek, 1996, p. 61).

A number of professional journals provide helpful reviews of information books – *The School Librarian, The Times Educational Supplement, Books for Keeps* and *English 4–11* – and there are a number of websites which include teachers' assessments of books and resources for the classroom. One example is Literacy Time which is part of the National Grid for Learning. There are age-group-related lists in Mallett's book *Young Researchers* and in *Core Books* (CLPE).

What is the likely future of the information book? In the United Kingdom the National Literacy Strategy gives considerable recognition to non-fiction genres which have a prescribed place in the Literacy Hour. On the other hand there may be less time for subjects like history and geography. So as a reviewer for several professional journals, I have noticed that fewer new titles, outside Literacy Hour needs at any rate, are being published. Then there is the impact of the new technology on print books. There is no doubt that there is a vast increase in the number of electronic texts and a greater use of the Internet as an information source with inevitable consequences on the demand for print books. However, new technology has brought about noticeable improvements in the format and layout of children's information books and a much higher quality of illustration. Dorling Kindersley, in particular, have contributed to transforming their look and appeal. Publishers are also bringing together the world of books and the world of computers in interesting packages. However, we have to apply the same criteria to these as we would to any other information text – making sure that pure entertainment does not compromise their educational work. I like The Interface series (Two-Can Publishing/ Zenith

Entertainment plc) for use with PC and MAC, which aims to link electronic extensions activities, puzzles and games closely with a book. The contents page in the book tell us 'What's on the disk' and 'What's in the book'. The package on 'Water' for seven to eleven year olds covers topics like The Water Cycle, Weather, Being Water Aware, Floating and Sinking and Surface Tension in double spreads in the book and 'disk link' boxes briefly explain the electronic extension activities. Thus the text for 'Being Water Aware' is matched with a computer game to reinforce the notion that 'every drop counts' and that we should save water at home. Reading print and reading on the computer are distinct experiences and I believe they will continue to exist side by side, increasingly complementing each other.

Arnold, Helen (1992) 'Do the Blackbirds Sing All Day? Literature and Information Texts' in Styles, Morag, Bearne, Eve and Watson, Victor (eds) *After Alice: Exploring Children's Literature* London: Cassell.

Ellis, Sue and Barrs, Myra (1996) *The Core Book* and *Core Booklists* London: CLPE.

Literacy Time website – http://www.vtc.ngfl.gov.uk/ resource/literacy/ index.html

Mallett, Margaret (1999) *Young Researchers: Informational Reading and Writing in the Early and Primary Years* London: Routledge (see Chapter 1).

Meek, Margaret (1996) *Information and Book Learning* Stroud: The Thimble Press.

Neate, Bobbie (1992) *Finding Out About Finding Out* London: Hodder & Stoughton.

Pappas, Christine (1986) 'Exploring the global structure of children's information books'. Paper presented at the Annual Meeting of the National Reading Conference, Austin, Texas.

Stones, Rosemary (ed.) (1999) *A Multicultural Guide to Children's Books 0–16+* London: Books for Keeps (see pp. 52–61 for reviews of multicultural information books).

Information and Communications Technology (ICT) & English

See also CD-ROM, e-mail, EXIT model, interactivity, interactive white board, Internet, non-fiction, visual literacy, websites

In the twenty-first century being literate will mean having the same facility in the use of computers as we have long expected to have in using other media. Computers have transformed our working lives and our leisure activities. Not surprisingly, ICT is perceived as a powerful tool for teaching and learning and there has been a great deal of investment in developing and promoting educational applications. The government in the United Kingdom requires that primary teachers use ICT in teaching the core subjects, English, Mathematics and Science (DfEE, 1998). This entry is concerned with how the computer and the Internet (See also under the Internet entry) can be harnessed to good practice in the English classroom. Although the four language processes are interwoven in all learning, for clarity this account first considers speaking and listening, second reading and third writing. In my analysis I will consider particularly how the teacher intervenes to maximise the learning achieved when children are using computers.

Speaking and Listening

Work using the computer is often collaborative and group based and this provides a good context for speaking and listening. One of the first decisions the teacher will make is about the size and nature of the group because its composition affects the kind of interaction. Three or four children is a good number for most activities, apart from those round 'text manipulation software' where larger groups are possible and sometimes more stimulating. The teacher will take account of gender, friendships and ability when grouping children for particular tasks. For example, teachers have found some girls adopt a passive role when in mixed groups, but their competence is now growing.

Speaking and listening get underway when children can be asked to create or read a text. They may begin a piece of group writing by word processing the fruits of a 'brainstorming'. Building on this, with one child acting as 'scribe', the group can develop their account on the screen. It is the interaction of pupil with pupil, listening and responding to each other's thoughts and ideas, which is so educative. The teacher's visits to the group will help the children review

progress and move them on by posing questions that challenge their understanding.

Another strong context in which to use discussion to support literacy is one with the umbrella term – 'DARTS' (Directed Activities Round Texts). A well-known example is 'cloze procedure' which involves making decisions about restoring words which have been deliberately removed from a text. Here children can be helped to acquire and use a meta-language to refer to aspects of language like 'meaning', 'text', 'letter' and 'word'. Use of this meta-language, encouraged by the teacher, leads to a heightened awareness of some of the features of spoken and written language which can transfer to other contexts, for example, evaluating a story. A version of cloze procedure is available in what is known as 'text manipulation software' (an example is *Sherlock – the Text Detector*). Typically, children work with a 'text' from which every letter has been omitted and which only retains the punctuation and dashes to represent the missing letters. Pupils can 'buy' or call up all the instances of one particular letter, usually beginning with the more common vowels and consonants. When these begin to replace the dashes, a pattern starts to emerge. The task becomes an absorbing game in which inference, prediction and hypothesising all come into play. Above all, the children share their thinking and 'guessing' as they reconstruct the text and from observation it will become evident that they are drawing on their knowledge of how texts are written. For a detailed analysis of the contribution of this kind of task to literacy, see Garvey, 2000, pp. 112–13.

Children have long enjoyed and critically evaluated literature without needing a computer to help them. However, having a poem or short story on screen for joint attention helps concentration and allows the teacher moving between groups to tune in quickly to what the children are discussing.

Valuable discussion can also arise from group work round software not directly linked to literacy. Searching for information from Internet sites and CD-ROMs can lead to lively discussion on topics and issues arising from history and geography. Where the group reports back to the rest of the class on what they have found, there are further opportunities for reflection. Questions from the teacher and other children will help those reporting back to sharpen their arguments and explanations. They can also be encouraged by the teacher to analyse how they learnt using this particular medium. They might, for example, talk about how scrolled and non-linear texts are structured and how animations and interactive diagrams help their learning (see DfEE, 1998). For further suggestions about strategies for encouraging talk round computers see Dawes and Wegerif, 1998. Shreeve (1997) discusses case studies showing how ICT can enhance English work from age seven to thirteen.

Reading

Large quantities of software have been developed to help with the teaching of reading. This software needs careful assessment and we need to be clear about the contribution a specific product makes to literacy learning. Computer-based reading resources tend to fall into two groups: first those that help children with the 'smaller shapes' – reading skills related to initial sounds and sound–symbol relationships and second those that support children's understanding of the 'big shapes' – the meaning and context related aspects of reading, by focusing on whole texts. Software supporting the text level aspects of reading, available from the early 1990s, takes the form of a story presented on screen using written text, speech and animation. These are often referred to as 'talking books'.

There has been criticism of both kinds of resource. Graham and Kelly point out that *Dr Seuss's ABC* (part of the 'Living Books' series), which teaches initial sounds through a question and answer approach together with amusing animations, proceeds at a slow pace even for beginners. We also need to keep our critical hats on when selecting electronic stories: sometimes the entertainment element is at the expense of their educational value. Nevertheless many are excellent. Here is Graham and Kelly's appreciative review of Sherston's much praised *Nursery Rhyme Time:* 'In this delightful CD-ROM chil-

dren can choose to sing along with, play with and hear read aloud any one of about a dozen nursery rhymes which they can select by clicking on an easily readable picture icon. Lively cartoon illustrations reflect a multi-cultural world and the English voice-over is easy on the ear' (Graham and Kelly, 2000, p. 50).

Research so far suggests that electronic talking books are best used alongside other teaching strategies. Medwell, for example, found that the greatest benefits were attained when the teacher first heard children read in a traditional way, and then set up small groups to use talking books (Medwell, 1998). In his summary of current views about talking books, Garvey stresses that it is the pleasure and liveliness of the electronic book context which seems to help children learn actively about features of text and particularly about some of the links between spoken and written language. To give one example, children come to understand the role of spaces and pauses 'which can be highlighted on the screen and related to the role of punctuation in clarifying meaning' (Garvey, 2000, p. 111). Thus the teacher can reinforce the ways in which a break in language is indicated in speech and writing – in speech we have a pause, in writing we have to put a comma or full stop.

So far I have been thinking about fiction when considering the software available to support reading but the best informational CD-ROMs also have considerable potential for helping children's progress. The multi-media nature of CD-ROMs – their use of sound and animation as well as written text – make them highly motivating and thereby provide an excellent context in which children are reading to learn. We do, of course, have to appraise them as rigorously as we would a print information text. The strategies for interacting with non-fiction set out by Wray and Lewis in the EXIT model – establishing purposes, locating information and so on – can be applied to research using CD-ROMs and the Internet. See more on this under the entries on CD-ROM, EXIT, encyclopaedias, Internet and information books.

The growth of the Internet raises some issues. While books and media programmes are usually independently edited, most websites are not and we need to be careful about children having access to material meant for adults and information where the content or language is of low quality. Many primary schools are taking a constructive approach by developing a 'book-marking' system of good websites.

Writing

The word processor and desktop publishing software have transformed how we approach writing tasks. This evaluation is personal and heartfelt! After writing a doctorate by hand, having it typed, then laboriously editing it and bringing it to final draft, my own output and efficiency increased enormously once I became word processor competent, and it must be the same for many others. Today's primary school children take word processing for granted and learn to type alongside learning to hand write. The advantages of the word processor over hand-writing are that:

- children can start to make marks on screen (perhaps using overlay keyboards) from the earliest stages. They can make marks on paper of course – but where their marks are put on screen, the adult can scribe to the child's dictation and they can expand the account together. Thus a child can feel like a writer early on.

- multiple copies can be printed out so that a child can have a personal copy of a piece of writing, one for the class library, one for a portfolio, one to take home and so on. This must be motivating as there is so much payoff from the initial effort.

- shared writing tasks are much more manageable – children in a group of three or four can focus jointly on the developing text.

- drafting is less time consuming as compositional and transcriptional changes can be made much more easily.

- because so many different choices about format can be made – children can produce professional looking posters, leaflets and reports using desktop publishing software. Attention is drawn to genre features and to how content and presentation reflect purpose and audience.

- multimedia authoring allows children to combine written text with graphics, video and animation to produce on-screen electronic books (Martyn, 1999).

- the professional looking presentation possible motivates children to see writing as a worthwhile and even exciting activity the fruits of which can be shared with others (Gamble and Easington, 2001).

Text manipulation software has been referred to earlier in terms of its contribution to reading progress. It can also help children's progress in writing since it can be adapted to supporting learning about grammar and spelling.

Three things press on me. First when children work with computers all the language processes come into play: they read what is on the screen, talk about how texts are structured at word, sentence and text level and listen to what each other has to say. Second the contribution of the teacher is critical in designing and focusing activities, challenging, questioning and extending what they are doing and celebrating success. Garvey reminds us that 'teacher questioning is critical in extending pupils' development of skills of inference, prediction and hypothesis testing' (Garvey, 2000, p. 113). Third, I agree with Wyse and Jones (2001) that exciting as the new technology is it is unlikely to replace books, pens and paper.

Dawes, Lyn and Wegerif, Rupert (1998) 'Encouraging exploratory talk: practical suggestions', paper in *Focus on Literacy Pack*, MAPE, Autumn 1998.

DfEE (1998) *Teaching: High Status, High Standards* London: HMSO (includes details of the ICT competence required by trainees in the use of ICT in the core subjects).

DfEE (1998) *National Literacy Strategy Framework for Teaching* London: DfEE. (see Year 4, text level 23).

Garvey, John (2000) '"Incredibly Creative Tools": using ICT and multimedia' in Fisher, Robert and Williams, Mary (eds) *Unlocking Literacy: A Guide for Teachers* London: David Fulton.

Graham, Judith and Kelly, Alison (2000, second edition) *Reading Under Control: Teaching Reading in the Primary School* London: David Fulton.

Martyn, Sarah (1999) 'Information Communication Technology. A Learning Revolution? in Riley, Jeni and Prentice, Roy (eds) *The Curriculum for 7–11 Year Olds* London: Paul Chapman.

Medwell, Jane (1998) 'The Talking Book Project: some further insights into the use of talking books to develop reading'. *Reading*. May.

Shreeve, Anne (1997) *IT in English: Case Studies and Materials* Coventry: National Council for Educational Technology (now BECTA: www.becta.org.uk).

Wyse, Dominic and Jones, Russell (1999) *Teaching English, Language and Literacy* London: Routledge, Chapter 28.

Information stories

See also biography, chronological non-fiction, factual genres, History & English, narrative, transitional genre

Teachers and children often refer to texts which follow a time sequence but which also impart facts and ideas as 'information stories'. The life cycles of plants and animals, journeys and historical events all have a natural chronology which is helpful to young readers and listeners who are familiar with the rhythms of story. This kind of genre is 'transitional' in that some of the features of the mature texts it is based on are modified. For example, fantasy elements may be brought in even though the function of the text is informational. Some teachers wonder if mixing text types might cause genre confusion! However, in my experience children understand which elements of texts are 'true' and which are devices to entertain us. For example, in *The Drop Goes Plop* by Sam Godwin and Simone Abel young children love the talking mother and baby seagull who take us on an exhilarating trip through the water cycle. Another favourite title in this series is *The Case of the Missing Caterpillar* which takes a first look at the life cycle of a butterfly into an intriguing detective story (MacDonald Young Books, M.Y. Bees series, 1998).

Not all information stories incorporate fantasy elements. Some have a number of features associated with children's non-narrative information books – fact pages at the end, carefully labelled diagrams and sometimes an index. Perhaps the best information stories are written by authors and illustrators with a personal foothold in a subject so that we benefit from their memories and feelings as well as 'the facts'. The Read and Wonder series (Walker Books) covers topics like apple trees, pigs, caterpillars, beavers and so on bringing a human dimension which strikes a chord with young readers. So we have, for example, *Spider Watching* by Vivien French and Alison Wisenfield which is based on the author's memory of persuading some other children not keen on spiders just how interesting these creatures are. It is not easy to write an information story for children that will truly make the young readers reflect and wonder. Karen Wallace and Mike Bostock manage this in *Think of an Eel*, another book in the Read and Wonder series, by sharing right at the beginning of the book the secret about the Sargasso sea. 'For thousands of years a secret lay hidden: this salt, soupy sea is where eels are born'. Yet 'no one has ever seen a wild eel lay eggs or an eel egg hatch'. The book appeals directly to the young reader's imagination through words and pictures. So we have the verbal image of the elver 'like a willow leaf, clear as crystal' and with 'teeth like a sawblade' and the perfectly matching illustration of the transparent creature.

A good example of the 'journey' kind of book is *River Story*, by Meredith Hooper and illustrated by Bee Willey (Walker Books, 1999), which takes us from the river's source high in the mountains, through valleys and fields, into the city and finally to the sea. A rhythmic text and wonderfully detailed illustrations impart much information about the river and the creatures and plants which inhabit it at each stage of the journey. Books like this often provide an inspirational start to a new topic before children use more conventional information books and resources: I cannot think of a more inspiring way to begin a study of rivers with children about six to eight years than to read this story out loud.

The story approach has a place across the curriculum and is particularly well established in history. Under the History & English entry there is an analysis of *Seeing Red* by Sarah Garland. The legend on which the story is based may be at least partially true and children up to about eight years learn about the eighteenth century from the landscapes, clothes and artefacts in the pictures as well as from the text (Anderson Press). For older juniors, Dorling Kinderley's Discovery series incorporates a story approach: each book tells the story of an exciting event and then gives an analysis of its significance. For example, in *Pompeii: the Day a City was Buried* we hear first of a dramatic series of events and then the impact of those events is discussed.

'Facts through story' kinds of text are likely to be represented in the class and school collections of primary schools. Of course, like other books, they vary in quality. Some can be banal, patronising to young readers and provide very little useful information in either text or illustration. When choosing, we should seek books which arouse curiosity and share, in a way young readers can appreciate, some careful observations, ideas and feelings about the phenomena involved.

Individualised reading

See also core books, independent reading

Rather than follow one reading scheme or stick to one publisher's selection of books for each age group, many teachers adopt a system where all the books (including those from schemes) are organised into broad bands of difficulty. Following the suggestions in Keith Moon's well-known book *Individualised Reading,* some schools colour code the books. In this system, young readers have a quick indication of which books they should be able to read independently. The teacher makes sure that children have read a good selection of books at one level before moving on to the next.

This system works well in many schools but not everyone is a fan. Some teachers feel that children might be prevented from trying books they would enjoy, because they have been limited to those marked at a particular level. Interest in a topic sometimes motivates a young reader to read above their normal level. There might also be some competition about which level children have reached (Browne, 1996).

Browne, Ann (1996) *Developing Language and Literacy 3–8* London: Paul Chapman.

Moon, Keith (updated each year) *Individualised Reading* Reading, Berkshire: Reading and Language Information Centre.

Initial Teaching Alphabet

The Initial Teaching Alphabet, ITA, was an attempt to help children learn to read more easily by regularising the sound-symbol system. Twenty extra symbols were added to the 26 letters of the alphabet. While the initiative arose from good intentions it cut young readers off from environmental print – a very powerful stimulus to getting meaning from print. It was also difficult for some young readers to change back to the conventional alphabet.

Inner speech

See also language and thought, metacognition

This is a term used by L.S. Vygotsky to refer to thinking. To understand what Vygotsky means by the sort of thinking he called 'inner speech' we have to be clear about his notion of the two different functions of language. First he believes a child has a strong urge to communicate with other human beings – so the first function of language is essentially social. But second, the very act of speaking and listening and in turn being addressed, informed and explained to by others allows language to become an instrument of thought and of self-regulation. What seems to happen is that the child internalises the ways of going about a dialogue with another person so that he or she can conduct such a dialogue with themselves as 'inner speech' or thinking. So what began as an urge to communicate becomes the means of a child developing their thinking and reasoning abilities.

Instructional texts – see procedural texts

'Interactive' reading model

See also big shapes, cue-systems, bottom-up reading approaches, phonics, reading, 'top-down' approaches to reading

'Interactive' reading models combine 'top-down'(emphasis on meaning) and 'bottom-up' (emphasis on code-breaking) approaches. In *The Teaching of Reading,* Jeni Riley promotes an 'interactive' model of learning to read, by both providing the theoretical underpinnings (Chapter 2) and then explaining classroom implications (Chapters 3–5).

The National Literacy Strategy's Searchlight model (DfEE, 1998) could be described as 'interactive' as it encourages the use of a range of strategies (or 'searchlights') to get at the meaning of a text. Informed reading practice in many parts of the world now seeks balance between a focus on larger units of language taking account of context and content and work on phonics and other word level skills (see for example Adams, 1993).

Adams, M.J. (1993) 'Beginning to Read: an overview', in R. Beard (ed.) *Teaching Literacy and Balancing Perspectives* London: Hodder & Stoughton.
The National Literacy Strategy *Framework for Teaching* DfEE, 1998 (see Introduction).
Riley, Jeni (1996) *The Teaching of Reading* London: Paul Chapman.

Interactive white board

This is a computer-linked device. The teacher writes tasks, notes and lists on an 'interactive white board' which the pupils can then download directly onto laptop computers. If these are personal lap-tops it will save laborious copying by hand and provide a useful record of all they have to do and learn.

Interactivity

This is a term applied to computer software which has been designed to allow the user to make choices about the information they want to access and in some cases to test their understanding as their learning proceeds This may involve, for example, clicking on links to get a fuller explanation of something not completely understood, to get more detailed information or to open up a new line of enquiry. Children can work at their own pace and be helped to tackle increasingly challenging concepts.

Internal rhyme

Most rhymes occur at the end of verse-lines but those that occur in the middle of a line are termed 'internal rhymes'. Abrams uses a line of Swinburne's poetry to demonstrate the internal rhyming of 'fleet' and 'sweet':

'Sister, my sister, O fleet sweet swallow.'

There is an interesting account of rhyme in Abrams, 1981 pp. 163–5.

Abrams, M.H. (1981 edition) *A Glossary of Literary Terms* New York: Holt, Rinehart & Winston.

Internet

See also e-mail, Information and Communications Technology (ICT) & English

The Internet is a world wide web linking information sites electronically to provide users with a mammoth database. It provides great opportunities for teachers and children to use it as a powerful resource for finding out about all manner of information to support learning. One of the most valuable features of the Internet for teachers are the reviews of fiction and non-fiction texts, both print and electronic. It also allows the sharing of good practice – the 'Literacy Time' site, for example, part of the National Grid for Learning, has many links to sites relevant to English teaching – http://www.teem.org.uk/. However, both teachers and children need to access the information they need competently and swiftly, and to know how to use the information when they find it. Elpseth Scott's booklet '*Managing the Internet*' (2000) focuses on the Internet as a whole-school, cross-curricular resource and illuminates aspects of managing the Internet.

We must remember that while technology can make possible some valuable learning experiences children also need to learn from interaction with other human beings. We are still developing a set of principles to guide the design of educational sites. In an interesting section in Chapter 2 of their book, Wyse and Jones (2001) suggest that a high quality of interaction is a feature of a good site for children. The BBC Teletubbies site, for example, included visual images, sound and speech and *encouraged* young children to investigate: 'Who spilled the Tubby custard?'

Teachers and children can add to the net as well as gaining information from it by creating a school website. (Software packages like *Web Workshop* Iona Software can guide this.) Some school websites serve the same purpose as a school prospectus while others offer web browser display boards showing children's work. The latter provide opportunities for sharing between schools and are often an incentive for children to write to others, perhaps in other parts of the country or in other lands. Schools are increasingly using networks like *European SchoolNet* and *Commonwealth Electronic Network*.

Commonwealth Electronic Network http:// www.col.org/cense

European SchoolNet http://www.eun.org

Scott, Elspeth (2000) *Managing the Internet* School Library Association and Reading and Language Information Centre.

Virtual Museums: www.cultureonline.gov.uk

Wyse, Dominic and Jones, Russell (2001) *Teaching English, Language and Literacy* London: Routledge.

Intertextuality

See also picture books

Intertextuality refers to the strategy of including allusions in one text to other texts. In children's picture books this means drawing on children's cultural knowledge to link ideas in different texts. In his book *The Tunnel* Anthony Browne includes images of Red Riding Hood, for example in a picture on the wall of the girl's bedroom. This makes readers reflect on possible thematic connections between one story and another. Other masters of intertextuality are the Ahlbergs. In their *Each Peach, Pear, Plum* each rhyming couplet refers to a different nursery rhyme character and in their *The Jolly Postman* letters are sent to fairy tale characters like Cinderella.

Intonation

This refers to the stress or emphasis placed on consonants, vowels and syllables by a speaker to give colour to their words and help listeners better understand their meaning and significance.

Intransitive verbs

An intransitive verb is a verb in a sentence which does not have a direct object as in 'She ran as quickly as she could.'

Inverted commas

See also quotation marks, speech marks

Inverted commas are commas placed to show where a quotation, a heading or a title begins and where they end. The marks may be either single, as in the example below, or double.

'As a storyteller Edward Ardizzone had the ultimate freedom of being both author and artist: he knew instinctively how to balance these skills and how to integrate words and pictures on the page.' (p. 6, *Books for Keeps,* No. 125, November 2000).

For a fuller account, see under 'quotation marks'.

Jargon

Jargon is those words and phrases used by all trades and professions as a shorthand way to describe or refer to technical matters. It can be used to communicate quite complex concepts, conditions or actions swiftly in a work context. Of course it can be quite irritating to an outsider to discover that something quite simple has been dressed up as something to sound complicated and difficult!

The world of education has its fair share of jargon – some of it useful in a school context, for example 'modelling' reading and writing, 'scaffolding' children's learning and inviting 'genre exchange'.

Journal – see diary, first person writing, reading diary/log

Journalistic writing – see advertisements, persuasive, visual literacy

Junior Years language and literacy

See also assimilation and accommodation, *Bullock Report*, child-centred learning, constructivism, Early Years language and literacy, English projects, hobbies & English, metaphors in education, History of English teaching, language and thought, *Plowden Report*, spontaneous and scientific concepts

There has been a tradition in the United Kingdom of viewing the 'Early Years' – up to the age of seven or eight – and the 'Junior Years' – from seven to eleven – as two distinctive stages of development each with its implications for classroom practice. Now the terminology has changed: the United Kingdom Government

identifies a Foundation Stage from three to six years, a Key Stage 1 from five to seven (see 'Early Years' entry) and a Key Stage 2 from seven to eleven. Thus the stage once known as the 'Junior Years', and now as 'Key Stage 2', still refers to children aged between seven and eleven (Years 3–6). The introduction of a terminology referring to 'key stages' went alongside the decision in the late 1980s, when the National Curriculum was introduced, to organise teaching in the primary years around subjects – English, Mathematics, Science, History and so on. This led to an emphasis on children acquiring subject knowledge, on target setting and on summative kinds of assessment and to less concern with child development and its implications for the classroom. This is now very evident in initial teacher education: what children have to achieve in the primary curriculum subjects and the teacher's own subject knowledge is at the centre of BA (Ed.) and Postgraduate Certificate in Education courses.

For many year dedicated Early Years practitioners and educationists have worked hard to maintain the long-established principles on which good practice in teaching the very young are based and they challenged innovations which, interpreted inflexibly, might threaten them (Hurst and Joseph, 1998). I believe teachers of children aged between seven and eleven should also proclaim and protect the principles at the heart of good practice. These principles draw on what we know about how children grow and develop physically, intellectually, socially and emotionally and it is important that they continue to inform practice within the prescribed frameworks. I have organised my thoughts about these principles under five headings, drawing out in particular some of the implications for

English, language and literacy in the years seven to eleven. These headings are: learning is active; learning is social and collaborative; language, learning and literacy are cross curricular; society's expectations can be met creatively; the role of adults is crucial.

Learning is active

Children can learn and make meaning actively, flexibly and imaginatively if given a sympathetic environment (Bruner and Haste, 1987; Egan, 1992). Learning is not just about absorbing information but about individuals transforming it to fit with and to extend their existing understanding. (The entries on 'constructivism' and on 'assimilation and accommodation' expand on this and you would also find Wells, 1986, helpful). In supporting children's learning we need to understand their intellectual progress alongside their physical, emotional and social development. For further discussion of cognitive development I recommend Wood (1988), Chapters 4, 5 and 6 and Chapter 1 in Riley and Prentice (1999) which discuss the theories of Piaget, Bruner and Vygotsky. English lessons – where we talk about fiction, improvise drama and write stories and poems – bring together actions, thoughts, feelings and collaborative effort in a particularly satisfying way. Drama and role play, now given welcome emphasis in the National Curriculum, at Key Stages 1 and 2, build on the play activities of the very young. Junior aged children still need to use language round practical and cooperative activities to remain absorbed and focused in their learning.

Learning is social and collaborative

Children learn best when they are working with others. It was Vygotsky and Bruner who drew our attention most powerfully to the impetus to learning provided by talk and cooperation. By seven children have settled into school and have some friends. They should be enjoying not just their growing competence in both physical and intellectual activities, but also their ability to relate to other children and to adults in school. Teachers of seven to nine year olds often remark on their sheer energy and enthusiasm for life. All

this vitality can be channelled into learning together through joint activities, not least language activities in which children share ideas and information and listen and respond to the points of others. In English, sharing ideas round books, and particularly stories and poems, is particularly enjoyable. We also need to reach out to parents and families as they play an important role in children's developing literacy – see the 'parents and families' and 'siblings and literacy' entries for the benefits of partnership with families.

Language, learning and literacy are cross curricular

Some of the most stimulating contexts for talking, reading and writing occur in lessons across the curriculum. Indeed speaking and listening, reading and writing are agents of learning in every lesson. Riley and Prentice (1999) argue strongly for a rich and flexible curriculum in the junior years and voice their concern that arts and humanities may be marginalised in an approach that privileges the three core subjects of the National Curriculum (see Riley and Prentice, 1999, Introduction).

Fiction – the stories and poems which are at the heart of English – can also bring a personal foothold to learning in other lessons. This is a major theme in the introduction to this encyclopaedia and in the entries linking English to art, design & technology, drama, geography, history, mathematics, physical education (and movement, music and dance), religious studies and science. For case studies celebrating children as young researchers, thinking deeply about their learning across the curriculum, see Mallett, 1999, and Brown *et al.*, 1999.

Society's expectations can be met creatively

Making progress involves meeting the expectations of the society in which a child is growing up. In her influential book *Children's Minds*, Margaret Donaldson emphasises the demands that developing a capacity for abstract reasoning, valued now in so many societies, make on young learners (Donaldson, 1978, Chapter 11). As children move through the junior years, they are expected to deal with increasingly complex materials as readers and writers. More of their learning is based on secondary sources. Today the sheer range of information is overwhelming. As well as dealing with books and other print sources children grapple with computer software and the Internet. It is important that they are not pushed into a passive role by the sheer weight of information. We want them to approach their learning creatively and to achieve their own 'voice' in what they say and what they write. We hope that during the later primary years they move forward in becoming critical and reflective readers, and writers who are not over reliant on any one source. This stands them in good stead to avoid being manipulated by advertising and propaganda in the mass media. The realisation that language is socially situated and that some forms enjoy a higher status than others also puts them in control.

The adult's role is crucial

The teacher's careful intervention remains vital to children's learning throughout the primary years. Careful planning, skill in interpreting the requirements of the official frameworks for a particular class, making lessons interesting and keeping careful records of progress are all the mark of a good practitioner. Selecting an exciting range of fiction is a particularly enjoyable responsibility. From about age seven or eight children are ready for longer, more complicated stories and poems. They can appreciate themes that reflect the complexity of many lives – to do with the disruption as well as the opportunities that change brings, coping with parents and families that are fallible and make mistakes and dealing with ambivalent feelings about friends and siblings. The texts themselves teach as Meek famously writes (Meek, 1988), but the teacher's sensitive intervention can help more than anything else make enthusiastic readers. It is the teacher whose comments and observations can inspire children's talk and thinking about literature whether in a class or a group context, in the literacy hour or outside it. Sometimes a question like – 'what makes you think that?' – encourages

a child to find evidence for their view in the text. But I have noticed that good teachers, whether students or more experienced practitioners, often offer a pertinent anecdote to the discussion and this seems to be more encouraging to some children than a question. I remember a student joining a group of nine year olds talking about Betsy Byers' *The Midnight Fox* and telling the children of her own confused feelings when her family moved from town to country and how writing letters to a friend helped. This led to involved talk by the children about their own experiences and those of others known to them. The student teacher skilfully led them into comparing how their experiences were similar to and different from those of the boy in the story. Talking about reading is one of the most important aspects of English teaching. Once again I recommend Aidan Chambers' inspirational book *Tell Me* in which he so eloquently makes this point and shows how teachers intervene to promote more profound discussion. The work of Vygotsky and Bruner consistently shows the importance of the role of the adult in accelerating children's progress in many learning contexts (Vygotsky, 1961; Bruner 1996; Bruner and Haste, 1987).

Teachers model and support children's writing too. Guidance material like *Grammar for Writing* (DfEE, 2000) aims to help, but it is the class teacher who can use the material in a way that takes the children in a particular class forward. Becoming a confident writer is a lot to do with finding a 'voice' and finding your own way of making sense of experience and information. For a most stimulating account of how a class of ten year olds were helped over the course of a school year to link their writing in English lessons with the study of literature – leading to writing in role, poetry and first person accounts – it is well worth reading *The Reader in the Writer* by Barrs and Cork. A review copy arrived on my mat one morning and I read it through in one sitting feeling thoroughly nourished and excited by the insights about the power of literature. I can think of few more rewarding books for any teacher of children in the junior years. One conclusion which matched with all I have learnt myself was that emotionally powerful texts, read well aloud by the teacher, can inspire passionate discussions and satisfying written accounts (Barrs and Cork, 2001). Books which inspired this class included *The Green Children* by Kevin Crossley-Holland which explores cultural difference in an interesting way, *The Lion and the Unicorn* by Shirley Hughes about the loneliness of a child evacuee in the Second World War and *Fire, Bed and Bone* by Henrietta Branford which, through the device of a dog-narrator, explores social issues at the time of the Peasants' Revolt. Literature in the junior years needs to support children's expanding ability to think and feel. Teachers can keep up with new books by reading journals like *Books for Keeps, English 4–11, The Times Educational Supplement* and *The School Librarian* and by looking at reviews by teachers and children on the Internet.

Good practitioners must ensure that teaching and learning are rigorous in the junior years. There are interesting but complicated issues to discuss, worthwhile but difficult books to read and some challenging writing tasks. The good teacher is able to show children that all this is worthwhile. As Mallett remarks: 'Above all, it is critically important to inspire, interest and foster that sense of wonder in the world and its phenomena that very young children bring naturally to their learning' (Mallett, 1999, p. 126).

Barrs, Myra and Cork, Valerie (2001) *The Reader in the Writer: The links between the study of literature and writing development at Key Stage 2* London: The Centre for Language in Primary Education.

Bruner, Jerome and Haste, Helen (1987) *Making Sense: The Child's Construction of the World.* London: Methuen.

Chambers, Aidan (1993) *Tell me* Stroud: The Thimble Press.

DfEE (1998) *The National Literacy Strategy Framework for Teaching* London: DfEE.

DfEE (2000) *Grammar for Writing* Guidance material London: DfEE.

DfEE /QCA (1999) *National Curriculum for English* London: DfEE and QCA.

Donaldson, Margaret (1978 edition) *Children's Minds* London: Fontana/Collins.

Egan, Kieron (1992) *Imagination in Teaching and Learning: The Middle School Years* Chicago: Chicago University Press.

Foot, Michael, Brown, Tony and Holt, Peter (2001) *Let Our Children Learn* Nottingham: Education Now Books.

Hurst, Victoria and Joseph, Jenny (1998) *Supporting Early Learning* Milton Keynes: Open University Press.

Mallett, Margaret (1999) *Young Researchers* London: Routledge.

Meek, Margaret (1988) *How Texts Teach What Readers Learn* Stroud: The Thimble Press

Riley, Jeni and Prentice, Roy (eds) (1999) *The Curriculum for 7–11 Year Olds* London: Paul Chapman.

Wells, Gordon (1986) *Learning Through Interaction: Children Learning Language and Using Language to Learn* London: Hodder & Stoughton.

Wood, David (1988) *How Children Think and Learn* Oxford: Blackwell.

K

Key stages – see Early Years Language and Literacy, Junior Years, Literacy Hour, National Curriculum

Key words – see look and say, Reading

Kinaesthetic strategies

This refers to the memorising of physical actions to help the forming of words. Eve Bearne argues that we are helped to internalise things through repeated movements so that, for example, a series of handwriting movements, if frequently carried out, would help a child memorise spelling patterns (Bearne, 1998). Literacy related tracing activities like writing over letters helps develop knowledge of shape and orientation.

Bearne, Eve (1998) *Making Progress in English* London: Routledge.

Kinds of writing – see genre

Kingman Report

See also Cox Report, grammar, LINC materials

Published in 1988, the Kingman Report on the Teaching of English in England and Wales aimed to produce a model which would inform the teaching of English language. Approaches based on the teaching of a grammar derived from Latin teaching were rejected. However, the report did recommend explicit teaching about the forms and functions of language and recommended that children be taught to use Standard English in appropriate contexts. The Kingman model has four sections: the forms of the language; communication and comprehension; acquisition and development; historical and geographical variation.

The *Cox Report* that followed set out how this approach could inform the English programmes in the National Curriculum which was being put in place for the first time.

While the Kingman Report did not please everyone – some felt the linguistic topics considered did not link into a coherent whole – it did encourage English teachers of all age-groups to increase their knowledge about language and how best to teach Language Study. The debate continues.

DES (1988) *Report of the Committee of Inquiry into the Teaching of English Language* (Kingman Report) London: HMSO.

Knowledge about language – see language and metacognition, metalanguage, subject knowledge

Language acquisition

See also communicative competence and performance, functions of language, language and thought, nativist approach to language acquisition

There are a number of theories to explain how the human infant acquires language. It is very much in the interests of teachers of all age groups to reflect on how children learn to represent their experience symbolically, above all through speech. How the very young child becomes a language user has important implications for teaching and learning in school. The usual pattern of learning to talk is generally agreed. In the first few weeks of life children 'babble' – they make sounds for the sheer pleasure of trying out their speech apparatus. The adults and older children around them respond to the sounds that most approximate to their mother tongue. Gradually the sounds that are most reinforced become organised. Children acquire a vocabulary of single words – naming the people and things important to them, and then as they approach two years they produce 'pivot' words which are the beginnings of sentences 'more milk', 'all gone', 'get book' and so on. From then on children will acquire more syntactic structures and a vocabulary of several thousand words by the time they start school at five years. If you want to read about the stages of acquiring the structures of language you would enjoy 'How Do we Do it? pp. 46–55 (Whitehead, 1997) or Roger Brown's book *A First Language* (1973).

In this short introduction I have pulled out what seem to me some of the main approaches to this fascinating but very complicated area of study: Behaviourist theory of language acquisition; Chomsky and the Language Acquisition Device; Cognitive theories; Social interactionist theories; Halliday's sociolinguistic functionalist model.

Behaviourist theory of language acquisition

Behaviourists believe that all behaviours are learnt and they extend this notion even to sophisticated behaviours like language. In his book *Verbal Behaviour* (1957) Skinner argued that language, like much early learning, was acquired by imitation. So the child might hear the word 'milk' said as his or her parent hands them a glass of milk. The word becomes associated with the context and the parent is likely to praise or 'reinforce' the child's appropriate utterance of the word. Of course imitation does account for some kinds of learning – we have to hear our mother tongue spoken in order to acquire a vocabulary – but the behaviourist theory is less convincing when we move on from content words like 'milk', 'ball' and 'Mummy' to words like 'yesterday', 'because' and 'when'.

Chomsky and the Language Acquisition Device (LADs)

One of the best known linguists contributing to our understanding of early language acquisition is Chomsky who believed with other nativists that language ability was genetically inherited. In his book *Syntactic Structures* (1957) Chomsky criticised the mechanistic approach to language acquisition of the behaviourists and pointed to the speed with which children acquire language without overt instruction. He suggested that children have an innate predisposition to make sense of the sounds they hear. This he termed a 'Language Acquisition Device' (LAD) – a grammar generating 'device' which processed fragments of language into a coherent system. If you listen to the conversation of very young children you soon find that imitation is only one strategy for learning language. In fact children seem to hypothesise and build up knowledge of syntactic rules. Interestingly it is the 'errors' young children typically make that suggest they are following rules and sometimes over generalise them. For example, as the past tense of verbs are normally inflected with an 'ed', children sometimes say 'heared' for 'heard' and as nouns often add as 's' to becomes plural they say 'mans' instead of 'men'.

Cognitive theories

Chomsky's theory has had its critics; Margaret Donaldson, for instance, thinks the notion of a language acquisition device can be just as mechanical as the behaviourist stimulus response model. Where, she asks, is 'the warm blood in the veins?' (Donaldson, 1973, p. 39). She refers to the view of John Macnamara who suggests that children do not have something as specific as a sensitivity to language, but rather they have a well developed capacity for making sense of situations involving direct human interaction. Macnamara, Piaget and other developmentalists leaning towards the cognitive view believe that language acquisition is part of general intellectual development. Piaget, for instance, believed that sensori-motor kinds of thinking (where the child feels his or her way round the environment and knows it through perception seeing, touching and tasting) need to be in place before verbal language can be acquired.

We have to be careful not to give the impression that all theorists under the cognitive umbrella think the same. Macnamara, for instance, gives much more emphasis than Piaget to the human element in situations in helping children make sense of them (Donaldson, 1973).

Social interactionist theories

These theories, which became influential in the late 1970s and 1980s, emphasise the social purposes of language. Although Vygotsky was no longer alive, the implications of much of his thinking was only now becoming assimilated. He believed that the impetus to learning language was essentially social. While Piaget had tended to stress the importance of learning from objects, Vygotsky saw the adult, whether parent or teacher, and other children as very much part of the social situation in which a child takes on both a culture and a language. Vygotsky's views on early thinking and concept formation and the implications for classroom learning are discussed in his best known book *Thought and Language* (1962).

Jerome Bruner is sometimes placed with the cognitive theorists. Like Piaget he suggests a number of overlapping stages in a child's development beginning with the enactive stage when the child makes sense of the world by movement and perception, progressing to an 'iconic' stage when the child can represent the world through images and finally reaching the symbolic stage when speech makes it possible to organise the thinking of the previous stages. In Bruner's theory we continue to learn through all three ways of representing the world. However, while he seems to stand with the cognitive theorists in believing some learning uses non-verbal cognitive abilities, he also insists on the powerful role of language, from an early age, in organising experience and thinking and communicating with others. Bruner, like Vygotsky, believes that young children's minds grow when they are stimulated and challenged by other children and adults. In this sense he leans towards a more interactionist view than, for example, Piaget.

Halliday's sociolinguistic functional model

Theories of early language acquisition have not only come to us from psycholinguistics. Sociolinguists have also taken an interest and one of the most influential is M.A.K. Halliday. Halliday asked a different question to the psycholinguists. He was interested in the functions for which children began to use language. In fact he began to study his own young child's attempts at communication long before he had words. Halliday suggests that the first six functions of language acquired by a young child are:

Instrumental	makes needs known
Regulatory	influences and manipulates others
Interactional	keeps relationships developing.
Personal	establishes a unique identity
Heuristic	sparks the will to learn
Imaginative	to do with playing games, role play and creating stories.

The seventh function – the *informational* or 'I've got something to tell you' function is evident after about twenty two months. The notion of telling somebody something they do not know is an advanced one and is usually dependent on words.

The books listed below give fuller accounts of theories of early language acquisition. As Whitehead remarks, no one theorist has answered all the questions about how children achieve the amazing feat of learning their language so quickly. Each perspective offers some insight. The behaviourists remind us of the role of imitation, while the nativists show that children actively construct their language. The cognitive theorists draw our attention to ways of making sense other than by verbal language and the social interactionists indicate the social and cultural functions of language. Sociolinguists like Halliday draw attention to the importance of having purposes so that language can serve functions in our social world. All these insights – not least the picture of the child as essentially an active meaning maker – have implications for teaching and learning in the primary school.

Britton, James (1970) *Language and Learning* London: Allen Lane, The Penguin Press, Chapter 2 'Learning to Speak'.

Chomsky, Noam (1957) *Syntactic Structures* Mouton: The Hague.

Donaldson, Margaret (1973) *Children's Minds* Harmondsworth: Penguin.

Halliday, M.A.K. (1975) *Learning How to Mean* London: Edward Arnold.

Vygotsky, L.S. (1962) *Language and Learning* Cambridge MA: The MIT Press.

Whitehead, Marian R.(1997) *Language and Literacy in the Early Years* London: Paul Chapman, Chapter 3.

Language Acquisition Device (LAD) – see language acquisition

Language across the curriculum

See also Art & English, factual genres, Geography & English, History & English, Information and Communications Technology (ICT) & English, information books, library skills, Mathematics & English, non-fiction reading and writing, reading, Science & English, study skills, speaking and listening, writing

The *Bullock Report* in 1975 brought formal recognition of the role of language in learning in every lesson. Good practitioners had always acted on this insight but the Bullock Report energised teachers' efforts to create a language policy for their school. In primary and secondary schools teachers met to decide on resources and teaching approaches to spelling, handwriting and grammar and to library and study skills, including note taking and making summaries. In secondary schools all teachers were encouraged to see a positive role in promoting children's development in language as well as their development of knowledge and understanding in a subject.

In the United Kingdom a subject centred national curriculum nudged away some language across the curriculum initiatives. However, primary teachers make links between the literacy hour and lessons across the curriculum, recognising that history, geography and other lessons provide strong contexts for kinds of non-fiction writing. Story, too, has relevance and importance beyond the English curriculum.

The principles behind the language across the curriculum initiatives still inform good practice. They include recognising that:

- it is helpful for each school to agree on a language policy, on how subjects are resourced, how the four language processes – speaking and listening, reading and writing – can be used to learn. A consistent approach to using the library and to study skills like note taking and summarising can be achieved.
- children's language development is promoted in every lesson. Part of learning history, geography, science and so on is learning to use and control the kinds of spoken and written

language involved. It is also true that some English objectives can be realised through other lessons. History provides good contexts for distinguishing fact from opinion, for example.

- listening and responding to what others say helps make learning social and collaborative and helps develop, change and extend a child's understanding of a topic.
- talk helps children get their language round concepts and ideas in every lesson. It reveals children's level of thinking and understanding at a particular stage so that the teacher can plan ahead in an informed way. History, geography and science can all provide the content to inspire meaningful and enthusiastic discussion of issues.
- subjects across the curriculum are the most appropriate and interesting contexts for particular kinds of reading and writing – the recount, report, instruction, discussion, persuasive and explanation genres of the National Literacy Strategy.
- visual kinds of literacy are best developed in a cross curricular way and a school language policy can help create a culture where teachers and pupils use language to illuminate the visual and the abstract.
- just as informational kinds of writing have a place in English, fiction can provide a personal foothold in lessons across the curriculum.

Hoodless, Pat (ed.) (1998) *History and English: Exploring the Links* London: Routledge.

Language and culture – see under bilingualism, multiculturalism, multilingualism

Language and thought

See also assimilation and accommodation, collaborative learning, constuctivism, critical discourse, language acquisition, metacognition, nativist approach to language acquisition, reflective reading, speaking and listening, spontaneous and scientific concepts, zone of proximal awareness

This entry introduces the interesting and complicated issue of the relationship between language and thought by looking at the ideas of some key contributors to the field. (There are links between issues here and early language acquisition – see 'language acquisition'.) All the positions are of interest, but the work of Vygotsky, Bruner and Donaldson is particularly relevant to the classroom because of the importance these developmentalists give to the role of instruction and the language used by both teacher and children.

The Sapir–Whorf hypothesis

This hyothesis proposes that language, and indeed the particular language we speak, affects our perception of the world. Whorf studied the differences between European and non European languages and formed the view that the vocabulary of a language has an impact on the way its speakers think. A language reflects what is important in a society – a hunter gather society is likely to have a particularly rich vocabulary of words to do with animals and plants. In western societies there is a developing vocabulary for the new technology – 'hyperlinks', 'e-mail', 'web browser' and so on in line with the increasing importance of these concepts in the culture. Whorf also noted that the syntax of languages varies: his work on the languages of Indian communities in north and south America revealed that the grammatical patterns for referring to concepts like time and home was distinctive. Some nomadic societies refer to a 'sheltering' rather than something permanent like a house. This led him to argue that the thinking of a child would be shaped by the language of their speech community.

Many take issue with the proposition that children are moulded by their language into a restricted way of seeing the world. (See under 'restricted and elaborated codes' for a consideration of variations within one language.) This does not fit with the experience of bilinguals or that of anyone who is able to communicate successfully with people from different cultures. Translation from one language into another is not mechanistic, but ways of expressing the full range of human experience can be found within the resources of every language. As Whitehead argues, while children are 'initiated into the language uses and the ways of thinking of their communities' this is far from a straight jacket and is best thought of as an open framework or supporting trellis (Whitehead, 1997, p. 57).

The cognitive theory of Jean Piaget

Piaget and other cognitive psychologists believe that there are kinds of thinking that are language free, including those that children use before they can speak. (see under 'functions of language' for comment on Halliday's work suggesting children 'mean' before they have verbal language). This position is a long way from the linguistic determinism of the more extreme interpretations of the Sapir-Whorf hypothesis, and tends to view language as one of a number of ways of making sense of experience. Piaget's adaptive model of learning, where new material is assimilated into an existing framework of knowledge which accommodates to take in the new knowledge, is described under the 'assimilation and accommodation' entry. I find this a valuable way of describing the learning process. Not least, it indicates the importance of organising prior knowledge before we introduce new learning. What is missing from Piaget's work is the recognition of the powerful role of language in learning from the earliest stages.

Piaget is also well known for his description of qualitative stages of development beginning with the sensory motor stage when the child knows the world through action and perception, the concrete operational stage characterised by practical thinking about what can be directly perceived (and which takes in most of the primary years) and the formal operations stage when children become able to hypothesise and deal with things that are not present. Piaget's theory of development has stimulated much discussion and further research. Donaldson (1978) questions his belief that children's reasoning abilities are limited before age eleven. She draws on Martin Hughes' reworking of one of Piaget's experiments to show that children's ability to problem solve is apparent if the task they are given makes sense in terms of their experience of the world. In her later work Donaldson modifies Paiget's stages of development, and her model allows for more flexible thinking during the primary years (Donaldson, 1992).

Social Interactionist approaches of Bruner and Vygotsky

These developmentalists place much more importance than Piaget on the role of language in the development of thinking and in the social situation in which learning takes place. Bruner's stages refer to ways of representing or thinking about experience: first comes 'enactive' thinking which takes place is through action and perception; second 'iconic' thinking which draws on images (of phenomena which may not be present) and finally the 'symbolic' – thinking through symbols which includes above all the ability to use language. Once a child reaches the symbolic stage, all three modes of representing experience interact in his or her learning and thinking.

Vygotsky also believed that children's development passed through a number of stages. Although convinced that thought and language have different roots, he considered that the child's mental functioning and powers of communication were transformed once the two systems come together. For Vygotsky the impetus for learning to speak is to be able to make contact with others. Through talking and writing children clinch concepts and internalise them. The role of the adult in the development of children's thinking is dominant in Vygotsky's work. There is more about this under the entries 'spontaneous and scientific concepts' and the 'zone of proximal development' and comment about Bruner's recognition of the power of adult intervention in augmenting the child's thinking and reasoning abilities under 'scaffolding'.

Developmentalists recognise the importance of becoming able to use systems of symbolic representation particularly for the more abstract kinds of thinking. Donaldson consistently shows the power of the written word to extend children's reasoning. Reading and writing seem to encourage the mind to grow in particular ways, ways which are valued in western societies and necessary to make headway in them. For an interesting analysis of the kinds of thinking needed across the primary curriculum I recommend Chapter 1 in Riley and Prentice, 1999. Under 'constructivism' I show how children learn actively – they do not pass through the developmental stages without effort or without guidance from parents and teachers.

Donaldson, Margaret (1978, second edition) *Children's Minds* London: Fontana, (Chapters 1–3).

Donaldson, Margaret (1992) *Human Minds: An Exploration* London: Penguin.

Riley, Jeni and Prentice, Roy (eds) (1999) *The Curriculum for 7–11 Year Olds* London: Paul Chapman Publishing (Chapter 1).

Whitehead, Marian R. (1997 edition) *Language and Literacy in the Early Years* London: Paul Chapman (Chapter 3).

Wood, David (1988) *How Children Think and Learn* Oxford: Blackwell (Introduction and Chapter 1).

Language change

See also functions of language, language variety

This is the modification to language which takes place over time, referred to by functional linguists as 'diachronic variation'. Language is essentially dynamic and so there are changes in how we pronounce words, in grammar and in vocabulary.

Change in pronunciation is gradual. We can detect quite subtle changes by comparing how speakers from a particular group spoke on film, television or on the radio with the present day speech of people from the same social group. The speech of upper middle class people in films like for example *Brief Encounter* was more rarefied than that of socially comparable people today. Younger and older members of the royal family speak differently from one another too. Something that fascinates me is the way in which regional accents endure: increased exposure to mass media has not so far resulted in a move towards standard pronunciation. This seems to be to do with group solidarity and identification with those with whom we feel comfortable.

Changes in grammar include the increasing acceptability of the split infinitive and modifications in verb forms like 'got, gotten'.

There is often resistance to change when it comes to vocabulary or lexis, particularly where a distinction between words is lost. A good example here is the loss of the distinction between 'uninterested' (not absorbed in something or curious about it) and 'disinterested' (an unbiased view or research study). But language changes relentlessly whether individuals approve or not. Changes in vocabulary include loan words from other languages (anorak, pizza) clipped words (like zoo), acronyms pronounced as words (UNICEF), cult words (like yuppy) and words that have changed their meaning (meat once meant any food but now means animal flesh). Changes in vocabulary often reflect cultural change – for example we have a richer vocabulary to talk or write about the new technology – microchip, multi-media authoring, digital animation and hotlinks. But sometimes there are attempts to make swift changes – for example feminist sociologists encouraged the use of 'Ms' to make it possible for women, like men, not to be defined by their marital status.

For a more detailed analysis and many interesting examples of language change, I recommend Rebecca Bunting's account in Chapter 1, 'Principles of language study', in her book *Teaching About Language Study in the Primary Years*.

Bunting, Rebecca (2000 edition) *Teaching About Language Study in the Primary Years* London: David Fulton.

Language functions – see functions of language

Language variety

See also accent, bilingualism, creole, dialect, field, functions of language, language change, mode, multilingualism, register, standard English, tenor

Language varies according to how speakers and writers use it. Functional linguists, for example Michael Halliday, recognise three main kinds of variation: dialectal, diatypic and diachronic. Dialectal variation recognises that within one mother tongue an individual may use a particular form of language – standard English or a regional or class dialect, sometimes called a 'sociolect'. There may also be variation according to gender, ethnicity and class. While 'dialect' is to do with variation in grammatical structures, 'accent' refers only to pronunciation – and may be 'received pronunciation' (RP) or a kind of pronunciation associated with a particular region or social group. This is normally a useful distinction but can become blurred in particular cases: Rebecca Bunting asks whether 'innit' should be regarded as a dialect feature of London English or as a feature of accent, as a pronunciation of 'isn't it' (Bunting, 2000 edition, p. 19). Angela Wilson draws our attention to emotional aspects of different accents and how advertisers exploit this on film and television – Dorset and Somerset accents being used to sell wholesome products and French accents to sell perfume (Wilson, 2001).

Diatypic variation refers to the adaptations we make in our language according to context and purpose. The 'register' of our language differs according to the formality of the situation – we would use language differently in a court of law or university seminar than in a pub or at a football match. Other factors also affect the 'register' or kind of language we use – the immediate context and the relationship between participants for example.

Diachronic variation refers to changes in language over time in vocabulary, grammar and pronunciation and is covered under 'language change'.

Halliday, M.A.K. and Hasan, R. (1985) *Language, Context and Text: Aspects of Language in a Social-Semiotic Perspective* Oxford: Oxford University Press.

Bunting, Rebecca (2000 edition) *Teaching About Language in the Primary Years* London: David Fulton (Chapter 1).

Wilson, Angela (2001) *Language Knowledge for Primary Teachers* London: David Fulton.

Left handed children – see handwriting

Legend

See also traditional tales

Legends are a category of traditional tale. McArthur tells us that they are generally 'unverifiable, usually fabulous stories passed down (often orally) in a community and widely accepted as in some sense true' (McArthur, 1992, p. 595). A traditional tale is a legend or 'hero tale', rather than a fable or parable for example, if it is about heroes and heroines – 'supermen who inspire marvel and wonder' (Steele, 1989, p. 11). Steele provides a helpful annotated list including Rosemary Sutcliff's *Dragon Slayer* (superbly illustrated by Charles Keeping in the Puffin edition) and *The Faber Book of Greek Legends* edited by Kathleen Lines. There are more excellent annotated lists in Rosemary Stones' *A Multicultural Guide to Children's Books* (1999). For a theatrical reading of tales based on the legend of Robin Hood I recommend the tape of Michael Morpurgo's book *Robin of Sherwood* (Hodder, 2000) which has a distinctive slant on the political and social aspects; for example Robin becomes committed to helping the poor after his mother dies of starvation. Kevin Crossley-Holland has written a trilogy about the legends of King Arthur which weaves the stories round the tale of another Arthur – a young boy in the year 1199 who longs to grow up and become a knight. Older juniors would find this an exciting retelling which recreates the texture of life in the Middle Ages with its hardships, challenges and distinctive sights and sounds (Orion Children's Books, 2000).

McArthur, Tom (1992) *The Oxford Companion to the English Language* Oxford and London: QPD with Oxford University Press.

Steele, Mary (1989) *Traditional Tales:* A Signal Bookguide Stroud: The Thimble Press.

Stones, Rosemary (1999) *A Multicultural Guide to Children's Books 0–16* London and Reading: Books for Keeps and Reading University Reading and Language Information Centre.

Letterland

Letterland is a reading programme developing phonological awareness and introducing letter shapes and sounds which was first published by Collins Educational in 1973 for three to seven year olds. The letter sounds are characterised by pictograms and the multi-sensory, interactive approach is thought to be particularly beneficial for children with reading difficulties. There is a range of materials – work books, Big books, videos and games – as well as a Teacher's Guide. As the materials reflect the phonics-based nature of the programme, it is recommended that they are used alongside other reading materials.

Letters

See also autobiography, first person writing

Letters are a kind of first person writing and lie on a continuum from the intensely personal to the strictly formal. Many literacy corners include a folder of examples of different types of letter for use in the Literacy Hour and in other English work. As children move through the primary years they appreciate increasingly that a letter's audience and purpose affect the degree of its formality. Letters are a helpful resource when children compare first person writing –autobiography – and third person writing – biography (NLS, Year 6, term 1). Younger children can be helped to write letters to recount, explain, enquire, congratulate and complain (NLS, Year 3, term 3). Some genuine contexts for letters arise – writing to invite parents and friends of the school to special events and thank you letters to guides who have taken them round a museum or art gallery. Other contexts can be created through stories. Children enjoy writing letters in the role of one character to another. The book which has helped greatly here is Janet and Alan Ahlberg's *The Jolly Postman* (Kestrel/Viking, 1986). *Dear Greenpeace* by Simon James (Walker Books, 1991) can also be used to inspire letter writing and books like Lisa Bruces' *Jazeera's Journey* (Methuen, 1991) show how letters can link lives. Children whose roots are in far off countries know how letters can sustain emotional links with relatives and friends. Drama is a motivating context for many kinds of writing and an authentic setting for letter writing often arises. A student inspired a Year 2 class to write letters with considerable enthusiasm by using Julia and Charles Snapes' *Giant* (Walker Books, 1990) in some drama work about conservation. When they reached the part of the story where the giant mountain moves away from the village, the children wrote letters to her asking why. To their delight they found a large envelope with a reply in the classroom the next day. So teachers too can write 'in role' and this often energises the children's approach.

Older primary children are able to attempt letters to persuade, criticise or protest (NLS Year 5, Term 3). Again, we need to find a strong context to make the task come alive. I worked with a nine year old class whose Literacy Hour had begun in the Shared Writing slot with an extract displayed on an overhead from an information book on the processing of household rubbish. One of the guided writing tasks was to write a letter in the role of a householder to the local council's environmental department protesting about the lack of sites for the recycling of rubbish and trying to persuade officials to take action. The children greatly enjoyed sharing their writing in the plenary. Other starting points might be a discussion on a current issue leading to letters taking up a viewpoint for a newspaper's correspondence column.

Johnson, Jane (1999) *My Dear Noel: The Story of a Letter from Beatrix Potter* London: Macdonald Young Book (For children of about seven years and above, this picture book shows how a friendship can be sustained through letters.)

Mallett, Margaret (1997) *First Person Reading and Writing in the Primary Years: Enjoying and reflecting on diaries, letters, autobiographies and first person fiction* Sheffield: National Association for the Teaching of English (NATE).

Letter–sound correspondence

See also bottom-up reading approaches, phonics, reading, spelling

When we teach phonics we teach children the relationship between letter symbols and sounds.

The National Literacy Strategy Framework for Teaching (DfEE, 1998) and support materials like *Progression in Phonics* (DfEE, 1999) set out a detailed programme of phonics teaching. To make progress, children need to acquire the skills of segmentation and blending, know the alphabetic code and how to use their knowledge of that code in reading and spelling. In this approach children are helped to hear individual vowel and consonant sounds which are called 'phonemes' and to recognise the written symbols for these sounds which are called 'graphemes'. But while there are 44 phonemes, there are only 26 letters of the alphabet. There are two ways of getting over this. First, letters can make more than one sound, for example the 's' sound in 'has' is different to the 's' sound in 'seal'. Second, letters can be combined to make certain phonemes – 'sh', 'au' and 'ph'.

One issue here is that teaching phonics can become rather abstract. In a detailed analysis Graham and Kelly put it like this: 'What is important, and this applies to whatever teaching skill you are focusing on, is that the child does not lose sight of the fact that reading is a purposeful and meaningful activity and that there are some small and large shapes to attend to' (Graham and Kelly, 2000, p. 12).

Graham, Judith and Kelly, Alison (2000) *Reading Under Control* London: David Fulton.

Level descriptions – see under criterion referenced assessment and National Curriculum

Lexical ties – see under cohesion

Libraries in primary schools

See also reading corner/areas, *Books for Keeps*, Dewey system, displays, library skills, writing area/corners

Most primary schools have both a central stock of books and resources and some classroom collections. Resources in the central stock are catalogued by title, author and subject in a card index system or, increasingly in computer form.

School libraries mostly use the Dewey system of classification or a simplified form of it. Quite often each class has a designated weekly slot in the library to carry out research for a lesson or to be taught library skills.

It is important that children also have more informal library use. So a good system ensures that the central library is accessible, open as often as possible to the children and that it creates an interesting reading environment with displays and areas where children can sit to take notes, browse and reflect.

Of course human resources are important and often it is the English Co-ordinator who orders books and resources, after consultation with other teachers, parents and most importantly the children. The skilled English Co-ordinator involves all the teachers in knowing how the library should develop. He or she can set up a staff room collection of journals which offer insightful reviews of books and resources, for example *Books for Keeps; The School Librarian* and *English 4–11*. It is also helpful to send round new acquisitions with some comments about the merits of the book and how it might be used. If there is a lively dialogue about books and resources and teachers are prepared to browse in local book shops, this is much better than just ordering books from catalogues. Nothing beats the hands on approach!

There are also good strategies for involving children in caring for the library. In quite a number of schools I visit, older primary children enjoy undertaking some light duties – replacing returned books to the shelves and helping younger children find their way round the library. Involvement in looking after their library is likely to encourage children to give reading priority in their lives. Primary schools can draw on the expertise of the school library services when creating a balanced collection of fiction, information books, audio-visual materials, CD-ROMs and software. The librarians will also usually visit to give talks to particular classes and groups of children about authors and illustrators and what the public lending library can offer them.

The books and resources in the classroom collections are usually centrally catalogued. English Co-ordinators usually consult with other teachers to agree a coherent approach to taking books into the classroom from the central library for special purposes. But each classroom in each year group needs a core of carefully chosen classroom books and resources, for example picture books, stories and poetry particularly appealing to the age range and appropriate reference books – dictionaries, encyclopaedias, thesauruses and atlases and other books which children and teachers need constantly to refer to. In the United Kingdom the literacy hour has increased the need for a diverse array of classroom resources including letters, articles, charts, posters as well as books and computer software. Please turn to 'reading corners' and 'writing corners' for suggestions about making the literacy area in the classroom inviting.

Chambers, Aidan (1991) *The Reading Environment: How adults help children enjoy books* Stroud: The Thimble Press.

Graham, Judith and Kelly, Alison (2000, second edition) *Reading Under Control: Teaching Reading in the Primary School* London: David Fulton.

Books for Keeps/School Bookshop Association (Tel: 020 852 4953).

School Library Association produces a helpful journal *The School Librarian* which includes reviews of all kinds of books and resources, articles on all aspects of setting up and developing a school library and a useful briefing section with news of recent development (Tel. 01793 791787).

Young Book Trust provide information about library resources (Tel. 020 8516 2977; website www.booktrust.org.uk)

Library skills

See also book area/corner, factual genres, libraries, retrieval devices, structural guiders, study skills

We should do all we can to encourage children to enjoy and be skilled at using the school library. When children are at work in the library it is an excellent opportunity for the teacher to observe children's reading behaviour. How are they getting on with finding books through the Dewey system? Do they know how to browse and how to swiftly sample a book by checking the cover and reading a page or two? These observations will inform how the teacher builds in helpful activities and teaching. So that we ensure that children progress in their ability to use the library the English Co-ordinator with input from other staff usually draws up a broad plan of what should be achieved by most children in each year group and how teaching will support this. This then feeds into the school's English policy and long- and short-term planning.

Specific skills like selecting books and browsing through resources can be modelled by teachers and older pupils. With encouragement, some children will be prepared to make themselves experts in library skills and general care of the library. This kind of involvement can be reinforced by inviting children to contribute an assembly item about what they have been doing.

Children enjoy making charts and labels to help others find their way round the books and resources. Charts can set out advice about using the numbers on the shelves to locate the books, and then going on to use the retrieval devices in the books to find exactly the aspect of the topic you need. And of course booklets on how to use CD-ROMs, software and the Internet are necessary as well. This kind of writing task has a very clear purpose and audience. Waters and Martin describe a most interesting case study in which older primary school children were systematically trained by teachers and classroom assistants in using library procedures consistent with an agreed approach. Adults took small groups for short teaching periods and trained them in putting books into alphabetic order according to author surname, dividing books into fiction and non-fiction and in social aspects of using the library. The social aspects included discussing what a pupil would do if they entered the library and found a plant knocked over, a book thrown on the floor or a group of children behaving in a silly way. Children often respond well to being asked to reflect in a mature manner. Short tests were built into the lessons and children who passed these were awarded a library licence which set out their competencies, which included: being able to use the Dewey system; following the library code; knowing what to do if you have a problem. Possession of the licence led to certain privileges like being allowed to enter the library alone and to supervise another pupil who has not yet achieved the licence (Waters and Martin, 1999, Chapter 8).

If children feel confident and comfortable using their school library it is much more likely that they will make use of all their local lending library offers, including the many holiday schemes and projects.

Waters, Mick and Martin, Tony (1999) *Co-ordinating English at Key Stage 2* London: The Falmer Press (Chapter 8).

Limerick

A limerick is an amusing verse often with an aabba rhyming pattern. Edward Lear (1812–88) made limericks popular with children with his entertaining rhymes with illustrations in *Book of Nonsense* (1877). Here is an example of one of his limericks:

> Bored by a Bee
> There was an Old Man in a tree,
> Who was horribly bored by a bee,
> When they asked 'Does it buzz?'
> He replied, 'Yes, it does!
> It's a regular brute of a bee!'

LINC materials

See also Cox Report, Kingman Report

The LINC materials (Language in the National Curriculum) were a government-funded, in-service resource produced by Professor Ronald Carter and his team to help implement language study programmes in response to the implications of the Kingman Report (1989). The 500-page pack was not for direct use in the classroom but to help increase teachers' own knowledge about language and language study so that they could plan, implement and evaluate appropriate lessons with the age-groups they taught. There were about 400 training courses and about 10,000 teachers attended them.

Then one of the most dramatic decisions in the history of the teaching of English was made: the Government of the day refused to publish the materials. In his book *Cox on the Battle for the English Curriculum,* Brian Cox (chair of the Working Group which created the first National Curriculum in English in 1989) sets out the background to this official censorship. Although most teachers, linguists and educationists considered the materials were based on a balanced view of issues like the teaching of grammar, Standard English and dialects some Ministers and journalists in some parts of the press thought otherwise. The language volcano, always simmering away in the background, had erupted! This shows what an emotional issue how we teach children about their mother tongue is and how much people care about it. The materials and several related books were eventually published by Nottingham University and the work of Professor Carter and his team continues to inform those concerned with language study in school.

Four principles underpin the LINC programme. First, teaching about language should build on children's implicit knowledge- on the rich linguistic resources they bring to the classroom. The next principle is to do with the relationship between reflecting on language and use of language. The LINC team believed that children use language before they begin to consciously reflect and analyse it in school. Later on they can be helped to use appropriate terminology to consider how they and other people use language and these insights can feed back into their use of language. Third, language is best analysed in purposeful settings rather than out of context. (This is where drama work with its wide potential for different kinds of language use can make a considerable contribution.) Finally teaching children about attitudes to language, its uses and misuses, can help children see through language to how it is used to communicate people's underlying attitudes and beliefs. (Cox, 1995).

Nothing stays the same and we now have new frameworks and teachers are obliged to meet new requirements. The DfEE guidance in *Grammar for Writing,* a National Literacy Strategy recommended text, reflects a more prescribed approach but we can still keep hold of the four principles enshrined in the LINC materials as a way of keeping our classroom work engaged and exciting.

Bain, Richard *et al.* (1992) *Looking Into Language* London: Hodder & Stoughton.

Carter, Ronald (1992) *Knowledge about Language and the Curriculum: the LINC Reader* London: Hodder & Stoughton.

Cox, Brian (1995) *Cox on the Battle for the Curriculum* London: Hodder & Stoughton.

Listening – see under National Curriculum, speaking and listening, story telling

Lists

See also factual genres, writing

Lists have purposes which even the youngest children can understand. They can remind us of things we need to do to feed the classroom snails or to bring to school the ingredients to make sweets or biscuits. When it comes to planning a piece of writing, a list can be the first step towards producing a longer account. Children working on their own information books are often encouraged to list the questions they want to consider – see for example the list of snail questions in case study 3.1 (in Mallett, 1999) which, with some rearrangement, became the contents page. As Barrs points out, a list can be one of the first kinds of writing children do that moves away from chronological organisation (Barrs, 1987). Lists can bring order to our experience and our thinking.

Children can be supplied with a special note book to jot down lists of things they want to include in their writing. There is a most interesting glimpse into a classroom where children are encouraged to have inquiring minds and to make lists in their 'wonder books' in Stephanie Harvey's book *Nonfiction Matters* (Harvey, 1998). Eight-year-old Jordan lists, with detailed illustrations, twenty-two topics he wants to research including 'volcanoes, dogs and cats, the human race, black holes and electricity'. Making lists of what they want to find out can be the first step for a young researcher, and lead to long term commitment to favourite topics and interests.

Barrs, Myra (1987) 'Mapping the world', *English in Education NATE,* Vol. 21. No. 3.

Harvey, Stephanie (1998) *Nonfiction Matters; Reading, Writing and Research Grades 3–8* York, Maine: Stenhouse Publishers.

Mallett, Margaret (1999) *Young Researchers: informational reading and writing in the pearly and primary years* London: Routledge.

Literacy corner/area – see under reading corner/area, writing corner/area

Literacy Hour

See also guided reading/writing, independent group work in the Literacy Hour, National Curriculum, phonics, plenary, reading, sentence level work, shared writing, speaking and listening, text level work, visual literacy, word level work, writing

The National Literacy Strategy Framework for Teaching (DfEE, 1998) builds on the National Curriculum English programmes for Key Stages 1 and 2. The main aim is to raise standards of reading and writing so that at least 80 per cent of eleven year olds achieve the standards expected for their age by 2002. During one hour each day teachers and children carry out structured reading and writing tasks, beginning with class-based, shared reading/writing and moving on to small group guided and independent reading/ writing before ending with a ten-minute plenary (see details under appropriate entries). There are clear termly objectives from Reception to Year 6 organised under the three headings 'word level', 'sentence level' and 'text level'. There is a steady stream of guidance for carrying out the literacy programme – for example *Progression in Phonics* (DfEE, 1999), *The National Literacy Strategy Spelling Bank* (1999), *Grammar for Writing* (2000) and *Developing Early Writing* (2001), and a number of training video films. Teachers also keep in touch with new developments by accessing the Standards website which has links between the Literacy Hour and other areas of the curriculum.

This entry considers some of the issues raised by a structure some would regard as over-prescriptive (see, for example, Wyse and Jones,

2001, p. 18) and suggests some of the strengths and possible limitations of the strategy. Many of the early criticisms of the Literacy Hour were of the kind that occur whenever a new strategy is implemented. If note is taken of the views of experienced teachers, drawing on their professional expertise and practical experience and if the move towards flexibility in its implementation is maintained, then I believe the Literacy Hour will help both teachers and children.

Although non-statutory, the inspectors from the Office for Standards in Education will need to be convinced that any alternative to the Literacy Hour is as good or better. Not surprisingly, most primary schools have chosen to work within *The Framework* Literacy Hour. Many teachers consider the framework helpful in making sure their literacy programme is comprehensive and, once familiar with the requirements, have found they can develop a good system for long- and short-term planning and evaluating and recording progress. Others question how comprehensive the framework is, pointing out that the organisation of the hour into segments makes it difficult to carry out drama, story telling, debates, extended listening (from a cassette or video film of a classic. perhaps) and sustained writing. For example making a website or writing an extended account are not activities capable of being fitted into a twenty-minute slot. Some teachers also feel that there needs to be time for the more active listening that leads to children's response and stimulates learning activities. These are all very important elements of a good English programme and are required to fulfil the National Curriculum English programmes. The challenge is to find time for these extended activities outside the Literacy Hour, as the writers of the strategy acknowledge.

What about the model of reading that informs *The Framework*? This is known as 'the search light' model: the metaphor of children bringing cue systems or 'searchlights' to bear when reading a text is a powerful one (see also under 'Reading' and 'Phonics'). The cue-systems are: phonic knowledge (sounds and spelling), graphic knowledge (word recognition), grammatical knowledge and knowledge of context. Some feel the

prescribed programme of phonics risks being rather abstract and difficult for children. However, the guidance material in *Progression in Phonics* includes many games and ways of teaching phonics in an interesting way. One of the most helpful accounts of how we can teach the phonic element required in *The Framework* is in Chapter 3 of Graham and Kelly's book *Reading Under Control* (2000). These authors show how we can do this while never losing sight of those bigger shapes that give point and meaning to learning to read.

Another issue about content is whether the multi-media flavour of the National Curriculum is carried over into the Literacy Hour or whether there is a risk of information and communication technology being marginalised. There is no need for this to be the case. Televisual texts, including advertisements, can have a useful place in the programme – not least in the area of visual literacy. The computer has much potential for group writing and focused work on spelling and directed activities round texts (DARTs).

Does the Literacy Hour make it possible and likely that teachers will be able to respond to the emphasis on drama in the National Curriculum through improvisation, role play and scripts? I hope so as the explicit recognition of the value of drama has been universally welcomed. It is well worth finding ways, both in the Literacy Hour and outside it, to ensure opportunities for drama in all its forms happens regularly – not least because this so often leads to extended speaking and listening.

The lack of time within the hour for sustained writing has been mentioned many times. Further, if we agree with the National Curriculum English guidelines that 'writing should be enjoyable in itself', pressure on time is not going to be helpful. Speaking more generally, Bethan Marshall, in her article 'The ice age stunneth' in the *TES*, 1 December 2000, urges us to resist the notion that 'the teacher is simply there to tip in the knowledge and move on' whether the children are ready or not. The emphasis on summative testing in the literacy strategy contributes to the feeling things have to be covered quickly and then tested. We need to make time for formative testing which gives a richer picture of children's progress and reveals more about how we can intervene to help their progress most effectively.

Although *The Framework* is, like the National Curriculum, genre based and sets out the full range of kinds of texts to be included from Reception to Year 6, teachers as reflective professionals, are free to choose the titles they consider their pupils would most enjoy and learn from. However, there is another risk to teacher's exercising their professional judgement. Publishers have tried to help resource the Literacy Hour making available big books, CD-ROMs, cassette recordings as well as the more traditional print books. Often huge packages promising everything you need from Reception to Year 6 in the way of materials are marketed. But adherence to one publishing programme, however good, risks taking the skill and creativity out of teaching.

Judith Graham raises the issue of the kind of resources we should use in the Literacy Hour. She suggests that some rather emotionally charged texts may not stand up well to the sort of 'dissection' required about language and literary devices. Rather, she would choose robust stories and picture books; Quentin Blake's *Mr Magnolia* she thinks, would survive. The rhymes – boot, rooty toot, flute, newt, suit, hoot, scoot, chute, fruit, salute and brute – all unleash Blake's inventive images and 'will bear examining and yield up their phonic irregularities with no loss of delight' (Graham, 1999, in Goodwin, 1999). Students returning from teaching practice enjoyed discussing the issue raised by Graham. There were different views but quite a number of students argued that it was when they introduced texts of some emotional power, particularly to older classes, the children became involved and wanted to talk about all aspects of the texts in depth.

Assessment based on the performance of pilot schools suggested that the implementation of the literacy strategy had improved reading standards, the rate of improvement being particularly notable in the case of girls and pupils speaking English as an additional language. This has been borne out by subsequent evaluations of schools beyond those involved in the pilot (see Sainsbury, 2000). OFSTED's interim evaluation pinpointed writing and independent group activities and teaching generally in Years 3 and 4 as aspects in need of improvement (OFSTED, 1999).

Two things are likely to contribute to the value of the Literacy Hour as a strategy to develop children's language and literacy. First, it will help if there is some flexibility over how the hour is organised and used. It may, for example, be helpful to reserve one 'Literacy Hour' each week for extended debate, reading or writing. Second, faced with this continuing challenge, teachers need to be motivated and encouraged by the support and interest head teachers and English Co-ordinators can provide.

Graham, Judith (1999) 'The Creation of Readers or Mr Magnolia meets the Literacy Hour. Will he survive?' in Goodwin, Prue (ed.) *The Literate Classroom* London: David Fulton.

Graham.J and Kelly, A. (2000) *Reading Under Control* London: David Fulton. Chapter 3.

Office for Standards in Education (OFSTED, 1999) *The National Literacy Strategy: An Interim Evaluation* London: OFSTED.

Sainsbury, Marian *Evaluation of the National Literacy Strategy Summary Report* National Foundation for Educational Research (Tel. 0845 6022260).

The Standards website: www.standards.dfee.gov.uk

Wyse, Dominic and Jones, Russell (2001) *Teaching English, Language and Literacy.* London: Routledge Falmer.

Literacy Land

Literacy Land is an up-to-date reading programmes which helps meet the requirements of the National Literacy Strategy and offers support to children's reading across the curriculum. It has three strands: story street, genre range and info-trail. Many of the books are by acclaimed authors.

Coles, Martin and Hall, Christine *Literacy Land* London: Pearson Education (Tel. 0800 579579).

Literary criticism

See also genre, history of children's literature, picture books, subject knowledge

Literary criticism is the study of literary texts. The term has usually been applied to the evaluation of texts for adults but, more recently, specialist critical theories and terminologies are being developed specifically in relation to children's literature (Hunt, 201, p. 2). The National Curriculum English programmes and the National Literacy Strategy *Framework for Teaching* require teachers to use a set of terms to discuss and think about the texts they use both in and outside the Literacy Hour. Not all the terms used will be appropriate to use with the children but they will be helpful to teachers when discussing their work with each other. The subject knowledge in both language and literature that teachers need is set out in *Circular 4/98* (DfEE, 1998). Teachers also find help on analysing texts, both fiction and non-fiction, in Chapters 9 and 10 of Angela Wilson's book *Language Knowledge for Primary Teachers* (2001) and in Medwell *et al.*'s *Primary English: Knowledge and Understanding* (2001).

Some of the terms are traditional ones like those to assign a work to a category – novel, drama, epic, sonnet. Others are technical expressions like iambic pentameters or rhyming couplets, or stylistic ones for example imagery, metaphor, simile, alliteration and onomatopoeia. The twentieth century brought new criticisms including structuralism and feminist criticism with whole new terminologies and concepts – deconstruction, intertextuality, meta-fiction and postmodernism. Obviously teachers need to know the distinguishing features of traditional tales, novels and ballads in order to teach about them. But do these later developments in literary theory have relevance to the teacher in the classroom? Interestingly, many teachers have been drawn into this world of literary theory through their interest in the children's picture book. The best picture books are original and highly sophisticated works of art which make considerable demands on the reader. For one thing the reader has to relate non-linear 'reading' of the picture to linear processing of words (Hunt, 2001, p. 288). In a story like Pat Hutchin's *Rosie's Walk* there is a thrilling mismatch between the blandness of the verbal and the threatened chaos of the visual. A new meta-language for discussing children's picture books is springing up. Jane Doonan, for

example, refers to pictures' 'schemes of colour', 'small and large patterning' and 'network of linear rhythms' (Doonan, 1993). David Lewis has produced a scholarly analysis of the postmodern elements in children's picture books (Lewis, 1990, p. 133) and, more recently, *Reading Contemporary Picturebooks* (Lewis, 2001).

Doonan, Jane (1993) *Looking at Pictures in Picture Books* Stroud: The Thimble Press.

Hunt, Peter (2001) *Children's Literature* London: Blackwell.

Lewis, David (1990) 'The Constructedness of Text: Picture Books and the Metafictive', *Signal*, 62, 131–46.

Lewis, David (2001) *Reading Contemporary Picturebooks: Picturing text* London: Routledge.

Medwell, Jane, Moore, George, Wray, David and Griffiths, Vivienne (2001) *Primary English: Knowledge and Understanding* Exeter: Learning Matters.

Wilson, Angela (2001, second edition) *Language Knowledge for Primary Teachers* London: David Fulton.

Literature across the curriculum

See also Art & English, Drama & English, fiction as a source of information, Geography & English, History & English, Mathematics & English, Music & English, Religious Studies & English, Science & English, Technology & English

In the primary years part of learning history, science and so on is to do with learning to think, speak and write in particular ways and with taking on a specialist terminology. Each subject is resourced with information texts, both print and on screen. But, particularly when we are beginning some new topic in one of the primary curriculum areas, it is important to help children gain a personal foothold. We do this when we help children to organise in discussion their existing knowledge and experience – what do you already know about magnets, volcanoes, the Vikings or patterns? Fiction can also help children get involved with a topic and it may help to read a book or poem at the start or finish of a topic or series of lessons or alongside the work. There are examples of fiction to awaken the imagination under the entries in the '*See also*' part of this entry. The very youngest children can learn about the past through story by looking at picture books like the Ahlbergs' *Peepo!* which shows the clothes and objects of an Edwardian childhood. Older children learning about the Second World War find inspiration in books about the impact of war on the young like Nina Bawden's *Carrie's War* and *Anne Frank's Diary* Other stories invite the sort of map work that would link with Geography, for example Beverley Naidoo's *Journey to Jo'burg*. The story would also be a sympathetic introduction to human and cultural geography (Marriott, 1995, p. 127). There is more about the potential of fiction in Stuart Marriott's *Read On* and in Lewisham's *Find That Book*.

As well as reading fiction, children sometimes write stories in response to work on a topic across the curriculum. There can be an interesting interplay between different texts and different ways of looking at topics. For example Nicola Moon's *Billy's Sunflower* could lead to the children's own stories about plants and to more science-based writing about observations as new seeds grow (*Find That Book*, 1999).

Find That Book: making links between literature and the broader curriculum Lewisham Education and Culture 1999 (available from Lewisham Professional Development Centre, Kilmorie Road, London SE23 2SP, Tel. 0208 314 6146).

Marriott, Stuart (1995) *Read On: Using Fiction in the Primary School* London: Paul Chapman.

London Reading Test

See also cloze procedure, reading age, Standardised Reading Tests

Published by the NFER in 1981 this group, written, untimed test with a score range of 6.0–12.0 years is for Year 6 (10–11 year olds). It is in the form of prose paragraphs and uses cloze procedure and comprehension questions.

Look and say

See also reading

'Look and say' is an approach to the teaching of reading which aims to build up a sight vocabulary. The stress is on the whole word and sometimes teachers using this method would hold up flash cards so that children could learn the pattern of the word. Often the 'look and say' and 'phonic' approaches were combined in a practice which was common up until the 1970s. Reading schemes, for example *Janet and John* and *Jane and Peter*, aimed to build up key words and to use a restricted vocabulary to reinforce them.

Traditional 'Look and say' teaching tended to place children in a passive role and reflected a behaviourist approach of stimulus and response- the stimulus was the word in book or on flash card and the response was the child's saying of the word. But learning the patterns of words and what the letter strings look like has a place in current reading programmes.

M

Magazines – see advertisements, comics, newspapers

Magic – see fairy tales, fantasy, traditional tales

Magic e

This refers to the 'e' at the end of a word (after a consonant) which gives a long value to the vowel before the consonant as in mope, make and site.

Management – see English Co-ordinator

Marking

See also assessment, composition, process approach to writing, proof reading, transcriptional aspects of writing, tick sheets, writing

Teachers make an oral response to children's writing whenever teacher and child look at a draft or fair copy together. This is a good context in which to intervene as teacher and child can see quickly whether they understand each other. In line with a 'process' approach, children can be helped to improve their work before it reaches final draft. Children also appreciate a written response on some of their work and this helps a child take an interest in which pieces of writing are placed in his or her portfolio to show progress. I have also found that parents are very interested in the teacher's comments when they look at work on parents' evening or open day. It gives them clear evidence of how you are intervening to help their child make progress. Older primary children are likely to write quite a lot each week and, as Wyse and Jones point out, there needs to be a whole-school marking policy

to make the job manageable (Wyse and Jones, 2000, p. 176). First the policy might attend to how to select samples for careful marking and perhaps others for skim reading acknowledged by a tick or teacher's initials. Range might be one criterion: it might be decided that during half a term the teacher will mark at least one piece of writing in each of the different genres introduced during that period. Second, strategies might be agreed for marking a piece of writing. Many teachers like to make a difference between secretarial corrections and suggestions for redrafting which involve reorganising the content or compositional aspect of the work. In the 'proof reading' entry I suggested that children might like to learn some of the conventional symbols for spelling and punctuation errors and omissions. This would be helpful if the teacher set up writing partners to look at secretarial aspects of each other's work.

The final comments might include – praise for the strong aspects of the work, for example 'an inviting beginning' or 'good, convincing dialogue', then advice about a weak point 'you need to keep up the pace of the action' or 'vocabulary needs to be more varied' and finally one or two clear 'next step' suggestions. These could be to do with global aspects of the writing' let us work on paragraphing together on your next draft' or with elements like characterisation or setting the scene. In *Writing Under Control* Liz Laycock mentions the practice of a teacher who asked the children to do some of their writing in a book, leaving one page blank for redrafting suggestions and attempts. This fits with Laycock's suggestion that we think less in terms of 'marking 'and 'correction' and more of 'feedback' and 'response'.

Graham, Judith and Kelly, Alison (eds) (1998) *Writing Under Control* London: David Fulton.

Wyse, Dominic and Jones, Russell (2000) *Teaching English, Language and Literacy* London: Routledge/Falmer.

Mass noun (uncountable noun)

See also count, grammar, noun, parts of speech

When a noun is not normally used in the plural we term it a mass or uncountable noun. They are rarely if ever used with the indefinite article – 'a' or 'an'. Examples include: greed, salt, cotton.

Mathematics & English

See also diagrams, language across the curriculum, visual literacy

There are two considerations here: how language helps children learn mathematical concepts through speaking and listening and reading and writing; how an 'English' approach to number and problem solving using stories, games and poems brings greater insight. Language used to discuss, question and speculate has an important role in mathematics as children learn about terms, concepts and the stages in solving problems. We want children to talk about mathematical ideas using their own language but there are important technical terms to learn which need good contextual support. We might praise a child for using the word 'oval' appropriately but add that mathematicians also use the word 'ellipse' to mean the same thing. Mathematical dictionaries or charts help to encourage children to check the meaning of words like 'mass', 'weight', 'tessellate' and 'estimate'. How mathematical texts – whether in print in the form of books, work sheets or work cards or on the screen – are written and presented is important. We want tasks that challenge and extend children's investigative abilities. We need to keep in mind that the children using them are at different stages in their reading development and will need different levels of mediation.

There was a time in the 1970s and 1980s when mathematics texts seemed to address children directly and this could be lonely for them because it reduced interaction with teacher and peers. Although there is a new emphasis on mental mathematics there is also recognition of the role of the teacher who intervenes to support, encourage and extend a child's thinking. Children enjoy working collaboratively to solve problems. So while there are non-verbal dimensions in mathematics, talk is a vital way of helping young children make sense of mathematics and relate it to real life experience. If you would like to read more about the role of talk in mathematics, particularly where children of six years and under are concerned, I recommend Janet Evans' article 'Five little dollies jumping on the bed'–Learning about mathematics through talk' (Godwin, 2001). There is welcome recognition for the role of talk in learning in the Qualifications and Curriculum Authority's *Curriculum Guidance for the Foundation Stage* (QCA, 2000) in which attention is drawn to the importance of children using talk to make connections between things. The centrality of talk in learning also underpins much of the National Numeracy Strategy (DfEE, 1999). Three types of talk are mentioned here: teacher's talk to introduce new concepts, teacher led discussion and children's task-focused talk with their peers. Mathematics texts may be used in the Literacy Hour to help children explore procedural and problem solving kinds of writing. Numbers, symbols, diagrams and verbal labelling all interact to make meaning and there are a number of very good big books to demonstrate all this. Where books show children engaging in mathematical activities we should ensure that girls and children from ethnic minorities see positive reflections of themselves as young mathematicians. Teachers and children often make their own mathematics materials – books and games – and add them to the classroom collection.

There is a creative, explorative side to mathematics which links it to the spirit of English and helps motivate children. For very young children there are imaginative number books which tell a story. For example, Simone Lia's *Billy Bean's Dream* (David & Charles) tells the story of the building of a rocket by Billy Bean and his friends and his friends' pets – there are so many things to count: the jellybeans, the work tools, the sandwiches and the stars as the rocket finally zooms into the sky. The book also shows how to work well in a team. In the school context, fiction – stories and poems – which includes vocabulary to do with size, measurement and money – help children secure mathematical kinds of thinking in an enjoyable way. For example teachers often use Browning's *The Pied Piper of Hamelin* in which there is much reference to size – the rats are lean, great and so on. Number songs like 'One Man Went to Mow' have much potential for singing and acting out. Each time another person enters 'the meadow' the children can pause and check the right number are there. These number songs can be reshaped by teacher and children to fit with current activities and preoccupations. Evans worked with four to five year olds on Ted Arnold's story-song *Five Ugly Monsters* (Scholastic, 1988) and soon the monsters became 'five little dollies' as the children had to hand some dollies they had been using earlier for an attribute exercise. In this work English and mathematics were truly entwined in an exciting way. The children enjoyed singing and acting out their own version of a story-song which was made into their own big book for shared reading. Their mathematical experiences included using the language of sorting and sets in context, counting from nought to five, exploring mathematical patterns and talking about number values (Evans, 2001, p. 76). Alongside the role play and practical work, the teacher scribed the story and included the numbers patterns. Let me give an example here. In one verse, four of the dollies are jumping on the bed and one dolly is on the floor – so the teacher wrote: 4 and 1 = 5. Writing the symbols clinched all that had been learnt through talk. For a most interesting account of how an interplay between practical activities and recording mathematical findings in symbols see Evans' book 'Have some Maths with Your Story' (Evans, 1995).

Children can be asked to estimate the number of days a fantasy journey in a book or poem might take. For example, working from Edward Lear's 'The Jumblies' (*A Book of Nonsense*, Dragon's World Publishers) they could estimate the amount of time the Jumblies were away,

using different clues. Or they might create their own notion of what Jumblie time might be like. Perhaps they have a different number of hours in the day?

DfEE (1999) *The National Numeracy Strategy: Framework for Teaching Mathematics from Reception to Year 6* London: DfEE.

Evans, Janet (1995) *Have Some Maths with Your Story* Liverpool: Janev Publications.

Evans, Janet (2001) 'Four little dollies jumping on the bed – Learning about mathematics through talk' in Godwin, Prue (ed.) *The Articulate Classroom* London: David Fulton.

The Mathematics Association (1987) *Maths Talk* Cheltenham: Stanley Thornes.

Media studies – see advertisements, CD-ROM, Information and Communications Technology (ICT) & English, newspapers, television and literacy, video-film, visual literacy

Medium-term plans – see English Co-ordinator, planning

Metacognition

See also constructivism, critical discourse, language and thought, non-fiction reading and writing

Metacognition is the awareness an individual has of how he or she has come to know something. Knowing oneself as a learner can lead to adopting more effective strategies and acting on them. For example, I find I need first to mark out a global structure, an overall plan, of the articles and reviews I write. Then I start working under each subheading. Being in control of our learning often involves some self-checking. As Riley and Prentice put it, 'being able to highlight for oneself those aspects of a learning task yet to be accomplished is emerging as one of the most valuable skills through which intellectual functioning can be enhanced' (pp. 8–9, Riley and Prentice, 1999). This active involvement in one's own learning strategies is close to the spirit of the constructivist model (see constructivism).

How do we help children develop the ability

to monitor their own learning progress? Discussion with children about their reading and writing over a period of time creates a context for talking about what they find easy and what they find difficult and what might help. To give a focus for such discussions it is helpful to have to hand perhaps the child's annotated reading journal or a selection of writing samples from which some are to be chosen, jointly, by teacher and child for their English portfolio. Children learn how to develop good strategies by observing the teacher and other children and from the feedback teachers provide (Galloway and Edwards 1991, p. 10). Searching for information is an area in which metacognitive abilities are particularly useful. It is not just a matter of hearing 'the facts' explained or reading them from one source. Teachers help children identify their purpose and then use all available resources – books, illustrations, CR-ROMs, the Internet, visiting experts – and sometimes their own first- hand observation. Then there are strategies to control like note taking, summarising and sharing findings in a way that will interest others.

Galloway and Edwards (1991) *Primary School Teaching and Educational Psychology* London: Longman.

Riley, Jeni and Prentice, Roy (1999) *The Curriculum for 7–11 Year Olds* London: Paul Chapman.

Metalanguage

See also Information and Communications Technology (ICT) and English, functions of language, reading, subject knowledge, visual literacy, writing

Metalanguage is a linguistic term which refers to language to talk about language.

The linguist M.A.K. Halliday proposed some functions for a young child's use of language (see under *Functions of language* entry). One of these, the heuristic function, enables a child to discover much about the world and their experience. One of things they find out about is language itself (Halliday in Wade, 1982). They hear parents comment on their developing language use – 'new word', 'a lot of questions' and so on.

When a child learns to read and write he or she will hear and use words like 'letter', 'sound', 'page', 'spelling', 'vowel', 'consonant' and 'phoneme'. Through the primary years he or she will learn to talk about different language forms and their features – the 'plot', 'setting' and 'characters' of a novel or story and the 'rhythm', 'rhyme' and 'metre' of poetry. The discussion of word meanings across the curriculum involves teachers and children in using a metalanguage to explain and discuss them. So in history we might talk about the concept of 'medieval', 'feudal' or 'chronology', in science about 'catalyst', 'chemical' or 'solution' and in geography about 'igneous' and 'sedimentary' rocks, 'environment' and 'boundaries'. Becoming more conscious of these terms and concepts also makes us more aware of our own learning processes and metalinguistic awareness therefore links with metacognition.

Changes in society bring about change in vocabulary as we need new terms to grapple with the new concepts. The need to acquire the ability to interpret and to create electronic texts has brought about new electronic literacies with their own concepts and terminology. Teachers use terms like 'computer literacy', 'network literacy' and 'online literacy' to refer to reading and writing using the new technology. Children now talk about 'hyperlinks' – a series of hot text links which enable users to navigate through a collection of screens or web pages – and to 'framing' – decisions about how much information is given to the viewer.

The need to explore the meaning of visual texts, still or moving, is giving rise to a vocabulary in which to discuss this kind of reading; for example we refer to 'composition' as the combination of the elements of an image into a whole text and to 'multi-modal' – to indicate a text that draws on a variety of communication modes – spoken, written, visual and spatial.

Halliday, M.A.K. (1982) 'Relevant Models of Language' in Wade, Barry (ed.) *Language Perspectives* London: Heinemann.

Metaphor

See also poetry, simile, subject knowledge

Metaphor permeates our use of language and it is difficult to imagine speaking or writing without this enrichment. While a simile makes the comparison between phenomena fully explicit – 'he fought like a lion' or 'she was a slight as a fairy' – a metaphor identifies two things with each other 'he was the lion of the team' or 'she was the fairy in the group'. So, in a metaphor, the qualities of the first thing carry over into the second.

Although metaphors occur in prose, they are more common in poetry and enjoying poems is a good context for introducing and learning about metaphor. While very young children tend to become locked into literal meanings by age seven or eight most children's thinking has become sufficiently flexible to understand metaphors.

Metaphors in education

See also apprenticeship approach to reading, child-centred learning, reading, scaffolding

Educational writing is rich in metaphor. We have the behaviourist view of the child as a 'sponge' or 'vessel' to be filled, while the child-centred philosopher will often refer to the child as a 'plant' which will grow given certain necessary conditions.

More interactive models of teaching and learning will see the child as an 'apprentice'. Bruner's metaphor of the adult 'scaffolding' a child's learning so that the joint achievement is greater than what the less mature partner could have managed alone also presents learning as a partnership. The good teacher 'lends' essentially temporary structure and support which, like a scaffold during building, can eventually be removed.

The reading process has also had its share of metaphors. Bussis thought of the cueing systems – syntactic, grapho-phonic and semantic – as instruments in an orchestra. The current model in the *National Literacy Strategy Framework for Teaching* (DfEE, 1998) takes as its guiding metaphor the notion of the cueing systems as searchlights on the reading process.

Metaphors are a powerful way of referring to particular ways of seeing the educational process and the only certain thing is that each one will fall out of favour and be replaced by another or others.

Bussis, A. *et al.* (1985) *Inquiry into Meaning: An investigation of Learning to Read* Hillsdale, NJ: Lawrence Erlbaum Associates.

Methods of English Teaching – see History of English teaching

Metonymy

This is a figure of speech in which something is brought to mind by mentioning something associated with it. So it is linked with the use of metaphor. Well-known uses of metonymy include 'crown' to suggest monarchy, 'bottle' to suggest alcohol and 'Downing Street' for the Prime Minister.

Metre

This refers to the poetic rhythm of a text determined by the number of feet, or beats, to the line and the nature of the stress on syllables. For example, an iambic meter uses iambuses which each consist of a stressed and unstressed syllable, for example,

'Bobby Shaftoe went to sea'

consists of four iambuses when 'sea' is pronounced 'see-ee'.

Miscue analysis

See also assessment, reading, record keeping and running reading records

Miscue analysis is a diagnostic reading procedure useful in helping to pinpoint children's strengths and weaknesses. It was devised by Goodman, 1973, who famously claimed it opened up a 'window onto the reading process'. There are a number of versions of miscue analysis, including a user-friendly one in Helen Arnold's book *Listening to Children Reading*. 'Running reading records' are a simple form of miscue analysis in which every word read correctly is marked with a stroke on a copy of the page.

There is detailed explanation of how to administer miscue analysis and of how to interpret the results in Graham and Kelly (2000, pp. 121–7) and Browne (1996, pp. 228–32). Rather than simply providing a stark score or reading age, miscue analysis – if conscientiously carried out – reveals which strategies the young reader controls well and where some support is needed. The use of the word 'miscue' rather than 'mistake' indicates a positive approach to a young reader's efforts to process the text drawing on different strategies.

Miscue analysis is usually carried out with newly independent readers or with older primary aged children who have a difficulty with reading. About 300 words of unfamiliar text, which makes some demands on the child without reaching frustration level, is usually chosen. You need a copy of the passage to mark in the miscues as the child reads out loud. Some teachers like to read with the child up to the selected passage so that he or she does not come to the task 'cold'. It is helpful to tape record the child reading and to explain you want to listen again so you can help them. Tell the child that you want them to try out any new words and that on this occasion you will not interrupt to help. (Of course it is best just to supply the word if children become confused and upset.) Teachers try to make the task as anxiety-free as possible and, when the analysis is complete, talk with the child about the meaning of the text, stressing the enjoyment element. Mark the photocopied text with symbols for omissions, substitutions, insertions, reversals, repetitions, hesitation and self correction (see chart below).

Symbols for marking miscues on photocopy of text read aloud by children

Omission	Circle the word/part of word which the child has missed out.
	e.g. 'Clara and Cliff⟨ord⟩ get on very well'.
Substitution	Write in word/part of word child has substituted above appropriate part
	of the text.
	mustard
	e.g. 'and mushy peas'.
Insertion	Write added word above a caret ^
	e.g. 'Clara Cliff takes ^ᵃ Clifford Climber'.
Reversal Use	transpositional symbol
	e.g. 'Cats', Clara says.
Repetition	Draw a line from left to right under the portion of text repeated.
	e.g. 'Yum yum!' says Clifford.
Hesitation	Place an oblique stroke over or next to word or phrase over which child hesitates.
	e.g. ' /lawful wedded husband'.
Self correction	Write SC over word or phrase child self corrects
	e.g. 'Fish and chips'. (Child said 'first and chips' and then quickly self-
	corrected to 'fish and chips').
Assistance	Write 'I' above a word or phrase supplied by teacher.

(Examples are from six-year-old Charlie's reading of Alan Ahlberg's 'Ms Cliff the Climber'.)

Then you can show the results of a miscue analysis in a simple diagram similar to the one below:

Diagram to summarise miscues

Name and age:
Date:
Book details:

Miscue types	Symbol	Number	Comment
Omission	⬭		
Substitution	write word		
Insertion	∧		
Reversal	⌐		
Repetition	⎯⎯		
Hesitation	/		
Self correction	SC		
Assistance	T		

Summary of child's strengths and limitations

Next step comment

Although the conversation between the child and the teacher afterwards is not part of the formal procedure, the child's comments may be useful in confirming aspects of the diagnosis – that he or she was reading for meaning, for example.

If the miscue analysis is to be placed in a child's portfolio, a brief summary should accompany it explaining the significance of the results. Does the child, for example, show good use of self-correction strategies using visual and phonic cues? Does he or she use cues from the general context of the passage? How did the results inform the teacher's planning?

Arnold, Helen (1982) *Listening to Children Reading* Sevenoaks: Hodder & Stoughton.

Browne, Ann (1996) *Developing Language and Literacy 3–8* London: Paul Chapman.

Graham, Judith and Kelly, Alison (2000, second edition) *Reading Under Control* London: David Fulton, pp. 121–8.

Mnemonics

A mnemonic is a word, phrase or rhyme which helps you remember something.

In spelling, for example, you might use the mnemonic – 'i' before 'e' except after 'c'; or an 'e' for envelope after the 'n' of 'stationery'.

Modal verb

See also auxiliary verb, infinitive, parts of speech

A modal verb is a sub-category of the auxiliary verb class. See the list below:

> can/could
> will/would
> must ought
> may/might
> shall/should

Modal verbs are used to indicate prediction (Roger *will* be in Rome soon), speculation (I *may* decide to go out) and necessity (You *must* leave now).

In these examples the modal verbs are 'will', 'may' and 'must' and the infinitives which follow each of them are 'be', 'decide' and 'leave'.

Mode

See also register

Mode is part of the abstract linguistic concept known as 'register' and refers both to the pattern of the text and to the medium in which a spoken or written message is given. Patterns in a text are achieved by combinations of grammar and vocabulary – for example a story has a temporal pattern while a science text may have a cause and effect pattern instead of, or as well as, a sequence of events. Understanding the different text patterns helps children appreciate the purpose of a particular text.

The medium for a written text might be a white board, a print or electronic work sheet or a book.

Models of English teaching – see under History of English teaching

Models of language – see communicative competence/competenes and performance, functions of language, language acquisition, language and thought, nativist approach to language acquisition, transformational grammar

Modelling (of language processes)

See also reading, speaking and listening, writing

'Modelling 'is a term used to describe the demonstration of a skill or means of going about something. It is often used in the shared reading part of the Literacy Hour to show children how to understand and apply the cueing systems which help us to read and skimming and scanning strategies in non-fiction reading. Enlarged texts are often used for this purpose. In shared writing, teachers demonstrate or 'model' how to plan, write and edit written texts, how to apply spelling strategies and how to proof read. When carried out well, it is in the spirit of Vygotsky's notion of the 'zone of proximal development' where the adult can, by the right kind of intervention, move young learners on further than they would

manage alone. It is also compatible with Bruner's proposal that we 'scaffold' children's learning.

Mood

In traditional English grammar there are three 'moods', expressed in clauses and sentences, which affect the meaning:

- the indicative mood which includes statements and questions as in 'He liked her' and 'He liked her?'
- the imperative mood expresses commands, requests, warnings or offers as in 'Sit down!', 'Please sit down', 'Look out!' and 'Have some more'.
- the subjunctive mood which expresses attitudes and wishes as in 'She preferred that it was not mentioned' or 'I wish my mother could have been here'.

Morpheme

See also reading

A morpheme is the smallest unit of meaning. A word might be one morpheme as in 'hand' or contain two or more morphemes as in 'handshake', 'handstands'. Prefixes (un, dis, in) and suffixes (ed, al, s) which can be added to change a word's meaning are morphemes.

Morphology

This is a linguistic term referring to the structure of words in contrast to 'syntax' which is the study of the order of words in the larger units of phrase, clause and sentence. The two kinds of morphology are: inflectional morphology which attends to how parts of speech are changed to indicate number, tense and so on and lexical morphology which is the study of word-formation.

Mother tongue

See also bilingualism, multilingualism

This usually refers to the language of a person's childhood home. Young emergent bilingual children need to go on developing their competence as speakers, readers and writers in their mother tongue while taking on their new language. If they do not, then they cease to be 'emergently bilingual' in a meaningful way. Researchers, like for example B. Mayor (1988), have linked children's intellectual development to their continuing progress in their home language. This progress may be sustained mainly at home or at community schools at the weekend. But home languages can still be respected and acknowledged in school – made visible in environmental print and in dual-language big books, and CD-ROMs and bilingual books. Tapes of books or songs in children's home or mother tongue languages are also a useful resource whether they are commercial or made by parents or older children. Interestingly, recent research suggests that all children, not just emergent bilinguals, benefit from initiatives to respect and recognise children's home languages (Thomas and Collier, 1998).

Mayor, B. (1988) 'What does it mean to be bilingual?' in Mercer, N. (ed.) *Language and Literacy from an Educational Perspective Vol. 1* Milton Keynes: Open University Press.

Thomas, W.P. and Collier, V.P. (1998) 'Two languages are better than one'. *Educational Leadership, Vol.* 55, pp. 23–6.

Motivation

See also big shapes, book making, collaborative learning, constructivism, English Co-ordinator, reading corner/area, shared writing, writing area/corner

'Motivation' is a psychological term to do with a person having the feeling that they want to do something, usually because they have a purpose and need for doing so.

Speaking of curriculum reform, Wyse and Jones comment: 'If higher standards are to be achieved, it is essential to fully involve those people who arguably are going to be most affected by the changes, namely the children' (Wyse and Jones, 2001, pp. 16–17).

There is a lot to cover in a modern primary English programme, including challenging work in gaining phonemic awareness in learning to read and understanding letter strings to improve

spelling. These aspects are important, but if they are over-emphasised we risk a narrow view of the English curriculum and lessons that do not fully involve and interest young learners. The necessary language skills or 'smaller shapes' are best set in the framework of wider intentions and purposes, sometimes called the 'big shapes'. Let us take the 'big shape' of helping children understand how stories work as tellers, readers and writers. There is everything to be gained from making sure the classroom is an encouraging environment by having displays of books and children's work. Experienced teachers also know that children's enjoyment of learning is increased by sharing and collaborating with their peers. Speaking and listening and particularly talking about texts is a powerful context for language development. Here works like Aidan Chambers' *Tell Me* show convincing examples of children extending their understanding of stories through talk with both peers and adults. Improvisation and role play also contribute to enthusiastic kinds of writing from a meaningful context. Shared reading provides the opportunity for the teacher to read stories in a way that will involve and excite the children. Retellings and discussion of the features of the stories and poems they are reading and later reading their own stories out loud help make work satisfying. Improvisation and language games are likely to enthuse children. When it comes to writing, we know that the 'process' approach of Donald Graves ensured high levels of motivation as children had some choice over what they wrote about and how they wrote it at each stage (Graves, 1983). If rich experiences precede children's writing, they are much more likely to have the will to write as well as they can, and to attend to the secretarial aspects that ensure their stories can be understood and enjoyed by others.

Teachers also need to feel interested and involved in their work and too much change and prescription can put their motivation at risk. Curriculum reformers need to involve them and consult them. It is the English Co-ordinator who can make the difference when it comes to teachers feeling part of a well-motivated team who are dedicated to supporting children's enjoyment of the process of becoming eager readers, writers and speakers.

Chambers, Aidan (1993) *Tell Me* Stroud: The Thimble Press.

Graves, Donald (1983) *Writing: Teachers and Children at Work* Portsmouth, NH: Heinemann Educational Books.

Wyse, Dominic and Jones, Russell (2001) *Teaching English: Language and Literacy* London: Routledge.

Moving images and literacy – see television and literacy, video-film and visual literacy.

Multiculturalism (or cultural pluralism)

See also bilingualism, carnival, dual-language texts, equal opportunities, multilingualism, traditional tales

The term 'multiculturalism' can simply mean the coexistence of several different cultures in one place but it usually has a political connotation. It can be used to refer to a socio-political ideal which encourages the cultural freedom and the development of different cultures in a plural society.

The term 'multicultural school' usually means a school which recognises in its curriculum and social policy making the diversity of cultures represented in the intake. This implies more than a few token gestures towards festivals across the world (although this might be part of it) and has to do first of all with attitudes, priorities and a belief that all the children and staff will benefit from strong links and activities involving the different communities. Some of the work in the National Curriculum programmes has thematic potential – journeys, ourselves, traditional tales – and multicultural dimensions can helpfully be explored. Schools following a multicultural approach, in more than a superficial way, make parents and friends of the school welcome and value their contributions – perhaps in making dual-language versions of books and advising on customs like tea ceremonies. The Carnival entry shows the cultural sharing that is encouraged in this kind of initiative.

As well as these positive attitudes, a school wishing to reflect multicultural values will put much thought into the range of resources provided; the English Co-ordinator nearly always has a key role to play. We want resources – both fiction and non fiction – which reflect the different parts of the world where the children have their roots. But all the children in the school deserve the very best texts from across the world. One of the most helpful guides to multicultural books is *A Multicultural Guide to Children's Books 0–12* edited by Rosemary Stones. This work is helpfully annotated giving critical evaluations of the materials, including dual-language texts (which vary in quality of translation) and including interviews by the different authors. Listening to, reading and telling stories from across the world crosses cultural boundaries and reinforces the values of the multicultural approach (see for example Gregory, 1997 and MacLean, 1996).

Gregory, Eve (1997) *Making Sense of a New World: Learning to Read in a Second Language* London: Paul Chapman (see Chapter 5).

MacLean, K. (1996) 'Supporting the literacy of bilingual learners: storytelling and bookmaking'. *Multicultural Teaching* Vol. 2, 26–9.

Stones, Rosemary (ed.) (1999 edition) *A Multicultural Guide to Children's Books 0–12* London: Books for Keeps and The Reading Language Information Centre.

Multi-layered texts – see under picture book

Multilingualism

See also bilingualism, dual-language texts, equal opportunities, language variety, mother tongue, multiculturalism

If a person is described as being 'multilingual' it usually means they control three or more languages. The degree of competence required in each language to qualify for the description is more controversial; it ranges from high competence to enough knowledge to meet particular purposes. In countries like India it would be unusual to be unilingual (or monolingual) but individuals may have different degrees of knowledge and understanding in each language. They might, for example, use one language in the home and another at work, another spoken but not written and another just read.

In the school context we have many children in British schools who control, to some degree, three or more languages and therefore are likely to have considerable linguistic ability which the teacher can build on. While their parents will want them to become confident in English as speakers and as readers and writers, they may also want them to develop in their own first languages as well.

Wyse and Grant (2001) remind us that multilingual children are not a homogenous group. Some children will be newcomers while others will have been born in this country and be second or third generation. Communities differ in how far they want their children to embrace British language and customs and how far they wish them to maintain their cultural identity within their new 'host' community.

There are suggestions for good practice in supporting young bilingual children in taking on their new language and culture under the 'bilingualism' entry.

Wyse, Dominic and Grant, Russell (2001) 'Supporting black and multilingual children' Chapter 29 in *Teaching English, Language and Literacy* London: Routledge.

Multi-media – see advertisements, CD-ROM, Information and Communications Technology (ICT) & English, television and literacy, video-film, visual literacy

Multi-sensory approaches

Multi-sensory approaches to reading use all the senses – touch, hearing, movement and sight – to help young children to recognise letters of the alphabet. They can make the letter shapes in sand, feel textured letters or find the right letter in a bag of wooden or plastic letters. The feel of different kinds of cloth and paper can be exploited in the interactive alphabet books teachers and children make.

Hearing as well as seeing 'onsets' and 'rimes' reinforces the patterns and when it comes to writing, the actual handwriting movement can help children memorise spelling patterns.

Music & English – see Physical Education & English

Myths

See also creation stories, traditional tales

Myths are culturally significant traditional stories about gods and heroes and the best illuminate problems of human existence. One important category is the creation story which attempts, within a particular cultural setting, to explain how the world began.

The imaginative power of many of the retellings and the possibilities for art, drama, writing and discussion make them a strong part of the English programme. Because their origins are often in the oral tradition they can be modified and adapted for different audiences and purposes. For a delightful tale seeking to explain why different animal species are unable to live together see Francesca Martin's *The Honey Hunters: a Traditional African Tale* (Walker Books, 1992). If you want a collection for younger primary children or less able older children Marcia Williams' *Greek Myths for Younger Children* (Walker Books) presents the stories of Orpheus, Perseus and other Greek heroes in amusing cartoon format. Myths often have quite complicated narrative structures and many collections of retellings are most suitable for older primary school children. Even then, they are often best read out loud and shared. Examples include the story based on a Zulu myth retold by Margaret Wolfson and entitled *Marriage of the Rain Goddess: a South African myth* (Barefoot Books, 1996) and *Ishtar and Tammuz: a Babylonian myth of the seasons* by Christopher Moore (Frances Lincoln, 1996) which explains the rhythm of the seasons. The Belitha Press collections of myths and legends include stories from

Africa, China, South America and Celtic tales. Each collection has an introduction putting the tales in a helpful context. There are further annotated booklists in Stones, 1999, pp. 27– 34 and Phinn, 2000, pp. 29–32.

Phinn, Gervase (2000) *Young Readers and their Books* London: David Fulton.

Stones, Rosemary (ed.) (1999) *A Multicultural Guide to Children's Books 0–16* London: Books for Keeps.

Narrative

See also fiction, genre, History & English, novels short stories, story, storytelling, text level work, writing

A narrative usually tells of events using the past tense. When the events are from the imagination we tend to call the narrative 'a story'. But of course even when we tell of real incidents, about our recent holiday to friends perhaps, we often reshape what happened to add interest! The recognition that narrative is a basic way of organising human experience through remembering, dreaming and planning is made in Barbara Hardy's 'Narrative as a primary act of mind' (in Meek, Warlow and Barton, 1977). Since, as Hardy reminds us, our very lives unfold through time, it is not surprising that children respond with interest to the narration of stories, told and read, from an early age. Stories tell us about human behaviour, about how people respond to events and challenges. The drive of the narrative makes us want to hear or read more and this is why stories have had such an important role in learning to read and write. The shape of a story, sometimes called a 'story grammar', includes an introduction to the setting and characters, a middle section of events and challenges and finally a resolution. This basic pattern becomes familiar and helps children use the semantic or contextual cueing system.

Stories, whether read independently or in shared contexts, are above all a source of enjoyment. Angela Wilson refers to the pleasure that children gain from making sense of a text (Wilson, 2001). There is, however, a balance to maintain between enjoying a story and analysing it as required by the text-level work which is part of the National Literacy Strategy in the United Kingdom. Wray and Medwell suggest a structure for analysing narratives like the fairy tale *Little Red Riding Hood* showing some of the elements necessary to give the story cohesion (Wray and Medwell, 1997). We have to be careful about assuming that any particular narrative structure can be universally applied.

The use of flashbacks and alternative tellings of familiar stories make classification problematic. It is also true that there are a number of ways of analysing texts. We might wish to examine the emotional impact of how the characters in the story respond to events and dilemmas. Or, as Wyse and Jones (2001) suggest, we may consider the social aspects of a story.

When it comes to children's writing they will certainly draw on the stories they have heard and read as well as on what they see on television and video film and events in their own lives. But there is an issue about expecting young children to conform to mature forms in their writing.

Hardy, Barbara 'Narrative as a primary act of mind' in Meek, Margaret, Warlow, Aidan and Barton, Griselda (eds) (1977) *The Cool Web: The Patterns of Children's Reading* London: The Bodley Head.

Wilson, Angela (2001 edition) *Language Knowledge for Primary Teachers* London: David Fulton.

Wray, David and Medwell, Jane (1997) *QTS English for Primary Teachers* London: Letts.

Wyse, Dominic and Grant, Russell (2001) *Teaching English, Language and Literacy* London: Routledge-Falmer.

Narrative non-fiction – see under auto-biography, biography, chronological non-fiction, History & English, information stories, procedural genre

National Association for the Teaching of English (NATE)

NATE is the association for the teaching of all aspects of English from preschool to university in the United Kingdom. As a member of the International Federation of the Teachers of English it both shares the experience of UK teachers and learns from teachers across the world. It aims to keep its members (about 5,000 in number) informed about new initiatives, and to provide them with a national voice. The association conducts research and welcomes involvement in curriculum development. It supports good practice in teaching and learning English through its annual conference, its journal *English in Education*, newsletter and its many books and professional development materials.

Among its committees are two covering the preschool and primary years: 0–7 and 5–11.

NATE Office
50 Broadfield Road
Sheffield S8 OXJ UK
Tel: 0114 255 5419
Website is http://www.nate.org.uk

National Curriculum

See also Literacy Hour

Since a National Curriculum was put in place in 1988 there have been several revisions, and in the nature of things, there will be changes in the future.

The National Curriculum (DfEE/QCA 1999) for English, like the other Primary Curriculum subjects, sets out 'Programmes of Study' stipulating what must be taught and then 'Attainment Targets' which describe levels of achievement.

English at both Key Stage 1 (5–7 years) and Key Stage 2 (7–11 years) is divided into En 1 Speaking and Listening, En 2 Reading and En 3 Writing. Each of these three elements is discussed under 'Knowledge, skills and understanding' and 'Breadth of study'. The 'Breadth of study' paragraphs indicate the range of activities, contexts and purposes through which the knowledge, skills and understanding should be taught.

You can access the English orders through the website or acquire a print copy from DfEE. There follow some observations and comments:

- Although the language processes are dealt with separately it is made clear that speaking and listening, reading and writing should be integrated.
- The orders are now compatible with the *National Literacy Strategy Framework for Teaching*, the latter being more detailed as termly requirements are set out.
- Notes in the margin link the programmes with the early learning goals.
- Collaborative work is encouraged in En1 and listening, often the neglected language process, is given consideration.
- Drama is given a welcome place in En1. Many early years teachers would like more recognition of the value of play.
- Children are taught a range of strategies to learn to read and there is recognition of phonological, syntactical and contextual (semantic) cueing systems compatible with the 'searchlight' model in the *National Literacy Strategy Framework for Teaching* (DfEE, 1998).
- It is implicit that language development is partly to do with controlling a large number of genre. Non-fiction reading and writing is fully recognised as well as the full range of fiction and both print and ICT forms of information texts are included.
- Children are to be taught about language variation, for example how language varies according to context and purpose and how talk and writing differ in form.
- Children must be taught about the structure of language and by Key Stage 2 (En 3) challenging concepts about grammar must be acquired.
- Children must acquire standard English forms in speaking and writing.
- There is recognition that the form of writing relates to the purpose and the audience.
- Teachers must help children plan and draft their writing. The SATs, however, require first draft accounts.
- Systematic teaching of spelling, punctuation and handwriting is required.

Website is www.nc.uk.net

National Curriculum for Initial Teacher Training – see subject knowledge

National Grid for Learning

This is a most important resource for everyone concerned with Education. It has a *Virtual Teachers' Centre (VTC)* providing book reviews, details of innovations and opportunities to share good practice. There are a growing number of sites including 'Literacy Time' which, amongst other things, has a CD-ROM section with reviews by teachers.

National Grid for Learning website: http://www.ngfl.gov.uk

National Literacy Strategy – see Literacy Hour

National Oracy Project

This project was established in 1987 by the School Curriculum Development Committee and later administered by the National Curriculum Council.

Over the four years of its development work many teachers in England and Wales were involved in establishing its priorities and direction. The work of the project and the belief in the centrality of talk in learning is explained and celebrated in *Thinking Voices*. The aims included:

- to enhance the role of speech in the learning process from age 5 to age 16 by encouraging active learning
- to develop methods of assessment through speech
- to promote recognition of the value of oral work in schools.

Norman, Kate (ed.) (1992) *Thinking Voices: The Work of the National Oracy Project* London: Hodder & Stoughton.

National Writing Project

The National Writing Project (1985–89) involved many teachers across the country and brought to a practical level the notion of writing for different purposes and different audiences One outcome was *Learning about Writing* by P. Czerniewska, director of the project. There was interest in writing across the curriculum as well as writing narratives and poems in English.

One of the strategies developed during the project was the idea of children acting as 'response partners' for each other's writing. The children usually needed some briefing from the teacher on how to comments on content and on spelling and punctuation in a constructive way. In *Responding to and Assessing Writing* there is a case study of two very young children – Reception age – helping each other in this way.

Czerniewska, Pam (1992) *Learning about Writing* Oxford: Blackwell.
National Writing Project (1989a) *Becoming a Writer* Walton on Thames: Thomas Nelson.
National Writing Project (1989b) *Responding to and Assessing Writing* Walton on Thames: Thomas Nelson.

Nativist approach to language acquisition

See also language acquisition, transformational grammar

Those taking a nativist approaches to language acquisition argue that human beings are programmed to learn language as long as they have a speech community in which to use and learn their mother tongue. One of the most renowned linguists taking this view is Noam Chomsky. He found unconvincing the behaviourist position of language acquisition – that children respond to stimuli in the environment and learn chiefly by stimulus responses and imitation (Chomsky, 1957). This seemed not to fit with observations of children's creative early utterances which suggested they were actively trying to make sense of the rules of the speech system. For example, as Marian Whitehead shows, children over-generalise. So that 'The mans are walking up the street' is a generalisation of how we usually make plurals. A child saying this is not imitating adult speech but actively trying to make rules which he or she will modify in the light of experience.

Chomsky's notion of LAD, or a Language Acquisition Device, was an internal capacity of the human infant to process the language he or she hears and to generate their own meaningful utterance.

As Whitehead (1997) and Donaldson (1978) have pointed out, Chomsky's theory does seem to underestimate the power of the social context and human relationship in making a child a communicator.

Chomsky, Noam (1957) *Syntactic Structures* Mouton: The Hague.

Donaldson, Margaret (1978) *Children's Minds* London: Fontana.

Whitehead, Marian, R. (1997) *Language and Literacy in the Early Years* London: Paul Chapman. See Chapter 3, 'Psycholinguistics: the big questions'.

Neale's Analysis of Reading

See also assessment, reading age, Standardised Reading Tests

This is a standardised reading test used widely by teachers, psychologists and researchers in the United Kingdom. First standardised and printed in 1958, the story content and the format was updated in 1988. The test is individually administered and assesses reading ages from six to thirteen years. Advantages of this test include the presentation of words, not just in a list as in for example the Schonell test but as part of a supportive context, and its appealing presentation with illustrations as well as prose text. The writers of the most recent manual show a broader notion of reading and point out that no test can sample all the components of the reading process. The revised test is based on a miscue analysis approach but rather than using it diagnostically a summative measure of the child's accuracy, comprehension and reading rate is provided. There have been some criticisms of the standardisation of the test but it remains popular for administering to very young readers as there are few other suitable individual tests available. In research where children are only to be compared with each other, as in Riley's case studies of children's progress during the first year of school, standardisation issues are of less importance (Riley, 1996, p. 104).

Riley, Jeni (1996) *The Teaching of Reading: The Development of Literacy in the Early Years of School* London: Paul Chapman.

News (writing of) – see diary

Newspapers

See also advertisements, Literacy Hour, persuasive genre, visual literacy

Newspapers are a useful resource for English and for lessons across the curriculum and amongst other things can be used to help children make distinctions between fact and opinion. Of course media texts in general need to be read critically and it helps if children learn to control a vocabulary to talk about newspapers including 'headlines', 'columns', 'features', 'front page' and 'captions'. All this helps when it comes to making their own magazine or newspaper. Microsoft Publisher and other desktop packages have contributed greatly to children's sense of achievement in producing professional looking texts (Fisher and Williams, 2000, p. 117). The easily managed changes that can be made in print size, insertions and so on leave children free to concentrate on the composition of their accounts. Activities using newspapers can be adapted for different age groups and include:

- using newspaper reports as models for children's own writing for a class or school newspaper. Children can look, for example, at how headlines help the reader. For younger children, some teachers find it helpful in getting the format right if teachers provide column-sized strips of paper on which to write. These also help children edit their work to fit a limited space (Guardian Unlimited site helps).
- interviewing adults and children in school using a note book or tape recorder for an article in the class or school newspaper.
- comparing the front pages of different newspapers and designing their own front pages using appropriate language and headlining and attending to where to start new paragraphs.

- looking at the purposes behind newspaper accounts – is a reporter trying to inform, persuade or make something sound sensational to sell more copies? How does the audience at which a newspaper is aimed affect its language and content.

- considering how reporters use direct speech and quotation to add interest to an article.

- studying the visual aspects – to see how photographs, maps and drawings communicate, explain, complement or extend the verbal element.

- using old newspapers as a primary source and where both English and History perspectives can be brought to bear.

- using reports, articles and letters about local or national matters of interest as a starting point for children's debates and persuasive kinds of writing (the Newswise Internet site helps here).

- improvising drama round what happens in a newspaper office: a teacher might be 'in role' as editor while children act as reporters and office staff.

Fisher, Robert and Williams, Mary (2000) *Unlocking Literacy: A Guide for Teachers* London: David Fulton.

Guardian Unlimited site: http//www.nesunlimited.co.uk/

Newswise Internet site: http//www.ndirect.co.uk/-sapere/Newswise

Non-fiction reading and writing

See also copying, Directed Activities Around Texts, diagrams, discussion texts, explanation texts, EXEL project, EXIT model, factual genres, information books, information story, language and thought, library skills, Literacy Hour, metacognition, motivation, non-narrative texts, persuasive genre, photographs, prior experience, procedural genre, projects, recount, referencing, reports, retrieval devices, spontaneous and scientific concepts, structural guiders, study skills, transitional genres, visual literacy, writing frames

The main functions of non-fiction reading and writing are to describe, inform, explain, persuade and instruct about aspects of the real world and all its phenomena. However, the best children's texts also often entertain and awaken a child's sense of wonder and curiosity. Learning to control the different kinds of non-fiction, whether print, software, CD-ROM or from the Internet, is a most important part of becoming literate. Supporting children's journey towards becoming confident readers and writers of non-fiction is a central requirement of both the National Curriculum English orders (DfEE, 1999) and the *National Literacy Strategy Framework for Teaching* (DfEE, 1998) in the United Kingdom. The six non-fiction genre referred to in these official documents – recount, report, discussion, instruction (procedural), explanation and persuasive–match with the work of David Wray and Maureen Lewis on the EXEL project and it is helpful to read one of their many books, for example *Extending Literacy: Children Reading and Writing Non-Fiction* (1997). At text level, helpful questions to ask about a non-fiction text are: what type of text is it – report, persuasive text and so on – how is the text structured; what kind of authorial voice is adopted and what are the graphic conventions used. Work at sentence and word level explores the syntax of the different non-fiction texts and their distinctive vocabulary. Some of DfEE's guidance material provides detailed advice about this, see for example, *Grammar for Writing* (DfEE, 2000). For a helpful analysis of how to go about studying non-fiction at text, sentence and word level I recommend the non-fiction chapters in Angela Wilson's book *Language Knowledge for Primary Teachers* (2001). In Chapter 12, 'Looking at Information Books', Jane Medwell *et al*. provide a comprehensive account of what trainee teachers need to know about the organisational features of the different non-fiction text types (Medwell *et al.*, 2001).

I have considered the different kinds of non-fiction and criteria for judging their quality in some detail under the separate entries. Study skills and library skills and the work of the Exeter Extending Literacy project are all covered under the appropriate entries. Here I consider some ways of helping children make progress in this difficult aspect of literacy. In doing so I use the model of non-fiction reading and writing set out in my book *Making Facts Matter* (1992) and discussed critically alongside the EXIT model in Riley and Reedy's book *Developing Writing for Different Purposes* (2000).

But just before I do this I want to mention some of the issues that arise when we start to think about which strategies best support this kind of reading and writing. Should the emphasis be on the teaching of study and library skills? Researchers of any age know these are essential tools to help us find out from secondary sources. The sheer amount of information that we can now access from print and electronic sources can be overwhelming and children certainly need skilful help to find what they need and then to use it and finally present it. The trouble is that too often this approach can lead to de-contextu-alised 'finding out' exercises which can be extremely dreary. Too much time spent on iden-tifying the genre features of different texts can also be mechanistic and joyless. Two very inter-esting and profound analyses help us get our minds round the issues here. First Margaret Meek's *Information and Book Learning* (1996) and second Helen Arnold's 'the blackbirds sing all day?' (*After Alice*, 1992).

An alternative approach starts from the young learners – their questions, comments, wonder-ings and curiosity about the topic in hand. The desire to know is a powerful motivator and work organised round this is likely to arouse a high level of interest and commitment. But we know that while much project work of the 1970s and 1980s was excellent, some lacked a clear enough focus and neglected to include teaching about necessary research skills and strategies (see entry on Cross curricular projects). The challenge is to combine the best of both these approaches by harnessing our teaching of study skills to chil-dren's concerns and purposes. The teachers and children in the classroom case studies in my book *Young Researchers* try to achieve this balance (Mallett, 1999). This brings me to another issue. So often it is lessons across the curriculum which provide the most exciting contexts for research and yet a great deal of children's reading and writing now happens in the Literacy Hour. Fortunately, a flexible approach allows for some of the same texts that the children are using for

research in history, geography and science to be explored from a language perspective in the Literacy Hour. Indeed this suggestion appears on page 13 on *The Framework for Teaching*. There is a strong example of children using their history research – on child labour in Victorian times – to produce letters 'in role' as protesting Victorian citizens in the Centre for Language in Primary Education's video-film *Communities of Writers*. The teacher of the Year 5 class involved, Clare Warner, considered this writing task provided the children with a standpoint from which to select their material (CLPE, 1999). I now offer a model for non-fiction reading and writing, newly expanded and annotated, for discussion and for comparison with the EXIT model which is more detailed in the later stages. Although my model is presented as linear, the stages overlap. As Riley and Reedy point out, 'it may be the discovery of a new piece of information that makes us reflect on our previous knowledge and thus raise ques-tions that need to be answered' (Riley and Reedy, 2000, p. 145).

A model for reading and writing non-fiction

Organising prior experience
Whenever a teacher begins a new topic it helps the children to organise what they already know by discussion and sharing. This is sometimes termed 'brainstorming' and making a topic web on a board or flip chart of all the ideas and issues may help. This involves the children in their own learning from the outset, but of course it is the teacher's skilful intervention which helps make the talk focused and valuable.

Offering new experience
The younger the children the less satisfactory it is to go straight to secondary sources.* Much better to offer an interesting experience which might be an outing, a talk by an expert, consideration of an artefact or reading a picturebook or poem. I used a BBC video-film about a baby squirrel reared by a cat with her kittens as the 'new experience' for a study of squirrels within a 'Living Things' science project (Mallett, 1992).

Formulating questions

The new experience combined with the 'prior experience' 'talk usually gives rise to a large number of questions. These questions can be displayed in the literacy corner or written down in children's jotters. The important thing is that they put the children in the driving seat and make it much less likely that they will be overwhelmed by the texts. I find it also makes children take up a critical approach: do these texts answer *my* questions? Children learn that some of the most interesting questions (sometimes ethical ones) can be the most difficult to find answers to. I remember a six year old trying to find some insight on 'Is it wrong to kill a spider that gets into your bath?'

Discussion and planning

The children begin to search in books and it is important to keep meeting together as a class to share findings and puzzles and to clarify purposes and ways of representing their findings. Collaborating over 'finding out' makes it less lonely and often infuses energy into the learning. It also recognises the powerful role of the spoken language in getting our minds round new and sometimes challenging ideas.

Study skills and retrieval devices

By now the children have much commitment to their work. They are ready for some modelling and demonstration of both library and study skills either in or outside of the Literacy Hour. Finding their way round the library and understanding how to use retrieval devices in print and electronic text are most important. I have found encouraging children to share their experiences and frustrations in group discussion very valuable here.

Summarising, reformulating and reflecting

This stage includes oral summary and learning how to make notes and bullet points to provide material for extended writing later on. Copying and closely paraphrasing from books is less likely if children work from notes. Teachers can use scaffolding strategies to support children's efforts to make oral summaries – 'what three main things did you find most interesting?' and also offer support like the 'writing conference' of the

process model and writing frames (see under entries on Process approach and Writing frames). In the case of the Squirrel work, the children's questions led to them creating contents pages which structured their findings.

Above all children enjoy sharing all they have learnt both orally and in writing. The nine year olds in the Squirrel Project referred to above made books to share with the six year olds in the school. The time spent reading their books aloud to the younger children and explaining the concepts was a highlight of the work.

* There are of course occasions in the Literacy Hour and outside it when children carry out worthwhile directed activities round texts (DARTs) sometimes using text on the computer.

Arnold, Helen (1992) 'Do the blackbirds sing all day?' in Styles, Morag *et al. After Alice* London: Cassell.

Communities of Writers: Writing at Key Stage 2 (1999). A video-film from the Centre for Language in Primary Education's Learning to be Literate series (CLPE, Webber Street, London SE1 8QW).

Mallett, Margaret (1992) *Making Facts Matter: Reading Non-fiction 5–11* London: Paul Chapman.

Mallett, Margaret (1999) *Young Researchers: Informational Reading and Writing in the Early and Primary Years* London: Routledge.

Medwell, Jane, Moore, George, Wray, David and Griffiths, Vivienne (2001) *Primary English: Knowledge and Understanding.* (Course book meeting 4/98 Standards) Exeter: Learning Matters.

Meek, Margaret (1996) *Information and Book Learning* Stroud: The Thimble Press.

Neate Publishing (2000), Literacy and Science series *A basic dictionary of plants and gardening,* Teacher and parent version with activity flaps, details from www.neatepublishing.co.uk

Riley, Jeni and Reedy, David (2000) *Developing Writing for Different Purposes* London: Paul Chapman.

Wilson, Angela (2001 edition) *Language Knowledge for Primary Teachers* London: David Fulton, Chapter 10.

Wray, David and Lewis, Maureen (1997) *Extending Literacy: Children Reading and Writing Non-fiction* London: Routledge

Non-narrative texts – see information books

Non-standard English – see Standard English, dialect, language variety

Norm referencing

See also assessment, Standardised Reading Tests

Unlike a criterion referenced test, norm tests do not serve a diagnostic purpose. Rather, as the results are set out in rank order, they make it possible to judge a person's performance compared with that of others. They work on the basis that in any assessment some individuals will do very well, some will have low scores, but most will be between the extremes. This expected pattern of results is called 'the curve of distribution'.

Noun

See also abstract noun, collective noun, common noun, count noun, mass noun, noun clause, noun phrase, proper noun

A noun is a part of speech (or word class) which names a person, a thing or a concept In the following sentence the nouns are in italics. 'When *Miranda* settled in the *countryside* away from the *crowd* in *London* she found *peace* at last.'

Noun clause

See also clause, grammar, parts of speech

A noun clause (or a nominal clause) works like a noun or pronoun. So while in the sentence – 'The claim was not justified' – we have a noun – 'The claim...', in the sentence – 'What he claimed was not justified.' – there is a noun clause – 'What he claimed...'.

Noun clauses usually include some form of verb while noun phrases do not.

Noun phrase

See also grammar, phrase, parts of speech

A noun phrase, like a noun clause, functions as a noun in a sentence. Examples of noun phrases are: the largest cabbage; a red dress; my favourite nephew. A noun phrase differs from a noun clause in that the former does not normally include a verb while the latter does.

Note-taking – see study skills

Novels

See also adventure stories, animal, fantasy, fiction, historical novels, history of children's literature, narrative, realism, school stories

As they move through the primary years children become able to enjoy longer stories or 'novels'. Like novels for adults, children's novels are sustained fictional narratives, long enough for the development of characters and a series of events. For suggestions for different age groups I recommend Stuart Marriot's *Read On* and, particularly for older children, Gervase Phinn's *Young Readers and Their Books.* Children's novels are very varied and include classics like Philippa Pearce's *Tom's Midnight Garden,* historical novels like Rosemary Sutcliff's *The Eagle of the Ninth,* adventures like Nina Bawden's *The White Horse Gang* and the rather surrealist and slightly disturbing kind of book, for instance, *The Daydreamer* by Ian McEwan. Some children greatly enjoy reading novels independently. The shared reading of a novel, probably outside the time constrained Literacy Hour, is a deeply educative experience. Amongst the benefits are that children:

- enjoy an imaginary experience
- learn from hearing the teacher's reading and discussion as a mature reader
- experience interactive learning as they discuss and enjoy the text together
- are exposed to different kinds of book language
- are introduced to a wide range of fiction that they might not have read on their own – adventure, historical novels, fantasy, realism
- develop empathy and understanding
- are helped to make links made between text and life and vice versa
- are helped to enjoy a building momentum and to develop cumulative insights over several sessions

- have the others in the class to provide a good audience for drama, writing etc.
- have their literacy developed in the widest sense.

In addition, teachers often find that children with special literacy needs can be encouraged to contribute and young learners of English as a second or additional language are placed in a supportive context.

Eight-year-old Cormac is not a bookish child but after hearing the teacher read Dick King-Smith's *The Sheep-pig* he remarked:

'I liked hearing the story because I could sit and listen and understand the story without having to read it myself. The teacher makes it sound funny and I can't wait for her to read the next chapter to find out what happens next. Sometimes I feel sad or scared for the character and sometimes I feel happy for them or they make me laugh. Hearing the story is one of my favourite things at school.'

Nursery rhyme

See also phonics, phonological awareness, poetry, reading, verse

This is a simple, traditional rhyming song or story. According to Townsend (1995, p. 105), the earliest known nursery rhyme collection was *Tommy Thumb's Song Book* published by Mrs Cooper of Paternoster Row in 1774. This collection included familiar rhymes like 'Sing a Song of Sixpence' and 'Hickory, Dickory Dock' as well as some rougher, cruder verses. But the Mother Goose anthologies – the first being *Mother Goose's Melody* – published, possibly by Newbery, in the 1780s – are the best known of the early collections.

The rhymes that survive in modern collections have their roots in different centuries and in different contexts (see Peter and Iona Opies' *The Oxford Book of Nursery Rhyme*, 1951). We must remember that the rhymes were often intended for the amusement of adults. Away from their original political and social settings they are often delightfully absurd.

This absurdity, and the subversion of the normal rules of the real world, seems to be one aspect that still appeals to the children of today.

Nursery rhymes can create special worlds of the imagination and wonderful opportunities for language play. Margaret Meek writes: 'They are memorable as speech, they also form the bedrock of all play, the alternative world. Jack and Jill, Old Mother Hubbard, Simple Simon, Polly, who put the kettle on are all there, ready to pop into stories, play-acting and a million children's books, generation after generation' (Meek, 1991, p. 84).

There is great variety in these short narratives we call nursery rhymes. Some tell of unpleasant events – Humpty Dumpty, Three Blind Mice and Jack and Jill all suffer grievous injury. In contrast, 'I had a little nut tree, Nothing would it bear, But a silver nut-meg, And a golden pear' is gentle and poetic. Whatever their theme they help prepare children for the imaginative world of fiction and for their own attempts at verse. You may know the landmark publication of the Opies – *The Lore and Language of School Children* – which celebrated the playground rhymes and culture of children in the 1940s and 1950s. Georgina Boyes has revisited the Opie's work and added evidence from her own research of the folklore of children brought up in a computer age. She shows how ancient rhymes are reworked and new ones added (Boyes, 1995).

As well as being hugely enjoyable for their own sake a number of research studies, notably those carried out by Bryant *et al.* (1989) and Goswami and Bryant (1990), link familiarity with nursery rhymes with success in learning to read. Children need to 'hear' separate sounds in the flow of spoken language around them if they are to learn to use the symbols of our alphabetic system to read and to write. Repetition of the nursery rhymes seems to help with a recognition of separate sounds which is called 'phonological awareness'. When children see the rhymes written down this brings to their attention some of different ways in which sounds are spelt. It is splendid that something as enjoyable as listening to and saying nursery rhymes should also be helpful in learning to read. I heartily recommend *Rhyme, reading and writing* edited by Roger Beard: the contributors explain recent research on the central role of rhyme and alliteration in the process of learning literacy and celebrate children's sheer delight in the linguistic playfulness of nursery rhymes.

Avery, Gillian and Kinnell, Margaret (1995) 'Morality and Levity' pp. 61–9 in Hunt, Peter, *An Illustrated History of Children's Literature* Oxford: Oxford University Press.

Beard, Roger (ed.) (1995) *Rhyme, Reading & Writing* London: Hodder & Stoughton (Chapter 8).

Bryant, P.E., Bradley, L., Maclean, M. and Crossland, J. (1989) 'Nursery rhymes, phonological skills and reading', in *Journal of Child Language,* Vol. 16, pp. 407–28.

Goswami, Ursula and Bryant, Peter (1990) *Phonological Skills and Learning to Read* Hove, East Sussex: Lawrence Erlbaum Associates.

Meek, Margaret (1991) *On Being Literate* London: The Bodley Head.

Opie, Iona and Peter (1959) *The Lore and Language of School Children* Oxford: Oxford University Press.

Townsend, John Rowe (1995, sixth edition) *Written for Children* London: The Bodley Head.

Observation – see research into Primary English

OFSTED (Office for Standards in Education)

This is a government body set up in 1992 to carry out school inspections so that standards can be monitored. It reports directly to the Secretary of State for Education.

123 and Away

This is a reading scheme for five to seven year olds first published by Collins in 1966 and revised in 1992. The books used in the scheme are narratives about the people living in a village and have a carefully controlled sentence structure and vocabulary. There are supporting resources which aim to develop word recognition and decoding skills. There are wooden figures and a video about the characters in the stories. Progression is built into the scheme. Some children like the stories but the scheme shares the imitations of others where the vocabulary is controlled and the characters unchanging.

Onomatopoeia

This is a figure of speech which refers to language where sound echoes sense, for example the 'squelch' of wet grass or the 'buzz' of a bee. Work round advertisements, strip cartoons and poetry introduces children to onomatopoeia.

Onset and rime

See also phoneme, phonics, phonological awareness

'Onset' is that part of the syllable which precedes the vowel while 'rime' refers to the vowel and final sounds. So in the word 'page', 'p' is the onset and 'age' is the rime. The research of Goswami and Bryant (1990) suggests that as children enjoy songs and rhythm, an approach to the initial teaching of reading which exploits this enjoyment is likely to be successful. Nursery rhymes, for example, are a rich source of single syllable words which can be tackled by beginning readers as onsets and rimes.

Goswami, U. and Bryant, P. (1990) *Phonological Skills and Learning to Read* Hove: Lawrence Erlbaum Associates.

Riley, Jeni (1996) *The Teaching of Reading: The Development of Literacy in the Early Years of Schooling* London: Paul Chapman, Chapter 2.

Oracy – see under collaborative learning, Drama and English, speaking and listening, story telling

Oxford Reading Tree

This reading package for children aged four to eleven was first published by Oxford University Press in 1985 and new materials are added regularly. At its centre is the imaginative evocation of a tree with different branches for each aspect of reading and its associated materials.

The package includes a wide range of books including stories in small and big book format, poetry and non-fiction. Other materials include photocopiable worksheets, guided reading cards and a teacher's guide with many suggestions for activities.

Strong points include the attractiveness and variety of the materials and the support provided for the different aspects of reading.

Oxford Reading Web from the same publisher

includes elements on phonics and grammar to support teachers' use of *The National Literacy Strategy Framework for Teaching*. It can stand on its own as a reading programme, or it can be used to supplement *Oxford Reading Tree*. Teachers of seven to eleven years olds welcome the addition of *Treetops* – top quality books including Chris Powling's *The Million Pound Mascot* (about football and superstition) and Margaret McAllister's *My Guinea Pig is Innocent* (about bullying).

PACT – see parents and families

Palindrome

This is a word or phrase which is the same whether read forwards or backwards, for example noon, peep, tat, Anna and madam.

Parable

See also the Bible, fable

A parable is a short story to make a moral point and is often associated with the teachings of Jesus in the New Testament. Well-known parables include the Good Samaritan, the Parable of the Talents and the Prodigal Son. A knowledge of parables is helpful in reading those books where some familiarity with them is assumed.

The term can also be used to describe some modern texts for adults and children. Perhaps Anthony Browne's *The Tunnel* can be read as a parable about sibling relationships.

Parables as a genre are included in the text types for children in Year 3, term 2 of the *National Literacy Strategy Framework for Teaching.*

Paragraphing

Paragraphing is a way of breaking up a text into topics and sub-topics. The beginning of a new paragraph is indicated by starting its first sentence on a new line and by indenting the first word.

Judging when to begin a new paragraph comes with experience. We get a sense as writers of when we have said enough about 'that' and need to move on to a new thought and therefore a new paragraph.

In direct speech, a new paragraph is often begun when a new speaker utters. Where a person speaks directly for several paragraphs the speech marks are usually placed at the beginning of the first utterance and the end of the paragraph with the last utterance.

Parents and families

See also bilingualism, emotional literacy, English Co-ordinator, family literacy projects, hobbies & English, multiculturalism, Primary Language Record

There is everything to be gained from schools and families keeping in close touch to support children's progress. We tend to use the word 'parent' as a shorthand but this should be taken to include a wider family involvement. Merchant and Marsh (1998) suggest that a term like 'partnership with families' might be appropriate in our ever changing society in which family groupings are varied and not always stable. Contact best starts early and may take the form of home visits and liaison with the local play group or nursery. Continuity is achieved in these crucial early stages if members of a family are encouraged to visit the school in the child's 'settling in' period.

Good home–school partnership is particularly important for children's developing language and literacy. Teachers benefit from extending their knowledge of children's literacy experiences at home and in the wider community. This is important for all the children and their families. When the school includes young 'emergent bilinguals' teachers benefit from some specific background knowledge. Eve Gregory lists some helpful initial questions; these include finding out in some depth about which languages the child speaks or writes and to what standard, and finding out about community-led classes and the pattern of tuition the child is used to. One very interesting aspect of Gregory's list is the emphasis given to the potential role of siblings in supporting each other's language development (Gregory, 1996, p. 102).

There are well-established ways of keeping in touch with families using letters, explanatory booklets about reading and English lessons, open days, meetings with staff and of course through the reading logs or diaries children take home. There is substantial research evidence about the value of children reading at home to parents, caregivers or siblings (see Wolfendale and Topping, 1995; Weinberger, 1996). A parent or another member of the family may be asked to write some comments on progress in the reading log or mark the page they have reached in the book. The Centre for Language in Primary Education's Primary Language Record and other similar record keeping formats include the opportunity for the parent to comment on their perception of the child's progress. This provides a good focus for discussion at meetings between parent and teachers. There is evidence that the interest of male family members in a boy's reading is helpful in encouraging positive attitudes towards literacy. Donald Fry describes the leap in seven-year-old Clayton's progress when his father read him Richard Adams' *Watership Down*.

The English Co-ordinator is best placed to organise the valuable contributions of parent volunteers who may work in the library, make resources like story bags or kits,* bring particular expertise like computer skills or providing home language text in book making and take part in story telling in some of the children's first language. In the classroom, parents can hear children read and will appreciate some sympathetic briefing. In the early years classroom parents can act as 'literacy partners' who read print and scribe for young children (Whitehead, 1999, p. 66). Much work goes into establishing and maintaining parent–teacher partnerships. Ann Browne provides good advice about the priorities and reminds us that, above all, we need to create openness and respect on both sides (Browne, 1996, Chapter 9).

* An example of the story bags which parents may help to create is the 'Storysack' described in Neil Griffiths' book *Storysacks*. (Reading: Reading and Language Information Centre, 2001). 'Curiosity Kits' are a non-fiction version of a storysack. Find out more from University of Plymouth Education Department (Tel. 01395 255473).

Browne, Ann (1996) *Developing Language and Literacy 3–8* London: Paul Chapman (see Chapter 9, 'Involving Parents').

Fry, Donald (1985) *Children Talk About Books: Seeing Themselves as Readers* Milton Keynes: Open University Press.

Gregory, Eve (1996) *Making Sense of a New World: Learning to read in a second language* London: Paul Chapman.

Merchant, Guy and Marsh, Jackie (1998) *Co-ordinating Primary Language and Literacy* London: Paul Chapman (see Chapter 11).

National Literacy Trust has a research report entitled *Parental Involvement and Literacy Achievement* (Tel. 020 7828 2435).

Weinberger, Jo (1996) *Literacy Goes To School: The Parents' Role in Young Children's Literacy Learning* London: Paul Chapman.

Whitehead, Marian. R. (1999) *Supporting Language and Literacy Development in the Early Years* Buckingham and Philadelphia: Open University Press.

Wolfendale, S. and Topping, K. (eds) (1995) *Parental Involvement in Literacy – Effective Partnerships in Education* London: Croom Helm.

Participle

'Participle' is a term in English grammar to refer to two endings of non-finite verbs. These are 'ing', the present participle, and 'ed', 'd' or 't', the past participle. The 'ing' ending appears in a number of forms. Used with the verb 'to be' it becomes the progressive continuous as for example in 'she was *teaching*'. In a participle clause it is used as a verb as in: 'After *talking* all through break, he was quiet when the teacher came into the classroom.' The 'ing' ending helps to form the future as in 'will be going' or the present, as in 'is talking'.

The past participle 'ed' is used in three ways. First it can be used with the verb 'to have' to form the perfect tense as in for example:

'The student has *produced* some excellent writing.'

Second, it can be used with the verb 'to be' to form the passive:

'He was *educated* at Kings College.'

Third, it can be used as the verb in an 'ed' participle clause:

> '*Questioned* for several hours, she still stuck to her story.'

For a particularly thorough explanation of participles, see Chapter 6 in Wilson, 2001, and pp. 751–2 in McArthur, 1992.

McArthur, Tom (1992) *The Oxford Companion to the English Language* London and Oxford: QPD Paperbacks and Oxford University Press.
Wilson, Angela (2001 edition) *Language Knowledge for Primary Teachers* London: David Fulton.

Parts of speech (or word classes)

See also adjective, adverb, article, conjunction, noun, preposition, pronoun, verb

Words are classified into categories which are known as 'parts of speech' or 'word classes'. The main parts of speech are named above and each is described under a separate entry. Words can belong to more than one category depending on their function in a sentence. For example, 'lift' can function as a verb in 'I lift the garage door each morning' or as a noun in 'I take the lift to the top floor'. The word 'that' can function as a determiner in 'I read that book last year', as a pronoun in 'what was that?' and as conjunction 'she claimed that she had written the book'. Another example of the flexibility in the use of words in English is 'love' which can be used in a sentence as a noun as in 'My love is like a red, red rose', as an adjective as in 'It was undoubtedly a love match' or as a verb as in – 'I love you'.

DfEE (September 2000) The National Literacy Strategy *Grammar for Writing* www.dfee.gov.uk
The Internet Grammar of English: http://www.ucl.ac.uk/Internet-grammar/home.htm
The Linguistics Association provides further information at http://www.art.man.ac.uk/English/staff/dd/reading.htm

Passive voice

See also verbs

The passive voice is a grammatical term used to refer to the form of the verb in which the recip-

ient of an action is the subject of the sentence: 'These teachers are being praised by the school governors for their excellence'. This contrasts with a sentence in the active voice: 'The school governors praised the teachers for their excellence'.

Many consider it best for writers to use the immediate, active voice whenever possible. However, there are times when the passive is appropriate, for example in some scientific kinds of writing where a tone of detachment is required, in cases where the doer is unknown as in 'We were burgled last night' and where the recipient of an action is more important than the doer as in 'The child managed to avoid being hit by the car.'

Pathetic fallacy

Like 'personification', 'pathetic fallacy' refers to the attribution of human feelings and characteristics to animals, plants and inanimate objects as a poetic device. 'Pathetic' refers not to pity, but to the awakening of emotional response to the comparisons. The term was used by Ruskin (*Modern Painters,* 1856) to criticise the falseness of imputing human characteristics to things in the world of nature even where personification adds to the literary quality of the language in a literary text. Sometimes 'pathetic fallacy' is applied pejoratively to the overblown or inappropriate use of personification. An example might be: 'The cruel stone landed on the suffering bluebell.'

Person

See also first person writing

This is a term that applies to pronouns and verbs and tells the listener or reader about the 'person' concerned. Turning to pronouns first, in English, only the third person singular has a distinct form – 'he', 'she' and 'it.' The first person singular 'I', the second person singular 'you', the first person plural 'we' and the third person plural 'they' all only have one form. Use of the first person gives an intimate flavour to a piece of writing. Use of the second person, too, can often give a friendly feel to a book for young children – 'Have you ever seen a squirrel crack a nut?' When it comes to using the third person we have to make sure children know that they have to look back in the text to find out who 'she' or 'he' or 'it' is. So we might have a series of sentences as follows. 'Leon gently lifted the mewing kitten from the tree. It was still trembling when he searched for its collar to find an address'. It is clear from the rhythm of the sentences and the context that 'it' is the kitten and Leon is the 'he' in the second sentence.

In some languages the 'person' is indicated in the verb, but in English only the third person singular of the present tense has a distinct form – 'he loves', 'she loves' and 'it loves'.

Personification

See also pathetic fallacy

This is a device in written and spoken language which links human beings metaphorically with the non human world of animals, plants and inanimate objects. It tends to be used in literary texts and particularly in poetry. Some uses of personification have become clichés – for example 'the cruel hand of time'.

Persuasive genre

See also advertisement, argument, critical discourse, discussion text, Literacy Hour, newspapers, non-fiction reading and writing, writing frames, visual literacy

Persuasive kinds of language present the case for one viewpoint and include advertisements and political propaganda. Visual texts can also be powerful in pressing one way of looking at things. In the UK in the *National Literacy Strategy Framework* a distinction is made between 'persuasive' texts which present one side of a case and 'discussion' texts which set out more than one viewpoint. Both of these kinds of writing involve argument and come late on in *The Framework* – in Year 5 when children are aged nine to ten years. This reflects a general assumption that developmentally narrative precedes argument and that 'recounts' will be the main kind of non-fiction writing before about nine

years. There have been some convincing challenges to this view. Mallett and Doyle found five year olds were alert to the environmental issues when learning about whales. The picture book *The Whales' Song* by Sheldon and Blyth contrasts the view of Uncle Fred that whales are valuable for their blubber and oil with the belief of Lucy and her Grandmother that whales are unique and beautiful creatures which should be protected. It is never too soon to discuss issues! (Mallett, 1999, p. 164). Riley and Reedy also used a picture book, Anthony Browne's *Zoo* in this case, to help children organise the arguments for and against keeping animals in captivity. They conclude that there are good reasons for including 'argument' in our teaching from the earliest years. The kind of thinking used in spoken and written forms of argument and persuasion seems to develop much earlier than was once thought. Where children are deeply interested in a topic their enthusiasm can be harnessed to acquiring a form to express it (Riley and Reedy, 2000, Chapter 8).

There are some things to bear in mind in developing this kind of thinking, discussing and writing throughout the primary years. First of all we need to plan the work round something likely to engage the children's interest and arouse strong feelings. Riley and Reedy's Zoo work came about within a bigger theme – 'Living Things'. Some kind of new experience can awaken a line of thinking – a letter, a picture or story. In the Riley and Reedy case study, a picture book was the trigger to thinking about some rather troubling issues. In Browne's book the mother thinks the lion looks 'sad' and children begin to reflect on why this may be so. The second thing to consider is how we support children's writing, how we direct all the excitement and feeling into an appropriate written form. Class or group discussion helps children consider the arguments and counter arguments of the issue. (Persuasive language presents one viewpoint but we do need to be aware of possible counter arguments in presenting the case powerfully.) Wilkinson got seven year olds to talk about the case for and against having playtime before asking them to write. The children were particularly encouraged to make a point and then elaborate it, and this structure was taken through to their written accounts later on (Wilkinson, 1990).

Sometimes it is helpful to put a structure on discussion by linking it to headings on a board or flip chart. In Riley and Reedy's 'zoo' case study the teacher organised the children's discussion under two headings on a flip chart: 'Good for animals' and 'Bad for animals'. Of course we must remember that much early writing is transitional and we do not want to press young children too quickly into mature forms (Barrs, 1987). The gentle shaping of thinking before writing used in the 'zoo' case study seems appropriate.

Are there some ways of helping older primary children to come closer to controlling the conventional ways of presenting argument? They still benefit from discussing the arguments first. When it comes to writing, they may need some help in creating a structure. Some children find the writing frames developed by Wray and Lewis helpful. These frames suggest that persuasive accounts or accounts setting out an argument begin with an opening statement defining the issue, go on to state the arguments using point and elaboration and end with a summary. A slightly different structure is suggested for discussion texts. These begin with a statement of the issue and also a brief preview of the main arguments. Then the arguments for the case are set out with supporting evidence, next the counter arguments get the same treatment and the writing concludes with a summary and recommendations (Wray and Lewis, 1997, p. 119).

The teaching challenge is of course to make sure the excitement and interest survives the writing tasks. It is well worth spending time on persuasive talking and writing, not least because understanding the ethical and controversial aspects of a topic takes children forward in becoming critical readers and writers.

Barrs, Myra (1987) 'Mapping the world' in *English in Education* NATE, Vol. 21, No. 3.
Mallett, Margaret (1999) *Young Researchers: Informational Reading and Writing in the Early and Primary Years* London: Routledge (Chapter 6, p. 164).
Riley, Jeni and Reedy, David (2000) *Developing Writing for Different Purposes* London: Paul Chapman (see Chapter 8, 'Developing control of the argument/persuasive genre').

Wilkinson, A. (1990) 'Argument as a primary act of mind' in *English in Education* NATE, Vol. 24, No. 1.
Wray, David and Lewis, Maureen (1997) *Extending Literacy: Children Reading and Writing Non-fiction* London: Routledge.

PETA, the Primary English Teaching Association, Marrickville, Australia

An independent association of professional educators and parents founded in 1972.
Website: www.peta.edu.au

Phatic communication

See also language functions

This refers to comments and questions whose function is more to do with reinforcing the relationship of the speakers than with conveying a meaning. Chat about the weather comes into this category as well as expressions like 'do you understand what I mean?'

Halliday, M.A.K. and Hasan, R. (1985) *Language Context and Text: Aspects of Language in a Social-Semiotic Perspective* Oxford: Oxford University Press.

Philosophy and literacy

See also constructivism, critical discourse, language and thought, metacognition, metalanguage, questions

The study of philosophy develops our ability to think and therefore our literacy. The journey towards becoming a critical reader involves becoming able to get past the literal meaning in a text and thinking about it at an analytical or conceptual level. Other entries have emphasised the importance of encouraging children to bring their own questions to a text, to read critically and to think creatively. Introducing children to philosophical thinking is one way of helping them to enquire, reflect and to reach their own conclusions.

One of the most interesting initiatives exploring the links between philosophy and children's literacy is the Philosophy in Primary Schools project. The project team have developed an approach in which children are helped both to 'care' – to take responsibility for their own thinking – and to 'collaborate' – to connect with the thinking of others through discussion and working together.

The researchers found that stories provide a sympathetic starting point for young children to be helped to think philosophically. Fisher explains how a teacher, who was a participant in the research project, read six and seven year olds a story called *The Monkey and her Baby;* she encouraged them to go beyond the literal meaning of the story to a discussion of issues like what it means to be beautiful. Using a story allows a philosophical approach to enrich work in the Literacy Hour. However, the research team consider such an approach might have a place in lessons across the curriculum. Teachers would of course need to have some support in learning how to develop children's thinking skills. Feedback has been positive from both teachers and children who have put into practice programmes like 'Stories for Thinking'. Children seem to have improved their achievements across a range of measures, including literacy, and when asked have said they enjoy the approach.

Two issues occur to me. First, might it be that children are moulded into a set way of thinking that might go against their own creativity? In fact, the approach encourages children to open up new areas of inquiry. Fisher gives two interesting examples of children taking the initiative. Tom, aged five, asked 'Where does time go when it is over?' A girl, after her father had finished a story with the words '...and they lived happily ever after', asked: 'What is happiness dad?' (Fisher, 2001, p. 72). So I think we can be assured that there is the possibility of children's thinking being expanded in a creative way.

Second, I think we need to remember that stories are not just for, or indeed mainly for, developing the intellect. Children, like adult readers, have an emotional and affective response to fiction and may sometimes want to read for sheer enjoyment. This is not to say that 'Stories for Thinking' is not an interesting way of developing literacy, but it is only one way of encouraging response to texts.

Fisher, Robert (2001) 'Philosophy in primary schools:

fostering thinking skills and literacy' in *Reading, literacy and language*. UKRA, Vol. 35, No. 2 July 2001 (this article reports on the 'Stories for Thinking' approach).

Teaching thinking journal site www.teachthinking. com

Phoneme

See also cueing system, digraph, phonics, phonological awareness

A phoneme is the smallest unit of meaningful sound. There are 44 phonemes in English including the five vowels and twenty-one consonants of the alphabet. 'Phonemic awareness' is to do with hearing and recognising the different phonemes within a word.

Phonetic

See also phonetic stage, spelling and the Initial Teaching Alphabet

If you spell phonetically, you consistently represent the same symbol for the same sound.

Phonetic stage

See also spelling

Children reach this stage in their approach to writing when they choose letters on the basis of sound and try to represent all the sounds in a word, for example 'cleen' for 'clean' and 'sesta' for 'sister'. Regional accent affects a child's pronunciation and therefore his or her attempts to spell phonetically.

Phonic knowledge

See also blends, onset and rime, phoneme, phonological awareness, phonics, segmentation and spelling

This refers to a reader's ability to segment a word into separate sounds and then to blend these sounds back together. This ability depends on knowing the alphabetic code and understanding the principles which inform the use of the code in reading and spelling. This ability is helpful when facing unfamiliar words and is the basis of word level work in the National Literacy Strategy *Framework for Teaching*.

Phonics

See also cueing system, grapheme, grapho-phonic cueing system, onset and rime, phoneme, phonological awareness

Phonics is to do with the correspondence between sounds (phonemes) and letters (graphemes). Recent models of the reading process tend to separate the graphic and phonic strands. You will come across the terms 'synthetic' and 'analytic' phonics and it is important to know the difference between them. The traditional phonic approach, one which assumed reading was a relatively simple matter of decoding, favoured synthetic phonics which begins at the level of the phoneme. Children were taught the sounds of the letters of the alphabet and the 44 phonemes; they sounded out the phonemes in words – 'm-a-t', 'ch-a-t' and so on. There are only 26 letters of the alphabet to make 44 phonemes. There are two ways in which all 44 sounds in English are covered. First, some of the same letters represent different sounds: for example, the 'g' in 'gift' has a different sound to that in 'gentleman'. Second, letters are combined to represent sounds not covered by single letters so we have, for example, the phonemes – 'th', 'ch' and 'ph'. The problem with a rigidly synthetic phonic approach came when children tried to decode irregular words. A newer approach to phonics, termed 'analytic phonics', encourages young readers to look at segments of words and at patterns in sounds and words: the identification of 'onset' and 'rimes' in words is typical of this approach. In the UK, the National Curriculum and The National Literacy Strategy require teachers to use both kinds of phonic strategy. The approach here is based partly on research by Goswami and Bryant which indicates that the key to reading is the ability to hear the separate phonemes in words. The framework for phonics teaching set out in *Phonics: Progression in Phonics: Materials for whole-class teaching* (DfEE, 1999) provides a systematic course in seven stages. Four skills are taught through activities: identifying sounds in spoken words; recognising written symbols for each phoneme; blending phonemes into words and segmenting words to help spelling. It is important that children develop a good understanding of the alphabet and how the alphabet code is used in reading and spelling (DfEE, 1999, p. 4).

The early part of the phonic programme requires children to recognise individual vowel and consonant sounds – in other words phonemes – and to match these with the written symbols we call graphemes. Learning to read and learning to spell are thus related. During what is often referred to as 'the phonetic stage' of spelling (Gentry, 1982) children spell words as they sound and this works well for a large number of words. But English is not entirely a phonetically regular language, and this is reflected in early spelling of, for example, 'eny', 'lite' and 'werk'.

In a particularly clear analysis, Graham and Kelly (2000, pp. 11–14) explain that children need to grasp that not all sounds can be represented by a single letter of the alphabet. Sometimes two letters are combined to make a new sound. So while 'c' and 'h' are both phonemes, when combined in a word like 'chin' they form together a new phoneme 'ch'. When children become more secure in their understanding of this they become more confident spellers as well as readers (Bielby, 1994). Dombey and Moustafa (1998) set out a phonics programme within a general philosophy of reading for meaning and purpose. The National Literacy Strategy support materials (for example the material for whole-class phonic/teaching which suggests a number of games and activities to help children make the link between sounds and written symbols) would be useful for anyone wishing to strengthen the phonological aspect of their reading programme.

The National Literacy Strategy's Three Principles about Phonics

1. Phonemes are represented by one letter or more letters like 'sh' and 'th'.
2. Phonemes represented by the same sound are not always written in the same way, for example the 'oo' sound is written differently in 'to' and 'shoe'. In 'bed' and 'said' the rime sounds the same but is spelt differently.
3. The same spelling can represent more than one phoneme, for example the 'ea' phoneme sounds different in 'mean' and 'deaf'. 'Said' and 'afraid' each have 'ai' when written down, but do not sound the same.

Phonological aspects of learning to read are given considerable weight in the UK National Curriculum English orders and the National Literacy Strategy. Teachers of children in the Foundation Stage (3–6 years) whether they are in a nursery school or in the Reception class of a primary school, are guided by the early learning goals. Sensitivity to speech sounds and patterns is encouraged by enjoying nursery rhymes and songs and children are helped to use their developing phonic knowledge to write simple regular words. There are some issues here. In their work on 'onset' and 'rime' Goswami and Bryant found that while young children could usually manage the initial sound (the 'onset') and the rest of the word (the 'rime'), coping with the middle parts was problematic. So they could manage for instance a split between l and ick making 'lick', but not with a separation into three phonemes as in l-i-ck (see Tyrrell and Gill, 2000 for an analysis of this issue in Chapter 4).

At Key Stage 1, phonic teaching mainly takes place in the 15-minute whole class work slot in the Literacy Hour. This is often followed up by activities in the guided or independent groups later in the literacy hour. For example, if the teacher has been concentrating on hearing phonemes in the final position at Phonic Step 4, as well as delighting in the wonderful story of Jill Murphy's *Peace at Last,* the children can demonstrate their new sound knowledge when they reach the phrase 'Tick-tock, tick-tock went the clock'. At Key Stage 2, phonic work tends to centre round more advanced spelling strategies. Some of the National Literacy Strategy support materials are helpful, for example *The National Literacy Strategy Spelling Bank* (DfEE, 1999).

Phonic practice can be rather abstract so the approach through games in *Phonics: Progression in Phonics* is helpful. Other cue systems, tuning into the syntactic and contextual aspects of reading, are also recognised as important in the National Literacy Strategy 'searchlight' model, reinforcing the important notion that we read above all to get meaning from text.

Bielby, Nicholas (1994) *Making Sense of Reading: The New Phonics and its Practical Implications* Leamington Spa: Scholastic.

DfEE (1999) *The National Literacy Strategy: Phonics: Progression in Phonics* London: DfEE (also in CD-ROM format).

DfEE (1999) *The National Literacy Strategy Spelling Bank* London: DfEE.

Dombey, H. and Moustafa, M. (1998) *Whole to Part Phonics: How Children Learn to Read and Spell* London: CLPE.

Gentry, Richards (1982) 'An analysis of developmental spelling in GNYS AT WRK' in *The Reading Teacher* 36, pp. 192–200.

Goswami, U. and Bryant, P. (1991) *Phonological Skills and Learning to Read* Hillsdale, NJ: Lawrence Erlbaum Associates.

Graham, Judith and Kelly, Alison (2000, second edition) *Reading Under Control: Teaching Reading in the Primary School* London: David Fulton, Chapters 1 and 3.

Tyrrell, Jenny and Gill, Narinderjit (2000) *Co-ordinating English at Key Stage 1* London: The Falmer Press.

Phonological awareness

See also cueing system, nursery rhyme, onset and rime, phoneme, phonetics, phonetic stage, phonics and reading

This refers to the ability to hear differences in sounds and is broader than 'phonemic awareness'. Children need to be able to hear phonemes, syllables and onsets and rimes to help them with the phonological aspect of learning to read. Conscious awareness of the features of speech sounds develops over a period of time. The National Literacy Strategy in the UK assumes that systematic teaching can accelerate this development. There is research evidence that sensitivity to phonemic structure of spoken words is linked with success in reading. (Bryant and Bradley, 1985; Goswami and Bryant, 1991).

Bryant, P. and Bradley, L. (1985) *Children's Reading Problems* Oxford: Blackwell.

Goswami, U. and Bryant, P. (1991) *Phonological Skills and Learning to Read* Hillsdale, NJ: Lawrence Erlbaum Associates.

Layton, Lyn, Deeny, Karen and Upton, Graham (1997) *Sound Practice: Phonological Awareness in the Classroom* London: David Fulton.

Phonology

See also phoneme, phonics

Phonology is the study of the sound system of a language.

Layton, Lyn, Deeny, Karen and Upton, Graham (1997) *Sound Practice: Phonological Awareness in the Classroom* London: David Fulton (Chapter 1).

Photographs

See also advertisements, Art & English, visual literacy

In school, children are most likely to come across photographs in the information and reference books they use. Photographs are used to illustrate and make immediate and real phenomena that would otherwise take many words to explain. In successful books the visual and verbal link effectively. Illustrators are using new technology in exciting way – photographs can be taken in almost every situation – from space to within the body. As well as imparting information photographs can have a strong emotional impact. Of course this is exploited in advertisements which is a good reason for helping children study or 'deconstruct' the social messages that may be imparted (Mallett, 1999, p. 102). It is never too soon to learn that we can be manipulated by the visual as well as the verbal! But this very power to move and effect is helpful in an educational context. In *School,* for example, one of the books in Wayland's *History from Photographs* series, the photographs of children in their Edwardian classrooms give us imaginative insight into the lives of individuals. The power of the photograph to illuminate social history is also shown in Waylands' *Migrations* series. In Hakim Adi's *African Migrations* we see family photographs showing ten-year-old Yemisi in Nigeria and then photographs taken after 1967 in London, the capital of her new country. The photographs show the difference between the two environments and the human issues involved in a way that even a huge amount of writing could not.

Of course a diagram or drawing is sometimes better for a particular purpose than a photograph as we see in David Macauley's drawing of the structure and function of machines in his book *The Way Things Work.* It is also true that photographs and other illustrations could not replace written contributions. Ten year olds who had been moved by a photograph of a Tudor sailor's shoe taken from the *Mary Rose*, observed that they needed to read about where and when the shoe was found and about Tudor shoe making to make full sense of the visual input.

If we give children the opportunity to take photographs to illustrate their own books, this takes them forward in understanding and appreciating the photographs they learn from in information books. In making or 'constructing' images they learn about the choices open to the photographer and this helps them study or 'deconstruct' the work of others. This can be a worthwhile collaborative activity with children learning to use the language of image making – 'close-up', 'mid-shot' and 'long shot' and talking about the social messages that can be communicated by the size and angle chosen to show people and objects (see Philip Hart's chapter in Callow, 1999, p. 82).

Callow, Jon (1999) *Visual Literacy: Visual Texts in the Classroom* New South Wales, Australia: PETA (see Chapter 7).

Mallett, Margaret (1996/7) 'Engaging heart and mind in reading to learn: the role of illustrations Exeter: Language Matters, Vol. 3, CLPE.

Mallett, Margaret (1999) *Young Researchers: Informational Reading and Writing in the Early and Primary Years* London: Routledge.

Phrase

A phrase is a unit in grammar which is between a word and a clause. It is a collection of linked words. There are six forms of phrase:

noun phrases have a noun as their headword as in 'famous people'('people' is the head word).

adjective phrases have an adjective as their headword as in 'very famous' ('famous' is the head word).

verb phrases have a verb as their headword as in 'was acting' ('acting' is the head word).

adverb phrases have an adverb as their headword as in 'very slowly' ('slowly' is the head word).

prepositional phrases begin with a preposition. In the phrase 'of a cake' *of* is a preposition.

genitive phrases include the participle 's' and usually modify noun phrases. In the following example 'the girl's big dictionary', 'the girl's' is a genitive phrase which is modifying (telling us more about) the noun phrase 'big dictionary'.

Students and children often ask how they can quickly tell a phrase from a clause. It is helpful to know that since a clause has a verb (while a phrase does not always have one) it is a more sentence like structure than a phrase.

Physical Education, Music & Dance and English

See also play, Language and Literacy

Physical education includes games, gymnastics, dance, swimming, athletic activities and outdoor and adventurous activities – all mentioned in the United Kingdom National Curriculum for the primary years. All this links with English in two main ways. First, as is the case with all learning, language is a crucial medium for teaching and learning. In physical education speaking and listening are used: to explain, 'narrate' a demonstration of a series of movements and to evaluate what children do. Because they need to plan and reflect on their performance, teachers and children develop a vocabulary to discuss movement and actions. In a useful taxonomy of language in physical education, Maude suggests we use vocabulary of body awareness (stretching), of space (moving forwards and backwards), of time (accelerating, stopping), quality (gracefully, running lightly) (in Bearne, 1998). The uniting of physical activity and language make physical education a lesson where there is a lot of collaboration and cooperation. For safety reasons a teacher needs to use their voice as a means of control too. There are also some opportunities for developing literacy – children may read a story which is the basis of a dance drama and

sometimes children are asked to write about their work.

Second, physical education links with English through play and the imaginative development of dance drama as a way of expressing human feeling. A dance drama round a story or poem creates the opportunity for many kinds of activity – language to plan, monitor and evaluate, physical activity shaped to tell the story and convey the emotions and aesthetic response to the music and the beauty of the movement. Costume and props may add to the visual impact. The roots of children's enjoyment of movement and music are in infancy. When we observe very young children we are struck by their urge to move from the earliest stages. As soon as they can stand, tiny children 'dance' and move to music. By the time they are nursery school age they choose physical activity as often as they can – skipping, running, climbing and riding little bikes and scooters. All this is highly enjoyable. Each new generation of children seems to recreate physical play for themselves and there may be some sort of 'play instinct' (Bailey, 1999, p. 32). This would explain both why children like their physical education lessons so much and why games and sport are so important in our society.

Bailey, Richard (1999) 'Physical Education: Action, play and movement' in Riley, Jenny and Prentice, Roy *The Curriculum for 7–11 Year Olds* London: Paul Chapman.

Maude, P. (1998) 'I like climbing, hopping and biking' – the language of physical education', in Bearne, Eve (ed.) *Use of Language Across the Primary Curriculum* London: Routledge.

Picture books

See also Art & English, fiction, history of children's lieterature, fantasy, visual literacy

Emerging during the last decades of the twentieth-century and the early years of the twenty-first, the children's picturebook has become an important cultural form. Each year more picture books, many of them excellent, pour out of the publishing houses. They have become the focus of academic study and there is a debate about whether it is the pictures that are central or whether we should be looking at the way in which the verbal and the visual interact to create meaning.

The best picture books have qualities which make them both hugely enjoyable and valuable in helping children learn to read. They are often narratives which encourage children to predict what might come next and sustain interest until the end.

But picture books are not just illustrated stories but highly sophisticated works of art. When reading picture books we have to relate 'non-linear' reading of the picture to the linear processing of words (Hunt, 2001, p. 289). Perhaps children today are helped by their experience of computer software, CD-ROMs and the Internet to be generally more visually competent 'readers' than earlier generations. Picture books are also sophisticated reading material because they work at different levels. So a book like *Oi! Get Off Our Train* by John Burningham may seem at first to be an exhilarating story about different animals joining Mr Gumpy and his children on a toy train that has magically become full size. But if we look more closely we see the animals are begging to get on the train because their habitats are being destroyed: as Townsend points out, the story can be read as a 'conservation fable' (Townsend, 1995, p. 335). Burningham's *Granpa* also works at deeper levels doing more than simply recounting a little girl's experiences and feelings during her grandfather's last months. The book is really telling us about the lack of communication between the generations because the experience of older people differs so much from that of the young. Burningham uses the visual to show us the mismatch between the grandfather's wishes and memories and the little girl. And Anthony Browne's *Voices in the Park* contrasts the friendly playfulness of children with the snobbish attitudes of older people.

Sometimes it is what the text does not say that matters. In Pat Hutchin's *Rosie's Walk* for instance, the young reader is drawn into the humour of the situation by the illustrations. The hen is oblivious of anything other than her progress across the farmyard, but the pictures show the predatory, although ultimately thwarted, fox following her. Meek shows how the author invites the reader to share the joke. It is this kind of reader/author collaboration that helps make readers (Meek, 1988). And there are of course picture books which tell the story through illustration alone. Examples here include Raymond Briggs' *The Snowman,* Pat Hutchin's *Changes* and Shirley Hughes' *Up and Up* – about a little girl's flying fantasy. The best wordless books have great imaginative appeal and provide rich opportunities for children to talk and speculate.

Another quality of picture books is their ability to draw on, indeed sometimes rely on, the reader's cultural knowledge (Cotton, 2001). The Ahlbergs' books do this particularly imaginatively. *Each Peach Pear Plum* tunes into a child's experience of nursery rhymes while *The Jolly Postman* brings in fairy tale characters as recipients of letters, postcards and catalogues. Anthony Browne also uses this 'intertexuality' with great success, for example in *The Tunnel* in which we see a picture of Little Red Riding Hood hanging in a young girl's bedroom. We see the same girl in a haunted wood later on.

Not only are picture books excellent reading material, they can also help children see the choices a writer can make by including different kinds of text. Shirley Hughes' *Chips and Jessie,* for example, tells five stories of the adventures of two young friends through cartoons and letters as well as the main narrative. *The Jolly Postman* with its different genres and audiences is often used as the starting point for children's writing.

Picture books are not only for the very young. The same books can be enjoyed in different ways by different age groups. I have seen work based on Anthony Browne's *The Tunnel* with seven year olds and with ten year olds. The younger children concentrated on the story while the older ones used it to explore their experience of and feelings about sibling relationships. Some picturebooks like Michael Foreman's *War Boy* have appeal for older primary children: words and pictures are skilfully used to bring alive a young boy's village childhood during the Second World War.

To extend your understanding of how picture books work I recommend David Lewis's *Reading Contemporary Picturebooks*. This is a challenging read but it illuminates the most recent thinking. It looks in depth at particular picture books – including favourites like Anthony Browne's *Gorilla* and Quentin Blake's *All Join In* and some interesting but slightly less well-known examples like Babette Cole's *Drop Dead* and David Pelham's *Say Cheese* – identifying their most important and interesting features. You would also find helpful Margaret Meek's analysis in *Texts that Teach* (1988), John Rowe Townsend's chapter 'Picture books in bloom' (Townsend, 1995) and Peter Hunt's succinct chapter 'Picturebooks' (Hunt, 2001). Marian Whitehead gives a detailed account of the response of very young children to picture books (see Chapter 5, 1997) and, with an eye on the Literacy Hour, Gervase Phinn has a helpfully annotated list of picture books in *Young Readers and Their Books* (Phinn, 2000).

Hunt, Peter (2001) *Children's Literature* Oxford: Blackwell.

Lewis, David (2001) *Reading Contemporary Picturebooks: Picturing Text* London: Routledge/Falmer.

Meek, Margaret (1988) *How Texts Teach what Readers Learn* Stroud: The Thimble Press.

Phinn, Gervase (2000) *Young Readers and their Books: Suggestions and Strategies for Using Texts in the Literacy Hour* London: David Fulton.

Townsend, John Rowe (1995 edition) *Written for Children* London: The Bodley Head (see Chapter 29 'Picture books in Bloom').

Whitehead, Marian (1997 edition) *Language and Literacy in the Early Years* London: Paul Chapman.

Plagiarism

See also quotation, referencing

This describes using someone else's work, and presenting it as your own. It usually refers to the

The Snail House by Alan Ahlberg, illustrated by Gillian Tyler (Walker Books Limited, 2000, reproduced by permission of the publisher) tells the story of three children who become small enough to live in a snail's shell. Grandma tells her story in a garden and words and pictures combine perfectly to bring alive the countryside and appeal to the young imagination.

unacknowledged use of another person's research, ideas or analysis in your own writing or in a lecture. It is entirely proper, and often desirable, to quote or paraphrase from both primary (original documents or research reports) and secondary sources (books and articles) provided you acknowledge them. Advice about this is under 'referencing'.

Planning

See also English Co-ordinator, English policy, Literacy Hour, National Curriculum

There are several levels of planning for Primary English. Let us begin with the most global aspects and move towards the weekly and daily planning that guide everyday practice. The school's agreed policy on English sets out the general principles on which the English curriculum is based and specifies the speaking and listening, reading and writing routines and resources for specific age ranges. The school's long-term plan provides more details about the programme, again on a term by term basis for each year group. It is from this detailed document that teacher's medium-term plans are developed.

Medium-term plans are sometimes called 'schemes of work'. The National Literacy Strategy *Framework for Teaching* refers to the three different aspects of medium-term plans – 'blocked', 'linked 'and 'continuous'. 'Blocked' work refers to a series of lessons on one aspects of English, like discussing the role of imagery in poetry or learning about the linguistic features of persuasive writing as readers and writers. 'Linked' planning joins English work with other areas of the curriculum. Children might be learning about different kinds of first person writing in English and looking at the role of letters and diary entries as primary sources in history. Planning for aspects of English like learning to spell, to handwrite and punctuate which need considerable practice may be termed 'continuous' planning.

Short-term plans for each week's work draw on medium-term plans. Teachers decide on a core of work together with appropriate resources

for everyone and then plan for differentiation based on what they know about the capabilities of particular individuals.

In the United Kingdom the Literacy Hour has shaped the way English work is planned. The National Literacy Strategy *Framework for Teaching* details term by term literacy work from Reception age five to Year 6 10–11 year olds.

Not all English takes place within the Literacy Hour. Teachers of older primary children need to find time for extended reading and writing. Sometimes particular kinds of reading and writing that fulfil English aims are appropriate in lessons across the curriculum. For example writing reports can flow from geography and history lessons and procedural writing is a major genre in science.

Anne Washtell gives a clear explanation of the intention behind the *Framework*. It is 'to ensure that all teachers have high expectations of their pupils and that children's experience in literacy follows a clearly defined, progressive and well balanced sequence' (Washtell, 1998). Particularly where it is followed with some flexibility, many teachers find *The Framework* helpful. However, it can inhibit a teacher from taking up learning opportunities that arise spontaneously and from spending more time on lessons where real progress is being made or where extra help is needed. For some teachers *The Framework* leans rather too much towards the prescriptive in its impact on planning and teaching for literacy.

DfEE, National Literacy Strategy *Framework for Teaching English* London: DfEE.

Washtell, Anne (1998) 'Routines and Resources' in Judith Graham and Alison Kelly (eds) *Writing Under Control* London: David Fulton.

Play and language and literacy

See also Drama and English

There is a strong link between play and early language and literacy. Imaginative play activities, drawing and games, often provide the opportunity to explore and experiment with both spoken and written language (Browne, 1996).

A picture book, story or poem can be particularly powerful in encouraging role play and discussion. In her chapter on 'Books and the World of Literature' Marian Whitehead explores children's playful exploration of pictures and written narratives (Whitehead, 1997). Let me give one example from my own experience of how a book can be the starting point for imaginative language and play. When asked to share with the seminar group the high points of her recent teaching practice a student who had been working with five year olds told us about her work round the Ahlbergs' picture book *Burglar Bill*. The home corner had been transformed into a room in the burglar couple's house and the children created their own role play round the story. Near the end of the practice, and with the class teacher's help, the student dressed as Burglar Betty and the children were invited to ask her about her behaviour, why she gave up being a burglar and what might happen in the future. It was a kind of 'hot seating' with the student teacher in the hot seat! The children were absorbed and their questions were interesting and profound. How, for example, would Burglar Betty stop Burglar Bill from slipping back to his old ways if money got short?

> *Edward the lion never comes out in the day,*
> *But when it gets all dark he goes out looking for his prey.*
> *Edward, Edward, Edward, Edward,*
> *He's a pretty lion,*
> *Edward, Edward, Edward, Edward,*
> *He's a lion you can rely on!*

Abbie experimented with words and rhymes on the computer at home and produced this poem when she was eight and a half. When it was read out at school, the other children liked the witty word play of 'lion' and 'rely on' in the last line.

Children enjoy language play round nursery rhymes and other verses. A playful approach to sounds can also encourage phonological awareness which helps children learn to read.

Because role play encourages involvement often over a period of time and throws up motivating contexts, it can be an excellent way of extending the range and the purposes for children's writing. Mallett evaluates a case study where nursery age children have made a pretend train in the home corner and feel the need to write out tickets and notices for the station. They are becoming aware through play of the social purposes of writing (Mallett, 1999, p. 34). Browne lists the varied kinds of writing that might result from setting up a post office: letters, postcards, invitations, notices, signs, posters, advertisements, stamp design, passports and writing addresses (Browne, 1996, p. 77).

There is now available a lot of software for the under sevens to encourage a playful, explorative approach to learning. For example the 'Max' series from Gauntlet Entertainment (01908 575 600) takes up a problem-solving approach. In *Max and the Secret Formula* children are invited to help Max find a hidden formula to save Auntie Lisa's leaning house. Of course we would not want these programmes to dominate – children can devise their own play situations – but the computer is part of our culture and we should exploit available software where it is helpful.

Older children also benefit from a playful approach to language. They still enjoy role play and improvisation – often round the themes in storybooks – and enjoy tongue twisters, limericks and comic verse. Some of the poems from Edward Lear's *Book of Nonsense* – 'The Jumblies' for example – can encourage both oral and written responses. For helpful advice about how to include play opportunities in planning for English see 'Play and Language' in Wyse and Jones, 2001.

Browne, Ann (1996) *Developing Language and Literacy 3–8* London: Paul Chapman.

Mallett, Margaret (1999) *Young Researchers* London: Routledge.

Whitehead, Marian (1997 edition) *Language and Literacy in the Early Years* London: Paul Chapman (See Chapter 6).

Wyse, Dominic and Jones, Russell (2001) *English, Language and Literacy* London: Routledge.

Playscript

See also Drama & English, Shakespearean drama for the primary school

Playscripts are texts in prose or in verse written for performance. They include stage directions, and sometimes notes about props. Improvised drama and role play, where the emphasis is on learning and cooperating rather than on performance, are more appropriate for younger children and continue to be important for older ones. However, writing and performing their own playscripts and using other people's is an important form of drama for children in the later primary years. Here they learn about the layout of a script on the page and about the strengths and the limitations of this kind of writing. They learn how everything is communicated through the words spoken by the actors and by gesture and facial expression. They can discover that playscripts differ from other kinds of fiction. A story or novel, for example, can provide some background and reasons why things have come about and people are as they seem in the play. However, we can explain that devices sometimes used by playwrights include a narrator or a soliloquy – a special kind of aside in which an actor confides his deepest thoughts to the audience.

Medwell *et al.* provide a helpful account of the structure, layout and organisation of playscripts in their book *Primary English, 2001.*

Medwell, Jane, Moore, George, Wray, David and Griffiths, Vivienne (2001) *Primary English: Knowledge and Understanding* Exeter: Learning Matters.

Plenary (at end of Literacy Hour)

This refers to the ten minutes at the end of the literacy hour when children are asked to report back to the whole class on their achievements in the group activities. This 'reporting back' might involve individuals in commenting on what their guided or independent group achieved or children may read aloud their writing. The teacher makes sure that, over time, each individual or

group has their turn. The plenary provides a good opportunity for children to reflect on what they have been doing and to share what they have learned. To give just one example: a group of ten year olds presented to the class a poster they had made which encouraged people to use the bins often placed at train or bus stations for glass, paper and cloth. The theme of the Literacy Hour was 'disposal of waste and rubbish' and the group were able to show how their group work related to the larger topic.

P-levels

These are skill descriptors for pupils attaining below level 1 in National Curriculum subjects. According to Senco Forum, P levels 1–3 outline progress in basic skills and understanding while P levels 4–8 indicate children's progress in specific subject skills in English and Mathematics.

Guidance on P scale descriptors for all National Curriculum areas is available at http://www.nc.uk.net/ld

Senco Forum is an electronic discussion group – e-mail: senco-forum@ngfl.gov.uk

Poetry

See also alliteration, ballad, creative writing, epic poetry, free verse, haiku, limerick, metaphor, nursery rhyme, personification, play, rhyme, rhythm, rime, simile, sonnet, verse

Poetry is a most important part of children's language experience. It is language with a distinctive form and pattern which manifests certain literary devices like metaphor and personification. Sometimes poetry is the most appropriate form in which to express certain insights and feelings. Teachers need to know about the different forms poetry can take and these are discussed under the separate entries named above. If you wish to strengthen your own understanding of the features of and categories of poetry you will find support in Medwell *et al.*'s chapter 'The Qualities of Poetry' (Medwell *et al.*, 2001).

Children start playing with language at the babbling stage when they repeat sounds for sheer pleasure. They are usually responsive to nursery rhymes and other verses which feature repetition and language play from the earliest stages. The shared experience of early verse and song and the actions which often accompany it, is what makes it enjoyable in the home, play group and nursery. As Wyse and Jones point out, its brevity makes it 'manageable and memorable' (Wyse and Jones, 2001, p. 259).

Once at school children continue their interest in sound and rhyme in the playground where they sing or chant to skipping games. In the early years classroom children learn nursery rhymes, verses and songs and will attempt to write their own. As they move through the primary years they will work with riddles, limericks and the kind of verse that appeals through humour. They will encounter traditional forms like ballads and sonnets. As well as poetry with

traditional forms and rhyming systems children will enjoy reading and hearing poems like those of Michael Rosen that have the natural cadences of conversation and everyday language. They will also have the opportunity to enjoy experimenting with free where they can concentrate on getting meaning across rather than on the form or pattern of the language. *The National Literacy Strategy Framework for Teaching* sets out the points at which different kinds of poetry are introduced. Teachers often read aloud to help children to enjoy a poem in its entirety whether it appeals to humour, tells a story or evokes memories of events and feelings. But they also want to explore how the poet has used language and images to affect us. Jo Naylor of Heber Primary School helps a class of seven year olds to explore the language of *Where Go the Boats?* She

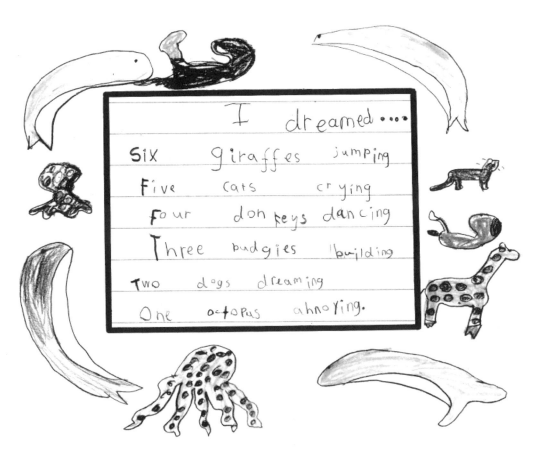

Children sometimes find that a poem they hear or read gives them a framework for their own poetry writing. A six year old at Castlecombe Primary School, Mottingham wrote her own alliterative poem 'I dreamed…' After hearing John Forster's 'Zoo Dream'.

manages to inspire the kind of discussion which encourages the children to enter imaginatively into the experience of the poem (*Becoming Independent* CLPE, 1999).

When it comes to children writing poems there are two main approaches in the primary school. The first is centred on the belief that children need strong experiences on which to base their own poems. Teachers often take children on visits to the countryside, seaside or pond for example or they brought in some objects like shells or fossils to inspire the children's writing. Sometimes the starting point might be a story or poem about a universal experience like a quarrel with a friend, loss of a relative or longing for a pet and children were asked to write from their own experience. Teachers working in this way tended to feel that children would find the linguistic resources to express strong feelings without direct help over patterning their poems. The second approach privileged technique above experience: the important thing was to show control over a poetic form like a haiku, sonnet or ballad. Perhaps the best known supporter of this way of approaching the writing of poetry in school is Sandy Brownjohn. Her books, for example *Does it Have to Rhyme?*, are full of interesting and practical ideas, often in the form of games to help children acquire the techniques to write particular kinds of poetry. 'The Furniture Game' for example invites children to choose an object and compare it to other things and then ask the other children to guess what it is. But does such an emphasis encourage children to structure genuinely felt ideas and emotions? One of the books which I have found most helpful in my poetry work is *Poetry in the Making* by Ted Hughes. He certainly thinks poetry is a disciplined activity but he also believes it has to shape strong feelings and ideas. Probably the best practice combines both these approaches as the teachers in the following case study did.

Sele First School's Angel Poetry

In 1999 children from Year 4 went on an outing to see and write about Anthony Gormley's *The Angel of the North,* a sculpture that towers above the motorway near Gateshead in the North East.

The teacher prepared the children by reading poems including Shelly's Ozymandias and they talked about how poets used powerful images to communicate their thoughts and feelings. Clipboards were taken on the visit so that children could clothe their impressions of the sculpture in words. There is no rush to get to the final drafts and the children are given time to reflect on the experience and to carve out a poem when back in school.

The children had the option of working in pairs and below are the poems of Emma and Sean and of Jessica and Hannah.

Angel of the North
by Emma Douthwaite and Sean Hanning

> The Angel casts its own shadow.
> It is rich in colours, brown and rusty red,
> Now it is clear to human eyes
> The angel rotates to face the sun,
> Feeling proud of itself.

The Angel
by Jessica Cusworth and Hannah Barrett

> The golden sun shines on the watching sentinel
> Towering over lengths of grass and houses.
> Its giant wings looking like a jet,
> Rippling ribs running down its body,
> A hard, cold, silent form.
> Earth, blood and clay all moulded into a sharp, pointed shape –
> The messenger of Gateshead.

I think you will agree the poems are vigorous and original. There is a strong metaphor in the second poem describing the Angel as a 'watching sentinel' and I very much like the personification of the sculpture in the line 'feeling proud of itself' in the first poem. In fact these and other poems have been the subject for an article in the *Times Educational Supplement* and were mentioned in a schools programme on Channel 4. Here are some observations – some aspects of the work that I think contributed to its success.

- there was helpful preparation for the visits including experience of how poets use images.
- the new experience – of a controversial piece of art work – was likely to lead to strong feelings and interesting thoughts.
- the children were encouraged to record their

very first reactions to the dramatic sculpture so that their notes would serve as mnemonic when they were writing their poems back in school.

- follow-up work included a display of the poems, photography and art work so that the children could share their work with the rest of the school – this raised their self-esteem as poets and encouraged younger children to feel confident about writing poetry.

- this work seems to combine something of the two approaches described earlier in this entry. It keeps children's responses to a striking, even moving experience, at the centre of the work while also providing opportunities for them to look at how other poets use language in particular ways to make their poems.

Following this success, it has become a tradition in the school that Year 4 go on a visit to the Angel and write poems which are displayed for everyone to enjoy. So a culture of writing poetry, an atmosphere where it is valued and built into the programme has become established.

Becoming Independent: Reading at Key Stage 1 (1999) Video-film in the Learning to be Literate series. Centre for Language in Primary Education (for an inspiring glimpse into how a teacher in a Southwark primary school helps children explore the language of a poem and enter imaginatively into its theme).

Brownjohn, Sandy (1980) *Does it Have to Rhyme?* London: Hodder & Stoughton.

Brownjohn, Sandy (1982) *What Rhymes with Secret?* London: Hodder& Stoughton.

Hughes, Ted (1967) *Poetry in the Making* London: Faber & Faber.

Medwell, Jane, Moore, George, Wray, David and Griffiths, Valerie (2001) *Primary English: Knowledge and Understanding* Exeter: Learning Matters.

The Poetry Library. Level 5, Royal Festival Hall, London SE1 8XX. Tel. 020 7921 0664 (houses a comprehensive twentieth century poetry collection for children and young people and provides a national information service for all concerned with children and poetry).

The Poetry Society. 22, Betterton Street, London. WC2H 9BU. Tel. 020 7420 9894. Website: http://www.poetrysoc.com. (The primary section of this organisation provides for members: news about new publications, poetry posters and specialist advice on all aspects of poetry.)

Rosen, Michael (1989) *Did I Hear You Write?* London: Andre Deutsch.

Pop culture – see advertisements, CD-ROMs, comics, television and literacy, video-film and visual literacy

Portfolios

See also English Co-ordinator, reading diaries, record keeping

Portfolios are folders or files in which representative samples of a child's work, the results of diagnostic tests and teachers' comments about progress, are kept. An English portfolio is likely to contain writing of different kinds, labelled diagrams and illustrations and cassette tape recordings of discussions showing the child's control over spoken language in different contexts. Running records or the results of miscue analysis are helpful in indicating reading progress. An annotated list of books read, perhaps in the form of a reading journal or log, and any dialogue book (a record of parents' and teachers' comments on reading at home or school during the year) are often included. Portfolios are valuable as a major way of showing a child's progress to future teachers, parents and the child himself or herself. Inspectors (for example OFSTED in the UK) also find portfolios a helpful source of evidence of coverage of the full range of work in the English curriculum including ICT and English. The English Co-ordinator will give guidance on the range of work which should be available in the children's portfolios. Inspectors will be looking for evidence of progression and continuity across the year group and will be interested in the quality feedback given to children by the teacher.

If you want to read more about the practical aspects of managing portfolios I recommend Tyrrell and Gill's book *Co-ordinating English at Key Stage 1*. They emphasise that portfolios should reflect teaching and not drive it and that children, however young, should be consulted about what is selected. If too much is kept, storage problems may arise. Many classrooms have a filing cabinet specially for the portfolios so that children and teacher have easy access. At the end of the year teacher and child usually discuss what should be sent up to the next class. As Tyrrell and Gill remark, if we are not selective 'portfolios could resemble suitcases by the time children reach primary six'. There is a trend towards using a networked computer system within the school to store data. The contents of portfolios can be scanned in and kept on disk solving space problems.

But portfolios are not just for children's work. Portfolios containing evidence of their classroom work are also kept by teachers sometimes because they wish to apply for accredited professional development courses. It is worth keeping evidence of children's work like writing samples and photographs of displays and reflections on the work. If you wish to read more about this, I recommend *Co-ordinating Primary Language and Literacy* by Merchant and Marsh (1998).

Tyrrell, Jenny and Gill Narinderjit (2000) *Co-ordinating English at Key Stage 1* London: Falmer Press.
Merchant, Guy and Marsh, Jackie (1998) *Co-ordinating Primary Language and Literacy* London: Paul Chapman.

Pre-communicative stage

See also spelling

This is the earliest of Richard Gentry's spelling stages; it refers to the period in a child's development when he or she does not yet make sound–symbol connections, but is beginning to recognise that symbols can be used to mean something. Children often write invented numbers and letters at this stage.

Gentry, Richard (1982) 'An analysis of developmental spelling in GYNS AT WRK', in *The Reading Teacher* 36(2).

Predicate

This is something said about the subject of a sentence. Thus in the sentence 'Janet has long, dark hair'. The subject is 'Janet' and the predicate is 'has long, dark hair'.

Prefix

A prefix is an affix which comes at the front of a word, for example *un*usual, *dis*appear.

Preposition

A preposition is a part of speech (or word class) which comes before a noun or pronoun to show its relation to another word – over, between, beneath, in and on. In the following sentence 'under' is a preposition: 'The key is under the doormat.'

Primary Language Record

See also Centre for Language in Primary Education, reading, record keeping

This is a format for recording children's progress and development in speaking and listening, reading and writing developed by Myra Barrs and the staff at the Centre for Language in Primary Education. It is used by teachers in the United Kingdom and in the United States and has had considerable influence on record keeping in general since *The Primary Language Record Handbook* was published in 1988. The handbook provides a helpful theoretical chapter on language and literacy development from three to eleven and detailed examples of teachers' records to show how the framework is used in the classroom. Teachers find that using this kind of record keeping system which gives a constructive picture of the child's progress indicates what is important in the whole area of language development. Thus planning, teaching, evaluation and then recording are combined in a coherent approach to the English programme. For example, if the record has space for using the spoken language for different purposes and audiences, this reminds us to reflect on and create opportunities for different kinds of talk. This comprehensive approach to record keeping notes the languages children use and whether English is being used as an additional language. It has also been praised for bringing the parent and the child into the assessment process. *The Primary Learning Record* is a cross-curricular development from the original *Primary Language Record* and sets out a systematic framework for the assessment of all the primary National Curriculum subjects and ways of collecting evidence of progress.

Barrs, Myra *et al.,* (1988) *The Primary Language Record Handbook* London: Centre for Language in Primary Education.

Barrs, Myra, Ellis, Sue, Hester, Hilary and Thomas, Anne (1993) *Guide to the Primary Learning Record* London: Centre for Language in Primary Education.

Prior knowledge

See also comprehension, concept mapping, non-fiction reading and writing

Prior knowledge is the existing understanding of a topic which we bring to learning about it. When teachers begin a new topic, they usually talk to the pupils to gain some insight into how much they already understand. This knowledge of where the pupils are conceptually at the start of the work helps the teacher plan and resource the lessons taking into account the needs of different children.

Procedural or instruction genre

See also factual genres, genre, recipes

Procedural or 'instruction' texts tell us how to do something. The chronological organisation of procedural text makes it a sympathetic genre for the very young, particularly when step by step instructions are given. One of the best books on the kinds of genre children read as they move through the school years is Alison Littlefair's clearly written *Reading All Types of Writing*. As with other kinds of writing, she looks at the 'register' of procedural writing. Register has to do with three things – what is written about ('field'), who is being addressed ('mode') and how the message is given ('tenor'). We would expect the tenor of procedural texts, both print and electronic, for early years children to be informal. An active form, using the second person, as in 'First you mix the flour and sugar together' is more

inviting than the passive form – 'first the flour and sugar are mixed'. As well as the recipes children read and write for simple cooking activity, the kinds of procedural texts common in the early years classroom include: how to look after the classroom tadpoles, how to mix paints to make different colours and how to follow the stages in a science experiment. The notices we find in the classroom can also a be a form of procedural writing, for example: 'Please wash your hands after using the paints'.

By the later primary years we would expect children to have progressed to more mature use of procedural texts. They may have the opportunity to read and write instructions for using computers, CD-ROMs, the Internet and atlases and to read and write stage directions and more sustained science experiments. Two examples of this kind of writing are Chris Oxlade's *Electronic Communication* and Catherine Chamber's *All About Maps,* both published by Watts. The latter

Dinomania: Things to do with Dinosaurs by Mick Manning and Brita Granstrom (Franklin Watts, reproduced by kind permission of the publisher), includes lists, labelled diagrams and insructions about games, models and plays. Children learn a lot about the different dinosaurs through interesting activities.

explains clearly how to read a map and how to construct one yourself. By the end of the primary years children can usually cope with procedural text with more formal features, for example the use of the passive.

We do need to check that instructions are clear for children of all ages. In a small-scale research study Littlefair found that the complexity of instructions in science books for children in the later primary years required careful teacher mediation.

Littlefair, Alison (1991) *Reading All Types of Writing* Milton Keynes. Philadelphia: Open University Press. Chapter 4.

Process approach to writing

See also conferencing, writing, writing area/corner

In a process approach to writing or 'process writing' attention is paid to the stages a writer goes through rather than just the end product. Writing is viewed as involving much thinking and reflecting and the teacher has an important role in helping the young learner shape meaning. The conversations in which a teacher, or sometimes another pupil, help a young writer to choose a fruitful topic (perhaps through brainstorming) plan and carry out a first draft, then edit and proof read and later appreciate the writing have been termed 'conferences' by Donald Graves a teacher and researcher in the USA.

Graves, and others in favour of the process approach, emphasise the importance of the quality of the whole writing environment and the aim of making the children feel part of a writing community. In the spirit of this teachers encourage a 'workshop' approach and often write for or with the children to model the writing process for them. Children may like to have writing partners for some of their work and to keep a writing journal of ideas and comments on their own progress. This notion of reflecting on their own writing and taking some responsibility for it is very much part of a process approach. Frank Smith, also associated with the process approach, urges us to help children to see themselves as writers so they feel confident and have a

strong self-image. Sometimes we have to 'scaffold' their early attempts until they can manage on their own and young writers often need to concentrate on 'composition', the content of their writing first and then on 'transcription' (secretarial aspects) and presentation (Smith, 1982).

If children experience a constructive approach to what they write at each stage, they are more likely to feel like mature authors and to have considerable commitment to what they have achieved. In an interesting article entitled 'Renters and Owners', Donald Graves suggests that we might usefully see process writing in terms of a metaphor of 'ownership'. If we own a property and tend it carefully we are likely to feel more commitment to it than if we just rent it. So the child who has been helped to become deeply involved in his or her work is likely to care about the quality of the final draft in terms of content and the secretarial and presentation aspects. This brings us to the 'publishing' aspects which are another feature of Graves' approach. The process approach brought a move towards 'publishing' some of children's work in hardback books with spines so that they were robust enough to join the school or class library – further reinforcement of the young writers' achievements. There was a commitment to writing for a clear purpose and a particular audience.

This dynamic approach to children's writing had great influence in America and Britain during the 1980s and into the 1990s. By the beginning of the twenty-first century Britain's National Literacy Strategy has brought a greater emphasis on grammatical aspects of writing and the English Standard Assessment Tasks assess end products rather than processes like planning and drafting. The issue here is whether knowledge of grammatical constructions transfers into children's writing to bring about an improvement. There is also concern about motivating young writers where tasks may be more prescribed. But concepts of purpose and audience, book making and the role of the teacher in supporting young learners as they write are all still recognised.

Graves, Donald (1981) 'Renters and Owners: Donald Graves on Writing' in *English Magazine*, 8, Autumn 1981.

Graves, Donald (1983) *Writing: Teachers and Children at Work* New Hampshire: Heinemann.

Smith, Frank (1982) *Writing and the Writer* London: Heinemann.

Programmes of Study – see National Curriculum

Progression in Phonics material (PIPs)

See also bottom-up approaches, phonics, reading

The National Literacy Strategy Progression in Phonics (DfEE, 1999) material sets out all the phonics and spelling work to be covered from Reception to Year 2. As Graham points out, it provides a useful structure to teach the requirements but needs to be used flexibly as children do not always progress in the exact order set out (Graham, 2000, p. 84).

Graham, Judith and Kelly, Allison (2000) *Reading Under Control* London: David Fulton.

Projects – see cross-curricular projects, English projects

Pronoun

See also cohesion, punctuation

A pronoun is a class of word used to stand in for a noun, or for a noun phrase. Often repetition of the name of a person, place or object can be avoided by using a pronoun. For example: 'Mrs Brown entered the classroom after break and sat down to read a report. She read it until the class returned.' The second reference to 'Mrs Brown' is by means of the pronoun 'she' and the second reference to the report is 'it'.

As pronouns require us to refer back to a previous unit, they contribute to the cohesion of an account.

McArthur, Tom (ed.) (1992) *The Oxford Companion to the English Language* Oxford and London: QPD Paperbacks direct & Oxford University Press.

The National Literacy Strategy Grammar for Writing Material London: DfEE, 2000.

Proof reading

See also drafting, editing, punctuation, spelling, writing

Proof reading is the stage in the process of producing a piece of writing where the secretarial errors are noted and corrected. Teachers can model the proof reading process in the context of shared writing. In many classrooms children help each other. Waugh (1998) considering punctuation, suggests that children might work in pairs to pinpoint each other's errors. Punctuation is to do with communicating meaning, so it may mean reading parts of the draft out loud to decide what kind of punctuation would be helpful.

Different categories of pronouns (adapted from Grammar for Writing, page 205 and The Oxford Companion to English Usage, page 810).

Personal pronouns:	I/me, he/him, she/her, we/us, they/them, it.
Possessive pronouns:	mine, yours, his, hers, ours, theirs, its
Reflexive pronouns:	myself, himself, ourselves, themselves
Indefinite pronouns:	someone, anything, nobody, everything
Interrogative pronouns:	who/whom, whose, which, what
Relative pronouns:	who/whom, whose, which, that
Reciprocal pronouns:	each other, one another
Demonstrative pronouns:	this, that, those, these.
Determiners as pronouns:	this/that/these/those

When it comes to spelling errors, some children find it helpful to look through their personal dictionaries of words they find difficult to remind them what to check.

Older primary children might like to learn some proof reading symbols used by professional proof readers.

Spelling error	cross through word and rewrite
Omission	^
New paragraph	//
Punctuation	mark to be included

Waugh, David (1998) 'Practical approaches to teaching punctuation in the primary school' *Reading*, 32(2): 14–17.

Proper noun

See also common noun, grammar, noun, parts of speech

Easily recognisable because it begins with a capital letter, a proper noun refers to definite persons, places and periods of time (for example: Richard, Paris, Christmas).

Prose

Prose is written language set out in sentences and in contrast to the stylised patterns of verse or poetry. For a detailed and most interesting account of different kinds of prose typical of different periods in history, for example Old and Middle English prose and Elizabethan and Jacobean prose, please see McArthur, 1992, pp. 814–18. When he considers trends in the twentieth century and beyond, McArthur notes that while every kind of prose is still evident – technical, legal and literary – the general trend is towards shorter sentences and relatively simple vocabulary as far as the subject allows.

When it comes to teaching primary age children how to write, there is a current stress in official UK documentation on changing writing style and vocabulary according to purpose and audience. More controversially, the teaching of grammar has been placed at the centre of teaching sentence level work on the assumption that making grammatical constructions explicit will build up knowledge that can be transferred to the young learner's writing (DfEE, 2000).

DFEE (2000) *The National Literacy Strategy Grammar for Writing.*
McArthur, Tom (1992) *The Oxford Companion to the English Language* London: QPD Paperbacks and Oxford: Oxford University Press.

Psycholinguistics and reading

See also big shapes, cue-systems, miscue analysis, reading

Psycholinguistics is a discipline created by joining psychology and linguistics. It is associated with a broader view of reading than just decoding print. In this approach children predict as they read but check these predictions against the actual words and letters on the page. Children make use of a number of cue-systems – the semantic, the syntactic, the grapho-phonic and the bibliographic. There is more under the separate entries cue-systems and miscue analysis.

Punctuation

See also colon, commas, dash, exclamation marks, full stops, question mark, semi-colon, sentence, speech marks

Punctuation refers to marks which serve as boundary markers in writing and which contribute to making meaning clear. Teachers in the United Kingdom have taught punctuation more systematically since the National Curriculum was first introduced. Since 1998, The National Literacy Strategy *Framework for Teaching* has set out when the different punctuation marks should be introduced from capital letters, full stops and questions marks in Year 1 to the very demanding knowledge and understanding of colon, semi-colon, parenthetic commas, dashes and brackets in Years 5 and 6.

Learning about punctuation is linked to children's developing understanding of some of the differences between speaking and writing and to their concept of what a sentence is. In writing, we need punctuation marks to serve the same function as stress, intonation, pause and gesture do in speech. For example, if we said 'You need some more pencils' we would indicate that this was a question and not a statement by using a rising tone. To make the same distinction in writing we would use a question mark: 'You need some more pencils?' Children are more likely to enjoy learning about punctuation and to see the point of it if we use examples from literature to teach it. Exclamation marks indicate how we should read a particular part of a text. In *The Giant Jam Sandwich,* by John Vernon Lord and Janet Burroway, a favourite book for reading out loud with under sevens, exclamation marks are used a lot show us when to raise our voice to bring out the full dramatic impact. After remembering that wasps love strawberry jam, Bap the Baker cries:

> 'Strawberry jam! Now wait a minute!
> If we made a giant sandwich we could trap them in it!'

Other punctuation marks indicate the boundaries of units like phrases, clauses, sentences and direct speech. Usage of colons, semi-colons, commas, full stops and speech marks is discussed under the separate entries. Children find some of these difficult to apply in their own writing. It helps if we are able to convince them that good punctuation helps them communicate their meanings to their audience, to those who read their work. I have also found that keeping their own notes with examples of using speech marks and apostrophes appropriately, perhaps at the back of their personal dictionary, gives a focus for discussing this aspect of their writing progress.

There are some issues to consider about teaching punctuation. As linguists like David Crystal point out, the conventions of punctuation have changed and will continue to change over time. Older primary children find it interesting to study this. We only have to look at how e-mail has brought about its own punctuation – as well as new spelling and grammar

forms – to appreciate how swiftly these changes can take place. Then there is the issue of whether punctuation which has such an important contribution to make to the overall coherence of a written account is a secretarial aspect of writing like spelling. For convenience, teachers usually plan and evaluate this aspect of children's writing development under the transcription or secretarial category and this seems sensible as long as the very real contribution punctuation makes to meaning is appreciated.

There had been relatively few research studies on this aspect of language until Nigel Hall and Anne Robinson began work on 'The Punctuation Project' in the Didsbury School of Education at Manchester Metropolitan University. Their publications include the scholarly book they edited, *Learning About Punctuation,* which brings together insights from research so far into how children learn to punctuate as well sharing the results of their own investigation. You might, however, like to start with their shorter publication *Teaching and Learning Punctuation.* I recommend also Alison Kelly's chapter 'Transcription: Spelling, Punctuation and Handwriting' in *Writing Under Control* which helps us appreciate punctuation is to do with meaning and part of writing as a whole. Another source of help is Waugh's article 'Practical Approaches to Teaching Punctuation in the Primary School' which suggests some enjoyable classroom activities like, for example, changing the speech in the bubbles of comic strips into punctuated text. Finally, the BBC *The Grammar Video,* includes an amusing programme on punctuation showing how it can help avoid ambiguity.

BBC Education (1998) *The Grammar Video (2).* Produced by BBC Education, BBC World-wide Publishing, videocassette.

Crystal, David (1995) *The Cambridge Encyclopaedia of English Language* Cambridge: Cambridge University Press.

Graham, Judith and Kelly, Alison (eds) (1998) *Writing Under Control: Teaching Writing in the Primary School* London: David Fulton.

Hall, Nigel (1999) *Teaching and Learning Punctuation* Reading: Reading and Language Information Centre.

Hall, Nigel and Robinson, Anne (1998) *Learning About Punctuation* Clevedon and Philadephia Multilingual Matters. For further information see

Website: http://www.partnership.mmu.ac.uk/punctuation/

Waugh, D. (1998) 'Practical approaches to teaching punctuation in the primary school'. *Reading* 32(2): 14–17.

Qualifications and Curriculum Authority (QCA)

See also assessment, Literacy Hour, National Curriculum, SATs

This is a government agency responsible for:

- producing standard assessment tasks/tests (SATs) and yearly handbooks for teachers on the administration of assessment procedures
- research on and evaluation of pupil performance.
- guidance on target setting and meeting the requirements of the National Curriculum and the National Literacy Strategy.
- advice on particular aspects of practice, for example *Teaching Speaking and Listening in Key Stages 1 and 2* (1999).

There has been concern about the emphasis given by government agencies to testing and particularly to summative kinds of assessment. However, QCA publications have been praised for their acknowledgement that not all assessment has to be written down (Wyse and Jones, 2001). They also provide helpful suggestions on formats for observation and record keeping.

QCA is based at 29 Bolton Street, London, W1Y 7PD. National Curriculum website is at www.nc.uk.net – includes QCA publications.

QCA (1999a) *Teaching Speaking and Listening in Key Stages 1 and 2* London: QCA.

QCA (1999b) *Standards at Key Stage 2: English, Mathematics and Science: Report on the 1999 National Curriculum Assessments for 11 Year Olds* London: QCA.

QCA (1999c) *Target Setting and Assessment in the National Literacy Strategy* London: QCA.

Questionnaires – see research

Questions – see non-fiction reading and writing

Quotation

See also direct and indirect speech, ellipsis, plagiarism, inverted commas, speech marks, quotation marks

I simply cannot do better than set down Tom McArthur's words. 'The concept of quotation depends on identifying (briefly or in detail) the source to which reference is made and from which words have been taken' (McArthur, 1992, p. 836).

In speech we simply say something like – as Iona and Peter Opie famously put it – a child who does not feel wonder is but an inlet for apple pie. If we are giving a formal talk rather than just mentioning the quoted words in conversation, we might add the name of the text and its date of publication.

In writing we use inverted commas to denote the beginning and end of the quotation.

As Iona and Peter Opie famously put it: 'A child who does not feel wonder is but an inlet for apple pie' (p. 17, *The Classic Fairy Tales* Oxford University Press, 1974).

Older primary children who wish to strengthen their argument in their persuasive writing or writing a history account can be helped to use quotations from a number of sources. It is never too soon to learn how to acknowledge the source of a quotation and avoid accusations of plagiarism – the use of others' words without acknowledgement! Books of quotations have a place in the staff room and school libraries. Teachers use such classics as *The*

Oxford Dictionary of Quotations (which includes quotations from major writers like Shakespeare and from texts like the Bible in alphabetical order) and the similarly organised *The Oxford Dictionary of Modern Quotations* to help children track down helpful quotes. There are also many anthologies of quotations, proverbs and words for children including the well liked *Quotations* (published by Kingfisher, 1992) which is full of modern quotations entertainingly illustrated and *The Children's Book of Words* (also by Kingfisher 1999) both by George Beal. These books encourage browsing and are nicely set out with clear print.

McArthur, Tom (1992) *The Oxford Companion to the English Language* London and Oxford: QPD & Oxford University Press.

Quotation marks

See also direct and indirect speech, inverted commas, quotation, speech marks

Quotation marks (also referred to as 'speech marks' or 'inverted commas') are punctuation marks which show the start and the end of direct speech or a quotation.

We teach the use of quotation marks as children make their way through the primary years. When direct and indirect speech is taught, teachers explain that the inverted commas are placed round what the speaker actually said. Even so, this seems difficult for some children. Sometimes taking a short play script or scripted dialogue and turning it into direct and then indirect speech helps.

Children, particularly when they are using direct speech in their stories, often need suggestions for synonyms for 'he said/she said'. Below is an example of dialogue where an attempt has been made to vary the verb:

'Do you want to take the part?' demanded the teacher.

Leon paused and then asked, 'Will it mean regular evening rehearsals?'

'Yes. But I am going to see if we can use some lunch times as well so that we can keep the evening rehearsals to just once each week', replied the teacher.

There are a few other ways in which quotation marks are used in addition to their use in direct speech and quotations from texts. They are often used to designate cited headings and book and article titles. For example: See Quentin Blake's article 'New Picture Books: Individual and Idiosyncratic' in *Books For Keeps* May 1999 No. 116. Putting a foreign or unusual word in quotation marks can alert the reader to its special status. For example – she showed a lot of 'savoir faire' during the project. We also sometimes use quotation marks to show that a word has been used by someone else and we are not sure we approve as in – these 'angels' seemed rather selective in the tasks they were prepared to take on.

I remember one very able eleven year old asking me how she could organise quotation marks where there was direct speech within direct speech. One way of coping with this is to use single commas for the main utterance and double commas for the quoted speech within it. For example: 'I heard Maria tell her little sister "You can eat the bun" and she did not need to be told twice,' insisted the girl.

Older children would also find it useful to know that where there are several paragraphs of direct speech, new paragraphs begin with opening quotation marks and closing marks are given at the end of the last paragraph.

QWERTY

See also alphabet, word processing

In the standard keyboard configuration on computer keyboards and typewriters there are four rows. The first part of the second row, on most machines for speakers of English, produces the letter-name QWERTY – hence our reference to a 'QWERTY keyboard'.

R

Readability – see individualised reading

Reading

See also cueing systems, genre, non-fiction reading and writing, phonics, phonological awareness, reading age, reading aloud, reading choices, reading conference, reading corner/area, reading diaries, reading environment, reading recovery, reading resources, reading schemes, responses to reading

A central aim of schooling is to help children become competent and thoughtful readers and writers. As a child becomes literate important kinds of thinking are developed and success in all parts of the curriculum becomes possible. Later, levels of literacy will affect job opportunities and contribute to competence in all areas of life. Literacy also enriches leisure whether a young learner's preference is for fiction or non-fiction.

Here we are looking at the reading rather than the writing side of the literacy coin. At its simplest, reading is to do with getting meaning from print. In the twenty-first century there are new kinds of literacy to control and children need strategies to read media texts – CD-ROMs, software and the Internet – as well as print texts – books, newspapers and articles.

There is no definitive theory about how children learn to read nor one practical method of teaching which is generally agreed to be the only, or best, approach. Teachers and student teachers need to understand the reasoning which underpins their own practice so that they can evaluate any proposed changes and assess the results of research. In a particularly lucid and comprehensive book Graham and Kelly describe principles and practice to help those who teach reading and want to be in control of the teaching and learning processes (Graham and Kelly, 2000).

This entry aims to give you a foothold this vast area, but of course you will need to consult other books and follow professional development courses on reading to keep up with the latest developments. Although there are many different theories and philosophies of reading and an array of programmes and resources, there are in essence only three methods of teaching reading.

Methods of teaching reading

First, there is the *alphabetic method*. Here the first step is for children to learn to name aloud the letters of the alphabet. Next they name the individual letters of syllables and simple words and then they learn and memorise the spoken form of written words. This method goes back to medieval times and survived into the seventeenth century. 'Horn books' used to teach reading by this method can be seen in museums. These are made of wood on which a layer of paper is placed and protected by a transparent horn film. They sometimes look rather like bats for ball games and feature religious texts and the letters of the alphabet. The alphabetic method is rarely used now, but the alphabet books and friezes found in modern primary classrooms reinforce the continuing importance of the alphabet in learning to read.

Second, we have the *phonic method* which replaced the letter naming approach of the alphabetic method. Here, children are helped to decode words by using sounds. This method came to the fore in the mid-nineteenth century although it existed earlier. In its historic form children learnt carefully graded sequences of sounds and applied this phonemic knowledge to reading simple texts. As the English language is not phonically regular children's early reading books or primers were limited to a vocabulary of phonically regular words. I remember being taught to read using a story called 'Tig is a Pig'. While phonically viable the tale was bizarre semantically – you need the magic of a Dr Seuss to make phonically restricted books exciting. In the UK, phonics has been given a new lease of life and current programmes are based on the results of recent research. Further issues here are covered under 'phonics' and 'phonological awareness'. The importance of the grapho-phonic cueing system in learning to read is well established but new approaches to developing phonemic awareness include games and activities rather than drills.

The third method, *look and say*, emphasises the visual aspect of learning to read. Children start by learning whole words, often from flash cards, before tackling them in a book. Reading books are graded to include an increasing number of key words. Just as phonic readers have a vocabulary carefully limited to sounds learnt so far, reading books based on key words have a controlled vocabulary with much repetition of key words. Aspects of the 'look and say' approach continue to inform current good practice. Since English is not phonically regular, some words have to be learnt by their shape, for example 'yacht' and 'salmon'. Children also benefit from having a sight vocabulary of key words to go alongside phonic and other strategies. Further, this method recognises that it is helpful to look at families of words, drawing attention to the change of shape in the stem word when inflexional endings are added.

Combinations of phonic and 'look and say' approaches were used during the twentieth century and, in reborn forms, are still used as part of reading programmes today. Those interested in a historical perspective will also want to know about two approaches which, while not actually reading methods, were manifestations of some philosophies and theories of reading dominant from about the late 1960s. These are called the 'language experience' approach and the 'whole language' approach. Both incorporated aspects of the phonic and 'look and say' methods but they were embedded in a different philosophy of learning to read. The 'language experience'

approach is associated with the provision of large collections of reading materials and resources and the principles and practice are carefully explained in a teacher's manual called *Breakthrough to Literacy* (David McKay, 1970). A key principle is that children's first reading materials are best based on their own oral language so that children's talk provided an impetus into decoding the written language. Using huge word banks, children and teacher built sentences together using plastic sentence-making stands. Just as phonic primers were limited to phonically regular vocabulary and 'look and say' materials to key words, reading books to accompany the *Breakthrough* materials were based on a particular kind of content – built from the research team's conversations with children on topics of everyday interest like 'The Loose Tooth' and 'The Lost Dog'. There were some fairy tales and adventure stories as well. Critics felt that while phonic kits were included in the materials, there was no class based, systematic approach to teaching the grapho-phonic cueing system. But its linking of reading and writing and its recognition of the value of talking about reading is enshrined in current good practice.

The 'whole language' approach, which is strongly associated with child-centred or progressive approaches to learning in general, was very much in evidence in some UK schools from the 1970s, but a similar approach was popular in the USA as early as the 1940s. All sorts of strategies were employed to help children to use all four language processes – speaking and listening and reading and writing – in their learning. There was emphasis on 'real books' rather than commercially produced reading schemes and children's own writing and book making was encouraged. Like the 'language experience' approach this one was criticised for undervaluing phonics. Its insistence on 'real' books is no longer such a great issue as the gap between reading scheme books and 'real' books has narrowed. The work of many 'real book' authors is now found in commercial reading programmes, and books used in learning to read are much more socially aware and linguistically interesting. The welcoming of parents as partners in learning, the benefits of paired reading and the importance of children's writing are all aspects of the 'whole language' approach that inform good current programmes.

So what is expected now of UK teachers helping children learn to read? They have to work within frameworks set out in a number of official documents. The National Curriculum English Orders 2000 link closely with the detailed reading programme for each term of each year from Reception to Year 6 in The National Literacy Strategy *Framework for Teaching*, 1998. There are also support materials and a major publication, with an accompanying CD-ROM, entitled *NLS Phonics: Progression in Phonics*. These official publications together with *Teaching: High Status, High Standards* (which sets out the subject knowledge needed for the primary subjects including for English, Annex C) are detailed at the end of this entry. At the centre of the current approach is the searchlight model.

The UK National Literacy Strategy Programme: The 'Searchlight' Model

The 'searchlight' metaphor with its connotations of shedding light on the text is an apt one for the reading process and entirely compatible with a 'reading for meaning' approach. Faced with an unfamiliar text, children 'search' for strategies by using the most appropriate of the cueing systems they have been taught. These are: the grapho-phonic cueing system which works well with words based on regular sounds and spellings; the syntactic cueing system based on young readers implicit knowledge of grammar which helps them make helpful predictions; the semantic cueing system which exploits children's prior knowledge of the topic and other similar texts. Some teachers add a fourth cueing system – the bibliographic – which draws on young readers' knowledge of different written genre. Previous experience of fairy stories or of information books, for example, helps children understand that different reading strategies are appropriate for different texts.

The National Literacy Strategy Searchlight Model based on the diagram in Phonics: Progression in Phonics

phonics
sounds and spelling
grapho-phonic cues

knowledge of context   **TEXT**   grammatical knowledge
semantic cues   syntactic cues

word recognition
and graphic knowledge
graphic cues

Requirements for work at text level, sentence level (grammar) and word level (phonics) are fully set out in *The National Literacy Framework for Teaching* and taught in the Literacy Hour. Of course some reading and writing takes place outside the literacy hour in lessons across the curriculum. Teachers are concerned about the difficulty of finding time for extended reading and writing opportunities outside the prescribed framework. This can be done by linking the literacy programme with other work across the curriculum.

Although the searchlight model includes all the cueing systems in the diagram above, the emphasis on teaching phonics is perhaps partly because this seemed to have been marginalised in approaches to teaching reading used in the recent past. The seven steps or stages of phonic knowledge are set out in *Phonics: Progression in Phonics* (DfEE, 1999).

Progression in reading over the primary years

Reading programmes, including the *Framework for Teaching,* help us to promote progression in children's reading abilities in several important respects. One aspect covered very thoroughly by *The NLS Framework for Teaching* is progression in phonics. The programme of phonic and spelling work from Reception to Year 2 is set out in great detail. Progression in phonics continues through Key Stage 2 where the emphasis is mainly on spelling development. Support here is available in the DfEE's *Spelling Bank*, 1999 and Laycock and Wastell's *Curriculum Bank*, 1996. Reading development is also to do with becoming able to understand a range of different genres or kinds of reading material, both fiction and non-fiction and in a range of media. This is covered under the 'Reading Range' entry. Of course, we would also expect there to be development within the main genres. For example, while a child in Year 1 would be able to enjoy a very simple fairy tale, by Year 6 an able reader would cope with a demanding fantasy like J.K. Rowling's *Harry Potter and the Philosopher's Stone*.

The quality of response to fiction develops so that by the upper primary years children can use inference to get at an author's more subtle meanings. We would also expect progress to be made in understanding and responding to more challenging kinds of non-fiction – texts featuring argument and persuasion. There is more about this under specific entries like Response to Reading and the different kinds of texts – Persuasive texts, Argument and so on. The next section considers the importance of attitude in children's journey towards wide, enthusiastic and reflective reading.

Attitudes helpful in learning to read

As well as developing a range of strategies to help children decode print and get meaning from it, teachers try to reinforce certain positive attitudes towards reading. Above all, we must communicate the sheer enjoyment reading can bring. Some kinds of reading are the means to an end – skimming through a train timetable or reading instructions to mend a fuse. But we need to convince children that many kinds of reading are deeply satisfying from a favourite story or poem to an information book about a historical period or about a creature's life cycle. Children are helped to discover this satisfaction by teachers who read aloud to them for sheer shared delight.

It is also important to cultivate a child's sense of confidence in their ability to learn to read and to use reading to learn about the world. Anxiety can be reduced by teachers and parents responding positively to what children are doing well. Quite small achievements are worth

commenting on – 'good – you stopped and tried again' or 'I like the way you broke that word up into chunks'.

Another useful attitude to cultivate in young readers is what we might term 'tentativeness' – a willingness to take risks and try things out and learn from mistakes. But in the end we have to direct a young reader to the words on the page and help them discover their meaning.

An attitude of openness to a range of reading experiences can be encouraged by creating a reading environment full of interesting and useful resources. Reading corners and displays exploiting the huge array of different kinds of text – in both electronic and printed form – support a breadth of reading experience. The resources work particularly well if used in a range of relevant contexts. For example, a display of work done in history lessons with reference books, artefacts and children's work supports both the learning of history and the achievement of literacy. When it comes to non-fiction reading and writing it is best to link these activities to real purposes rather than used as a vehicle for decontextualised exercises. This is not to say that DARTs (Directed Activities Around Texts) are not sometimes helpful and interesting.

Assessment and record keeping

Some reading assessments are summative and like the National Curriculum SATs take place at the end of an age phase (see entries on assessment, SATs and standardised reading tests). However, for a fuller and richer picture of a child's developing reading abilities we need to integrate assessment and recording into the planning, teaching and learning cycle and to keep evidence of progress. Formative tests, those which have a diagnostic element, are useful in informing our next round of planning for particular children.

Most schools have a portfolio system to store samples of children's work (see entry under Portfolio). So – what would a good reading section of the English portfolio be likely to contain?

- a summary of the results of a miscue analysis. Many teachers carry out this procedure or the simpler version known as a 'running record' with each child about once a term to assess which cueing systems they are using well and where some support is needed (see details under miscue and running record entries).

- informal but systematic teachers' records of children's progress in a diary format. The teacher might make dated entries after observing children reading in different contexts. In the CLPE 's *The Reading Book* (Section 10) there is an excellent matrix which can serve both as a planning tool and a record. It would help make a teacher's approach systematic as it covers all the reading contexts (choosing books, reading aloud, reading silently, developing print awareness, discussing texts, using information texts, reading in drama and story telling) and the social contexts (reading alone, in pairs/small groups, child with adult, small group with adult and large group with adult) that we need to provide.

- evidence of children's involvement in their progress. Sometimes children keep their own reading logs or journals, dating when they read books and adding some comments in a format agreed by teacher and children. Teachers might add a comment on the child's remarks, making the log interactive. The child's perspective is also often recorded when teachers write summaries of what are sometimes called, rather grandly, 'literacy conferences' – planned discussions between teacher and pupil covering their reading preferences, response, needs, opinions and agreeing an action plan to help further progress. The teacher will need to scribe for younger children while older ones may write up their own notes for the portfolio.

- comments from the parent or caregiver. Children's reading books and reading diaries go from school to home and back and parents are usually invited to make comments on children's progress. What parents have observed is also shared on parents' evenings and recorded by the teacher.

- teachers' notes on how children are doing in the different parts of the Literacy Hour. It saves time if comments can be swiftly written down in a simple format. For guided reading,

for example, all that is needed is the name of the reading group, the date, the text and the teaching focus at the top of the page and a comment box for each child with a section at the bottom of the page to note aspects to consider for the next reading session.

From time to time all this evidence needs to be summarised and presented in a helpful and easy to use format, agreed by the English subject manager or Co-ordinator with the other teachers. The format should be designed to make communication with parents and the next class teacher easy. One well-known and much-praised format is the Centre for Language in Primary Education Language Record which provides space for the views of parents and the child and notes if English is being acquired as a second or additional language. The latest version, The Primary Learning Record (incorporating the Primary Language Record) is a welcome development for many teachers as it simplifies and unifies the whole record keeping process across the curriculum (details from CLPE, Webber Street, London SE1 8QW).

Some teachers find the National Curriculum reading levels in some respects rather schematic. To help here, the team at the Centre for Language in Primary Education has devised some reading scales to use alongside the official levels of reading attainment. Children from six to eight are placed on a criterion referenced continuum from the dependent beginner reader to the exceptionally fluent reader who 'has strong established tastes in fiction and non-fiction' and enjoys pursuing their own reading interests independently.

Another well-thought-of reading profile which shows a child's progression at text level, making use of context and making meaning at word level is the First Steps Reading Development Continuum from Australia. This profile takes us through six phases – Role Play Reading, Experimental Reading, Early Reading, Transitional Reading, Independent Reading and Advanced Reading. Information from both the CLPE Reading scales and the First Steps profile feed directly into good planning for individuals and can be summarised on a record keeping format like the Primary Language Record at the end of the school year.

If you work with the foundation age group (three to six years) your records will take account of children's progress in the reading element of the Early Learning Goals. Objectives to do with reading include broad understandings like recognising the elements of stories and knowing how we use non-fiction texts as well as word-level skills like linking sounds to letters. You may also find the Croydon Early Years Development Record helpful in filling out the picture. It provides evidence for the Entry Profile and is designed to reflect competencies in the child's home language as well as in English. Devised by a working party of teachers from Nursery and Infant schools in Croydon and Lewisham, the Record has statements which can be highlighted, ticked and initialled. Statements are organised under Attitude to Books and Stories, Rhythm and Rhyme, Reading Illustrations and Print Awareness (contact The Schools Advisory Services Croydon or Raising Standards, Lewisham Education).

Into the future

Language is dynamic and changes whether we wish it to or not. New literacies are created as society and technology moves on. How children are taught to read in the future will depend on the findings of educational researchers and on cultural developments including innovations in technology. What one wonders will be the effect in the classroom of innovations like voice recognition computers? My own prediction is that we will soon need to attend much more in the classroom to visual kinds of literacy from 'reading' diagrams and graphics of all kinds in print and electronic form to understanding purpose and meaning in photographs and images on video film and the Internet.

Barrs, Myra *et al.* (1988) *The Primary Language Record* London: Centre for Language in Primary Education (www.rmplc.co.uk/orgs/clpe/index.html).

Barrs, Myra *et al.* (1991) *The Reading Book* London: Centre for Language in Primary Education.

DfEE (1998) *The National Literacy Strategy Framework for Teaching* London: DfEE.

DfEE (1998) *Teaching High Status, High Standards (Circular number 4/98).* London: DfEE,.

DfEE (1999) *The National Literacy Strategy, Phonics: Progression in Phonics* London: DfEE.

DfEE (1999) *The National Literacy Strategy Additional Literacy Support Module* London: DfEE.

DfEE (1999) *Spelling Bank* London: DfEE.

DfEE/QCA (1999) *English, The National Literacy Strategy for England* London: DfEE.

DfEE/QCA (1999) *Early Learning Goals* London: DfEE/QCA.

Early Years Reading Development Record London: Schools Advisory Service, Croydon with Lewisham Education.

First Steps: Indicators For Reading Development Continuum (1994) Education Department of Western Australia. Published by Longman Australia.

Graham, Judith and Kelly, Alison (2000 edition) *Reading Under Control: Teaching Reading in the Primary School* London: David Fulton.

Laycock, L. and Washtell, A. (1996) *Curriculum Bank: Spelling and Phonics Key Stage 2* Leamington Spa: Scholastic.

Reading age

This is established by a child taking one or more standardised reading tests which make it possible to compare individual performance with that of a large number of other children of the same chronological age. Thus a child's reading age found by that comparison may be above or below his or her chronological age. If a criterion referenced test is used a reading profile emerges, but where the test is norm referenced there is no diagnostic element. In either case, in addition to the test score more informal evidence of a young learner's reading strengths and limitations and reading behaviour is needed to give a balanced picture of progress.

Reading aloud

See also novels

Before children learn to read independently and silently they read aloud to the teacher who supports and monitors progress. Even when children become independent readers they continue to do some reading out loud. Contexts for reading aloud include guided reading sessions in the Literacy Hour, reading directly from the text to give evidence for an opinion about part of a poem, novel or other piece of literature, reading in assembly or at school concerts and as a way of communicating information from texts in every lesson.

The value of teachers reading to children from all kinds of texts has long been recognised. As a mature reader the teacher models important aspects of the reading process. Younger children enjoy hearing picture books, poems and stories read by the teacher. Teachers of older primary children often read a class novel for all the children to share and enjoy. Some children are by this means able to enjoy books they would not manage on their own. For suggestions for a range of books particularly suitable for reading out loud and some ideas for activities, see Goodwin and Redfern, 2000. Among the suggestions for Key Stage 1 are Quentin Blake's *Fantastic Daisy Artichoke* and Ahlberg and Amstutz's *Fast Fox/ Slow Dog*. At Key Stage 2 recommended books include *Unusual Day* by Sandi Toksvig and Brain Patten's *Beowulf and the Monster*. *Unusual Day* is decribed by Goodwin and Redfern as a 'bridging book' which has short chapters and a line drawing per page as an introduction to longer novels for children.

The present writer joins the many teachers who believe passionately that new demands and more prescription must not be allowed to threaten time allowed for this profoundly enjoyable and educative experience.

Goodwin, Prue and Redfern, Angela (2000) *Reading Aloud to Children* Reading: The Reading and Language Information Centre.

Reading choices

See also reading, reading resources

The Library Association carried out a survey of the reading choices of 2,300 children between four and sixteen in 1993 and found that Roald Dahl, Enid Blyton, Judy Blume and Dick King-Smith were the most popular writers. The appeal of Blyton's world of the 1940s and 1950s – *The Famous Five, The Secret Seven* – for modern children surrounded by television, computers and the world of technology puzzles many. The outdated language and attitudes of the Famous Five led to the rejection of the books by some teachers, parents and libraries in the 1980s. But editors made some changes – for example 'a nasty common voice' became 'a nasty mean voice'. Children seem to respond to the safe world Blyton creates and to some simple but good stories.

In 1993 the Library Association's survey found that half of the children surveyed visited a library once a week and 70 per cent once a fortnight.

For the findings of other research see the research into children's reading at the turn of the century carried out by the Roehampton Institute. One of their findings was that contemporary novels and fantasies like the *Harry Potter* books were favoured much more than other novels, for example history novels.

Make Friends with Books: http://www.anholt. co.uk
Young People's Reading at the Turn of the Century. (1999) The Children's Literature Research Centre, The Roehampton Institute.

Reading conference

Reading conferences are conversations between a teacher and child about the child's reading progress, reading choices and response to reading. These conversations need to be built into the programme and summarised in the reading record as they are an opportunity to find out about a child's out-of-school reading and use of information sources like the Internet, CD-ROMs and computer software. The value of 'conferences' with each child (and from time to time with their parents) about attitudes, reading preferences and reading progress has long been recognised in the philosophy of the staff at the Centre for Language in Primary Education. The conferences are an opportunity for children learning English as an additional language to make known to the teacher the wide range of literacy experience they may have outside the classroom.

Now that 'guided reading' has to some extent replaced a child's one-to-one reading to the teacher, reading conferences are important contexts for helping to widen a child's reading repertoire.

Gregory, Eve (1996) *Making Sense of a New World* London: Paul Chapman (informs us about the wider literacies in minority communities).

Reading corner/area

See also displays, library, reading environment, reading, writing corner/area

The reading corner is usually combined with a writing area and provides a quiet place for children to read, browse and work. The amount of space available varies but children need a literacy area in their classroom from the nursery years right through to Year 6. Bearing in mind the age group, teachers try to make the corner inviting by providing simple seating and display areas. There are many attractive books and materials for children of nursery age and we would expect there to be alphabet and word books, nursery rhymes, big books, picture books, folk and fairy stories and illustrated early non-fiction books. The 'starter list' at the end of Chapter 3 in Marian Whitehead's book *Supporting Language and Literacy Development in the Early Years* provides many suggestions for enjoyable books for the Foundation Stage.

From Reception to Year 6 most schools follow the National Literacy Strategy and the collections in each classroom include examples of the text types children are using in the Literacy Hour for that term or year (see 'The Summary of the Range of Work', pp. 66–8, *The Framework for Teaching*, 1998). Children need to be helped to move from enjoying picture books, story books, short poems and simple non-fiction to classic fiction and poetry, full-length novels and more demanding kinds of non-fiction suitable for the later primary years. There is also a need for dual-language books and for books made by the children themselves. As well as books the corner should include video-films, video cassettes, CD-ROMs and computer software, posters, magazines, newspapers and collections of advertisements and letters. I recommend Chapter 2, 'Resources for Reading' in Graham and Kelly (2000) for a detailed discussion of the kinds of books and resources for each year group. They remind us what experienced teachers know – that if we want children to feel involved in the book corner it is necessary to involve them in setting it up. Discussions about how to house the books – on shelves or in simple plastic containers – and how to categorise and label them are valuable. If the teacher uses some reading scheme books these could be stored separately.

The reading area should be a resource that is built into the work of the class. The books and resources should be those used each day and there should be fair ways of making sure all the children have equal access.

DfEE (1998) *The Framework for Teaching* London: DfEE.

Graham, Judith and Kelly, Alison (second edition, 2000) *Reading Under Control: Teaching Reading in the Primary School* London: David Fulton.

Whitehead, Marian (1999) *Supporting Language and Literacy Development in the Early Years* Buckingham: Open University Press.

Reading diaries

See also portfolios

Keeping reading diaries (sometimes called logs or journals) with the titles of the books they have read at school (and possibly also at home) during a particular period of time involves pupils in record keeping. The diaries have many different formats but entries are always dated and usually annotated. It becomes tedious to have to write about plot, characters and so on every time and often just a short comment is all that is needed – nine-year-old Adam put 'brilliant story, interesting characters and tells us about friends' about Gene Kemp's *The Turbulent Term of Tyke Tiler* (Penguin, 1979).

However, teachers sometimes require more detailed reviews of both fiction and non-fiction as a helpful indicator of how a pupil's critical faculties are developing. A selection of the longer reading entries could be photocopied, written out again or copied using the printer if the work has been word processed and placed in the port-folio. If you want detailed suggestions about a format for these longer reviews, I recommend Judith Graham's response sheets (NATE, 1997). As the author herself makes clear, the six sheets are a starting point for teachers and pupils and not everything should be included in every review a child writes.

Children find it satisfying to present their reviews to the class and to leading discussion. This is an opportunity for the teacher to assess a child's progress in speaking and listening as well as reading and writing. It also encourages the children to think of themselves as a community of readers and writers.

Graham, Judith (1997) *Cracking Good Books: Teaching Literature at Key Stage 2* Sheffield: National Association for the Teaching of English (NATE).

Reading environment

See also displays, fiction, libraries, reading corner/area, response to reading, USSR, writing area/corner

The 'reading environment' is to do with the social context of reading. Where we read is important as is having the reading materials we want. Our mood, the time we have, the reasons for reading and of course our more general atti-tude to it all affect the quality of our reading. These are the factors that decide how far we are willing, avid, and – most important of all, thoughtful readers – factors explored by Aidan Chambers (1991) in one of the most inspiring books ever written on the Reading Environ-ment.

At the heart of his book is the notion of the Reading Circle with the Enabling Adult at the middle, the Selection of Resources at the top and Reading (Reading time) and Response (book talk) at each side.

Chambers, Aidan (1991) *The Reading Environment: How adults help children enjoy books* Stroud: The Thimble Press.

Reading range

See also under separate entries for fiction – novels, playscripts, poetry, short stories and non-fiction – discussion, explanation, instruction, persuasive, recount, report, visual literacy

Good practitioners provide a collection of books and resources for children to read, listen and respond to and children often add the books they have made themselves, both hand-written and using the computer. Schools reflect changes in the culture and in addition to a wide selection of books we now include computer software, CD-ROMs, media texts and access to the Internet. Teachers working in the United Kingdom build up resource boxes of materials including adver-tisements, articles and newspaper letters to fit with the requirement that journalistic and persuasive kinds of text should be made available to older primary children. Pages from texts are often presented on the overhead projector to meet a particular requirement. Particularly in the case of fiction, it is best if children have a chance outside the Literacy Hour to read or hear the text in its entirety. There is a summary of the range of texts for each term for each year group, fiction and non-fiction, on pages 66 and 67 of the UK National Literacy Strategy *Framework for Teaching* (1998a). It is recommended that there is free flow between texts used across the curriculum and texts or parts of text used in the Literacy Hour.

Graham, Judith and Kelly, Alison (2000 second edition) *Reading Under Control* London: David Fulton (Chapter 2).

Mallett, Margaret (1999) *Young Researchers: Informa-tional Reading and Writing in the Early and Primary Years* London: Routledge.

Reading records – see under portfolios, reading, reading diaries and record keeping

Reading recovery

See also miscue analysis, reading

'Reading recovery' is an early intervention programme to help children with reading difficulties. It is associated with Marie Clay, a reading expert working in New Zealand, who has achieved international recognition for her contribution to our understanding of the teaching of reading and writing. Her programme to help struggling readers, how to diagnose children's difficulties and how to put supportive teaching strategies in place, is set out in her book *The Early Detection of Reading Difficulties* (1979).

Wyse and Jones admire the way Marie Clay 'mixes down-to-earth practice with rigorous research' (Wyse and Jones, 2001, p. 97). A reading recovery programme based on Marie Clay's work was put in place in the United Kingdom in 1992 but funding was withdrawn in 1995 (see QCA, 1998; Wright, 1998). It was expensive to train teachers in the method and labour intensive to run the programmes. Nevertheless many of Clay's ideas are used by schools and teachers in a modified form (Wyse and Jones, p. 99). In her book *The Teaching of Reading*, Jeni Riley shows how teachers can use Clay's approach to observe the reading strategies of all the beginning readers in the class (Riley, 1996, p. 51). Clay prioritises the cue-systems important in the 'searchlight' model of reading used in *The National Literacy Strategy Framework*. Key elements in the 'reading recovery' approach to struggling readers are:

- early identification of children who would benefit (Clay's running record, a modified version of miscue analysis, helps diagnosis of reading difficulty)
- one-to-one teaching
- using texts with natural language rather than the controlled vocabulary of some scheme books
- encouraging children to make 'locating responses' about the direction of text and pages by pointing
- looking carefully at print and carrying out word analysis
- hearing sounds in words
- linking sound sequences with letter sequences
- engaging children in sequencing tasks – reassembling a story cut into parts
- encouraging children to write stories

- helping children to monitor their own reading strategies by, for example, asking 'how did you know that word?' and reinforcing their successful strategies with a comment like 'I liked the way you worked that out for yourself'.

Clay, Marie (1979) *The Early Detection of Reading Abilities* Auckland: Heinemann.

Institute of Education University of London. Reading Recovery National Network: http://www.ioe.ac.uk/cdl/readrec.html

Qualifications and Curriculum Authority (QCA) (1998) *The Long-term Effects of Two Interventions for Children with Reading Difficulties* London: QCA.

Riley, Jeni (1996) *The Teaching of Reading* London: Paul Chapman.

Wright, A. (1998) *Evaluation of the First British Reading Recovery Programme.* NISS EBSCO MasterFILE Service. *British Educational Research Journal,* 18(4): http:www.niss.ac.uk/EBSCO-MF/cgi-bin/n

Wyse, Dominic and Jones, Russell (2001) *Teaching English, Language and Literacy* London: Routledge (see Chapter 10 'Reading Recovery').

Reading resources – see display, history of children's literature, reading environment, reading range, reading schemes, writing area/corner and under the many different text genres – fiction, information stories, transitional genre etc.

Reading schemes

See also big books, core books, individualised reading, look and say, resources for English, and under individual reading schemes and programmes like 'Story Chest', Oxford Reading Tree, Cambridge Reading

Reading schemes consist of books and other materials arranged into difficulty levels for teaching reading from about age five to age ten or eleven. In the 1970s and 1980s there was much debate about whether children should be taught to read using a reading scheme, with its controlled vocabulary, or using what were termed 'real books'. The reading schemes available at the time often had a stilted text and were criticised on linguistic grounds. There were also objections to the social messages in of some of the books which tended to show adults and children from one particular group in our society. Gender roles were shown as more fixed than in real life and children from some groups rarely saw themselves described or pictured in the books. This was all the more worrying as many schools insisted on the children making quite a lot of progress through the scheme before they were encouraged to read other books.

Publishers of reading schemes have responded positively to such criticisms and many of their books are now by quality authors so the old accusations of linguistic poverty in the books no longer apply. Characters and settings are more representative of all the groups which make up our society and both boys and girls are shown taking up a range of activities. They have also introduced other media – posters, audio cassettes, CD-ROMs and software. Increasingly writing activities as well as reading activities are built in. Also of note is the introduction of non-fiction titles – this kind of literacy has been given welcome recognition in *The Framework*.

More recently another factor, the emphasis in the Literacy Hour on shared rather than on individual reading, has shaped the design and content of reading schemes and reading packages. For example, many publishers now include big books which are sometimes enlarged versions of existing books. *Story Chest* started to produce these many years ago but others – *Cambridge Reading* and *Oxford Reading Tree* – now have strong examples. Also in tune with *The Framework*'s requirements are initiatives like *Oxford Literacy Web,* a programme with materials organised under 'Letters Sounds and Rhymes (phonological knowledge),' 'Fiction', 'Non-Fiction', 'Poetry' and 'Launch into Literacy, Grammatical skills in context'). This can stand on its own as a full literacy programme or fit alongside *Oxford Reading Tree*.

Despite the improvement in the quality of reading schemes in the recent past, it remains essential for teachers to assess them carefully before committing the school to the considerable cost of a particular scheme. Another issue is the possible effect on teacher's professionalism and self-esteem of accepting ready selected and organised materials to meet detailed official requirements. Publishers have increasingly sought help from leading experts in explaining how their resources should be used and the advice for practitioners is often very sound. This and the sheer comprehensiveness of these schemes can both beguile and terrify! We need to remember that part of the satisfaction of being a teacher is to work with colleagues to select materials for literacy that meet the needs of the children in the school you work in. Many schools prefer a flexible approach in which they use one or more schemes, or parts of schemes, together with books and resources chosen for different ages and stages by the teachers. In building resources for a reading programme there is guidance in, for example, Cliff Moon's *Individualised Reading* and the Centre for Language in Primary Education's '*The Core Book*' and '*Core Book lists*'.

Ellis, Sue and Barrs, Myra (1996) *The Core Book and Core Book Lists* London: Centre for Language in Primary Education.

Moon, Cliff (published each year) *Individualised Reading* Reading: Reading University Reading and Language Information Centre.

Reading tests – see under individual texts and SATs

Reading time – see ERIC, independent reading

Realism (in children's fiction)

See also domestic and family novels, fiction, history of children's literature, short stories

'Realism' or 'social realism' in children's books refers to the use of themes and characters close to preoccupations in contemporary life and events which could happen. These cover almost every topic including sensitive ones like teenage pregnancy, drugs, assault, terminal illness and abandoned children. Peter Hunt traces the 'realism or fantasy' debate to the 1970s when the 'teenager' became a 'distinct cultural category' (Hunt, 1995, p. 298). Of course there were 'realistic' novels for young people before this – Salinger's *Catcher in the Rye* (1951) and Paul Zindel's bleak novel about children betraying their elderly friend – *The Pigman* (1968).

But what about social realism in books for primary aged children? The book that stands out as an early example of 'social realism' for the young is Eve Garnett's *The Family from One-End Street* (1937). Children still find it highly entertaining but some have felt it patronised people from a particular social group. By the late 1970s there was much debate about whether social criteria as well as literacy criteria should be used to judge books for children. On the one hand some critics felt concern about sexual, racial or social bias in books for the young while on the other hand others feared this could lead to both censorship and recipe-written books portraying the world as it ought to be rather than as it is. I think it is also a question of looking at the whole book collection in a school library and checking that as a whole there are not too many books about children with nannies and ponies and too few reflecting children from different social groups and communities. This debate is taken up in the chapter on 'Contemporary Children's Literature' in Hunt (1995).

Perhaps the emphasis in Nina Bawden's books puts the raw side of life in perspective: social problems arising from divorce, cruelty and poverty are explored but these elements are firmly embedded in a fully realised story. So we have a theme of loneliness in a young child in *Squib* (1971) and how other children respond to it. Older primary children enjoy her book *The Peppermint Pig* (1975) which is about an Edwardian family left to cope without the father when he seeks his fortune in America. The story centres on a year in the life of Poll, the youngest of the four Greengrass children. The year in question is also the life span of the piglet, Johnnie, who becomes a pet but meets his end, as pigs tend to, when the year finishes. The story is about a child becoming able to cope with the sad aspects of life. In another of her books, *Carrie's War* (1973), events and characters – neither of which are shown in a 'cosy' way – are seen very much from the point of view of two young evacuees.

Philippa Pearce tackles the tension between what children want and what their parents find acceptable with a touch of humour in her book *The Battle of Bubble and Squeak* (1978). Two pet gerbils stretch the mother's patience to the limits. Another pet story is *A Dog So Small* (1962) in which Ben longs for a dog – but when dreams come true there is often a price to pay. The book also explores the impact of broken promises by people a child trusts.

Gene Kemp's book *The Turbulent Term of Tyke Tiler* (1977) is a humorous school story with a surprising end but as one perceptive ten year old told me 'it is really about friendship and Tyke really caring about Danny and his learning difficulties'. Jan Mark's is another distinctive voice in 'realism' for older primary children and her books appeal to boys in particular. *Thunder and Lightnings* (1976) is also about a friendship – between middle class Andrew and the less advantaged Victor. As John Rowe Townsend points out – although we hear things from Andrew's viewpoint, 'the book is more about Victor, who is supposed to be backward but who has hidden depths' (Rowe Townsend, 1992, p. 264). Janni Howker has been writing stories about the North of England since the beginning of the 1980s. Older primary children enjoy the five short stories in *Badger on the Barge* (1984) which are partly about relationships between the old and the young.

What about books reflecting our diverse multicultural society and what it might be like to join it? For help here I suggest you look at the fiction sections, which are age range presented, in *A Multicultural Guide to Children's Books* edited by Rosemary Stones.

Lisa Bruce's series of books about Jazeera and her family whose roots are in India are sometimes set in London – *Jazeera's Journey* (1993) and *Nani's Holiday* (1994) and sometimes in India *Jazeera in the Sun* (1995) – is enjoyed by independent readers of about eight to ten but can be read out loud to younger children. A favourite collection of short stories, again about the impact of Indian culture in Britain, is *Grandpa Chatterji* by Jamila Gavin – for children from about five to eight years.

Mary Hoffman's picture books about Grace, *Amazing Grace* (1991) and *Grace and her Family* 1995) some of whose family are still living in The Gambia, have a life-enhancing message – that you can achieve things if you really set your mind to it. In *Grace and her Family* Grace has to take on a new culture and cope with her ambivalent feelings about her father's new family. The best books are not recipe written and they share profound things about human nature that transcend class, gender and ethnicity. As we move through the twenty-first century, children seem to prefer fantasy – the work of writers like Roald Dahl, R.L. Stine and J.K. Rowling. But there will always be a place for those short stories and novels which we term 'realistic', the best of which take on those human issues that matter to children.

Hunt, Peter (ed.) (1995) *Children's Literature: An Illustrated History* Oxford: Oxford University Press.

Stones, Rosemary (ed.) (1999) *A Multicultural Guide to Children's Books 0–16+* London and Reading University: Books for Keeps with The Reading and Language Information Centre.

Townsend, John Rowe (1990) *Written for Children* London: The Bodley Head.

Received pronunciation

See also accent, usage

Received pronunciation is a term used in linguistics and language teaching to describe the accent associated with educated British speakers. It is the form of pronunciation usually taught to those learning English as a second or additional language and, until recently, was the typical accent of readers of the news on BBC television.

People speaking English with a received pronunciation use standard English dialect, but not all users of standard English dialect use received pronunciation. It is possible to speak standard English with a regional accent and this is socially acceptable in all but the most rarefied stratas of society.

Recipes

See also genre, non-fiction, procedural writing

Recipes are a sub-category of procedural writing which explains how to make or use something or how to carry out a science experiment. Cooking is a favourite activity for young children and they are often helped to follow simple recipes for biscuits and cakes in the nursery or Reception class. Recipes provide a list of ingredients and then provide instructions for making the dish, often written in the second person 'First you take one egg….'.

There are many good cook books for children, including Jane Asher's *Round the World Cookbook* London: Dorling Kindersley, 1997.

Record keeping

See also assessment, portfolios, reading, reading diaries, sampling, speaking and listening and writing

It is generally acknowledged that children's progress in English needs to be carefully monitored. In the CLPE Reading Book Barrs and Thomas pinpoint some characteristics of a good record keeping system. They are thinking of reading, but the principles apply more generally. A good record keeping system needs to:

- be based on sound educational principles
- rely on the collection of different kinds of evidence
- be a cumulative picture of a child's progress over time
- communicate clearly to other teachers and to parents and the children themselves
- be a collaborative process involving teachers, parents and children.

Barrs, M. and Thomas, Ann (1995) *The Reading Book* London: Centre for Language in Primary Education.

Recount

See also genre, non-fiction reading and writing

A recount is a chronologically ordered retelling of events. Children's early recounts may be in the form of their 'news' writing, describing what they did at the seaside, at Grandma's house or in the park. Recount is one of the six non-fiction genres in *The National Literacy Strategy Framework for Teaching* (DfEE, 1998).

In looking at progress in recount writing, Liz Laycock assesses the work of eight-year-old Martin. His later recounts as he moves through Year 2 show greater control over chronology and the ability to link his sentences with connectives like 'first', 'then' and 'next' (see Graham and Kelly, 1998, p. 117).

Laycock, Liz (1998) 'Monitoring and Assessing Writing' in Graham, Judith and Kelly, Alison (eds) *Writing Under Control* London: David Fulton.

At just five years Rowan is able to write a recount of a visit made to the school by a storyteller.

Recurring principle

The idea that writing consists of the same shapes constantly repeated is known as the recurring principle. Many teachers and educationists have observed that very young children produce lines of recurring shapes which will later be used in their writing. Children understand and experiment with this feature of writing from an early age and soon detect the difference between drawing and writing (Clay, 1975; Browne, 1993, p. 7).

Browne, Ann (1993) *Helping Children to Write* London: Paul Chapman.

Clay, Marie (1975) *What Did I Write?* London: Heinemann.

Referencing

See also plagiarism, quotation, research into language and literacy

The most widely recommended reference style is called the Harvard system. In this system writers record the quoted author's surname, year of publication and, if a direct quotation is used, page number. For example: 'In discussing the results of the Elmswood study, Jo Weinberger suggests that 'there is scope for increasing and enhancing the communication of parents and teachers over literacy' (Weinberger, 1996, p. 115). This style of referencing allows the reading to flow in the main text. Full details of all references are provided at the end of the essay, article or book in an alphabetically organised list or bibliography. There is a detailed account with many examples of how to reference academic work in Mallett and Mallett, 2000.

You may need to seek the permission of author and publisher if you wish to quote more than about 200 words. A fee may be charged for work which will be published, but this is usually waived when the long quotation is needed for an academic essay or thesis.

Mallett, Margaret and Mallett, Anna (2000) 'From starting point to fair copy: reading, writing and thinking' in Herne, Steve, Jessel, John and Griffiths, Jenny, *Study to Teach: a guide to studying in teacher education* London: Routledge.

Reflective practitioner

See also research (into Primary English), metacognition

A 'reflective practitioner' is someone in any professional field who thinks deeply about their practice rather than just delivering it to prescription (Schon, 1989).

When it comes to people preparing to teach, it is helpful for them to get to know themselves as learners. This knowledge of one's own learning strategies and processes is often termed 'metacognition'. A good way of organising one's thinking is to share it with others and to respond to their comments. So those who educate teachers – college and school tutors – need to provide opportunities for students reflect on their developing practice and to encourage them to listen and respond to all the 'voices' involved (Kendall, 2000; Whitty, 1995).

Once students qualify, they should continue to see themselves as learners. Lawrence Stenhouse urged teachers to take an active part in research and curriculum development (Stenhouse, 1975). More than ever we need to evaluate the materials and teaching strategies we use and to insist on being part of decisions on curriculum change. In the area of language and literacy, for example, it is only classroom teachers who will make the literacy hour a powerful means of developing children's reading and writing.

Kendall, Sue (2000) 'Professional working relationships' in Herne, Steve, Jessel, John, Griffiths, Jenny (eds) *Study to Teach* London: Routledge.
Schon, D.A. (1989) *Educating the Reflective Practitioner: Towards a New Design for Teaching and Learning* San Francisco: Jossey-Bass.
Stenhouse, Lawrence (1975) *An Introduction to Research and Development* London: Heinemann.
Whitty, Geoff (1995) 'Quality Control in teacher education', in Kerry, T. and Shelton, Mays, A. (eds) *Issues in Mentoring* London: Routledge.

Reflective reading

See also critical discourse, language and thought, metacognition

We read in different ways and at different intensities, depending on the context and on our mood and purpose. Reflective kinds of reading, in contrast to the quick scanning of a passage of text for a date or name or skimming to get a rough 'gist' of the content and ideas, implies understanding what we are reading in a deep way and evaluating it. The Bullock committee refer to 'interrogating the text' by which I think they mean challenging taken-for-granted facts and bringing all our critical faculties into play.

For a clear and interesting account of thinking and reading across the curriculum I recommend Lunzer and Gardner's book *The Effective Use of Reading*. When reading non-fiction children need to develop the judgement to understand the status of what they read. Is it fact or opinion?

Reading literature calls for a different kind of reflection. As well as enjoying the story or poem, the mature reader is also judging the behaviour of the characters by their own experience – does what this character thinks and does ring true? We also judge the quality of the language – the success of any dialogue in telling us about characters and situations, the author's ability to create a setting. Does the author make us think deeply about some aspect of the lives of human beings caught in particular dilemmas and circumstances? Children also learn to think and talk about the features of particular kinds of text – the first person voice of the autobiography or the distinctive structure of a traditional tale.

One thing does press on me – all my experience tells me that children do not learn to read and then to read reflectively. Through talk about books with adults and other children they enter into a discourse of critical thinking and transfer this to their reading.

Very young children sharing the picture book *The Whales' Song* were able to discuss the very different attitudes of the uncle and the grandmother towards non-human species.

An older class were able to talk about the subtleties of sibling relationships after reading Anthony Browne's *The Tunnel*.

So to make possible reflective thinking about texts we need quality materials that themselves teach us (Meek, 1988) and the opportunity to think deeply and to share our thoughts with others.

Lunzer, Eric and Gardner, Kenneth (1979) *The Effective Use of Reading* London: Heinemann.
Meek, Margaret(1988) *How Texts Teach What Readers Learn* Stroud: The Thimble Press.

Register

See also field, mode, tenor

Register is a linguistic term referring to the way in which language varies according to the situation in which it is used. There are three aspects of register. 'Field' is the topic, 'mode' is who is being spoken or written to and 'tenor' refers to the way in which the message is given – how formal or informal it is. If you would like to read further about 'register' I recommend Alison Littlefair's book *Reading All Types of Writing* which shares new thinking about both register and genre and the educational implications. For a more challenging read you might try one of the books by the linguists M.A.K. Halliday and R. Hasan, for example *Language, context and text: aspects of language in a social semiotic perspective.*

Halliday, M.A.K. and Hasan, R. (1985) *Language, context and text: aspects of language in a social-semiotic perspective* Oxford: Oxford University Press.

Littlefair, Alison (1988) *Reading All Types of Writing* Buckingham: Open University Press.

Relative pronoun

A relative pronoun introduces a relative clause. Commonly used relative pronouns are 'who', 'whom' and 'which'. 'That' can also function as a relative pronoun.

In 'the teacher who came to lunch', *who* is a relative pronoun in the clause *who came to lunch.*

Religious Education & English

See also Bible, epiphany, Literacy Hour, sacred texts

As is the case in other lessons, children and teachers use language to understand information and ideas in religious education. But English also links closely with religious studies because both subjects involve us in thinking deeply about our experience as human beings. Both fiction and non-fiction texts help here and we can link texts used in the Literacy Hour with those in religious studies. Factual texts about different religions and religious observances can be used in religious studies to inform children's developing understanding, while in the Literacy Hour the same texts could be looked at as examples of the different kinds of non-fiction genre. In *Find That Book* Margy Burns Knight's book *Welcoming Babies* is recommended for children in Year 1, five to six year olds. This information book shows how babies are welcomed into Muslim, Jewish and Christian families and links with children's own experiences can be made both in the Literacy Hour and in religious studies. But what about religious texts that are organised as stories? The texts used in the Literacy Hour are broadly divided into fiction (a text which is invented by a writer or speaker) or non-fiction. As Margaret Cooling writes in 'Scripture's place in the literacy hour' (TES, 4 December 1998, p. 21) many people would be offended at their sacred texts being described as 'invented'. But there is a problem about automatically placing them with other non-fiction materials. Cooling's suggestion is that we replace the categories 'fiction' and 'non-fiction' with 'narrative 'and 'non-narrative'. 'Narrative describes the style rather than the status of a story and can cover a range of stories from historical to invented.'

I recommend *Find That Book* as an excellent source of suggestions about how narratives can be used to link work in the Literacy Hour and religious studies. For children in the first term of Year 3, eight to nine year olds, Penelope Harnett's book *Lives and Times – St Francis* is suggested. There are imaginative suggestions for work both in the Literacy Hour, distinguishing between fiction and non-fiction for example, and in religious studies lessons – talk about what makes a 'good' person.

In both subjects we encourage pupils to make connections between the events and issues in stories and their own experience as growing human beings. It is the significance and meaning of religious stories that will be central in the Literacy Hour as well as in religious studies.

Find That Book (1999) London: Lewisham Professional Development Centre.

For advice about RE materials and the Literacy Hour write to Margaret Cooling at The Stapleford Centre, Stapleford, Nottingham NG9 8DP, e-mail: admin@stapleford-centre.org

Reports

See also genre, information books, non fiction-reading and writing

Report, one of the six kinds of non-fiction text in *The National Literacy Statergy Framework for*

Teaching (DfEE, 1998), differs from recount as it is organised non-narratively. It usually starts with a general introduction moving on to the main characteristics of the subject, often finishing with a summary. The typical children's information book on one subject like 'Spiders', 'River' or 'The Romans' is organised as a report.

Research (into Primary English)

See also bilingualism, Bristol Language at Home and School Project, Early Years (Language and literacy), EXEL, EXIT, History of children's literature (includes details of centres where research is carried out), National Oracy Project, National Writing Project, reflective practitioner, siblings (and literacy)

Educational research takes many forms including large-scale surveys and statistical analyses as well as more qualitative studies based on the classroom, the home and the community. We must not forget that library-based philosophical studies can also be valuable, investigating as they do such issues as assessment, the purpose and value of official documentation and studies of areas of the curriculum.

There have been a number of funded studies into aspects of Primary English, language and literacy some of which are considered under the entries listed above. The most recent and influential include the Bristol Language at Home and School project, The National Oracy Project, The National Writing Project, research from the Roehampton Institute Children's Literature Centre, The Punctuation Project (Manchester Metropolitan University) and the Exeter Extending Literacy Project. Research studies are regularly carried out by National Foundation for Educational Research and by staff at The Centre for Language in Primary Education in London and by those at Reading University's Reading and Language Information Centre. Teachers also need to feel informed about the research studies carried out by government bodies like OFSTED to monitor initiatives like the National Literacy Strategy Literacy Hour.

It is very much part of a teacher's professional role to keep in touch with research findings to inform their work in the classroom (Kershner

and Chaplain, 2000). Many of the entries in this encyclopaedia refer to recent research and summaries are available in professional journals like *Reading, language and literacy* (UKRA), *Language Matters* (CLPE) and the *Times Educational Supplement*. These journals often include articles by practising teachers, and the section which follows suggests how teachers can contribute to knowledge through classroom research.

The teacher as researcher

Here I am thinking of the small scale, qualitative* studies of Primary English, language and literacy which can be carried out by teachers and by student teachers writing dissertations. Any curriculum, including the language and literacy curriculum, develops and changes and it is important that teachers are part of the development process (George, 2000, p. 93). Undertaking classroom research confirms the status of teachers as professionals and reflective practitioners and discourages a view of us as technicians delivering the requirements of others. The kind of research known as 'action research' is particularly suited to the classroom for the following reasons. First it is essentially practitioner-led, although there is no reason why teacher researchers should not involve others like college tutors and student teachers. Colleagues too can assess the findings to reduce subjectivity.** Second it can address those issues which have come up in everyday practice. Topics my students have investigated, often in collaboration with their teachers in partnership placements, include: how far exploring a text through drama can lead to improved range and quality in children's writing; the progress of groups of children in persuasive forms of writing with and without writing frames; the role of the computer in promoting group writing; teacher-led talk about particular fairy tales as a way of helping children control the genre as readers and writers; strategies to promote confident story telling. Third, action research, like teaching, is cyclical and can enrich practice as it goes forward. There is the formulation of a question or hypothesis, planning, teaching and evaluation, and then the fruits of the research are taken into the next round of planning and so on. However, although it has much in common with good teaching, action research involves a more than usual amount of time at the planning and evaluation stages. When well planned, it should be as systematic as any other kind of research. Collection of data has to be meticulous and includes making tape and video-recordings of classroom work, producing transcripts of children's talk, collecting examples of writing, formulating and assessing questionnaires, recording interviews and making notes of careful observations in research diaries. There needs to be careful attention to the dates on which things happened, who was involved and the time spent on particular activities.

The next challenge is to write up the story of the research, the findings and conclusions in a rigorous and lucid way. This will involve a section, a literary review, which situates the study in the context of other relevant research and thinking. Support here can be found in Judith Bell's well-known book *Doing Your Research Project* (1993) and in Chapter 6 of *Study to Teach* (2000) which gives detailed advice about structuring essays and dissertations and about referencing. While the challenge of taking on these projects alongside all the other things a teacher has to do must be recognised, sharing the fruits of the work with others is usually satisfying and enjoyable.

* Qualitative researchers use texts, written and spoken, (questionnaires, interviews, writing samples and lesson transcripts), and observations of what people do as a basis for its conclusions. It is systematic in the gathering of data.

In contrast, quantitative approaches 'collect facts and study the relationship of one set of facts to another' (Bell, 1993, p. 5). They often involve large-scale surveys with substantial samples to produce quantifiable conclusions which can be generalised.

Many researchers use both qualitative and quantitative approaches within one study.

** This is known as 'triangulation'.

Bell, Judith (1993) *Doing Your Research Project* Buckingham: Open University Press.

George, Rosalyn (2000) 'Starting your research project' in Herne, Steve, Jessel, John and Griffiths, Jenny (eds) *Study to Teach: a guide to studying in teacher education* London: Paul Chapman.

Kershaw, Ruth and Chaplain, Rowland (2000) *Understanding Special Educational Needs: A Teacher's Guide To Efffective School-based Research* London: David Fulton.

Mallett, Margaret and Mallett, Anna (2000) 'From starting point to fair copy: reading, writing and thinking' in Herne, Steve, Jessel, John and Griffiths, Jenny (eds) *Study to Teach* London: Routledge.

Research awards and databases

The Government gives awards for 'sharply focused research' in key areas of classroom practice (www.dfee.gov.uk). Grants are also available from the Teacher Training Agency (www.canteach.gov.uk) for small-scale classroom based enquiries.

Some educational trusts will consider funding teacher research, for example The Farmington Trust (Tel. 01865 271965).

The National Literacy Trust has a research database www.literacytrust.org.

The National Foundation for Educational Research has a database of research studies www.nfer.ac.uk

British Educational Research Association – www.bera.ac.uk.

Journals that publish research articles by teachers include:

Reading, Literacy and Language. Journal of the United Kingdom Reading Association (UKRA). Teresa Grainger, editor, Christ Church University College, Canterbury. Kent CT1 1QU. e-mail: t.m.grainger@cant.ac.uk.

English 4–11. Primary Journal of The English Association, University of Leicester, University Road, Leicester LE1 7RH. e-mail:engassoc@le.ac.uk.

The Primary English Magazine (NATE). 50, Broadfield Road, Sheffield. S8 0XJ Website:www.nate.org.uk.

Resources for English teaching – see CD-ROMs, displays, history of children's literature, individualised reading, reading, reading environment, reading schemes, writing area/corner and also under the different text genres like advertisements, comics, recipes, recount, reports

Response to reading

See also enabling adult, fiction, reading environment, zone of proximal development

We respond to different kinds of reading – fiction, non-fiction, environmental print and so on – in different ways. Children are most likely to respond deeply to literary reading. We know children have enjoyed a work of fiction if they want to read the book again or seek another one by the same author. We can help children become thoughtful readers by creating opportunities for them to share their response to a book that has moved, excited or delighted them. The role of the adult as mature reader is also of great importance. Aidan Chambers considers that however helpful learners are to each other, in the end young readers 'depend on knowledgeable grown-ups because there are some things about every art and craft – that you only know from experience and can only be passed on by those who've learned them by experience' (Chambers, 1991, p. 15).

This has implications for how we educate primary teachers: Children's Literature should, I believe, be a core area of study.

Chambers, Aidan (1991) *The Reading Environment: how adults help children enjoy books* Stroud: The Thimble Press.

Retrieval devices

See also information books, library skills. non-fiction reading and writing

'Retrieval devices' are those parts of a text, the contents page and index, which help direct the reader to the exact information he or she needs. They also indicate the scope of a text. Publishers of children's information and reference books nearly always include satisfactory retrieval devices and teachers model retrieval strategies in the shared reading part of the Literacy Hour.

Rhyme

This is a literary term to refer to words which are the same or similar in sound.

Rhythm

A poem's rhythm is its beat and gives it form and pattern. The rhythm of a poem contributes to its meaning by contributing to the mood and 'colour'.

Rime – see onset and rime

Role play – see Drama & English

Running reading records

See also reading, record keeping and miscue analysis

Running records are a simple kind of miscue analysis which enable the teacher to observe how a young reader processes a text. There are different approaches and while some teachers choose an unfamiliar chunk of reading, others use a known but not-known-by-heart text. The important thing is that the procedure shows how the child reconstructs meaning, uses available cues and integrates strategies.

This procedure is usually carried out with newly independent readers who read out loud to the teacher from a book. Using a photocopy of the paragraphs to be read, the teacher marks each word read correctly with a stroke. Some of the symbols for miscue analysis are used to identify words read incorrectly. For example missed-out words are circled, substituted words are written above, words supplied by the teacher are marked 'T' and 'SC' identifies parts of the text where the child self-corrected his or her reading. New Zealand's leading reading specialist, Marie Clay, gives detailed advice about every aspect of carrying out and interpreting running records (Clay, 1985). It is important to mark every miscue and to reflect on the child's strategies carefully to arrive at an accurate diagnosis. Do the child's miscues suggest he or she is cueing into the visual aspects of reading and not also searching for meaning? A child's comments during the reading are worth noting as they may confirm aspects of the diagnosis. There are interesting examples of filled in running records in the appendix of Riley (1996).

Clay, Marie (1985, third edition) *The Early Detection of Reading Difficulties* Auckland: Heinemann.
Riley, Jeni (1996) *The Teaching of Reading: The Development of Literacy in the Early Years of School* London: Paul Chapman.

Salford Reading Test (Sentences)

First published in 1976 by Hodder & Stoughton, this oral, individual, untimed reading test covers an age-range from 6.10 to 11.9. The test assesses the young reader's ability to read progressively more difficult sentences.

Sacred texts

See also the Bible, parables, religious studies & English

In a plural society we have to respect texts which are sacred to the different groups which make up our community. There are a number of books which explain the world's major religions including Christianity, Judaism, Islam, Hinduism, Sikhism, Buddhism, Shinto and Tao. *What I Believe* by Alan Brown and Andrew Langley (Macdonald) describes the main beliefs, practices and festivals for these eight religions for children of about seven to ten years. It is difficult to explain all aspects of different faiths to children – indeed some scholars spend a lifetime studying only one of them. But perhaps a book like this would provide some background for stories from different parts of the world where some understanding of a particular faith is helpful. For further consideration of these issues please see under Religious Studies & English.

SATs (Standard Assessment Tasks)

See also assessment, reading, record keeping, running reading records, writing

The format of the UK National Curriculum Standard Assessment Tasks/Tests (SATs) has been stable over a number of years. It is important to recognise that this is an essentially criterion refer-enced approach to assessment, using the UK National Curriculum Attainment Target levels which are set out in the English Orders of the 2000 National Curriculum. Teachers, parents and children regard these tests as more formal than the assessments carried out by the teacher in the course of everyday work.

Key Stage 1

At Key Stage 1 (5–7 years) teachers estimate the child's progress in reading using the NC Attainment Target Levels. A child estimated by the teacher to be at level 1 will read out loud from one of a list of four books. There will be some general questions first to establish the child's knowledge about books and print. Where the child seems to be around level 2, he or she must then go on to read particular passages identified in particular books and the teacher uses a 'running record' approach to judge the child's strategies. Like 'miscue analysis', a 'running record' identifies the child's degree of success in using 'phonic', 'graphic', 'syntactic' and 'contextual' cues. A child's accuracy is judged as 2A, 2B or 2C; the teacher also notes if the child can retell the story and comment on its meaning. Children achieving levels 2A, 2B or 2C take a further reading comprehension test which is in the form of a short story and an information text set out in a booklet.

There is a teacher's guide giving instructions about both administering and marking the test. Children judged by the reading aloud tests and the reading comprehension tests achieving level 2A take a further comprehension test to establish whether or not they have reached level 3.

The assessment of writing at Key Stage 1 is carried out by asking children to carry out a task rather than by a formal test. Starting from a book read to the child, the teacher decides on an appropriate linked writing task. This may take one of a number of forms including an account that develops ideas and language patterns in the book or one which is in the form of a letter or a review. The writing is usually done on one occasion lasting about an hour. Thus the task is very much like the writing children do every day but it is 'first draft' writing. The teacher assesses the writing using sample assessment sheets and the current guidelines in QCA's *English Tasks Teacher's Handbook*. Children also take a formal spelling test set out in an illustrated booklet. The words to be written are dictated by the teacher.

Key Stage 2

Year 6 children (at the end of the primary years), who are operating in the teacher's estimation at level 3 or above take unseen timed tests over a week in May. The reading tests are in the form of a booklet of a set of readings of different genres, some of which are linked to a theme. Children read through the extracts and questions for 15 minutes and then for the next 45 minutes answer the comprehension questions in an answer booklet. Children judged to be working at level 6 proceed to a sixty-minute extension test in the same sort of format but which requires an extended written response in the last question.

The writing test at Key Stage 2 is timed, allowing fifteen minutes for planning and forty-five minutes for writing. There is a choice of about four different titles in an illustrated booklet. Recent essays titles include 'The School Trip' (in the form of a newsletter) and 'Changes' and 'Journeys' – short story themes. The teacher reads through the planning booklet at the beginning of the test and points out the prompts which give reminders about the structure of the different writing tasks. External assessors mark the tests with regard to two categories: purpose and organisation and grammar (including punctuation). Spelling and Handwriting are not part of the criteria as they are assessed in a separate test. In the latter test the teacher reads out a passage and children put in the required spellings in the gaps in the passages in their test booklets. Children who are judged to be working at

National Curriculum level 6 take a further test which assesses their 'extended writing' ability. For a fuller account of the writing SATs please see Graham and Kelly, 1998, Chapter 6, 'Monitoring and Assessing Writing'.

What are the issues raised by the SATs?

The tests make considerable demands on the children who have to cope with different kinds of reading material in a short space of time.

A number of important issues are raised by the SATs. Where the results of an assessment are fed into published league tables teachers, children and parents experience considerable anxiety and teachers might 'teach to the test', causing a narrowing of the curriculum. The possible bias of the tests towards gender or ethnicity are also a concern even though the Qualifications and Curriculum Authority trial each test with special regard for these aspects. Boys seem to achieve slightly higher scores with certain kinds of text. For example, the 1999 short, large-type poem *Spinners* – which was illustrated with cartoons – seemed to be one factor in raising boys' reading scores. Many teachers have reservations about the 45 minute story writing task at Year 6. Sue Palmer, for example, fears coaching for the test may 'distract attention from real creative writing, an activity from which children really benefit, since it gives them the chance to explore and express their ideas'. The government's assessment procedures are under constant review. Palmer suggests placing the emphasis on non-fiction kinds of writing plus some focused creative options – for example writing a character study or a short prose piece on a theme like 'The Sea' (Palmer, p. 12, 2001). A number of other teachers and educationists have considered the SATs in the context of wider assessment issues, (see for example Wyse and Jones, 2001, Chapters 11 and 19 and Graham and Kelly, 2000, Chapter 4).

We must also remember that the SATS are only one snapshot of a child's reading and writing competence and may not reflect his or her true achievement. 'This means that teachers' ongoing assessments, even if they have to be modified, still have an important role in providing a fuller picture of a child's reading as well as evidence of what has been accomplished and information on which to base planning for the child's future needs' (Graham and Kelly, 2000, p. 133). Other ways of assessing and recording reading and writing are under entries on portfolios, reading, record keeping and writing.

DfEE/QCA (1999) *English: The National Curriculum for England* London DfEE.

Graham. Judith and Kelly, Alison (1998) *Writing Under Control* London: David Fulton (see Chapter 6).

Graham, Judith and Kelly, Alison (2000, second edition) *Reading Under Control* London: David Fulton.

Palmer, Sue (2001) 'Dear *English 4–11*' on 'Issues' page in *English 4–11*, Summer 2001, No. 12.

Qualifications and Curriculum Authority (QCA) (1998) *English Test Mark Schemes* London: QCA.

Qualification and Curriculum Authority (QCA) (1999) *Target Setting and Assessment in the National Literacy Strategy* London: QCA.

School Curriculum and Assessment Authority (SCAA) (1995) *Exemplification of Standards: English* London: SCAA.

Wyse, Dominic and Jones, Russell (2001) *English, Language and Literacy* London: Routledge Falmer.

Scaffolding

See also metaphor, zone of proximal development

This is a metaphor used by Jerome Bruner to indicate the support the older person gives to the younger person in a teaching situation. Like Vygotsky, but unlike Piaget, Bruner developed a theory of instruction alongside his developmental stages. Both Vygotsky and Bruner believed that intellectual development could be facilitated and that children could achieve more if supported by skilful practitioners.

Just as scaffolding on a building is a temporary support, so the help given by the adult is expected to be needed for a limited time; the aim is for the young learner to achieve independence as soon as possible.

Bruner, Jerome (1966) *Towards a Theory of Instruction* Cambridge, Mass: Harvard University Press.

Scan

To scan involves a kind of reading in which the eye travels down the page seeking out a name or a date.

Schonell Graded Word Reading Test

See also Standardised Reading Tests

This widely used individual test, which was re-standardised in 1972 (Oliver and Boyd), requires the child to read out loud from a list of progressively demanding words. The test, which is untimed, produces reading ages from 6.06–12.06 years.

The test is easy to administer and inexpensive. However, more recent tests are often now preferred since they take a broader view of reading and tend to use sentences and paragraphs to read and understand rather than single words to decode.

Schonell Graded Word Reading Test (1972) London: Oliver and Boyd.

School Development Plans – see English Coordinator

School stories

See also history of children's literature

School stories are an important category of children's fiction, popular throughout the twentieth century. There are stories for boys about boys' schools but it is a genre that appeals mainly to girls from about eight to thirteen. In 1925 the very successful *Chalet School* series of books by Elinor Brent-Dyer began and the books remain in print. In the 1940s and 1950s Enid Blyton's adventures of Malory Towers, a girls' school in Cornwall, dominated the reading choices of many girls.

School stories are often in series: this is not unconnected with their marketing success as Victor Watson points out in *Reading Series Fiction*. He goes on to show us the development in the school story and other books in series as they made their way through the twentieth century. I have found Gene Kemp's stories about Cricklepit Combined School appeal to both boys and girls. The comic situations in *The Turbulent Term of Tyke Tiler* continue to amuse each generation of children (Puffin, 1977). Boys and girls seem to like Tyke's adventurous spirit combined with a genuine concern for the less bright Danny and the surprise at the end never fails to amaze the first-time reader of the book.

As schools reflect wider cultural changes, the school story will also change.

Auchmuty, Rosemary and Cotton, Joy (compilers of 2000 edition) *The Encyclopaedia of School Stories* published by Ashgate (two volumes, one on girls' school stories the other on boys' school stories).

Watson, Victor (2000) *Reading Series Fiction: From Arthur Ransome to Gene Kemp* London: Routledge Falmer.

Science & English

See also CD-ROMs, diagrams, factual genres, genre, information books, language across the curriculum, non-fiction reading and writing

In science, like other lessons, children and their teachers use language – speaking, listening, reading and writing – to discuss, explain, question and understand concepts and to encode them in writing. We think of science involving much practical work and recording using diagrams, but even in these contexts language helps organise the learning achieved. Part of learning in science is to do with acquiring a technical vocabulary to clinch the concepts. This vocabulary is used and explained in the non-fiction texts children use in science lessons – work cards, reference books like science dictionaries and encyclopaedias and in information books and software on topics like Electricity, Water and Magnets. The Internet is also a source of a great deal of information. So children's literacy is developed through their work in science; this link between science and literacy has been strengthened by the use of science texts in the shared reading and writing part of the Literacy Hour as an example of scientific genre.

We need to look for certain qualities in the science materials we select for children of different ages, interests and abilities and the criteria we might keep in mind for information books and CD-ROMs are discussed under the appropriate entries. Let me just say that I think a good science book, as well as scoring well on accuracy, clear format, quality of writing and illustration, needs to encourage an enquiring mind and a curiosity to find out more.

Perhaps we are less likely to think of fiction as a source of inspiration for science, but stories and poems can link science and English in a fruitful and sometimes exciting way. There is some evidence that girls in particular find a story approach to science humanises the subject for them and makes it more attractive (Frost, 1999). In her interesting book *Creativity in Science* Jenny Frost describes how five and six year olds enjoyed hearing a Masai story called *Who's in Rabbit's House* told by Verna Aadema (1978). The story tells how Rabbit returns to his house to hear some rather puzzling sounds inside. The tale was used as a starting point for making Rabbit's house out of cardboard and then developing a listening activity; some children made noises using shells, pencils and so on and asked the other children to guess which implement is making the sounds. Each child speaker held a large conch shell when it was their turn to guess. One outcome was a wonderful hard-backed book with charts showing the results of the listening activities. Another source of inspiration for linking science and fiction is *Find that Book,* which reminds us that Ted Hughes' modern fairy tale *The Iron Man* can stimulate an interest in magnetism and, for younger children, Verna Aadema's *Bringing the Rain to Kapiti Plain* can reinforce the understanding that plants need water and light to grow (Lewisham Professional Development Centre, 1999).

Of course there are many aspects of science which fiction tends not to relate to. I think the most promising areas for poems and stories arise from environmental and animal welfare issues. There are many works of fiction that reach out to children's love of and interest in wildlife and the natural world. If we want scientists who care about the environment deeply and about wildlife we should not underestimate the role of fiction in awakening concern and interest in issues of conservation. After all it is often scientific interference which causes problems. Younger children enjoy Beatrix Potter's *The Tale of Squirrel Nutkin* (Frederick Warne) and reading this would be a good preliminary to reflecting on the fate of the red squirrel, once prolific but now rare in the British Isles. Since the turn of the century we have lost much of the woodland that was this creature's habitat. The same sort of problems have affected the animals introduced in fictional guise in the children's classic Kenneth Graham's *Wind in the Willows* (Methuen). The book creates the riverbank environment before pollution wrought its havoc. In *The Willows and Beyond*, William Horwood has created sequels to the original stories in which the Wild Wood has been cut down by housing developers. Texts like Ted Hugh's *The Iron Woman* and Barbara Jeffers' *Brother Eagle, Sister Sky* (a retelling of an American Indian legend) are also used to bring home environmental issues, and manage to take on the complexity of these.

Poetry too can link science and English. Children aged about 5–8 years would like Adrian Henri's *H25* – a three-verse poem about hedgehogs and the poet's wish to save them and badgers, frogs and toads from death crossing the motorway (this is one of the poems in Roger McGough's *Ring of Words,* Faber & Faber). Referring to this poem in *Child Education,* January 1999, Sian Hughes of The Poetry Society comments that the idea of a hedgehog motorway is not so far-fetched: there are underpasses built for animals under busy roads in some places and groups of people go out at night to carry toads across dual carriageways safely to their ponds. The poem could be the start of lively discussion about how we can help as well as study animals and might also lead to children's writing. For a leaflet about helping hedgehogs survive send an SAE to British Hedgehogs Preservation Society, Knowbury House, Knowbury, Shropshire SY8 3LQ. Poems for older children that encourage the questioning of certain environmental strategies include Judith Nicholls' selection *Earthways:*

poems on conservation (Oxford University Press, 1993).

Find that Book: Making Links between Literacy and the Broader Curriculum London: Lewisham Professional Development Centre.

Frost, Jenny (1997) *Creativity in Primary Science* Buckingham: Open University Press.

Hughes, Sian (1999) 'Hedgehogs' in *Child Education,* January.

Scribing

In a teaching context, this refers to the role of a teacher, parent or older child in writing down what a young child dictates, enabling them to 'compose' like a more mature writer. Seeing what they say written down can be a motivating experience.

Sometimes the teacher scribes in the shared writing part of the Literacy Hour, writing down the children's suggestions. In a group writing context one child may take up the role of scribe, either handwriting or using the computer.

Semantic cue-system

See also big shapes, critical discourse, cue-systems, miscue analysis, reading, top-down reading approaches

This is one of a number of cue systems or 'search lights', as they are called in *The Framework for Teaching* (DfEE 1998), on which a reader draws. The others are explained under 'syntactic cue system', 'grapho-phonic cue-system' and 'bibliographic cue-system'. When drawing on the semantic cue-system, the search for the meaning of a text is paramount. But not only does the reader draw on meaning in the text, he or she also draws on their knowledge from everyday life and the other reading they have done. In a miscue analysis, the teacher can check whether or not a child is using the semantic cue-system well. If a child says 'home' when the actual word is 'house' we know they understand the gist of the story even though the actual word read out is not correct. If they substituted 'hole' for house it would indicate they were not cueing into the meaning successfully.

Semi-colon

See also punctuation

A semi-colon is a punctuation mark with three main uses:

* instead of two short sentences or a conjunction to link two parallel statements: Children need to have some breakfast; it gives them the energy to concentrate during morning lessons.
* to link two independent clauses* within a compound sentence** when a conjunctive adverb*** connects them:

    The teacher remarked that she had never taken a music lesson; however, she added that she had always taught in schools where a specialist took responsibility for music.

* to separate items in a list often after a colon:

    The basket contained: a story book for the lesson after break; some spare pencils; a cartridge for the printer; a carton of fruit juice.

* an independent clause is one which is sentence–like in its construction, having a subject and an object.
** a compound sentence has two or more main clauses.
*** a conjunctive adverb has a connective role, as 'however' has in the example.

Semi-phonetic stage in spelling

This is the second stage of a child's spelling development according to Richard Gentry's stages; it refers to the time when there is some evidence of making sound–symbol connections.

Gentry, Richard (1982) 'An analysis of developmental spelling in GNYS AT WRK' in *The Reading Teacher* 36(2) (for a helpful summary of the stages, see Graham and Kelly, 1998, *Writing Under Control*, Chapter 5).

SENCO – see under Special Educational Needs

Sentence

See also grammar

A sentence is a group of words which make sense. There are three main kinds of sentence:

* a simple sentence has only one clause with one subject and one verb. (Anna loves fruit).
* a complex sentence has one main clause and one or more subordinate clauses. (Anna loves fruit, particularly the kind you can pick in the countryside in the Autumn).
* a compound sentence has two or more main clauses which could stand as short sentences. (The rain fell and the wind blew.)

Within a sentence are smaller groups of words which also make sense and these are called clauses. Clauses are made up of phrases.

The smallest building blocks are words, next come phrases, next clauses and finally sentences. For more about sentences and how to help children structure them, see *Grammar for Writing* (DfEE, 1998) and Chapter 5 in Medwell *et al.*, 2001.

Medwell, Jane, Moore, George, Wray, David and Griffiths, Vivienne (2001) *Primary English: Knowledge and Understanding* Exeter: Learning Matters.
The National Literacy Strategy *Grammar for Writing* (2000) DfEE.

Sentence level work – see Literacy Hour

Shakespearean drama (in the primary years)

See also drama & English, playscript

Why do teachers use the work of Shakespeare in the primary years when many adults find the language and themes of the plays difficult? Probably there are two main reasons. First, many of the stories round which the plays are built are exceptionally engaging for any age group – a king giving away his kingdom, the confused adventures of jealous lovers in a wood where magic is at work, people shipwrecked on a strange, enchanted island. As we all know, Shakespeare often got the bare bones from other sources but he developed the characters and situations to produce works that come fully to life when they are performed. Second, we want children to enjoy, as early as possible, Shakespeare's unsurpassed ability to use language, both prose and poetry, to bring situations and the thoughts and feelings of characters alive for us.

The National Literacy Strategy *Framework for Teaching* suggests study of classic fiction, including where appropriate a Shakespeare play, in Year 6, term 1. Reading and perhaps performing a complete Shakespeare play, even in considerably abridged form, would be a challenge for any Year 6 class. Many teachers and children prefer to work with single scenes or their own scripts drawing on the plays. In my experience, where children in Year 6 are to be able to take on the challenges of 'the study of a Shakespeare play' (DfEE, 1998, p. 68), English coordinators working with their colleagues have created a culture where the children have been exposed to his work from an early age. How is this achieved? Perhaps the first thing to say is that there are some implications for teachers' subject knowledge here. You might find helpful 'The Qualities of Drama', Chapter 11 in Medwell *et al.* 2001 which includes sections about writing playscripts and about Shakespearean drama. Sedgwick's *Shakespeare and the Young Writer* would also provide good background (Sedgwick, 1999). How then do we involve children with Shakespeare's work? A good way in for younger children is through stories based on Shakespeare's plays. There are a number of good collections including Garfield's *Shakespeare Stories* (1988). I have sometimes started with such a story and added some quotations from the play when I have read to a class. Having a grip on some of the stories will be very helpful to children later on – but the stories are enjoyable in their own right. When it comes to appreciating Shakespeare's language and particularly his poetry, introducing it as part of telling the story of one of the plays helps make it meaningful for the children – the fairies' chant to Titania in the context of the story of *A Midsummer Night's Dream* for example. In the first term of Year 5, sonnets are one of the

forms mentioned in *The Framework* and teachers often use 'Shall I compare thee to a summer's day' as an introduction to this form of poetry. Another way in which the school builds a tradition of work on classic drama is in the context of working with texts for drama. Children enjoy reading a scene from a Shakespeare play and then adapting the script for their own purposes. Colleen Johnson has provided a very helpful list of activities round Caliban's 'The isle is full of noises' speech from Act III, Scene ii, Shakespeare's *The Tempest.* Including the fruits of this kind of work in assemblies and on open days for parents makes Shakespeare's work accessible to children. It has an impact on the children presenting the work and on the younger children who see what will be expected of them when they are older. In some schools part of the expectation will be that when they get to Year 6 it will be their turn to work with a complete Shakespeare play and to perform part or all of it for others.

One inspiring case study known to me involved Years 5 and 6 (nine to eleven year olds) in work on Shakespeare's *Cymbeline.* The play was chosen because of its strong characters and compelling story. The teachers involved downloaded a text and edited, manipulated and copied it to suit their purposes. Almost all the plot was included but the play was reduced to 'a child and audience friendly one and a half hours running time' for performance to the school and visitors (Alexander, 2000, p. 8). Some modern speech narrative was used to help understanding of the plot through the device of two narrators dressed as Shakespeare who announced the locations of the different scenes and assembled the characters. You need to read this case study for yourself to appreciate the richness of the project – it was so much more than just the school play. It fed into National Curriculum English and *The Framework* requirements well, but also spread into extra-curricular activity and the daily life of the school. Fred Sedgewick, author of *Shakespeare and the Young Writer* (1999), worked with the children on the 'Fear no more' song from *Cymbeline* and one of the results was some moving writing by the children on a person they had lost. This was one of many examples of extension work which helped the children become fully involved in the themes and undercurrents in the play.

You might also like to read about another imaginative use of a Shakespeare play, this time *A Midsummer Night's Dream* with nine to eleven year olds, evaluated in Chapter 3 of *The Prose and the Passion* (Styles *et al.*, 1994). The many exciting lessons drew on their knowledge of popular culture in understanding the appeal of the play: the jealousy of the lovers, for example, was linked to the shenanigans of characters in television soap operas. Work on the 'rude mechanicals' scenes led to children telling tall stories to get 'under the skin' of Bottom the Weaver. A huge amount of learning was involved – about Shakespearean times and particularly Shakespearean theatre, about comedy, the function of sub-plots and the use of magic in plays. After work on the character and motivation of Puck the teacher heard the children playfully chanting some of his lines – 'I am that merry wanderer of the night' and 'I go, I go, look how I go/ swifter than an arrow from a tartar's bow'. The many activities and sustained work through drama involved the children imaginatively and emotionally. Yes: this is the point – if we truly involve children in work of this quality, as Styles remarks, children can rise to 'the difficulties involved – unfamiliar language, complicated plot, and challenging demands on acting and memory' (Styles, 1994, p. 51).

Alexander, Catherine (2000) 'The Cymbeline Project' in *English 4–11* No. 9, Winter 2001. (This project was carried out at St Andrew's Primary School, Stanstead Abbotts.)

Garfield, Leon (1988) *Shakespeare Stories* London: Heinemann.

Johnson, Colleen (2000) 'What did I say?: speaking, listening and drama' in Fisher, Robert and Williams, Mary (eds) *Unlocking Literacy* London: David Fulton.

Matthews, Andrew (2001) *The Orchard Book of Children's Stories* London: Orchard Books. (Retelling of eight plays with atmospheric illustrations by Angela Barrett.)

Medwell, Jane, Moore, George, Wray, David and Griffiths, Vivienne (2001) *Primary English: Knowledge and Understanding* Exeter: Learning Matters.

Sedgwick, Fred (1999) *Shakespeare and the Young Writer* London: Routledge.

Styles, Morag (1994) '"Am I That Geezer, Hermia": Children and "Great Literature"' in Styles, Morag, Bearne, Eve and Watson, Victor (eds) *The Prose and the Passion: Children and Their Reading* London: Cassell.

Shared reading – see under text level work and also under class reader, fiction, Literacy Hour, novel, short stories, story time, text level work

Shared writing

See also Literacy Hour, text level work, writing

The term 'shared writing' refers to any collaborative writing task. For example, a group of children may write a story together with or without the teacher's help – on a white board, flip chart or on the computer.

The term is also used to refer to the class-based shared writing activity taking place in the first half of the Literacy Hour and intended to move children towards becoming independent writers. (This part of the Literacy Hour may focus on shared reading or shared writing.) Teachers draw on text, sentence and word level objectives from the National Literacy Strategy *Framework for Teaching*. Shared writing gives the teacher an opportunity to model the writing process, for example by encouraging the children to rehearse sentences orally before committing them to the page. The children reread what has been written to ensure a flow from one sentence to another and to put right errors. There can be valuable discussion on punctuation and on why one writing decision is better than another. As with any writing task, teacher and children need to be clear from the outset about to whom the writing is addressed and its purpose. The concept of 'audience' and 'purpose' was at the heart of the work of Jimmy Britton and his colleagues on The Schools Council Writing Projects of the 1970s. An issue for teachers is how to make shared writing tasks more than exercises, the 'dummy runs' Britton refers to. One way is to draw on work which has engaged and interested the chil-

Class Writing Project: The Story of Cocoa the Brown Bear

Elaine Shiel, an Edinburgh primary teacher, wanted to create an exciting context for children's writing. While on holiday in London she bought a little brown bear from Hamley's and brought it to school to show her class of seven year olds. Her intention was to base story telling and story writing round the bear's pretend adventures. The children's imaginations shifted into top gear as they reflected on what it must have been like for Cocoa when he was pushed to the back of the shelf when no-one wanted to buy him. Night time was worst as he could not see a thing.

The children and teacher began to construct stories about his adventures and his thoughts and feelings as he adjusted to life in Primary 3's hut. The scene was set for the teacher to direct the children's interest and enthusiasm towards different kinds of writing. There were stories about visiting the teacher's home and meeting Happeny the puppy, Posh Giraffe and One-eyed Duck and about going on holiday. One day when the class came into school Cocoa had disappeared. This led to a flurry of activity and meetings to decide how to track him down. Then the children made posters asking for his return and they put up notices, sent messages and wrote letters asking the school secretary and the caretaker to help find him.

On another occasion the children wrote about Cocoa going to A Teddy Bears' Picnic at Corstorphine Fair with the children's teddy bears.

After a while the children wanted to make a book about Cocoa and the teacher took up the role of editor. Their joint work led to the children learning about chapters, how to engage the reader's interest and how to match illustrations to the narrative. This was the final structure of the book.

Chapter 1

Once upon a time there was a little teddy bear who lived, all squashed at the back of the shelf in a big toy shop. Poor teddy bear!

It was the biggest toy shop in the world. It was called Hamleys. Hamleys was in London.

The little brown bear was squashed at the back of the shelf. He was stuck by an octopus that kept pushing the bear back with all his hands. A giraffe kicked brown bear too. Polar bear was a mean teddy too. No one cared.

At the back of the shelf it was hot, very hot. At night time it was dark, very dark. Brown bear could not see any light.

Page 1

The Adventures of Cocoa
Chapter 1. In the Toy shop
Chapter 2. The Journey to Scotland and Primary 3's hut
Chapter 3. A weekend at Miss Shiel's house
Chapter 4. Meeting Happeney, Posh Giraffe and One Eyed Duck
Chapter 5. Cocoa Disappears.
Chapter 6. Cocoa tells of his Adventures
Chapter 7. Cocoa Acquires a Rug
Chapter 8. Cocoa's Camping Holiday
Chapter 9. A New Friend
Chapter 10. The Teddy Bears' Picnic

And to give a flavour of this work the first page of chapter 1 is displayed here. For a more detailed account of this interesting project see E. Shiel's article in *English 4-11*, No. 9, 2000.

dren in other lessons to give real purpose to the Literacy Hour tasks. The children writing about Cocoa the Bear felt great committment to their work (see case study).

Britton, James (1970) *Language and Learning* London: Allen Lane, The Penguin Press.

DfEE (1998a) *The National Literacy Strategy Framework for Teaching* London: DfEE.

Short stories

See also creation stories, fairy tales, fiction, folk tales, narrative, realism in children's books, traditional tales

Short stories are a genre in their own right and those specially written for children share many of the characteristics of the versions for adults. The setting and the characters have to be communicated swiftly and there is not space for the long descriptions of scenery and introspection possible in a full-length work. Nevertheless, good short stories offer insights into the human condition and can awaken children's own wish to write.

They provide a bridge between the picture-books for the very young and the novels enjoyed by older primary children. Their relative shortness allows teacher and child to look at global aspects of the text – the development of the characters and the situation for example. A number of teachers have mentioned to me that the stories in *The Practical Princess and Other Liberating Fairy Tales* by Jay Williams seem to encourage discussion with different age groups. Gervase Phinn's annotated short story suggestions for younger children include tales about a range of human experience. There is Philippa Pearce's entertaining collection – *Lion at School and Other Stories,* Dick King-Smith's animal stories – *Sophie's Snail* and Berlie Doherty's lively *Tilly Mint Tales* (Phinn, 2000).

For older children there are fantasy collections, for example Nicholas Fisk's edited *The Puffin Book of Science Fiction* and, for a mixture of different genres by well-known children's writers – *The Turning Tide and Other Stories* edited by Gervase Phinn. When older primary school children have enjoyed many folk tales from around the world they become able to identify common themes that interest and 'speak to'

human beings everywhere. Oxford University Press has reissued its well-known collections of folk tales in paperback, for example Kathleen Arnott's retelling of *Tales from Africa* and Philip Sherlock's retelling of *Tales from West Africa.*

Phinn, Gervase (2000) *Young Readers and Their Books: Suggestions and Strategies for Using Texts in the Literacy Hour* London: David Fulton.

Short-term plans – see English Co-ordinator, planning

Siblings (and literacy)

See also parents and families

Brothers and sisters are very much part of a child's life at home and there is evidence that they extend each other's literacy experiences in important and interesting ways. The impact of siblings on each other's literacy development was one of the aspects studied in the Elmswood research which Jo Weinberger has described and evaluated in her book *Literacy Goes to School.* She looked at children's literacy development from three to seven years and concentrated on the adult who provided the 'parent' as opposed to the 'school' perspective on children's literacy learning. Half of the sixty children in the study had an older brother or sister and during the interviews Weinberger found that there were a number of positive ways in which siblings enriched each other's literacy. Turning to reading first, younger children benefited from being with their older siblings when they were read to by adults and older siblings quite often enjoyed reading to their younger brothers and sisters. A child with older siblings was also likely to have access to a wider range of books and materials than 'only' or firstborn children. Younger children were also involved in writing activity earlier than they might otherwise have been as older children were effectively 'models' for writing behaviour. One mother commented that 'when we help Joanne to write, Sarah pretends to write too…' (Weinberger, 1996, p. 57). All that we know about early writing suggests that children who see the purposes of writing early are at a considerable advantage in learning to write. Most of the children in the Elmswood study were monolingual. What might be the role of siblings when children are learning to read in a second or additional language? Eve Gregory illuminates the issues here in her book *Making Sense of a New World*. In Gregory's research we see a culture of sibling support developing in some families: eleven-year-old Fatima remarks that she was teaching her little brother and sister to read in English just as her older brother had taught her. Gregory comments:'Older siblings are excellent 'brokers' of a new language because they are able to link school and home reading practices' (Gregory, 1996, p. 176).

Are there any disadvantages, from the literacy point of view, as a result of being a younger child? It is possible that some parents are not able to give younger children the quality and amount of time that they gave to their eldest child and that this may have had an effect on their literacy development. Older children may also encourage distractions away from literacy – like watching television and playing computer games. In the Elmwood study the positive aspects of the contribution of older siblings seemed to outweigh the possible negative ones. Perhaps the most enjoyable context in which help was given was when older children read out loud to younger ones.

Gregory, Eve (1996) *Making Sense of a New World: Learning to read in a second language* London: Paul Chapman.

Weinberger, Jo (1996) *Literacy Goes to School* London: Paul Chapman.

Silent letters

Some letters are used to spell a word but they are not pronounced when the word is said. They may be at the beginning of a word like the 'k' in 'kneel', at the end like the 'e' in 'nose' or in the middle of a word, for example the silent 'l' in salmon. Silent 'e' at the end of a word often makes another vowel sound long.

Silent reading – see under ERIC, independent reading, USSR

Simile

A simile is a figure of speech which makes a comparison nearly always using either 'like' or 'as'. Some similes have lost their power through constant use – 'as white as snow', 'as pleased as Punch'. The challenge for a young poet is to find new and startling ones. Learning to recognise and talk about similes and other figures of speech is helpful in the context of enjoying poetry but opinions differ about whether or not we should encourage children to contrive them in their own writing. If you want to read about an approach where children are encouraged to practise techniques to apply later in their writing you would find interesting Sandy Brownjohn's book *What Rhymes with Secret?* (Brownjohn, 1994). To help children with simile and metaphor, Brownjohn has developed 'The Furniture Game'. Children think of someone known to the others in the class and help them to guess who it is by comparing them to a piece of furniture, a plant or a type of food (see p. 19). Brownjohn takes up a playful approach to language, but believes that children need to control the techniques so that they are free to write the sort of poem they want to.

Similes can be used in everyday speech and in factual writing as well as poetry: nine-year-old Jarinder uses a simile in his account of the Spanish Armada. 'Then I saw the Spanish Armada scatter around us like a bunch of rats being chase by a cat' (Laycock, in Graham and Kelly, 1998).

Brownjohn, Sandy (1994) *What Rhymes with Secret* London: Hodder & Stoughton.

Laycock, Liz (1998) 'Monitoring and Assessing Writing' in Graham, Judith and Kelly, Alison (eds) *Writing Under Control: Teaching Writing in the Primary School.* London: David Fulton.

Singular and plural

When a noun or verb refers to one thing, it is said to be 'singular'. Uncountable nouns like 'cotton' or 'envy' tend to be regarded as singular to match with the verbs they are used with. 'Singular' contrasts with 'plural', the latter showing there is more than one thing. There are a number of exceptions in forming the plural of nouns in English which children are encouraged to learn. For example:

child   children
salmon   salmon
mouse   mice.

Skimming

Skimming refers to a reading strategy where we read quickly through a passage or article to get the gist of the argument swiftly. Lunzer and Gardner contrast this kind of reading with the more reflective kind when we evaluate a set of facts or ideas. The flexible readers know when to apply each reading strategy.

Lunzer, Eric and Gardner, Kenneth (1979) *The Effective Use of Reading* London: Heinemann.

Slang

See also language variety, language change, standard English

Slang refers to informal words and expressions often thought to be inferior to standard forms of language. But perhaps it is more to do with what is appropriate in a particular context. Slang is used to identify us with an age group or a social group. People who normally use standard English may use slang words and phrases if they are relaxing with a group of people with whom they share activities and attitudes.

Although some 'slang' words become accepted into language and even into dictionaries, the colloquial expressions in vogue change constantly.

Socio-economic groups and literacy – see under elaborated and restricted codes

Software – See CD-ROM and Information and Communications Technology

Sonnet

This is a poem of fourteen lines with a regular rhythm and rhyming pattern. Two well known types of sonnet are the Petrachan or Italian sonnet and the Shakespearian sonnet. The Petrachan sonnet has two parts, the first of eight lines and the second of six; each part has a separate rhyming pattern. The Shakespearean sonnet does not separate the 14 lines into separate parts and has a different rhyming pattern to the Petrachan one: ababcdcdededgg – three quatrains and a rhyming couplet.

The sonnet is one of the kinds of poetry children following *The Framework* read in Year 5. Teachers usually find examples from Shakespeare's 154 sonnets a favourite being *Shall I compare thee to a summer's day?* William Wordsworth and, more recently, W.H.Auden and Dylan Thomas are also writers of sonnets. There are some examples of children's sonnets in Sandy Brownjohn's book *Does it Have to Rhyme?*

Brownjohn, Sandy (1980) *Does it Have to Rhyme?* London: Hodder & Stoughton

Speech – see Speaking and listening

Speaking and listening

See also accent, Bristol Language at home and School project, Bullock Report, collaborative learning, conferencing, dialect, discourse analysis, discussion, drama, language acquisition, language and thought, National Oracy Project, response to English, slang, speech act, storytelling

> 'All learning across the whole curriculum, could be said to begin and end with speaking and listening. It would be almost impossible to introduce any new topic or revise an old one without some form of questioning or discussion by the teacher or children.' (p. 64 in Grugeon *et al.* (1998) *Teaching Speaking and Listening in the Primary School'*

This entry concentrates on speaking and listening in the classroom. I have begun with a quotation from Grugeon *et al.* because they remind us of the central place of oracy in all learning. What is written here is best read in conjunction with the entries on language acquisition and language and thought, where you will find some analysis of the theoretical contributions of the developmentalists Piaget, Vygotsky and Bruner and the socio-linguistic perspective of M.A.K. Halliday.

In the classroom, it is helpful to keep in mind that speaking and listening have three main aspects: social, cognitive and linguistic. These elements are present in all episodes of speaking and listening, but often one dominates. A teacher may aim to stress the social aspect by encouraging children to take turns in putting their points and listening to each other. On another occasion the cognitive function of talk might be uppermost, if for example children are hypothesising, summarising points, inferring or referring back to previous points. The linguistic element is always present, but comes to the fore when teachers encourage children to rephrase to make their meaning clearer or to show flexibility in their language use according to context.

We must also remember the teacher's use of language is of great importance. Not only have instructions to be clear and intervention helpful – sometimes the teacher has to sharpen the focus with a question or comment – the teacher also provides a model of mature language use. It is the teacher's role to create contexts where children will feel comfortable and able to contribute. The teacher's own ability to tell anecdotes and stories is of great value.

Planning for speaking and listening
Children use their speaking and listening abilities in every lesson. In English much talk centres round children learning to read and write, responding to literature and creating roles and incidents in drama. Story telling is an ability worth nurturing as it is a source of great enjoyment and satisfaction and helps children develop a sense of characterisation, pace and sequencing of events. Evaluation of all that they do is achieved through discussion. Although teachers often work within official frameworks there are some general planning questions which will always be helpful. The following planning diagram is adapted from that in *Teaching Talking and Learning* by Kate Norman (1990).

1. What do you want the children to learn?
2. What are the stages in the activity and the time scale?
3. What is the role of speaking and listening in the learning?
4. Is the work to be done collaboratively?
5. What kinds of groupings (issues of special needs, gender and young learners of English as an additional language to be considered here)?
6. What resources are needed?
7. If the work is in groups how will the reporting back to an audience be organised?
8. How will the children's evaluation of what has been achieved be built into the work?
9. How will I record the work?

The Early Learning Goals
These are objectives children are expected to meet by the end of the foundation stage in the UK (3–6 years). As far as speaking and listening is concerned: by age six years children should be able to: enjoy listening to and using spoken (and written) language, using it in their play and learning; explore and experiment with sounds, words and texts; listen with enjoyment and respond to stories, poems and so on and make up their own; use language to imagine and recreate roles and experiences; talk to organise, sequence and clarify thinking, ideas, feelings and events; sustain attentive listening, responding to what they have heard by relevant comments, questions or actions; interact with others and take turns in conversations; extend their vocabulary and retell narratives drawing on the language patterns of stories; speak clearly and audibly with confidence and show awareness of the listener; hear and say initial and final sounds in words, and short vowel sounds within words; link sounds to letters and name and sound the letters of the alphabet.

The National Curriculum
The Year 2000 National Curriculum English Programmes divide En 1 (and En 2 and En 3) into two parts: knowledge, skills and under-

standing; breadth of study. At Key Stage 1, teachers help children to build on the early learning goals in supporting children's development as clear, confident speakers and thoughtful listeners, aware of the needs of others in the group and of their audience. Language is used in imaginative ways to express feelings as well as thoughts in class and group discussion as well as in drama and role play. Children learn to use some of the main features of spoken standard English and about language variation according to context and audience. At Key Stage 2 they progress to in speaking in a wide range of contexts with increasing sensitivity to purpose and audience. They take up a variety of roles as speakers and listeners in class and group contexts and think about the language used as well as the content and sense of what is said. Progress is made in becoming able to use different ways to summarise main points, reviewing what has been said, clarifying, drawing others in, considering alternatives and anticipating consequences. Teachers help children gain further control over standard English and to go deeper into how language varies between standard and dialect forms and between spoken and written language. Drama activities are important in giving the opportunity for children to create different roles and to use dramatic techniques to explore characters and issues.

The National Literacy Strategy and the Literacy Hour

There are opportunities for speaking and listening, particularly exploratory and presentational talk, within the structure of the Literacy Hour at Key Stages 1 and 2. Shared text work with the whole class provides a context for exploratory talk about texts and about writing. Focused word and sentence work encourages children to explore patterns in language and to contrast and compare. Group work with and without the teacher is accompanied by talk about texts and about writing tasks while the whole class plenary is a good context for presentational talk to share what particular children or groups have achieved.

Gender issues

Although there are quiet boys and exuberant girls, teachers often find that boys are more dominant in discussion, particularly where activities are organised round technology like the computer. Because boys seem more noisy and demanding – more of a threat to classroom order perhaps – teachers sometimes unwittingly reinforce such behaviour by giving boys more opportunities to participate in discussion. In a much-quoted research study, Swann and Graddol (1988) provide evidence for this. We can use strategies in our planning to achieve more balance: girls can be encouraged to be more assertive by direct invitation of their views and boys can be praised when they interact with other children in a group discussion and listen to contributions. Some teachers set up non-stereotypical role play for younger children's interactions in the home corner and older children's role play in drama. It is a matter of making sure that some contexts encourage girls to be more forthcoming while boys are given the chance to 'engage in activities that will enable them to use the quiet, sensitive, caring aspects of their natures' (Browne, 1996).

Sometimes it is appropriate to make issues about boys' and girls' language development explicit by discussing them. Two books which I have used to encourage thoughtful conversation with older primary children are *The Turbulent Term of Tyke Tiler* by Gene Kemp and *The Tunnel* by Anthony Browne. Literature has a wonderful distancing effect, enabling children to talk about issues without making direct reference to themselves unless of course they want to.

Children learning English as a second or additional language

A young bilingual child's receptive English may be ahead of his/her productive English and this needs to be kept in mind when talk contexts are planned. Teachers also need to record information about the languages spoken in the child's home.

Special Educational Needs

Pupils who appear to lack concentration and involvement in small group talk may suffer from a physical disability, for example hearing loss or speech impairment. Visual disability may mean children miss facial expression and gesture which give meaning to what other pupils say. Such pupils need support, possibly by the sympathetic understanding of other pupils who can repeat instructions if necessary. Other children may be reluctant talkers because of lack of confidence. After raising the matter with the child and his or her parents, teachers may place a child with a sympathetic partner so that they feel confident to speak. Sometimes children who are shy are much more forthcoming when they use a puppet allowing them to talk 'in role'. A Year 6 girl who had literacy difficulties was encouraged to tell stories to younger children using a puppet. She greatly improved her skill and her general self-image as a learner was transformed (see *Teaching Talking and Learning in Key Stage 2* by Kate Norman (1990)).

Teaching and learning contexts

Suggestions for developing chldren's speaking and listening appear in a number of entries. 'Drama and English' introduces the powerful kinds of talk which can accompany improvisation. Entries which consider fiction as a starting point for talk include: 'Fiction; choosing and using'; Play & Language and Literacy'; and Storytelling'. Talk round the computer is discussed in the 'Information, Communications Technology & English' entry. I recommend two inspirational books which illuminate examples of classroom talk. They are Gordon Wells' *The Meaning Makers*, Hodder & Stoughton (1986) and Aidan Chambers' *Tell Me*, The Thimble Press (1993).

Assessing and recording progress in speaking and listening

Many otherwise good schools seem to have a problem with assessment. Yet once you have a good system working it becomes part of the teaching and learning cycle. A good approach in my view is systematic, economic of teachers' and children's time and worked out and monitored collaboratively within the school. There are two main aspects when we turn to the assessment of speaking and listening: assessment *of* speaking and listening and assessment *through* speaking and listening.

Assessment of *speaking and listening*

This is to do with assessing pupils' capacity to use the spoken language and their listening skills for different audiences and a variety of purposes. Schools choose or create a format for summarising children's progress over a period of time; such assessment is *formative* in that it helps the teacher give help where it is needed. But it can also provide the basis of a *summative* assessment as it is a record of achievement.

Let us look at the main stages in the learning and assessing cycle. We begin planning for a range of speaking and listening contexts across the whole curriculum. And then we introduce them into the teaching programme. We establish routines for observing and recording the progress of individuals in some different settings. Some teachers use a ring binder file for notes, allocating several pages to each child; others prefer a box file. These notes (and perhaps evidence from photographs, short transcripts or even occasional video film) can then be summarised, perhaps twice a year, in a useful format. What is a useful format? One which a school constructs collaboratively and which communicates effectively the achievements of each child. Many schools use the speaking and listening part of the Centre for Primary Language in Education's primary language record or a similar system. One of the many strengths of this record is that there is space for the views and observations of the children's parents. There is also a slot for the child's own perception of his or her progress. The notes, and the record which summarises them, provide an evidence base which shows us what has been achieved so far and provide useful information about how we might help a particular child to progress further. Thus the assessment of progress feeds into our planning and the next round of teaching. Where a summative assessment is required, the information on the record can be matched with level requirements. In the United

Kingdom, primary children's level of achievement is judged at seven and eleven years according to brief descriptions of six achievement levels in the statutory orders. Class teachers often work with the English Co-ordinator or another colleague to establish common standards of comparison. The notes and observations and the summarising record provide rich material to share with parents on open evening.

But so far we have not considered exactly what we are looking for. When observing speaking and listening, three overlapping categories are helpful: social, cognitive and linguistic. Social aspects include the ability to listen to and value what others say as well as making a contribution to the discussion. In the cognitive area we look for a growing ability to use talking to think through and organise ideas and to build on what we have heard others say. Articulation of how children feel about important issues also fits here. Linguistic aspects are to do with becoming able to express ideas and thoughts clearly in appropriate language. But of course all three aspects come into play in most discussions and conversations. If a group of ten year olds are arguing a case, perhaps about how we can preserve the environment, and from time to time summarising their viewpoints they need to draw on their intellectual or cognitive ability to organise the ideas, their social skills to respond to others as well as to attract and keep their attention and their communicative ability to clothe their ideas and feelings in appropriate language. From these three main headings, more detailed lists can be drawn up. For example, under 'cognitive' at Key Stage 1 (5–7 year olds) we might include 'listening to others' reactions' and 'taking different views into account'. At Key Stage 2 (7–11 year olds) we might include giving/responding to instructions, asking/answering questions, summarising an argument, planning a group activity and responding to a story or poem. Teachers following the national curriculum often organise the items listed in the orders under the main headings of social, cognitive and linguistic.

We will also need to make sure our observations of the children's speaking and listening cover different kinds of groupings – whole class, small groups and pairs. Some groupings will place the children in a more formal setting than others.

Assessment through *speaking and listening*

Here we are concerned with a pupil's progress in understanding skills and concepts in an area of study. Often we can judge their linguistic development at the same time. The focus of our assessment depends on our purpose at the time. We can judge children's degree of knowledge and understanding in every lesson by what they say. However, we have to keep in mind that children may know more than they are able to articulate. This is especially the case where children are very young, where the context is unfamiliar and where children are at an early stage in learning English as a second or additional language.

Teachers judge children's prior knowledge of a subject by helping them organise their ideas through talk before beginning new work. Work on amphibians might begin with the teacher asking if anyone has touched a frog or toad and what the skin felt like. These discussions show a teacher where the children are in relation to the topic and helps inform good planning of how to proceed. This process of listening to what children say as they go about their work contributes throughout the learning and assessing cycle. Both closed questions (those where there is a definite answer) and more open questions (those where several different answers or opinions are welcomed) often encourage children to reveal what they know and where some help is needed, perhaps with a particular concept. Where the emphasis is on sensitive intervention, assessment is of a formative kind and the teacher helps the children by improving their learning opportunities. At the end of a series of lessons teachers often seek evidence about what individual children have learned by setting up class and group discussions. Here, children often find it satisfying to evaluate their own learning and the quality of the resources they have been using.

A final thought

This entry has had to refer to the speaking and listening requirements in the official frameworks. Over prescription – the sheer anxiety of meeting termly objectives – can risk sapping the vitality of teachers' planning and practice. But as good teachers put the requirements into effect they take control and interpret what is set out flexibly and creatively. They insist on keeping talk in a central role in promoting reading and writing. They make time for the kind of discussions that generate excitement and energy, keeping alive what Chris Powling calls 'the rumour of magic' in the classroom (Powling, 1998, p. 1).

Browne, Ann (1996) *Developing Language and Literacy 3–8* London: Paul Chapman.

Grugeon, Elisabeth, Hubbard, Lorraine, Smith, Carol and Dawes, Lyn (1998) *Teaching Speaking and Listening in the Primary School* London: David Fulton.

Norman, Kate (1990) *Teaching Talking and Learning in Key Stage One* and *Teaching Talking and Learning in Key Stage 2* National Curriculum Council and the National Oracy Project. (Although these works have been published some time, they include the insights of many excellent practitioners who took part in the National Oracy Project in Great Britain. They also make a valuable contribution to our understanding of how children can be helped to use spoken language effectively and imaginatively to communicate and learn.)

Scottish Committee on Language Arts (1982) *Mr Togs the Tailor* (although this was written a long time ago it is one of the most inspiring accounts ever written about situating children's talk, listening and learning in a strong human context).

Swann, J. (1992) *Girls, Boys and Language* London: Blackwell.

Swann, J. and Graddol, D. (1998) 'Gender Inequalities in Classroom Talk', *English in Education*, Vol. 22, no. 1, 48–65.

Special Educational Needs (SEN) in language and literacy

See also Code of Practice dyslexia, miscue analysis, parents and families, P-levels, reading recovery, running records, *Warnock Report*, zone of proximal development

This entry considers 'Special Educational Needs' in the area of literacy under two main headings. First I consider the needs of children who struggle with learning to read and write. What is included here links with the entries on the *Code of Practice* (which covers the process by which some children are provided with a 'statement of special educational need'), on dyslexia and on

Reading Recovery programmes. Second I turn to the additional literacy needs of children who are achieving well above what seems usual for their chronological age and discuss the kind of support and resources which will keep pace with their swift development.

Communication is essential: meeting these individual needs requires liaison between the class teacher, the Special Educational Needs Co-ordinator (SENCO) and the English Co-ordinator as well as the involvement of the children and their parents. The strategies the school adopts in this very important area of co-operation also need to be written into the school's policy. There are of course a number of issues which never seem to be completely resolved. For example, at which point do we consider a child's intellectual abilities are so impaired that the best option seems to be a special school? Where children with quite severe language difficulties are in an ordinary primary school, are they best withdrawn from the class for special help in reading and writing? The trend at the moment is to keep children together with their age group and offer support within the classroom.

Struggling young readers and writers – how can we help?

Difficulties with reading and writing can affect children's progress across the curriculum and lead to low self-esteem. So it is important that those with this kind of special need are helped as soon as possible. This is very much the philosophy of Marie Clay whose intervention programme is explained under the 'Reading Recovery' entry. There is a vast literature about this important challenge for teachers; I have selected some books and information sources which I hope will help. In the list below I recommend two sound general books, Gross (1999) and Moss (1995), and some books to help with provision for struggling readers and writers and children with a range of physical and intellectual impairment in the literacy hour (Berger and Morris (1999) and Berger and Cross (eds) (1999b)). Out of a number of excellent books on literacy special needs I have listed two: Tony Martin's *The Strugglers* (1989) and Bentley and Reid's *Supporting*

I found out

I found that the female mors lys eggs. The caterpillars eggs haiched and it has terd into an caterpillar. The caterpillar turns into a chrysalis. Then the chrysalis turns into a beautiful butterfly. The butterflies hide in bushes and trees.

Well done Shannon ★ kraht ✓
L2C

Butterflies

I found that the female, lays eggs. The caterpillars hatch. Then the caterpillar turns into a chrysalis. Then the chrysalis turns into a beautiful butterfly. The butterflies hide in bushes and trees.

By Shannon

Children who struggle with writing often gain great satisfaction from seeing their work in print. Shannon from Year 2 word processed her informational piece from a draft written in science in the ICT lesson,

Struggling Readers (1995). Tony Martin's book presents an unforgettable case study of the how the author helped Leslie, a nine-year-old boy, break through to literacy. Martin explains simply how his version of an approach called 'paired reading' helped Leslie. In a 'paired reading' context an adult begins by reading a book to a child, next the adult reads it with the child joining in and then gradually withdraws support as the child gains confidence and competence. This book was written long before the National Literacy Strategy came about, but more than any other this book shows that the first challenge is to find how to help a struggling reader improve their attitude towards reading. I also keep Bentley and Reid's book close at hand. My students and I appreciate the practical and constructive approach of the authors, an approach which is underpinned by sound principles.

The rest of this entry draws on all these texts

in suggesting some strategies for the classroom. The first task is to diagnose the child's problems for yourself, even though there will already be reading records on file. A miscue analysis, perhaps in its simpler 'running record' form, will help show which of the cueing systems seems to be posing most difficulty. Is the child, for example, always guessing from the context or only using grapho-phonic correspondence which will not work in the deciphering of all words? This guides us in planning a programme to help.

Anything we can do to improve a child's understanding of the purposes of reading and the pleasures it can bestow is helpful. Talking about books and discussing the illustrations can be a good starting point. Parents and family members can be encouraged to help at home, linking with the teacher's efforts. Good language recording systems like *The Primary Language Record* have space for reports based on regular discussions with parents about their child's reading progress.

Building on a sight vocabulary of commonly used words – 'a', 'and', 'be', 'I', 'in', 'is', 'it', 'of', 'that', 'the', 'to', 'was' and so on helps confidence. Bentley and Reid believe over-dependence on 'sounding out' can be helped by games to support a sight vocabulary.

We also need to give careful phonic teaching. The work of Goswami and Bryant indicates that many struggling readers need to improve their phonic awareness. Bentley and Reid believe that some children find it easier to make sound–symbol correspondences if they work with larger units like rhyming words rather than with letters, digraphs and blends alone.

Marie Clay recommends that we praise these young readers with difficulties, pointing out specific achievements, saying perhaps something like 'good, you looked at the beginning of the word' rather than a more general 'well done'.

Interesting and appropriate resources are important for all children but especially so for children with special literacy needs. It is not so much that the latter need different books, but rather that they need imaginative help to appreciate and respond to them. A multi-sensory approach using drama, story board tellings and music can awaken interest and response. Many teachers find that talking topic books are enjoyed by children of all abilities. In *Young Researchers* Chapter 6, there is a case study showing how some Year 1 and Year 2 children benefited from Sherston's '*Look ! Here!*' software on Pets (Mallett, 1999).

Less forward older primary readers do not like to be given books which are very obviously for a younger age group. Collections of short stories are helpful, including traditional tales from all parts of the world. These are often well illustrated and have a clear plot and set of characters for discussion. You will find many suggestions in the Centre for Language in Primary Education's *Core Booklist* and Rosemary Stones' *A Multicultural Guide to Children's Books*. Humorous and subversive tellings like Scieszka and Smith's version of *The True Story of the Three Little Pigs* often intrigue even the most reluctant reader. One of Young Booktrust's selective booklists is 'Fiction for Reluctant Readers'.

Teachers also seek strategies to encourage reluctant writers and try to give help at the planning stage and support throughout the task, but no-one pretends it is easy to enthuse the more reluctant young writers. Finding a topic that inspires a child is the first step and an exciting story can often awaken interest. Writing frames, either adapted from Lewis and Wray's work (see for example Scholastic, 1996) or structured by child and teacher together for a particular task can help provide a scaffold. Struggling writers often feel more supported in a collaborative context. The computer can be helpful here as two or three children, perhaps with the help of the teacher, can produce a joint effort. The transcriptional aids that the word processor provides are also appreciated. In her research on *Software in Schools* (NFER/NCET, 1995) Christine Preston found that young readers and writers were able to concentrate for longer on the computer than working traditionally.

Able young learners – what are their additional needs?

Children who advance quickly as young readers and writers need to be challenged and supported if they are to make progress commensurate with their promise. This means building on the core programme of work in the Literacy Hour, and outside it, and agreeing with the SENCO and other colleagues on some differentiated activities appropriate for this group of learners. Bear in mind, however, that many of the activities which benefit all children are suitable for the gifted language user if we adapt them to make greater demands.

When it comes to reading, able children enjoy the challenge of more difficult fiction and non-fiction texts and more advanced activities responding to those texts. Forward readers from the Reception class upwards are able to understand the language features of different genres and benefit from talk with the teacher about these features. As well as enjoying the picture books liked by all young children – Raymond Brigg's *The Snowman*, Maurice Sendak's *Where the Wild Things Are* for example – able young children can also rise to the challenge of the layers of meaning and interesting illustrations in more complex works such as Anthony Browne's *The Tunnel* and *Voices in the Park*. By Key Stage 2 all children, and particularly the more able, are ready for the challenge of an exciting range of fiction from classic novels and poetry to traditional tales. There are some excellent ideas for supporting a range of fiction reading and extending it into writing in Barrs and Cork's *The Reader in the Writer*. Young Booktrust have reading suggestions for abler readers of 10 years and over.

There is also thought-provoking non-fiction to inspire able young readers. Imaginative illustrations and interesting text combine to raise environmental issues in Jeannie Baker's *Where the Forest Meets the Sea*. Sometimes the profundity of the questions young children ask mean that we have to read aloud to them from texts intended for much older readers. This need for advanced texts is explained in Doyle and Mallett's case study about the work on whales by a Reception class. The interest of all the children was engaged by a visit to the National History Museum. What was interesting was that the questions of the more able children obliged the teacher to seek out, and read aloud, some much more advanced books than those written for the age group. (Doyle and Mallett, 1994; Mallett, 1999). By the later primary years able readers are ready to tackle more advanced kinds of non-fiction themselves, for example full-length autobiographies, biographies and travel books intended for older readers. They are likely too to be able to understand and reflect on difficult arguments in more controversial areas to do with environmental, social and political issues. One way of supporting this reflection is to encourage them to read quality newspapers and magazines where there will be features and correspondence of interest and challenge.

Texts other than books can also nourish thinking and writing. In his exceptionally valuable book *Challenging the More Able Language User*, Geoff Dean argues that video texts can help all children, and particularly gifted children, to reflect more deeply on the themes of the books they have sprung from. He refers to interesting work with able children at Key Stage 1 who studied John Burningham's picture book *Granpa* alongside a video based on the book, made by TVS and Channel 4. The children first read the book and were then asked what a director would need to keep in mind when making the video. They enjoyed talking about music and sound effects and how the illustrations in the book might be built on in the animation process (Dean, 2001, Chapter 7). Older children also benefit from this combined study of book and video. Sometimes more than one video version of a book exists so that children can consider the choices made by different directors, say for example by the directors of Frances Hodgson Burnett's *The Secret Garden*. Other media have potential for stretching able learners: planning and recording 'radio' programmes is one example.

Many of the texts mentioned above, and the reflection on them, can lead to writing tasks which enthuse and stretch the able. Forward writers control the genre features of different texts more quickly than other children. This ability to approach the same subject matter using different kinds of writing can be exploited both in the Literacy Hour and in other areas of the curriculum. Children might present the content of a factual account as a letter, diary entry, advertisement, e-mail or newspaper article. Information technology develops language abilities in ways we are still discovering, but not least in the area of writing where children can use word processing and desk-top publishing systems to present work in interesting and novel ways. My students at Goldsmiths College have enjoyed working with multi-media authoring programmes like hyperstudio and have taken them into school to help children integrate written text with sounds, pictures and video clips.

Teachers need to bear in mind that their abler pupils often have a particularly flexible 'zone of proximal development' and are likely to benefit from some quality one-to-one teaching. This is valuable at the planning stage of a piece of writing and at the various stages of drafting.

Their work can be shared with peers either by being read aloud with invitations for questions or displayed in the literacy area of the classroom. We must remember that able children, like others, need to have their efforts recognised and praised.

Barrs, Myra and Cork, Valerie (2001) *The Reader in the Writer* London: CLPE.

Bentley, D. and Reid, D. (1995) *Supporting Struggling Readers* Widnes: UKRA.

Berger, Ann and Morris, Denise (1999, second edition) *Implementing the Literacy Hour for Pupils with Learning Difficulties* London: David Fulton.

Berger, Ann and Gross, Jean (eds) (1999) *Teaching The Literacy Hour in an inclusive classroom: supporting Pupils with Learning Difficulties in a Mainstream Environment* London: David Fulton.

Booktrust (and Young Booktrust) www.booktrust.org.uk

Dean, Geoff (second edition, 2001) *Challenging the More Able Language User* London: David Fulton in association with NACE (The National Association for Able Children in Education, PO Box 242, Arnolds Way, Oxford, OX2 9FR. Tel. 01865 861879. E-mail is: info@nace.co.uk.)

Doyle, Kathleen and Mallett, Margaret (1994) 'Were dinosaurs bigger than whales?' TACTYC *Early Years Journal,* Vol. 14, No. 2, Spring.

Goswami, U. and Bryant, P. (1991) *Phonological Skills and Learning to Read* Hillslade, NJ: Lawrence Erbaum Associates.

Gross, Jean (1999) *Special Educational Needs in the Primary School* Milton Keynes: Open University Press. (Recommended as practical and on sound principles.)

Hancock, Susan (with Jenny Kendrick and Kimberley Reynolds (1999) *Young People's Reading at the End of the Twentieth Century: Focus on Children with Special Educational Needs.* (BNB Research Fund Report 93. British Library).

Mallett, Margaret (1999) *Young Researchers* London: Routledge.

Martin, Tony (1989) *The Strugglers: Working with Children who Fail to Learn to Read* Milton Keynes: Open University Press.

Moss, G. (1995) *The Basics of Special Needs: A Routledge/SPECIAL CHILDREN Survival Guide for the Classroom Teacher* London: Questions Publishing Company/Routledge.

National Association for Special Educational Needs (NASEN), Tamworth. See publication list sincluding books/leaflets about language develop-ment and special literacy needs. Journals include *Support for Learning, British Journal of Special Education* and *Special!* (Website: http://www.nasen.org.uk.)

Stainthorp, R. and Hughes, D. (1995) 'Young early readers: a preliminary report on the development of a group of children who were able to read fluently before Key Stage 1', in Raban-Bisby *et al. Developing Language and Literacy* London. UKRA. Trentham Books.

Special Educational Needs Co-ordinator (SENCO) – see Code of Practice, Special Educational Needs, Warnock Report

Speech act

A 'speech act', according to philosophers of language, for example J.L. Austin, is an utterance that performs an act. So an apology – 'I apologise for arriving late' performs the act of apologising and a promise 'I will send the letter tomorrow' performs the act of promising.

Speech marks

See also inverted commas, quotation marks

Speech marks are punctuation marks used in written texts to show when we are indicating direct speech or a quotation from another source. For a longer explanation with examples, please see under 'quotation marks'.

Spelling

See also transcriptional aspects of writing, writing

How do children gain the knowledge to become good spellers? We now have quite a lot of research to help us support children at each stage in their development. Much information is available about how spelling and reading are linked and the most promising kinds of teacher intervention are suggested in O'Sullivan and Thomas' *Understanding Spelling* (2000). Another book which gives practical help for spelling at Key Stages 1 and 2 is Norma Mudd's *Effective Spelling* (1994).

The research of Margaret Peters, set out in her book *Spelling: Caught or Taught,* was one of the first systematic accounts of children's spelling development. The book was first published in 1967; she wrote another edition in 1985 which contains a similar message to the first: that teachers need to intervene to help individual children develop their spelling competence and that visual strategies are needed as well as those based on sound. Phonics helps us with regular words but we need visual strategies to help us learn the exceptions. For many years teachers have referred to the magic 'e', the split digraph which lengthens the vowel. Some children have a strongly developed visual memory and remember the 'look' of words easily and this helps them benefit from their reading when it comes to spelling. We have to help children whose visual memory is less developed to acquire useful strategies. The National Literacy Strategy requires us to link spelling to phonics work as well as developing the visual strategies (DfEE, 1998).

Richard Gentry's work and that of others indicates that spelling develops in stages. Children begin by writing something that creates the flow of adult-type writing. Then they realise there are different letter shapes – in the precommunicative stage. When they begin for example to use 'r' for 'are' we know they have arrived at the prephonetic stage. The next stage is the phonetic stage where there is better control over sound/symbol relationships. Visual strategies strengthen at the 'transitional' stage. Individuals may not go neatly through the stages.

In the United Kingdom the National Literacy Strategy team have targeted writing as a new priority because National results for 11 year olds suggest the Literacy Hour has raised reading but not writing standards. Teachers of all five to seven year olds are required to use 'Developing Early Writing' (from DfEE, ref. 0055/200 Tel. 0845 602 2260) which suggests that fifteen minutes should be spent each day on spelling and handwriting. This has to be 'unlinked to story writing' and the concern of some early years teachers is that motivation is lowered if children carry out too many decontextualised tasks. If we want children to use their minds to explore the spelling

system we have to allow them to risk sometimes being wrong.

Department of Education and Employment (DfEE, 1998) *The National Literacy Strategy Training Pack, Module 2 Word Level Work* London: DfEE.

Gentry, Richard (1982) 'An analysis of developmental spelling in GNYS AT WRK'. *Reading Teacher,* 36: 192–200.

Mudd, Norma (1994) *Effective Spelling: a practical guide for teachers* London: Hodder & Stoughton.

O'Sullivan, Olivia and Thomas, Anne (2000) *Understanding Spelling* London: The Centre for Language in Primary Education.

Peters, Margaret (1985 edition) *Spelling: caught or Taught: A New Look* London: Routledge & Kegan Paul.

Spiral curriculum

See also prior knowledge, spontaneous and scientific concepts

This concept is associated with the work of Jerome Bruner who challenged the view that learning is in a simple sequence (Bruner, 1975). Rather we get a foothold in an idea or piece of information when we are first introduced to it and then refine our understanding, perhaps relating it to a structured set of relationships, when we revisit it on possibly several later occasions. Two things are useful to keep in mind, particularly when we help children get a first grounding in an area. First, incorporating firsthand and practical experience into the lessons, encourages an intuitive sense of what is involved. So in science children might work with simple series circuits using batteries, wires and bulbs and get a 'sense' of how electricity behaves. As older pupils they will build on this when they learn about the laws and sophisticated application of electric power. Second, language can be used by teacher and pupils to support understanding about objects, processes and concepts each time a topic or idea is visited. Children's talk and writing about real experiences and purposes takes their understanding forward at each stage. Talk about ideas and information helps children share and organise developing knowledge.

The National Literacy Strategy Framework

encourages a spiral curriculum approach to literacy by revisiting different kinds of reading and writing at different levels – for example recount appears first in Year 1 term 3 and is revisited in the first term of Year 5.

Bruner, Jerome (1975) *Entry Into Early Language: Spiral Curriculum* Swansea: University College of Swansea.

Spoken language – see speaking and listening

Spontaneous and scientific concepts

See also prior knowledge

The difference between 'spontaneous' concepts which are acquired through everyday experience – cup, pleased, dog – and 'scientific' concepts which are formally taught – feudal, solution, igneous – was first pointed out by the developmentalist Jean Piaget and later used by Vygotsky. In *Thought and Language* Vygotsky explains how part of the role of the adult is to help children make helpful connections between the two kinds of concept. Mallett and Newsome (1977) apply Vygotsky's theory to an analysis of a primary school science lesson on igneous and sedimentary rocks.

When introducing a new topic it is helpful for a teacher to keep in mind that children will have some common sense or spontaneous concepts about it. This is often referred to as 'prior knowledge'. School learning connects this prior learning or spontaneous concepts with related 'scientific' concepts. So in a study of frogs, children might bring prior knowledge – frogs live in or near ponds, can live on land and in water and start life as frog-spawn – which can be developed into scientific concepts like habitat, belonging to a class of creatures called amphibians and life cycle.

Mallett, Margaret and Newsome, Bernard (1977) *Talking, Writing and Learning 8–13* London: Evans/Methuen.
Vygotsky, L.S. (1986 edition, ed. A. Kozusin) *Thought and Language* Cambridge Mass: MIT Press.

Standard English

See also dialect, language variety

Standard English enjoys a high social status and is the form of English usually used in writing. It is not linguistically superior to non-standard dialects but for historical and cultural reasons it became the form used in speech and writing by people of high social and educational status. It is associated with BBC voices, royalty and is the form of English learnt by people from abroad.

It is important to realise that, like other dialects, it has a distinctive grammar and vocabulary but need not be expressed in 'received pronunciation'. Standard English can be spoken in any accent.

As Medwell *et al.* point out, the English language changes constantly in both its oral and written forms, and therefore 'There can never be an absolute statement of correct standard English – the aim is appropriate use of English' (Medwell *et al.*, 2001, p. 9). This 'appropriateness' is constantly negotiated by the speakers of the language.

The notion of 'appropriateness' is helpful in the sensitive area of helping children to use standard English in speech and writing. Many teachers feel concern that if they correct children's regional dialect the implication is that their family and community speak an inferior form of language. But if the emphasis is on appropriateness rather than correctness a much more positive approach can be taken. We can agree that in writing and in formal situations like interviews and lessons, the standard form is most appropriate, not least because it has become the dialect most people can understand most easily.

The National Literacy Strategy encourages teachers and children to study dialect forms in writing. This could be achieved through looking at songs and poems in the local dialect and talking about dialect used in direct speech in children's books.

Medwell, Jane, Moore, George, Wray, David and Griffiths, Vivienne (2001) *Primary English: Knowledge and Understanding* (Course book meeting 4/98 Standards) Exeter: Learning Matters.

Standardised Reading Tests

See also assessment, reading, reading age and under names of particular tests

Standardised reading tests provide a summative picture of aspects of children's reading progress. The reading activities in the test booklets aim to identify particular skills like decoding, word recognition, accuracy, comprehension and fluency. From the results, the teacher or educational psychologist work out the child's reading age which enables comparisons to be made between children and with national norms. Some tests, for example the very well-known *Schonell Graded Word Reading Test* (restandardised in 1972), require the child to read a list of separate words which become progressively more difficult. Others present sentences – like the *Salford Sentence Reading Test,* Bookbinder, 1976. More recent tests – *Group Reading Test* (Young, 1980 version) for example – tend to assess understanding as well as decoding skills. There is a growing recognition on the part of test constructors that no one test can assess all aspects of reading progress. *The Edinburgh Reading Test* (Godfrey Thompson Unit, 1977–1981) and the *Effective Reading Tests* (Vincent and De La Mare, 1986) both aim to tap into a number of aspects of reading including comprehension. We think of 'miscue analysis' as a diagnostic test but the revised *Neale Analysis* (1988) uses the approach to produce a summative measure. This test has been used by researchers, for example Riley (1996), to make comparisons of the progress of children in different early years classrooms since it produces reading ages from six years.

The past assumption that these tests, even the most recent and sophisticated, are more objective than a teacher's judgement of progress has often been challenged. We now accept that a number of different ways of assessing progress, both summative and formative, are needed to gain a full and balanced profile of a child's developing reading abilities. The other issue we need to keep in mind is that the cultural and linguistic bias of any test, particularly those which have not been revised for some time, may disadvantage children from minority groups.

Graham, Judith and Kelly, Alison (2000, second edition) *Reading Under Control* London: David Fulton (explains the issues about standardised tests and reading ages clearly in Chapter 4).

Riley, Jeni (1996) *The Teaching of Reading: The Development of Literacy in the Early Years of School* London: Paul Chapman (see pp. 104–5 for details about the use of *Neale Analysis*).

Stanza

This is a verse in a poem usually consisting of at least four rhymed lines.

Story books – see fiction, narrative, short stories

Story Chest

See also reading, reading schemes

This is a set of reading resources, first published by Kingscourt in 1981 and revised in 1996, for the 3–11 year old age range. It is organised into stages: stages 1–7 for Key Stage 1 (5–7 year olds) and stages 8–11 for Key Stage 2 (7–11 year olds). This publisher was one of the first to produce quality big books with clear text and attractive and helpful illustrations. Favourites are the humorous and rhythmic stories *Mrs Wishy Washy* and *The Hungry Giant.* There is a pleasing range of different formats and genres for older children, including non-fiction, poetry, plays and traditional tales. This helps teachers meet the objectives of the National Literacy Strategy.

Story grammars – see narrative

Story props

See also story telling, speaking and listening

These are pictures of characters and scenery from story books mounted on small magnets so that they can be placed on a magnet board. Alternatively Blu-Tack can be used on a non-magnetic story board. The teacher or one of the children tells or reads the story and the items are placed on the board at appropriate points in the narrative.

Story telling

See also anecdotes, drama & English, fiction, historical novels, History & English, narratives, picture books, short stories

Story telling by both teacher and children can be a most enjoyable part of English work and plays a significant role in the development of children's oral language. It contributes particularly to children's ability to use narrative as a way of organising ideas and experiences. 'Story telling' covers a range of activities from the short anecdotes children share to the performance of a gifted adult story teller.

We have a rich treasure house to draw on: not only have we our own store of United Kingdom traditional tales, riddles, sayings and nursery rhymes which can be told as well as read, we can also draw on stories from oral cultures across the world. The arrival of children in our schools whose roots are in cultures rich in story telling has heightened our interest (Graham and Kelly, 2000). Teachers often model story telling, sometimes using story props – characters and scenery – on a felt story board. Some children are eager to take a turn at telling stories to the group. As well as retellings from stories they have heard others tell or those based on book stories, children with some encouragement tell anecdotes about their lives both inside and outside the classroom. With a new class or group I have found telling my own anecdotes – the day I lost three guinea pigs – often encourages the children to share their tales. Children also come to school with stories about their family's history – when they lived in another country or another part of the country or when Grandad or Grandma went to a Beatles concert in the 1960s. Student teachers I have worked with have, once they tried story telling activities in the classroom, often been surprised at the rich resources children are able to draw on. Medical emergencies including true tales of being admitted to casualty wards after accidents seem to be told with particular relish. Of course, with practice, children develop over the primary years in their control over a narrative, how they select and sequence the events, what they decide to emphasis in the char-

acters to enhance the tale and how they bring the tale to a satisfying resolution.

In their book *Reading Under Control* Graham and Kelly set out one approach to first using story telling in the classroom. They cover the preparation you will have to do if you begin by telling a story to the class yourself and suggest you might base it on a written-down story with lots of humour and action. How you tell the story depends on the age of the children but you need to keep the pace up and include direct speech to keep it lively.

Hopefully the children will comment at the end without you asking them a question. Then, they could be invited to retell the story, perhaps several children telling part of it each (Graham and Kelly, 2000).

One very strong context for group story telling is drama and role play. An interesting book on drama and traditional tales shows how events in stories are given new meaning and significance when children take on the roles and 'voices' of the characters. For example, the linguistic resources of a group of very young children were extended when they took on the role of the staff of building suppliers selling materials to the three little pigs to construct their houses (Toye and Prendiville, 2000). In early years settings in particular, the teacher needs to help the children develop the narrative, often by taking a central role.

The storybox approach is a way of drawing children into a fictional world which has considerable appeal to the very young. Developed, used and evaluated by Helen Bromley, it involves early years teachers in placing some objects in a shoe box which provide the bare bones of a story (Bromley, 2000). The children can build on miniature settings for the objects, choosing all or just some of the objects to tell a story. One box much favoured by the girls in the class Helen Bromley worked with, presented a vet's surgery and had Playmobil people and some animals ready to be patients. Three boys chose a 'Science Fiction' box which, when the lid was lifted, looked like the inside of a moon crater and included space ships and moon rocks. The children, with a little encouragement, involved themselves in imaginative play and spoke in the roles of the people and animals, using language appropriate for the various situations. This proved to be a window into children's thinking and therefore indicated what they knew and understood.

Story telling links with the development of literacy in several important ways.

An introduction to the features of stories in oral form help children understand the same features when they occur in written form and in other media like film and television. All stories have a setting, characters and a sequence of events or plot. Usually there is a conflict to be resolved. Being exposed to these features in a told story helps children bring a set of expectations about form, structure and events when they read from books. Older primary children can be helped to consider how told and written-down stories differ. What, for example, replaces tone, pitch, pace, gesture and facial expression in a written-down story?

Certainly a knowledge of traditional stories gained through oral tellings helps children enjoy fully books like Hoffman and Binch's *Amazing Grace* and *Grace and Her Family* published by Frances Lincoln. These written-down stories draw on the ancient tales in all sorts of subtle ways: in the latter book Grace is shown reading a book about fairy tales when her stepmother offers her food. Other examples of intertextual stories are *I Like Books* (a book about genre for very young children) and *The Tunnel* both by Anthony Browne and *The Jolly Postman* by Allan and Janet Ahlberg.

Story telling is not only for very young children. A Year 5 class told their own stories to the class about sibling relationships (or relationships with friends) after hearing *The Tunnel* read out and savouring and talking about the pictures. The stories could be 'true' or from the world of the imagination. Later some of them adapted their stories into written form. So this series of lessons moved naturally from listening, to reading to telling and then back to writing again.

Story telling can stretch out across a number of subjects – dance and drama of course but also history, geography, science and even mathematics – but in English lessons it is a valuable activity in its own right from the earliest years onwards.

Bromley, Helen (2000) 'The Gift of transformation: Children's talk and story boxes' in *Language Matters* Journal of the Centre for Language in Primary Education, Winter 2000.

Graham, Judith and Kelly, Alison (2000, second edition) *Reading Under Control* London: David Fulton (see Chapter 3 for a section on how telling stories can help develop literacy).

Grainger, Teresa (1997) *Traditional Storytelling in the Primary Classroom* Leamington Spa: Scholastic.

Grugeon, E. and Gardner, P. (2000) *The Art of Storytelling in the Primary Classroom* London: David Fulton.

Howe, A. and Johnson, J. (1992) *Common Bonds: Storytelling in the Classroom* Sevenoaks: Hodder & Stoughton.

Toye, Nigel and Prendiville, Francis (2000) *Drama and the Traditional Story* London: Routledge/Falmer.

Story time

See also fiction, reading, response to reading, story telling

This is a designated time, often at the end of the day in nursery and Reception classes, for telling or reading stories to the whole class. The advantage of choosing an earlier time is that other activities like role play and drawing can follow during the day (Browne, 1996). Teachers seek quality stories – there are so many wonderful ones in picture book form – and try to ensure that over a period of time the stories cover a range of types and present different experiences. Fortunate are the children whose teacher is able to tell or read stories in a spellbinding way with pace and enthusiasm, a feel for mood and atmosphere and with different voices for the direct speech. In the Reception class stories are read during the Literacy Hour but it would be sad if stories were not read for sheer pleasure at story time as well. Last time I joined a Reception class at story time the children were enthralled by one of the books in the Mr Men series – *Mr Small*. They asked the teacher to read it again. They laughed in all the same places and there was an atmosphere of complete harmony and shared enjoyment in a class of children that had had their fair share of squabbles during the day.

Reading and telling stories out loud is not just an activity for the very young. Older primary children greatly enjoy hearing the teacher read a novel over several weeks. It provides a valuable shared experience for all the children and helps make the class a community of listeners and readers. I remember the profound discussion which accompanied a Year 5 teacher's reading of *The Midnight Fox* by Betsy Byars. Tom had just confessed to Aunt Millie and Uncle Fred that it was he who let the baby fox escape after the chickens had been killed. The class talked about the conflicting interests of the farmers and the fox and Tom's difficult combination of loyalties. I hope reading out loud to the whole class, whatever their age, will always be part of good practice in Primary English.

Browne, Ann (1996) *Developing Language and literacy 3–8* London: Paul Chapman.

Structural guiders

These are the headings and subheadings which sometimes organise an information book. For more about structural guiders and other global aspects of non-fiction, see Bobbie Neate, 1992.

Neate, Bobbie (1992) *Finding Out About Finding Out* London: Hodder & Stoughton.

Structuralist model of language

Those linguists taking up a structuralist approach see language as a sort of web in which every part is related to the whole. The American structuralist, Leonard Bloomfield, aimed to set down a catalogue of elements in a language and the positions in which they can occur. The structuralist position was challenged by Noam Chomsky who developed 'generative linguistics' which went far beyond a description of elements (see under 'communicative competence and performance' and 'transformational grammar').

Study skills

See also CD-ROMs, copying, encyclopaedias, Directed Activities Around Texts, Dewey system, dictionaries, factual genres, information books, Information s and Communication Technology, Internet, library skills, non-fiction reading and writing, note-taking, retrieval devices, structural guiders, summaries

'Study skills' is a term referring to all the strategies researchers of any age use when finding out about a topic. As well as learning how to use the library, and usually the Dewey system of cataloguing, children need to be taught how to find the information they want by using the retrieval devices – the contents pages and index of books – and how to access material from databases and sites on the Internet. As well as locating information, children need to learn to make useful notes and summaries of key passages. These will be the basis of their own writing. The acquisition of study skills is built into *The Framework for Teaching* (DfEE, 1998) and is part of teaching non-fiction kinds of literacy. In the shared reading and writing part of the Literacy Hour teachers 'model' for example how to find one's way round a reference book or CD-ROM. Acquiring study skills helps make a young learner independent. We need to teach them, but too many decontextualised exercises can risk making the 'finding out' process seem dull. Learning to research is satisfying if it is linked to finding out what we need and if we want to take our knowledge and understandng of a topic further (Mallett, 1999).

If you seek detailed guidance on researching for essays and dissertations and on referencing you would find Chapters 6 and 7 in Herne *et al.* (2000) helpful.

Herne, Steve, Jessel, John and Griffiths, Jenny (2000) *Study to Teach: A guide to studying in teacher education* London: Routledge.

Mallett, Margaret (1999) *Young Researchers* London: Routledge.

Subject knowledge

See also alliteration, cohesion, digraph, ellipsis, factual genres, fiction, genre, grammar, grapheme, history of children's literature, imagery, metaphor, morpheme, onset and rime, parts of speech, onomatopoeia, phoneme, poetry, prefix, punctuation, Shakespearean drama, simile, spelling, suffix, syllable (and entries on different genre – persuasion, narrative and first person writing, on parts of speech – verb, adverb, noun and syntax – adverbial clause, sentences, finite and non-finite verbs, clauses and phrases)

Teachers have always needed a background of knowledge in language and literature to teach English in the primary school. Now the United Kingdom has a National Curriculum and a National Literacy Strategy the requirements for teachers' knowledge and understanding of English in its own right as well as in relation to children's learning have been formalised. For teachers and student teachers and tutors in college and university departments concerned with teacher education, DfEE Circular 4/98 entitled *Teaching: High Status, High Standards* specifies the essential core knowledge, skills and understanding about subject knowledge required for qualified teacher status. Annex C of this document deals specifically with English and sets out the subject knowledge required under the headings 'lexical', 'grammatical' and 'textual'. 'Lexical' study includes phonology (the sound system), graphology (the writing system) and morphology (word structure and derivations). 'Grammatical' study consists of the grammar of spoken and written English and punctuation. 'Textual' study takes in cohesion, layout and the organisation of different kinds of text. Part of the task is to learn the meanings of the technical terms for all three areas of study and to be able to use them appropriately.

If you are a student teacher the following strategies may help you to meet the requirements:

- Carry out the English audit your college provides or a similar published one – see for example Wilson (2001 edition) or Challen (2001) and identify the areas where you feel you need to strengthen.
- Use a self-study aid or book to take forward your knowledge (for example, Wray and Medwell, 1997; Crystal, 1996; King, 2000; Medwell *et al.*, 2001; Wilson, 2001). Useful websites include: www.ucl.ac.uk/internet-grammar;http//webster.comment.edu/grammar/index.htm;www.standards.dfee.gov.uk/literacy
- Talk about your studies with a colleague or colleagues in college and school – collaborative study can be more enjoyable for something like this.
- Be pro-active in seeking advice from colleagues, teachers in school and your tutors.
- Research aspects of subject knowledge before working with children in school.

For example, if you are telling and reading traditional tales with six year olds it is helpful to research the features of this genre. In preparation for a study of poetry with older pupils you could check through different types of form like haiku, ballad and free verse and secure your grasp of terminology like alliteration, metaphor and personification.

A huge pile of books, articles and CD-ROMs, including a good number on language study and grammar, have been my companions as I have worked on this encyclopaedia. Some of these are written in an accessible way and are likely to be useful for anyone wishing to build their knowledge. Bain and Bain's *The Grammar Book* is written for secondary-aged children, but I find this useful as is Shiach's *Grammar to 14*. Angela Wilson in *Language Knowledge for Primary Teachers* writes with a welcome touch of humour and covers all three required areas – lexical, grammatical and textual thoroughly. Her insights about ways into understanding the genre features of both fiction and non-fiction are particularly valuable and enjoyed by students and teachers. Mark Smee's *Grammar Matters* also brings some humour to the topic – through the illustrations to the eight units which progress from 'words' to 'sentences' to 'paragraphs and whole texts'. There is also a teacher's manual with extra examples and answers to some of the tasks in the text for students. If you want an alphabetically organised grammar reference book you might like *Collins School Reference Grammar*. David Crystal's book

Discover Grammar explains challenging notions in a clear way. When it comes to terminology, I find the glossary of language terms in DfEE's *Grammar for Writing* both helpful and easy to use.

Primary English: Knowledge and Understanding (a course book by Medwell *et al.* meeting 4/98 Standards) suggests detailed and pertinent information, provides interesting tasks and has useful pedagogical links – to promote good classroom practice.

For more advanced study and for reference purposes I recommend Tom McArthur's beautifully written and scholarly *The Oxford Companion to the English Language*. This is especially helpful over literary terms and text types.

For those who would like to learn more about linguistics, I recommend David Crystal's *Cambridge Encyclopaedia of Language* and John Seely's *The Grammar Guide*.

Bain, R. and Bain. E. (1993) *The Grammar Book* Sheffield: NATE.

Challen, D. (2001) *Primary English Audit and Test* Exeter: Learning Matters.

Crystal, David (1996) *Discover Grammar* London: Longman.

DfEE (1998) *Teaching: High Status, High Standards* Circular 4/98 (obtainable by telephoning 0845 60 222 60 or by downloading from the Internet at: www.canteach.gov.uk/info/standards). (Revised Spring 2002).

DfEE (2000) *Grammar for Writing* London: DfEE.

King, G. (2000) *Collins Wordpower: Good Grammar* London: Collins

McArthur, Tom (1992) *The Oxford Companion to the English Language* Oxford: Oxford University Press.

Medwell, J. Moore, G. Wray, D. and Griffiths, V. (2001) *Primary English: Knowledge and Understanding.* Exeter: Learning Matters.

Seely, John (1999) *The Grammar Guide* London: Heinemann.

Shiach, Don (1999) *Grammar to 14* Oxford: Oxford University Press.

Smee, Mark (1999) *Grammar Matters* (with an accompanying teacher's resource pack by John Drayes). London: Heinemann.

Wilson, Angela (2001, second edition) *Language Knowledge for Primary Teachers* London: David Fulton.

Wray, David and Medwell, Jane (1997) *English for Primary Teachers: An audit and self-study guide* London: Letts International.

Suffix

A suffix is an affix which ends a word, such as 'ful' in 'useful' or 'ed' in 'acted'.

Summary (or précis)

See also Directed Activities Around Texts, non-fiction reading and writing

This is a shortened version of a longer text containing the most important points. The National Literacy Strategy *Framework for Teaching* requires children to write summaries in text level work in Year 3, term 3 (DfEE, 1998). However, before this children can be helped to practise activities which prepare them for summary writing; for example underlining main points in a text and then developing the underlined points into notes in the shared writing part of the Literacy Hour.

Mallett suggests another promising strategy: read a section from an information book that is being currently used for work in any lesson or the Literacy Hour, and ask the children to write down about five key points – about 'the Diet of the Ancient Greeks' or about 'Young and Old Rivers'. Children usually enjoy the opportunity to read out their list for constructive criticism. They learn to reflect on the status of particular pieces of information and from skeleton notes they can write summaries (Mallett, 1999, p. 108).

A summary at the beginning of a dissertation or academic article is called an abstract.

Summative assessment – see assessment, SATS, standardised tests

Sustained Silent Reading (SSR) – see ERIC and USSR

Syllable

See also phoneme, phonological awareness

A syllable is part of a word which is pronounced as one beat. In the word 'subject' there are two syllables 'sub' and 'ject'.

Synonym

See also thesaurus

A synonym of a word means the same thing as that word. There is some doubt about whether any two words can ever have an identical meaning. McArthur, for example, writes that some linguists consider 'no two words have the same distribution, frequency, connotation or language level'. Nevertheless a thesaurus works on the principle that it is useful for a speaker or writer to know synonyms for as many words as possible. *Chambers School Thesaurus,* for children over ten years, includes panels of important words for extended treatment 'anger', 'difficulty', 'money', 'health' and 'happiness'. Many dictionaries also include lists of synonyms at the end of definitions.

Children increase their knowledge of synonyms through listening and reading from an early age. They are mentioned particularly in the vocabulary extension work in Year 3, term 3 of *The National Literacy Strategy Framework for Teaching* (DfEE, 1998).

McArthur, Tom (1992) *The Oxford Companion to the English Language* London and Oxford: QPD Paperbacks and Oxford University Press.

Syntax – see grammar

Syntactic cue-system

See also cue-systems, miscue analysis, reading, grammar

When using this cue-system, readers draw on their knowledge of grammar and language to get a sense of what is coming next. Young readers know for instance that if they read at the beginning of a sentence 'the teachers' the next verb will be plural, and an adjective like 'beautiful' will often be followed soon by a noun, such as 'horse'.

The other cue-systems are semantic, graphophonic and bibliographic.

Synthetic phonics

See also phoneme, phonics

This approach to teaching phonics involves young readers in first separating out the phonemes in a word and then blending them together to read the word. This way of perceiving phonics contrasts with 'analytic' approaches in which larger segments of words are analysed and patterns across words detected.

T

Talk – see under speaking and listening

Talking books

'Talking books' are interactive reading aids. Children focus on the written text and look at the pictures as a voice speaks the words. Teachers also use software in shared writing sessions to produce their own talking books with the children. Some of the books used in the Literacy Hour can provide a framework for children's first efforts at making their own talking book.

Taped books – see under audio books/tapes/cassettes

Target setting

See also assessment, portfolios, SATs

Often the statutory assessments (SATs) at the end of key stages are a stimulus and guide to teachers' target setting. The senior management team and the governors compare their results in reading and writing with the national figures, especially those for schools that are similar in intake and facilities. Targets are set to raise attainment gradually. Once realistic targets are agreed, everyone concerned needs to have a clear understanding of the action needed to achieve them. This needs to be built into any target setting chart. So we might have column headings as follows, which are based on the diagram in Tyrrell and Gill 2000, p. 159: Standards at; Projected Target; Success Criteria; Action to be Taken; Standards at. The Success Criteria will be drawn from the NC and NLS objectives.

The challenge of increasing the children's attainment over time and measuring progress against projected targets is now build into educational culture. However, there are some issues that the English Co-ordinator and class teachers need to bear in mind. First there is the problem of pupil mobility so that input is not the same as output over a number of years. Tyrrell and Gill estimate that for some schools there may be inwards and outwards transfers of 50 per cent, making target setting somewhat imprecise. They conclude that too much reliance on figures risks misunderstanding the nature of schooling 'and shows a lack of awareness of anything other than the stereotypical childhood where a little boy or girl sets off to Reception and stays in the school until they leave at the end of Year 6' (Tyrrell and Gill, 2000, p. 158).

Another difficulty arises if we think schools are like businesses which can increase output by economies in employee numbers and resources. After a couple of years of considerable effort, schools may reach a plateau and in spite of excellent teaching, performance levels according to fairly crude measures are unlikely to show large rises. It is also the case that cohorts of children can vary in their levels of motivation and ability so that 'dips' in performance may occur.

As Graham and Kelly point out, in a target-setting climate teachers need to have some richer evidence than just test scores of a child's progress. They are very much in favour of building up portfolios with annotated samples of writing and other evidence and of involving children in setting targets. Where a number of key targets are identified each term or half term these can be shared with the children 'who then decide…how far the targets have been achieved, before moving on to set new targets' (Graham and Kelly, 2000, p. 133). So an eight year old might for a half term be working on some particular letter strings to

improve reading and spelling and on strength-
ening the use of dialogue in stories. Teacher and
child would talk about progress, focused on the
child's reading and writing samples at the end of
the half term.

Graham, Judith and Kelly, Alison (2000) *Reading Under
Control* London: David Fulton.

Tyrrell, Jenny and Gill, Narinderjit (2000) *Coordinating
English at Key Stage 1* London: David Fulton.

Teaching English – see under history of English teaching

Teacher Training Agency (TTA)

See also English Co-ordinator

The Teacher Training Agency is a government
body which sets standards for all aspects of school
teaching. They have, for example, set up national
standards for subject leadership which stress that
coordinators need to work towards high-quality
teaching in every classroom, effective use of
resources and the improvement of standards of
achievement for all pupils.

Teacher Training Agency, Tel. 020 7925 3700.

Television and literacy

See also – advertisements, cartoons, CD-ROM,
Internet, video-film, visual literacy

Watching television (unless it was educational
television) was, until relatively recently, thought
to be a much more passive activity than reading
print. Apart from concerns about the possible
effect on children of watching 'unsuitable'
programmes intended for adults, there have long
been suspicions that watching a lot of television
could make children less likely to spend time
reading. Research, for example that carried out
by Brown (1999), tends to show that children's
perceptions are that both parents and teachers are
against 'watching too much television'. But
opinion is now swinging towards the positive
contribution that viewing film, video-film and
television can make to children's developing
literacy (Marsh and Millard, 2001). Indeed

dramatic technological changes have expanded
the ways in which meanings can be carried. So
there are exciting new literacies to develop and
support, not least visual literacy. It is these new
literacies that we need to develop in the primary
classroom alongside print literacy if we want children to be imaginative and flexible thinkers in a
technological culture. But teachers have to know
how to use the medium effectively. I consider the
role of video-film, and particularly videos of children's stories, in developing children's literary
competence under the 'video-film' entry. This
entry looks more specifically at the educative role
of television programmes first in the home and
then in the school context.

The home context

If you watch very young children while they are
viewing their favourite programmes – *The Teletubbies, Sesame Street, The Tweenies* or *Playdays*
you are likely to be struck at how active their
response is. They jump up, sing, dance and ask
questions. In her qualitative study of the role of
televisual texts in children's development, Naima
Brown observed that children did not always
respond to adult presenters' explicit invitation to
'join in and sing along' but made their own decisions about how to participate. Often they
insisted on seeing a favourite video over and over
again. Brown believes the lively response of such
young children shows the potential of television,
or as Brown terms them 'televisual texts', as a
starting point for role play, story telling and, later
on, writing.

Perhaps because of time constraints, parents
do not often seem to watch television with their
children, so opportunities to answer questions
and generally mediate between child and
programme are limited. Brown did find some
families who watched programmes together. For
example five-year-old India told the researcher
that she and her seven-year-old brother and their
parents watched *Coronation Street* before the children went to bed (Brown, 1999, p. 63).

There has been concern about children who
spend long periods in front of television without
any talk or interaction with others. Some studies
suggest children's listening skills are unlikely to

develop under such circumstances. Sue Palmer points out that family rituals of singing nursery rhymes may be a casualty of a television-dominated home (Palmer, 1997). But it does seem to be the lack of interaction which is the problem here. Not surprisingly, Brown found that in contexts where there was lively talk about programmes, children were more likely to extend the experience through story telling and play. There are many examples of the creative response of her own child, see for example her retelling of *Pollyanna* at age 5.6 years (in Appendix F of Brown, 1999). Rehana sings a made-up tune at the beginning of her story – as she has heard introductory music on the many story and video-tapes she has heard.

The new emphasis on televisual texts from mainstream television in school may change parents' perceptions of television to more positive ones.

The school context

A teacher's television resources fall into two main categories. First there are the school programmes on every subject which may be watched live or pre-recorded for greater flexibility. Second there are the pre-recorded programmes from mainstream television in video-film form. The latter may be factual programmes on wild life or geographical themes for example but the 'English' collection is more likely to be television serials of children's stories. (Teachers also use television advertisements for analysis of persuasive texts and this is covered in the Advertisements entry.) The second of these is discussed in the 'video-film' entry so I turn mainly to the first in the discussion below, Over the years there have been a large number of educational programmes to support the teaching of English, some of them of high quality like *Storyworld* and *Words and Pictures* for younger children and *Living Language* and *The English Programme* for older ones. Many of today's television programmes help develop children's literacy – *Look and Read* for example, and can be recorded to use at the most appropriate point in the teaching programme. In his study for the Independent Television Commission, Paul Kelly found that

teachers preferred to use pre-recorded programmes so that they could stop the video machine to highlight points or invite discussion (Kelley, 1998). The programmes are usually interactive, inviting children to call out the names of letters, to predict and sometimes to join in other ways like singing. Very often there are programme notes for the teacher and booklets for the children and, increasingly software packages. The linking of the different media through which teaching is planned and carried out makes demands on the practitioner. But the careful use of television programmes can prove an enjoyable whole class activity and link home and school.

For older children there are programmes about the use of English and to promote reading and writing; sometimes such programmes are presented by children's writers and poets like Michael Rosen. There is no doubt that many programmes provide inspiration for literacy work as they provide whole works or extracts from literature ranging from Shakespeare and Aesop, classic poetry and ballads, traditional tales from different cultures and modern fairy tales and popular fiction. In the 'video-film' entry I suggest that children can be helped to compare how aspects of the same narrative can be stressed in different media. In her chapter in Jon Callow's book *Image Matters,* Annemaree O'Brien suggests that we help children to discuss the features of a televisual text, including the acting, settings, lighting, use of sound and music and the angle of camera shots (Callow, 1999, p. 48). As well as televised stories specifically for children, teachers are now including for older primary children examples of popular television including carefully selected episodes of soap serials, cartoons and sports commentaries and, as mentioned above, advertisements. With help from the teacher, children can develop their thinking about important issues and expand their understanding of how a particular medium carries its meanings.

Film Education's webpage: www.filmeducation.org

Brown, Naima (1999) *Young Children's Literacy Development and the Role of Televisual Texts* London: Falmer Press.

Kelley, P. (1998) *The Future of Schools' Television* London: Independent Television Commission.

Marsh, Jackie and Millard, Elaine (2001) *Literacy and popular Culture* London: Paul Chapman.

O'Brien, Annemaree (1999) 'Reading TV: a basic visual literacy' in Callow, Jon (ed.) *Image Matters: visual texts in the classroom* Marrickville, Australia: PETA (Primary English Teaching Association).

Palmer, Sue (1997) 'Turned on and Switched off' *Times Educational Supplement*, 18 April.

Tenor

See also register

To understand what 'tenor' means we first have to consider 'register' of which 'tenor' is an aspect. 'Register' is an abstract linguistic concept which refers to the way in which language varies according to the situation in which it is spoken and written. 'Tenor' is to do with the way in which the message is given. An informal use of tenor might include the active voice and the use of the pronouns 'I' and 'you' while the passive voice indicates a more formal expression of the message.

Tense

See also verb

The tense of a verb is a grammatical feature that situates in time the events, feelings, conditions and so on, expressed in a sentence. All finite verbs have a tense. See examples under 'verb'.

Terminology (of Primary English)

See also Cox Report, LINC materials, metalanguage, phonics, reading, speaking and listening, writing

Primary school teachers have always needed a vocabulary to enable them to talk to children, colleagues and parents about the aspects of language and literature they have covered in the English programme. To understand how we have arrived at the more formal requirement for teachers' knowledge about language or 'subject knowledge', which includes an ability to use a technical vocabulary, we need to take a brief look at recent history. As part of the move towards a

National Curriculum during the late 1980s, a committee, chaired by Sir John Kingman, was set up to explore models of how language works and to consider what pupils needed to be taught. After *The Kingman Report* (DES, 1988) was published, another committee, chaired by Brian Cox was set up to build on the work of Kingman and to devise programmes for study and attainment targets to use in The National Curriculum. The first report of this committee was published in 1988 (DES, 1988) and concentrated on Key Stages 1 and 2. A whole chapter on linguistic terminology was included. The second version, sometimes referred to as *Cox 2*, included proposals for the teaching of pupils at Key Stages 3 and 4 in addition to primary-aged children. There was an even more detailed chapter on 'knowledge about language' and reference to the fact that the government had set up a project to produce training materials to support the teaching of Language in the National Curriculum. These were known as the LINC materials and the story of how these were received by the government of the day is told under the LINC and Cox report entries. The work of the two committees and their reports had given rise to an explosion of interest in what children should be taught about language and many people took up entrenched positions on the teaching of grammar.

These debates about issues like whether a knowledge of grammatical structures transfers into children's writing still simmer away but what primary teachers in the United Kingdom must cover in English is now formalised. As well as following the programmes of the National Curriculum, teachers work with the *National Literacy Strategy Framework for Teaching* (DfEE, 1998) which includes a substantial glossary of technical terms. It was decided that intending teachers needed to achieve a high level of subject knowledge to enable them to cover the official requirements. *Circular 4/98, Teaching: High Status, High Standards* (DfEE, 1998) lays down the statutory requirements for courses of initial teacher training and specifies the subject knowledge teachers need at their own level. This subject knowledge is set out under three categories: Lexical, Grammatical and Textual. The technical vocabulary required to cover this is made fully explicit. As well as the better known terms to refer to reading and writing – 'consonant', 'vowel' and 'letter' teachers are also required to control terms like 'onset and rime', 'split digraph' and 'affix'. In addition, there is a vocabulary to talk about texts, for example to refer to the different kinds like 'fable', 'sonnet' and 'fantasy' or, in the non-fiction categories, texts like 'recount', 'report' and 'instruction'.

Knowing these terms and the concepts they express is helpful for teachers. Judging when and if particular terms are used with children is more of an issue. Too technical an approach too early might inhibit the spontaneous enjoyment of learning about language and enjoying stories and poems. And there is still that question about whether knowing about grammatical constructions and what they are called is likely to transfer to children's writing.

Of course UK teachers need to read the official documentation but there are also a number of publications which help them become secure in their knowledge of terminology and I hope the following suggestions will be helpful.

Bain, Elizabeth and Bain, Richard (1977) *The Grammar Book* Sheffield: NATE.

Crystal, David (1996) *Discover Grammar* London: Longman.

Graham, Judith and Kelly, Alison (2000 edition) *Reading Under Control* London: David Fulton (see glossary of literacy terms).

Medwell, Jane, Moore, George, Wray, David and Griffiths, Vivienne (2001) *Primary English: Knowledge and understanding* Exeter: Learning Matters.

Wilson, Angela (2001 edition) *Language Knowledge for Primary Teachers* London: David Fulton (has a welcome light touch while covering the essentials well).

Wray, David and Medwell, Jane (1997) *English for Primary Teachers: An audit and self study guide* London: Letts.

Texts

See also CD-ROM, fiction, genre, history of children's literature, illustrations, information texts, non-fiction reading and writing, television and literacy, video-film, visual literacy

'Text' is used to refer to a continuous piece of writing such as a poem, a playscript or a novel. The term is now used more widely to refer to spoken as well as written language so that a conversation, for example, could be regarded as an oral text. Linguists examining everyday utterances tape record speech in a context and refer to it as a 'text' for the purpose of study. The coming of new technology has brought into the sphere of texts – electronic and multi-media texts, which have visual, auditory and spatial features as well as visual ones.

Text level work

See also fiction, genre, information texts, Literacy Hour, National Curriculum, National Literacy Strategy, reading

'Text level work' helps develop children's understanding of and response to the global features of different texts. In the case of a story or a novel, text level aspects would include the plot, characterisation, setting and language style. The National Literacy Strategy expands on the National Curriculum English orders' requirements for helping children to respond to texts. Detailed requirements for text level work in the Literacy Hour for each term of each year group are set out in *The National Literacy Strategy Framework for Teaching* (DfEE, 1998).

TGAT Report

See also assessment, reading, record keeping, speaking and listening, writing

This report was an outcome of the work of a group appointed to consider how the National Curriculum programmes should be assessed. Their recommendation that attainment in each subject was to be measured against a ten-level scale proved unmanageable and a slimmed-down Dearing version was introduced in 1995.

Many teachers found the most positive aspect of the TGAT report was its view that assessment should not only occur at the end of phases of work. Rather, it should be an integral part of the educational process and incorporated into planning and teaching strategies. This attitude to assessment was in line with assessment and record keeping approaches like the Primary Language Record of the Centre for Language in Education.

Report of the Task Group on Assessment and Testing (DES. 1987) London: HMSO.
Primary Language Record (PLR) 1988 London: Centre for Language in Primary Education.

Theme – see cross-curricular projects, English projects

Thesaurus (plural can be either 'thesauri' or 'thesauruses')

See also dictionary, genre

A thesaurus provides lists of antonyms and synonyms, either arranged alphabetically or thematically. The best ones for children reinforce a belief that language is essentially creative and adds to the range of options a speaker or writer can select.

Publishers of children's dictionaries – Chambers, Usborne, Oxford University Press, Collins – nearly always also include thesauruses on their title lists. There is now a children's version of Roget's Thesaurus. In his introduction to his Oxford Children's Thesaurus (1991), Alan Spooner – compiler of thesuaruses for different age groups – expresses his view that a good thesaurus for any age group should have a wide enough vocabulary to make it interesting and thought-provoking. The Usborne Illustrated Thesaurus, for children of about ten years and over, has 60,000 words and fully labelled illustrations which make it a good browse. Chambers School Thesaurus goes up a gear for the over tens and offers panels giving extended treatment to words where synonyms and antonyms are particularly important – for example 'get', 'happy', 'nice'. Whether a thesaurus is built into a word processing package or in print form its function is to offer us an exciting range of options to express our meaning.

Thinking – see critical discourse, language and thought, metacognition, philosophy and literacy, reflective reading

THRASS (Teaching Handwriting, Reading And Spelling Skills)

See also phonics, phonological awareness and spelling

This organisation produces resources in print, audio, video and software form to help teach children and adults (including teachers and parents) about what they term 'the building blocks' of reading and spelling, that is, the 44 phonemes (speech sounds) of spoken English and the graphemes (spelling choices) of written English. The products are used in 8,000 institutions world-wide.

Davies, Alan (2000) 'The Phoneme Test: Should All Teachers Pass It?' in Dyslexia Review, The Journal of the Dyslexia Institute Guild, Vol. 11, Nos 4, 9–12, Summer.
Davies, Alan and Ritchie, Denyse (1998) THRASS Teacher's Manual http://www.thrass.co.uk

Tick sheets

See also assessment, marking, portfolios

Tick sheets in print or on screen might show children's names down the left-hand side and detail tasks across the top. Lines are drawn so that boxes can be ticked when tasks are completed. So a tick sheet on writing might tell us that Scott has made a plan, written a list and drafted a story. An individual child's reading tick list might have a column with the names of books written on the left-hand side with ticks against those the child has read. Another kind of tick list for reading might indicate a child's progress in reading strategies with categories like 'uses semantic cues', 'sounds out words' and 'looks for letter strings'. These check lists are useful as quick reminders of a child's achievements for busy teachers. However, if too much reliance is placed on them they can lead to a superficial view of a child's progress, to a 'board game mentality' (Tyrrell and Gill, 2000, p. 142). Tick lists can give the impression that assessment is something that happens at the end of learning rather than, as the TAGT report (1987) suggested, a process that threads through planning and teaching.

We need to know what was good about Scott's story and how we might intervene to help him. By involving him in the process of evaluation we make it much more likely that he will have a pride in his best work and an idea about how to improve further. The tick list of books read could lead to a child thinking progress was a matter of rushing through as many books as possible when we really want to show we are in favour of talking about books and sometimes revisiting favourite ones for sheer enjoyment. Even the reading strategy check list which can give a helpful profile of a young reader's progress nearly always needs annotation to give a full picture.

Report of the Task Group on Assessment and Testing (DES, 1987) London: HMSO.

Tyrrell, Jenny and Gill, Narinderjit (2000) *Co-ordinating English at Key Stage 1* London: Routledge-Falmer.

Timelines

See also diagrams, History & English

Timelines are vertical or horizontal representations of a journey through time. They can cover a thousand years or the events of a day or even an hour. They always involve careful selection of what to include and what to leave out. Events can be denoted by words or by pictures or both.

In English lessons we often chart a journey of a character or characters through time, for example the journey through war torn Europe to find their parents of the children in Ian Seraillier's *The Silver Sword*.

Children enjoy making timelines of fantasy characters like The Jumblies (see Edward Lear's *A Book of Nonsense*, Dragon's World Publishers) using words and perhaps some illustrations bringing English and Art together.

Timelines are most often used in history lessons to show the events of a monarch's reign or the movement of a people through the centuries across the globe. In preparation for the millen-

nium many teachers and children constructed their own timelines of the past 1,000 years. During 1999 *The Times Educational Supplement* kept in touch with the work of many schools and noted that many of the time lines constructed by children in the UK included key events: the coming of the Normans in Britain, building of Notre Dame Cathedral, the arrival of the Renaissance, the Industrial Revolution, Art Deco images of the1920s and 30s, the technology revolution of the present day. However children did not echo adult views of history and some of the liveliest most interesting timelines showed an emphasis on their own regional, ethnic and religious communities. Some children concentrated on music, sport or environmental issues and developments.

Choices had to be made from all the possibilities and children learnt that for a project like this you have to select, as all historians do, when telling the story of the past. In one school I visit often children in each year group were responsible for a particular period of time or aspect, the youngest children taking up aspects of the present or recent past.

The talk, discussion and writing involved linked history, English and art in fruitful ways.

From TES … *Florence Nightingale Timelines* (www.drai.com/-bomeo/nightingale/index.html) One of many hundreds of timelines on the Net with a focus on Nightingale as the first modern war nurse. Illuminates her particular qualities and abilities which made possible her great contribution.

'Top-down' approaches to reading

See also big shapes, bottom-up reading approaches, cue-systems, interactive reading model, reading

'Top-down' approaches to reading emphasise the role of searching for 'meaning' rather than the role of 'code-breaking' in the initial teaching of reading. Frank Smith (1978) and Goodman and Goodman (1979) are associated with the theoretical underpinning to approaches favouring 'top-down' strategies for decoding based on prediction and guessing. Jeni Riley defines the strong point of these approaches as follows: 'Meaning provides the dynamo for the whole activity of reading, giving it purpose' (Riley, 1996, p. 23). However, she joins other critics of extreme forms of the model in pointing out that 'whole reading' or 'top-down' approaches do not help teachers with the systematic teaching needed at the initial stages. There needs to be some carefully planned work at letter and word level ('bottom-up' approach) as well as attention to context and whole text aspects ('top-down' approach).

The entry under Interactive reading model explains how important aspects of 'top-down' and 'bottom-up' approaches can be combined.

Goodman, K.S. and Goodman Y.M. (1979) to read is natural. In Resnick, L.B. and Weaver, P.A. (eds) *Theory and Practice of Early Reading*. Vol. 1, Hillside, NJ: Lawrence Erlbaum Associates.

Riley, Jeni (1996) *The Teaching of Reading* London: Paul Chapman (Chapter 2).

Smith, Frank (1978, second edition) *Understanding Reading* New York: Holt, Rinehart & Winston.

Topics – see cross-curricular projects, English projects

Traditional tales

See also creation stories, fable, fairy tales, folk tales, legend, myths

'Traditional tales' is an umbrella term for all the kinds of story named above which are discussed under the individual entries. These ancient stories were told many times and passed down the generations. Some of the same universal themes are found in stories all over the world. Such stories are an important part of the fiction collection in the primary school and they thread through the English programme. They impart much of importance about human nature in general and are an excellent way of learning what is valued in cultures different from out own. Here it may be helpful to explain the emphasis of each kind, although there is much overlapping.

- *Creation stories* are tales in a cultural context which try to explain how the earth and all its objects, people and creatures came about.
- *Fables* are stories ending with a moral prin-

ciple. They often involve animal characters as in Aesop's Fables.

- *Fairy tales* always include an element of magic and often magical folk like elves, gnomes, sprites and fairies (see Carpenter and Prichard, 1984 for a substantial account of the history of the fairy tale).
- *folk tales* are mainly about the lives, trials and tribulations of ordinary people from every part of the world. Some contain fairytale elements such as characters being granted three wishes or people being transformed by magic.
- *legends* are usually about heroic characters, for example King Arthur and his knights. They may be based on historical characters and events that actually happened, but they tend to be embroidered with detail and supernatural elements.
- *myths* are ancient stories of gods and heroes, often about the origins of life and issues of deep human concern. (Creation stories are often thought of as a category of myth because of their emphasis on how things began.) Greek myths concentrate on stories about the gods, for example the story of Persephone, the daughter of Zeus who spent half the year on earth and half in the underworld. But there are myths from all over the world and there are many excellent collections of retellings.

Excellent annotated lists of collections of the different kinds of traditional tale are found in *Tales for Telling* (2000) a file from The Centre for the Children's Book and in Steele (1989), Stones (1999) and Phinn (2000).

Carpenter, Humphrey and Prichard, Mari (1984) *The Oxford Companion to Children's Literature* Oxford: Oxford University Press.

Phinn, Gervase (2000) *Young Readers and their Books* London: David Fulton.

Stones, Rosemary (1999) *A Multicultural Guide to Children's Books* London: Books for Keeps.

Steele, Mary (1989) *Traditional Tales: A Signal Bookguide* Stroud: The Thimble Press.

Tales for Telling: A Journey Through the World of Folktales. (2000) Newcastle on Tyne Centre for the Children's Book. (Tel. 0191 274 3949).

Transactional writing

See also factual writing, genre, non-fiction reading and writing

The term 'transactional writing' was used by James Britton and his team on the Schools Council Writing Project (carried out in the 1970s) to refer to factual kinds of writing. Britton suggested that we relate to our experience in two ways: either as participants seeking to act directly in the world or as spectators, reflecting on and reorganising all that happens to us. Transactional kinds of language are the outcome of relating to our experience as a participant.

Britton, James N. (1970) *Language and Learning* London: Allen Lane, The Penguin Press (Chapter 3, 'Participant and Spectator').

Transcriptional aspects of writing

See also handwritimg. paragraphing, punctuation, spelling

These include spelling, punctuation, capitalisation, legibility and paragraphing. The distinction between compositional and transcriptional (or secretarial) aspects of writing was made by Frank Smith (1982). Noting the physical effort young children put into spelling and handwriting, Smith suggested teachers encourage them to concentrate first on what they wanted to communicate (the composition of the content of their writing) and second on bringing the transcriptional aspects to a good standard. This approach was intended to prevent the inhibiting of the content of the writing by premature worry about the secretarial matters. The distinction is recognised in the National Curriculum English programmes where transcriptional aspects are referred to as 'presentation'.

Smith, Frank (1982) *Writing and the Writer* London: Heinemann.

Transformational grammar

See also communicative competence, language acquisition, nativist approach to langauge acquisition

Transformational grammar refers to the way in which language structures can be changed (or transformed) while keeping their essential meaning. The concept is associated with the influential linguist, Noam Chomsky, of the Massachusetts Institute of Technology who revolutionised thinking about language and how we acquire it.

To come closer to understanding Chomsky's view we need to know about certain universal and fundamental properties of language – of all known languages – and their link with how human beings think. The proposal that there are language universals adds weight to Chomsky's theory that human beings have a genetic predisposition to language. First, every sentence has a subject–predicate relation – the predicate tells us something about the subject. In: 'The teacher read the picture book with the scarlet cover' 'The teacher 'is the subject and the rest of the sentence is the predicate. Second, every sentence has a verb–object relationship which gives a logical relation between cause and effect. In the same example, 'picture book' is the object of the verb 'read'. Third, there are elements in a sentence that add to the meaning called 'modification'. In the sentence above 'with the scarlet cover' is the modification.

Chomsky observed that the basic sentence could be expressed in different ways. One obvious alternate would be to put the sentence in the passive tense. So our sample sentence could be expressed as 'The picture book with the scarlet cover was read by the teacher'. Here what Chomsky refers to as the 'surface structure' has changed. But he contrasts this transformation of the 'surface structure' with the stability of the 'deep structure' – the profound meaning.

Chomsky made a clear distinction between what he called 'competence', a language user's knowledge of the rules and potential structures of their language and 'performance' by which he meant the actual utterances made by particular speakers. If you would like to read a clear introduction to the work of Chomsky I recommend either Chapter 4 'Language and Learning' in David Wood's book *How Children Think and Learn* or Chapter 65 'Linguistics' in David Crystal's *Cambridge Encyclopaedia of Language*.

Wood, David (1988) *How Children Think and Learn* London: Blackwell.

Crystal, David (1987) *The Cambridge Encyclopaedia of Language* Cambridge: Cambridge University Press.

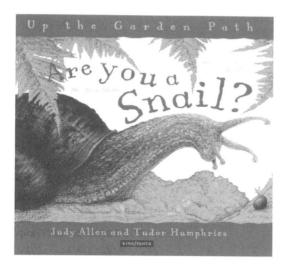

Are you a Snail? by Judy Allen and Tudor Humphries, Kingfisher, is an inviting early information book for children aged six years which has wonderful detailed illustrations and a lively written text. The cover illustration is reproduced by permission of Kingfisher Publications plc. Copyright Kingfisher Publications 2000. All rights reserved.

Transitional genre

See also faction, information story

This term refers to texts, usually for young children, which modify some of the features of the maturer forms they are based on. For example, non-narrative texts may have a more conversational tone and a more appealing format than those for older children. Other transitional texts are organised, like stories, in a narrative form and sometimes called 'faction' because they use some devices more typical of fiction. They may, for example, like *The Drop Goes Plop*, have characters that seem to have escaped from a fairy story – in this case a talking mother and baby seagull who nevertheless cover some basic concepts about the water cycle by following the journey of a drop of water. Structured round a sort of adult–child conversation – the mother's utterances are quite a good introduction to information book language. 'When the cloud gets heavy, the drops fall out as rain. If it's really cold, the drops freeze and fall as snow or hail'. The concept of how the water cycle works and the dynamic nature of the process comes through well. A sense of movement is achieved by making some of the text wave along the page with the flow of the water. A group of seven year olds told me this kind of text was 'an information story'.

Baker, C.D. and Freebody, P. (1989) *Children's First School Books* Oxford: Basil Blackwell.

Godwin, S. and Abel, S. (1998) *The Drop Goes Plop* London: Macdonald Young Books.

Mallett, Margaret (1999) *Young Researchers: Informational reading and writing in the early and primary years* London: Routledge.

Transitive/intransitive verb

See also verb

Transitive verbs have objects as, for example, in 'He enjoyed the holiday' or 'Which one do you want?' Intransitive verbs lack objects as in, for example, 'She's tripped over' or 'They gesticulated'.

A verb may be transitive or intransitive according to its function in a sentence. So while the verb in 'The girl is playing' lacks an object and is therefore intransitive, if we add the object 'netball' the same verb structure becomes transitive in the sentence 'The girl is playing netball'.

Trigraph

See also digraph, reading

A trigraph is made up of three letters which make one sound, for example 'tch' in 'batch'.

United Kingdom Reading Association (UKRA)

See also reading

UKRA is the professional association for teachers of language and literacy and it aims to promote research, innovative practice and debate about issues.

There are three publications. *Reading* is a refereed journal published three times a year containing articles on all aspects of literacy work including the description and evaluation of classroom work. It is read by practitioners, teacher educators and student teachers. *Journal of Research in Reading,* also refereed, provides a forum for researchers into reading in Britain and Europe. The articles report on empirical studies in reading and related fields. *Language and Literacy News* is a quarterly newsletter which provides up-to-date information about conferences, research projects, new books and resources and awards as well as short articles on topics of current interest.

The website provides accessible information about UKRA research projects, publications, awards and conferences.

UKRA website is www.ukra.org.

Usage

See also accent, dialect, grammar, parts of speech, punctuation, received pronunciation, spelling, standard English

The term 'usage' when applied to use of English issues is to do with customary practice. So we might speak of 'standard usage' in spelling, grammar, pronunciation and punctuation, and all the '*See also*' entries above include a consideration of this.

Primary school teachers in the United Kingdom are, more than ever, expected to know about conventional usage so that they can help children acquire standard forms in speaking and reading. But what is acceptable adapts to changes in society. As pointed out many times in this encyclopaedia language is dynamic and 'correct' usage at a particular period in history depends on a social consensus of educated people. There are a large number of books on usage in English, but the best known is still Fowler's dictionary which McArthur describes as 'a blend of prescription, tolerance and idiosyncrasy' (McArthur, 1992, p. 1076).

At one time split infinitives and ending sentences with prepositions were avoided, but both are now accepted in informal usage. The double negative, on the other hand, while being part of some non standard dialects, is still not acceptable in standard English. Purists also keep an eye on word meanings and many struggled to keep the original meaning of 'nice' as 'precise' rather than submitting to its contemporary meaning – 'affable' or 'pleasant'.

There are interesting social and moral factors in usage, for example the use of 'Ms' instead of 'Miss' or 'Mrs' is an attempt to avoid language-driven continuance of gender prejudice. We still lack a generally accepted third person, gender-neutral pronoun. In spoken language, there has been an interesting change in what is grammatically acceptable: many people disobey the normal rules of concord (agreement between parts of speech), using a plural form to avoid saying 'he or she' or 'him or her'. For example we might say 'If any child arrives late, please ask them to report to the school secretary'. For a thorough discussion of this and many other issues see McArthur's entries on 'Usage' and 'Usage Guidance and Criticism'.

Fowler, H.W. (1965 edition) *A Dictionary of Modern English Usage* Oxford: Oxford University Press.

McArthur, Tom (1992) *The Oxford Companion to the English Language* London: QPD & Oxford: Oxford University Press.

USSR (Uninterrupted Sustained Silent Reading)

See also ERIC, independent reading, reading, reading environment, response to reading

Silent, quiet or independent reading helps children extend the range and variety of their reading. Because they choose the books they develop their own tastes and critical standards. To achieve these things they need to read a lot and to respond directly and independently to the books. At home, the time spent at the computer and on other hobbies and activities may lessen the sustained reading a child does. All the more reason then for teachers to insist on quiet reading time in the classroom even though we face increasing demands on the curriculum. In an assessment-based school culture how do we convince others of the worth of an activity that has no immediate physical end product? Steve Marriott asserts that 'books work in mysterious and subtle ways…and reading the book of one's choice for a prolonged period is of just as much, if not more, value than other classroom activities that appear to be more immediately productive' (Marriott, 1995, p. 71).

Those of us who believe passionately in the value of reading time insist that it is *uninterrupted* because we are trying to help the children to achieve a special kind of engrossment, *sustained* so that there is time to achieve intense concentration and *silent* to avoid anyone being disturbed. Very young children may not achieve the last of these.

Aidan Chambers has good advice about encouraging newly independent readers, reluctant or inexperienced readers to enjoy reading time. '…read aloud for part of each session, because this draws everyone together and tunes their minds into story. For the rest of the session the children read their own books for a period of time that is gradually lengthened as they get used to the activity and their stamina grows' (Chambers, 1991, page 38).

Chambers, Aidan (1991) *The Reading Environment: How adults help children enjoy books* Stroud: The Thimble Press (Chapter 8, 'Reading Time')

Marriott, Stuart (1995) *Read On: Using fiction in the primary school* London: Paul Chapman (Chapter 4, section on Silent Reading).

Utterance

See also discourse analysis, speaking and listening

An utterance refers to something said whether word, phrase or sentence. Used in linguistics, 'utterance' tends to mean something said which has more or less the syntax of a written-down sentence.

V

Verbs

See also clause, parts of speech, sentence

A verb expresses an action, a process or a state. Often thought of as a 'doing' word (The boy *runs* to the playground each day), a verb may also indicate 'being' (The head teacher *was relieved* to learn of the successful results.)

Sometimes two or more words make up a verb phrase, for example 'had been hoping', 'did not think' and 'will be running'.

Verbs (except modal verbs like 'can' or 'will') have four or, in some cases five, different forms:

- Infinitive: to ride
- Continuous present: rides/am riding
- Present participle: riding
- Simple past: rode
- Past participle: ridden

In their finite forms, verbs can be active or passive, they have a tense and a person, have agreement with their subject and may be main or auxiliary verbs. I look at each of these aspects in turn.

Active or passive?

Verbs may be active (Anna *made* a cake) or passive (The cake *was made* by Anna).

The sentences seem to be saying the same thing, but in the first one the attention is on Anna, and in the second on the cake. When we use the passive tense we use the verb 'to be' together with a past participle. In the second sentence above 'was' is a form of the verb 'to be' and 'made' is the 'past participle' of the verb 'make'. Another thing to note is that in a passive sentence the 'doer' or 'agent' is often indicated by the use of the word 'by' as in the second sentence above which tells us the cake was made by Anna. At other times the agent is not identified as in

'The house has been renovated'.

When we teach children about different levels of formality in writing, we draw attention to the passive as a formal and impersonal style often used in scientific, official or legal documents.

Verbs have a tense

I now set out the main tenses in English using the verb 'to run'.

- Present: I run
          I am running (continuous)
- Present Perfect: I have run
          I have been running (perfect continuous).
- Past: I ran
          I was running (past continuous).
- Past perfect: I had run (perfect).
          I had been running (perfect continuous).
Future: I will run
          I run

Verbs have a 'person'

Verbs must have 'agreement' with their subject. So the pattern changes in the verb 'to be' as follows:
    I am happy/ I was happy
    You are happy/ You were happy
    She is happy/ She was happy
    They are happy/ They were happy.

Main or auxiliary

There are some forms of verbs whose definitions most of us need to check from time to time – auxiliary verbs, modal verbs, present and past participles, transitive and intransitive verbs and I consider these below.

An 'auxiliary' verb is used together with other verbs in a verb phrase. So in 'Tom has departed'

– the main verb is 'departed' and the auxiliary verb 'has' supports this main verb. The most common auxiliary verbs are 'be', 'have' and 'do' but they can also sometimes be main verbs. I find it helpful to ask myself which is the main verb, and then I know that the other verbs in the verb string are supporting it as auxiliaries.

Modal verbs

A 'modal' verb is a special kind of auxiliary verb which modifies the meaning of a sentence or clause by expressing possibility, speculation and necessity. The modal verbs are can/could, will/would, shall/should, may/might and must/ought. They are followed by the infinitive as in 'I shall stay', or by 'to' plus the infinitive as in 'I ought to go'.

Participles

Verbs have a present participle and a past participle. The present participle ends in 'ing' (playing, seeing, making) and is used in present continuous forms (she is bringing) and past continuous forms (she was bringing, she would have been bringing). The past participle often ends in 'ed' as in 'gambled' and 'moved' but there are many irregular forms like 'shown' and 'kept'. Past participles are used after 'have' (he has waited) to make the perfect form and after 'be' to make passive forms (it has been taken).

Transitive and intransitive verbs

'Transitive verbs' are verbs followed by an object – 'She enjoyed the outing' or preceded by their object 'What are you doing?' 'Intransitive verbs' are verbs without objects – 'He ran home'.

Sources

In my analysis I have drawn on the definitions in *Grammar for Writing* (DfEE, 2000, for further detail see in this text under 'verb', 'agreement' and 'participle') and on McArthur (QDP & Oxford University Press, 1992 – see under Verb for futher explanation). As Angela Wilson remarked, when she kindly cast her eye over this entry, it is sometimes difficult to know whose terminoloy to use. What used to be 'parts of speech' is now often termed 'word classes', and

recent DfEE literature calls 'verb phrases' – 'letter strings'. The linguist David Crystal prefers to refer to the 'ing' and 'ed' participles, while *Grammar for Writing* refers to 'past' and 'present' participles. For interesting discussion of this last issue, see Crystal's book *Rediscover Grammar* Harlow: Longman, 1988, p. 71.

In her article 'Finding your feet in the grammar minefield', Sue Palmer (who has written and lectured extensively to teachers about teaching grammar to primary children in an interesting way) argues that understanding of verbs may be helpful in a number of ways. For example, we can help children become aware of the rich range of verbs so that commonly used ones like 'went' and 'got' can be less overworked. Teaching about verbs can also reinforce spelling rules like the endings 'ed' and 'ing' and the spelling patterns of irregular words. Knowing about verbs also helps us decide whether a group of words is a clause – it is if it has a subject and a verb (TES, 22 January 1999, English Curriculum Supplement, p. 20).

For an activity-based approach to verbs see the appropriate sections in *The Primary Grammar Book* by Richard Bain and Marian Bridgewood. For example, there are cards on which sentences with different verb tenses are written and children are invited to sort these and to explain to each other how verbs change to form past, present and future. It is this invitation to make their understanding explicit which is particularly beneficial.

The National Literacy Strategy Grammar for Writing (DfEE, 2000) guidance also suggests activities to explore parts of speech, including verbs, in sentences (see, for example sentence level activities for Year 4, Term 1).

Verse

See also ballad, nursery rhyme, poetry

In everyday usage 'poetry' and 'verse' may be used interchangeably. Verse describes a stanza of a poem and a distinctive metrical structure like 'iambic' verse. However, in traditional literary criticism 'verse' tends to apply to technique and can be a pejorative term implying that some forms are not worthy of being called 'poetry'.

Verse is a familiar form in the modern world and the tradition of nursery rhymes and ballads continues in the rhymes children repeat and those they make up in the playground, and in the jingles used in radio and television advertising.

Video-film

See also television and literacy, visual literacy

Video-film, films at the cinema and television are all important cultural media and are likely to have a considerable effect on children's developing literacy. One obvious link between books and screen are the films of children's picture books (John Burningham's *The Snowman*) and the serials of children's stories (E. Nesbit's *The Phoenix and the Carpet* and, more recently, Clive King's *Stig of the Dump*) on mainstream television. Good resource collections for English work now include a range of video-films, some featuring advertisements and extracts from factual programmes and others based on children's novels and picture books. For more about the use of advertisements please see the appropriate entry. There is also a separate entry on television and literacy. Here I want to reflect on the reasons many teachers have for helping children enjoy and evaluate video-films of stories, often alongside reading the print versions in the English lesson. First, it is a motivating experience for most children to study a medium which is so central in our culture. Seeing a video-film of a story links the sitting room with the classroom in a life enhancing way (Parker, British Film Institute).

Second, the visual image can sometimes awaken powerful emotions that can lead to enthusiastic story telling, role play and writing (Brown, 1999). A study carried out for Film Education suggests that boys particularly enjoy writing on themes from film. Such a highly visual medium is also likely to be helpful to children learning English as an additional language,

Third, there are useful 'tie-ups' between books and video-film: children may see a video-film

version of a story and be drawn into reading the book or vice versa. Brown found in her study *Young Children's Literacy Development and Televisual Texts* that generally girls have a more wide ranging viewing pattern in terms of genre and types of narrative than boys. Girls favoured books and video-films which had a strong emotional impact – Hans Anderson's *The Little Mermaid* and E. Nesbit's *The Railway Children* – or those with an intriguing or unusual set of events like Frances Hodgson Burnett's *The Secret Garden* or Mary Norton's *The Borrowers*. Boys had far fewer 'tie-ups', the most mentioned in Brown's research being Roald Dahl's *The BFG*, Rev. W. Awdry's *Thomas the Tank Engine* and Rudyard Kipling's *The Jungle Book* (Brown, 1999). Imaginative teaching, using a wide range of narratives in video-film and print form, might help boys appreciate some of the narratives they would not choose to view or read independently.

It is clearly worth persevering with these 'tie-ups' as evidence is building that experiencing a story in more than one medium leads to more refined understandings of both forms. In his research for the British Film Institute and Kings College, London University, David Parker found that seven year olds who had worked with both the book and the film version of Roald Dahl's book *Fantastic Mr Fox* were able to answer more insightfully in written tests than those who had only read the book. Teachers can show how, in a print version of a narrative, the written word carries the full weight of plot and characterisation. This can be compared through careful observation and discussion with how in film features – the nature of the acting, the camera angles, the lighting, the settings, the sound and the music – all contribute to the impact.

For all these reasons we need to recognise the potential of English work round video-film. The work does need sensitive handing and Richard Hoggart in *The Way We Are Now* urges us to keep in mind that reading a book and watching a film are distinct experiences and one cannot replace the other.

For teachers just starting to work in this way, particularly with older primary children, I recommend *Reel Lives* a helpful resource which includes video-film based on stories. It shows clips from many well-known children's films and television programmes including adaptations of the classics – *The Borrowers, The Wind in the Willows* and *The Animals of Farthing Wood.*

British Video Association (1999) *Reel Lives.* London: British Video Association. Website is: www.bva.org.uk (video extracts are used to explore issues like bullying and care of the environment).

Brown, Naima (1999) *Young Children's Literacy Development and the Role of Televisual Texts* London: Falmer Press.

Film Education's website: www.filmeducation.org

Graham, Judith (1996) *The English Curriculum: Media 1: Year 7–9 (updated edition).* London: English and Media Centre (for secondary-aged children but principles can be applied to the primary years. Hans Anderson's *The Little Mermaid* is considered in Disney film form and as a book.)

Marshall, Bethan 'Review of *Reel Lives*' in *Guardian Education* Tuesday 8th June 1999, p. 5.

Virtual Teacher's Centre (VTC)

See also The National Grid for Learning (NGfL)

The Virtual Teacher's Centre is part of the National Grid for Learning (NGfL) and includes websites which support the teaching of English – 'Literacy Time' for example, presents reviews of children's books and author profiles.

Literacy Time (part of the National Grid for Learning):http://www.vtc.ngfl.gov.uk /resource/literacy/index.html

Visual literacy

See also advertising, cartoons, Art and English, CD-ROM, charts, diagrams, drawings, illustrations, photographs, picture books, television and literacy, video-film

Visual literacy is to do with 'reading' images of all kinds and seeing the connections between picture and print. Today's children live in a society where images – in entertainment, advertising and in information sources – are a very important part of the culture. So becoming literate is no longer a matter of just learning to read and write – but is also to do with interpreting and evaluating both static and moving images in different contexts. Children bring to school considerable knowledge

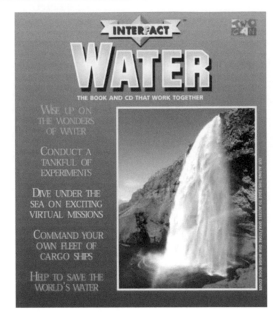

Interact Water by Bryan Murphy is designed to use with PC and MAC. It combines an information book with a disk with extension activities. The text and photographs in the book are well extended by the dynamic visual opportunities on the disk. The cover is reproduced with permission of the publisher, Two-Can Publishing, a division of Zenith Entertainment plc.

and experience about visual images since they are likely to have watched television, viewed video-films and have been surrounded by print images. However, if they are to develop their capacity to use and evaluate the visual and see how it complements and extends the verbal, this kind of literacy needs to be brought explicitly into the curriculum.

The cultural context of images

In many ways reading a visual text is similar to reading a written text; in his introduction to *Image Matters* the Australian academic, Jon Callow, observes that both kinds of reading are dynamic processes involving 'not only a text (verbal or written) but the person reading/viewing, the authors, and the wider cultural context of all three' (Callow, 1999, p. 2). Visual images can pass us by, remaining implicit and unevaluated: this is why it is so helpful to explore with children the meaning of images in advertisements and other mass media where they can be used to manipulate. They can lead us to assume certain interpretations of the world are universal or 'the norm' while in reality they represent the favoured view of one group. Getting behind images to intentions helps put the young viewer in control. The increasingly 'multimodal' nature of classroom texts, drawing as many of them do on spoken, written, visual, spatial and musical modes is exciting but can also be overwhelming. Even print texts for young children sometimes assume they are familiar with the typical icons on the computer screen. We can help children by making time to explore and evaluate the different strands of such rich input together. (These issues are discussed by Kress and van Leeuwen in *Reading Images,* 1996.)

Ways of representing experience

In order to explore how we make sense of a visual world I want to look briefly at the work of the developmental psychologist, Jerome Bruner. He identified three main ways in which the growing child represents the world: enactive, iconic and symbolic. The baby knows the world through doing and through experience and this is termed 'enactive representation'. The roots of many later activities are here, including acquiring the skills to operate all the technology to be found in a typical home or classroom or by using dramatic improvisation to explore how people lived in another historical period. As infants grows older they begin to have mental images of familiar objects and places, even if they are not present; for example 'teddy in bedroom' or 'Peter Rabbit plate in the kitchen'. This Bruner termed the 'iconic' mode: from early beginnings this is the way of representing the world that develops into all kinds of visual literacy – how we make sense of maps, photographs and paintings and of moving images. The last mode of representing experience to develop is the 'symbolic' – this includes the ability to use language to express ideas and information. By the age of about five years a child is using all three modes of representation in making sense of and acting in the world. So when we think about visual literacy, we also need to consider how Bruner's three ways of representing experience interrelate in the child's learning.

A framework for teaching visual literacy

One of the most helpful frameworks in which to plan the teaching of visual literacy is suggested in *Image Matters,* edited by Jon Callow. There are chapters by teachers and academics on different image contexts in the classroom – including information books, picture books, television programmes and CD-ROMs. The framework for teaching visual literacy described in his introduction is a good starting point for classroom work with any age group. It suggests that learning about images parallels learning about language. We learn language from early childhood and refine and develop our verbal ability, we use language to learn about all manner of subjects both in and out of the classroom and we learn about language as a system with structures and functions. Let us see how becoming visually literate links with this analysis.

- *Learning images* – here the child learns to recognise symbols and patterns that represent the things they come across in everyday life and tries to make his or her own representations. So a sort of visual vocabulary is acquired.

- *Learning through images* – these help children learn in every part of the curriculum – in science, the humanities and the arts and about every aspect of our culture. Children's own productions – electronic and print books, models and diagrams help make learning active.

- *Learning about images* – this involves knowing how to comment on and evaluate their cultural and contextual aspects and also (following the arguments of Kress and van Leeuwen, 1996) coming to understand the 'grammar' inherent in images. For many of us this is a new area of understanding and we need to learn alongside our pupils how images work and 'mean'.

Explaining how the three aspects of this framework for organising visual literacy relates to print pictures and information texts, to the moving image in video and CD-ROMs and in television would take a whole book to explore thoroughly. The books in the reference section of this entry will help build your understanding. You might like to take to your reading some thoughts about the different kinds of visual image children encounter.

Print images

A major art form in many countries is the children's picture book where text and pictures can relate in exciting ways – sometimes to illustrate the action in a story, sometimes to extend the written text and occasionally to contradict it in a tantalising way (Arizpe and Styles, 2002). Some picture books like John Burninghams's *The Snowman* and Shirley Hughes' *Up and Up* – a cartoon about a little girl's flying fantasy – are wordless and rely on quite young children's cultural knowledge to gain meaning. Both these books yield their meaning through action. The sophistication of the best picture books make them valuable contributors to children's literacy, both verbal and visual (see picture book entry).

Pictures have always provided powerful ways into bodies of information. Visual media can convey concepts that might be difficult to explain in writing. Harnett (1998, p. 72) reminds us that medieval paintings showed the mysteries of heaven and hell, with beautiful angels and terrifying demons, to non literate people. Even in our more literate society, advertisers exploit the power of pictures to move, persuade and excite. The money spent shows how much advertisers believe in the power of the visual image to effect people's views and actions. How teachers might approach a study of advertisements to put children in control of their viewing is discussed further under the Advertisements entry.

Children's information books make considerable demands on children's visual literacy as they feature a rich variety of illustrations including photographs, drawings, diagrams, maps and portraits. These need to integrate well with the written text so that they are illuminating and not obscuring or misleading. Children themselves enjoy discussing how useful the illustrations are in particular books they have been using. The increase in variety of illustrations has come about since the end of the Second World War. Those of us of a certain age well remember the distinctive black and white line drawings in Unstead's history

series along with a few coloured pictures. Artists' drawings continued to dominate in the 1960s and 1970s. Since then there have been vast improvements in reprographic techniques and, while artists 'illustrations are still used a great deal, photographs are equally favoured. Books and CD-ROMs show animals in their environments and wonderful close ups of creatures. In the United Kingdom, the National Curriculum programmes have included visual literacy. For example, in history the role of photographs of objects and buildings as a valuable source of historical information has been stressed. The potential role of diagrams in 'explanation' texts is also recognised.

There is interesting research on children's use of pictures in history; Blyth (1988) found that children by about the age of nine years could be helped to understand abstract concepts like change and power with the help of pictures. Seeing a number of pictures of people and objects from a particular period helps children make generalisations about, for example, what people wore and the objects they used. Harnett (1998) found a development in children's competence in using pictures as information sources. Around age five years, children talked about all the details in a picture while as they neared eleven years they were able to look more broadly at a series of pictures and draw specific conclusions. Sequencing abilities in both history and in English can be developed by looking at a series of pictures and ordering them.

What comes through particularly powerfully in Harnett's study is the way in which children supported each other in making sense of visual input. Some children were looking at a portrait of Elisabeth 1 and a child said the queen had a 'heart shaped frill' on her back. Another child explained that it was not really a heart shape 'it just goes round like a semi circle'. The social, collaborative side of history work links it with English. A study of portraits through the ages helps children understand how 'image 'is constructed and put them in a position to question the way today's media images manipulate us.

Moving images

We encounter the moving image in CD-ROM texts, televisual texts and on film. CD-ROM versions of information texts have the advantage of being able to show function as well as structure. A print version of a diagram of the blood system could indicate the direction in which the blood is flowing using devices like arrows, but the electronic version could show the system in action. Concepts like the water cycle, migration, earthquake and so on can be brought to virtual reality. These dynamic texts are discussed further under the 'CD-ROM' entry.

Turning to watching television and film, while many people of all ages are frequent viewers of serials and other narratives, they tend not to have a profound understanding of the medium. There is, however, an evolving language to talk about the moving image. Annemaree O'Brien in her chapter in *Image Matters* (1999) edited by Callow entitled 'Reading TV: A basic visual literacy' argues that learning to 'read' television texts can start early and can help develop visual literacy and analytical and critical thinking abilities.

O'Brien identifies two key aspects to reading television. First we need to understand how visual and sound techniques create meaning in television and film stories and how they influence how we interpret them.

Second, it is important that we help our pupils to understand that television programmes are created to affect the viewers in particular ways. Programme makers make choices about scripts, locations, dialogues, the order in which events are shown, colours used and sounds. Like other texts there may be multiple layers of meaning and bias. There is more about this under the 'advertisements' entry.

For more about the benefits of children experiencing the same story in both print and in film form please see the entry under 'video-film'.

Arizpe, Evelyn and Styles, Morag (eds) *Children Reading Pictures: Interpreting Visual Texts* London: Routledge.

Blyth, Joan (1988) *History 5–9* London: Hodder & Stoughton.

Callow, Jon (ed.) (1999) *Image Matters: visual texts in the classroom.* Marrickville, Australia: PETA (Primary English Teaching Association).

Hall, James (1974) *A Dictionary of Signs and Symbols in Art* London; John Murray.

Harnett, Penelope (1998) 'Children Working With Pictures' in Hoodless, Pat (ed.) *History and English: Exploring the Links* London: Routledge

Kress, G. and van Leeuwen, T. (1996) *Reading Images: The Grammar of Visual Design.* London: Routledge.

Morris, Susan (1989) *A Teacher's Guide to Using Portraits* English Heritage.

National Portrait Gallery (Tel. 020 7306 0055 ext. 212) Courses for teachers and children on decoding period and contemporary portraits.

Welton, Jude (1993) *Eyewitness Art: Looking at Paintings* London: Dorling Kindersley

Vocabulary – see word level work

Voice

In ordinary usage we may describe someone as having for example a cultured voice or a shrill voice. There are three more technical aspects. First the notion of 'voice' in phonetics where the 'voiced' sounds are b d g z and the 'voiceless' sounds are p t k s. Second, in grammar, we speak of the 'active' or 'passive' voice. Third, the 'narrative voice' is a literary term for the narrator or the character who 'speaks' in a story.

Vowel

See also digraph, diphthong, phoneme, phonics

The vowels are a,e,i,o,u with 'y' functioning as a vowel as in 'ay', 'ey' and 'oy'. Vowel sounds are produced with a steady flow of air from throat, tongue and lips.

When children begin to learn to read using the phonic approach they are taught to hear individual vowel and consonant speech sounds – phonemes. Then they learn the written symbols for these sounds – graphemes. The graphophonic system is not regular and children need to understand that while words can usually be sounded out, sometimes there are exceptions to the usual rules.

Useful terms to understand when teaching about vowels include: the 'short vowel' sound, for example 'rag', 'peg', 'fig', 'dog' and 'tug'; the 'long vowel' sound which is the name of an alphabet letter – 'A', 'E', 'I', 'O', 'U'; the 'diphthong' which is a single sound made of two vowels, for example 'ee', 'oa' and 'au'; the 'split digraph' which is a 'vowel digraph' where there is a consonant between the two vowels that make the phoneme but it keeps its sound as in 'pine' (ie) and 'complete' (ee). Some teachers explain 'split digraphs' to children by referring to the 'fairy e' rule which makes the preceding vowel sound its name – as 'i' in 'line'.

The National Literacy Strategy Phonics: Progression in Phonics (DfEE, 1999) sets out (in List 3) the phonics and spelling work that children need to cover from Reception to Year 2. As experienced practitioners will know, the guidance materials suggest some helpful teaching strategies. For example, when teaching about 'split digraphs', it is suggested that individual children are given large cards with a letter on so that they can physically represent the letter strings. So three children might make the word 'tie' and then a fourth, carrying an 'm', can split the digraph by standing between the 'i' and the 'e' to make 'time'. As well as helping with graphophonic relationships in reading, this kind of approach also supports spelling.

Warnock Report

See also Code of Practice, Special Educational Needs, SENCO

The Warnock Report of 1978 recommended that children with learning difficulties should have a statement of 'special need' which set out what was required to help them benefit from the curriculum. *The Code of Practice* (1994) developed further the recommended strategies requiring that school-based assessments should lead to an Individual Education Plan (IEP).

Another important recommendation of *The Warnock Report* was that children with special needs should, whenever possible, be educated in mainstream schools. The report was also the beginning of a trend in the United Kingdom towards providing extra support to children within the classroom rather than withdrawing them for their special help.

Teachers vary in their views on this. Some feel that many struggling young learners benefit from the quietness of a separate special needs room, particularly when they are receiving help with their reading. On the other hand, many consider that there are advantages in not being singled out as 'special' and yet often still receiving help from an extra teacher in the classroom who is in tune with what the class teacher is doing.

Websites and Primary English

See also Internet

Websites

BBC Education: http://www.bbc.co.uk/education/schools

BECTA: http://www.becta.org.uk

Booktrust: http://www.booktrust.org.uk

British Library: http://www.bl.uk

British video association: http://bva.org.uk

CD-ROM reviews http://www.teem.org.uk

Centre for Language in Primary Education: http://www.clpe.co.uk

DfEE Standards: http://www.standards.dfee.gov.uk

English Association: http://www.le.ac.uk/engsoc

Literacy Trust: http://www.literacytrust.org.uk

National Association for the Teaching of English: http://www.nate.org.uk

National Curriculum website: http://www.nc.uk.net

National Grid for Learning: http://www.ngfl.gov.uk

Newswise: http://www.ndirect.co.uk/-sapere/Newswise

OFSTED: http://www.ofsted.gov.uk

Peters Library Service: http://www.peters-books.co.uk

Reach:National Resource Centre for Children with Reading Difficulties: http://www.reach.reading.demon.co.uk

Reading Recovery National Network (Institute of Education University of London: http://www.ioe.ac.uk/cdl/readrec.html

Reading and Language Information Centre: http://www.ralic.reading.ac.uk

Reading Online: http://www.readingonline.org

School Library Association: http://www.sla.org.uk

Schools Online: http://www.bbc.co.uk/schools

Standards Unit DfEE: http://www.standards.dfee.gov.uk

TES Learnfree: http://www.learnfree.co.uk

TES Primary: http://www.tesprimary.com

The Federation of Children's Book Groups: http://www.fcbg.mcmail.com

The Internet Grammar of English:
     http://www.ucl.ac.uk/internet-
     grammar/home.htm
The Poetry Library:
     http://www.poetrylibrary.org.uk
United Kingdom Reading Association:
     http://www.ukra.org
Virtual Teachers' Centre:
     http://www.vtc.ngfl.gov.uk
Young Book Trust: http://www.booktrust.org.uk

Whole class teaching

See also discussion, shared writing

When teachers plan for and organise English work they decide when to teach the whole class and when to help the children to learn in groups or on an individual basis. Teachers have always tended to work with the whole class when introducing new topics, reading the class novel, short story or a series of poems out loud and when bringing children together for class discussion.

In the United Kingdom there has been a new approach to some kinds of class teaching since the establishment of the Literacy Hour in line with National Literacy Strategy requirements. The major part that shared reading and shared writing take in the Literacy Hour arises partly from a belief that children learn more in class-based contexts. However, the idea of using texts, often enlarged texts, with a group or class is also in the spirit of Don Holdaway's belief that the teacher could demonstrate reading strategies while also emphasising the enjoyment and satisfaction reading can bring (Holdaway, 1979). In current practice in the United Kingdom, sometimes the teacher and at other times the children, read aloud from enlarged texts. Not only can the teacher give support to word recognition skills and sentence structure, he or she can also encourage children's comments on and response to textual features. Valuable experience of speaking and listening in the relatively formal context of the whole class setting is gained. Many teachers believe that children's individual reading is enriched by their application of what they have learnt in the class reading context. Similarly, the practice of shared writing helps children learn useful strategies to take to their individual writing assignments.

While reading, writing, listening and speaking in class-based contexts has an important place in the English programme, certain kinds of learning are best supported in individual and group settings. For example, children benefit from learning to express a view or ask a question in a small group before speaking out in front of the class. Indeed many of the National Curriculum Speaking and Listening objectives are best achieved in the small group context. For more about these other settings, please see the following entries: collaborative learning, ERIC, speaking and listening and writing.

Holdaway, Don (1979) *The Foundations of Literacy* London: Ashton Scholastic.

Word – as a unit of meaning

One of the first things the beginning reader has to acquire is an understanding of that most fundamental of language units – the word. When we speak, spaces between words are not always evident but in writing the spaces separating words from one another are fundamental. One of the most interesting analyses of a young child's efforts to make sense of the reading and writing systems is *GNYS AT WRK* by Glenda Bissex. Bissex noted that her young son Paul at just over five years of age tended to concentrate on whole words when he was reading but on sounds when he was writing.

For a detailed and challenging account of concepts of 'word' for your own background knowledge I recommend McArthur, 1992.

Bissex, Glenda (1980) *GNYS AT WRK: A child learns to write and read.* Cambridge, Mass: Harvard University Press.
McArthur, Tom (1992) *The Oxford Companion to the English Language* London: QPD and Oxford: Oxford University Press.

Word books – see alphabet, dictionary

Word classes

See also under parts of speech, adjective, adverb, conjunction, noun, preposition, pronoun, verb

The main word classes are discussed in detail under the entries mentioned above under '*See also*'. Words can belong to more than one class. *Grammar for Writing* page 215 reminds us that, for example, 'play' can be either a verb – I play, or a noun – a play; 'that' can be a determiner – that book, a pronoun – who did that? or a conjunction – she said that she.

The National Literacy Strategy Grammar for Writing
DfEE, 2000.

Word level work

See also antonyms, bottom-up reading approaches, cue-systems, dictionary, homonyms, language change, onomatopoeia, parts of speech, poetry, phonics, reading, slang, synonym, thesaurus, writing

Word level work involves helping children to understand how words can be read and written and aims to help children extend their vocabulary. There are links between word level and sentence level work, for example the terms for parts of speech have grammatical implications as well as being the names of units. Indeed, the careful selection of and placing of individual words can have a cumulative effect on a whole text, creating atmosphere, mood and making a contribution to its identification with a particular genre. While phonics is to do with how a word or phoneme sounds, graphics is the study of the recognition of written forms of words and letter strings. In the United Kingdom, teachers are required to follow prescribed programmes when teaching about the grapho-phonic cueing system. There is more about this in this encyclopaedia under 'phonics' and 'grapho-phonic cueing system. You would also find useful, before turning to the official publications I am about to mention, the sections on 'Phonics and phonological awareness' in Chapter 1 and 'Teaching phonic and graphic knowledge in Chapter 3, in Graham and Kelly, 2000. These authors are amongst those who feel strongly that, while following the requirements, teachers should be allowed some flexibility in the order in which they teach phonemes, for example.

The word level requirements are organised under phonics, spelling and vocabulary on the left-hand side of each page of objectives in *The National Literacy Strategy Framework for Teaching* (DfEE 1998). There are also supplementary publications, including *Phonics: Progression in Phonics* (1999), *The National Literacy Strategy Additional Literacy Support Module* and *The National Literacy Strategy Spelling Bank* (DfEE, 1999).

There are lists of words, a 'technical vocabulary' for use with each year group in *Phonics: Teaching About Phonics* (DfEE 1999). There is considerable discussion amongst teachers about when it is appropriate to help children to use terms like phoneme, vowel and consonant. The teacher is best placed to know how to introduce these terms to the children in his or her class.

Other vocabulary to clinch concepts includes antonyms, synonyms and onomatopoeia. A good way of introducing these is by sharing examples from literature and encouraging children to write down their own examples. The use of dictionaries and thesauruses, print and on screen can be modelled.

Another aspect of work at word level involves children in making collections of words with particular origins. In a very helpful video-film made by The Centre of Language in Primary Education we see eight to nine year olds tracking down words with Greek roots. As well as helping children grapple with word meanings this kind of research makes them more conscious of word structures and spellings (CLPE, 1999).

An excellent context for learning about words in a playful way is poetry and verse. The youngest children enjoy nursery rhymes and we know from the work of Goswami and Bryant that attention can be drawn to grapho-phonic patterns (Goswami and Bryant, 1991). Older children go on to experiment with riddles, haiku and rhymes which highlight poetic devices in an enjoyable way. Children enjoy constructing 'Shape' poems making the words follow an appropriate pattern to match themes like fire-works, climbing a hill or the dance of a bee. I have often seen good results when poems have started from subjects like feeling hot or cold or chasing an escaping hamster. These are more than word games as children can be helped to a more sensitive use of vocabulary. I remember an eight-year-old girl being very pleased to discover and use in her poem the word 'tepid' to describe water that was neither very hot nor very cold. Another memory from the classroom presses on me when I think about language play and activities with words. A class of eight year olds made a wonderful 'language thermometer' which was made of silver paper and stretched along a whole wall. They started by placing 'cold' words at one end and then created a continuum with increasingly 'warm' words ending up with sizzling. The most striking thing was the quality of the discussion of the order of words according to intensity of heat and cold. For example, is 'tepid' hotter than 'warm'? And is 'frozen' colder than 'icy'?

One concern about the National Literacy Strategy's very challenging requirements for older primary children is that the new vocabulary and concepts may be taught out of context. A powerful context for refining and extending vocabulary will always be the reading of literature – novels and poetry. If we want motivated and enthusiastic young learners we need to find ways of making language learning interesting and relevant.

Communities of Writers: Writing at Key Stage 2 (1999), a video-film in the Learning to be Literate series of the Centre for Language in Primary Education (see 29.35 for work on word roots). (CLPE)

Goswami, Ursula and Bryant, Peter (1991) *Phonological Skills and Learning to Read* Hillsdale, NJ: Lawrence Erlbaum Associates.

Graham, Judith and Kelly, Alison (2000) *Reading Under Control: Teaching Reading in the Primary School* London: David Fulton.

McArthur, Tom (1992) *The Oxford Companion to the English Language* London: QPD Paperbacks & Oxford: Oxford University Press.

Word processing – see Information and Communications Technology & English

Worksheets

See also constructivism, non-fiction reading and writing

Worksheets: are they manacles or wings? The answer is – it all depends on what you mean by 'worksheet'; it is one of those umbrella terms under which quite a collection of different resources are gathered. It is usually a sheet, card or small, stapled booklet with headings and subheadings, numbered tasks and illustrations. Whatever form the worksheet takes and whatever subject it supports, the following criteria may be helpful:

- does it fit into current work or extend it in a coherent way?
- is the language at an appropriate level for the children and are any new terms explained or evident from the context?
- are diagrams carefully drawn and labelled?
- do at least some of the activities require thought rather than just a 'right' answer?
- is there some opportunity for collaborative work?

In science and mathematics work cards or sheets (either commercially produced or made by the teacher) usually meet the first of these criteria. They guide children through the stages of an experiment or practical activity that is linked to the theme of a series of lessons. In science it might be 'Grouping and classifying materials' and in mathematics 'Using and applying shape, space and measures'. Often laminated to make them sufficiently robust to stand up to constant use, if worksheets meet the other criteria of clear language and helpful diagrams they can be good models of procedural writing.

In subjects like English, history, religious education and geography, teachers have often structured some of the work by using worksheets that guide the children's independent or group research. When a lot of content has to be covered, particularly with older primary classes, the worksheet has a role so it is unfortunate that worksheets, particularly in the humanities, have acquired a negative connotation. What are some of the criticisms? Used too often for independent learning, they can cut children off from the energising effect of interaction with the teacher and the other children. Questions can be rather dull and require 'right' answers rather than stimulating thinking – thus assuming a transmission model of learning where children respond to stimuli rather than a constructivist approach where children are active learners. The same worksheet is unlikely to challenge the ablest children and be at the right reading level for the less forward readers. All these criticisms can be met if worksheets are carefully constructed, not used too often and the same core of work adjusted for the different ability levels in the class.

A glimpse of an actual example of good practice might help here. A Year 6 class teacher had covered core history work on the Tudors using pictures and videofilm to accompany her own account over a number of lessons. She wanted to give the children the opportunity to carry out some work in groups to go a little deeper into some of the topics. Groups of four children each had a worksheet with suggested activities, some groups chose 'Tudor Buildings', others chose 'The *Mary Rose*' or topics like 'Crime and Punishment'. There was a space at the bottom of each worksheet for the group's own ideas for tasks or modifications to one of the suggested tasks. The other interesting thing about these worksheets was the request to 'make some notes on any issues you think your study has raised'. Each group had some folders of pictures, contemporary documents and access to information books in the library and to the Internet. Judging by the lively work and the group presentations that followed these worksheets were 'wings' rather than 'manacles'.

In English, worksheets can provide a starting point for interesting research into language change, dialect and traditional tales. I have also seen workcards used imaginatively to develop drama and to focus discussion on a text or topic. There are, however, less interesting examples – passages taken from longer texts with rather dull comprehension, like questions to answer or uncontextualised dictionary work. Children may, for example, be asked to look up the meanings of words and to put them in sentences.

In short, a worksheet is as good as the tasks and activities it invites and their relevance to children's learning.

World Wide Web – see Information and Communications Technology (ICT) & English, Internet and websites and Primary English

Writers for children – see History of children's literature

Writing

See also composition, copying, creative writing, critical discourse, diary, Early Learning Goals, editing, emergent writing, EXEL Project, expressive talk and writing, factual writing, fiction, first person writing, gender, genre, grammar, handwriting, Information and Communications Technology and English, independent group work, letters, Literacy Hour, marking, National Curriculum, persuasive genre, poetry, proof reading, punctuation, purpose, scribing, shared writing, spelling, transactional writing, transcriptional aspects of writing, word processing, worksheets, writing area/corner and writing frames

Writing is one of the four language processes – the other three are speaking, listening and reading. It is a powerful organiser of thinking and reasoning and enables us to communicate meaning in a relatively permanent form to an absent audience across space and time. In an increasingly complex society people need to be able to write effectively to meet many different purposes. So it is not surprising that learning to write is a major component of the primary curriculum. However, the journey towards becoming a competent and enthusiastic writer is a demanding one and children need skilled and imaginative support on that journey. Many books have been written about helping children to write; some are referred to in the further reading for this entry and others are mentioned in the many other related entries listed above. This entry serves as an introduction to what has always been a very challenging task for teachers. I raise what, for me, are some of the most pertinent issues and show where to find further help, support and insight. I have taken a developmental approach because this allows me to focus on what is significant at different stages in the primary years, looking first at what is important for Beginning Writers and second at what is important for Developing Writers.

Beginning writers (3–7 years)

Early representation

Young children in literate cultures are surrounded by print in their environment – print on signs, notices and shop fronts outside the home and on food packets, instructions on household machines and toys inside. They soon try to 'write' themselves – we have all seen the wavy lines which are the first attempts of very young children at writing. Then they start to make links between letters and sounds – as they do in reading. Most importantly they grasp that the names of objects – and these names are arbitrary – are symbols of the real things they stand for. To emphasise the symbolic nature of writing, early years teachers encourage children to write their own names for all sorts of purposes – on their work, their pegs and their belongings. Children come to realise that their name symbolises them, who they are in all their complexity – see under Emergent writing for a more detailed account. There are a number of books on these early stages of writing and I particularly recommend Chapter 7 'Early representation and emerging writing' in Marian Whitehead's book *Language and Literacy in the Early Years*. This sets out important principles to guide our support of very young writers, drawing on research findings and including interesting examples of early writing. Another particularly helpful book is Temple *et al.*'s *The Beginnings of Writing*.

Writing from 5–7 years (Key Stage 1): purpose and audience

In many books about writing, including statutory and guidance material, you will find your attention drawn to two major dimensions. First, children need to have real purposes and second they need a sense of the audience they are writing for. This raises some important issues. It certainly suggests that children should not be obliged to carry out mere exercises – what James Britton (1970) referred to as 'dummy runs' – but from

the earliest stages to have reasons or purposes for their writing. Skilled practitioners use their imagination to create contexts strong enough to nourish the urge to write. Inviting children to write lists for a real use can be an interesting and not too difficult task for young children just acquiring some confidence as writers. This is what the teacher of a Reception class had in mind when she asked the children to help her write a shopping list for food for the classroom snails. The children's suggestions – apples, green beans and lettuce – were written on a flip chart. Labelling some of the things in the classroom is another strong purpose for writing. I remember visiting a student in a Year 1 class in which children studying the classroom tadpoles wrote about their development on labels and placed these on the side of the tank.

The second aspect mentioned above is 'audience' – who is the writing for? The teacher and the other children can provide a strong audience and children often like to be invited to read their work out loud. There are also wider audiences for children's work – letters to museum guides, parents and writing for the school magazine.

The enabling adult

As children try to gain control over their writing teachers need to make sensitive interventions. They talk about writing, and sometimes demonstrate round a computer with one or two children or with the help of a flip chart for a group or the whole class. Both the National Curriculum and the NLS *Framework for Teaching* encourage an interactive approach in which the teacher demonstrates many of the features of writing. (For more about this see the Shared writing and Guided reading/writing entries.)

When considering how we can intervene it is helpful to make a distinction between two different aspects of the writing process, the 'compositional' and 'transcriptional' aspects – a distinction made by several authors, perhaps most memorably by Frank Smith in his book *Writing and the Writer*, 1982. 'Compositional aspects' have to do with content and with being a writer creating for a purpose and an audience. Our purpose and audience affect how we organise what we are composing, whether it is a story to share with others or a notice for the classroom asking people not to disturb the tadpoles. At this stage we search for ideas, select a vocabulary to convey our thoughts, feelings and those ideas and use the syntactic constructions available to us. 'Transcriptional' or 'secretarial' aspects have to do with spelling, capitalisation, paragraphs and with handwriting or word processing. Shared writing is a context where the teacher models writing for the children, folding in their contributions and suggestions to the developing account on the white board or flip chart. Here the teacher supports both the compositional and the transcriptional aspects during these shared sessions.

Inspiration for composition – stories as a starting point for writing

When helping children write fiction, the stories read to them can be an excellent 'scaffold' or support. In exciting classroom work shown on the video-film *Gaining Control,* we hear that one of the snails in a Year 1 classroom had climbed out of its tank and had started to eat a book about snails on the display table. This was a wonderful example of life imitating art. When the teacher asked the children if this reminded them of a book they had enjoyed they all shouted out – *The Very Hungry Caterpillar.* Using the structure of Eric Carle's book, the children wrote their own stories about the very hungry snail.

Another book which seems to inspire lively writing is Jeannie Baker's picture book *Where the Forest Meets the Sea,* now in big book format. It appeals to children of different age groups and of different abilities. The book tells of a young boy's visit to the Australian rain forest. After showing him enjoying the natural beauty of the forest, the final picture shows the ghost of the future where hotels and service stations replace the trees, plants, animals and birds of a unique environment. Children usually enjoy taking on the issues in the book in discussion and writing. Sensitive intervention and encouragement from the teacher help children to shape their ideas into satisfying stories.

Encouraging informational kinds of writing: first hand observation and experience

There are a number of ways in which teachers can support children's informational writing. For example, when children hear information books read out loud it helps them become accustomed to the flow of the language and familiar with the way such a text is structured. This helps them begin to control this kind of writing. Another important way of moving children forward is to demonstrate the features of non-fiction texts in shared writing contexts. But children need not only knowledge about the form of the writing, they also need some inspiration to provide the content. The things children see and do – practical experiences of all kinds – provide an excellent starting point for talk and writing. The children learning about the classroom snails mentioned above commented on their 'delicate shells and tiny eyestalks' and on 'the tininess of the babies' shells' when they hatched out of their eggs. Jane Bunting, the teacher, understood that these careful observations were worth writing down. So the children saw their contributions written down on the flip chart as the first stage in making a joint book. We need this sort of sensitive help which allows children to explore and take risks without fearing criticism (*Gaining Control.* CLPE video-film). Please see more about this aspect of writing under the extended entry 'non-fiction reading and writing'.

Supporting transcriptional aspects

I have already mentioned that shared writing contexts help teachers demonstrate both compositional and transcriptional aspects of writing. Beginning writers need help to develop their understanding of spelling, punctuation and handwriting. In becoming able to spell, the child explores the system and many teachers and educationists have identified stages through which each young learner moves. Gentry's model is particularly well known and includes precommunicative, pre-phonetic and phonetic stages. By the phonetic stage a child has a better grasp of the sound/symbol relationship. Spelling is partly to do with sound but visual aspects – getting to know the look of words – are also important. Teachers both combine teaching of spelling and phonics and draw attention to visual patterns in words. Using dictionaries and their own word books also helps reinforce visual aspects. In some classrooms part of the wall becomes a huge dictionary so that the children can track down the words they want to spell. For further discussion of the issues in the teaching of spelling, punctuation and handwriting see under the appropriate entries.

There have been some recent government initiatives which aim to support children's writing development. The Early Learning goals, set out in *Curriculum Guidance at the Foundation Stage,* include requirements for supporting children's early writing. Detailed guidance is also given in The National Literacy Strategy *Developing Early Writing* manual which has been distributed to all state school teachers in the United Kingdom who teach five to seven year olds. It requires fifteen minutes' focused work on spelling, phonics and handwriting, trying to develop speed and accuracy. Work is initially with the whole class, rehearsing sentences and the children writing them down. This guidance material is meant to help but teachers of young children are concerned that too much worry about accuracy could inhibit writing which genuinely engages children.

Out of a large number of good books about writing from about age five to seven I find Ann Browne's book *Helping Children to Write* particularly comprehensive with strong chapters on young bilingual writers and on gender issues in children's writing. Pam Czerniewska's book *Learning About Writing* explains some of the differences between spoken and written forms and how this informs good practice.

Developing writers (7–11 years)

Audience and purpose are still important
By about seven most children are developing some confidence as writers. Nevertheless, writing continues to be one of the most challenging activities in school. What can we do to support children's writing development over these later primary years? Just as in the case of younger children, it is a strong sense of 'purpose' – why am I writing this – and of 'audience' – who am I writing this for – that makes all the effort seem worthwhile. Being in control of purpose and audience helps decide the text type (the type or

'genre' of the writing) and the sort of language features that are appropriate. The writer's self-image is strengthened if the teacher responds first to the content or 'composition' of the writing. Then help can be given with the transcriptional aspects – spelling, punctuation and paragraphing – so that the writing communicates clearly to others. In the later primary years we are above all trying to help children develop a distinctive authorial 'voice'. Donald Graves writes, memorably, that: 'Voice is the imprint of ourselves in our writing…the dynamo in the process' (Graves, 1983, p. 227).

Helpful intervention

Planning
Everyone has their own idea about what is a helpful plan and, while we can make suggestions, I do not think imposing a particular format for planning is always appropriate. I have come across children who prefer to have a plan 'in their head' and this works well for them. Others like to make their planning visible – either in a list of ideas with main points underlined or in the form of webs to sort out the different elements.

Teachers help with planning in shared writing contexts where children can collaborate by sharing developing ideas and information. There is nothing like talk for helping children organise their ideas and feel some enthusiasm for the writing task. In this way some of the valuable aspects of what Donald Graves termed 'conferencing' can be included.

Drafting and composing
Writing is a complicated process in which planning, composing and drafting can intermingle. Thinking about your writing as you draft involves throwing bits away and putting bits in – all of us who struggle to write well know how complicated a process it is. Often it is only when we start to struggle with a topic that we find out what we actually think and feel about it. Drafting becomes more demanding as children move through the primary years for the simple reason that they are learning to control more genres each with particular features. One of the most challenging genres children work with from about Year 4 onwards are the genres known as 'persua-

sion' and 'discussion'. Under the entries on these subjects I look at how focused discussion and writing frames can help children develop a standpoint from which to structure their accounts.

As I pointed out in the first paragraph of this entry, one important function of writing is to organise our thinking. We need to convince children that the grammatical structures they select help structure their thoughts and belong to the compositional aspect of the writing task. Think, for example, how syntax can help put the emphasis where it is needed. Children can be shown how a point in the form of a question can alert the reader and add variety to the page. A short sentence with an exclamation mark can add to the energy that inhabits a dialogue. Making a sentence active rather than passive often infuses life into writing.

Once the first draft is written older children can be encouraged to work further on the content and how it is ordered and expressed. Particularly when it comes to informational kinds of writing we will want to help children to find the clearest ways of expressing information and their ideas about the issues the information raises. Children seek something that excites them and which seems worth sharing with an audience. Purpose is bound up with a sense of audience: part of becoming a mature writer involves having the imaginative insight to have the readers' needs in mind. Children need help in dispensing with parts of their accounts which seem repetitive or of little interest while adding to and developing the parts that seem successful and likely to appeal to readers. Let us not underestimate the challenge of this task. Children find it difficult to make more than superficial changes to their writing without a great deal of help.

DfEE's guidance material *Grammar for Writing* examines sentence level aspects of writing and how we can support children's developing control over different genres. There is an issue here: too much stress on grammatical construction might interfere with fluency. It is a matter of finding a balance between technical and creative aspects. (Many teachers like the playful approach to grammatical constructions taken in Bain and Bridgewood's materials in *The Primary Grammar Book*.)

Transcriptional aspects

There is a full account of how to support children's developing control over transcriptional aspects of writing under the entry of that name and under Spelling, Punctuation, Handwriting and Proof reading. In the Information and Communications Technology entry, I point out that word processing with its spell check systems makes these drafting processes much easier. So there is everything to be gained by helping children have confidence on the keyboard.

When children start to bring a piece of writing to final draft we need also to draw their attention to punctuation and help them understand how this can enhance the communication of meaning. Teachers can help here as model writers in shared writing contexts showing for example how a colons and semi-colons are used by thinking aloud as they make notes on the flip chart or white board.

Learning about genre

Children have always developed an understanding of the features of different texts as they move through the primary years. This has been formalised in the National Curriculum English programmes, in the National Literacy Strategy and in the requirements for teachers' knowledge in *Teaching: High Status, High Standards*. In the Literacy Hour children move systematically through a range of texts. But this sensitivity to different texts, not only print but across a range of media, begins very early as children begin to have an intuitive and often quite sophisticated grasp of texts in different media. Watching television and video-film they may see cartoons, cooking programmes and science fiction and while they might not be able to articulate the differences, they are aware of them. It is on all this intuitive knowledge, which includes the beginnings of visual literacy, that the teacher can draw when promoting children's writing as well as their reading.

We need to reinforce children's understanding that genres are not static – new forms of writing emerge to reflect social need – e-mail, for example – and they soon grasp that different genres enjoy different statuses. And as they move towards the end of the primary years children develop sensitivity to the different levels of formality required in writing. Next I want to make some observations first on fiction and then on non-fiction kinds of writing.

Enjoying writing fiction

Children need the opportunity to try out some different kinds of writing and often a story, comic strip, poem or factual account can be a starting point. Teachers of older primary children would find inspirational *The Reader in the Writer*, a book about how we can use the links between reading literature and writing to help children make writing progress. It describes and evaluates the literacy work over a year of some Year 5 classes. The examples of writing 'in role' are particularly interesting. Nine-year-old Yossif wrote a letter as one of the characters after hearing the teacher read aloud Kevin Crossley-Holland's book *The Green Children*. There is no doubt that this writing task helped him reflect profoundly on the themes of the book. A major finding from this research was how important it is to select texts of emotional power to awaken the desire to write as well as reflect and discuss; among the many books used were: *The Midnight Fox* by Betsy Byars, Shirley Hughes' *The Lion and the Unicorn* and *Goodnight Mister Tom* by Michelle Magorian (Barrs and Cork, 2001). Interestingly, a report published by the Basic Skills Agency found that in schools where children's writing achievements were particularly good, time was found to read whole texts, not just the extracts which the Literacy Hour format seems to lead to. And the nourishing of writing with reading was another practice linked with success. You will find suggestions for encouraging children's writing of stories and poems under the following entries: 'fiction: choosing and using', 'novel' and 'poetry'.

Supporting non-fiction kinds of writing

When it comes to non-fiction writing there are a number of ways of helping children plan, draft, edit and present their work. One outcome of Wray and Lewis' Extending Literacy project was the EXIT model which shows how support can be given at each stage. Entries in this ency-

clopaedia which aim to advise on this important aspect of literacy include 'prior knowledge', 'process writing', 'editing', 'summaries', 'proof reading', 'writing frames', 'non-fiction reading and writing' and the entries on kinds of texts like 'recounts', 'reports', 'explanation' and 'persuasive genre'. A main challenge is to teach about study, research and presentational skills while keeping up high levels of involvement and interest. In Chapters 4 and 5 of *Young Researchers* there are suggestions for helping place note taking and study skills within the broader framework of children's intentions and purposes (Mallett, 1999).

First-hand experience continues to be a strong context for writing across the curriculum – experiments in science, work with artefacts in history and outings to see rivers and valleys in geography. But writing about what has been seen or done often needs to be enriched by information from secondary sources. Uniting input from first-hand and second-hand sources coherently stretches most of us. This is where a strong urge to make sense of issues and information helps greatly. Let me give one example. Year 6 children saw a Tudor sailor's shoe found when the Mary Rose wreck was raised. The effect of seeing this artefact with evidence, as one child remarked, that 'the little toe might have had a corn that pushed the leather out of shape' was considerable. Committed research into Tudor shoes followed to enrich the children's writing.

Just as reading and writing fiction are connected, so reading and writing non-fiction are linked activities. Sometimes it is an inspirational book that is not only the spur to children's research and writing but which also shows new and exciting ways of presenting information. Nel Marshall's *Letters to Henrietta* about a young girl's letters to and from her bothers at the front in the Second World War indicates how social history can be presented in a powerful and involving way. There is more about the role of texts in developing children's interest and control over informational writing under 'information books', 'factual genres', 'first person writing' and 'persuasive genre'.

Assessing writing and recording progress

There are two purposes in assessing children's writing. We may wish to use children's writing, as indeed we do with their speaking, to assess their progress in lessons across the curriculum. In this case we are using writing to monitor their grasp of historical, geographical or scientific information and concepts or their powers of observation during an educational visit. But in this entry we are concerned mainly with the assessment of writing more generally as a means of organising, making sense of and communicating experience and information. There are a number of ways of doing this, each of which tells us something different about a young writer's development. Ways of assessing writing and keeping records need to be economic of the time of both teachers and children. Too complicated a system risks taking the pleasure out of children's writing and teachers' support.

The writing SATs (see under the entry of that name) children take at seven and eleven years (that is at the end of Key Stage 1 and Key Stage 2) give us a summative assessment – a snapshot of what a child has achieved at a particular time. As this is 'first draft' writing any plan has to be made in the head. Writing for the SATs is awarded a grade on the National Curriculum levels of achievement. Evidence from teacher-assessed sampling of children's writing can also contribute to a summative judgement.

But sampling also helps us make a formative assessment, highlighting what a young learner is doing well and where they need some intervention to make progress. Formative assessments of writing, using a sampling strategy, are diagnostic and we are interested not just in the products but also in the processes – how the child goes about the writing process, making plans, drafts and perhaps notes. Most teachers either make a comment orally to the child or write down some constructive comments – see under Marking. Sampling, if carried out thoughtfully, helps us chart a child's progression as a writer both in terms of increasing the range of genres they control and their increasing skill within a genre.

The English Co-ordinator usually takes the lead in producing sampling sheets to help teachers make their sampling systematic. Sampling sheets usually have space to give the date the writing was done and the context in which it arose. There is usually a heading to do with how the young writer goes about their task – the process of writing – and nearly always sections to comment on compositional – (expressing and communicating meaning, and transcriptional or secretarial aspects, including spelling, punctuation and presentation. Often the child will be invited to give their own comment on their progress. One of the most valuable parts of the sampling sheet will be to do with the 'next step' or target. Teachers make notes on their observations of children's writing progress during shared, guided and independent writing sessions. They also select, often together with the child, a range of dated and annotated writing samples to include in the child's English portfolio. The children's progress using the National Curriculum English levels of achievement and the National Literacy Strategy objectives (perhaps enriched by using the CLPE's Writing Scales which are more detailed), evidence from the samples in the portfolios, together with SATs results, can be recorded in a system like The Primary Language Record of the Centre for Language in Primary Education (Barrs *et al.*, 1988), see the Record keeping entry. The samples and summaries of progress help the English Co-ordinator discuss any strengths or weaknesses in a class teacher's approach to writing. It also helps the Co-ordinator have background knowledge for meetings about the school's success in supporting writing.

In the United Kingdom there is a culture of target setting. In *Grammar for Writing* (DfEE, 2000) it is suggested that writing targets can be adapted from the National Literacy Strategy objectives and made into 'We can…' statements. For example 'We can plan our writing carefully by thinking up and collecting ideas and using charts and story boards' (Year 3). These statements could then be used to structure some plenary sessions in the Literacy Hour, helping children feel involved in their progress. They can also be a focus for discussion with parents and could inform records of achievement as the child moves through the school years.

Final thoughts

What I want to leave you with at the end of this entry is first that, although writing is one of the most challenging things we ask children to do, we should encourage them to see it as useful, creative and satisfying. The second is that the teacher can be a powerful enabling force. In her preface to *The Reader in the Writer* Margaret Meek writes: 'When young writers believe that teachers are interested, really interested, in what they want to communicate they will do all they can to get their meaning across…'. (Barrs and Cork, 2001). It is the quality of the encouragement they receive and the chance to write about something important to them that helps young writers find a distinctive 'voice'.

Bain, Elspeth and Richard (1996) *The Grammar Book: Finding Patterns, Making Sense* Sheffield: NATE.

Bain, Richard and Bridgewood, Marion (1998) *The Primary Grammar Book: Finding Patterns-Making Sense* Sheffield: NATE.

Barrs, Myra *et al.* (1998) *Gaining Control: Writing at Key Stage 1* Centre for Language in Primary Education with Southwark Education.

Barrs, Myra and Cork, Valerie (2001) *The Reader in the Writer: the links between the study of literature and writing development at Key Stage 2* London: CLPE.

Britton, James (1970) *Language and Learning* Harmondsworth: Allen Lane, The Penguin Press.

Browne, Ann (1993) *Helping Children to Write* London: Paul Chapman.

Czerniewska, Pamela (1992) *Learning About Writing* Oxford: Blackwell.

DfEE (1998) *Teaching: High Status, High Standards* (Circular 4/98) London: DfEE.

DfEE (1999) *English in the National Curriculum* London: HMSO.

DfEE (1999) *Early Learning Goals* London: QCA Publications.

DfEE (2000) *Curriculum Guidance for the Foundation Stage*. London: QCA.

DfEE (2000) *Grammar for Writing* London: DfEE.

DfEE (2001) *Developing Early Writing* London: QCA. (ref:0055/200. Tel. 08455 602 2260. Website: www.dfee.gov.uk).

Frater, Graham (2001) *Key Stage 2 Writing*. Survey for The Basic Skills Agency (Tel. 0870 600 2400).

Graham, Judith and Kelly. Alison (eds) (1998) *Writing Under Control: Teaching Writing in the Primary School* London: David Fulton.

Mallett, Margaret (1999) *Young Researchers: Informational Reading and Writing in the Early and Primary Years* London: Routledge.

Qualifications and Curriculum Authority (QCA) (1999) *Target Setting and Assessment in the National Literacy Strategy* London: QCA.

Temple, C.A., Nathan, R.G., Burris, N.A. and Temple, F. (1988, second edition) *The Beginnings of Writing* Boston, Mass.: Allyn & Bacon.

Whitehead, Marian (1997, second edition) *Language and Literacy in the Early Years*. London: Paul Chapman (Chapter 7, 'Early representation and emerging writing').

Wray, David and Lewis, Maureen (1997) *Extending Literacy: Children Reading and Writing Non-fiction* London: Routledge.

Writing Scales (Information available from CPLE, Webber Street, London SE1 8QW).

Writing area/corner

See also displays, reading corner/area, writing

Reading and writing are complementary and mutually enriching activities. So the classroom writing area is nearly always part of the reading area or next to it. A special area for writing in relative privacy, whether alone or as part of a small group, is appropriate and desirable for every year group from nursery to the final year, although naturally the emphasis in resources and activities changes.

Space may be limited but the area must look attractive. One Reception teacher known to me displays enlarged pictures of the children at work on their writing: this helps their self-image as writers and is a good talking point. Displays help make the area inviting and are likely to include, for every age group, examples of the children's best work, clearly labelled and annotated. Children's reviews of both fiction and non-fiction are often included. Posters showing writing routines, advice about note making and the principles of paragraphing are helpful reminders.

Examples of the kinds of writing named in the *National Literacy Strategy Framework for Teaching*

(DfEE, 1998) for a particular term can be diplayed for reference. For example, children in Year 4 and above will need to learn about the format of some journalistic and persuasive kinds of writing, such as newspaper reports and advertisements.

When it comes to writing implements, young children like to have pens, pencils, crayons, chalks, writing brushes, while older children will appreciate the addition of biros, felt tips, pastels and calligraphy pens. Materials to write on include paper and card of different sizes, shapes, colours and textures, an assortment of envelopes, some ready-made sewn books of different proportions, concertina books and book making materials like hard covers and book spines. Other items to have to hand are sellotape, display folders, staplers, paperclips, rulers, rubbers and glue. Word books, dictionaries and thesauruses, at the right level of difficulty for the children, are necessary and of course a word processor, a printer and, if possible, access to the Internet.

To be effective a writing area must go beyond just looking good: it needs to both reflect the work of the class and be referred to in everyday work. Children's input to the planning and setting up of displays is important. Some teachers have a rota of helpers to put up displays and to keep the writing corner tidy. A developing display – one that is constantly modified and extended – reflects the dynamic nature of children's learning. The best displays include work which is a genuine outcome of current work. Experienced teachers make time for children's writing to be read out loud and discussed as well as displayed.

Good organisation and sensitivity ensures fair access to the relative privacy of the area for individuals and groups. The good writing area provides a space where children can experiment, take initiative and enjoy their writing.

Writing frames

See also EXEL project, genre, non-fiction reading and writing, scaffolding, writing

Writing frames are frameworks provided by the teacher to help children structure their writing.

The children are launched into their writing by 'sentence starts' like 'I want to explain why' and supported by 'connectives' such as 'moreover', 'next' and 'then'. This strategy became widely known through the work of Wray and Lewis on the Exeter Extending Reading Project in the 1990s. They have published several books on writing frames, including *Writing Frames: Scaffolding Children's Non-fiction Writing in a Range of Genres,* 1996. The frames arose out of classroom-based research during which they identified six different kinds of informational writing. These six genres have been used to inform the non-fiction objectives of the *National Literacy Strategy Framework for Teaching* (DfEE, 1998a). These are: recount, report, instruction, explanation, discussion and persuasion. One of the persuasive frames has the following headings: 'I think that', 'because', 'another reason is', 'moreover', 'because', 'these facts/ arguments/ ideas show that'.

Writing frames have been put forward as one answer to the challenge of a genre-based national curriculum English and National Literacy Strategy. Even older primary children find it challenging not only to have to wrestle with new hierarchies of facts and ideas but also to control a particular format. The researchers consider that when it comes to a new genre, having a skeleton structure, often with a vocabulary that drives the writing on, leaves the children free to concentrate on the content. It is not recommended that the frames are used to teach children about the different genres in decontextualised exercises. They should be used in the context of meaningful writing tasks where there is an understanding of purpose and audience.

There is no doubt that some children benefit from the organisational and linguistic support a frame can provide. Young learners who struggle with the writing process are particularly likely to find the prop useful to get started. But of course we want children to learn to organise their own written accounts and Wray and Lewis would be the first to say that the frames are a temporary aid not to be used too long or too mechanistically. Nevertheless there is still some concern that too enthusiastic a use of the frames might jeopardise a young writer's spontaneity and delay their effort to structure their own writing. Barrs is concerned about too genre-based an approach particularly where young children are concerned. She was not making her point by discussing writing frames but argues that children need to be encouraged to use 'provisional and informal genres' – lists, memos, logs and journals. These more accessible kinds of writing are likely to help young learners use language as a tool for thinking (Barrs, 1987, p. 2). So while the frames have a role to play, hopefully their use will not be prescribed and teachers will use their professional judgement to decide if and when to use them.

Lewis, Maureen and Wray, David (1996) *Writing Frames: Scaffolding Children's Non-fiction Writing in a Range of Genres.* Reading: Reading University Reading and Language Information Centre.

Writing resources – see under writing corner

Young's Group Reading Test

See also assessment, Standardised Reading Tests

This is a timed, written attainment test given to groups of children. First published by Hodder & Stoughton in 1968, it covers an age range from six and a half to just over twelve years. The later versions, including that published in 1980, include sentences in which the children fill gaps to indicate some understanding of what they are reading.

Graham, Judith and Kelly, Alison (2000, second edition) *Reading Under Control: Teaching Reading in the Primary School* London: David Fulton (gives a clear account of the different reading tests, and the issues they raise, in Chapter 4, 'Monitoring and Assessing Reading).

Z

Zone of proximal development

See also collaborative learning, language acquisition

This is the area of a child's emerging abilities. A standardised test gives a summative score but with help from an adult or older pupil, a child's level of working may be raised. The gap between what a child can achieve on their own and what they can achieve with help was termed the 'zone of proximal development' by the great Russian developmentalist and psychologist L.S. Vygotsky in *Thought and Language* (1987). The zone of proximal development can vary considerably in children of the same age who have a similar set of standardised scores: one child may have a much more elastic potential and be able to benefit from a level of teaching for which the other child is not yet ready. One child needs to be challenged while for the other teaching may be best aimed just beyond present achievements.

The theory supports a social interactionist view of learning since it suggests that interaction with others – both peers and adults – can further children's progress. The right kind of teacher intervention, carefully adjusted for individual learners, can provide vital support in a child's journey towards competence, not least in language and thinking but also in other areas of development.

Vygotsky, L.S. (1987) *Thought and Language* Cambridge, Mass.: MIT Press (revised and edited by A. Kozulin).

Wood, David (1988) *How Children Think and Learn* London: Blackwell (Chapters 1 and 7).

A Who's Who in Primary English

ADAMS, MARILYN J.
An American specialist in cognition and education, she has published a number of books and journal articles on learning to read, including *Beginning to Read: Thinking and learning about print* (Cambridge Mass.: MIT Press, 1990). Adams makes a clear distinction between graphic and phonic cue systems in learning to read and this approach is taken up in the National Literacy Strategy 'searchlight' model of reading. She is often cited to support phonic approaches, but she believes reading skills should be situated in a programme of good quality and interesting reading materials.

ARNOLD, HELEN
During her career she was a teacher, lecturer, adviser and researcher into children's literacy development. She is known best for her books *Listening to Children Reading* (1982, Hodder & Stoughton) and, with Vera Southgate and Susan Johnson, *Extending Beginning Reading* (London: Heinemann, 1980). Her work on non-fiction reading and writing is wise and useful, not least her chapter 'Do the Blackbirds Sing All Day? Literature and Information Texts' in *After Alice* M. Styles, E. Bearne and V. Watson (eds) (London: Cassell, 1992). She believed children deserved the very best quality non-fiction texts and that these relate to their own questions and their own experience.

BAIN, RICHARD
With co-author M. Bridgewood, he wrote *The Primary Grammar Book: Finding Patterns, Making Sense* (Sheffield: NATE, 1998) which contains many suggestions for language games and activities to help children enjoy learning about syntax and parts of speech.

BARNES, DOUGLAS
Although his main experience was in secondary schools, Barnes' work on the role of talk in classroom learning, particularly in small groups, made an impact on primary practice. The ideas from *Language, the Learner and the School* (1969, Harmondsworth: Penguin), written with co-authors James Britton and Harold Rosen, influenced the Bullock Report which reached a wide audience of primary practitioners and researchers and still supports best practice.

BARRS, MYRA
Myra Barrs is Warden of the Centre for Language in Primary Education (CLPE, Webber Row, London SE1 8QW). She and her colleagues stress that they work as a team and some of those who have made a considerable contribution include: Sue Ellis, Hilary Hester, Clare Kelly, Anne Thomas, Olivia O'Sullivan and Moira McKenzie who was an earlier Warden. The centre is known for its superb reference library and many courses on all aspects of Primary English for teachers. As well as its journal, *Language Matters,* the centre has produced many useful and influential publications including *Testing Reading* (1989), *The Reading Book* (1991), *Boys and Reading* (1998) and *The Reader in the Writer* (2001). Above all, Myra Barrs and her colleagues at the centre are known for *The Primary Language Record Handbook for Teachers* (1988) which provides a record keeping format which informed and inspired approaches to record keeping world wide.

BEARD, ROGER
Known by primary teachers for his work on the development of literacy, Roger Beard communicates the issues clearly in books like *Children's Writing in the Primary School* (1984, London: Hodder & Stoughton) and *Developing Reading 3–13* (1990 second edition, London: Hodder & Stoughton). He has also produced in-service packages and edited a large number of books, for example *Teaching Literacy, Balancing Perspectives* (1993, London: Hodder & Stoughton) and *Rhyme, Reading and Writing* (1996, London: Hodder & Stoughton). He is a critic of extreme interpretations of 'apprenticeship' approaches to reading and 'process' approaches to writing.

BEARNE, EVE
Eve Bearne is known for her work on children's literature (*After Alice, The Prose and the Passion*) with her colleagues Morag Styles and Victor Watson at Homerton College, Cambridge where she is Assistant Director of Research. She has written about a number of topics in Primary English, see, for example, her book *Making Progress in English* (London: Routledge, 1998).

BEIRETER, CARL AND SCARDAMALIA, MARLENE

These are American educationists, best known for their research into the development of children's writing. They believe the challenge is to encourage young writers to transform information rather than just recall it. See their main arguments set out in *The Psychology of Written Composition (*1987, Hillside, NJ: Lawrence Erlbaum Associates).

BENTLEY, D. AND REID, D.

They are known particularly for their publication *Supporting Struggling Readers* (Widnes: UKRA, 1995) which provides an excellent analysis of reading difficulty with clear practical advice for classroom strategies.

BERNSTEIN, BASIL

Berstein was an international figure in the world of sociology and education from the early sixties. Based at the London Institute of Education, where he became professor in 1967, he influenced large numbers of teachers on postgraduate courses. In an obituary in *The Times Educational Supplement* (6 October 2000, p. 27) his first PhD student, Dennis Lawton, comments that: 'His major contribution was to demonstrate how nearly every aspect of a child's life was affected by the language used by its parents.' He was interested in the role of language in all kinds of social interaction and as a means of social control. But he is best known for his work on the distinction between elaborated and restricted codes. In his earlier work he seemed to be saying (although he modified this later) that while middle class children had control over elaborated forms of language, including academic discourse, as well as over more personal speech forms, working class children only had access to the latter more restricted code. It is not difficult to see how this led in some cases to a deficit model which linked working class under-achievement at school to inadequate use of language. Many found this model determinist and abhorrent, although it did lead to much discussion, research and argument.

BIELBY, NICHOLAS

Nicholas Bielby has written about the theoretical aspects of literacy and has explained the underpinning to 'the new phonics' in his book *Making Sense of Reading: The New Phonics and Its Practical Implications* (1994, Leamington Spa: Scholastic Publications).

BISSEX, GLENDA

She is known for *GNYS AT WRK (GENIUS AT WORK): A child learns to write and read* (1980) (Cambridge Mass.: Harvard University Press) This is a seminal work named after a sign the author's young child, Paul, hangs on his door. The case study of a child's writing and reading behaviour at home from age five years shows the importance of motivation in a child's progress and has implications for how we support children's writing in school.

BLAKE, QUENTIN

He is the first children's laureate and illustrator of a large number of poetry and storybooks. His economical style is both distinctive and versatile. His work in Michael Rosen's poetry books is much loved by children and many of his books, for example *Mister Magnolia* (1980, Cape), have become classics.

BRICE-HEATH, SHIRLEY

She is an American educationist, anthropologist and linguist whose study of children's language development in different cultural and social contexts is clearly explained in *Ways with Words: Language, Life and Work in Communities and Classrooms* (1983, Cambridge University Press).

BRITTON, JAMES

Best known for emphasising the role of talk in learning and for his classification of writing modes, James Britton helped draft the Bullock Report. A secondary teacher of English, a publisher and then an academic at the London University Institute of Education, he was also Dirrector of a Schools Council Project on Writing, 11–18. Later, he was appointed Professor of Education at University of London Goldsmiths College. He had a deep concern for and interest in children's language development at the primary stage. His book *Language and Learning* (Allen Lane, 1970) remains a seminal work.

BROWNJOHN, SANDY

Author of a number of books on the teaching of poetry including *Does it Have to Rhyme?* (1980), *What Rhymes with Secret?* (1982) and *To Rhyme or not to Rhyme, Teaching Children to Write Poetry* (1994) (all published in London by Hodder & Stoughton), she believes that children need to be taught the techniques to write different kinds of poem. These strategies, which can be learnt through play and games, will encourage children to play with language and to control what they say. An inflexible interpretation might risk contrived lessons, but many teachers have found her work helps both them and the children they teach enjoy and feel confident about reading and writing poetry.

BRUNER, JEROME

He is an American educationist and developmentalist known for his research into very early human communication and the language and thought of school aged children. He argues that the young child first knows the world through sensation (enactive stage), then becomes able also to make sense of experience through images (the iconic stage) and finally through symbols, including language (symbolic stage). A good book to start with is *Making Sense: the Child's Construction of the World* (1987, Methuen, written with co-author Helen Haste), moving on to *Actual Minds, Possible Worlds* (1986, Harvard University Press).

In his early work he tends to concentrate on cognitive development, but his later books recognise the importance of developing an inner world of the imagination – not least through story.

BRYANT, PETER

Educational researcher with a special interest in how children make inferences, Peter Bryant has also turned his attention, with his colleague Ursula Goswami, to phonological aspects of learning to read. See, for example, *Phonological Skills and Learning to Read* (1990, Lawrence Erlbaum Associates).

BUTLER, DOROTHY

Author of *Babies Need Books* (1995, Harmondsworth: Penguin), Dorothy Butler drew in her writing on her experience as a New Zealand bookseller and a mother of a large family of children and grandchildren.

CARTER, RONALD

Ronald Carter is Professor of English Studies at the University of Nottingham. Known for his work on knowledge about language for teachers and school age children his best-known book is *Knowledge about Language and the National Curriculum: The LINC Reader.* (London: Hodder & Stoughton, 1990). For an analysis of the controversy over the publication of the materials dee LINC material's entry.

CHAMBERS, AIDAN

Co-founder with his American wife, Nancy Chambers, of The Thimble Press, Aidan Chambers has published fiction for children and a number of inspiring books for teachers including *Tell Me: Children, Reading and Talk* (1993) and *The Reading Environment* (1991). These books are about the pleasure reading can provide and how teachers can help children become enthusiastic readers.

CHAMBERS, NANCY

Editor and founder of The Thimble Press which has published many well-regarded publications on all aspects of children's books and reading as well as the journal *Signal*.

CLARK, MARGARET

She drew attention to the role of the adult and of the library in supporting children's attitudes to reading before they receive formal instruction. Her book *Young Fluent Readers: what can they teach us?* (1976, London: Heinemann Educational) examines the case studies of 32 children who read at an early age.

CLAY, MARIE

She is a leading reading specialist in New Zealand, well known for her work on Reading Recovery and a large number of books on literacy, such as *What did I Write?* (1975, Heinemann). Her work has been adapted for reading recovery programmes in the UK.

CLEGG, ALEX

Creative writing flourished in the 1960s and one of the outstanding books celebrating children's work was Clegg's *The Excitement of Writing* (1964, London: Chatto & Windus). The book is based on the belief that children write powerfully and imaginatively out of their own experiences and using their own choice of language.

The creative writing approach has had many critics and it can lead to children keeping to a rather narrow range of writing. Nevertheless Clegg's work is still an inspiration and a reminder that some of the writing children do should arise from their own lives and wishes.

CLIPSON-BOYLES, SUZI

A major contributor to our understanding of educational drama and its potential role in children's developing literacy, see for example her book *Drama in Primary English Teaching* (1997, David Fulton). She directed the Catch Up Project, a literacy intervention programme for struggling readers in Year 3, at Oxford Brookes University.

COX, BRIAN

Chair of the Cox Committee which produced the two Cox Reports on Primary English and laid the foundation for the first National Curriculum English orders, he has been a critic of the more prescriptive revisions of the English Orders – see, for example, his book *Cox on Cox: An English Curriculum for the 1990s.* (1991, Hodder & Stoughton).

CRYSTAL, DAVID

David Crystal is a leading linguist and author of a large number of books and educational materials on language for different age groups. Perhaps his three best-known books are *Child Language, Learning and Linguistics* (1987, Harmondsworth: Penguin), *The English Language* (1988, Harmondsworth: Penguin) and *The Cambridge Encyclopaedia of Language* (1987, Cambridge: Cambridge University Press). The last two of these are useful reference books for teachers wishing to refine their knowledge about language.

CZERNIEWSKA, PAMELA

Director of the *National Writing Project* and author of many books and articles on children's writing development including *Learning About Writing* (1992, Oxford: Blackwell).

DOMBEY, HENRIETTA

Professor of Education at the University of Brighton, Henrietta Dombey has taught, lectured and researched in the area of children's reading. She is a widely respected expert in the field and is never afraid to appraise new initiatives in literacy with a critical eye. Her book with co-author H. Moustafa, *Whole to Part Phonics: How Children Learn to Read and Spell* (1998: CLPE), argues we should encourage phonological understanding in the context of whole texts. She also edited a book with M. Robinson, *Literacy for the Twenty First Century* (1992, Brighton Polytechnic Literacy Centre).

DONALDSON, MARGARET

Educational researcher and developmentalist based for a number of years at Edinburgh University, Donaldson has lectured and written about children's intellectual development. Just a very few education books are truly exciting and ground-breaking and, for many teachers and students, this is true of *Children's Minds* (1978, Fontana). Here she argued that children under eleven coped best when learning made 'human sense'. She suggests a number of strategies to help the successful teaching of reading and writing and shows how becoming literate can bring about a special kind of intellectual growth.

EDWARDS, VIV

Viv Edwards has made a major contribution through books like *The Power of Babel, Teaching and Learning in Multilingual Classrooms* (1998, Stoke-on-Trent: Trentham Books) to our understanding of how we best support young learners who speak two or more languages. Her colleages on the Multilingual Resources project include Urmi Chana and Sue Walker. She worked with Sue Walker on dual-language texts and this work is described and evaluated in their book *Building Bridges: Multilingual Resources for Children* (1995, The Multilingual Resources for Children Project, University of Reading: Multilingual Matters).

She is director of the Reading University Reading and Language Information Centre and other team members include Sue Abbas, Pam Brown, Prue Goodwin, Chris Routh, Barbara Shaw and Judy Tallet.

EGAN, KIERAN

Like Jerome Bruner, Egan sees children as active meaning makers rather than storers of symbols in the mind for later retrieval. His books, such as *Imagination in Teaching and Learning* (1992, Chicago University Press), emphasise the creativity at the centre of all learning and share exciting examples of children's work in science and history.

FISHER, MARGERY

An expert on children's books of all genres and author of *Intent upon Reading* (1964, Brockhampton) which was one of the first surveys to view children's books as part of mainstream literature, she was also one of the first to recognise the importance of offering children quality non-fiction – see *Matters of Fact* (1972, Brockhampton Press).

FOX, CAROL

Carol Fox has shown us the influence of experiences of the real world and of the world of books on young children's narratives. Her analysis in *At the very edge of the Forest: The Influence of Literature on Storytelling by Children* (1993, Longman) suggests that we see young children's stories as forms of verbal symbolic play. Children use 'story language' from books for retelling their own stories. (Those interested in cultural influences on young children's literacy would also find interesting Naima Brown's *Young Children's Literacy Development and the Role of Televisual Texts*, Falmer Press, 1999, in which she illuminates how young children's literacy is enriched by watching video-film and television.)

FOX, GEOFF

Co-author (with M. Benton) of one of the most inspirational book ever written on English teaching *Teaching Literature 9–13* (Oxford University Press, 1987), Geoff Fox co-edits the journal *Children's Literature in Education* based at Exeter University. He shares a love of children's books in *Celebrating Children's Literature in Education* (1995) (London: Hodder & Stoughton).

FROEBEL, FRIEDRICH

An educator who had great influence on child-centred approaches to educating young children, Froebel recognises the importance of stories in a child's development – not least as a way of understanding the circumstances of others in different times and places – in his book *The Education of Man* (1887, Appleton Century Croft).

GENTRY, RICHARD

Gentry is best known for setting out a model of developmental stages in spelling – see 'An analysis of developmental spelling in GNYS AT WRK', *Reading Teacher*, 36:192–200. The stages are included in N. Mudd's comprehensive book on spelling *Effective Spelling: A Practical Guide for Teachers* (London: Hodder & Stoughton, 1994).

GIPPS, CAROLINE

She has examined the theoretical underpinning to good primary practice and has a special interest in the issues raised in assessment – see for example her book with P. Murphy *A Fair Test?: Assessment, Achievement and Equity* (1994, Buckingham: Open Books).

GOODMAN, KENNETH

Kenneth Goodman argued over many years that learning to read is a natural development and not essentially different from learning to speak. In fact he saw spoken language as a key tool in deciphering new words. Children were helped to make out an unfamiliar word by the meaning of the rest of the sentence and other contextual clues. His views had enormous influence and his references to reading as 'a psycholinguistic guessing game' and miscue analysis as 'a window onto the reading process' are familiar to many (see Goodman, K. (1973), 'Miscues: Windows on the Reading Process' in Goodman, K. (ed.) *Miscue Analysis: Application to Reading Instruction*. Urbana, Illinois: ERIC Clearing House on Reading and Communication, NCTE). There are several revised versions of Goodman's original miscue analysis task which are easier to use in the classroom, for example Cliff Moon, 1984, and Helen Arnold, 1982. See under the Miscue analysis entry for more detail.

The opposite view of reading requires that children be taught letter-sound relationships as a basis for learning to read and write. In practice, most people who favour the latter approach also understand there is more to reading than decoding. Similarly, Goodman accepted there is a phonological cueing system playing its part alongside the contextual, semantic and syntactic systems. It is a matter of emphasis. While more value is given to the teaching of phonics in the National Curriculum and National Literacy Strategy programmes, Goodman's influence is still evident in the searchlight model which takes in a number of cueing systems.

GOODWIN, PRUE
Author of *The Literate Classroom* (London: David Fulton, 1999), she is a reading specialist whose research is in reluctance to read in the primary years.

GOSWAMI, USHA
Author of *Rhyme and Analogy, Teacher's Guide* (1996, Oxford: Oxford University Press), Ursula Goswami has worked with Peter Bryant on how children develop phonemic awareness. She argues that children use their awareness of rhyme to make rime analogies which draw attention to phonemes.

GRAHAM, JUDITH
Teacher of children and students, Judith Graham is Principal Lecturer at Roehampton Institute and author of many influential books on literacy, including *Pictures on the Page* (1990, NATE) and *Reading Under Control* (with Alison Kelly, David Fulton, 1997, 2000). She has been particularly effective in helping student teachers interpret the National Literacy Strategy requirements in a flexible and creative way.

GRAINGER, TERESA
Editor of UKRA journal *Reading,* Teresa Grainger has written on all aspects of primary English and is known particularly for her book *Traditional Storytelling in the Classroom* (Leamington Spa: Scholastic, 1997).

GRAVES, DONALD
Researcher and author who has made a considerable contribution to our understanding of writing as a process, Donald Graves draws attention to the importance of 'conference' – talking to children about the content and organisation of their writing before and during the task – and of 'publishing' – presenting children's writing in books to make their work attractive and permanent – see his book *Writing: Teachers and Children at Work* (1983, Heinemann)

GREGORY, EVE
A former teacher of young children, now Professor of Language and Culture at Goldsmiths College, University of London, Eve Gregory carried out major research projects on the literacy practices of ethnic minorities and the effect on their children.

Her research drew teachers' attention to the fact that young bilingual children do not bring certain culturally acquired knowledge (for example, words that go together like 'fish and chips' and 'bread and butter') to their reading in a second language. This has implications for how the teaching of reading and writing is best approached with young bilingual children. (See *Making Sense of a New World: Learning to Read in a Second Language* 1996, London: Paul Chapman.)

She has extended her research to 'city literacies' – to the literacy practices of several different communities in inner London – and to the role of siblings in children's developing literacy.

GRUGEON, ELIZABETH
A specialist in primary English, she has written a number of valuable books including, with P. Gardner, *The Art of Storytelling for Teachers and Pupils* (2000) and *Teaching Speaking and Listening in the Primary School* (1998), both published by David Fulton.

HALL, NIGEL
He is known both for his work on the literacy of young children and for his role as co-director (with Anne Robinson) of The Punctuation Project, Manchester Metropolitan University.

Hall and Robinson set out the first attempt to offer a comprehensive account of the issues involved in learning and teaching punctuation in their book *Learning About Punctuation* (1996, Clevedon, Philadelphia and Adelaide: Multilingual Matters).

HALLIDAY, M.A.K.
Halliday is a systemic-functional linguist who has investigated how language changes according to a particular social context. In his book *Language as Social Semiotic* (1978, London: Arnold) he shows how, as we express meaning through language, we recreate social reality. For teachers of young children, Halliday's most relevant book is *Learning How to Mean* (1975, London: Arnold) in which he presents a case study of his own child as he manages to 'mean' before he has verbal language. So Halliday sees the human infant as essentially a meaning maker who communicates before he or she has words. The social impetus into speech is stressed – 'to take on a language is to take on a culture'.

Functional linguists are more interested in the functions or uses to which we put language than the structure of the system. Halliday's functions of language model (see under Functions of language entry) has had great influence on how we construe the young child's language development.

HEATHCOTE, DOROTHY
Dorothy Heathcote has made an outstanding contribution to the development of educational drama with many different age groups. Her work with primary aged children has often been connected with history. Children are invited to 'put themselves in somebody else's shoes' whether they are a Saxon villager coping with a failing harvest or a Viking about to invade. In her many articles, lectures and demonstrations she has pointed to the potential of the teacher-in-role. By adopting this position the teacher can comment, question and help inform and shape the children's improvisation in a natural way. Gradually some of the responsibility can be shifted to the children and they then take over what Heathcote terms 'the mantle of the expert'.

The potential of drama as a tool for learning and imagining across the curriculum, explored by Heathcote with Gavin Bolton who is also distinguished in the field of educational drama is set out in *Drama for*

Learning: Dorothy Heathcote's Mantle of the Expert Approach to Education. (1995, Portsmouth, NH: Heinemann).

If you want to read a case study carried out by Tom Stabler, a former student of Heathcote at Newcastle University, see Mallett, Margaret and Newsome, Bernard (1977) *Talking, Writing and Learning 8–13* Evans/Methuen for the Schools Council, pp. 52–61. The range of writing encouraged by participation in the improvisation on conflict in a Saxon village is impressive.

HOLDAWAY, DON

Holdaway is known for his books both about the parent's role in encouraging literacy and the use of enlarged texts to demonstrate aspects of the reading process to children in the classroom. Much of his wisdom is contained in his book *The Foundations of Literacy,* 1979 (London: Ashton Scholastic). We must remember that Holdaway's aim in using large texts was to make available to a group or even a class the special benefits of individualised reading. He was very much in favour of teacher and children making some of their own reading materials, including big books.

The shared reading part of the Literacy Hour when done well is a realisation of Holdaway's principles.

HYNDS, GEOFF

A specialist in children's reading development across the key stages, Geoff Hynds is known for his belief that children should have quality books and resources. One of his intiatives was the Geoff Hynds Bookshop.

JONES, RICHARD

He is the author of an exciting book *Fantasy and Feeling in Education* (1972, Penguin) which gives a central place to play, dreams and story telling in the educational process and is inspiring to teachers of any age group.

HUGHES, TED

As well as producing many books of stories and poetry for children, including *The Iron Man* – a modern fairy tale – Ted Hughes wrote books and articles for teachers, for example *Poetry in the Making* (1967, Faber & Faber) about teaching poetry, and articles, for example 'Myth and Education', in (*Children's Literature in Education,* 1, March 1970) about the cultural importance of myth.

LEWIS, DAVID

David Lewis is a leading scholar on the nature and importance of children's picture books. His insights on studying and understanding picture books are shared in a number of articles and in his book *Reading Contemporary Picturebooks: Picturing Text* (2001, London and New York: Routledge Falmer).

LEWIS, MAUREEN

After many years teaching in primary schools, Maureen Lewis became Research Fellow for the Exeter University Extending Literacy Project (EXEL). With David Wray and a team of classroom teachers, she produced a framework for reading non-fiction which had considerable influence on the *National Literacy Strategy Framework for Teaching* (DfEE, 1998). The work of the EXEL project is explained in a number of books including *Extending Literacy: Children Reading and Writing Non-fiction,* 1997, Routledge which Maureen wrote with co-author David Wray.

LINDLEY, MADELEINE

In 1988 Madeleine Lindley left her post as primary adviser for the Manchester Literacy Project to open a book shop in the family garage – Madeleine Lindley Ltd. She wanted to provide quality books for different age ranges and interests. She sent out carefully selected books by mail order. The business expanded and moved to The Acorn Centre at Oldham and then on to the Broadway Business Park at Chadderton where there was enough space to have showrooms to browse in. Soon a thousand visitors were turning up each month to browse through books and resources of all kinds – poetry books, story books, picture books, children's short story collections and novels of all categories. She or one of her colleagues was always available to give advice on choosing books for different parts of the National Literacy Strategy. There were training days and days when authors of children's books came to talk about their work. Madeleine gave inspiration and practical help to many primary teachers across the nation.

LITTLEFAIR, ALISON

She is the author of *Reading All Types of Writing* (1991, Open University Press). The book provides a useful taxonomy of the kinds of writing children learn to control as they move through the school years. It is compatible with the genre-based approach of the National Curriculum English orders and is a particularly clear account.

MACKAY, DAVID

He is best known as one of the authors of the book and materials known as *Breakthrough to Literacy* (1970, Longman), which showed an approach that based children's early reading on their own sentences made in plastic sentence makers from folders of letters and syllables.

MARSHALL, BETHAN

She has a distinctive 'voice' on many important issues – setting homework and the danger of over-prescriptive frameworks for literacy and English lessons, see, for example her chapter 'English teachers and the third way', in Cox, B. (ed.) (1998) *Literacy is Not Enough: Essays on the Importance of Reading* (Manchester University Press and Book Trust).

MARSHALL SYBIL

Sybil Marshall taught in a village primary school during and after the Second World War. She found that children produced writing of great vitality when it was linked with music and art. One of her books – *An Experiment in Education.* (1963, Cambridge: Cambridge University Press) – described and evaluated the truly creative teaching that is possible when cross curricular connections are forged by a creative practitioner. Times change and so do priorities, but Marshall's account is still inspirational.

MARTIN, J.R., CHRISTIE, FRANCES and ROTHERY, JOAN

These three university teachers and researchers are the main figures in the Australian 'genre theory' school. They had reservations about 'process' approaches to writing, associated with Donald Graves and Frank Smith, and believed that different kinds of writing have distinctive global structures and linguistic features about which children needed to be directly taught. Their research in Australian schools showed that children wrote more fiction than non-fiction and that there tended not to be any direct teaching of how to write in the different genres.

There have been opposing voices. Myra Barrs (1994), for instance, considers that the genre approach does not fit with what we know about children's development as writers. Children seem to learn through using 'transitional' genres including lists and 'expressive' kinds of writing.

In their paper, Social processes in education: a reply to Sawyer and Watson and others' (1987, Centre for Studies in Literary Education, Deakin University, Victoria) Martin, Christie and Rothery replied to their critics.

The Australian genre theorists have had considerable influence in and outside Australia and their work continues to stimulate heated discussion. Wray and Lewis adapted some of the writing categories in their EXEL project and the National Curriculum and National Literacy Strategy have a genre-based emphasis.

MARTIN, TONY

Head of the Education Department at the College of St Martin and former president of the United Kingdom Reading Association, Tony Martin is best known for his excellent book on reading and special needs *The Strugglers* (1989, The Open University). In a powerful case study about Leslie, a young learner with reading difficulties, Martin shows how he was able to help by a strategy of paired reading.

MEEK-SPENCER, MARGARET

Margaret Meek-Spencer is a leading scholar in the area of the links between literature and literacy. She has written extensively about becoming literate, children's literature and the power of fiction in children's learning and development. Her books include *On Being Literate* (London: The Bodley Head, 1991) and *How Texts Teach What Readers Learn* (Stroud: The Thimble Press, 1988) – which must be one of the most influential books on literacy ever written. With Aidan Warlow and Griselda Barton she edited *The Cool Web: The Pattern of Children's Reading* (1977, The Bodley Head) which is a collection of 50 chapters by distinguished authors who are bound by their belief that stories are a major way of making sense of our experience. Her book on information texts – *Information and Book Learning* (1996, The Thimble Press) has contributed considerably to our understanding of this difficult aspect of literacy.

MILLARD, ELAINE

She has written about several aspects of Primary English, including reading in the middle years, but is particularly known for her book on gender and literacy in which she argues that the very act of reading is often seen as 'gendered' – *Differently Literate Boys, Girls and the Schooling of Literacy,* (1997) (London: Routledge-Falmer).

MINNS, HILARY

She has written on all aspects of language and learning and is particularly well known for her study of the emergent literacy of five four year olds – *Read it to Me Now! Learning at Home and at School* (Buckingham: Open University Press (1997 edition)).

MISKIN, RUTH

She believes in the systematic teaching of the alphabet to children in Reception and Year 1 and of phonics, both 'synthetic' and 'analytic'. Her forceful views have brought critics as well as admirers and are expressed in 'Fast Track to Reading', *The Times Educational Supplement. Primary Magazine* and in a 'good practice' video from OFSTED, 22 January 1999.

MOON, CLIFF

Author of many publications on reading, Cliff Moon is known particularly for *Individualised Reading* (1998, Reading University Language and Information Centre) which is updated yearly. Moon places books in twelve colour-coded categories based on their 'readability' but is cautious about assigning ages to stages. He offers the lists to teachers as a rough guide and believes that a child's interests are a factor in selecting a book.

MORRIS, JOYCE

Joyce Morris is known for her belief in phonics as the basis of learning to read. She describes the phonics work in her reading programme as 'linguistically informed' (see, for example, her chapter entitled 'New phonics for old' in Thackray, D.V. (ed.) *Growth in Reading* (London: Ward Lock, 1979). The current approach followed in the United Kingdom, based on the National Literacy Strategy searchlight model, recognises the role of the phonological cueing system Morris has always championed. Morris took issue with the Goodman-Smith notion that learning to read is 'natural'. If you want to read further about the debates round reading issues I recommend Wray and Medwell's *Teaching Primary English: The State of the Art,* 1994 and Roger Beard's *Teaching Reading: Balancing Perspectives,* 1993. When thinking about Joyce Morris' position on whether or not learning to read is 'natural' I am always reminded of Keith Gains' entertaining analogy that learning to read is about as natural as 'a vegetarian hedgehog flavoured pot noodle' (chapter on special literacy needs in Beard (1993) *Teaching Literacy, Balancing Perspectives*).

NEATE, BOBBIE
Author of *Finding Out About Finding Out* (London: Hodder & Stoughton, 1992), Bobbie Neate is a writer of children's information books, editor and reviewer. She has written about the structures and registers of children's information texts and has firm views on what 'good' non-fiction texts should be like and how children are best helped to acquire study skills.

OPIE, IONA AND PETER
They are compilers of anthologies of poetry and nursery rhymes (*The Oxford Dictionary of Nursery Rhymes,* 1951) and fairy stories (*The Classic Fairy Tales,* 1974, Oxford University Press) and researchers of children's playground rhymes (*The Language and Lore of School Children,* 1959, Oxford University Press).

The Opie Collection of Children's Literature is housed in the Bodleian Library, Oxford.

PALMER, SUE
A former teacher and head teacher, Sue Palmer is known for her creative and flexible approach to interpreting current requirements in primary English. She lectures, reviews books for teachers and children and writes books and articles on educational topics, particularly grammar and spelling. Her series of articles on these topics in *The Times Educational Supplement* (1997–1978) 'From A–Z' are clear and entertaining and she is the author of six books on phonic skills for Scholastic.

She is the originator of the Time to Teach initiative which challenges the story-writing task in Year 6 SATs. The concern is that too much time is spent on mechanistic preparation for the test.

PERERA, KATHERINE
Has worked as a teacher, journal editor and as Professor of Educational Linguistics at Manchester University. A member of the Cox Committee, she has written many books and articles on aspects of Primary Language, for example *Children's Writing and Reading: Analysing Classroom Language* (1984, Oxford: Basil Blackwell) and is the editor of the *Journal of Child Language*.

PETERS, MARGARET
She is author of one of the most influential books on an aspect of children's language – *Spelling: Caught or Taught?* (1967, Routledge). It was published in a second edition as *Spelling: Caught or Taught – A New Look* (1985). Peters believed that good verbal ability, interest in words, good visual perception and careful handwriting all seemed to be linked with good spelling.

PIAGET, JEAN
A developmentalist and psychologist who described stages of development but did not write directly about classroom matters, Piaget nevertheless exerted considerable influence on teaching approaches. His view on language – in a nutshell – was that it is one important way of dealing with experience alongside other kinds of mental functioning. After about age eleven years, when children hypothesise about phenomena not actually present, Piaget considered language took on a more important role.

In stressing the importance of a stimulating environment in which a young child can learn by using objects, the role of interaction with adults and peers was sometimes undervalued by educators influenced by his work. The work of both Bruner and Vygotsky restored language to a central position in children's learning. One of Piaget's clearest considerations of his view of the role of language is in Chapter 5, 'Language', in *Six Psychological Studies* (1968, Random House, New York: Vintage Books).

His adaptive model of learning remains useful. The metaphor is of the digestive system: we *assimilate* any item of new learning (by altering it to fit with existing frameworks just as gastric juices prepare food intake) and *accommodate* our existing knowledge base to take in the new (just as the organs of digestion reshape to accept food). For me, this is one of the most powerful models of how we learn. We must also remember that the distinction between 'spontaneous' concepts – those that we learn through everyday living (mother, cup, happy) and 'non-spontaneous' or 'scientific' concepts – those usually acquired through formal education (solution, feudal, igneous) was made by Piaget although the ideas were usefully extended by Vygotsky.

Piaget has also contributed to our understanding of children's play as an essentially assimilatory activity. In his book *Play, Dreams and Imitation in Childhood* (Routledge & Kegan Paul edition, 1962) he links the satisfactions children get from telling stories and reading fiction with play and daydream. There are links here between Piaget's thinking and the work of Freud, 1908, Winnicott, 1972 and Britton, 1971.

PLOWDEN, BRIDGET HORATIA
Bridget Plowden chaired the committee which, in 1967, produced the 1,100-page report on primary education known as The Plowden Report. The proposals included setting up 'educational priority areas', the expansion of part-time nursery education, greater parental involvement in school and the abolition of corporal punishment. However, Lady Plowden is remembered most for the child-centred approach to teaching and learning she recommended. She believed learning should be active and that while direction by teachers and the practice of skills should be included in

the programme, too much formal work was inappropriate for children under eleven. Her views had a major influence on primary practice and the creators of the first National Curriculum orders reacted to what some felt was too unstructured an approach by imposing a subject-centred curriculum. Her critics have felt that she tended to project infant practice into the later primary years encouraging teachers to plan work round projects and themes. While the best project work awakened children's interest and produced lively talk and writing, the less successful work lacked a clear content and focus. Classroom organisation for children's activities in English and other lessons has also been a contentious issue. The Plowden Report praised individual and group work and this has attracted criticism that some learning is best achieved in class-based teaching. This concern has led to requirements for some class teaching in both the National Curriculum, in all its editions, and the National Literacy Strategy.

The educational climate has changed considerably since the Plowden Report was published and a much more systematic model of teaching primary English is now in place. Nevertheless, the notion that children should be active in their learning and that school activities should be enjoyable is one that we would do well to hang on to.

POWLING, CHRIS

A former teacher, head teacher, college lecturer, Chris Powling continues to write inspiring books for children and professional texts for teachers. He is a former editor of *Books for Keeps.* With co-author Morag Styles he edited *A Guide to Poetry 0–16,* (London and Reading: Books for Keeps and The Reading and Language Information Centre, 1996).

RILEY, JENI

The tutor in charge of Primary English at the Institute of Education, University of London, Jeni Riley is a leading specialist in the literacy of young children. Two of her best-known books are *The Teaching of Reading* (1996, London; Paul Chapman) based on her research into reading in Reception classrooms and, with David Reedy, *Developing Writing for Different Purposes* (2000, London; Paul Chapman).

ROSEN, CONNIE

She and Harold Rosen were directors of the Schools Council Project 'Language in the Primary School', one outcome of which was *The Language of Primary School Children* (1974, Penguin). This book, full of examples of lively, creative language work showing the links between language and learning, inspired many students and teachers. It belongs to a time when we spoke about Primary Language work rather than English work.

ROSEN, MICHAEL

He is author of many books of poetry with the rhythms of natural speech and about the everyday concerns of children, including *Wouldn't You Like to Know* and *You Can't Catch Me* and picture books such as *We're Going on a Bear Hunt* (Walker Books) illustrated by Helen Oxenbury. Michael Rosen is also known for his broadcasting – he is presenter of 'Treasure Islands' on Radio 4 – and speaks and writes about wider aspects of literacy, see, for example, his book for teachers and parents *Did I Hear You Write?* He visits schools and works with children of all age groups throughout this country and overseas.

SASSOON, ROSEMARY

A specialist in educational and medical aspects of handwriting, Rosemary Sassoon has made a major contribution to our understanding of the factors that effect children's handwriting. She has lectured all over the world and produced many publications including *Handwriting: A new perspective* and *Handwriting: A way to teach it,* both published in 1990 by Stanley Thornes.

SMITH, FRANK

Smith, together with Kenneth and Yetta Goodman, is associated with the psycholinguistic approaches to the teaching of reading influential in the 1970s and 1980s. The starting point for this model is the young reader's expectations about the text. Then he or she is encouraged to test out these expectations or predictions. Mistakes are regarded as 'miscues' and systematic attention to these – 'miscue analysis' – helps teachers give appropriate support. Thus the reading process is seen as essentially interactive, predictive and to do with getting meaning from text. Among his many publications are *Understanding Reading,* 1971 and *Psycholinguistics and Reading,* 1972, both published by Holt, Rinehart & Winston. Smith fell out of favour because of his unwillingness to recognise the role of phonics in teaching reading. His argument was that a phonics approach does not provide an entirely reliable word decoding system and meaning tends to be marginalised. Smith's positive legacy is twofold. First he has helped keep in our minds the importance of quality materials to make children feel reading is worthwhile. The term 'real books approach' has often been used pejoratively, but there is no doubt that it has encouraged the publication of excellent books and resources both inside and outside structured reading approaches. More recently, the gap between quality books and reading scheme books has narrowed. Secondly, Smith is one of those who has emphasised the crucial role of the adult as expert reader to model the reading process. He will always be associated with the 'apprenticeship' metaphor. The importance of the adult's role continues in current approaches to the teaching of reading.

When it comes to writing, Smith will be remembered for drawing attention to 'composition' and 'transcription' as two different elements in the process (see Smith, 1982, *Writing and the Writer*). These terms are still used frequently by teachers and educational writers and used in assessment and record keeping materials. Smith recommended that children concentrated first on 'composition' – the organisation of what they want to say – and then on 'transcription' – the secretarial aspects including spelling, punctuation and presentation. The practice of encouraging children to plan their writing and to write first and second drafts is encouraged in the National Curriculum En 3 at Key Stages 1 and 2. However, the writing required for SATs requires a first draft response.

STYLES, MORAG

Known for her work on poetry (*The Books for Keeps Guide to Poetry 0–16*), she was editor of two books on children's literature – *After Alice* and *The Prose and the Passion* (London: Cassell, 1992) with her colleagues at Homerton College – Eve Bearne and Victor Watson.

SWANN, JOAN

She is known for her work on gender and race issues, see for example her book *Girls, Boys and Language* (Blackwell, 1992). The emphasis has changed from a concern for girls' possible disadvantage in talk contexts, very evident in Swann's work, to worry about boys' achievements in literacy.

TIZARD, J. AND HUGHES, M.

Their work on the important contribution to learning made by the home environment, see *Young Children Learning: Talking and Thinking at Home and at School* (1994, London: Fontana Press), has been most influential. They contrasted the lively demeanour of children in their research when they were in the home environment compared with a less linguistically active one in the nursery.

In his later work, with Greenhough, Hughes has studied how schools can encourage quality conversations at home, see in 'Parents' and Teachers' interventions in children's reading', *British Educational Research Journal*, 1998, 24(4): 283–398.

TOWNSEND, JOHN ROWE

Writer for both children and adults. See the definitive sixth edition of *Written for Children: an outline of English-language children's literature* (1995, The Bodley Head) for an inspiring contribution to the study of children's literature.

TUCKER, NICHOLAS

Based in the Educational Psychology Department of Sussex University, Nicholas Tucker is a major contributor to our understanding of children's response to books and to concepts of childhood at different times in history. He reviews books for journals and newspapers, is a frequent broadcaster and lectures at conferences throughout the world. In one of his most influential books – *The Child and the Book* (1981, Cambridge: Cambridge University Press) – he relates children's response to reading to their intellectual and affective development. He writes from careful observation of how children approach books rather than how adults think they should.

VYGOTSKY, L.S.

His best-known book *Thought and Language* (1986, Kozulin edition, Cambridge, Massachusetts: MIT) is about concept development but has relevance to all aspects of language and thinking, including those pertinent to reading and writing.

Primary practice benefits particularly from the following aspects of Vygotsky's work.

First he stresses the social nature of learning – interaction with other human beings accompanies all aspects of development including of course language development. This supports practice which includes much collaboration, co-operation and discussion between pupils. Second he recognises that it is verbal communication through talk and writing that makes possible the higher order kinds of thinking and meaning making. Control over the word 'meaning' helps a child clinch understanding of a concept. Language is needed to make links between the 'spontaneous' concepts children bring to school and the 'scientific' concepts that are part of formal learning. A child might bring to school the spontaneous concepts 'frog' and 'pond' where he or she might, in the science lesson, add the related scientific concepts 'amphibian' and 'habitat'. Third, he recognises the importance of adult intervention in children's learning. The adult's skilfully judged comments and questions can extend a child's thinking. Part of successful teaching is to do with estimating a child's 'zone of proximal development' – the space between where he or she is intellectually at present and where they could be with the right sort of adult help. Bruner extends Vygotsky's 'zone of proximal development' theory by using the metaphor of 'scaffolding' to describe the enabling role of the teacher, or parent.

WADE, BARRY

He is the author of many books on reading including the influential *Reading for Real* (ed.) (1990, Open University Press) and a director of a project on books for babies which led to the publication of *Baby power.*

WATERLAND, LIZ

Liz Waterland was an infant teacher who found inspiration in the Goodman-Smith model of reading. In her book *Read With Me* (1985, Stroud: The Thimble Press) she promoted an approach to reading which regarded the young learner as an apprentice who would read alongside the teacher who modelled the process. She was also in favour of 'real' books rather than those written for a reading scheme. Since her book was written the climate has changed. Publishers use respected authors to write books for their programmes so the social stereotypes and the linguistic impoverishment of reading schemes is largely a thing of the past. Research into phonological aspects of learning to read (for example by Bryant and Bradley, 1985; Goswami and Bryant, 1991) indicates that children need to be helped to acquire phonemic knowledge and understanding as well as the 'big shapes' of reading.

Nevertheless, Waterland drew attention to the importance of quality books and the search for meaning as an important basis for learning to read.

WATSON, VICTOR

An editor with his colleagues at Homerton College of *After Alice,* 1992, he is also a specialist in books for children in the eighteenth and nineteenth centuries and reviews for the *TES* and for *Signal.* He is editor of *The Cambridge Guide to Children's Books in English* (2001).

WELLS, GORDON

Director of the 'Bristol Language at Home and School' longitudinal research study, Wells studied the spontaneous speech of children and caregivers. In his books, for example *The Meaning Makers* (Hodder & Stoughton, 1987), he identifies talk as a major means of making sense of experience and school learning. Story and talk about stories were shown in his research to be linked to success at reading and writing at school. One of his clearest accounts of the role of talk is his essay 'The Centrality of Talk in Education' in *Thinking Voices,* a book about the National Oracy Project, edited by Kate Norman and published in 1992 by Hodder & Stoughton.

WHITE, DOROTHY

The 'message' of some books survives through time and this is true of children's librarian Dorothy White's fascinating diary of her daughter's early book experiences – *Books Before Five* (1956, New Zealand Council for Educational Research). The account emphasises the interplay between characters and incidents in the books read and real life incidents. For example, when Carol has been given a little smack – she and her mother find it helpful to read about Beatrix Potter's *Tom Kitten* whose mother also loses patience. The comforting message is – parents still love their children even when they make them, temporarily, cross. (A more recent example of a single case study is R. Campbell's (1999) *Literacy from Home to School; Reading with Alice.*)

WHITEHEAD, MARIAN R.

Her publications, including *Language and Literacy in the Early Years* (1997, Paul Chapman), stress the enjoyment involved in supporting young children's development as speakers, listeners, writers and readers. Her belief in the role of picture books, nursery rhymes and stories as crucial, imagination-developing resources in the early years classroom comes through strongly. There are of course a number of others who have written illuminatingly about early years language and literacy – Anne Browne, Robin Campbell, Diane Godwin, Cathy Nutbrown and P. Hannon, Margaret Perkins – to name a few – but Marian Whitehead was one of the first to do so.

WILKINSON, ANDREW

Wilkinson is known particularly for his research into children's writing development and the assessment of progress. The study produced what has become known as the Crediton Model of writing assessment and the findings are set out in his book with authors G. Barnsley, P. Hanna and M. Swann in *Assessing Language Development* (1980, Oxford: Oxford University Press). Writing was assessed mainly in terms of its meaning and analysed in terms of categories like thought, feeling and social awareness. However, the growth of syntax from the simple and literal to more elaborate syntax and cohesion was included.

WILSON, ANGELA

Known by primary teachers for her work on subject knowledge, her book *Language Knowledge for Primary Teachers: A Guide to Textual, Grammatical and Lexical Study* (London: David Fulton, 2001 edition) is both sound and entertaining.

WRAY, DAVID

Now Professor of Language and Literacy at the University of Warwick, David Wray was co-director of the Exeter Extending Literacy Project (EXEL) funded by the Nuffield Foundation. This 'grass roots' research was school based and the findings were the basis of the National Literacy Strategy's non-fiction programmes. Building on research in Australia (for example that of Martin and Rothery, 1986), Wray and his team proposed six non-fiction writing types – recount, report, instruction, explanation, persuasive and discussion – each with distinctive features and purpose. The work is also known for its help in showing how teachers can use writing frames (structured writing plans) and genre exchange (writing in one genre following reading in another) to develop children's writing.

The use of writing frames has caused some controversy. Wray and Lewis never intended the frames to be used to teach genre and they would be the first to advise against mechanistic or too frequent use.

David Wray has written many books and articles on all aspects of literacy some jointly with Jane Medwell (for example *Teaching Primary English: The State of the Art,* Routledge, 1994) and others with the co-director of EXEL, Maureen Lewis (for example *Extending Literacy: Children Reading and Writing Non-fiction,* Routledge, 1997).

WYSE, DOMINIC

He has been a teacher and English Co-ordinator and is now a university lecturer and researcher into aspects of primary English, particularly writing. His book, with Russell Jones, *Teaching English, language and literacy* (London and New York: Routledge-Falmer, 2001), indicates the issues the reflective practitioner should keep in mind.

List of entries in the Encyclopaedia

Extended entries are highlighted in **bold**

Participle
Parts of speech (or word classes)
Passive voice
Pathetic fallacy
Person
Personification
Persuasive genre
PETA, the Primary English
    Teaching Association,
    Marrickville Austalia
Phatic communication
Philosophy and literacy
Phoneme
Phonetic
Phonetic stage
Phonics
Phonic Knowledge
Phonological awareness
Phonology
Photographs
Phrase
Physical Education & English
Picture books
Plagiarism
Planning
Play & Language and literacy
Playscript
Plenary (at end of Literacy Hour)
P-levels
Poetry
Portfolios
Pre-communicative stage
Predicate
Prefix
Preposition
Primary Language Record (The)
Prior knowledge
Procedural or instructional genre
Process approach to writing
Progression in Phonics material
    (PIPs)
Pronoun
Proof reading
Proper noun
Prose
Psycholinguistics and reading
Punctuation

Qualifications and Curriculum
    Authority (QCA)
Quotation
Quotation marks
QWERTY

Reading
Reading age
Read aloud
Reading choices
Reading conferences
Reading corner/area
Reading diaries
Reading environment
Reading range
Reading recovery
Reading schemes

Realism (in children's fiction)
Received pronunciation
Recipes
Record keeping
Recount
Recurring principle
Referencing
Reflective practitioner
Reflective reading
Register
Relative pronoun
Religious Education and English
Reports
Research (into Primary English)
Research Awards and Data bases
Response to reading
Retrieval devices
Rhyme
Rhythm
Running reading records

Salford Reading Test (Sentences)
SATs (Standard Assessment
    Tasks)
Scaffolding
Scan
School stories
Science and English
Schonell Graded Word Reading
    Test
Scribing
Semantic cue-system
Semi-colon
Semi-phonetic stage in spelling
Sentence
Shakespearean drama (in the
    Primary Years)
Shared writing
Short stories
Siblings (and literacy)
Silent letters
Simile
Singular and plural
Skimming
Slang
Sonnet
Speaking and Listening
**Special Educational Needs (SEN)
    in language and literacy**
Speech act
Speech marks
Spelling
Spiral curriculum
Spontaneous and scientific
    concepts
Standard English
Standardised Reading Tests
Stanza
Story Chest
Story props
Story telling
Story time
Structural guiders
Structuralist model of language
Study skills

Subject knowledge
Suffix
Summary (or précis)
Syllable
Synonym
Syntactic cue-system
Synthetic phonics

Target setting
Talking books
Teacher Training Agency (TTA)
Television and literacy
Tenor
Tense
Terminology (of Primary
    English)
Texts
Text level work
TGAT Report
Thesaurus
THRASS (Teaching Hand-
    writing Reading And Spelling
    Skills)
Tick sheets
Timelines
'Top- down' approaches to
    reading
Traditional tales
Transactional writing
Transcriptional aspects of
    writing
Transformational grammar
Transitional genre
Transitive/intransitive verbs
Trigraph

United Kingdom Reading Asso-
    ciation (UKRA)
Usage
USSR (Uninterrupted Sustained
    Silent Reading)
Utterance

Verbs
Verse
Video-film
Virtual Teacher's Centre (VTC)
Visual Literacy
Voice
Vowel

Warnock Report, The (1978)
Web sites and Primary English
Whole class teaching
Word- as a unit of meaning
Word classes
Word level work
Worksheets
Writing
Writing area/corner
Writing frames

Young's Group Reading Test

Zone of Proximal Development